Changing Maine

1960–2010

Edited and with an introduction by Richard Barringer
Illustrated by Jon Luoma

Tilbury House, Publishers   Gardiner, Maine

Changing Maine
1960–2010

New England Environmental Finance Center
Muskie School of Public Service University of Southern Maine Portland, Maine

Tilbury House, Publishers
2 Mechanic Street
Gardiner, Maine 04345
800–582–1899
www.tilburyhouse.com

Muskie School of Public Service
96 Falmouth Street
Portland, Maine 04104–9300
207-780-4150
www.muskie.usm.maine.edu

First printing, June 2004 • 10 9 8 7 6 5 4 3 2 1

Cataloging in Publication Data
Changing Maine, 1960/2010 / edited by Richard Barringer ; illustrated by Jon Luoma.
   p. cm.
 Includes bibliographical references and index.
 ISBN 0-88448-264-2 (pbk. : alk. paper)
 1. Maine—Social conditions. 2. Maine—Economic conditions. 3. Maine—Politics
and government—1951- 4. Quality of life—Maine. I. Barringer, Richard E.
HN79.M2C53 2004
306'.09741—dc22

                              2004008179

Cover illustration and design by Jon Luoma, Alna, Maine.
Text designed on Crummett Mountain by Edith Allard, Somerville, Maine.
Layout by Nina DeGraff, Basil Hill Graphics, Somerville, Maine.
Copyedited by Judith Robbins, Whitefield, Maine.
Scans by Integrated Composition System, Spokane, Washington.
Covers printed by the John P. Pow Company, South Boston, Massachusetts.
Printing and binding by Maple Vail, Kirkwood, New York.

To friends John Cole (1923–2003) and Peter Cox, their gifted spouses, Jean Cole and Eunice Cox, and the team of splendid writers they gathered at the *Maine Times*. Without them, much of what is recorded here, and more, would not have come to pass.

Acknowledgments

Changing Maine, 1960–2010

and the public lecture series on which it is based have been made possible
with the generous support and contributions of

Maine Community Foundation

Muskie School of Public Service

Maine Public Radio

Nancy R. Masterton

Maine Humanities Council

New Century Community Program

U.S. Environmental Protection Agency

FIFTEEN YEARS AGO the Edmund S. Muskie School of Public Service, with support from the Maine Savings Bank, sponsored a series of public lectures entitled, "Changing Maine." It was my pleasure then to organize and host the series, broadcast over radio by the Maine Public Broadcasting Network, and, subsequently, to edit the book of the same title, published by the University of Southern Maine (USM).[1] The first *Changing Maine* was prompted by a shared belief among its contributors that the Maine we knew and loved was at a crossroads and under assault from a variety of forces—demographic, economic, and technological—and that caring and deliberate choices might turn these forces better to Maine people's advantage.

A dozen years later I was approached once again to assess where Maine has come in this new century, how we arrived here, and where we are going as a community of people. The result is this new volume, *Changing Maine, 1960-2010.* It is the product of more than two years' work among its contributors, who met together in a series of seminars in which we shared outlooks on these questions and approaches to the compelling issues facing Maine and shaping our shared future. The lecture series was delivered throughout the fall and winter of 2003–04 in the Moot Court Room of the University of Maine School of Law, and was again broadcast to its listeners by Maine Public Radio. The lectures were subsequently revised and edited into the form in which they appear here.

I am especially grateful to each of the author/lecturers for their devotion to this effort, and to those whose generosity and support made it possible: the Maine Community Foundation; the Muskie School of Public Service; Maine Public Radio; Nancy R. Masterton, in memory of her late husband, Bob Masterton; the Maine Humanities Council; the New Century Community Program; and the U.S. Environmental Protection Agency (EPA). Charles Beck, Barry Darling, and Mary Mayo of Maine Public Radio made possible the popular broadcast of the entire lecture series. Rosemary Monahan, Diane Gould, Vera Hannigan, and Vanessa Bowie of the EPA afforded valuable support; and Colleen Khouri, Barbara Gauditz, Lisa Yaeger, and Elizabeth Worley of the Law School were unfailingly generous in making their facilities available.

Muskie School olleague Bruce Clary offered the original suggestion for the second *Changing Maine* series, and Bob Woodbury and Karl Braithwaite provided continuing encouragement and support. Many Muskie School colleagues made indispensable contributions, among them Sondra Bogdonoff, Jennifer Hutchins, Tom Wood, Sam Merrill, Evan Richert, Alison Barker Deb Arbique, Linda Grace, and Kimberly Bird. Barry Darling and, under his expert tutelage, Jennifer Hutchins recorded the lectures for radio broadcast, and brought their personal warmth to many a cold winter's night gathering. USM's Robin McGlauflin made the lectures available to the Internet audience on the Muskie School's website. Linda Grace, Deb Arbique, and Kimberly Bird helped translate and edit the lectures into the text that follows, for which I am especially grateful. Frank O'Hara of Planning Decisions, Inc., was, as ever, unfailing in his editorial suggestions, good humor, and readiness to party!

Teague Morris and Tessy Seward, graduate students in the Muskie School, contributed happily—he, in organizing, recording, and make meaning of the seminars among our contributors; she, in making the lectures hospitable to the general public and, in particular, writing the abstracts that precede each of the chapters below. Their personal commitment was essential to keeping matters in hand and on track, and I am deeply obliged to both. All of the seminars save one were conducted at the Maple Hill Farm B&B in Hallowell, Maine, and we are indebted to its gracious hosts, Scott Cowger and Vince Hannan. The early seminars were facilitated by Martha Freeman with her accustomed presence and wit. The last seminar before the lecture series was held at the Blaine House in Augusta, and we are most grateful to Governor John E. Baldacci for his generous hospitality and inspiration, and to Kim Gore of his staff for the necessary arrangements.

The readiness of Tilbury House, publishers of Gardiner, Maine, to produce this volume, even before the first lecture had been delivered, and to do it so quickly, was a great incentive and singular contribution to the success of this effort. Jennifer Bunting offered timely advice and encouragement throughout, and made light the many possible burdens that accompany so complicated a publication project. The wonderful illustrations that grace the cover and pages that follow are the work of Jon Luoma of Alna, Maine. Jon, too, participated in the seminars and offers these renderings as his own personal essay on Maine today—even as he did in the first *Changing Maine*. It is, as ever, a joy and a privilege to work with so fine a person and keen and caring an observer of Maine. Special thanks to Gary Crocker, Alice Kirkpatrick, and Karen Hamilton of the Maine Community College System, and to Ed Haddad of South Freeport for use of their materials in the illustrations. Finally, Richard Kelly of Augusta created the fine Maine maps throughout the text, and did so as a generous contribution to this project.

Thank you for all your help, your collaboration, and your warm support.

R. B.
May 2004

Contents

THREE

Toward Greater Ecological Integrity

Maine Transformed
An Introduction

RICHARD BARRINGER

Much about Maine has changed since 1960.

In 1960 Maine people were driving Chevy Impalas down the new stretch of turnpike from Augusta to visit family and friends in Massachusetts and Connecticut. Annual log drives dominated life along the Androscoggin, Kennebec, Penobscot, Machias, Allagash, and St. John rivers. An endless stream of high-quality wood, agricultural, and fish products flowed from Maine to regional and national markets. Young men and women of Maine continued to serve their nation in disproportionate numbers, as they had always done.

School superintendents puzzled over how to respond to the new Sinclair Act that offered them incentives to abandon hundreds of one-room schoolhouses for greater student achievement and lower costs, in something called "school administrative districts." A summer resident along Maine's midcoast, wildlife scientist Rachel Carson, worked on a manuscript that, upon its publication two years later, would forever change the world.

Maine's junior senator, Edmund S. Muskie of Rumford and Waterville, traveled by Eastern Airlines' Electra prop-jet to Washington and congratulated his Senate colleague, John F. Kennedy of Massachusetts, on his election to the nation's highest office by the narrowest of margins. JFK would return to Maine three years later, just weeks before his untimely and tragic death. Arriving by helicopter to grace a splendid fall afternoon on the University of Maine campus, President Kennedy would speak of a first, important step to calm Soviet-American relations after the Cuban missile crisis, a nuclear test ban treaty, and the terms of "a genuine and enforceable peace."

In 1960 Americans in general were celebrating the domestic achievements of the post-World War II national economy. The pent-up demand of fifteen years of depression and war had driven prosperity in the nation that was unprecedented in human history. Education, housing, and highway construction led the way, as veterans returned from national service to create the baby boom and be educated in unprecedented numbers by the GI Bill. President Dwight D. Eisenhower signed the National Defense Highway Act, the progenitor of a national interstate highway system that would permanently alter the face and character of American life.

Through the reverse telescope of today's mass media, America in 1960 is viewed as Roger Maris and Mickey Mantle, Marilyn Monroe and Brigitte Bardot, pillbox hats and bikini bathing suits, ranch-style houses and suburban subdivisions, drive-in theaters and restaurants, Ford Thunderbirds and Chevy

Corvettes, a limitless prospect of material plenty and leisure pastimes, and the dark specter of a possible nuclear war with the Soviet Union.[1]

A visitor to Maine forty years ago encountered a different, hardscrabble place—one outside the American mainstream and grappling mightily with problems of industrial decline, widespread and visible poverty, and chronic fiscal stringency. Maine's traditional manufacturing industries, save pulp and paper, were under massive, deadly assault from the South's cheaper labor, energy, and transportation costs; farm acreage was in precipitous decline; disaster impended in the commercial fisheries due, it was thought, to the arrival of foreign factory ships on the fishing grounds; and the poultry industry was about to founder upon its own rising costs, environmental outrages, and ineffectual management practices.

Maine in 1960 enjoyed a generations-old reputation as an exporter of young people who, after some military service, would labor a lifetime in Connecticut factories and others across the nation, to save money enough to "come home" for retirement; as a source of regionally inexpensive land, labor, and energy on which its own, once-prosperous mill towns and cities had been built; and as a quaint, safe, and serene haven for summer refugees from the cities of the Northeast and their growing populations and problems of neglect.

Today, after the demise, deregulation, and globalization of Maine's traditional industries, this static image of Maine has been overtaken by events. In the intervening years long-familiar, mainstay companies vanished from the Maine landscape and the first substantial wave of in-migration in a century washed over Maine, with impacts in every corner and sphere of life. Looking backward from the perspective of forty years, it is impossible not to recognize the impact of the ideas of JFK's "New Frontier" and, even more, the programs of President Lyndon B. Johnson's "Great Society" throughout Maine. State and local government became growth industries. Following a failed war and presidential resignation, the hopefulness of the Kennedy–Johnson era gave way to a general cynicism toward government, beyond traditional skepticism, that lingers to this day. All this and more—much more—has literally *transformed* Maine, the Maine landscape, and Maine's prospects for the future.

In the pages that follow, the story of this transformation is told in three parts that are intended, as the reader will see, to create a coherent, unifying whole among interconnected parts. In the first, we examine the growing complexity of Maine's economy and its interpenetration with the public sector.

Toward Greater Economic Viability

From the earliest days of the republic, the nation's founders recognized the importance of consistent information about who we are, of census-taking as a tool of governance and policy-making for both public and private purposes. How many of us are there? Where are we? Where did we come from? What do we do? The answers to these and similar questions help define our shared needs and shape business priorities and public policy.

The most recent decennial census was taken in the year 2000 amid much political controversy. As its results have been released, our newspapers and magazines have filled with the news that Maine is today among the oldest states in the nation and the slowest growing; that unlike the 1960s and '70s, few youths and young families are moving into Maine today, even as they leave our rural places in alarming numbers for more urban settings; and that for want of normal in-migration, we have become the lily-whitest state in the nation.

What do these findings portend? We have learned from the great migrations of the past, such as that from Ireland in the nineteenth century, that it can take generations and, especially, new economic and political institutions to rebuild a lost workforce, and from populations like those in Arizona and Florida, that rapid aging can exert a powerful influence on the political culture and behavior of a state. Demographers Richard Sherwood and Deirdre Mageean help us understand the changing characteristics of Maine people—our aging, the persistence of the "two Maines," and the "missing populations" that cast a shadow over our future.

Charles Colgan then documents the profound "structural" changes in the Maine economy over these decades and what he describes as the "urbanization" of the Maine economy. Maine's urbanization is a difficult idea to swallow for people long-accustomed to a rural self-image and national reputation. At one time as many as four out of every five of us depended for a living on Maine's rural land and water resources. In our agricultural heyday, around 1880, as much as one-third of the entire Maine landscape was cleared for farming. Today more than five-sixths of that land has reverted to forest, making Maine the most forested state in the nation. Colgan's novel thesis questions our very eyesight, then—even as it offers a new and useful understanding of the regional economic forces that shape the prospects and challenges before us.

We have observed that in 1960 Americans were generally celebrating the unprecedented power and beneficence of the postwar national economy. Then, in 1962, author and social activist Michael Harrington struck a responsive chord in the nation with his book, *The Other America: Poverty in the United States*.[2] In it he argued that tens of millions of our fellow citizens, from Mississippi to Maine, remained mired in poverty, trapped in what he termed a self-perpetuating "culture of poverty." Harrington urged a national response to these conditions and the direct result was President Johnson's "War on Poverty," which flourished for a time and, together with an expanding economy, reduced poverty in Maine and the nation by fully 20 percent within a decade.

Here, Lisa Pohlman discusses the dogged persistence of poverty in Maine in the past generation, despite the dramatic inroads made during the 1960s and '70s, and asks, "What of those who have been left behind as Maine has joined the nation's flight from basic manufacturing to a services- and knowledge-based economy?"

Of all the Maine "quality of life" issues today—housing, health care, and education—none is more basic than access to decent, affordable housing. The access that housing affords to transportation, to education and health care, to jobs and services, to nature and social activity is well-documented and clear for all to see. Affordable housing today is at the very center of our concern for Maine's future growth and development.

We have come a long way in housing Maine people in recent decades— much of it for the better, some for the worse. Prior to World War II most Maine housing lacked full indoor plumbing and electricity. All this has changed, due in large measure to enlightened public policy and action. Today, again due in large measure to public policy and action, it is *all but impossible* to build in any Maine city or town the kind of compact, economically efficient, and socially rich neighborhood in which most of us grew up. Today some have more housing than they might need, while others cannot find housing they can afford, where they need it. Frank O'Hara helps us sort out these complex and compelling issues and points to how we might provide the housing we need to help Maine grow, to build a housing future for Maine people that is at least as good as the recent past.

We then address the compelling and confounding issue of health care. In the late 1960s my family was vacationing in Stockton Springs, at the head of Penobscot Bay, when I came down with a terrible fever that had me bedridden for two days. My wife called the local doctor in Bucksport, who came out to visit later that day, examined me, prescribed an antibiotic that he took from his bag, and left a bill for all of *seven* dollars.

In the intervening decades, as Peter Mills argues in a later chapter, health care has become a dominant, highly technologized, and largely bureaucratized industry, and health care costs in the United States have, accordingly, gone from just over 5 percent of the nation's gross domestic product to some 14 percent today. Experts predict they will consume two to two-and-a-half times this share of *all* national wealth in coming decades, as the baby boom generation retires.

How did we get from the cottage industry of a generation ago to a place where, in Mills's words, health care has become virtually a semi-public utility, from which most people expect to receive services when they are needed, regardless of cost or ability to pay? By general agreement, there are three interrelated challenges today to effective health care policy: quality of care, access to care, and cost of care. Solving any two of these challenges is possible if the third is ignored; solving all three at the same time has proven elusive up to now, if not impossible. Still, Maine state government is today attempting this very feat! Elizabeth Kilbreth, one of the central participants in this effort, tells this dramatic story.

We next examine the largest of all cost drivers in the Maine public purse, public education. David Silvernail reviews the remarkable record of elementary and secondary public education in Maine since 1960, one that has transcended Republican, Democratic, and Independent administrations in Augusta. It is a tale of great investments of hard work, imagination, and money; of great collaborations among teachers, parents, administrators, and political leaders; and of great promise for all Maine people. Indeed, these changes over the last generation have made our public schools among the very finest in the nation today.

At the same time, public higher education in Maine, with all its abiding trials and tribulations, has proven remarkably resistant to changing times and needs. In 2003 the Maine Community College System finally came into existence, some three decades after many of the states we admire made this sensible move to overcome financial and psychological barriers to higher education. In 2004, and in response, the chancellor and board of trustees struggled mightily to create an affordable vision and effective strategy for the University of Maine System. Terrance MacTaggart offers his analysis of this institutional stasis, as well as his recommendations for ways and means to assure that higher education meets the needs of all Maine people in the twenty-first-century "knowledge" economy.

Finally, Peter Mills—state lawmaker and foremost among the students of Maine's much-maligned tax system—addresses the questions, "Where did all this government come from, and how did we pay for it?" The answer to both questions, of course, is *our taxes!* In the 1950s our modest state and local governments were all paid for from a 2 percent state sales tax and the local property tax, a portion of which went directly to the state, much as we pay for county government today. The great growth in both state and local government—and the extension of their services to new areas of concern—was made possible *only* by the advent of the state income tax, which was justified initially (as are all new Maine taxes) by the need to strengthen the public education of our children. Having recounted the history, Mills offers proposals to stabilize Maine's wildly erratic revenue stream, assure fairness in the burden of taxes, and restore common sense to the ongoing fiscal debate.

Toward Greater Community Vitality

Here we examine the connection between our economic and social well-being, and observe the increasing difficulty of distinguishing the two in today's world. We begin with the extraordinary changes in Maine's state and local governments since 1960. In this time, of course, Maine's land mass has not changed by a square foot, despite New Hampshire's best efforts to annex Seavey Island and the Portsmouth Naval Shipyard! Maine's population has grown by just 31 percent, to some 1.3 million persons. At the same time, state government employment has grown by 240 percent, and local government employment, by no less than 300 percent!

Put another way, in 1960 we had one state government employee for every ninety-four Maine citizens; today it is one for every fifty-one. In 1960 we had one local government employee for every fifty-one citizens; today there is one for every twenty-two citizens. This explosive growth in state and, especially, local government employment reflects a sea change in our society and in the roles our state and local governments play in our lives—with all their attendant benefits and costs.

Kenneth Palmer attempts to answer the question, "What does all this public sector growth *mean* for Maine?" What has been gained? What has been lost? What abides in Maine's civic life? In particular, Palmer finds the key to Maine's political culture in the abiding tension between "citizen participation" and professionalism in government—a tension we have yet to resolve happily.

We consider Maine civic life further by exploring Maine's *civic culture*—that is, the web of civic values and commitments we share and that tie us together as a community of people. The Maine traditions of community involvement and engagement go deep into our history and culture and are a source of both personal pride and community strength. It is impossible to imagine a Maine without the voluntary efforts Maine people have made at every level to build the lives of our communities, our institutions, our state and nation.

This is, I believe, a tale that grows in large measure out of the geographic isolation of Maine historically, of the frontier lives Maine people led for so long, and of their determination to build a better society of all, by all, and for all. This spirit of voluntarism is more than a matter of simple neighborliness, however; it is, in scholar Robert Putnam's mind, the key to building civic life and "social capital," the very foundation of economic prosperity.[3] To tell this important story and explain its implications, we have one of Maine's most acute observers of New England rural life and culture, Mark Lapping.

In 1960 Maine still had more than a million acres in farmland; today, that number is barely one-half as great, and the rate of change is accelerating. The State Planning Office reports that in the five years between 1992 and 1997 we converted some 34,000 acres *each year* to development, a rate four times that of the previous decade, and an amount greater than all the cropland in nine of our sixteen counties. Greater Portland was recently cited in a national survey by the Brookings Institution as among the ten most "sprawling" metropolitan areas in the nation, converting more land per capita for development than Nashville, Tennessee, and Orlando, Florida![4]

What does this change on the landscape we so love mean for Maine's future? Rachel Carson is rightly regarded by many as the intellectual source of the modern environmental movement, and, like all important change agents, Carson stood on the shoulders of others who had gone before her. One of these was the great forester and conservationist Aldo Leopold of Wisconsin. In his 1949 classic, *A Sand County Almanac,*[5] Leopold wrote that our very survival as a species depends upon our developing and embracing a "land ethic," one that enlarges the boundaries of our caring community to include soils, water, plants, and animals—or, collectively, the land.

"We abuse the land," Leopold continued, "because we regard it as a commodity belonging *to* us; when we see the land as a community to which *we* belong, we may begin to use it with love and with respect." As much as any in this nation, Maine people grasp Leopold's point and strive to live by it. How *are* we doing in this regard? Evan Richert discusses the past forty years of change on the Maine landscape and its unhappy implications—fiscal, ecological, and social—if we continue our present, inefficient land-use ways.

Maine today attracts more than 26 *million* out-of-state visitors each year. Beyond our diverse landscape, part of what attracts them is the rich heritage we enjoy of fine, applied, and performing arts; of crafts of all kinds; of civic, domestic, and commercial architecture—of what we know, love, and enjoy as *the creative arts and culture* in Maine. Soon after his election in 1964, President Johnson made the arts an important part of his Great Society program, and the new National Endowment for the Arts found no more lively arts community anywhere in the nation than here in Maine. Today, the fine, applied, and performing arts are more than a source of local pride and pleasure; they are increasingly understood as an engine of economic and community development all across Maine. Their importance to our well-being is growing, even as is our appreciation of them.

Alden Wilson recounts the growth and development of Maine's arts infrastructure and explores its potential as an economic driver for Maine's future. We learn that what we once thought of as the sole province of our nonprofit institutions is now of central importance to Maine's economic future.

The nonprofit sector of our economy—sometimes called the "third" sector, along with the private and public sectors—has grown remarkably in recent decades. Recent studies indicate that full-time employment in Maine's third sector now almost equals that in the manufacturing and tourism sectors, making it Maine's *third largest* source of employment today—with average annual wages *higher* than they are in the private sector as a whole, and in the local government sector, as well.

Today the nonprofit sector is a major economic, social, environmental, and political force in Maine life, and it is more so in Maine than in the nation as a whole. Dahlia Lynn tells the story of the growth in Maine's nonprofits, and a truly remarkable story it is—one that is little understood in terms of its scope and impact on our lives, and of the needs of the thousands of organizations that make up this important "third" sector of our economy.

Where were Maine *women* in 1960? Where have they come in the decades since? What did the women's movement of the 1970s achieve in Maine, and what is left undone today? No examination of Maine life since 1960 would be complete or meaningful without consideration of the dramatically altered roles of women in our everyday lives. In 1960 the civil rights movement had yet to reach its fullness in the land, to achieve its profound effect in American law and life—and, then, to give birth and momentum to the environmental, Native American, women's, and gay and lesbian rights movements.

In many respects the women's movement found fertile ground in Maine, with its cultural traditions and values of independence and neighborliness, of tolerance and fairness. At the University of Maine School of Law, by way of but a single example, there were *no* women in the graduating class of 1960; just two decades later, fully 48 percent of the graduating class of eighty-six new lawyers were women, and this rough parity continues to the present. The struggle for women's rights and equality in Maine, told here by Marli Weiner, is a remarkable and unfinished story of extraordinarily hard work, discipline, and devotion.

It is no exaggeration to say that in 1960, Native Americans were Maine's *forgotten* people—out of the mainstream, marginalized, often ostracized, their lot in life little publicized. Inspired by the civil rights movement of the 1960s and its accomplishments, Native Americans inserted themselves into the nation's consciousness and politics in unprecedented ways, and Maine's Native Americans were no exception. The Maine Indian Lands Claims case of the mid-'70s shook Maine to its very roots, and the 1980 Settlement Act marked the beginning of a new and more mature relationship between the races that has yet to reach its fullness. It is a powerful and continuing story told by Barry Dana, chief of the Penobscot Nation.

Finally, in the early 1950s the late Edmund S. Muskie and a small company of Democratic friends broke the lock the Republican Party had on Maine politics since before the Civil War. At every election time in his later years, the former governor, senator, and secretary of state was fond of remarking that when he ran for the governorship in 1954, the entire budget for his own campaign *and* that of the three Democratic candidates for the U.S. Congress was less than $20,000! (Maine had three seats in the U.S. House of Representatives at the time; if demographic trends continue, we may expect to have but one in 2020.) Today that 1954 figure is regularly exceeded by a single candidate for the Maine legislature, and to be "credible," a candidate for the governorship must demonstrate the ability to commit seven-figure amounts of his or her own or other people's money!

It is a sea change brought about by new expectations, new technologies, and new forms of political organization and communication in Maine elections. Chris Potholm addresses what all this means for our political culture and institutions.

Toward Greater Ecological Integrity
In the third and final part of the book we consider Maine's environment and the legacy of natural resources that have so long sustained us—and their abiding connection to our economic and community well-being. In 1960 public policy on the environment was limited largely to federal research and state monitoring of drinking water quality. This was before the era of state advocacy groups, when national conservation groups were occupied largely with fighting the construction of hydroelectric dams in some of the most pristine areas of the American West, along the Colorado River, and before the 1962 publication of *Silent Spring* by Rachel Carson, a summer resident of Southport Island.[6]

Carson's book would invoke the wrath of the nation's vast chemical industry and prompt President Kennedy to appoint a special commission to assess her assertions about the deadly impacts of chemical pesticides on *all* of life. Within a decade, amid mounting evidence that the human species was fouling its own nest, Republican and Democratic leaders in Washington forged a consensus that strong air and water quality laws were needed, and the U. S. Environmental Protection Agency was created by executive order of Republican President Richard M. Nixon.

Here in Maine a similar bipartisan effort produced a series of laws between the late 1960s and early '70s, during the administration of Democratic Governor Kenneth Curtis, that placed Maine squarely in the forefront among the states in environmental management and protection. There are several dozen Maine men and women—some no longer with us, the rest now getting along in years—whose names will forever be associated with this remarkable achievement: Edmund Muskie, Ezra Briggs, Marian Fuller Brown, Harry Richardson, John Martin, Sherry Huber, Jon Lund, John McKernan, Joseph Brennan, Bob Cummings, and Phyllis Austin are just a few of the best-known among them. There are *many* others, however, whose contributions were every bit as important and in some cases even more so. Orlando Delogu, who tells this story, is among them.

No sphere of Maine life has witnessed more dramatic events and change in the past forty years, or more volatility in response to changing market conditions, than that of energy. Waterpower fueled the nineteenth-century industrial revolution in Maine, which brought with it unprecedented prosperity for Maine people and unprecedented concentration of political power in the hands of Maine's public utilities and their leaders. This political power reached its zenith in the 1960s, and the ensuing decades brought repeated upheavals to challenge Maine industry, Maine lawmakers, and Maine citizens.

It is a tale of markets old and new, of energy sources come and gone, of government policies born and discarded, of private companies built and dissolved, of personal careers made and unmade. It is, in other words, a tale well worth the telling, as it is here by Cheryl Harrington, herself a witness to and thoughtful participant in much of the story.

Lloyd Irland next tells the bittersweet story of Maine's forests and the industry they have sustained from the time of earliest European settlement. John Sinclair, former president of the Seven Islands Land Company, once told me that if you wish to understand the Maine character, you must go into the Maine woods where that character was formed. Europeans first came here for cod, and what they found in great abundance was not just protein, but wood—the pine and spruce and birch that became the foundation of commerce and manufacturing by which we built our early prosperity, around which we built our towns and cities, and upon which we built a national reputation for making products of quality.

From Saco, Bath, Thomaston, West Paris, Norway, Skowhegan, Wilton, Bangor, and a hundred other Maine cities and towns came an immense variety of products from wood that the nation and world found not only useful but beautiful and lasting—and which made Maine one of the leading manufacturing states in the nation in the late nineteenth and the first half of the twentieth centuries. It is a fabulous story of resource use, human ingenuity, entrepreneurship, and community-building unsurpassed in the nation's history. In many ways, it made our state what it is today.

In the past generation, and especially in the last decade under the impact of a globalizing economy, as many as a thousand wood manufacturing businesses have disappeared from the Maine landscape, often with dire consequences for the communities of which they were part. As a result, the Maine wood products industry today faces challenges as great as any in its fabled history—as do many of the communities that historically organized around them and grew off their prosperity.

Little Spencer Mountain,
East Middlesex Canal Grant

Stewart Smith addresses the plight of one of our most treasured assets, and the very foundation of the landscape that has so strong a hold on the national imagination of Maine—agriculture. For more than a generation, national statistics have told a discouraging tale of Maine agriculture—one of steady decline in terms of both the total acreage of our farms and the number of families practicing farming on a full-time basis. These numbers mask a far more complicated picture, however—one that holds the promise and prospect of a resurgence of Maine agriculture in a new and more complicated form, if it is nurtured and helped along properly.

The Maine natural resource that is today under the greatest possible stress—as are the communities that have traditionally depended upon it—is Maine's fisheries. From the historic days of cod too abundant to imagine, today's disputed science, inept regulation, and rapacious technologies have brought many of Maine's fishing communities to the threshold of collapse. How could Maine—with some 400 years of fishing traditions, experience, and skill—have come to so unhappy a place? Two generations ago such a state of affairs was unimaginable to everyone involved—fishermen, politicians, and scientists, alike. It is a painful and, as yet, a not very promising story. James Wilson tells it and offers us hope in the form of a new ecosystems-based, decentralized, and "heterogeneous" approach to managing the Maine and New England fisheries.

Last—and hardly least—we turn to an industry that depends uniquely for its health and well-being upon that of Maine's natural resource base—Maine tourism. It is little appreciated that while farming, fishing, and forestry provide the necessary backdrop for Maine tourism, tourism affords more full-time equivalent jobs than all these natural resource-based industries combined. In 2001 tourist spending generated nearly 7 percent of *all* Maine's personal income, more than any sector except health care and the paper industry, and tourism's 78,000 full-time equivalent jobs make it Maine's second largest source of employment today.

With the steady decline in manufacturing jobs, many Maine communities look to tourism as one possible engine of their economic futures. For all of us who love Maine—including the many millions of visitors who come each year—the challenge has become, "How can we make the best of tourism and still avoid loving Maine to death?" David Vail has thought a lot about this question and offers a practical vision for "Vacationland" that will sustain both the tourism industry and the character of the communities that depend increasingly upon it.

Some Questions and Learnings
Thirty years ago, while researching a book on the relationship between Maine's natural resources and economic development prospects, A *Maine Manifest*,[7] I

asked my friend and colleague Arthur Johnson, then professor and later president at the University of Maine, what Maine might look like in another ten years. Johnson's response reflected the general mood of acceptance of the economic stasis that had characterized most of Maine, most of the time since World War I: "If you'd like to know what Maine will look like ten years from now," he observed, "just take a look at it now, or even ten years ago."

Today, as the world and the nation have changed, so has Maine. No longer structurally disadvantaged or culturally insulated by its geographic position "at the end of the line," Maine has been overtaken by the events of the past four decades to an extent that leaves many natives shaking their heads at the degree of the "Americanization" of Maine life. In a surprisingly brief time, the twentieth-century consumer economy and culture have spread across Maine's nineteenth-century agricultural landscape with effects in every city and town, every hamlet and village, every remote forest outpost and township.

Modern communications and transportation have left Maine no less vulnerable than any other place in the nation to changing demographics, economic cycles, and cultural influences: the aging of the baby boom, the decline of American manufacturing, the growth of the service sector and "knowledge" economy, the two-wage-earner household, the costly effects of sprawling development, the "graying" of our population, the ubiquity of television and the Internet, and the blurring of regional differences in everything from food and architecture to language and dress.

What are Maine's prospects amid all this change? Are we today at the mercy of accelerating history and global capital markets? Or can we, as individuals and as a community, take active steps and fashion measures to shape Maine's future? The only thing that can be said with certainty about the future, of course, is that it will bring *yet more* change. In light of this, the question becomes, "Can we shape the change upon us to advance the values and build the community we share?" It is useful to begin by asking what we can take away from the evidence of these forty years of a changing Maine.

We begin by remembering that there *are* things we want to improve and will continue to work to change: the persistence of poverty and the "two Maines" of opportunity and participation in the fullness of Maine life, both of which remain real and compelling; the precarious nature of the hard-won gains in Maine civil, women's, Native American, and gay and lesbian rights, which are not yet wholly part of our shared ethical mandate; the accelerating fiscal, environmental, and social costs of our sprawling land development patterns, especially in southern and south coastal Maine; the ineffectual policies that have left Maine fisheries and aquaculture in a shambles; the health care non-system that burdens our economy and leaves tens of thousands of Maine citizens without access to its benefits; the continuing barriers to higher education for too many of our people, denying them access to the new economy upon us; and the lack of nimbleness in response to changing conditions among too many of our public institutions.

Systems theory, of which I speak more below, teaches us that in the face of great changes, healthy systems survive not by clinging to outdated forms, structure, and behaviors, but by identifying *core values* and adapting forms, structures, and behaviors to ensure *their* survival. That is, to the extent that we value Maine's "different-ness," the quality of our small town life or landscape, or the "local control" of our governance, we must together examine the institutions and behaviors designed for another time and ask if they are adequate to the time in which we find ourselves. Where they are found wanting, we must seek the wisdom, the leadership, the courage, and the resources to change, if these values are to endure for the benefit of another generation of Maine people.

In one sense, after a generation of heroic effort and investment Maine people are better prepared for an uncertain future than ever before. Our transportation and communications systems have, in general, never been stronger compared to the rest of New England's and the nation's. A strong civic life persists at the core of Maine's communities. A vibrant and greatly expanded nonprofit sector has been built to "fill in" the many gaps left between the competencies of the private and public sectors. Maine's governing institutions remain among the most open, honest, and accessible of any in the world.

Still, this government operates best when it is at its most pragmatic, dealing effectively with the practical concerns and problems Maine people face in their everyday lives, where the private sector is found wanting. When it is driven by ideology and intransigence, as it was in the state government shut-down of 1991, the result is the unhappy imposition of New England's only legislative term limits law,[8] and the decade of largely hamstrung government that has followed on its heels.

It is increasingly clear that Maine's future prosperity will depend equally upon the vitality, efficiency, and effectiveness of all *three* sectors—the private, the public, and the nonprofit—working together for the good of all. New global markets have brought great changes to Maine's private sector—new technologies, new management techniques and practices, new structures and networks to support the complexity of operations needed to compete and survive today. Meanwhile, Maine's "third sector" has grown dramatically without, in most cases, benefit of these innovations from which it, its clients, and its sponsors would benefit. It is time the university system addressed the compelling need for something within its legitimate jurisdiction—for information, knowledge, and best-practice and technology transfer to Maine's overburdened and increasingly important nonprofit sector.

It is clear in the public sector, as well, that rising costs have run head-on into voter unhappiness and the inability of state and local government, alike, to adapt their form and structures to assure the preservation of important values, especially those of citizen participation and accountability. For its part, state government has clung to a hierarchical and largely centralized view of its role and failed to adequately fashion its delivery systems to meet the diverse needs of this highly various state and to engage local citizens effectively through them.

At the local level, almost 500 local governments conceived in the eighteenth century prove increasingly too numerous to be efficient and too small to deliver effective "local control" over economic markets—for land, labor, and customers—that are today invariably regional in nature. Whether state and local governments will respond to the challenge of greater regionalization of their organization and service delivery will largely determine the outcome of Maine citizens' efforts to meet the challenges of this new century.

Finally, a word about the one, indispensable ingredient in all democratic change—leadership. These forty years speak clearly to the point that *leadership matters*, and the nature of leadership *changes over time*. Throughout what was perhaps the most creative period in the history of Maine government—the two gubernatorial terms of Democrat Kenneth Curtis—both branches of the legislature were controlled by the Republican party. Notably, leaders of both chambers and the executive branch took an expansive view of the public good beyond partisanship and seized upon repeated opportunities to overcome differences and work to that end. The result was historic progress for the people of Maine. How different was this from the unhappy events two decades later that closed the doors of state government in apparent indifference to the needs of Maine people!

In 1959 Duane Lockard, the pre-eminent student of New England politics in his time, wrote of Maine:

> In few American states are the reins of government more openly or completely in the hands of a few leaders of economic interest groups than in Maine.... The abundance of timber and water power in Maine has created Maine's number one political problem: the manipulation of government by the overlords of the companies based on these resources.... Two groups (timber companies and paper manufacturers, and the developers of hydroelectric power), combined with the textile and shoe manufacturers, have done more than merely "influence" Maine politics; "control" is probably a more accurate term.[9]

Lockard's influential and enduring thesis was founded upon a set of assumptions that—with the demise, deregulation, and globalization of Maine's traditional industries—have been overtaken by reality. And what has emerged to take its place?

The evidence here suggests that we in Maine have moved from what one might call a corporate or "heroic" model to a more democratic, diverse, and diffuse model of leadership. This new model is based less upon the "movers and shakers" of old and the idea of leadership as the property of a single individual, and more on relationships among empowered actors and the idea of leadership as a *shared* act. Where once leadership consisted literally of an "old boys' network" who could "get things done," leadership in Maine lies now with *advocacy groups* and temporary alliances among them, based as much upon convenience as shared values and interests. Because it must, this new leadership relies less upon corporate leaders and more on assembling the essential functions of leadership from where they can and bringing them to bear on the purpose at hand.[10]

This is a formidable task, and it is not clear that this new model of leadership is adequate to the demands of the historic changes upon us; indeed, the evidence to date suggests otherwise. Still, scholars of American history from both the right and the left agree that while it may serve for good or ill, "democracy will stand or fall on the quality of its leadership."[11]

Toward the Fourth Era in Maine History

In the past three decades I have often heard, from leaders of one cause or another, the glib assertion that "Maine is at a crossroads!" (Indeed, it is the very first sentence of *A Maine Manifest.*) The expression evokes Robert Frost's imagery of the road "less traveled by," of the possibility of effective choice, self-determination, and control over a world we are about to enter.[12]

From the evidence here, however, it is apparent that the crossroads metaphor is not appropriate to Maine today; that Maine has been literally *transformed* by the events of the past forty years; that we have come fully into a new world, a new time—a new political-economic era, if you will. This new era, like previous eras in Maine history, will require of us new ways of thinking, new ways of understanding, new ways of organizing ourselves as a community of people—if the values and culture we share and cherish are to endure. Unlike forty years ago, none of us is any longer certain what the future will hold—except that it *will* be different.

It helps to recall that since European settlement, Maine has enjoyed (more or less, at various times) three, distinct political-economic eras. The first and harshest—extending from around 1600 through the 1780s—was a time of insecure and interrupted settlement in places like Damariscove and Richmond Islands, the Pemaquid and Georgetown peninsulas, and York and Falmouth (today's Portland). These settlements were all characterized by a largely coastal economy, foreign market domination for our products, and various defensive compacts for sheer survival of the scattered communities. Indeed, we went so far at the time as to join Massachusetts!

The second period followed the creation of the United States, which put to rest once and for all the governance and security questions. For, after all, it is hard to invest one's life and fortune when it is not clear just who is in charge and whether disputes will be resolved peacefully! Within a generation Maine's population increased ten-fold, from some 30,000 persons to more than 300,000, and Maine became a state of its own. What followed has been characterized as Maine's "Golden Age" of agriculture and cottage industry, extensive settlement up the great river valleys of the Androscoggin, the Kennebec, the Penobscot, and the St. John, and the growth of our highly decentralized and individualistic local governments.

The third period, beginning after the Civil War and lasting through most of the twentieth century, was a period of industrial rise and decline, of what has been called "managerial capitalism" that was capital intensive, largely urban, highly centralized and hierarchical in its nature, and increasingly non-Maine in its ownership and control. Its corporate structure was largely replicated in the state government that grew during this time; its dirty industrial processes eventually drove people from our cities into a now-sprawling suburban landscape.

Several "operating principles" of economic and community development were established in this third era and generally embraced by Maine's political elites: first, that more and bigger is generally better; second, that community development will naturally flow *from* economic development, regardless; third, that the economy and the environment may, at best, be held in a "balance" that would not kill us in the end; fourth, that whatever environmental problems exist are in fact the corporate managers' responsibility, and not our own, personally; and, finally, that the public and private sectors are uneasy allies at best, if not natural enemies![13] Thirty years ago, then, Maine agonized mightily over the idea of an aluminum smelter in Trenton, oil refineries in Machiasport and Searsport, and similar development proposals that might capitalize on a unique resource (such as deep-water ports) and provide the "big bang" or "magic bullet" our rural communities needed to reverse their fortunes.

Today we have come into a new era, in need of a *new* organizing principle— a new language, a new *story*, if you will—a new narrative for our continuing development as a community of people. For much of the 1990s and into this century, it has appeared that unbridled greed might offer this principle for the nation as a whole, "and the devil take the hindmost." For much of the past decade, as well, many of the contributors to this volume and others have been asking the question, "Can the idea of *sustainable development* contribute to the new narrative Maine needs?" Many of the authors make reference to this idea in their chapters, so it is worthy of some discussion here.

During the nation's first great wave of environmental policy making in the late 1960s and early '70s, most of the problems we dealt with were local, the products of individual discharge pipes and smokestacks. Environmentalist Garrett Hardin gave the nation and, especially, the U.S. Congress the idea of "the tragedy of the commons," to which his recommended solution was "mutual coercion mutually agreed upon."[14] The end result was the strict regulation by government of these pollution sources to clean up our rivers, our lakes, and our air. As private industry responded to public coercion and the environmental movement gathered momentum, the public's attention shifted in the 1980s to the national and international scenes—to global population growth, acid rain, the destruction of tropical rainforests, depletion of the ozone layer, and global warming.

Research soon made it clear that the causes of this "second generation" of environmental concerns lay not in exhaust pipes and smokestacks, but in the very nature and organization of our everyday human activities—especially in North America and Europe. One report after another concluded that much of what we do, many of our efforts to make what we call "progress," cannot and will not be sustained indefinitely on this planet of limited resources. We cannot indefinitely continue in our ways of using energy, transporting goods and people, managing forests and farmlands, protecting plant and animal species, managing suburban sprawl, and producing industrial goods without inevitably compromising our natural heritage and bankrupting the future!

In light of the growing evidence to this effect and the prospect of these practices spreading worldwide, the United Nations General Assembly in 1984 appointed a World Commission on the Environment and Development, chaired by Norwegian Prime Minister Gro Harlem Brundtland. The commission's report, known as the *Brundtland Report*,[15] borrowed the idea of "sustainable development" from the work of economist Herman Daly and adopted it as the central theme of its recommendations. It defined sustainability, simply, as *a continuing process of social and economic development that meets the needs of the current generation without compromising the ability of future generations to meet their own needs*. It is founded upon the commonsense notion that one cannot indefinitely live off the principal of one's heritage or endowment, that this will exhaust itself in time. Instead, one can only live, grow, and prosper indefinitely off the interest on this principal, through prudent savings and careful, timely investments.

In 1987 the U.N. General Assembly adopted the commission's report and commended it to the member governments. In July of the same year the G–7 Summit, including the United States, called for the "early adoption, worldwide, of policies based on sustainable development." In April 1991 the International Chamber of Commerce drafted a "Business Charter for Sustainable Development" that has since been endorsed by many hundreds of corporations worldwide, including 3M, Chevron, Alcoa, Interface, Dow Chemical, and DuPont. In 1992 the United Nations World Conference on Environment and Development in Rio de Janeiro, known as the Rio Earth Summit, adopted a model local sustainable development plan known as Agenda 21. It is today being used as a guide to sustainability by nations and communities around the globe, with the notable exception of the United States. Governments in Japan, Malaysia, New Zealand, India, Australia, Denmark, Belgium, the Netherlands, Germany, Sweden, Canada, and elsewhere have made serious national, provincial, and local commitments to its principles and practice.

The concept recognizes that economic activity and natural resources are inextricably linked; that the quality of present and future life rests on meeting basic human needs without compromising the natural systems on which all life depends; and that new forms of dialogue and collaboration among government, business, and society-at-large will be needed to achieve the goal of a sustainable society. It requires not just a current understanding of economics and efficiency, but a shared vision and an ethic based upon inclusion not only among people and nations, but between the generations.

First and foremost, sustainable development means a break once and for all with the ancient mindset that has pitted economic opportunity against the environment and placed human and community concerns on the sidelines of the struggle for "progress" and "a better life." This is the basis for what is known as the "three-legged stool" of sustainability, connecting economic, ecological, and social well-being.

Toward More Sustainable Maine Communities
Several years ago my colleague and contributor to this volume, Charles Colgan, studied the Canadian national and provincial "roundtables" established by government to prepare a sustainable development strategy.[16] He found that sustainable development is not an inevitable replacement for traditional approaches to development, even (especially?) when it is prescribed from above. Political cycles do not conform to economic cycles, and new governments do not necessarily "own" their predecessors' strategies and policy commitments.

Nor does the commitment to sustainable development, in itself, resolve the continuing conflicts that emerge between economic development and environmental values. It does, however, force the issues to the table and test whether the existing mechanisms for resolving these conflicts are adequate to the task. While much of what the roundtables recommended made sound policy sense, Colgan found, policy recommendation does not equal policy adoption or implementation. *Knowing the right thing to do is not the same as doing it!*

Here in the United States the President's Council on Sustainable Development learned from the Canadian experience. In its 1997 report the council recognized the interdependence among economic, environmental, and social health and well-being, and, importantly, that sustainable development for the nation means, first and foremost, sustainable development of the places in which we live our daily lives—that is, *sustainable communities*.[17] The council provided no single definition of a sustainable community or description of one type of city, town, or region. What it did find in common among the communities it studied is a new kind of "ecosystems thinking" applied to *all* of their development efforts.

What *is* systems thinking? First, it involves the shift from discrete objects to relationships—from thinking separately about things like the economy, the environment, and the community, as if all three were not intimately and lastingly connected. It is the *relationship* between them that is of interest and concern to the systems thinker—that is, *the network* they create and the flow of communication and information between them that allows the system as a whole to learn, to organize and reorganize itself, and to adapt to changing circumstances and requirements.

The Second Law of Thermodynamics teaches us that *all* systems tend toward disorganization, or entropy, without the infusion of energy; that is, unless they are tended to *as a system*, they will disorganize of their own accord! Finally, in all healthy systems, competition, dominance, and control coexist with communication, cooperation, and collaboration in their maintenance. As a result, all competition, all the time, is not system development; it is chaos!

The "three-legged stool" of sustainable development links its three constituent elements as shown in this flow diagram:

Economic
Viability

Ecological
Integrity

Community
Vitality

What does all this mean for Maine? For some time now my students at the Muskie School and I have been looking at places like Canada, New Zealand, and the Netherlands; at North American cities like Toronto, Seattle, San Diego, Austin, Jacksonville, Chattanooga, and Burlington; at island and mainland communities here in Maine; and at private businesses—companies like Guilford Industries of Maine—that have organized serious, ongoing efforts around this systems approach.

We have learned that "sustainable development" remains today less than a full-blown theory; it lacks, for example, the formal elaboration that Adam Smith accorded capitalism, itself, in his classic *Wealth of Nations*,[18] from the vantage of a couple hundred years of experience with it in the Netherlands, Scotland, and elsewhere. We have, however, begun to observe what we might call ten useful *principles of sustainable community*. They include:

1. *The Novelty Principle.* First, sustainable development is *not* just old wine in a new bottle; it is a fundamentally new and different way of thinking about the world and how it works when it is both healthy and just. Not a "magic bullet" or a substitute for private markets, it is new way of understanding the market economy, its important role in society, and its requirements as a long-term generator of both private wealth and public good.

2. *The Unity Principle.* Second, and as is well-understood by Maine's island communities, it starts from a profound and simultaneous commitment to *economic viability, ecological integrity, and community vitality*—which are *not* to be balanced against one another but to be effectively *married* in a single, enduring unit.

3. *The Diversity Principle.* Third, sustainability is not a road map to a single, certain destination or outcome, but a framework that leads to a class of possible outcomes—like life, itself, with its warm- and cold-blooded creatures, vertebrates and invertebrates, and so on. Getting there is less a matter of technical knowledge or structural issues than of appropriate policies, institutions, and personal behaviors.

4. *The Nimbleness Principle.* Further, while there is no one way to achieve sustainability, it does require flexibility, creativity, and adaptability to changing market and environmental conditions—that is, *nimbleness* in personal, business, and policy responses to change.

5. *The Pragmatic Principle.* Fifth, it is facilitated by a certain set of attitudes or dispositions on peoples' part: a slight (but not debilitating) dissatisfaction with the present; a positive attitude toward experimentation; a well-regulated private market system; effective planning for fragile or scarce resources; high levels of intra- and inter-community discussion and decision-making; and a history of effective implementation of these decisions.

6. *The Systems Principle.* Sixth, marrying the three core elements requires what is called "systems thinking" and an understanding of its basic needs: a shift from objects to relationships; high levels of information sharing and feedback; high levels of cooperation, even among competing actors; and a readiness to adapt form and structure to preserve and protect core values. Successful "intentional" communities, like the Benedictines and Amish, understand this well.

7. *The Community-First Principle.* Seventh, the traditional way *into* the unbroken economy–environment–community circle has been seen as economic growth, regardless of its quality: more jobs will kick the system into action. We have come to believe that effective and lasting access is gained first and foremost through increasing community vitality and competence. That is, as Putnam has argued, social capital *precedes* rather than follows upon general economic prosperity.[19]

8. *The Discontinuous Principle.* Eighth is an understanding—even a faith—that system change generally does not occur as a continuous event, but comes as a discontinuous occurrence when a "tipping point" is reached.[20] Do we know when? Well, we do know something of the economics and ecology of tipping points, but we know much less about the social and community factors involved. We are learning, however, that things like acknowledged fairness, widespread trust, and mutual give-and-take play very large parts in it.

9. *The Persistence Principle.* Ninth, sustainability is *not* easy work or for the faint-hearted or the non-persevering. It involves *change*, profound change in the ways that we gather information, we know, we understand, we envision, we relate, and we go about our daily lives. It is at once as simple and as difficult as understanding that prosperity and success lie less in quantity than in quality, less in objects than in relationships, less in outward form than in personal outlook and commitment to values.

10. *The Here and Now Principle.* Tenth, we can only start toward sustainability from where we are! Creating the successor to industrial capitalism as a world view and building sustainable communities means spreading the word; making it safe for change agents and opinion leaders to try, to fail, and to succeed; and concentrating on early successes and building on them at every opportunity.[21]

Much about Maine has changed since 1960, and much has persisted, as well. As a result, Maine is well suited today to this more "sustainable" way of building our shared future. Maine people share the core values of a deep and abiding respect for nature and its *own* requirements, one that long pre-dates modern environmentalism; long-standing habits of industry, thrift, innovation, adaptation, and pragmatism; and, perhaps above all, mutual trust and lifelong devotion to community, fairness, and democratic decision-making. Now the task is just to *marry* these values in *all* our development efforts.

How do we overcome the present to achieve a sustainable Maine? What of the vested interest we have in doing things as we have done them for the past century or more, holding community vitality, economic viability, and ecological integrity largely separate from one another? Well, dear reader, read on— and recall the words of my favorite economist, Joseph Schumpeter, who once remarked that the power of vested interests is vastly exaggerated when compared to the gradual encroachment of ideas. Not in the near run, surely, but sooner or later it is ideas that rule the day, that make the difference in how we live our lives! "We are all," Schumpeter observed wryly, "the captives of some defunct philosopher."

The authors of this book share the conviction that ideas make a difference; that there is nothing so powerful as an idea whose time has come; and that in a democracy, dialogue and discourse are the best means we have of testing its truth and durability.

Much about Maine has changed since 1960, and more change is headed this way, like it or not. If we do not get it right, we may surely anticipate the relentless march of the larger, homogenizing American culture across the Maine landscape, the continuing departure of our young, the decline of our rural communities, and the erosion of our natural heritage.

If, on the other hand, we do get it right, we may look forward to an era of a more decentralized and responsive state government; more effective and efficient (if a little more distant) local government; an economy built upon high standards of quality and high-end products and services; new, compact villages in which to raise our children and renew community life; a new stream of leaders from the nonprofit sector to fill the void left by our changed corporate structure; a community college system that eases the passage of every high school graduate and adult learner to the world of opportunity and responsibility; high-speed rail connections to and from Boston and an efficient, multimodal transit system to move goods and people throughout Maine; a thriving arts and culture sector that drives the revitalization of our downtowns; and a natural environment that remains accessible to all and the envy of the nation.

The challenge is nothing less than to reinvent ourselves in this new era— not our values, which may abide, but the outward forms and structures that give expression to them in out everyday lives. The final and ultimate question, then, is, "How do we recreate ourselves in order to assure the preservation of what we cherish most?" The choice, as we begin this new era, is ours to make. It is a daunting and exciting prospect!

*E*ducated at Harvard College, the University of Massachusetts, and MIT, Richard E. Barringer served in the administrations of Governors Kenneth Curtis, James Longley, and Joseph Brennan. Since 1987 he has served as consultant on strategic planning and public policy development to various organizations, and as co-founder and director of three nonprofit research and public education organizations in Maine. In 1987–88 he was visiting professor of economics at the University of Maine, after which he became professor and founding director of the Edmund S. Muskie School of Public Service at the University of Southern Maine. He is now research professor at the Muskie School and director of the EPA/New England Environmental Finance Center. He is the author or editor of six books, numerous articles and reports, and many landmark Maine laws in the areas of education, the environment, energy, economic development, and fiscal policy. Before moving to Maine in 1973 he taught at the John F. Kennedy School of Government and co-founded a successful non-profit firm in government program evaluation.

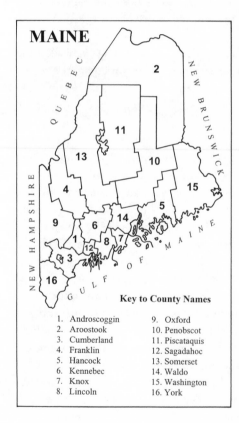

MAINE

Key to County Names

1. Androscoggin
2. Aroostook
3. Cumberland
4. Franklin
5. Hancock
6. Kennebec
7. Knox
8. Lincoln
9. Oxford
10. Penobscot
11. Piscataquis
12. Sagadahoc
13. Somerset
14. Waldo
15. Washington
16. York

County Locator Map

ONE
Toward Greater Economic Viability

FIVE DEMOGRAPHIC FORCES critically affect Maine society today and tomorrow: the aging and passing of Maine's "baby boomers"; the changing composition of our family households; our lack of diverse populations; the trend toward low-density living arrangements; and the geographic divergence of employment opportunities. The results of these trends include heightened demand for housing despite slow population growth, a sprawling landscape, and increased concentration of the state's population along and near our shores and coast. Young people leave the state in large numbers even as retirees move in. As Maine looks to the future, the policy implications of these trends will demand the most careful consideration and creative responses.

1 Demography and Maine's Destiny

RICHARD SHERWOOD and DEIRDRE MAGEEAN

Five aspects of Maine's recent demographic history shape our destiny—today, tomorrow, and for the foreseeable future. They may be characterized as: the passage of Maine's baby-boomers; Maine's changing households; Maine's missing populations; Maine's suburbanization; and, finally, Maine's geographic divergence. These changes in our population offer important insights not only into our past, but into our shared future.

Our approach in this chapter will be to outline the demographic facts of these changes, then to pose some of the issues and questions that these facts suggest to us. To provide the reader with historical context for these recent changes, we begin with some comparisons between Maine and the nation, to which we shall return later.

- Maine had just under a million residents in 1960, and a million and two hundred seventy-five thousand in 2000, a one-third increase in population. The U.S., including the new states of Alaska and Hawaii, had slightly fewer than 180 million residents in 1960, and slightly more than 280 million in 2000, an increase of almost 60 percent.

- In 1960, the average age of the Maine and U.S. populations was twenty-nine, with the Maine population a fraction of a year younger than the U.S. The U.S. median increased to age thirty-five in 2000, while Maine's increased to thirty-nine, making it the third oldest state in the nation after West Virginia and Florida.

- The Maine and U.S. crude birth rates—that is, births per thousand residents—were almost identical in 1960, with the Maine rate just slightly higher than the U.S. Both rates fell between then and 2000; but Maine's fell further, and was 25 percent below the U.S. rate in 2000.

- Maine's crude death rate in 1960 was somewhat higher than the U.S., with one and one half more deaths per thousand residents. Both rates fell between then and 2000, but Maine's fell slightly further, so that in 2000 it was only one death per thousand higher than the U.S.

- Maine's rate of natural increase—that is, the number of births per thousand residents minus the number of deaths—was nine-tenths that of the U.S. rate in 1960. As a result of the changes we have noted in birth and death rates, however, Maine's rate of natural increase had declined by 2000 to less than two-tenths the U.S. rate.

- Both Maine and the U.S. experienced positive net migration over the forty years from 1960 to 2000; that is, more people moved to the U.S. and to Maine than left. In the case of the U.S., the migration was to and from destinations overseas; while in the case of Maine, it included movements both to and from overseas and to and from the other forty-nine states.

In summary, Maine's birth rate, which was similar to the U.S. rate in 1960, has since fallen substantially below the U.S. rate. Maine's death rate, which was higher than the U.S. rate in 1960, has fallen further than the U.S. rate, but still remains above it. While both Maine and the U.S. had net positive migration over the forty years from 1960 to 2000, it contributed less to Maine's population growth than to the growth of the U.S. The combined effect of all this is that Maine's population has grown at only a little more than *one-half* the U.S. rate.

The Passage of Maine's Baby Boomers: A Mighty Wave
1960 marked the crest of the post-World War II baby boom, which lasted from 1947 to 1964. After 1964 the number of births declined rapidly due to, among other things, the widespread adoption of the birth control pill and the legalization of abortion. Maine, which averaged 22,000 births a year during the baby boom, has averaged only 16,000 a year since. Indeed, in 2000 and the five years preceding, births have been below 14,000 a year, the fewest since we started keeping records in 1892, when Maine's population was only half its present size. Births since 2000 have remained below 14,000.

The baby boom was not a surprise to demographers; baby booms often follow wars. They occur as people catch up on the marriages and childbearing that have been deferred by war, and respond to the more optimistic outlook fostered by postwar social and economic conditions. What *was* a surprise was the duration and magnitude of the baby boom—seventeen years, with a total of 72,000,000 births in the U.S., and 400,000 in Maine. People were not only making up for the lost war years, but also for the prior Great Depression, when economic conditions discouraged marriage and family formation.

One can visualize the baby boom as a wave forming far out at sea and rolling in towards the beach, over several decades. Immediately ahead of it, closer in, is a trough, representing the 40 percent fewer births during the Great Depression and World War II. Further out, twenty-seven years behind the baby boom, is the crest of a following, smaller wave. Sometimes described as the baby boom echo, this wave is made up of the baby boomers' children. Between the baby boom and their children is another trough, containing the few children of the Depression and World War II birth cohorts. In the coming decade, a third wave—the baby boomers' grandchildren—will begin to form. However, it is projected to be still more attenuated, a faint echo of an echo.

The wave metaphor suggests that we think of social institutions as boats tethered to a jetty which extends out into the water. Tethered farthest out are the boats (or institutions) that the wave first encounters: the individual's family of orientation, his or her play group, day care center, and nursery school. Then come religious instruction, elementary school, middle school, high school, trade school, and college. Next are workplace, commercial and financial institutions, the individual's family of procreation, civic groups, political and governmental institutions, and so on. Still further inshore are the institutions addressing the later years of life: pensions, retirement communities, elderhostel, Medicare, assisted living, and so on. As a wave or trough rolls toward shore, it successively passes the clusters of moored boats, although its strength or force is attenuated and gradually depleted.

Pursuing our metaphor, an important feature of the wave-like character of population fluctuations is that the passing waves and troughs set the boats to pitching and rolling and straining at their tethers, always at risk of damaging their hulls on the jetty or even of parting their lines and being swamped. It is important, therefore, to allow enough slack in the lines for the boats to fall and rise with the passing waves and troughs.

Figure 1. Passage of the Baby Boomers: 1960

Number of Maine Residents

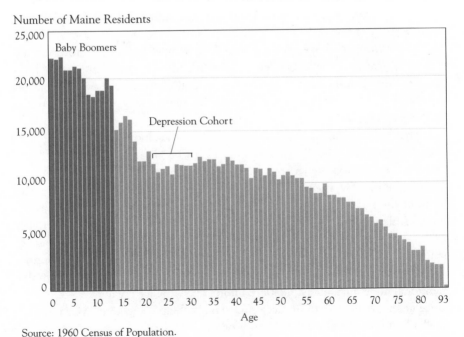

Source: 1960 Census of Population.

Demography and Maine's Destiny

In 1960 the baby boomers were under age fourteen, with the oldest just about to enter high school, with more than 100,000 still to be born in Maine; some forty years later, in 2000, they were between the ages of thirty-six and fifty-three. Comprising as it does such a large portion of the population, the baby boom wave dragged the median age of the Maine population upward ten years from twenty-nine in 1960 to thirty-nine in 2000. It would have pulled the median even higher, were it not for the following wave of baby boomer children. The baby boom generation also pulled the U.S. median upward in 2000, but by much less—a point to which we shall return later, when we discuss Maine's missing populations.

After the end of the baby boom in 1964, births declined for a dozen years and then swelled as the baby boom women reached childbearing age and began having their own children. Although the boomer women had fewer children per woman than had their mothers and older sisters, the following wave was still large because of the many potential mothers in the original baby boom. This wave crested at 17,500 births in 1989, when the baby boom women were between the ages of twenty-five and forty-two. Then, births fell to fewer than 14,000 a year in the nineteen-nineties, as the older baby boom women began to enter menopause. Today, in 2003, the youngest baby boom women are thirty-nine and nearing the end of their childbearing years.

The trough following the end of the baby boomers' childbearing years has already roiled educational institutions and will continue doing so into the future. By 2000, public school enrollments in kindergarten through grade five had fallen as result of the decline in births after 1989. Projections by Sherwood to 2015 show this grade-level continuing to decline until 2007, then growing very slightly thereafter as the baby boomers' grandchildren begin to enter school. Middle school enrollment has now begun to decline, which Sherwood projects will continue until 2011, after which it will resume growing at an anemic one-third of one percent per year.

High school enrollments will follow, starting to decline in 2005 as the trough continues towards shore. Projections to 2012 by the National Center for Education Statistics show a similar trend, with *total* Maine public school enrollment declining until 2009, then leveling off. Some already-small schools in rural areas confront the possibility that these declining enrollments will force them to close. While enrollment of traditional undergraduates may decline as this trough rolls past age eighteen, the University of Maine System has other constituencies which can allow it to continue growing. Enrollment in graduate school, continuing education, and Senior College are all healthy and can offset declines in the traditional undergraduate population. Efforts to encourage greater college attendance among Maine youth, if successful, can also help compensate for the smaller numbers of eighteen- to twenty-two-year-olds ahead.

Figure 2. Passage of the Baby Boomers: 2000

Number of Maine Residents

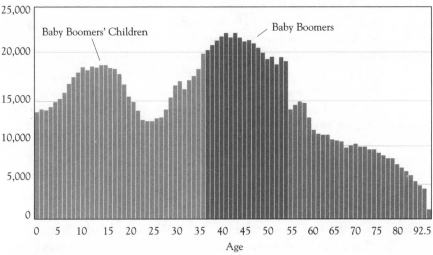

Source: 2000 Census of Population.

The baby boomers were too young in 1960 to move out of their parents' homes and establish independent residences; by 2000, all were old enough, and nearly all had. Thus, the maturation of the baby boomers created a demand for an additional 91,000 homes in 2000—a number equal to a third of all homes in 1960. What had been two households in 1960 with perhaps three children each had become five households in 2000: the two parental households, plus the three created by the marriages of the children. This does not include the additional homes resulting from changing lifestyles and occupancy patterns that we shall discuss later.

About the time the first baby boomers were turning eighteen and leaving their parents' homes in the mid-1960s, Maine's migration flow unexpectedly reversed itself. For the preceding quarter of a century, more people had been leaving Maine than entering it. Indeed, if one overlooks a small net in-migration of fewer than 3,000 people during the 1930s (most likely Mainers who had left the state earlier, and returned home to wait out the Great Depression with relatives), then Maine had had nearly continuous out-migration since 1910.

This 1960s reversal of the historic rural-urban migration flow was not peculiar to Maine; it occurred in New Hampshire and Vermont, as well. It occurred in Virginia just beyond the other end of BOSWASH—the Boston to Washington megalopolis; and it occurred around the fringes of all the megalopolitan areas in the Midwest and on the West Coast.

Several factors contributed to the new urban-rural flows. One was the completion of the interstate highway system. Now, one could live in rural Maine or Vermont or Virginia and be but a two-, three-, or four-hour drive from Boston or New York. A second factor was cheap housing and land. Decades of rural out-migration had held down demand for rural land and housing and kept prices low. This would have been particularly attractive to young baby boomers starting out in life.

The third factor was a back-to-the-land movement among the baby boomers. This was one of several ways the baby boomers sought to live a more authentic lifestyle than that of their parents. The back-to-the-landers were undoubtedly a tiny percentage of the boomer population, but given the enormous pool of boomers, the back-to-the-landers still represented a sizable *number* of individuals. Furthermore, once here, they offered potential contacts for other baby boomers who were not themselves back-to-the-landers but who were casting about for suitable places to settle. For it is the case universally that most migrants choose destinations where they have friends or relatives.

Maine had a net flow out-of-state between 1980 and 2000 of people right out of high school and in their twenties, and a countervailing in-flow of people thirty to forty-four. These flows of young adults out and older adults in have been important sources of the aging of the population over these two decades.

Many of the young adults leaving were the children of baby boomers, while many of the older adults moving in were baby boomers themselves. One wonders how much both flows were shaped by the initial in-migration of baby boomers in the 1960s and '70s. How many of the young people leaving Maine in the '80s and '90s were the children of baby boomers who moved to Maine earlier? Were the decisions by these young people to leave related to the fact that their in-migrant parents had family and friends out of state who provided contacts for the young people? How many of the thirty- and forty-year-olds moving to Maine in the 1980s and '90s were baby boomers? Were their decisions to come influenced by contacts with relatives and friends who moved to Maine in the earlier in-migration of baby boomers? Certainly, migration has markedly increased the links between Maine and other states since 1960. The proportion of Maine residents born in other states, and likely to have family or friends there, more than doubled between 1960 and 2000.

The baby boomers began entering the labor force in the early 1960s. By 2000, they had twenty to thirty-five years of work experience and made up almost half the working-age population. One might have expected that their work experience and large numbers would pull the average earnings of the overall labor force upward, just as they have pulled the average age of the population upward. The law of supply and demand, on the other hand, would suggest that the potential labor supply represented by the boomers should have kept wages low; and, indeed, that seems to be the case. Average labor force earnings in constant dollars were no higher in 2000 than they had been in 1970, even though the 2000 labor force had a much larger percentage of very experienced workers. Exerting additional downward pressure on wages has been the increased labor force participation of baby boomer women. Between 1960 and 2000, the percentage of women in the paid labor force almost doubled.

The baby boomers began turning age forty-five in 1992. For most people, the age range from forty-five to fifty-five or sixty is the lifetime peak of earnings and savings. They are established in their careers. They have purchased and furnished their homes. Their children have left or are leaving home. Expenses are declining, while their incomes are as high as they're ever going to be. On the other hand, after age sixty or sixty-five, most will spend more than they earn, as they draw down their pensions and life savings in retirement. The bull market of the 1990s, the ready availability of capital, and low interest rates throughout the decade and beyond were surely connected to the pool of savings accumulated by the baby boomers as they began to pass age forty-five. One might hypothesize, as well, that some of the recent gains in labor force productivity reported for the nation are due to the large number of baby boomers who now have twenty or more years of work experience.

Figure 3. Passage of the Baby Boomers: Projected to 2025

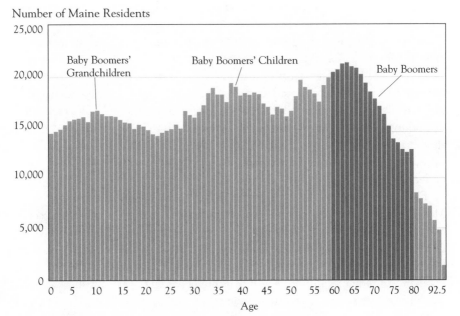

Source: U.S. Census Bureau A-Projections. Issued October 1996.

As the baby boom wave continues on, it will begin to roll past age sixty-five in 2012. By 2029 it will have entirely passed sixty-five, and the leading edge will be beyond age eighty. Pessimism is frequently expressed about the ability of the economy to produce all the goods and services society will need, if the large labor force of baby boomers is allowed to retire. Will subtracting that many workers from the economy create labor shortages and force up wages?

A statistic called the "dependency ratio" allows one to compare the burdens different age structures impose on the economy. The ratio is based on the existence of age-graded activities: on the fact that society encourages or discourages selected activities at different ages, and that participation in the labor force is one of those activities. Forbidding children to work in factories is an example of labor force age-grading; so is providing pensions that encourage seniors to exit the labor force, to retire. This, by the way, was an explicitly stated motive for the creation of Social Security in the Great Depression, namely, to encourage seniors to quit work, so the young could find jobs.

Generally, our society discourages full time labor force participation before high school graduation, or about age eighteen, while full Social Security benefits are available at age sixty-five, with many private pensions available even earlier. The dependency ratio tells us how many potential dependents there are (persons under eighteen or over sixty-five) for every hundred persons of working age (eighteen to sixty-four). Since there are some persons under eighteen and over sixty-five in the labor force and some persons eighteen to sixty-four not in the labor force, the dependency ratio gives only an approximation to the burden imposed by age grading.

As you might guess, the 1960 dependency ratio was high. There were eighty-eight potential dependents—persons under eighteen or over sixty-five—for every hundred Maine residents of working age. The baby boomers, all of whom were under fourteen, accounted for two-thirds of the potential dependents. By 2000 the baby boomers were between the ages of thirty-six and fifty-three, all of working age, and the dependency ratio had declined by a third. (In 1990 there was relative generational balance between the two dependent populations, the increase in the elderly population being offset by the decline in those under age eighteen.)

The year 2025 is the farthest out for which there are age projections for Maine, to allow us to calculate a dependency ratio. By then, four-fifths of the baby boomers will be over sixty-five and potential retirees. While the projected 2025 dependency ratio is higher than that of 2000, it is still one-fifth less than the 1960 ratio. This suggests that the effect on the labor force of the baby boomers' retirement will not be as dire as predicted by the pessimists, and that we shall be able to say, "Been there, done that, and more, in 1960."

By 2025, at least *a fifth* of the total Maine population will be over age sixty-five. With this in mind, Governor Angus King, Jr., adopted a policy of fostering the growth of the retirement industry in Maine. To our surprise, we found that there are retirement flows to relatively cold weather areas such as Cape Cod, and that Maine already has an edge, with more people moving here to retire than the number of Maine retirees leaving for warmer climates like Florida and Arizona. The retirement industry has several desirable features. It is a clean industry. It brings new money into the state from the pensions and Social Security and health insurance benefits migrant retirees have earned elsewhere. And the expansion of retirement services here is likely to dissuade some Mainers from taking their retirement income and benefits elsewhere when they retire.

The legislature, partly to encourage this industry, has exempted up to $6,000 of retirement income from taxation. The goal is to someday exclude all retirement income from taxation. It will not be all gain, though. There are costs associated with an elderly population. The federal government bears a smaller share and state government, a higher share of those costs than is the case for costs associated with children.

Maine's Changing Households
In both 1960 and 2000, 3 percent of the Maine population lived in group quarters, that is, school and college dormitories, rooming houses, nursing homes, military barracks, jails and prisons, convents and monasteries, homeless shelters, etc. The remaining 97 percent lived in individual homes and apartments. While the population living in them increased by only one-third, the number of occupied homes and apartments almost doubled between 1960 and 2000. Several factors contributed to the rapid growth in occupied units. None were peculiar to Maine; all were common to the U.S. as a whole. As was mentioned earlier, the maturation of the baby boomers alone increased the demand for housing by fully 40 percent.

A second factor was the increase in the over sixty-five population, which grew three times as fast as the younger population. Housing the senior population requires more units than housing an equal number of younger adults because many seniors live alone, having outlived their spouses and partners. The homes of most younger adults, on the other hand, house two spouses or partners. This effect of aging will become even more important as the baby boomers age further.

The age at marriage has increased, with the concomitant likelihood that some who have postponed marriage will never marry. Evidence from national samples suggests that not only are people postponing marriage, but many married couples are also not cohabiting; instead of moving in together, more "couples" are retaining their separate houses and apartments. The percentage of divorced and separated individuals, not including those who have remarried,

Figure 4. Changing Households 1960 and 2000

Percent

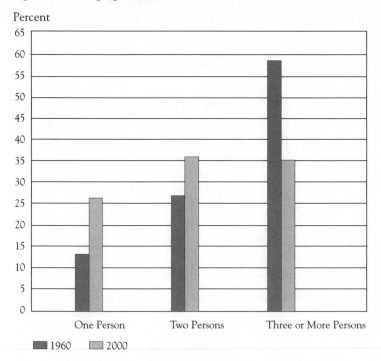

One Person   Two Persons   Three or More Persons

■ 1960   ▧ 2000

Source: 1960 and 2000 U.S. Censuses of Population.

increased five-fold between 1960 and 2000. Separation and divorce, of course, mean the occupation of two units, where only one was occupied before.

The net effect of all these changes is that the number of homes and apartments required to house a thousand Maine people increased from 300 units in 1960 to 400 units in 2000. Or, another way to think about it: *Had the average number of occupants per home remained constant from 1960 to 2000, there would today be a surplus of some 150,000 homes in Maine!*

The average size of the new homes has not declined, even though there are fewer occupants; if anything, the new homes are larger than those in 1960. Certainly, many of the homes in which the baby boomers grew up, and where many of their parents still live, were the small, Cape Cod-style houses built for World War II veterans. Since it took 300 homes to house 1,000 people in 1960, and 100 more homes than that to house 1,000 people in 2000, we may conclude that the decline in average household size has increased housing costs per occupant by at least a third (+100/300). This does not include any run-up in land and housing prices caused by increased demand.

For municipal governments, the decline in average household size has increased per capita costs for water, sewer, trash pickup, and police and fire protection. Even in a community where the population remained constant from 1960 to 2000, real costs for these services would have risen by a third or more, as the residents spread out over more units requiring the services. Indeed, the *per capita* increase in municipal costs may contribute more to the perception that property taxes are too high than the increase in the cost per home. A 1960 tax bill of, say, $2,000 in today's dollars would have been equivalent to $600 per capita (or per occupant) while the same tax bill in 2000 would have been equivalent to over $800, because of the smaller household.

On the other hand, educating children is usually the biggest municipal cost; and the increase in the number of homes to be taxed combined with the decrease in the number of school age children has helped hold down tax rates. In 1960, there were eighty-five school-age children to be educated for every hundred occupied homes; in 2000, there were only forty-four.

To live together is to share each other's burdens; when everyone lives alone, however, with whom may we share? Before we reach that unlikely extreme, we might ask if there is a cost to us and to society of relying on paid outsiders to provide the intimate assistance to the ill, the infirm, and the aged, which the other members of our households used to give. Is this "building alone" syndrome a symptom of dissociation, and a distancing of Maine people from one another?

Maine's Missing Populations
The Memoirs of Sherlock Holmes record that when Inspector Gregory asked Holmes in the "Silver Blaze" case, "Is there any other point to which you would wish to draw my attention?" Holmes referred to "the curious incident of the dog in the nighttime."

"The dog did nothing in the nighttime," responded Gregory.

"*That* was the curious incident!" remarked Holmes.

In a similar vein, two of the curious demographic facts about Maine are the populations that *aren't* here. The first are minorities. In 2000, one in three U.S. residents, and just one in twenty-nine Maine residents was non-white or Hispanic; this makes Maine the *whitest* state in the nation. There is an historic reason for this: Maine has had no large employment centers like Boston, Chicago, or Detroit to attract African-American migrants in the 1940s and '50s, and Hispanics more recently.

The second missing population is immigrants. One in nine U.S. residents was an immigrant in 2000, but only one in thirty-five Maine residents. Maine had a *larger* proportion of international immigrants than the U.S. in 1960, when more than 80 percent of the foreign-born in the U.S. were from Europe, the Soviet Union, and immediately adjacent Canada. Maine is closer to all of

Figure 5. Maine's Missing Minorities in 2000

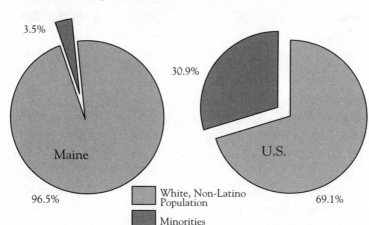

3.5%

30.9%

Maine

U.S.

96.5%

White, Non-Latino
Population

Minorities

69.1%

Source: 2000 U.S. Census of Population.

these than most of the U.S., and more than 95 percent of the foreign-born in Maine in 1960 were from these points of origin. By 2000, on the other hand, over three-quarters of the foreign born in the U.S. were from Asia and Latin America; and Maine is as far from those places as one can get in the U.S.

The implicit, operative principle is that the greater the distance between origin and destination, the smaller the migration flow. Another factor has been the concentration of the flow of international immigrants into six major U.S. debarkation cities, and the gradual dispersal of the immigrants in short moves outwards from those cities. Maine has no such city, Boston being the closest one; and with many opportunities for resettlement closer to Boston, few recent immigrants have reached Maine.

It is important that Maine has so *few* immigrants and minorities, for several reasons. First, minority populations contribute disproportionately to population growth, because they have higher birth rates and lower death rates than the non-Hispanic white population. Their death rates are lower because they are younger on average than the non-Hispanic white population. Their birth rates are higher partly for the same reason, and partly because they tend to have larger completed families. Immigrants, of course, contribute directly to population growth by moving to the U.S.; but they also tend to be younger with higher birth rates and lower death rates.

We noted earlier that Maine's median age increased by ten years between 1960 and 2000, while the U.S. median increased by only six years. The difference is largely due to the larger proportion of immigrants and minorities in the

Kwabena Owusu, Augusta

U.S.. Because they are younger, on average, than the native, white population, immigrants and minorities have kept the U.S. median age from rising as far as Maine's has.

Minorities accounted for half the total population increase in the U.S. between 1960 and 2000, while immigrants accounted for a fifth of the increase. The two categories are not mutually exclusive, of course.

Some minorities are also immigrants, and vice versa. So, we cannot add their separate contributions to derive their combined effect on population growth. However, immigrants and minorities together certainly accounted for something over half the total U.S. growth between 1960 and 2000. If this is the case, then, without the contribution of immigrants and minorities, the U.S. growth rate during those forty years would have been no faster than Maine's. Indeed, the U.S. rate would probably have been slightly slower than Maine's. From this, we may infer that without substantial numbers of immigrants and minorities, Maine is unlikely to grow at anything near the U.S. rate—with important consequences for our economy.

A second potential consequence of Maine's sparse population of immigrants and minorities is that their absence may well be a barrier to business recruitment and economic development. Iowa's racial and ethnic mix is very similar to Maine's. Several years ago *The New York Times* reported that major U.S. corporations were bypassing Iowa, choosing not to locate facilities there, because they had executives who were themselves minorities and uncomfortable at the idea of living in an all-white state. Since then, Iowa has begun recruiting overseas, to encourage immigrants to move to the state.

James Tierney, the former Maine attorney general, suggested in his 2002 TIAA/CREF Distinguished Honors Graduate Lecture at the University of Maine still other ways in which a lack of ethnic diversity slows population growth. His talk was prompted by the controversy in late 2001 over the migration of Somali refugees to Auburn and Lewiston. After talking about Maine's slow population growth rate and the out-migration of youth, Tierney said, "Many of our best Maine kids move away—perhaps for education or perhaps for work—and find a level of energy and excitement elsewhere, in places where diversity is the rule and not the exception. And they like it." Unstated, but implied is his conclusion that because of the state's lack of diversity, many Mainers who leave and might one day return never will, after experiencing the energy and excitement of a pluralistic culture.

Tierney points out that he himself has chosen to teach at Columbia University in New York instead of the University of Maine Law School "in part because I cannot imagine teaching a class of all-white students. It just wouldn't be as much fun for me." He goes on to cite three examples among his family and friends, of Mainers living out of state who would like to return but have married immigrants and minorities who, because of our lack of diversity, don't want to live here.

Tierney argues that we must recognize the importance of diversity to our future, talk about it, and find ways to encourage immigration. Particularly important is changing the way we support newcomers and making state government responsible for resettlement costs, rather than individual municipalities.

One wonders how readily Maine's culture will adapt to a flow of new immigrants, particularly minorities from Africa, Latin America, and Asia. Tierney suggests we begin not with recruiting immigrants, but by talking to each other about why it's necessary. The response by Mainers to attempts to stir up hate and resentment for the Somali immigrants was reassuring in this regard.

The Suburbanization of Maine
Over half of all Maine residents lived in urban areas in 1960; yet, 95 percent of the growth between then and 2000 took place in rural areas. As a result, the share of the population living in urban areas declined to 40 percent in 2000. This was no movement back to the farm, however; the farm population actually declined more than 75 percent between 1960 and 2000.

The Maine State Planning Office, in *Economic Distress and the Changing Nature of Rural Maine*, published in 1979, described the Maine population as an "urban labor force living in a dispersed rural settlement pattern." The office found that about half of the four hundred fifty towns identified by the U.S. Census as rural in 1970 were actually suburban in character with many residents commuting elsewhere to work. Census 2000 supports this observation, reporting that over three-quarters of Maine workers living in rural areas commuted to jobs outside their towns of residence. Their livelihoods were obviously not rooted in the natural resources where they live. There is a delicious irony here: people moving to rural areas in order to turn around and commute back to jobs in the cities.

The decennial census lacks a "suburban" category, classifying everything as either urban or rural. In Maine, half the towns identified by the census as rural are such *only* in the sense of having low residential densities. Speaking somewhat loosely, we shall use "rural" and "suburban" interchangeably here, but, of course, that is not strictly true. There are many rural communities whose residents do not commute, and who make their livelihoods growing or harvesting the local natural resources. Also, in what follows, we shall use "urban" to include densely settled villages, even though their populations may not be large enough to qualify them as cities. The village of Wiscasset, for example, has too few inhabitants to be a city, but its dense settlement pattern is still similar to the mixed-use neighborhoods found in cities.

We are sure everyone can visualize what we mean by "suburbanization." It is a house or mobile home located every hundred yards along the secondary roads of Maine; since 1960, there have been over 200,000 homes sited there. Contrast this with the 75,000 homes added to the urban housing stock during the same period. People have shown an overwhelming preference for supposed "rural" living. We suspect, too, that the reader realizes that another name for suburbanization, as we have described it, is "sprawl." In the past half-dozen years, the subject has become a major concern in both Maine and the nation—although sprawl elsewhere means a five-hundred-home development every couple of miles on a major artery, not a new house every hundred yards down a back road.

After studying the effects of sprawl, the State Planning Office reported that, "This outward movement has had unanticipated and unintended consequences." In particular:

It has increased local and state taxes in three ways. First, it has required new and redundant infrastructure in remote areas; for example, state taxpayers have paid for over $300 million in new rural school capacity [and for other increased educational costs, as well], even though the student population statewide has declined. Second, it has required the lengthening of service routes for police, fire, emergency, road maintenance, and plowing; towns are losing economies of scale. Finally, it has left older city and town centers

Figure 6. Suburbinization 1960 and 2000

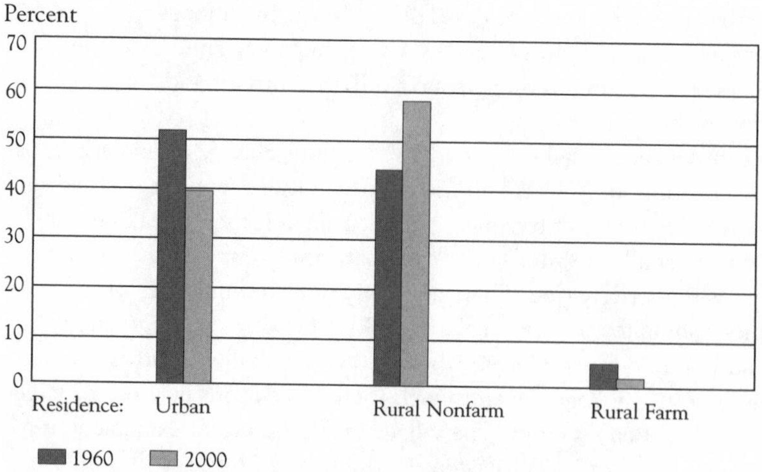

Source: 1960 and 2000 U.S. Censuses of Population.

saddled with a declining population and an underused infrastructure. The ironic result is that even while rural taxpayers are pitching in to build new capacity, in-town residents are paying more (on a per-family basis) just to support the old capacity.

The costs go beyond dollars and cents. Spreading out also creates more air pollution from automobiles, more lake degradation from development run-off, and more fragmentation of wildlife habitats. There are social costs, such as the isolation of the poor and elderly in cities, and the disruption of traditional farming and forestry activities in the countryside. (*The Cost of Sprawl*)

The State Planning Office has tried to address these costs of sprawl in several ways. In 1997 it published a report outlining the personal, social, and environmental costs of sprawl. In 1998 it surveyed recent movers and people planning to move, to ascertain who was moving where and why. It has proposed and supported legislation and administrative actions to discourage sprawl and strengthen Maine's service centers. It has hosted conferences to acquaint both the public and the building industry with the issue, and sponsored a design competition to overcome some of the drawbacks of urban living that people cite as reasons for moving to the country.

In a referendum in summer 2003, Scarborough voters rejected the construction of Dunstan Crossing, a development specifically designed to reduce sprawl by clustering buildings in a compact settlement that included a mix of residences, offices, and stores. This suggests Mainers are not ready to return to a more dense, urban lifestyle.

The decrease in household size we discussed earlier has been an important source of sprawl. You will recall that, because of declining household size, it required a hundred more homes to house a thousand people in 2000 than it did in 1960. This is demand over and above that required to meet the one third increase in total population.

Since land in rural areas is sparsely settled and has low monetary value for economic activities, it is considerably cheaper than the densely settled urban land. This has made rural land attractive for siting the additional units needed to house the smaller households. There is also the bonus to the homeowner of the initially lower rural tax rates. However, these lower rates do not generally derive from greater municipal efficiency, but from providing fewer services. Because of their densities, urban areas are able to deliver services more efficiently. Their higher tax rates result from their offering more services and from aging infrastructure.

When we look at who lives in the cities and who in the country, we find that young adults (nineteen- to twenty-four-year-olds) and the elderly (people over eighty) are more likely to live in urban than in rural areas, while people

Washington County

twenty-five to seventy-nine are more likely to live in rural areas. This makes intuitive sense. The city, with its dense population, makes it easier for the young to meet one another and congregate. The sparse population of the suburbs works against this. Thus, young adults, until they have children, enjoy the urban lifestyle, particularly its nightlife. Maine's lack of major urban areas is a factor contributing to our inability to retain our young people.

Seniors, on the other hand, value the city less for its social life than for its convenience. They often have health problems requiring frequent visits to health care providers who are usually located in urban areas. Their health problems may, in addition, make impossible that quintessential suburban activity, driving. Moving from suburbia to the city at that point in life may make great sense: medical and other services are closer at hand, and alternative means of transport are available. Further, an important reason for the original move to the suburbs—cheap housing for raising a family—is no longer salient. Per square foot, urban housing will be more expensive than rural housing but, with their children gone, the elderly can compensate for this by moving into smaller city apartments. They may even be able to rent subsidized senior housing.

The baby boomers will begin to turn eighty in 2026. Will large numbers of them leave the suburbs to move back to the cities after that date? Will there be enough one- and two-person urban apartments to accommodate them? Enough subsidized senior housing? Will the flow of the elderly baby boomers back to the cities depress suburban land and home values and drive up urban prices? Will that, in turn, encourage even more families in the middle years to flee urban life for the suburbs?

Maine's Geographic Divergence
Regional population trends diverged in Maine between 1960 and 2000. Eight of our sixteen counties increased their shares of the total state population, while the shares of the other eight either declined or remained constant.

Maine's southwestern coast has always been more densely settled than the rest of the state; but the disparity between its density and that of the rest of the state became even greater in the forty years from 1960 to 2000. Well over half the total statewide population increase during those years was concentrated in the two westernmost, coastal counties of York and Cumberland. Fully 80 percent of the statewide increase was concentrated in those counties and the five other southwestern coastal counties, stretching from Sagadahoc to Hancock. Census Bureau estimates since 2000 show this concentration continuing, and projections by the State Planning Office out to 2015 forecast no slowing of the trend.

Among the coastal counties, only the easternmost one, Washington, failed to increase its share of the state population between 1960 and 2000; its share declined. Among the inland counties, only Franklin in western Maine increased its share of the State population. Two inland counties—Aroostook and Piscataquis—had absolute population losses, although Piscataquis's was but a nominal 144 persons.

There are two sources of change in a population: natural increase and net migration. Natural increase is the difference between births and deaths. Net migration is the difference between those moving to an area and those leaving it. When we look at the sources of change for the southwestern coastal region, we find that most of its growth came from net migration—more people moving in over the forty-year period than leaving. Every county in this region had net positive migration, although two-thirds of the gain was concentrated in York and Cumberland Counties. Of the nine other counties in the state, four had a small net in-migration; only about a tenth that along the southwestern coast. One county, Androscoggin, lost out-migrants to a suburbanizing area in adjacent Oxford County. The remaining four counties—Piscataquis, Penobscot, Washington and Aroostook—which form a contiguous northern block, all had out-migration over the forty years. Most of that was from Aroostook.

The increased concentration of the population along the coast continues a trend begun in the mid-nineteenth century, when agriculture in Maine reached

Figure 7. Geographic Divergence 1960 to 2000
(Differential Regional Growth Rates)

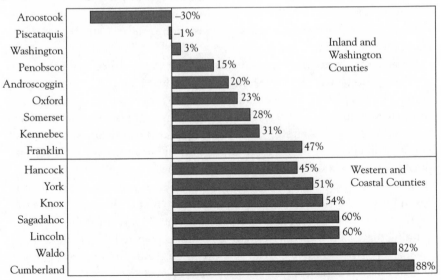

Population Growth 1960 to 2000

Source: 1960 and 2000 U.S. Censuses of Population.

its greatest geographic extent. Settlement during the seventeenth and eighteenth centuries was largely confined to the coastal areas. After the Revolution, settlement rapidly expanded up-river and inland, as land was cleared for farming. However, the opening of the Erie Canal, the availability of land in the American West, and competition from those more productive western lands first slowed and then reversed the movement of the Maine population inland. Mechanization on the farm and in the woods during the twentieth century further reduced the demand for labor in inland Maine. (We noted when discussing suburbanization that Maine's farm population fell more than 75 percent in the forty years between 1960 and 2000.) Today, increasing productivity and competition from abroad continue to erode job opportunities in the factories of small town, inland Maine, as manifested in the closure of shoe, textile, and paper mills.

Kenneth Roberts, the novelist who chronicled early New England, claimed that Maine does not begin until one crosses the Kennebec River. He said everything west of there is an extension of Massachusetts. There is increasing merit in his observation, at least in regard to York County. In 1980 the U.S. Census Bureau documented the emergence of a new metropolitan statistical area centered on Portsmouth, Rochester, and Dover, New Hampshire, and identified five towns in southernmost York County as part of this area. When the bureau identifies a town as part of a metropolitan area, it is because the available economic information, in particular that on commuting patterns, indicates the town is economically integrated with the central city or cities. In other words, the bureau was saying in 1980 that these five towns were no longer part of the Maine economy, but were aligned with an economic region centered on the three New Hampshire cities.

In the 2000 census, the bureau reclassified the twenty-three cities and towns making up this metropolitan area, including the five York County towns, as part of a Consolidated Metropolitan Statistical Area centering on Boston. The Boston metropolitan area had spread outward to include part of southern Maine! A couple of statistics from the 2000 census support this conclusion. Almost half the workers living in these five towns worked outside Maine in 2000, presumably in New Hampshire and Massachusetts, and one in five residents was living in another state five years earlier. Statewide, only one Maine resident in eleven lived out-of-state in 1995. Are we going to find in the 2010 census that the Boston metropolitan area has crept further into Maine? Probably. When planning the 2000 census, the Census Bureau was prepared to extend the boundaries of the Boston metro all the way to Portland. After reviewing the data, however, it concluded that this hasn't happened—yet!

Besides participating in the long, slow decline in the demand for rural labor, the Aroostook and Penobscot County populations were also subjected to the closing of the Dow (Bangor) and Presque Isle Air Force bases in the 1960s, and Loring Air Force Base (Limestone) in the 1990s. When Loring closed, for example, the federal government packed up 8,000 military, their dependents, and civilian employees of the Defense Department, and moved them out-of-state. They were followed by additional residents who left in response to the downturn in the local economy caused by the base closing. Should the Naval Air Station at Brunswick or the Naval Shipyard in Kittery close, we may expect a temporary slowing, at least, in the increasing concentration of population in York and Cumberland counties. A cutback in navy contracts at Bath Iron Works would have a similar effect on mid-coast and central Maine. Any slowing of growth in the southwestern coastal region is likely to be comparatively short, however, if we go by the example of the closing in the 1980s of Pease Air Force Base, just across the line in coastal New Hampshire.

Retirees have been an important source of the in-migration to Maine's coastal region. This agrees with the finding that most people, in moving or considering a move at retirement, want to settle near water. For people living near the coastlines of the country, this has meant the ocean. For those in the middle of the country it has meant lakes. (The attraction of the Rangeley Lakes to retirees is one reason Franklin County increased its share of the state population between 1960 and 2000; other reasons are enrollment growth at the University of Maine at Farmington and employment growth at Franklin Memorial Hospital.) We mentioned former Governor King's support of the retirement industry when discussing the passage of the baby boomers. If successful, promotion of this industry will accelerate migration to the western coastal region.

Retirees confer several benefits on an area. First, they reduce volatility in the local economy because pensions and Social Security benefits provide a stable flow of cash unaffected by the economic cycle. Second, they can increase the availability of health services when the general population is too small, too young, or too poor to create effective demand for less frequently used services. Retirees, because of their age, consume more health services and, with their access to an outside funding source—Medicare—can support services the general population cannot, but from which it will benefit. In 1960 volunteer work and the maintainance of community organizations were carried on largely by women. With the doubling of the percentage of women working outside the home for pay, there has been a decline in the proportion of women available for these activities. Retirees, particularly the younger, more affluent sort attracted to Maine, are filling this gap

We said earlier that for some fifty years from 1910 to the mid-1960s, there was an almost continuous net outflow of people from Maine, the exception being a very small in-migration during the Great Depression. In the mid-'60s this changed, and Maine has since had a net inflow. But, that's not true for the four northern counties—Aroostook, Piscataquis, Penobscot and Washington—which have continued to hemorrhage people, more than 20,000 a decade between 1960 and 2000. Population projections by the State Planning Office out to 2015 forecast no change in this.

Most of these out-migrants were young. Between 1980 and 2000, a net outflow of 50,000 people between the ages of eighteen and thirty or thirty-one left the state. Furthermore, this flow accelerated from the earlier to the later decades. Most would have been from the four northern counties. The young are the ones who usually leave because they are freest of ties and obligations. The middle-aged own homes, have obligations to aging parents, and participate in a complex web of social relations.

Out-migration may be as hard or harder on those who stay as it is on those who leave. Those who go, after all, carry the hope that their move will open doors and improve their circumstances. Those who stay wonder what's wrong with them that they remain behind. Do they lack "the right stuff"? They watch the social life of the community gradually atrophy and the storefronts empty. Parents see their children leave. The young see their siblings and friends leave. None of this is peculiar to northern Maine. The same thing is happening throughout rural America, wherever the decline in the number of farms and factories and their respective work forces is reducing the need for labor. To address the issue of youth out-migration, Governor John Baldacci announced in his inaugural speech that he will convene a youth summit to seek ways to keep young people in Maine and bring back those who have left.

There has been talk since at least the late 1970s about the existence of "two Maines" and how to make the economy of the second Maine viable. Despite all the talk, the situation remains essentially unchanged. The young continue to leave. Some states and provinces, Iowa and Pennsylvania among them, have programs to lure their out-migrants back. But, what is the sense of that if the economy cannot absorb them? Or are those correct who say that, if there is an educated and skilled workforce, it will attract good jobs? What proposals will Governor Baldacci's youth summit advance? Is James Tierney's proposal to increase diversity a solution? How would one increase diversity in northern Maine? Should we follow Iowa's approach of recruiting immigrants from abroad? Would an east-west highway really boost the northern Maine economy as much as its proponents claim?

Closing Thoughts
Today, Maine's population is almost evenly divided between the southwestern coastal region and the rest of the state—just under 51 percent along the coast, just over 49 percent elsewhere. As the population concentrates more and more

along the coast, it will become harder to muster either the political will or the electoral power to address conditions in the "other" Maine. With a declining share of the state's workforce and consumers, it will also become increasingly difficult to attract business investment there.

In 1960 Maine had three representatives in Congress; today, we have two. If we remain a native, all-white enclave, our slow population growth will continue to erode our influence in the nation. This may not take the form of another lost Congressional seat; at least not right away. It will mean decreasing national attention to those interests and issues—whether political, economic or social—that are peculiar to Maine and the other slow growth, rural states.

Maine's average age increased ten years between 1960 and 2000. The Census Bureau projects it will increase another two years by 2010. Has this aging of the population made Maine less attractive to the young? Has it created a middle-aged society and culture they find dull? Is James Tierney correct? Are we losing our young people and failing to attract others because Maine doesn't offer the energy and excitement they find elsewhere?

In 1960 one household in eight was a single person living alone. By 2000, that had doubled to one in four. If we widen our focus to include households with children but only one adult, then one household in three had but a single adult in 2000. The trend in the U.S. is similar. Should we be concerned about this? Can we afford to pay the mounting governmental and environmental costs of dispersing our population across so many homes? Are there implications for social cohesion? What, if anything, might reverse this trend?

One thing is clear: these are major policy issues, which will require for their remedy the engagement of *all* our institutions—public and private, profit and non-profit, local, state, and federal.

---

*R*ichard Sherwood was born in Portland, moved to Bath with his parents when he was three, and grew up there. He left Maine after high school and spent sixteen years out of state, attending college and graduate school and serving in the army and his first professional positions. He returned to Maine in 1969 to teach at Ricker College. In 1974 he joined the State Planning Office where he spent most of his professional career, as state demographer. He is a sociologist by training, and his principal areas of concentration are research design, demography, social inequality, and community sociology.

Educated at Queens University of Belfast, Ireland, the University of York, and the Open University of England, Deirdre Mageean is associate vice president for research, dean of the graduate school, and former director of the Margaret Chase Smith Center for Public Policy at the University of Maine. Dr. Mageean teaches in the areas of demography, quantitative research methods, and community and economic development. Her research interests include how humans critically affect the natural environment, rural poverty and development trends, and residential mobility patterns.

IN THE LAST FOUR DECADES Maine's economy has evolved from a manufacturing-based, rural economy quite distinct from that of the rest of the nation to one that today is essentially identical to that of the rest of the United States. If trends continue, future growth in employment and output will be concentrated in services and related industries, and this growth will take place primarily in Maine's more urban areas. Thoughtful planning and investment will be essential to manage this ongoing transition happily. The choices Maine communities make about land-use patterns, transportation, design standards, and land conservation will determine the extent to which they will remain desirable places to live and to work.

2 Maine's Changing Economy
The Rise of "Urban Maine"

CHARLES COLGAN

Any discussion of the Maine economy that begins with the term "urban Maine" is destined to provoke a reaction somewhere between mild amusement and downright hostility at the thought that anything in Maine could be described as "urban." Such a reaction is not surprising. Since the arrival of the first "rusticators" in the post-Civil War era, Maine has seen itself as the quintessential *anti*-urban society. This view intensified when, in the 1930s, we declared ourselves as "Vacationland," defining our territory as the place to which weary urbanites from benighted regions to the south might flee each summer for relaxation and restoration. It continues to this day, in our invocation of the dreaded "sprawl" as the justification for stopping, or drastically limiting, anything that looks like growth.

The rise of urban Maine has occurred for a number of reasons, deriving primarily from the economic changes that have washed over in Maine in recent decades. These changes have dramatically altered what we do in Maine for a living, where we do it, and the incomes we earn from it. Together, they have brought a Maine economy that is today indistinguishable in structure from the nation's, significantly raised the incomes of Maine people, and permanently changed Maine from a rural- to an urban-dominated society

Because it so conflicts with the time-honored image of Maine—among Mainers and non-Mainers, alike—the last change to which I refer causes the strongest reaction and the greatest disbelief among people. Because of this, and because our understanding of this issue will shape what we would become far into the future, it is the major focus of this chapter exploring Maine's twenty-first-century economy.

Setting the Stage: Maine's Economic Growth and Change, 1970-2000[11]
Over the thirty years between 1970 and 2000, the Maine economy grew at rates that few, if any, would have envisioned at the end of the '60s. (See Table 1.) During this period, population grew in Maine from less than a million to over a million and a quarter, an increase of nearly one third. Even more remarkable was employment, which grew almost *three times* the *rate* of population growth. While population grew by 29,000, employment grew by 239,000, a 62 percent increase in thirty years. This rate of increase in employment compared with population was made possible largely by an increase in the labor force, primarily from the addition of women.

Table 1. Economic Change, 1970–2000

	1970	2000	Change	Percent Change
Agriculture, Forestry and Fisheries	11,421	10,092	–1,329	–11.6%
Construction	18,659	31,181	12,522	67.1%
Durable goods Manufact.	33,802	43,149	9,347	27.7%
Nondurable goods Manufact.	76,770	42,481	–34,289	–44.7%
Transport, Communications/Utilties	17,324	24,671	7,347	42.4%
Wholesale and Retail trade	67,155	154,175	87,020	129.6%
Finance/Insurance/ Real Estate	12,433	31,776	19,343	155.6%
Services	60,149	186,700	126,551	210.4%
Government	84,492	97,071	12,579	14.9%
Total Employment	384,175	623,296	239,091	62.2%
Population	996,784	1,286,670	289,886	29.1%
Personal Income (Thousands)	$1,871,337	$32,866,505		
Personal Income (Nominal $)	$1,931	$25,544		
Real Personal Income (2000 $)	$10,891,181	$32,866,505		202%
Real Per Capita Personal Income (2000 $)	$11,237	$25,544		127%

The increase in employment was accompanied by a dramatic increase in personal wealth. In 1970 per capita personal income was $15,198 in 2000 dollars (adjusted for inflation by the consumer price index). In 2000 per capita personal income was $25,544, an increase of 68 percent. Total personal income, in inflation adjusted dollars, more than *doubled* over the period.

This growth in population, employment, and wealth was accompanied by equally dramatic change in the *structure* of the Maine economy. Figure 1 shows the distribution of employment in Maine in 1970 and 2000, by major sector. The most important change is a dramatic shift *away* from natural resource extraction and manufacturing, and *toward* the non-manufacturing sectors. Together, natural resources and manufacturing accounted for more than one job in three in 1960; by 2000, fewer than one job in six was in these sectors. Together, almost 45,000 jobs were lost in these sectors, which means that other sectors added a total of over 346,000 jobs. The largest gains were in services, which accounted for 40 percent of all the net jobs created. Next were wholesale and retail trade/government.

The loss of Maine manufacturing jobs is an oft-told tale that is confirmed by the raw data from 1960 to 2000; but the tale is only partially true. Nondurable goods manufacturing employment declined by 34,000 jobs, or 44 percent. Almost all of this job loss was in shoemaking, apparel, and textiles, and most of

Figure 1. Employment in Maine 1970 and 2000

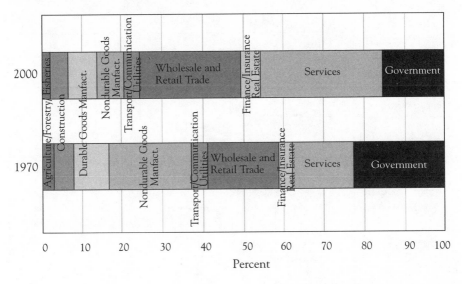

those jobs were lost in the 1980s. There were also job losses in the pulp and paper industry, and in food processing. At the same time, the durable goods manufacturing industries grew by 29 percent, or nearly 10,000 jobs. The manufacturing industries which grew included electrical and electronic equipment, shipbuilding at Bath Iron Works, and metal fabrication.

The largest growth rate of all was in government employment; and the vast majority of this was in local government, especially in school systems. State government expanded, as well; the federal government expanded somewhat in civilian occupations, but declined significantly in the military with the closing of the air force base at Loring and many smaller facilities.

The result of these shifts was that *by 2000 the Maine economy was largely indistinguishable from the U.S. economy in its structure.* Figure 2 shows the difference in employment specialization in the major sectors for the United States and Maine in 1960 and 2000. A bar pointing to the right shows that Maine was, at the time, more specialized in a sector than the U.S.; a bar pointing to the left denotes specialization in the U.S. The width of the bars shows the degree to which Maine and the U.S. differed. The most important point to note is that the differences between Maine and the U.S. in specialization have dramatically diminished since 1960. Today, Maine is slightly more specialized in nondurable goods manufacturing and trade, and slightly less specialized in the other sectors; but the differences are now virtually negligible.

Figure 2. Maine and U.S. Employment Specialization, 1970 and 2000

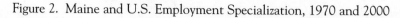

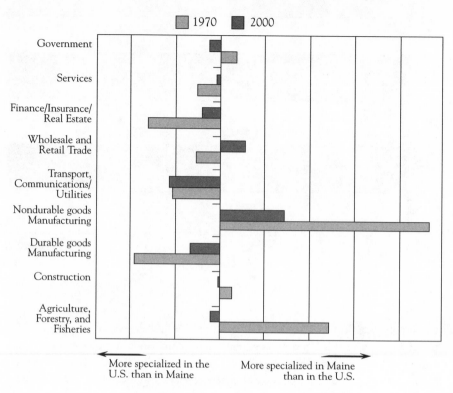

More specialized in the
U.S. than in Maine

More specialized in Maine
than in the U.S.

The shift in the Maine economy to essentially the same basic structure as the U.S. is also reflected in a shift in the *geography* of Maine's economy. The "two Maines"—generally, north and south—has been widely used to describe the Maine economy for more than twenty years; but the other two Maines— urban and rural—has received little attention. This is too bad, because the change in the industrial base of Maine also marks—and masks—the change to an *urban economy*.

Urban Jobs, Suburban Living
On the surface, describing Maine as an "urban" economy would appear unusual, if not a contradiction of common sense. After all, even in 2000 over half of Maine's employment was located outside the Census-designated metropoli-

tan areas; and the proportion of the population in metropolitan areas in Maine was only 40 percent, compared with over eighty percent for the U.S. as a whole. However, the simple division between "metropolitan" and "nonmetropolitan" obscures the real nature of change in Maine, and in the U.S. as a whole.

To see the real story, we need to trace the evolution of Maine's urban areas, and their role in the Maine economy.

For federal statistical purposes, metropolitan (or, metro) areas are defined as central cities and their surrounding suburbs. Maine has three such areas: Portland, Lewiston–Auburn, and Bangor. Parts of southern York County are also included in the Portsmouth–Rochester–Dover metropolitan area. From 1969 to 2001 the proportion of Maine's employment in metro areas increased from 45 percent to just under 50 percent, using the 1990 definition of metro areas. This increase of almost 5 percent compares with an increase of employment in metro areas of just over 1 percent in the U.S. over the same period.

Over this same period, the proportion of Maine's total personal income earned in metro areas increased from 43 percent to 44 percent. More importantly, per capita personal income in Maine's metro areas rose from being 6.8 percent *above* the statewide average in 1969 to 11.2 percent above in 2001; meanwhile, average wages in the metro areas rose from being 3 percent above the state average to nearly 7 percent above the state average.

Over the past thirty years, much ink has been spilled over Maine's placement in the rank ordering of the states on per capita personal income. The fact that over the last decade we declined from twenty-fifth in the nation to thirty-seventh (in 2002, to thirty-fourth) has been a cause of great angst. If you look not at our ranking but at the size of Maine's per capita personal income relative to the U.S., however, Maine has risen from 81 percent of the U.S. average in 1969 to 88 percent of the U.S. in 2001; and it was the metro areas that led the way, increasing to 92 percent of the U.S. per capita personal income.

These long-term trends, moreover, have been accelerating significantly over the past decade. The proportion of Maine's personal income in the metro areas was 40 percent in 1990, rising to 44 percent in 2001; the proportion of employment in Maine's metro areas was fairly constant at 43 percent up to 1991; the surge to nearly 50 percent has occurred since 1992.

Over the last decade, Maine employment growth was even more concentrated in its metro areas than the U.S. Employment in Maine's metro areas grew 29 percent faster than in the non-metropolitan areas, while in the U.S. the differential in growth rates between metro and nonmetro areas was only 15 percent. On the other hand, personal income grew much faster in the U.S. metro areas than the U.S. non-metropolitan areas, compared with Maine.

The one statistic that is not consistent with these trends is population. The proportion of Maine's population in the metro areas actually declined, from just over 41 percent to just over 40 percent between 1970 and 2001. Population growth was actually slower in Maine's metro areas over 1990–2000, while the reverse was true in the U.S. Therein, as they say, lies a tale. To understand that tale we need to consider the areas that comprise Maine's metropolitan areas.

With the expansions of the metro areas following the 2000 Census, which was released only in June 2003, a more accurate picture of the role of urban areas becomes clear, and the actual proportion of population in metro areas is seen to have grown, not declined.

The expansion of the metro areas in Maine can be attributed in part to changing definitions of what comprises a metro area; but the primary driving factor has been the *expansion* of the urban areas, as more and more of the economy has been concentrated in urban areas, and more and more people move farther out from the central city. This brings us to the issue of sprawl.

An Economic Explanation of Sprawl

Sprawl is a term with numerous definitions. One is disproportionate growth outside the central city of a metro area. Another is low density residential growth wherever it occurs. A third is, "any growth I don't like." There is no doubt that by the first and second definitions, Maine has been affected by sprawl; nor is there much doubt that the third definition has become the most influential and widespread, at least in southern Maine.

The explanations for sprawl are also numerous. In Maine, fingers are pointed in all directions. The usual suspects rounded up in any discussion of sprawl include property taxes, the school funding formula, local planning, lack of local planning, building codes, the lack of building codes, and, of course, transportation policy. If there are not enough explanations here in Maine, we may turn to federal policies, including the construction of the interstate highway system, the urban renewal policies of the 1960s, the mortgage interest tax deduction, and other federal housing policies.[2]

The problem with all of these "explanations" is that they make it seem like sprawl is somehow unique to Maine, or even to the U.S. To listen to many people attribute sprawl to the imperfections in Maine's tax system, real as they may be, is to fall into the trap of the hammer and nail. If all you have is a hammer, everything looks like a nail. That is, tax policy is something we might be able to fix (though we have been singularly unsuccessful so far); so, tax policy *must* be the key.

The problem is that what we call "sprawl" is actually characteristic of almost all of the U.S., major parts of Canada, and most of Western Europe. If one were

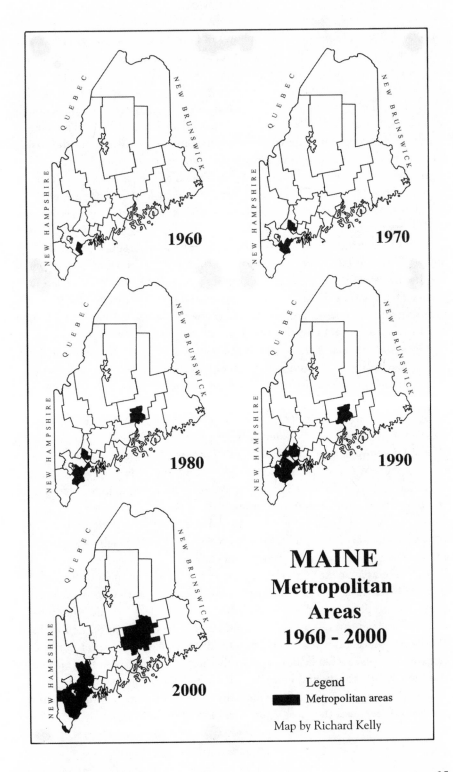

1960

1970

1980

1990

2000

MAINE
Metropolitan
Areas
1960 - 2000

Legend
■ Metropolitan areas

Map by Richard Kelly

blindfolded and dropped into the suburbs of Paris, Bordeaux, Copenhagen, Amsterdam, or London, and the blindfold removed, it would scarcely be possible to tell whether one were in Maine, somewhere else in the U.S., or Europe until seeing the language of directional signs. The subdivisions are there. So are the strip malls, the office complexes, the limited-access highways coursing through farm land, the single family houses on dead-end streets, and the traffic jams.

There are important differences across regions and countries; but the basic point is that a phenomenon which can be observed in so many different places at the same time cannot reasonably be attributed to the particular quirks of any one locality's transportation or tax system. *Something larger is going on here.*

That something larger is the evolution of what urban theorists have come to call the polycentric urban region.[3] This concept has two critical implications. The first is that the idea of "urban" no longer applies to a single political jurisdiction called a "city," but to an entire *region*, the shape of which is determined by the interaction of the living-working-shopping patterns of people who live there. That region will have not a single central city, but multiple centers of employment, commerce, and residence. While the largest of these centers may be the historic central city, this is not by any means inevitable.

Does this concept of the polycentric urban region fit Maine? Quite well, actually. We have already seen how the metro areas of the state have expanded from a small core of towns around Portland to cover large areas of the state. Consider also the commuting patterns.

A few years ago we conducted a study of commuting patterns in the Portland area, in preparation for a recently released regional transportation plan. In that study of residents of Portland, South Portland, Falmouth, Cape Elizabeth, Scarborough, Westbrook, and Gorham, we found that only 10 percent of the respondents live and work in the same town—while more than four-fifths work in one of those towns and live in another town. Many of these are people who live in a suburb and commute to Portland; but many of the Portland residents commute outside of Portland to South Portland or Scarborough to work, and many are people who live in suburbs and commute to suburbs.

In fact, employment opportunities are widely spread throughout the urban regions. If we think of cities as places where people come to work, as concentrations of employment, then one measure of "urban-ness" could be the ratio of total employment to residents in a community. One would expect a place like Portland to have more employees than residents, which it does. Yet Portland is not the only place where this occurs in the metro area. It is also true of South Portland, Scarborough, and Freeport, with Westbrook, Falmouth, and Yarmouth having about equal numbers. In terms of the ratio of employment to residents, Freeport is the most *urban* area in the Portland region.

Another example of larger urban trends affecting Maine is offered by Joel Garreau's concept of *edge cities*.[4] In 1990, Garreau notes the emerging phenomenon of growth of commercial and office space outside of the centers of metropolitan areas. Describing such areas as Tysons Corner near Dulles Airport in Northern Virginia, Route 128 around Boston, and Las Colinas in Dallas, Garreau noted increasing concentration of daytime activities like shopping and offices outside the central cities, but without any residential space.

The location of these areas is usually determined by the intersection of interstate highways, and often cut across municipal boundaries. This may be observed in Maine, where the Maine Mall region in South Portland has developed as a major edge city, cutting across the boundaries of Portland, South Portland, Westbrook, and Scarborough. Other examples in Maine include the burgeoning area at the Route 27/Belgrade exit from I-95 in Augusta and the Bangor Mall area, again along and around the interstate highway.

There are numerous reasons that the polycentric urban region has developed as the dominant urban form here, and elsewhere. To be sure, the various explanations that have been offered for sprawl have their elements of truth. Federal, state, and local policies have played their roles—but as exacerbators of more fundamental forces, rather than as causes in their own right. Those fundamental forces are primarily related to the evolution in the economy, and may be grouped into four categories: relative land prices, rising incomes, transportation, and the shift to a service economy

The first and simplest reason for the spreading out of urban areas is that as population and the demand for housing grows, the tendency is to seek the cheapest land to develop, and land tends to be cheaper, the farther it is from the city. This was shown nearly 200 years ago by a German named von Thunen, who developed a "bull's eye" model of urban land use based on land prices.[5] In the center was the city, where high demand meets very limited supply, and the price of housing rises quickly. On the fringes of the city, where farmland predominates, there is abundant land, meaning that housing costs will be lower.

This classic pattern of land prices has met two other, more recent trends. One is transportation. Much has been made, and rightly so, of the rise of the automobile and its associated infrastructure, in shaping the large urban region; but the pattern was actually fixed in the early twentieth century, with the first major public transportation system: the electric streetcar. The inner suburbs around Boston—such as Newton, Malden, and Melrose, which became known as the "streetcar suburbs"—all grew as the progenitors of sprawl.[6]

In Maine, a similar pattern emerged in the pre-automobile era—though it did not last long—with such towns as Turner functioning as streetcar suburbs to Lewiston. Ironically, the automobile killed the streetcar and restored Turner to its predominantly rural character until recent years. The remnants of this

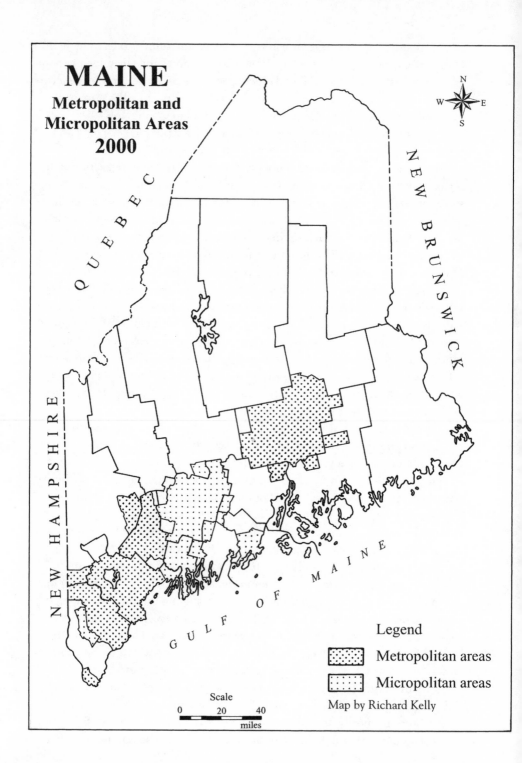

MAINE
Metropolitan and
Micropolitan Areas
2000

QUEBEC

NEW BRUNSWICK

NEW HAMPSHIRE

GULF OF MAINE

Legend

Metropolitan areas

Micropolitan areas

Map by Richard Kelly

Scale

0   20   40

miles

system still exist today at the Seashore Trolley Museum in Kennebunkport, which operates its historic streetcars on the old lines connecting southern Maine towns.

The other major trend contributing to sprawl is rising incomes, which increase both the desire for more housing space and the means to pay for it. Factors such as the G.I. bill and the mortgage interest deduction increased the resources available for expanded housing. Rising incomes and demand looked for the lowest-price housing; and improved transportation, particularly the automobile (which was subject to the same trends) made it very likely that housing demand would be met not by building up in cities, but by building out, away from the cities. To these economic forces were added the demographic force of the baby boom, with larger families looking for more space "for the kids."

These factors explain why residences moved away from the city, and so created the expanded urban region. These factors are present in *all* regions of the U.S., so that population growth in metro areas over the past decade was more than three times faster in the portions of these areas *outside* their central cities. In New England, all of the population growth in metro areas occurred *outside* the central cities.

These factors do not, however, explain the polycentric nature of the urban region, with multiple centers of employment. Two additional factors were critical to this development. The first is the shift of the economy from manufacturing to services. Maine's shift toward more of a service economy was described earlier. What is not clear from the mere fact that the shift occurred, is why and how it impacted the spatial distribution of economic activity in Maine. The rise of the polycentric urban region here and elsewhere occurred in distinct phases that replicated here what was happening elsewhere.

First, the people moved out of the city in search of more housing on cheaper land. As the residential areas grew outside the cities, companies providing personal and retail services followed the population to be near their customers. Then firms in other service industries followed both to be nearer their employees as traffic congestion increased. As new firms grew in industries like finance and insurance, transportation, and health care, they, too, began to look for cheaper land on which to expand, and they found it in the same place that those seeking to build residences did—outside the central cities.

The increasing size of the average American house was noted as part of the trend in residential growth. A similar trend also occurred in the growth of the new service economy, because firms in service industries need a much larger land base from which to work. This is partly because services often are clustered near one another, due to the need for interaction among them, like banks, lawyers, etc.

North Berwick

It is also because of a second, fundamental characteristic of the service industries. While manufacturing companies are able to expand output while using fewer employees through the application of more efficient capital equipment, firms in the service industries have generally been able to expand only by adding *more* employees, because the ratio of output to employee has remained constant. From 1980 to 2000, value added per employee in manufacturing in Maine increased by $39,000, while during the same period value added per worker in services increased by $2,500, and actually fell by $300 in retail.[7]

With 21,000 fewer jobs in manufacturing, the contribution of manufacturing to the economy could grow without any additional space being used (though some was, of course). On the other hand, the 250,000 additional employees in retail and services had to go somewhere; and they had to have roads, parking spaces, green spaces, and other land-consuming accoutrements, often dictated at a high level (especially in the case of parking) by local zoning codes.

These economic forces explain the origins of the polycentric urban region, the reasons why it is so widespread across post-industrial societies, and they suggest that there is no effective policy response that will *reverse* these trends. Nor should we necessarily want to. If we hypothetically stuck all the population growth in the Portland metro area back into Portland, South Portland, and Westbrook, the population of each of those cities would be more than double its current size, with Portland having more than 120,000 people in it. Would Portland, which recently had a major revolt over a modest apartment complex on Munjoy Hill, be enthusiastic about such a result? The question answers itself.

The Choices Before Maine

The lesson in all this is that no post-industrial economy we know of has grown without spreading out across the landscape to some degree. The question before us, then, is not whether we shall spread, but how and how much. If the Maine economy is to remain competitive in a global economy, it will only do so in ways that are consistent with further growth in its urban areas and, just as importantly, further decentralization of those regions.

It is easy to imagine the reaction to this idea that Maine's destiny lies in becoming more urban. In northern and eastern Maine, it will be seen as one more example of how the people in Portland are willing to let rural Maine wither on the vine. In southern Maine, it will be seen as a prediction that Maine's future lies in becoming at best Boston, and at worst, the dreaded New Jersey.

This is far from the case, however. First, the trends influencing the increasing concentration of the economy in urban areas do not speak to the question of *how* development will occur within those areas. While more and more of

Maine may become part of urban regions, this does not mean that all of Maine will be comprised of cities. Indeed, *Maine has an extraordinary opportunity: to develop an urban society for the twenty-first century that is built on and preserves the best features of an extraordinary natural environment.*

Maine today is a very, very long way from being either Boston or New Jersey. While its metropolitan areas have greatly expanded, the proportion of Maine that is actually settled at a high density (that is, more than 500 people per square mile) is much smaller than the U.S. metro areas as a whole; and is easily the smallest proportion in the Northeast. (Figure 3.) This means that most of Maine's urban life lies in the future, and that we still have choices to make about what to do with our urban areas that have been largely foreclosed in other states. Those choices fall into several categories.

Patterns of Residential Growth

Maine has pretty much followed the path of every other major urban region in the U.S. by encouraging, even insisting on, low-density residential growth separated from commercial areas. Abundant evidence accumulated in Maine and elsewhere over the past twenty years makes clear that this pattern is death by a thousand house lots. The only alternative is increasing patterns of residential density, combined in some instances with mixed-use development. Such growth is resolutely resisted in Maine, proving that when it comes to patterns of growth, Mainers, like Americans elsewhere, know what they hate: both sprawl and density.

This view of density is laden with irony. Here are New Englanders, who adopted what many consider to be the most harmonious and attractive form of settlement, the New England village,[8] turning their backs on the past and rushing to gobble up the countryside. Equally ironic is that by refusing denser development because it looks "urban," the result will not change. Maine will still have urban regions; but they will be ones choked with traffic and spread out over more and more of the precious landscape we are so keen to preserve.

One of the opponents to the proposed mixed-use development at Dunstan Corner in Scarborough said that defeating it was essential to preserving the "small town character" of Scarborough. The problem is, Scarborough is already an urban center; and it is likely to become Maine's fifth or sixth largest city in this decade, whether or not that particular development were approved.

Patterns of Commercial Growth

Everyone hates strip malls—except when it comes time to build them. Some concentrations of retail and consumer service establishments is essential to the very nature of these industries. We want shopping to be in concentrated areas,

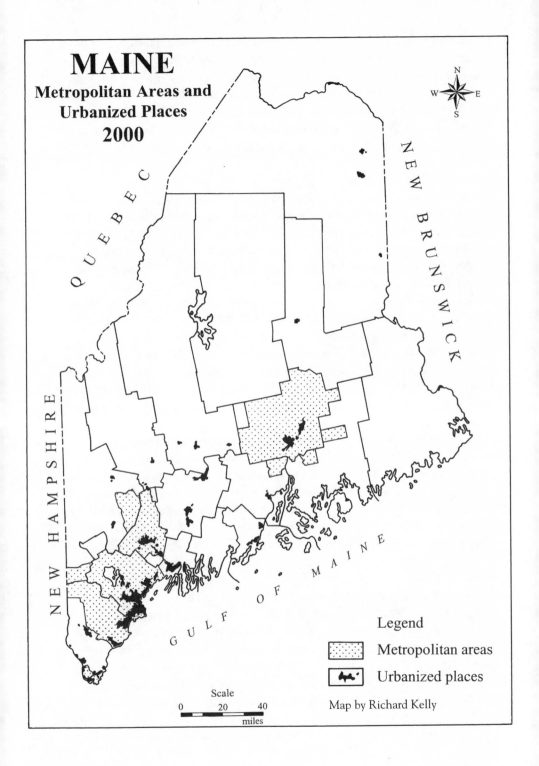

MAINE
Metropolitan Areas and
Urbanized Places
2000

QUEBEC

NEW BRUNSWICK

NEW HAMPSHIRE

GULF OF MAINE

N
W E
S

Legend

Metropolitan areas

Urbanized places

Scale
0   20   40
miles

Map by Richard Kelly

to maximize our choices and minimize the costs of time and travel; but we have so rigorously separated commercial from residential that we have virtually guaranteed massive traffic jams, as every purchase requires a car trip. We need to re-integrate some commercial development with residential areas, while making sure that other commercial development is properly sited and that transportation is managed the way Falmouth has done along Route 1, where a secondary road was built behind the shopping venues to reduce traffic on Route 1.

Commitment to Good Design

Overarching everything we do with commercial and residential development must be a commitment to better design. Mainers are terrified that someone else will tell them what their house should look like, preferring to retain the option to keep at least one snowmobile in the front yard, year-round. The consequence of this steadfast preservation of the right to be ugly is the guaranteeing of a lot of really ugly development.

Some years back, the citizens of Manchester turned down a design ordinance for commercial development along Route 202. When the Irving Oil Company proposed building a new Mainway store and service station using its standard concrete box design, some of the citizens tried to persuade Irving to build a more attractive building. Irving's response, quite properly, was that they were building according to the town's codes and did not see the need to do anything differently. Of course, there are exceptions. Falmouth was able to improve the appearance of their Wal-Mart by judicious use of design codes, and the McDonald's in Freeport has been a national example for nearly two decades of how commercial and community interests can be made to work together.

Mainers by and large are far more passionate about the natural environment than the built environment. Nothing will more surely guarantee the failure of Maine's urban growth than this attitude. A strong commitment to developing a Maine sense of design for the built environment, as architects such as John Calvin Stephens did, will make all the difference in Maine's urban society.

Transportation

If one of Maine's great opportunities lies in the relatively small areas that are today densely urban, this also presents one of our major challenges. For, we do not really have the density, and will not likely have it in the next several decades, to warrant major investments in large scale public transportation, particularly fixed route networks such as light rail. Our existing public transportation systems will continue, and may grow modestly; but our urban society is going to remain far more dependent on the auto than other urban areas.

This means that more and more attention will have to be paid to the transportation and land-use connection. It also means that we are going to build more roads, and existing roads are going to be expanded. Some transportation problems simply cannot be handled in any other way. However, we will not be able to build highways, alone, as the way out of our transportation problems. It may be that such systems as BRT (Bus Rapid Transit), which provide many of the advantages of rail systems at a fraction of the cost, will play a role in the next few decades. One Portland company has already won a national design award for a concept called "RoadRail."[9]

New capacity will also have to be supplemented by better use of existing capacity. Intelligent transportation systems, such as varying the synchronization of traffic signals to improve the flow of traffic, will have to play a major role. The network of traveler information signs installed by the Maine Turnpike will have to be expanded to major non-turnpike roads to keep people informed about optimal travel routes.

Land Conservation Choices
The most frequently cited example of Maine's commitment to preserving its special natural environment is Baxter State Park. Unfortunately, this example actually proves the wrong point. Percival Baxter was unable to get the state to make the investment in preserving Mount Katahdin, so he did it himself. Mainers long had a real reluctance to set aside areas from development. Happily, this has already begun to change substantially. Mainers have approved quite large bond issues for the Land for Maine's Future program, which has already purchased interests in 115 separate parcels of exceptional land. Many local governments have raised money through bonding and taxing to purchase land. The private, non-profit land trusts flourish in Maine, like the Nature Conservancy and the Maine Coast Heritage Trust.

Which land do we conserve? Some areas, like Baxter State Park, are easy to spot; others are less clear. Often in recent years, the desire for land conservation has become yet another excuse to stop or limit development, rather than a strategic choice about what kinds of landscape and habitat most need protection. As Maine's urban regions grow, nothing will be more critical to the state's ability to retain what is uniquely Maine than good choices about where to invest the scarce resources available for land conservation. The desire to conserve land is certainly there; whether there is sufficient wisdom to do it right remains an open question.

Governance
Finally, there is the question of who gets to make what decisions about how Maine's urban regions will grow. Obviously, the key decisions will be made by the towns, which raises a number of questions about "regional" versus "local" perspectives. While the traditions and structures of local government in Maine

Dustin Day and Joshua Whitelaw
at Work in Bucksport

are strong, inevitably frustrating attempts to plan from a regional perspective, these issues are not unique to Maine.

Urban regions worldwide struggle with these same issues. You can hear many of the same concerns—in virtually the same terms—in the very archetype of the polycentric metropolis, Los Angeles. The problem of regional versus local decision making is so much a part of the urban region, that sometimes drastic changes are undertaken. Some regions such as Toronto and Montreal have attempted to solve the problem by simply creating consolidated governments, made up of the central city and its suburbs—as was done five years ago when five towns and the City of Toronto were consolidated.

What is interesting about the Toronto example is that this is the second consolidation of governments in Toronto. The first one, in the 1960s, was hailed as the very model of metropolitan governance. Yet that model could not contain the forces of decentralization; and thirty years later, another major change in governance, this time encompassing an even larger area, was needed. The urban region waits upon no fixed political boundary.

The point is that there is not likely to be a single solution to the problems of regional governance in the urban region. Matching political boundaries with economic and natural boundaries is one possible approach, but it is not the only one. All of Maine's metro areas, especially Portland, have been able to look at one of the key features knitting the urban region together—transportation—from an increasingly regional perspective.[10] Moreover, such a regional perspective is widely supported by the public. A recent survey showed that Portland area residents preferred transportation improvements that benefited the region by a four to one ratio over those in their own town. It will be possible to address many regional concerns within current governance structures, though we should be open to the idea that changes may be needed for some issues.

In each of these regards—patterns of growth, design, transportation, land conservation, and governance—Maine has already begun to make changes in response to the forces of urbanization and decentralization. The choices that will be made in the next few years will determine whether Maine evolves into an urban society that is economically vibrant while retaining a high degree of livability. In the alternative, Maine will become like so many urban regions in the nation and Western world, with a growing economy in a region that fewer and fewer people want to call home.

And what of rural Maine? Is this argument about the central importance of Maine's urban areas simply another way of consigning rural Maine to stagnation and poverty? Not at all, for two reasons. First, the development of Maine's cities does not change the fundamental balance between Maine's urban and rural regions. Maine's rural areas have relied on the growth and development of our urban areas for more than a century. Maine's agriculture, forest products, and marine resources have prospered only to the extent that they found urban markets. As Maine's rural areas diversified into tourism and recreation, they became even more dependent on people—and the incomes earned—in cities.

Just as important, there are numerous development opportunities for Maine's smaller cities—what the State Planning Office defines as our service centers.[11] The economies of Maine's rural regions are highly dependent on the success of the economies of the smaller cities. Washington County depends on Machias and Calais; Somerset County on Skowhegan; Aroostook County on Presque Isle–Caribou. Clearly, these communities face different challenges than does a Portland or a Bangor, but the differences should not obscure the fact that Maine's rural regions will depend on the economic health of their urban centers as much as the state as a whole.

The predominant trends of the last three decades have seen Maine evolve from an economy that was quite distinct from that of the rest of the nation, to one that is, both structurally and spatially, essentially like that of the U.S. today. The long-term outlook is that these trends will continue, and may even intensify. Manufacturing will remain an important part of the Maine economy; but most of the growth in employment and output will be concentrated in services and related industries, and these will shape, and be shaped by the state's urban areas.

Thirty years hence, a reasonable forecast would see Maine's population increasing by as much as 50 percent, or more than 600,000 people. Fully four-fifths of this growth will be in counties that are part of metropolitan or micropolitan areas in 2000. The same trends will see an addition of more than 400,000 jobs, with nearly 70 percent of the jobs in the same counties. It is likely that counties such as Hancock and Waldo will be defined as micropolitan areas or incorporated into metropolitan areas by then; and *most* of Maine's land area and population will be within some form of urban region.

As it has been over the past decades, Maine's economic future will be bound up in the fate of its urban areas. As in the past, the forces affecting Maine are part of larger forces affecting the economies of New England, the U.S., and other nations. A recent study of world growth shows how increasingly important urban regions are to the fate of *all* economies.[12] Maine cannot escape these forces in the future, any more than it did in the past.

The whole notion of "urban Maine" is unsettling, in part because it so conflicts with the mental images we all carry around, about what it means to be in Maine and not in Massachusetts, or someplace else. We are a state where the vast majority of us work in cities, live in cities or suburbs, and everyone thinks they're in the middle of "the country."

It is also unsettling because the basic implication of these economic growth patterns is a paradox: *to retain Maine's special character as a place that feels closely* connected with the natural environment, Maine people will have to pay much, much more attention to the built environment. Put another way: to keep what is special about its natural environment, Maine must decide how best to become more urban.

C harles Colgan is Professor of Public Policy and Management in the Muskie School of Public Service. Educated at Colby College, the University of Pennsylvania, and the University of Maine, Professor Colgan is Chair of the Ph.D. Program in Public Policy and Management at the Muskie School, and Associate Director of the University of Southern Maine's Center for Business and Economic Research. He served in the Maine State Planning Office from 1976-89; has served as chair of the State of Maine Consensus Economic Forecasting Commission since 1993; and is currently Chief Economist for the National Ocean Economics Project.

THOUGH LESS VISIBLE than in states with greater income inequality, poverty is and always has been a reality in Maine. Fewer elderly people are now poor than were poor forty years ago, thanks to Medicare, Medicaid, and Social Security, but more working families earn incomes below the federal poverty level. The minimum wage has not kept up with inflation, the costs of housing and childcare have risen dramatically, and federal support for anti-poverty programs has suffered drastic cuts. Public policies such as deregulation and trade liberalization have accelerated wage and income inequality in Maine. More than ever before, we understand that income inequality incurs steep social costs, including negative effects on health, children, the environment, and community life. In recent years, Maine government has taken ground-breaking steps to help reduce poverty in the state, but federal tax cuts and a slowing economy point to a future that will continue to challenge Maine's poor and policymakers.

3 Being Poor in Maine
Working Hard, Falling Behind

LISA POHLMANN

There is a traditional image of Maine people: of sturdy men, women, and children toughing it out with a lot of Yankee ingenuity in a nice rural setting, piecing together seasonal work, growing food, and tinkering with old cars to keep them on the road.

A 1969 Lewiston *Sun-Journal* article on poverty in Maine captures this image. Among the photographs in the article is one of "slum" children skipping rope on the crowded streets of New York City; in another, two strapping young boys haul lobster traps, under the kicker, "Lucky Boys Having Fun." The article reads, "These Maine boys live on the coast and their families no doubt gain much of their living from the sea as well as from growing vegetables in their garden; but still, the family may be one of those considered at the poverty level…. At least the youngsters are luckier than slum children, for they enjoy fresh air, warm sun, and the nearby sea, as they prepare to cart the family lobster traps to the water."[1] This idyllic image endures today, and masks a grinding level of poverty that many Mainers simply have not been able to escape

What Is It Like to Be Poor Today?
What it means to be poor has changed with the times. Items once considered luxuries for the wealthy are now considered basic necessities. In the 1950s only about half of Maine homes had plumbing and a telephone, let alone a television. Today, most poor households have these items, and probably some kind of a vehicle. Informal modern styles and cheaper clothing prices allow poor people to dress like everyone else. These changes have made poverty less visible but no less present.

Here is how you might experience poverty today. You have no financial security. You work in a series of low-wage, part-time, or seasonal jobs, with a layoff just around the corner. You work two or three jobs in order to stay afloat, and don't have much time with your kids. Your budget drives you to buy cheap food with low nutritional value, or you run out of food altogether before the next paycheck.

You have more debt than assets. Your car is old and unreliable, and the next breakdown could cost you your job, again. Your residence needs major repairs you can't afford, or the landlord won't pay for. You try to pacify bill collectors to keep the lights on. You lost your housing this year because you got so behind, and you had to move in with your sister, and then you had to take the whole family to stay at a shelter.

You have no savings for an emergency, let alone for your children's college education or your retirement. You have no health insurance. You can't afford even over-the-counter medicines for a chronic skin rash or an asthma attack. And after years of dealing with the stress of poverty and the lack of regular health care, you have more health problems than your well-to-do neighbors.

You feel like you are living outside the mainstream. There is not enough money for the kids to go on school trips, to take a family vacation, or to pay for the gas or child care necessary for you to join a club or to attend community meetings. In short, being poor means lacking the resources to meaningfully participate in the society in which you live, and experiencing each day the toll this deprivation takes on you and your family.

Who Is Poor in Maine Today?

The experience of poverty is not easily captured in official determinations about who is poor. The poverty rates that are generally cited in the media are based on a measurement called the federal poverty threshold. In 2002 the threshold for a single person was an annual income of $9,183; for a single parent with two children, it was $14,494 per year.[2]

The federal poverty threshold offers the only available historical trend analysis; but it is important to remember that federal poverty rates consistently underestimate the number of people struggling to get by. When this measure was first developed in the 1950s, it was estimated that food made up about one-third of household expenses; thus, the federal poverty threshold was calculated by multiplying by three the cost of a minimum food budget and adjusting it for inflation each year.

This same method is used today. Over the years, however, the cost of food has declined as a proportion of everyday expenses, while other costs —such as housing and child care—have risen dramatically. Many researchers today estimate that a family requires at least two or two and a half times the income at the federal poverty threshold to meet its basic needs.

Since the 1960s there have been several major changes in terms of who is poor in Maine. The biggest change has been the reduction of poverty among the elderly. Prior to the 1960s, it is estimated that over 30 percent of all elders were poor, and they made up some of the most destitute people in the nation. The creation of Medicare, Medicaid, and the automatic inflation adjustments in Social Security benefits have been the most important elements in dropping the rate of poverty among the elderly in the U.S. as a whole to about 10 percent overall.[3] (See Figure 1.) Maine's elderly and non-elderly poverty rates according to the 2000 Census were 10.1 and 10.9 respectively.

Figure 1. U.S. Poverty Rates by Age: 1959 to 2001

Note: The data points represent the midpoints of the respective years. The latest recession began in March 2001. Data for people 18 to 64 and 65 and older are not available from 1960 to 1965.
Source: U.S. Census Bureau, Current Population Survey.
1960–2002 Annual Demographic Supplements.

The second change is both demographic and cultural. According to the 2000 Census (used in all of the following poverty rates), one in four Maine households is a single-person dwelling; and nearly half of such households are below poverty. In some counties, the elderly account for half of the poor single-person households, which is related to the aging of Maine's population. These households might include a widow who lives on a minimal Social Security income because she and her husband had low earnings throughout their working lives.

The third change is the significant increase in female-headed households, which began in the 1970s. About one in five Maine households below the poverty threshold is headed by a single mother. In fact, well over *one-third* of all female-headed households with children in Maine are living below poverty. Nearly 14 percent of all Maine children live in poverty and half of them live in single-parent families. Managing as a single parent with two children is difficult for anyone, but nearly impossible on an income of $14,500 or less.

In some ways, regional poverty has not changed much since the 1960s. Washington County still has the highest rate of poverty, at 19 percent, followed by other northern and western counties; while southern counties have the lowest rates. Cumberland County's poverty rate of 8 percent masks the reality in Portland, Maine's largest city and service center, where the poverty rate is 14 percent. Meanwhile, poverty has decreased significantly in Knox, Lincoln, Waldo, and Hancock counties due to coastal development and the in-migration of upper-income retirees.

Ethnic minority populations in Maine, while small, are at least twice as likely to be poor as those who are white. While a little over 10 percent of the white population is living below poverty, over one-quarter of African Americans, one-fifth of Asian Americans and Hispanics, and one-third of Native Americans live below poverty in Maine.

Nearly one-fifth of people with disabilities live below poverty. These include many individuals who previously lived in institutional settings and are now living independently, some with community support services. Those with no income other than Supplemental Security Income (SSI) live at about 75 percent of the poverty threshold.

The most dramatic change of all is the rise in number of the *working poor*. This began in the 1970s and accelerated in the 1980s, when Maine began to lose good paying, often unionized manufacturing jobs that were replaced with low-wage service sector jobs. Table 1 shows that from 1982 to 2000, Maine lost 22 percent of its manufacturing jobs; they had an average weekly wage of $680 in 2000. At the same time, Maine saw a 72 percent increase in retail sales jobs;

Table 1. Average Weekly Earnings and Job Growth by Maine Industry

	Number of Jobs, 1982 (thousands)	Number of Jobs, 2000 (thousands)	Percent Change, 1982–2000	Average Weekly Pay, 2000
Total Nonfarm	415.5	604.1	45%	$525
Mining	0.1	0.1	0	$484
Construction	16.7	29.6	77%	$601
Manufacturing	108.6	85.2	−22%	$680
Transportation, Communications, Public Utilities	18.5	24.3	31%	$653
Wholesale Trade	18.8	27.4	46%	$697
Retail Trade	71.7	123.0	72%	$323
Finance, Insurance, Real Estate	17.5	32.3	85%	$731
Services	81.5	182.4	124%	$502
Government	82.1	99.9	22%	$571

Source: U.S. Department of Labor, Bureau of Labor Statistics

Changing Maine

they had an average weekly wage of $323 in 2000.

If the working poor are defined as having income up to 185 percent of the federal poverty threshold—or about $26,800 for a family of three—then, they are working in many of the jobs we encounter everyday. They are hanging up shirts on department store racks; ringing up gas at quick stops; wiping down cafe counters; making hotel beds for tourists; taking care of the elderly so they can stay at home; and taking care of children so others can go to work. They are teacher aides, library aides, office clerks, corrections officers, rehabilitation counselors, cashiers, and telemarketers. In some cases, their wages are so low that they still qualify for and need welfare assistance.

Why Aren't People Earning Enough to Get By?
Barbara Ehrenreich, a well-known national journalist, came to Portland to live for a few weeks as a low-skilled worker during the economic boom of the late 1990s. In her acclaimed book, *Nickel and Dimed*, she describes her experience as a maid cleaning plush homes during the week, and as a nursing home dietary aid serving meals and loading dishwashers on weekends. Her brief foray into low-wage life with two jobs, no days off, and not enough income to cover food and housing, led her to conclude, "Something is wrong, very wrong, when a single person in good health, a person who in addition possesses a working car, can barely support herself by the sweat of her brow. You don't need a degree in

Figure 2. Real Value of the Federal Minimum Wage,
(2001 dollars), 1960–2002

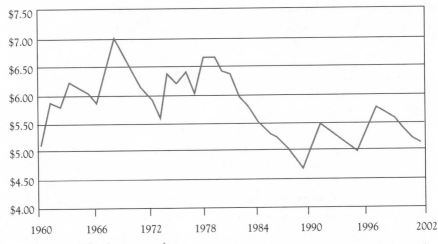

Source: Economic Policy Institute analysis.

economics to see that wages are too low and rents are too high."[4]

The value of the minimum wage, for starters, has not kept pace with inflation. If there was a time when a family could actually make ends meet on the income of one minimum wage earner, it was in the late 1960s when the minimum wage reached its highest real value.[5] (See Figure 2.) Since then, the value of the minimum wage has continued to decline due to lack of regular raises by the Congress.[6] The last federal increase—to $5.15—was in 1997, and by 2001 it had lost 10 percent of its buying power.[7] Like many states, Maine has raised its minimum wage above the federal minimum, and it is currently $6.25 and will increase to $6.50 by October 2005. While this is a step in the right direction, minimum-wage workers in Maine still do not have anywhere near the buying power they had in the 1960s.

Minimum wage earners contribute an average of 54 percent of their families' weekly earnings.[8] Most are adults supporting families, not teenagers just getting their feet wet in the job market. Sixty-eight percent of the workers who would have benefited from an hourly wage increase to $6.65 in 2003 are adults.[9] Studies have also determined that the 1996-97 federal minimum wage increases caused no loss of jobs, even among the most vulnerable workers, and contributed to the first decrease in the gap between middle- and low-income workers in almost twenty years.[10] It has been suggested that job loss did not occur because employers could absorb some of the increased costs through higher productivity, lower recruitment and training costs, decreased absenteeism, and increased worker morale.[11]

Over the last decade, researchers across the U.S. have been estimating a so-called "livable wage" based on today's actual living expenses. These "basic needs budgets" use a market-basket approach, and calculate actual living expenses—including housing, transportation, child care, health care, and taxes—and take into account regional variations and family make-up. Economic self-sufficiency is defined as making ends meet without public assistance, with the exception that some budgets include eligibility for Medicaid.

Using this method, it is estimated that the livable wage for a single-parent with one child in 2002 in Maine was $13.94—over twice the current minimum wage, and nearly two and half times the federal poverty threshold.[12] Housing, child care, and health care accounted for well over half of most basic needs budgets, while food was only about 13 percent. This is why it is argued that the federal poverty threshold, still based on the assumption that food makes up 33 percent of people's living expenses, now significantly underestimates the number of families who are unable to get by in today's economy.

The perception that many Maine families are struggling is accurate. The median hourly wage in Maine for all occupations was $11.93 in 2001.[13] That means well over half of Maine workers earn less than a livable wage, and strug-

Changing Maine

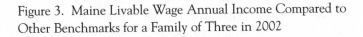

Figure 3. Maine Livable Wage Annual Income Compared to
Other Benchmarks for a Family of Three in 2002

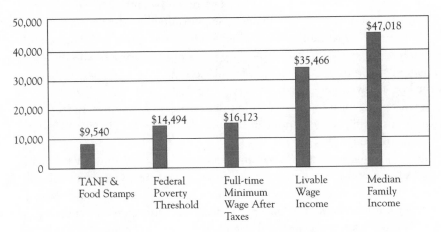

Source: Author's analysis.

gle to get by if they are the sole earner in their household. To put the livable wage measure in context, it is helpful to compare it to other measures. Figure 3 shows a livable wage income and various annual income benchmarks, including welfare cash grants (Temporary Assistance for Needy Families) and food stamps, the federal poverty threshold, a full-time minimum wage income (at Maine's 2002 rate of $5.75), and the median family income for all Maine families.[14] (The average family size in Maine as of the 2000 Census is 2.9 persons; thus median family income approximates a three-person family.) Figure 3 challenges the myth that families who receive public assistance or who work in minimum wage jobs are able to get by, let alone get ahead.

Maine's transition away from a manufacturing base has also meant that wages have become much more segregated by education. Until the late 1970s, a young person could graduate from high school, get a job at a mill, and support a family in Maine. That possibility is pretty much gone today. Nationally, between 1973 and 2001 (in 2001 dollars), the hourly wage of college graduates increased by $3.09 an hour; the hourly wage of high school graduates declined by $.55 an hour; and the hourly wage of high school dropouts declined by $2.16.[15]

During the 1970s and 1980s women entered the workforce in large numbers, making up for some of the wage losses experienced by men. In the 1990s, wives' hours of work grew much more slowly than in the 1980s, indicating that families were reaching the limit of hours they could spend in the workforce.[16]

There is a common belief that anyone can make it up the ladder to success in America, even if you start out at the bottom. It is true that some families only have low income for a few years, such as a young couple just graduating from college, with a very good chance of moving quickly into the middle class; but many more families do not see their income rise over time.

One way that income trends can be examined is by putting all families in the U.S. or in a state on a continuum by income, dividing the continuum by five, and then comparing the fifths, where each group represents 20 percent of all families. Between 1969 and 1994, 41 percent of those earners who started out among the bottom 20 percent of families on the basis of income were still at the bottom twenty-five years later. Another 25 percent had only moved up to the next rung, or into the second lowest 20 percent of families. In fact, the chances of starting at the bottom and staying there increased between the late 1960s and the early 1990s.[17]

Many have suggested that job training and education, presumably for highly technical or professional jobs, is the key to assuring livable wages for workers. However, most of the service occupations that have become the bulk of Maine's job opportunities require little advanced education. Unless we raise their wages, we cannot reduce poverty among the large working poor population.

These *wage issues* have been the chief factors in the growth of Maine's income inequality over the last thirty years. In this way, we have mirrored the nation. The economic prosperity following World War II, fueled by Roosevelt's New Deal and Johnson's Great Society, led to greater equality as Americans across the income spectrum saw their incomes rise significantly through the 1970s.

In Figures 4 and 5 the bars represent the growth rate of average income by fifth of families. For the U.S. as a whole, income for the 20 percent of families with the lowest incomes grew the most, at 120 percent between 1947 and 1979, while income of the 20 percent of families with the most incomes grew the least, at 94 percent.[18] (See Figure 4.)

After 1980 income growth slowed for everyone but more so for those at the bottom, fueled by economic restructuring, program cuts for the poor, and tax cuts for the wealthy during the Reagan Administration. The annual growth of family income of the bottom fifth of families actually declined by 1 percent between 1979 and 1999, while incomes of those in the top 20 percent grew 42 percent. (See Figure 5.) The top 1 percent experienced even faster growth in this period, with the help of capital gains and executive bonuses.

Maine's income growth pattern has been similar in the last 20 years. Since the late 1970s in Maine, the average income of the bottom 20 percent of families along the income spectrum has increased 22 percent, while the average income of the top 20 percent of families has increased 55 percent. (See Figures 6 and 7.) The exceptionally low unemployment rates during the boom of the late

Figure 4. U.S. Family Income Growth by Fifth of Families. 1947–79

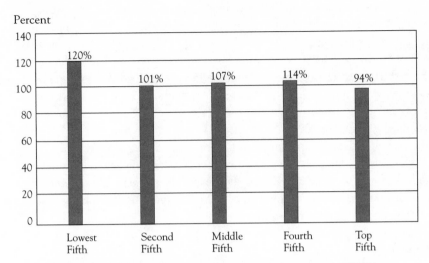

Source: Economic Policy Institute. The State of Working America 2000/2001.
(Analysis of U.S. Bureau of the Census data).

Figure 5. U.S. Family Income Growth by Fifth of Families. 1979–99

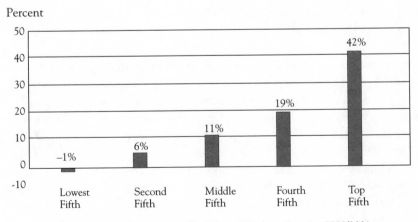

Source: Economic Policy Institute. The State of Working America 2000/2001.
(Analysis of U.S. Bureau of the Census data).

'90s brought some gains to low-wage workers, but high-income families still gained the most by far.

This rise in income inequality may also be seen by comparing the average income among families in the top 20 percent with those in the bottom 20 percent. Using this measure with three-year averages, Maine inequality grew from a ratio of 6.6 in 1978-1980 to 7.6 in 1988-1990 and to 8.3 in 1998-2000, now ranking thirty-fifth among states in income inequality by this measure. National rates of inequality grew even faster.[19] In the late 1990s, the average family income for the top fifth of families in Maine was $133,000 while in the bottom fifth it was $16,000.[20]

Public policies have contributed to the increase in wage and income inequality, including deregulation and trade liberalization; inadequate minimum wage increases; the weakening of the social safety net; the failure to have effective labor laws regulating the right to collective bargaining; and changes in federal, state, and local tax structures.[21]

What Is the Social Cost of Poverty?

Maine remains a place where people of all incomes interact, due in large part to our historically small income divide. Take a ride down most rural roads, and there will be mobile homes next door to new split-levels, next door to old farmhouses under endless repair. Go to town meetings and people from all walks of life will be gathered to assert their opinions, loudly and colorfully. Most children attend classes together in public schools. This kind of shared community has been to our great benefit as a state, but times are changing. As the income gap widens, there is more class separation

People with modest incomes along the southern and mid-coast have begun to retreat inland, as the wealthy have bought up seafront property at increasingly high prices, raising overall valuations. There is a growing gap between the poverty in the northern and so-called "rim" counties (bordering Canada), as compared to the relative wealth in southern coastal counties. In Portland, low-income people in the center of town are increasingly unable to find or afford housing, as evidenced by the dramatic increase in numbers of intact families coming into homeless shelters, and the flight to neighboring communities of those who can afford to move.[22] Many negative results arise from these trends.

Income inequality is bad for our health. Researchers have shown that income and status, work environments, social support networks, education, and other social indicators are the greatest predictors of our health status.[23] Material deprivation and social exclusion that diminish participation in common activities and civic decision-making contribute to poor health.[24] People living in states with high income equality live longer than people living in states with great income inequality. This goes for the wealthy, too. It appears that the *level*

Figure 6. Maine Family Income Growth by Fifth of Families,
Late 1970s to Late 1990s

Percent

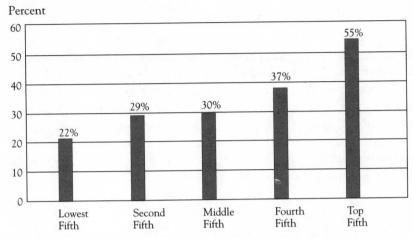

Source: Economic Policy Institute & Center on Budget & Policy Priorities.
2002. Pulling Apart.
(Analysis of U.S. Bureau of the Census Current Population Survey data).

Figure 7. Maine Family Income Growth by Fifth of Families,
Late 1980s to Late 1990s

Percent

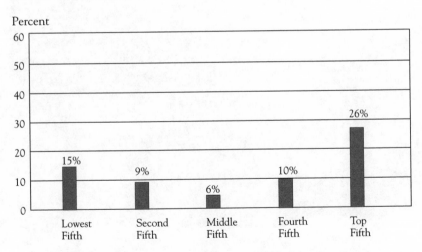

Source: Economic Policy Institute & Center on Budget & Policy Priorities.
2002. Pulling Apart.
(Analysis of U.S. Bureau of the Census Current Population Survey data).

of equality matters even more for the life expectancy of everyone, than how much wealth a state has.[25]

Poverty and income inequality can harm our children. Poor children may not receive enough nutrition to support normal growth.[26] Their cognitive and verbal skills are often reduced.[27] They have less exposure to toys, books, stimulating experiences, and successful role models. Conflict between economically stressed parents and the pressure of debt provokes anxiety and weakens self-esteem in their kids.[28] Regional segregation by income increases disparities in the quality of education available to poor children, as Maine has experienced. The patterns of social interaction created by the neighborhoods and the quality of schools that kids grow up in structure the opportunities and constraints they perceive when it comes time to decide whether or not to continue their education beyond high school.[29] Maine's economic future is at risk if we tolerate this reduction in human capital among our children.

Lewiston

Maine's growing income inequality threatens our community life and social cohesion. As people segregate more and more by income, fear and resentment grow. People are more likely to be concerned about the well-being of a family down the street whom they know and see every day, and to take both private and public actions to help them, than they are likely to be concerned about a vague notion of the "poor" or "rich" living in some part of town or some region of our state they never see. The poor are becoming concentrated in neighborhoods and communities. And while we have yet to see gated communities in Maine, the wealthy enclaves at the end of southern coastal roads are not much different.

As workers slip from the middle class to the ranks of the working poor, it is common for them to become resentful of and distance themselves from the very poor who need public assistance. A bumper sticker on an old pick-up stating, "Just Another Slave to the Welfare State" exemplifies this tendency to scapegoat the poor rather than the very wealthy who have benefited disproportionately from tax cuts and "corporate welfare." Meanwhile, many wealthy people have become so far removed from everyone else that their impression of community well-being relies primarily on stock market performance.

Growing income inequality has reduced trust in government. Hard working families who once felt supported by government now feel that something is wrong with "the system," because they are falling farther and farther behind. Poor parents have seen family assistance reduced, as welfare rules have tightened or subsidized housing has diminished. They feel frightened and frustrated when they get a low paying job and then lose all public assistance long before they make enough to meet expenses. It is no surprise that they feel "the system" is working against them, as well.

It is not just poor families who need the safety net. Many have lost sight of the fact that public assistance to struggling families puts cash in the hands of people who need it and will spend it during economic downturns. The economy needs fiscal policies that sustain demand when unemployment rises, so employers will have an incentive to maintain production. Welfare and other income maintenance programs such as unemployment insurance and food stamps help smooth out the economy's ups and downs.

The current anti-tax fury in Maine has made an ironic alliance between many people at the bottom and at the top of the income spectrum; both believe that their taxes are too high. The reality is that taxes are too high for those at the bottom precisely because taxes have become relatively lower for those at the top. Yet, this nuance is usually not articulated in the ongoing headlines about Maine's tax burden.

So, government is now more often seen as the problem rather than the solution. This was not always the case.

The Federal Role in Addressing Poverty

In the economic expansion following World War II, millions of people across the U.S. and in Maine moved out of poverty and into the middle class; by the 1960s, however, there were still millions of people left behind.

President John F. Kennedy was moved by the poverty he saw during his campaign and by authors such as social activist Michael Harrington, who brought to light the lives of poor people still struggling from the Mississippi Delta to Appalachia to rural Maine.[30] Kennedy's anti-poverty proposals were later implemented in President Lyndon B. Johnson's War on Poverty, announced in 1964. This resulted in a dramatic expansion in social welfare policies and in the domestic federal budget.[31]

Medicare, Medicaid, Community Action Programs, and Head Start were all created during this period. The Food Stamp Act was passed. Benefit levels were increased in Social Security for the elderly and eligibility was broadened in Aid to Families with Dependent Children (AFDC). Social Security disability benefits and coverage, introduced in the 1950s, were expanded. Housing assistance was extended through the Farmers Home Administration to provide low interest mortgage and home repair loans for low-income rural families.[32] Several years later, in 1973, the Comprehensive Employment and Training Act (CETA) was enacted, to provide public service jobs and on-the-job training to disadvantaged workers.

In the 1960s, government fostered the ideals of shared prosperity. When President Johnson announced the War on Poverty, he declared that the poor were not to blame for poverty and that the nation was responsible for giving them a lift up, toward self-sufficiency. The welfare reform movement of that time was about helping poor families get such assistance. As a result, at least some of the stigma that had attached to welfare disappeared. As Harrington later stated, "It was no longer dishonorable to claim rights to which one had been entitled all along but never used out of a sense of shame."[33]

In Maine, federally funded community action agencies started operations, like PROP in Portland and Penquis CAP in Bangor. They worked to help low-income neighborhoods organize themselves and to advocate for their needs. They offered new programs and services. Pine Tree Legal Assistance, with federal funding, helped ensure that eligible low-income parents were able to enroll in AFDC, and represented poor people's interests to the state. One of Pine Tree Legal's early victories in 1967 brought about the end of debtors prison in Maine, exemplifying a turning away from penalizing people because they were poor.

The War on Poverty reduced poverty among the elderly, but did so at considerable expense by providing Social Security and Medicare benefits to *all of the elderly*, even those who were not poor. Hindsight indicates that the policymakers of the time, despite their honorable intentions to eradicate all poverty, did not recognize the enormity of the challenge and the level of continuing investment it would take to do the job.

In the 1970s oil price shocks, multiple recessions, industrial restructuring, and the cost of the Vietnam War curtailed the War on Poverty, and halted the dramatic drop in overall poverty rates.[34] Unemployment rose. Conservative administrations that followed attacked social welfare programs on the premise that they were encouraging dependence on the federal government, marital breakups, and "out-of-wedlock" childbearing. The poor, especially single mothers, came under attack. There was a growing emphasis on "fraud and abuse" within the system, and a return to distinctions between the "deserving poor" and those who were supposedly "taking advantage of the system." This rhetoric has remained an entrenched part of the public discourse about welfare ever since, despite mounds of evidence to the contrary.

During the Nixon Administration, the public policy emphasis shifted to enhancing benefits only for those who were working. The idea of a guaranteed income level was discarded; and, instead, the Earned Income Tax Credit (EITC), a refundable tax credit for low-income workers, was adopted in 1973 and has enjoyed bipartisan support ever since.

In the early 1980s the most severe recession since the 1930s raised the overall U.S. poverty rate to about 15 percent and the child poverty rate to more than 20 percent. In 1981 President Ronald Reagan imposed 60 percent of his budget cuts upon the poor, cutting AFDC eligibility, food stamps, subsidized housing, and employment and training programs.[35] During his administration, Reagan instituted significant tax cuts intended to advance economic growth and create a "trickle down" to the poor through increased employment and earnings. Except for an expansion of the EITC, there was very little trickle down at all; rather, as we have seen, most of the benefits flowed to people at the top of the income scale.

By the 1990s the welfare reform debate was focused on reducing eligibility and cutting back assistance. In 1996 President Bill Clinton fulfilled his campaign pledge to "end welfare as we know it," by turning AFDC into a block grant program that ended the federal guarantee of family assistance for states. The new program, called Temporary Assistance for Needy Families (TANF), has a five-year lifetime limit on receipt of federal cash assistance. For the first time, welfare recipients are required to work, no matter what their circumstances, in order to receive benefits. TANF allows just twelve months of training activities, and the program emphasis is on "work first."

Across the nation, and in Maine, caseloads dropped by half. Most of these single mothers went into the low-wage job market with few skills and expanded the number of the working poor. Many came back on welfare when their job ended, or a sick child or broken car led to a job loss. Further, workforce training programs were cut through the Workforce Investment Act. The only significant new help for low-income families was another expansion of the EITC. By the late 1990s there was more funding for the EITC than for cash welfare.[36]

In the late 1990s the longest economic expansion since WWII produced another time of plenty. This time, however, the federal government did not dedicate itself to trying to share this prosperity and eradicate poverty, as it had done during the 1960s. Rather, the administration of President George W. Bush has pressed for more hours of work from single parents receiving welfare assistance, of whom about one-third have disabilities or are taking care of children with serious disabilities.[37] They have recommended flat-funding for TANF with no inflationary increase, shifting more of the cost to states for workforce supports that help low-income workers stay in the workforce—such as transportation, child care, and remedial education.

Meanwhile, the prominent policy debates of the day revolve around reducing taxes for the wealthiest Americans, instead of broadly distributing benefits for all. *When it comes to addressing the plight of the poor, federal leadership in policy setting is paramount*; in this way, we are much farther behind than we were in 1960.

What Has Maine Done to Help the Poor?
Despite federal cutbacks in social welfare over the years, Maine has remained a bright light, and at times has been a shining star. With our limited state resources, Maine's policy leaders by and large have retained a deep commitment to helping their fellow citizens in need.

Maine expanded family assistance in several areas during the Administration of Governor Joseph Brennan in the 1980s. Maine's AFDC benefit levels have traditionally been the lowest in New England; during the 1980s, however, Maine passed AFDC benefit increases almost every year, allowing them to at least keep pace with inflation. During this period, the state took over a significant portion of General Assistance funding, a program of emergency relief administered by municipalities. The Maine Resident Homeowners and Renters Property Tax Relief Program was created for elders in the 1970s, and expanded in the 1980s to other adults. This is a state-funded program providing a property tax or rent refund to eligible low-income households, and is commonly referred to as the property tax "circuit breaker."

In Maine as in many states, the deep recession of the early 1990s brought calls for spending cuts, many of them targeted at programs for the poor. Maine experienced some of the deepest AFDC benefit cuts in the nation, bringing them back to 1988 levels. The state cut its contribution to General Assistance from $22 million to $6 million. The property tax circuit breaker was reduced in the early 1990s, although modestly improved later in the decade. Cash support for nonworking adults in 2001, and for those working adults still eligible for

Changing Maine

welfare, had about two-thirds the buying power of what it would have had in 1969.

After the 1996 federal welfare reform legislation, many states tightened their welfare eligibility even more than required by federal legislation, by enforcing shorter time limits and adding "family caps"—denying assistance for children born while a parent is receiving welfare benefits. Maine, however, was an exception. During the Administration of Governor Angus King, Jr., Maine implemented one of most compassionate and effective welfare reform programs in the country. It includes state-funded access to two- and four-year college degrees for women on welfare, the Parents as Scholars program; individualized services for families, to help them succeed in the workplace; expanded Medicaid coverage for low-income children and their parents; child care and transportation supports for working parents; and a state commitment to continue benefits beyond the sixty-month federal limit for needy families who "play by the rules."

Equally important, Maine's tax system has remained relatively less regressive than many other states. This means that we recognize the logic that people with greater financial capacity should contribute more to public resources than those with the least ability to pay. In recent years, various efforts have helped maintain Maine's tax fairness, including strengthening the property tax refund program; reducing the sales tax; increasing the threshold of liability for income taxes to $10,000; and enacting a state Earned Income Tax Credit.

More recently, Governor John Baldacci's commitments to help reduce poverty include expanded eligibility for unemployment benefits for part-time workers, a minimum wage increase, the creation of a low-cost community college system and the promise of health care access to even more working poor families through the passage of Dirigo Health. Maine can be proud of these and many public policies that contribute to our overall quality of life. Despite our relatively low per capita income, the Fordham Institute for Innovation in Social Policy ranked Maine fourth among all the states in 2002 on numerous indicators of "social health," including income equality, infant mortality, child abuse, high school completion, health insurance coverage, and homicides.

There remain challenges ahead, however. Maine, like most states, is now experiencing budget shortfalls, as the impact of federal tax cuts and the slowing economy settle in. Federal deficits are predicted for the foreseeable future, and will likely result in spending cuts. If recent history repeats itself, federal programs for the poor will take the biggest hits, and states will be faced with making up the difference. In the years to come we will have to decide again and again how much we are willing to collectively invest to make sure that all Maine people have equal access to opportunities to build our shared future.

Maine, like the rest of the country, will also become more ethnically diverse. Our stable commitment to the poor is due in part to the relative homogeneity of Maine's population. In many other states, ethnic minorities make up a much larger proportion of the population and, as such, are a more significant portion of the poor. Black women on welfare have been the targets of "welfare-bashing" for many years in this country. Since the poor are mostly from the racial majority in Maine, it is not so easy to construe them as "different" from the rest of us. Still, the fact that ethnic minorities in Maine are already at least twice as likely to be poor than their white neighbors indicates that we are not exempt from institutional racism in this state. Recently, the resistence by some in Lewiston to the influx of Somali immigrants gave us a blatant indication of what can happen if a population of a different race is perceived to be competing for scarce public welfare resources.

Conclusion

Many policy leaders have proclaimed that, "A rising tide lifts all boats." The widespread prosperity of the post WWII years did raise living standards, but still left millions trapped in poverty. Lyndon Johnson, and Franklin D. Roosevelt before him, recognized that *both a robust economy and deliberate policy interventions are needed to lift up those at the bottom.*

The federal government must lead if we are to make serious inroads into poverty reduction. Without federal leadership and resources, the states can only work at the margins. Maine has done a very good job of this, and remains one of the best family assistance laboratories for our federal system.

It is not by accident that resentment towards the poor has coincided with the manufacturing decline across the country, under the impact of globalization and free trade agreements. Some political leaders have managed to deflect the legitimate fears and anger of vulnerable workers, families, and communities onto the poor who seek public assistance, especially when they are in the ethnic minority. This cycle of victim blaming and lack of public will legitimizes the lack of real poverty reduction strategies and actions at the policy level.

We can and must do better, for all our sakes. With the help of our Congressional delegation, we must break through the ideological blockade in Washington that blames the poor for being poor, and continues to unravel the safety net. We need national economic policies that support working families, an adequate safety net for times of need, and affordable, accessible education and training to help bring all workers along in this ongoing restructuring of the economy. In Maine, we need to maintain and strengthen our commitment to help the poor in all the ways we can.

Each one of us will have to work harder to reach across the income divide. We have a responsibility as good citizens to generate public understanding of the terrible effects of poverty that permeate our communities. To do this, we need a new image of the poor that recognizes their struggles and their strengths.

Heidi Hart was a welfare recipient who participated in the Parents as Scholars (PaS) program and graduated from the University of Southern Maine in 2001. She was quoted in a report about the success of PaS graduates, saying: "I feel really lucky that I lived in Maine where people agreed that education should be part of welfare reform. The day that I graduated, my eight-year-old daughter walked across the stage with me. I felt so proud!"[38] This is the kind of image that will move us to support the potential in all Maine people, and ensure a prosperous future for everyone.

L isa Pohlmann is Associate Director for the Maine Center for Economic Policy, an independent, nonpartisan research organization. MECEP's mission is to advance public policy solutions to achieve a prosperous, fair and sustainable economy. Lisa has written on livable wages, welfare reform, affordable health care, and sustainable development. She has a master's degree from the School for International Training in Vermont and a Masters in public policy and management from the Muskie School of Public Service. Lisa has lived and worked in Maine for twenty-five years.

OUR HOUSING STOCK has increasingly provided decent shelter and solid financial value to Maine people over the past four decades. Especially in recent years, however, it has not been so successful in providing access to jobs and services, and in fostering community. No- and slow-growth policies have limited the construction of needed multi-family housing, and facilitated the suburbanization of land use known as sprawl. Maine communities must re-evaluate these policies and practices, especially to meet the needs of young workers in our service centers and those of isolated older people living in suburban communities. For its part, the state must see itself as building communities, not just individual residential and commercial structures. With stronger state leadership, a more complex approach to distinguishing housing markets, and a bottom-up decision approach, Maine can ensure that our housing will once again foster access and community as well as shelter and financial security.

4 Housing for a Changing Maine
It's Not Working!

FRANK O'HARA

Housing has many dimensions. Just consider your own home or condominium or apartment. At a minimum, your housing provides you with shelter, economic value, access to services, and community.

It provides you with physical shelter. It prevents rain and snow from falling on your head. It protects from cold winds and hot sun. It supplies running water. It affords privacy. It has door locks for safety. We take all of this for granted until the roof leaks or the plumbing breaks or there's an ice storm. Then, we are reminded that physical shelter is the most basic function of the home.

Second, your home is an investment; it represents financial value. Even if you are a renter, housing is the biggest single expenditure you will make in your lifetime, and choosing wisely will affect your entire financial outlook. If you are an owner, your home is likely your biggest financial asset. If you can't afford your home or apartment, you will find yourself unable to buy other necessities, such as health care and education. On the other hand, if you're a homeowner, and you've chosen well, you may make a windfall when you sell. You can test the importance of housing as an economic investment yourself. At your next neighborhood party, say in a loud voice, "You know what the Smiths' house down the street sold for?" Then, stop and listen as the room grows quiet.

A third function of housing is to provide access to society's goods. Your home address is a ticket to good schools, to paved and cleared roads, even to the eligibility to vote. Beyond these public goods, your location also provides you with access to places of employment, places to buy goods and services, and places to enjoy culture and the arts. Your home address matters.

The fourth and last function of housing is to foster community. Your home or apartment or condominium sits in some relationship to other homes and apartments and condominiums. This cluster creates your neighborhood, your village, your section of town. From your neighbors, you receive companionship, support, and security. With your neighbors, you sustain churches, sports leagues, arts associations, reading groups, corner stores, and restaurants. Your neighbors watch your home when you are away, shovel your sidewalk in winter, and watch out for your children. This is why, when you refer in conversation to your "home," you are often talking about much more than a simple building.

So, these are the four dimensions of housing: physical shelter, financial value, access to jobs and services, and community. Now, if I may, let me step back from your individual home and look at the broader picture. How well has Maine's housing stock done in providing all four dimensions—shelter, value, access, and community—over the last half century? What is the outlook for the future? And what might Maine state government do about it?

Housing as Shelter

The economist David Birch once defined a house as a "nearly weather-tight box with pipes in it which will not freeze in the winter."[1] Maine's and the nation's performance in improving   er since World War II is, truly, a great public policy success story.

In 1940, at the beginning of World War II, two out of five homes in Maine (39 percent) had no indoor toilets.[2] Over half (55 percent) lacked some basic plumbing facilities—if not the toilet, then hot-and-cold piped water, or a bathtub or shower. By 1960, a third (30.5 percent) lacked some basic plumbing facilities. And by 2000, fewer than one in a hundred homes lacked all the elements of indoor plumbing (0.9 percent). So in sixty years, Maine has gone from 55 percent lacking complete plumbing to less than 1 percent.

It's the same story in heating. In 1940, eight out of ten homes were heated entirely by wood and coal stoves. By 2000, nine in ten had central heating. In 1940, one in seven families lived in overcrowded circumstances (more than one person per room); by 2000, the proportion was down to one in 100.

Further along I will make some critical observations about recent housing policy. Whatever the shortcomings, however, the achievement is plain: in the two generations since World War II, we have made spacious, heated, uncrowded physical shelter the *norm* rather than the *exception* for Maine people.

This is not to say that the need continually to repair, rehabilitate, and upgrade our housing has gone away. Maine has the *oldest* housing stock in the nation: nearly a third of our housing units are more than 60 years old. Anyone who owns an old home knows that they eat money; you can spend all you have, and there is *always* more to do.

At least those of us who own our houses are motivated to keep up on repairs. Landlords are not always so motivated; and even when they are, the rent levels are not always adequate to pay back their investment. There are 50,000 Maine households in apartments built over sixty years ago.[3] Many are three-deckers in mill towns like Lewiston, Waterville, Rumford, and Sanford. They often lack insulation, have outdated electrical service, and present fire safety risks. Without government action, we may expect to lose many of these buildings in the next few decades.

Besides old urban apartments, there is also substandard rural housing. The modern incarnation of the tarpaper shack is the old trailer, built before federal manufactured housing building and safety codes were implemented in 1976. There are at least 5,000 rural Maine families living in these old trailers; and it seems every few months there's a news story about a fire in such housing.[4]

Finally, considering our housing stock in its physical aspect, there is an emerging challenge that Maine must face in coming years: how to adapt our old, walk-up, small-room, narrow hallway housing stock, to an aging population. Already in 2000, the Census reports that over 100,000 Maine people have physical disabilities that limit their ability to move around a house.[5] These numbers will grow substantially as our population grows older. This means another generation of adaptations will be needed for Maine's old three-deckers and extended farmhouses.

In short, when it comes to shelter, we've made great strides in the last half century. Yet, many poor people still live in substandard apartments and trailers; and adapting our housing to an aging population will be a challenge.

Housing as Economic Value
The second dimension of housing is its economic value. The median value of a single-family home in Maine was just $4,900 in 1950. If you were looking for a bargain, you could drive to Washington County and pick up a median home for $2,275. Even after factoring out inflation, the 2000 Census-reported Maine median value of just under $100,000 represents a *tripling* in real value. If you can see ocean water outside of your window, the likelihood is that your home's real value has increased fully ten times.

So, the value of the investment is up. Moreover, the proportion of us who have such an investment is also up. In 1950, two out of three Maine households (63 percent) owned their own homes. By 2000, three out of four of us (74.5 percent) owned our home, giving Maine one of the highest homeownership rates in the nation.

What is it all worth? In 2000, the value of owner-occupied homes in Maine was $32 billion; add in another $6 billion or so for non-residents, and the total housing stock is worth about $38 billion. A third of owners in Maine own their homes outright, with no mortgage or debt whatsoever. Another third have one mortgage only. The last third have a mortgage plus a second mortgage or equity loan as well, enabling them to use the asset value of their home to make major purchases such as cars or college tuitions or home improvements.[6] So, more of us own homes than in 1950, and the homes we own are more valuable. That's good news.

The bad news is that the price of houses has increased faster than incomes over this time. In 1950, the median home cost about 2.2 times the median household income. In 2000, the median home cost 2.7 times median household income. Today's mortgage tools are much more sophisticated than were available in 1950—with subsidized rates for first-time buyers (through the Maine State Housing Authority), variable rates, longer terms, lower down-payments, and more detailed credit reviews. As a result, people can buy a given home with less income than was true then, which explains why the ratio of income to housing price has changed.

Renters have had a better deal, as well. In current dollars, average monthly rents have risen from $286 to $497 in Maine from 1950 to 2000, a pace that is 27 percent slower than the growth in incomes. This is one of the reasons we have had so few private apartments built in the last few decades: rents have not increased as fast as single family home values; so, builders have concentrated on the latter. Even in Southern Maine, where rents now have reached the thousand-dollar-a-month level, relative to incomes they're no worse than they were in 1950.

Amazingly, after all of these changes—after we have gone from three-deckers to condominiums, from small Farmer's Home ranches to three-car garage colonials; after we've moved to the suburbs and out into the country—the proportion of Mainers who experience a problem with affordability is pretty much the same as when it was first calculated in 1980. About one in seven Maine owners pay over a third of their income for housing, and about one in four renters do the same.

One of the reasons the affordability picture has remained stable is that *the federal government once played a major role in helping people get apartments and homes*. The Farmer's Home Administration helped tens of thousands of rural Maine families buy a first home in the 1970s; in 1984 one in thirteen Maine owners had an FMHA mortgage. Likewise, almost all rental housing construction in that period was subsidized by the federal Department of Housing and Urban Development; for example, in 1984, one in five renters received HUD subsidies.[7] Today, these federal programs no longer are building more than a handful of homes and apartments in Maine. In fact, the initial mortgages from subsidized apartment projects built in the 1980s are now being paid off, and the threat exists that some may be converted to more lucrative private use.

So, as with shelter, the overall historical picture on affordability is pretty good. More of us are owners; houses provide a lot more savings to all of us; and most of us aren't paying any more than we used to.

Of course no one lives in this "big picture;" we all live in individual houses, and it is in the details that the picture gets more complicated. Here are a few particulars:

- There are several thousand Maine people who are homeless each year, including families with children. While reliable information about comparative rates of homelessness is unavailable, informed observers say that overall there has been an increase over the years. Contributing factors include the deinstitutionalization of people with mental health problems; more mobility for individuals; the weakening of the bonds of the extended family; the disappearance of inexpensive, in-town rooming houses; alcohol and drug addiction; reduced rental vacancy rates, allowing landlords to be more choosy; and the high cost of security deposits.

- On the coast, fishing and farming families have seen their property values rise, and their property taxes along with it; and many have had to leave family homesteads and move inland, to the other side of Route 1.

- In the north, the problem is exactly reversed: the decline in population in some towns has led to a reduction in housing prices, resulting in a loss in assets for individual families. Many Millinocket families are facing the loss of a lifetime of savings, as they watch their home values plummet.

- In contrast, in the south, one in three renters in Greater Portland paid more than a third of their income for rent; and as rents have jumped again since the Census year, the proportion may be approaching closer to half of all renters today. The Kittery-York homeownership market has been identified by the National Association of Homebuilders as one of the ten least affordable housing markets in the United States; and the only one of the ten outside California.[8]

So, we have some markets in Maine where home values have gone down so much that people have lost their savings; and others, where inflation in cost is so out of hand that few can afford to buy a home.

This variability of local conditions is one reason *it is important that state government have different housing goals and policies for different parts of the state.* Up north, where demand is low, the challenge is rehabilitation and preserving the stock; new construction there will only lead to abandonment of old housing. Down south, where demand is high, new construction is needed; and rehabilitation assistance is largely wasted, since the private market is accomplishing this, anyway.[9]

One final question: Is this housing market on a bubble, about to collapse as it did in the late 1980s? There *are* similarities. I remember doing housing market studies in the late 1980s for over-eager developers; and I have had similar experiences again in recent years. Sometimes, it feels like housing prices become unhinged from people's ability to pay. The *Economist* magazine has argued for some months this is the case in housing markets worldwide: namely, that housing prices are in a speculative bubble similar to that of high technology stocks a few years ago, and that a collapse in prices is imminent.[10]

Certainly housing prices will stabilize for a time. The economy is still fragile; interest rates are rising; and the stock market is attracting more capital—all trends that tend to weaken housing investment. Despite this, I don't think Maine prices will fall, for several reasons:

- From a historical point of view, rent levels today are no higher (and in some areas of the state are lower) than they were in 1950, relative to incomes;

- Home prices in the interior of Maine are still very reasonable, relative to incomes;

- Home prices on the coast today are influenced not only by the incomes of local residents, but also by the incomes and assets of retirees moving here from Massachusetts. In the second quarter of 2003, the median sales price of a home in the Portland area was just under $200,000, and the median sales price of a home in the Boston area was twice as high, just over $400,000.[11] Home inflation in coastal Maine will not abate while prices in Boston remain high.

In sum, then, the big picture in housing finance in Maine is that more people own houses, and the houses are worth more. Yet, at a micro level, people are having problems both in markets that are too cold—such as Millinocket, where home values are disappearing—and in markets that are too hot—such as Portland and York, where costs are out of sight. In a state with so many varying, local conditions, this is where averages are not always helpful—just as people can drown in a lake with an average depth of 6 inches.

Housing as Access

Now, let us turn to housing's role in providing access to services and jobs. The good news is that the *electronic* access of our homes is much better. In 1960 over a quarter of Maine homes lacked a telephone. Today 99 percent have a phone and 60 percent are wired to the Internet. In these respects, the modern home is more open and accessible to the wider world.

In a second respect—physical location—access is worse. Our houses are farther away from each other, from our places of work, from our shopping, and from our recreation and culture. To give just one example: In a recent meeting I attended with Gardiner landlords, they said that their fastest growing market consisted of Portland area commuters.[12] Charles Colgan and Evan Richert have addressed the issue of sprawl in detail in prior sections of this book. What I will focus on here is one aspect of the problem, the relationship of affordable housing to economic development.

Take Greater Portland. This region was the job engine for the *entire* state during the 1990s, accounting for one in three new jobs statewide, and 23,300 new jobs in all. More importantly, for a state facing the out-migration of our young people, the Portland area provided an in-state alternative to Boston and points south. In fact, the Census reported in November of 2003 that the City of Portland ranked tenth in the country in attracting young, single, college-educated people.[13]

During this same decade, however, Greater Portland added only 3,000 new apartments. That's 23,000 new jobs, and only 3,000 new apartments. Not surprisingly, the vacancy rate dropped from 8 percent to 1 percent, and rents have passed the $1,000 mark. The obvious question is: *How long can Greater Portland continue to sustain job growth for Maine's young people if there are no places for them to live?*

Apartment construction is particularly important. Young people are mobile. They are trying out different jobs, careers, friends, lifestyles, and regions. Mobile people tend to live in apartments. Furthermore, as young people like to live near the action, near night life, the apartments are typically downtown.

Greater Portland is not exceptional in not providing new apartments. For several years in the late 1990s, Maine as a whole ranked *last* among the fifty states in new multifamily construction. The question remains, however: If we in Maine don't build housing for young people in the one geographic region where there has consistently been economic opportunity, and where young Mainers have consistently moved to, then where do we expect our young people to go? We all know the answer: straight to Boston, by-passing southern Maine.

Here's one last fact to consider about apartments and young people: In the 1970s and '80s, Maine added 50,000 rental units, and had a *net in-migration* of people under thirty-five. During the '90s, Maine added just 8,000 apartments, a third of the prior rate, and had a *net out-migration* of people under thirty-five. As former New England Patriots end Terry Glenn once said, "You do the math."

Why aren't we building apartments? Part of the reason is the withdrawal of the federal government from housing. During the Reagan administration, federal subsidies for the new construction of affordable apartments and homes were cut back to nearly zero. At the same time, the tax code was revised to treat apartment investments less favorably. Today, outside of a limited tax credit program (building 150 to 200 apartment units in Maine a year), the federal government is largely *out* of the construction business.

That's half of the story. The other half is that communities in growing areas have chosen to try and slow growth by adopting policies that discourage or prohibit multifamily housing. So we have the paradox in southern Maine of communities actively seeking property tax-producing businesses, while at the same time denying housing for their workers. This is a formula that, if allowed to continue over time, will choke the economic growth of southern Maine, which in turn will reverberate throughout the entire state economy.[14]

I have chosen to speak about housing's role of providing access to jobs with regard to young people. I could just as easily have discussed *other* groups who are experiencing access problems in the same detail, such as:

- Fishing families who can no longer live on the ocean side of Route 1;

- Police, firefighters, and teachers who can't afford to live in the town where they work; and

- Retirees who can't afford to stay in the homes they have lived in their whole lives:

In the other dimensions of housing which I have spoken about—the quality of shelter and the financial value of homes—there has been measurable improvement since 1950. In the area of *access*, Maine has taken a step back: It is harder today than it was then to find apartments and homes on the coast and in southern Maine.

Housing as Community

The lack of access has implications for the fourth dimension of housing, housing as community.

A year ago I conducted several community visioning sessions in towns around the state. At these sessions, fifty to a hundred residents would come and spend a day talking about what they wanted for their town's future. I particularly remember a man in Ogunquit.[15] He stood up after everyone had spent most of the day trying to think of ways to protect the town from traffic and houses. He said that the last grade school in town was about to close due to lack of students, because families with young children couldn't afford to live in Ogunquit any more. He asked if his fellow citizens wanted to live a town where everyone had white hair, where there were no sounds of children playing on the street corner, where everyone who drives the police cars was from someplace else. There was a moment of silence after he spoke. His concern had struck a chord felt by people living all up and down the coast of Maine.

Yet, despite this concern, people still have a hard time making the connection to housing. The connection in fact is simple: *To have a diverse population— young and old, working and retired, large families and singles—a town must have a diverse housing stock*—single and multifamily, in town and in the country, manufactured and stick-built. It is as simple as that.

In recent years, many town officials in Maine have tended to view housing development as an extension of property tax policy—to let in the houses that they think pay more in taxes than they cost in services, and to prohibit those that they think don't. In practical terms, this has meant permitting senior housing and seasonal housing, and restricting apartments and starter homes where young families might live.

This fiscal approach to residential development is short-sighted on two counts. First, the various state-aid funding formulas around school aid and other services make many prevailing assumptions about the tax impacts of housing projects simply wrong. For example, with regard to school children, if a commu-

Changing Maine

Senior Citizens' Center, Fort Kent

nity has a stable or declining student population—which is true of most Maine cities and towns—then state revenue gained from additional students is usually a net fiscal benefit, not a loss, to the community. My firm, Planning Decisions, is currently studying this issue and will be issuing a report in early 2004.

Second, this strategy drives towns towards only approving that new housing that serves people of the same income and status. It is making many Maine communities far less diverse and colorful than they were a generation ago. This *social segregation* is one more cost of sprawl, to go along with the loss of land, the disruption of habitat, and the increased cost of municipal services.[16]

Maine did better in generations past. The small town centers—with their greens and Civil War statues and general stores, with their white church spires and their clapboard houses crowded together—created lively spaces for people of all kinds. The urban three-deckers along the trolley lines in Maine's mill towns of a century ago were at times crowded and dirty; but they were places where families and neighbors watched over each other.

Charles Colgan argues elsewhere in this book that we are in a period of the "rise of urban Maine." I would note that urban Maine has risen before. In the second half of the nineteenth and first half of the twentieth centuries, more Maine people lived in mill towns and urban neighborhoods than on farms or islands or in logging camps—even though, as Colgan points out, at the same time we were selling ourselves as "rural vacationland." It is this tradition that Evan Richert has sought to recapture in the idea of "Great American Neighborhood." It is not something new. Rather it is a return to what we used to do before World War II, before public policy became focused on making the world convenient for automobiles.

Interestingly, the one new housing innovation in Maine in the last twenty years captures this community value. It is the retirement housing—the complexes of single-family cottages, condominiums, and assisted living facilities that have been built from York to Blue Hill along Maine's coast, and inland to Orono and Augusta. These projects are built to be walkable—to have good access to health services and recreation, to arts and culture, and to shopping. The residences are energy-efficient and low-maintenance. There are common rooms for eating and visiting and social activity. These planned communities appeal to the market; they are generating a demand that no one thought was achievable in Maine twenty years ago.

If you were to ask young people what *they* want, you would hear many of the same things: walkable, accessible to recreation and social activities, etc. The difference is that they tend to look in urban centers rather than along the coast.

Some say that Maine people cannot afford these retirement projects and that, therefore, there is nothing to be learned from them. It is true that the average retired Mainer cannot afford to spend several hundred thousand dollars for a condominium unit, and another thousand per month for services; but that is missing the point.

Maine already has houses that are close together, that are near health services, that have sidewalks, that are close to arts and cultural and recreational activities, and that are inexpensive. They are in urban neighborhoods throughout Maine. Recently planner Holly Dominie and I worked with the West Side Neighbors in Augusta to identify ways that their neighborhood could become more friendly and inviting to older people. The group found many ways that traffic could be calmed, that sidewalks could be made more safe and passable, that community activities could be enriched, that health and shopping services could be brought close together.

This is the Great American Neighborhood, all over again. In central and northern Maine, the Great American Neighborhood model must be, in the first instance, one of rehabilitating and restoring existing town and city centers. In southern and coastal Maine, the model must also involve building new housing in compact neighborhoods.

Implications for State Policy

In sum, then, there are four functions of housing: to provide shelter, to provide a financial asset, to provide access to services and jobs, and to provide community. Since World War II Maine has done well at the individualized functions of providing decent shelter and good investments; but is doing worse in the social functions of providing access to jobs and community. What does all this mean for state policy?

Let me start with some background.

For thirty years the federal government led housing policy in the United States, and in Maine. The Housing Act of 1949 declared it a national goal to provide a "decent home and suitable living environment for every American family." This led to Urban Renewal, Public Housing Authorities, Section 8 apartments, Farmer's Home housing, and Community Development Block Grants. These programs, in retrospect, had mixed results. They certainly contributed greatly to the improvement of the quality of housing, and in some cases they also caused the loss of housing and neighborhoods. Regardless of the varying results, however, the message was clear: The federal government was leading the effort to improve housing in the United States.

Congress has not formally retracted the goal of the 1949 Act; but there is no question that, since the Reagan years, the wind has gone out of the sails. For twenty years there has been a void. State governments in Maine and elsewhere have continued to see their housing role as limited and specialized, namely, to sell tax-exempt bonds for the purposes of helping first-time homebuyers, and helping affordable apartment developers.

It has been long enough. The federal government has not resumed its former role in twenty years, and is unlikely to do it soon. Maine has too much at stake in terms of economic development and quality of life to remain passive about housing. It's time for the State of Maine to accept a leadership role. This will not require massive new expenditures. Maine will never be rich enough to replace the generous subsidies once provided by the federal government. However, Maine already spends several hundred million dollars each year on transportation, housing, and community planning and economic development; and a more intelligent and coordinated use of these funds can have powerful results.

There are two areas where the state can and should assert leadership.

First, *the state should manage overall supply and demand in Maine's thirty-five local housing markets.*

Housing is unlike other consumer goods, in that there is generally a lag between supply and demand. If a book is popular, the publisher runs a new edition; if a car is popular, the automakers extend production runs. However, if housing is in high demand, it usually takes several years before land, builders, municipal governments, and financers can organize to respond.

The result is that housing markets are topsy-turvy, sometimes too hot, sometimes too cold, never just right. Some housing markets in northern Maine have been too cold for decades; they have a surplus of housing, high vacancy rates, and high rates of deterioration. Some housing markets in southern and coastal Maine have been too hot for a long time; they have high prices, low vacancy rates, and many homeless people.

Maine state government could prevent human suffering and help economic development by becoming proactive. In hot markets state government can focus its community development and transportation funds on assembling land, getting town approvals, extending infrastructure, and selling it to developers to create affordable housing. In cold markets state government can provide rehabilitation help.

This is a role for state government that goes beyond helping individual homeowners and individual project developers. It is a role beyond that of just helping low-income families. It assumes a responsibility for monitoring the overall supply/demand picture, and for finding ways to channel private investments to redress market imbalances. The alternative of continuing to stand by passively as prices get out of hand in southern Maine, as young people head over the border, as employers pick up and move away to find a workforce, is unacceptable and unnecessary.

The second leadership role is related to the first. It is that *the state government, in all of its agencies, must see itself as being in the business of building communities, not just individual structures.*

Right now we have one state agency that builds roads; another that builds houses; another for business parks; another for schools; another for parks and recreation. Each has its own internal decision-making rules focused on creating the best possible structures. As a result we in Maine have sturdy roads, safe houses, well-equipped business parks, full-service schools, and beautiful parks. But they are all arranged in a haphazard, hodgepodge fashion across the landscape. As a result, we are creating fragmented living and working spaces.

Maine can no longer afford to keep paying for expensive structures with the hope that, someday, with good luck, they might fit together, somehow. We need to make the criteria of *fitting together* the first consideration in what we build. This again, is the "Great American Neighborhood" idea. It should guide every infrastructure investment that state government makes.

This is not a simple task. My former boss at the Maine State Planning Office—one Richard Barringer—is fond of stating that, "Coordination is an unnatural act." To truly achieve a holistic perspective on making infrastructure investments in Maine communities, the organization of decision-making must also change. It is not enough to set up a "coordinating committee." These are already rife in state government; and, as Barringer's comment suggests, they are largely a waste of time.

What is needed, instead, is a bottom-up decision-making structure. It starts with the way people wish their communities and regions to look and feel—identifying where the affordable housing and business growth and retail growth should go.[17] This local and regional vision would then be responded to by state professionals in transportation, housing, and land use. Is the local/regional vision practical, achievable, cost-effective? The vision would go back and forth until it met both local/regional desires and state practical tests. Then all state agencies would have to revise their programs to support the implementation of the regional/local visions; and cities and towns would have to revise their local ordinances and policies to achieve the same purpose. This is the way to break down the fragmented decision-making process, and introduce a broad and holistic investment policy.

What if cities and towns do not cooperate in implementing the agreed-upon vision? Then the city or town would not be eligible for state investment funds, nor would it be allowed to access Tax Increment Financing or state development grants. It will take a partnership of towns and state agencies. The most likely organization to lead such an effort would be the regional councils, or reformed counties. Such an effort, by the way, would complement other efforts underway to create more regional cooperation and efficiency in service delivery.

Maine state government can lead in balancing housing market supply and demand, and in building communities, without large infusions of new money. It will, however, take a long-term perspective and a willingness to stick with it through a multi-year reorganization process.

Historical Precedents

For Maine state government to take a strong leadership role in housing and community development is not a radical suggestion. Maine has done it before.

After the Revolutionary War, the Massachusetts legislature wanted more people to move to Maine. Maine, you may recall, was a part of Massachusetts at the time. The state government sent surveyors to lay out townships (six miles square) and lots. Then they sold the lots to Revolutionary War veterans. One hundred and fifty acres along a river went for a dollar an acre. One hundred acres inland was free. The only requirement was that the family had to clear sixteen acres in four years, or the land would revert to the state.[18] Massachusetts also held land lotteries. A fellow named William Bingham from Philadelphia put in $300, and today a whole town is named after him.

This housing and economic development policy was highly successful. In the sixteen years between the end of the Revolutionary War and 1800, Maine's population tripled from 56,000 to 152,000—the fastest rate of growth in its entire history. The policy was so successful, in fact, that Maine soon had enough people to break away from Massachusetts and form its own state—yet another illustration of the law of unintended consequences in public policy!

This land and housing policy kicked off the great agricultural era in Maine. A similarly forward-looking housing policy helped kick off the industrial era, one hundred years later. That policy was driven by private business, in the form of company housing provided by mill owners. I will take just one example. In 1890 an enterprising businessman named Hugh Chisholm founded a power company, then a paper company, in Rumford, Maine. Within fifteen years, these enterprises created 3,000 jobs.[19]

But where were the people to live? Chisholm took the proactive approach. As he later wrote, "The inadequate supply of dwellings, in the face of constantly increasing demand from the mill operatives, and the desire to give suitable homes for these people, who were pioneers in the growing town, and upon whom its future character so much depended, let me set apart a section across the river, to be used for small houses, that should be at once attractive to the eye, of reasonable rental, and possessed of all up-to-date conveniences."

Chisholm hired Cass Gilbert, one of the nation's leading architects. He told him "We will build of brick and stone and slate, and we will provide not merely for a house, but for comfort, elegance and social gratification of those who dwell here." This is Strathglass Park, a place you can still visit today. Like a Great American Neighborhood, it had a mix of housing types: two wooden rooming houses, five brick single family homes, twenty-eight wooden houses, sixty brick two- to six-unit structures. In all, Chisholm developed 266 units in three years.

Rumford's Strathglass Park in 2000[20]

Chisholm did not, however, see his role as simply providing affordable shelter. He was interested in building community as well as houses. "(Our) leaders," he wrote, "should realize the importance of conservative growth and careful investment, and they should not forget that the town's growth cannot be permanent unless the children and young people, who will soon be leaders in the community, are given every advantage, which those in older communities enjoy. The library should be built up, means of healthy recreation afforded, safe places of evening amusements furnished for the young people of the town. Given the proper regard for the well being of those upon whom the future of the town rests, I can see no element lacking, that is needed to assure Rumford Falls an increasing prosperous future...." So Chisholm built the Mechanics Institute to hold books and recreational activities.

In sum, Maine is today embarking on another economic transition. As it once made the transition from a hunting/trading economy to an agricultural economy, and from an agricultural to industrial economy, both with the help of strong housing and community development policies, so, today, Maine is passing from an industrial to a service economy. We need a proactive housing policy today with the same level of ambition and excellence that guided Maine in the past.

In the last half century, we have done well in improving housing conditions and in making ownership more affordable. Now, in the coming decades, we must do more to ensure access to jobs and services, and to create lively and diverse communities. We need to build new homes and new communities today for the same reasons that our predecessors built them: because building a home is the ultimate act of faith in Maine's future, and because building a community is the ultimate gift to Maine's future generations.

A graduate of Haverford College and the Yale Divinity School, Frank O'Hara has worked in the housing and community development field in Maine since 1975 at the local level in Portland; at the regional level, for the Greater Portland Council of Governments; at the state level, for the Maine State Planning Office, the Maine State Housing Authority, and the Office of the Governor; and, for the past sixteen years, as a private consultant and co-owner of Planning Decisions of South Portland, where he works in the areas of housing, community development, workforce development, and strategic planning. For the past dozen years Frank has also been an adjunct faculty member at the Muskie School of Public Service, teaching in the areas of communications and community economic development. He is also a former, award-winning writer and commentator for the Maine Times.

THE DEVELOPMENT OF HEALTH POLICY in Maine over the past fifty years mirrors that of the nation at large. If it succeeds, Maine's innovative Dirigo Health Plan may lead the way for the entire nation in this era of needed health care reform. Research and development in medical science have combined to create a level and pace of change in health care delivery that requires skillful and innovative policymaking to address people's needs. How did a small state with a limited tax base reach the front of the pack in health policy? Maine's unique strengths include an intimate political arena where all the major players can and do interact regularly; leadership from a governor committed to universal access to health care, for both economic and humane reasons; and a strong consumer advocacy community that facilitates communications between legislators and constituents. Maine creatively pursues a time when all people will have access to quality, affordable health care.

5 Health Policy in Maine
Recurring Themes, Persistent Leadership

ELIZABETH KILBRETH

Health policy is today among the most dynamic and complex areas of public policy. The health sciences—medicine, technology, pharmaceuticals, genetics—develop and change at breathtaking speed, requiring policymakers to confront issues not imaginable fifty years ago. The ethics of gene therapy, privacy concerns regarding personal medical information, and medical wills and "do not resuscitate" orders are all policy concerns thrust upon us today by innovations in medical science and information technology.

Health policy is also peculiarly complex because of the unique and frequently strained partnership that has evolved in the nation between the public and private sectors to manage health care. Some policy areas concern services that are ceded to the public sector. Social Security, for example—offering a universal benefit and requiring mandatory participation—stands alone in the service it offers. To the extent that businesses and unions offer pension plans, these are viewed as supplemental to Social Security, not in competition with it.

In other policy arenas, government serves a narrow, regulatory role, setting rules for activity within the private sector. The Occupational Health and Safety Administration (OSHA), for example, sets rules for workplace safety and inspects worksites but does not produce safety equipment or offer businesses and workers any services or alternative workplace settings.

The government funds health care research, training, and infrastructure development, regulates providers and drug safety, and is a direct provider of health benefits to substantial segments of the population. Meanwhile, we view the delivery and financing of health care as primarily a *private sector* activity. The majority of Americans get health benefits through a commercial insurer, or an employer- or union-sponsored health plan. Federal and state government entered the arena as safety-net providers, assuring health care availability to the elderly, disabled, and indigent. Over the years, however, the private system has faltered, and public programs have expanded so that our health care system is today *a mosaic of public and private programs.*

The growth of public sector programs has put both the federal and state governments in the position of being, simultaneously, competitors with private insurers in seeking out cost-effective health care providers, and regulators who set the rules of the game. The term "crowd-out," coined to describe the transition of populations from private coverage to public coverage, is symptomatic of the sense of uneasily shared space felt by the various players in the health care field.

Finally, health policy maximizes the complexity of our already intricate federal system, where the national government and states divide authority. Both the states and the federal government fund and operate health programs—separately, and in partnership. Regulation of providers and insurers has traditionally been an area of state authority; but, increasingly, Congress is stepping in with regulatory laws that complicate or pre-empt state regulation.

The development of health policy in Maine over the past fifty years mirrors the experience of the nation at large. It is a story of growing administrative capacity and sophistication in state government, and of rapidly accelerating infrastructure and technology development in the health care delivery system.

However, health care is also an area where *Maine stands apart from other states in policy leadership.* Increasingly, over the past twenty years, the Maine legislature and executive leaders have kept Maine in the forefront of developments as the health policy community struggled with each new challenge. Today, Maine is at the threshold of what may be a new era of government activism in health care.

A Snapshot from Fifty Years Ago

The practice of medicine fifty years ago seems a quaint cottage industry, compared to the muscular industry of today. In 1960, Marcus Welby typified the family doctor. General practitioners went directly from a hospital internship to practice without the lengthy residency training programs that all physicians undertake today. Doctors carried the tools of their trade in small black bags; they made house calls; and they worked singly, in small offices, with perhaps one assistant, usually a nurse, who managed both clinical support and all administrative functions.

Polio had only recently been conquered, and reminders of its scourge were still frequently seen in children and adults who had permanently lost the use of limbs. Children lined up at local schools every year to get the polio vaccine. Measles and mumps were considered a normal childhood rite of passage.

While contagious diseases were still a source of dread, the public was blithely oblivious to the health risks associated with low-level exposures to toxins. The Marlborough Man was seen in his heyday as an icon of the self-confident, virile, and, of course, healthy American. The issue of radiation exposure, which would galvanize many communities located near nuclear power plants in later years, wasn't an issue, even among health professionals.

Children's shoe stores, as a marketing device, used x-ray machines that allowed children to view a green image of the bones of their feet. Similarly, public consciousness was very limited about long term strategies and behaviors that might improve health in later years. No one jogged or watched their intake of high cholesterol foods. Battles raged in communities around the nation over whether fluoridated water was a health promotion measure or a subversive Communist plot.

Growing Responsibility in State Government
In the early '60s, state government played a far more limited role in health policy than it does today. Responsibilities were encompassed within three domains: public health, provider and insurance regulation, and funding and operation of state institutions. These domains have changed and expanded in response to shifting health priorities, technological changes, and political demands from providers and consumers.

Maine, like other New England states, never adopted a model of public health services that partnered with counties to build a direct service infrastructure of county hospitals and health clinics. A well-developed town nurse system was in place fifty years ago, and Maine's Health Department could turn to it for help with programs targeted to the health of mothers and infants, funded under the federal Title V Maternal and Child Health Block grants. Beyond these federally funded programs, medical care in Maine was an exclusively private enterprise. Excepting these direct medical care services, however, Maine's Health Department was left with traditional public safety functions, such as assuring drinking water safety and tracking incidence of infectious disease.

The activities and responsibilities of state government have burgeoned in the past forty years. Now, in 2004, Maine's Bureau of Health has eight separate divisions that encompass at least twenty separate programs. The Division of Community Health reflects the growing importance we place on chronic disease, and the encouragement of health behaviors that can prevent or ameliorate some of these diseases. The division supports these specific programs, for example: a diabetes control project, a cardiovascular health program, a breast and cervical health program (targeting early cancer detection), and a program to reduce use of tobacco products.

The Division of Disease Control's list of high priority diseases for education and monitoring also signals the constantly shifting challenges within the health care field. On their top-ten list of current threats are three diseases that had not been identified by medical science in 1960: HIV, Lyme disease, and West Nile virus.

The division that may take the prize for the most unanticipated change in focus and mission is the Office of Emergency Preparedness. Until 2001 the major concerns with regard to public health emergencies were possible infectious epidemics such as the flu or radiation hazards from a nuclear power plant malfunction. Now, the one document listed on the office's website is Maine's training plan for a bio-terrorism public health emergency.[1]

Fifty years ago, public support for care and treatment of persons with mental illness or with developmental disabilities was weighted toward custodial care in large institutions that served more to isolate these individuals from society than to provide therapeutic treatment. As early as 1948, the federal government provided funding to states to build outpatient mental health clinics; but funding levels were fairly modest.[2] The range of treatment for mental illness was far more limited than today; moreover, it hampered the ability of persons with chronic mental illness to remain in the community. The federal Mental Retardation Facilities and Community Mental Health Center Construction Act of 1963 greatly hastened the development of increased capacity for treatment within the community.

Even as the state developed a greater range of treatment options within communities, however, the most seriously disabled languished in the large state institutions in Maine—the Augusta Mental Health Institute (AMHI), Bangor Mental Health Institute (BAMHI), and Pineland Institute for the Mentally Retarded. In 1950, for example, 1,600 patients were housed at AMHI, a facility designed to hold a maximum inpatient population of 1,270.[3]

Deinstitutionalization began in earnest in the 1970s, but, ultimately, it was class action lawsuits brought on behalf of residents within these facilities and subsequent court orders that hastened the process, mandated a broader range of community-based services, and closed the Pineland Institute.[4] Pineland closed in 1995, and the number of residents within AMHI and BAMHI has shrunk to less than 200. A new mental health hospital is currently under construction in Augusta, which will replace the badly deteriorated AMHI facility.[5]

Changes in public health and mental health have been dramatic. Yet the policy area that has persistently demanded the attention of the Maine legislature over the past fifty years is the financing and regulation of health coverage for basic and comprehensive medical care.

The 1964 enactment of the federal Medicare and Medicaid programs let loose a force that stimulated huge growth in state administrative capacity and changed forever the face of state government. The growth in the health care system, greatly stimulated by federal policies and programs, has also drawn the state into a role as referee, both to navigate disputes among different provider groups and to safeguard consumer interests in the rapidly evolving private insurance market. To understand fully the shifting role of state policy in the health care arena, it is necessary to start with a review of the impact of several federal policy initiatives.

The Federal Impact on Maine Health Care
The story begins shortly after World War II when, in the face of a perceived shortage of health care providers, Congress acted to increase as quickly as pos-

sible the number of doctors and hospitals. Federal funds were dedicated to developing new physician training programs, and to educational loan programs for doctors in training. The Hill-Burton Act, passed by Congress in 1946, stimulated an unprecedented spurt of hospital construction that carried through the '60s. Congress allocated $75 million each year for new hospital construction.

States willing to develop surveys and plans for locating new hospitals could tap into these federal dollars. Federal policy also promoted the expansion of the nursing home industry and community mental health centers. These federal initiatives led to an enthusiastic building spree in Maine. At the height of the hospital expansion push, at the end of the '50s and early '60s, there were eighty hospitals operating in Maine, compared to the thirty-nine today.[6]

The other major federal initiative of the post-World War II era was funding medical research. Between 1941 and 1960, federally funded medical research grew from $3 million to $400 million annually.[7] This emphasis on research and new technology promoted the growth of major academic medical centers and encouraged the proliferation of medical specialties. This burgeoning, new, hospital-based health industry contributed to dramatic advances in the treatment of important diseases. The overall age-adjusted death rate in the U.S. in 1950 was about 145 deaths per 10,000. Now, in the twenty-first century, the rate has dropped to 85 per 10,000. The mortality rate from heart disease, alone—the number one killer in America—has dropped by more than half.[8]

In a rural state like Maine, these federal capacity-building initiatives resulted in major increases in access to care all across the state. The number of physicians practicing in the state has more than doubled in the past thirty years. We have seen the introduction of advanced treatment options for heart disease, cancer, childhood cancers, and organ transplants, and significant advances in the treatment and care of high-risk, low birth weight babies.

All this advancement in medical technology—all this federal largesse—has had its down side, however. With attention and resources flowing to research and construction of a technologically sophisticated medical infrastructure, some fundamental needs were neglected—notably, assuring access to basic medical services. Emphasis was placed on finding cures to dread diseases rather than on prevention. Primary care—the treatment at the point of entry into the health care system for most patients—was neglected by medical training programs as mundane and unimportant.

The financing of health care services for citizens was left to the private sector; and high technology care is expensive. Physicians operated as self-employed, entrepreneurial small business owners who charged for their services as they saw fit; hospitals, at their own initiative, created Blue Shield insurance plans to assure a reliable payment mechanism for the more expensive inpatient-care services.

The Impact of Medicare and Medicaid

Over the years, as health care services have become both more effective in improving the quality and length of life and more expensive, all industrialized nations have added health benefits to their government-sponsored social security systems. All nations, that is, except the United States. The issue of universal health insurance for this country is not new. It has been debated in Congress four times, and defeated four times. Instead, we have continued to rely, for the most part, on private insurance coverage, largely available as a work-related benefit. This system—never intended to meet everyone's needs—had troublesome gaps from the start. In 1960 about 78 percent of all full-time workers were covered; but among retired persons, only 43 percent were insured, and among housewives coverage was just 32 percent.

It was primarily the plight of the elderly that galvanized action. Medicare, the federally funded and operated health insurance program that covers almost all Americans over age sixty-five, was enacted in 1964. Ironically, it was the efforts of the American Medical Association and others to limit Medicare to a means-tested program for low-income elderly that resulted in the enactment of Medicaid—not *instead* of Medicare, but in addition to it. Faced with two competing proposals, Congress decided to pass both. When first enacted, Medicaid provided comprehensive health insurance for families on income assistance programs (welfare) and individuals with disabling conditions that prevented them from working. Over the years, eligibility criteria have been gradually expanded so that now, all very low-income children are eligible, regardless of the employment status of their parents or guardians, and states may, at their discretion, extend eligibility to various categories of low-income adult populations.

The enactment of these two programs is probably the single most important policy decision in health care in the last fifty years. It set in motion a series of dynamics that continue to reverberate throughout the health care system, affecting cost, infrastructure, and availability of care. First and foremost, of course, these programs extended a safety-net to some of our most vulnerable citizens. Early studies of the impact of Medicaid, for example, found that poor children, whose access to and use of health services before Medicaid was abysmally low, quickly caught up to affluent and insured children once they enrolled in Medicaid. The Medicare program had a comparable impact on the elderly. The enactment of these two programs was a significant step forward in the struggle to assure adequate health care to all Americans.

An important side effect of Medicare and Medicaid, however, was that these programs thrust everyone—states, health care providers, hospitals, patients—into a new relationship with the federal government. The American Medical Association (AMA) had seen this coming. They fought "tooth and nail" against the passage of Medicare and Medicaid, precisely because they feared their free-

Northeast Cardiology Associates, Bangor

dom to practice as they chose would be compromised. An AMA-sponsored recording sent to physicians' spouses all across the nation in 1962 provides a flavor of the association's fight to oppose Medicare. The tape ends this way:

> Write those letters now.... If you don't, this program, I promise you, will pass...and behind it will come other federal programs that will invade every area of freedom as we have known it in this country. Until one day.... we will awake to find that we have socialism. And if you don't do it...one of these days you and I are going to spend our sunset years telling our children and our children's children what it was like in America when men were free.[9]

As an aside, it is interesting to note that the person who recorded this message on behalf of the AMA was an actor who has since become more widely known, Ronald Reagan.

The Medicare and Medicaid programs did not, of course, open the door to socialism in America, but they did insert the government into shaping our health care system. This process was slow to start. Medicare's authorizing legislation contains language that disallows government interference with the practice of medicine, and commits the program to paying for medical services on the basis of what is "reasonable and customary."[10] The impact of this commitment to pay "reasonable" charges, without bargaining or review, was reminiscent of the likely outcome of an indulgent parent handing a credit card to a teenager, saying, "I won't review or second guess what you use this card for, and it has no credit limit—but *please* be reasonable with it."

The health care sector transformed into a market with ever-expanding demand and a seemingly unlimited payment source. With the impetus already given to hospital-centered, high technology medicine, and this major new revenue source for payment of patient services, the results were astounding. *Health care became the Godzilla that ate the national budget.* In 1960, total health care spending in the United States was about 5 percent of the economy; now, it is close to 15 percent. In 1960, we spent, on average, $638 per person on health care; in 2003 the average spent per person was $5,440.[11]

As Congress grew more worried about rising costs within the Medicare program, the "hands-off" commitment gave way to increasingly prescriptive strategies to contain costs. Under direction from Congress, the Health Care Financing Administration (HCFA, the agency that administers Medicare), adopted a hospital reimbursement system that paid a lump sum per admission, based on diagnosis. This reimbursement approach motivates hospitals to conserve resources since—regardless of services provided or resources consumed—payment remains the same.[12] Later, HCFA established a restructured fee schedule for physician services and adopted prospective reimbursement strategies for other services (such as home health care services).[13]

Changing Maine

Just as the initial federal largesse within the Medicare program profoundly impacted the health economy at the state level, the revised policies targeted to slowing the growth of health care costs are felt locally, as well. Because persons over age sixty-five consume the largest share of health care services, Medicare services comprise about one half of the volume of care at most hospitals. Medicare changes, thus, dramatically affect hospital revenues. Attempts by hospitals to maintain their revenue streams when Medicare cuts back often result in substantial increases in charges to private insurers and self-paying patients.

Medicaid, unlike Medicare, is administered by states. Federal law establishes program guidelines and rules, and the federal government pays more than half of each state's program costs; but states have some discretion in how their program is structured and administered, and have full responsibility for program operations. Medicaid is a large and complex program. It requires state government to screen eligibility, track enrollment and dis-enrollment, pay medical claims, review the credentials of participating physicians, oversee the quality of nursing homes and other residential facilities, and manage an enormous budget. In 2003 Maine Medicaid, or MaineCare, provided health coverage to almost 343,000 individuals. Total program expenditure exceeded $1.2 billion. The program processed around 6 million provider claims, not including bills for pharmacy services.[14]

State government has grown enormously in the last fifty years—from an entity with little infrastructure and few program administrative responsibilities—to a large organization with the capacity to manage complex programs and maintain sophisticated understanding of a variety of policy areas. Medicaid was one of the primary engines that fueled this change. The start-up of the Medicare and Medicaid programs ushered in the modern era in health policy at the state level, a time when the policy debate has been dominated by two issues: cost control and appropriate access to care. *In this era, Maine moved to a leadership position among states in trying innovative policy responses.*

State Policy Efforts to Contain Costs

The cost problem was the first to catch the attention of policymakers. It took only ten years from the start of the Medicare program for national health care spending to double from $115 billion to over $230 billion (in 1990 constant dollars).[15] Suddenly, government enthusiasm faded for funding hospital construction and training more doctors. The health care economy, we discovered, did not follow the basic law of economic markets—that is, of supply and demand. Increased competition among a larger number of providers did *not* reduce prices; instead, increased capacity just seemed to generate increased use. Demand for health care services appeared insatiable.

Maine first addressed this issue in 1978, by starting a state health planning process and instituting a "Certificate of Need" (or, CON) program.[16] The State Health Plan tried to establish objective, population-based measures of need for services and facilities; and to determine which areas in Maine were under-served and which, over-served. Certificate of Need gave the State regulatory power to approve or disapprove new hospital services and hospital capital expenditures exceeding a specified cost-threshold.

In a second cost-containment initiative, Maine joined a small cadre of states trying more aggressive strategies for taming health inflation. The Maine Health Care Financing Commission (MHCFC, pronounced McFick)) was established in 1984 with the regulatory authority to establish limits on each Maine hospital's revenues on an annual basis. The MHCFC had several objectives. In addition to slowing the growth of hospital expenditures over time, the commission was charged with rationalizing payment rates among different payers and assuring that hospitals were made whole for uncompensated services from bad debt or charity care services.

The MHCFC regulated Maine's hospitals for twelve years. During this period, comparative analyses of rate-setting states with other states indicate that this regulatory system had some success in slowing the rate of growth of hospitals' costs.[17] However, Maine hospitals chafed under the regulatory structure. Hospital administrators felt the system was too rigid and cumbersome, and that it inadequately recognized the changing environment and costs hospitals had to contend with.

Many hospitals spent considerable time and resources locked in disputes with the regulatory agency—appealing rulings and trying to make cases for exceptions to the MHCFC's formula-driven standards. Repeatedly, the Hospital Association tried to introduce legislation to dismantle the MHCFC. In 1987 a Blue Ribbon Commission to Study Hospitals was established and, as part of a larger health reform package, hospital regulation under MHCFC was phased out in 1996.

Access Strategies
While the struggle for cost containment was underway, Maine was also one of the states providing leadership in efforts to expand access to care. These two issues, of course, are inextricably linked. The more health care costs rise, the more insurance premiums rise. With each hike in costs, fewer people can afford to maintain coverage.

Coverage started to erode in the aftermath of the exuberant cost increases of the '60s and '70s. Overall, the number of Americans without insurance coverage had held steady at about 26 million during the 1970s, then began to climb. It was 32 million by 1985, 36 million when President Bill Clinton introduced his health reform bill in 1992, and, has since continued to climb. Estimates are that about 44 million persons are now uninsured; Maine's current share of those is about 136,000.[18] Both within Maine and nationally, the numbers continue to creep up despite expansions in public coverage through the Medicaid program. Unfortunately, private coverage has been eroding at a faster rate than public coverage programs have been able to absorb the vulnerable uninsured.

Maine policymakers were trying to address the access issue as early as 1974 when the Maine legislature enacted a Catastrophic Illness Program to provide resources to individuals who exhausted insurance and personal finances due to a major illness. The Catastrophic Illness Program operated until 1984 and, at its height, served about 2,500 people over the course of a year.[19]

In 1986 the legislature commissioned a study to look at the scope and causes of medical indigence, and to propose various responses. The next step on the arduous journey toward comprehensive coverage in Maine was a High Risk Insurance Program, enacted in 1987. This program, modeled on similar initiatives in other states, offered health insurance coverage to individuals who could not obtain private insurance at normal premium costs because of pre-existing medical conditions. The program was a response to a problem caused by underwriting practices in the private insurance market. These practices, today remedied through insurance regulation, generated some of the most horrific examples of barriers to care.

Insurers routinely excluded coverage of pre-existing health conditions for applicants purchasing individual or small group coverage. In addition, insurers could, at their discretion, refuse to renew the contract of a prior enrollee. An individual who might have been faithfully paying premiums throughout a working career could find herself without coverage midway through treatment of a major illness, like cancer, if her insurer chose not to renew her contract. Incidents like this were not uncommon in the 1980s.

The High Risk Pool was open to individuals who had either been refused coverage or provided only limited coverage, due to pre-existing medical conditions. The program offered a comprehensive health benefit at a price set at 150 percent of the average, non-group health insurance premium price. Although expensive, the coverage was broader and better priced than available alternatives for many individuals. Since the targeted enrollment group was expected to include individuals with potentially catastrophic health expenses, legislators anticipated that premium revenue would not cover program costs. Premiums were supplemented by a .03 percent assessment on hospital revenues to ensure adequate reserves.

The Maine legislature followed the lead of about eight other states in establishing the High Risk Pool; Maine went a step further than other states, however. For built into Maine's program was a sliding-scale premium subsidy for low-income individuals, so that price barriers as well as underwriting barriers would be removed. Policymakers also hoped that the program would help stabilize the small-group and non-group insurance markets. The expenses of pool participants, ostensibly among the costliest citizens in the state, would be spread across a very large funding base. The small assessment on hospitals was expected to be recouped through a negligible increase in hospital charges.

In 1988 Maine's Department of Human Services sponsored a three-year demonstration project to try expanding health coverage among small businesses in Maine. The legislature appropriated $3 million to cover the costs of subsidizing the premiums of low-income workers in businesses of fewer than fifteen and the self-employed, on a sliding scale based on income. Although popular among participating businesses, the program was never brought to full-scale, and was phased out during a state budget crisis of the early '90s.

Despite these incremental steps, uninsured and consumer concern continued to grow, and, in 1989, the legislature confronted both vociferous consumer demand for action and the hospitals' intensified campaign to deregulate hospital financing. Hospitals bolstered their argument by pointing to the growth in managed care and to employer interest in it as a strategy to increase competition in the insurance market. Hopes were high that competition among managed care plans would rein in prices and improve quality in health care—thus removing the need for regulatory controls.

Among consumer activists, momentum had gathered for a more comprehensive response to the health care access problem for low-wage workers and others. Sympathetic legislators sponsored a bill for a state-funded program that would cover everyone in the state whose income was below 150 percent of the federal poverty level. The public hearing on this bill drew a crowd so large that it had to be moved to the Augusta Civic Center. All day, citizens came forward to tell their stories of hardships caused by not having health insurance.

Legislators put these two issues—hospital deregulation and access expansion—together in a single bill. The Maine Health Program was enacted, and the hospital finance commission was dismantled. The new legislative reform package was funded at $20 million for the first year, with two-thirds of the funds earmarked for the Maine Health Program, and one-third set aside to help hospitals that could show hardship related to bad debt, charity care, and underpayments by Medicare and Medicaid.

As ever, the enactment of the two major initiatives produced unintended consequences. The health care system in Maine was infused with $20 million in new public funds at the same moment that hospitals were deregulated. Managed care entities had made a valiant effort to get a toe-hold in the state, to change utilization patterns and bargain down prices; but they largely failed. So, what happened, in retrospect, seems inevitable. It is, in many ways, on a mini-scale, similar to what happened when Medicare was enacted. Utilization increased and prices soared. The Maine Health Program, itself, was the first victim of the jump in health care costs, lasting only through 1992. The combination of higher than expected costs, a down-turn in the economy, and soaring state budget deficits doomed it.

In hindsight, it is clear that the attempt to rely on market competition for cost control was a failure. After dismantling the hospital regulatory commission, the Certificate of Need Program became the only remaining vestige of a regulatory approach to cost containment. Maine's major initiative at significantly expanding health coverage also went down to defeat. Medicaid expansions and, under the Clinton administration, the creation of the State Children's Health Insurance Program (SCHIP), which significantly expanded coverage for low-income children, provided limited venues for Maine to expand its health care safety-net.

In the race between rising costs, eroding private coverage, and access expansions, however, coverage was slowly losing. These circumstances set the stage for Maine's most recent round of policy activism, discussed in the last part of this chapter.

Insurance Market Regulation: From Laissez-faire to
Comprehensive Management

The health policy initiatives discussed so far have been aimed at expanding public coverage programs, regulating provider costs, or both. States have another weapon in their policy arsenal, namely the licensing and regulation of the commercial health insurance industry. Maine policymakers have spent a considerable amount of energy using this regulatory authority to assure that private health insurance coverage is as widely available as possible.

Historically, regulatory oversight of health insurance has had two focuses: assuring industry solvency, and protecting consumers from fraud and unfair business practices. For many years, these relatively narrow concerns required limited intervention and oversight by Maine's Bureau of Insurance. The bureau sets minimum risk reserves levels that insurers must maintain as protection against unexpectedly high claims. Bureau staff review policy contract language and company marketing material to make sure that consumers are not misled by the "small print" they are unlikely to read or understand. The bureau maintains an investigative unit to look into consumer complaints.

However, with the exception of Blue Cross and Blue Shield of Maine (Maine's only not-for-profit insurer, and no longer extant), insurers have been free to price products as they wished and to market a variety of benefit plans. Health insurance has been considered a competitive market where consumer choice would correct for unfavorably priced or unpopular products.

Until the mid-1980s, legislators intervened in insurance market regulation only to specify required benefits. Starting in the '60s, the lawmakers responded to pleas from patient groups, provider groups and, sometimes, public health officials, to require that insurers include certain benefits in all their health insurance policies. Among the first mandated benefits was a requirement that insurers automatically extend coverage to babies born to persons with family coverage policies. Prior to this requirement, some insurers required a separate application for newborns, allowing the company to avoid neonatal intensive care costs for babies born with significant health problems, and to deny coverage to babies deemed a significant risk because of congenital health conditions.

Other service gaps where the Maine legislature has mandated coverage to meet the needs of particular patient groups include coverage of alcoholism treatment and treatment for drug addiction. More recently, consumer advocacy groups and public health officials have successfully lobbied to mandate inclusion of various preventive health measures, such as mammography for women and other screening tests. Provider groups have prevailed upon the legislature to mandate that insurance companies recognize and reimburse their services if they provide a service that would be covered when provided by a physician. Chiropractors, nurse practitioners, and licensed mental health care providers are among those who have gained access to third-party reimbursement through legislative mandates.

Over the past decade and a half, tremendous change and increased complexity within the insurance industry has stimulated more expansive and refocused interest by legislators. In 1960 Blue Cross and Blue Shield of Maine essentially had unobstructed control of the private health insurance market. Most large commercial insurance companies had, at most, a toe in the market, and where they did, they were interested exclusively in large business groups.

Blue Cross and Blue Shield was a nonprofit entity, exempt from state taxes, and, in some respects, functioned on the model of a *public utility*. Rates were established on a community basis, and had to be reviewed and approved by the Bureau of Insurance. This meant that anyone in a given region of the state who purchased a policy from Blue Cross and Blue Shield paid the same premium price, regardless of their age, sex, or health status.

Commercial insurers who entered the market in the '60s and '70s introduced experience-rating and medical underwriting—marketing and pricing strategies that gave them a competitive edge in the market. Experience-rating allowed employers with young, healthy workers in low-risk occupations to pay premiums lower than the community rate because their "experience"—the dollar value of medical claims reimbursed on their behalf over the course of a year—was lower than the community average, which, of course, included older and sicker individuals.

In the small business and individual insurance markets, commercial insurers devised rating schemes that, again, allowed them to under-price Blue Cross and Blue Shield. The insurers set rates "by the book," using actuarial tables to establish different rates according to age and sex. Further, the companies devised lists of types of businesses that they would "red-line"—that is, refuse coverage—based on a perceived risk associated with the type of industry.

Some businesses—those with heavy equipment operators, for example—had a difficult time finding insurance because of the risk of serious accidents and trauma to their workers. Other businesses, such as restaurants, might be excluded because the high turn-over rate of employees adds heavy administrative costs to the insurer. Individuals and very small businesses also faced medical underwriting, where medical histories of the applicants were required as part of the application process, and persons might be refused coverage based on a chronic medical condition or costs associated with a previously treated condition, or face waiting periods for coverage.

The universal adoption of experience rating and medical underwriting across the commercial insurance sector had dire and unforeseen consequences. First, consumer choice became very constricted because of the uniformity the rating practices. Many individuals, whether employed by a small business or purchasing non-group coverage, found they could not find affordable coverage that met their health care needs if they had a history of a major illness.

The competition from the commercial insurance sector took a toll on Blue Cross and Blue Shield of Maine, as well. To keep its tax-exempt status, the company was required to hold to a policy of turning no one away. Because commercial insurers offered advantageous prices to young and healthy individuals and workforces, those who remained with Blue Cross and Blue Shield tended to be the older and less healthy, who did not get attractive rates from the commercial sector. As a consequence, within the Blue Cross and Blue Shield insurance pool, average, per-person costs crept upward and upward, and the community rate soared.

Starting in the late 1980s, the murmurs of public discontent with segmentation and barriers in the health insurance market rose to a threatening roar. Legislators heard from constituents saddled with insurmountable debt from medical expenses, because they had not been able to find or maintain coverage. Small business owners complained about the churning in the insurance market caused by what they perceived as bait-and-switch tactics, when an insurance company that offered them a very favorable initial rate, then increased premiums 20 or 30 percent in the following contract period.

Blue Cross and Blue Shield of Maine also let it be known that they could not continue to offer community-rated coverage in the face of current insurance market practices. If the rules governing market competition were not changed, the company announced, it would have no choice but to adopt the same underwriting strategies as their competitors (a strategy already adopted by other Blue Cross and Blue Shield plans around the country).

Policymakers in Maine took a series of steps to re-stabilize the insurance market. In 1989 they enacted legislation creating a High Risk Pool, as discussed earlier. Next, the legislature addressed marketing and pricing practices in the non-group and small group market. In 1993 legislators passed a law that established mandates for insurance portability and guaranteed issue. The portability provision stated that any individual who applied for insurance coverage within thirty days of losing prior coverage due to a job change (or other reason not related to defaulting on premium payment or fraud) could not be denied by the applicant company. Moreover, to the extent that an individual had met pre-existing condition waiting periods under prior coverage, new waiting periods could not be applied by the subsequent carrier.

The guaranteed issue provision outlawed the practice of denying coverage to an individual within a group, if the rest of the group was to be offered coverage. Finally, the law set limits on price differentials within the small group market, gradually narrowing the differential between high risk groups and low risk groups, so that the market would achieve a community-rating structure after five years. Maine was among the first states to undertake regulatory reform of the small group insurance market, and implemented its reforms several years before Congress mandated similar changes on a national level, through the Health Insurance Portability and Accountability Act (HIPAA).

Medicare, Medicaid, and Managed Care
In the 1990s, the rise of managed care organizations and the initiation of cost containment strategies by insurers instigated a policy debate and legislative action that fundamentally changed the nature and scope of insurance regulation in Maine. For a decade, at the federal level, Congress had struggled with establishing rules governing the oversight of managed care provisions for Medicaid and Medicare recipients. Much of Congress's concern stemmed, however, from the facts that the Medicaid and Medicare programs serve particularly vulnerable populations, and that enrollees have little choice as to care arrangements.

People who get coverage in the private sector can vote with their feet if they dislike the quality of services of their current insurance provider. Public program enrollees have nowhere else to turn. The earliest efforts of states to contract with managed care providers for the provision of health care services to Medicaid recipients resulted in widely publicized abuses. There were instances of denial of clearly needed medical care. Individuals were assigned to physicians who were hours away by bus or other public transportation.

The Medicare program experienced a different but equally troubling set of problems. HMOs, offered as a choice to Medicare recipients, adopted questionable marketing strategies. In some instances, plans sent representatives door to door, representing themselves as government officials and asking recipients to sign enrollment forms without making clear that enrollment was voluntary. In other instances, plans targeted enrollment to young and healthy seniors by advertising in health and sports clubs, and establishing enrollment offices accessible only by climbing a flight of stairs.

Because HMOs were paid a formulaic rate that used average Medicare costs as its base, by selectively "cherry-picking" healthy enrollees, these plans made large profits in their early years. Congress responded to these abuses by developing an intricate regulatory apparatus, specifying access-to-care standards, consumer appeals processes, quality-of-care standards, allowable marketing strategies, and substantial reporting requirements to document compliance with all the rules.

Until the mid-1990s, the growth of regulatory constraints on managed care organizations by the public sector appeared to both Maine's legislature and Bureau of Insurance as irrelevant to the private insurance market. Here, the faith was that market competition would motivate quality and efficiency and drive out bad actors. However, as large employers increasingly turned to managed care plans to tame their ballooning health benefits costs, both consumers and providers raised the alarm.

Most employers contract with only one carrier (even if they offer a choice in benefit levels), resulting in very limited choice for the majority of consumers, even those unhappy with coverage arrangements. The initial shift to a managed care plan requiring a primary care "gate-keeper" for referrals to specialists was frequently plagued with problems. Employees of the State of Maine, for example, when enrolled in a managed care plan for the first time, found that there were not enough primary care physicians in the areas where most state employees live, for everyone to easily select a primary care provider (PCP).

Providers raised their own set of concerns. One major strategy of managed care plans is to use selective contracting with providers to negotiate contracts with favorable rates. In essence, the plans promise to send their patients—guaranteeing a full case-load—to providers who will give them discounts on their usual fees.

Suddenly, physicians were confronted with a threat to their traditional, professional privilege. Through control of licensing, credentialing, and hospital privileging, physicians have had, since the beginning of the twentieth century, major control of market access among their peers and other providers. Now, when managed care companies threatened to cut off a physician's or hospital's access to patients through selective contracting, they were, in essence, effectively superceding state medical associations as the gateway to a successful practice. Physicians took the issue to the legislature as a threat to quality-of-care for patients. What if health plans contracted with the lowest-cost doctors rather than the doctors with the best outcomes? Wasn't it likely that the providers most willing to offer discounts would be those who had the most difficulty in maintaining a busy practice in an openly competitive market?

Hearing concerns from both consumer advocates and providers, the Maine legislature launched into a policymaking initiative that fundamentally changed the nature and scope of health insurance regulation and the responsibilities of Maine's Bureau of Insurance. The Health Plan Improvement Act, the Health Plan Accountability Act, an Act to Establish a Patient's Bill of Rights, and provisions governing utilization review and grievance procedures are all now consolidated in Rule 850 of the Insurance Code.

The level of detail governing health plan behavior is a complete turn-around from the old, hands-off regulation that limited regulatory oversight to licensure, solvency, and fraud. Rules now specify, for example, that health plans must file an annually updated access plan. The plan must specify the current and projected enrollment by county of residence. It must provide the projected ratio of primary care and specialty care providers to enrollees by county, and a map subdivided by town, indicating the distribution of providers and contracted facilities.

Rules specify (with certain exceptions) that primary care services must be available within thirty minutes travel time by automobile from each enrollee's home, and that specialty and hospital care must be available within sixty minutes travel time. This travel time is spelled out in mileage for primary roads, secondary roads, and interstate highways. Rules specify the maximum acceptable wait-time within a physician's office and the maximum acceptable appointment scheduling-time for different visit types. There are regulations detailing consumer appeals processes, and provider rights with regard to plan-credentialing procedures.

Momentum Builds for Dirigo Reform

Throughout the decade of the '90s, as managed care transformed the organization of health care in other parts of the nation, we saw consolidation in both the health insurance industry and in hospital networks in Maine. Thirty-one of Maine's thirty-nine hospitals are now affiliated with one of four hospital networks. Physician specialty practices have consolidated. Several insurers have left the state or were purchased by larger insurance companies, so that now Maine has only three insurers with any measurable share of the market. The largest insurer holds 95 percent of the individual insurance market and 54 percent of the overall insurance market.

Health care costs, on a per capita basis rose faster in Maine than in any other state in the nation over the past decade.[20] The State of Maine, which is thirty-seventh in average income in the country, rose to tenth in average health care spending.[21] These increases show up in employers' and individuals' insurance premiums. One of Maine's large employers had increases in health benefits costs of 60 percent over three years. Maine's University System saw costs jump by 49 percent at the end of a two-year contract—an increase that translated to close to a 10 percent reduction in overall budget resources for other purposes. Small businesses have seen comparable increases, and individuals who have to buy their own coverage have been hardest hit. Comprehensive policies in Maine now cost families $20,000 to $25,000 a year.[22] The cost of comprehensive coverage has become almost a moot issue. Insurers are actively marketing only policies with high deductibles (minimum of $5,000 per person) in the non-group market, now, and are aggressively pushing these policies among small businesses, as well.

These market trends are signs of an industry in trouble. High deductible policies hasten the breakdown of insurance pools, the necessary ingredient for insurance to work. Many moderate-income, healthy individuals consider paying about $4,000 a year in premiums for coverage that requires an additional out-of-pocket expenditure of $5,000 before they realize any benefits from the policy, to be an unwise choice for the use of their limited funds. They choose to "take the chance" and go without insurance, reasoning that they are likely to spend less than $5,000 a year in health costs, so why pay the premiums? On the other hand, high deductible policies leave individuals with chronic illnesses particularly vulnerable, because they face repeated high expenditures as deductible requirements are renewed each contract year. When the healthy are siphoned off, either into the ranks of the uninsured or into high deductible policies, the insurance pool tips into a death spiral—one where costs and limited benefits increase incentives for the healthy to forego coverage, and the worsening demographic and health profile of the insured drive premium costs higher still.

These are the circumstances that, once again, galvanized Maine to step into the leadership on health reform—this time, to take on health care costs and expanded access to care simultaneously. The stage was set for the Dirigo initiative by two exploratory studies and several incremental health reforms authorized by Maine's legislature. In 2000 Governor Angus King, Jr., established a Blue Ribbon Commission to Study Health Care Costs.[23] In 2001 the Maine People's Alliance sponsored a referendum campaign in Portland to advance the "Creation of a System of Universal Health Care." The initiative was widely debated, drew fire from Anthem Blue Cross, and finally passed.

Later that same year, the legislature appointed a committee to study the feasibility of a single-payer, universal health care system, and to develop recommendations for its design and implementation. The speaker of the house of representatives sponsored successful legislation to develop a program to assist small businesses and their employees in securing health coverage; and the president of the senate sponsored a reform bill based on consumer choice and purchasing pools, which also passed.

Health reform was clearly back on the front burner and John E. Baldacci, as a gubernatorial candidate, pledged to make this a priority of his administration. His first act as governor was to create a Governor's Office of Health Policy and Finance, charged with developing a proposal that would encompass universal access, cost controls, and measures to enhance quality. The governor convened a task force—the Health Action Team—with representation from consumers, providers, the insurance industry, business, and labor—to provide a sounding board for ideas on reform strategies.

Baldacci brought a comprehensive proposal before the legislature within 100 days of taking office, and the legislative leadership convened a select, bi-partisan committee to "work" the bill. Bringing together members from the standing committees on health and human services, banking and insurance, and appropriations, the special committee was designed to streamline review of the legislation by including representatives from all the committees of jurisdiction.

Features of the bill were controversial, and negotiations for change and compromise were intense between the governor's office and various interested parties, including hospitals, physicians, the insurance industry, business groups, and consumer advocacy groups. The various interest groups were able to agree, however, on an amended bill that encompassed changes to meet the various concerns. Once all these constituent groups signed on, bi-partisan support was possible in the legislature. The bill was moved out of committee with a unanimous "ought to pass" recommendation. With such strong, bi-partisan support, the bill moved easily through both branches of the legislature.

Dirigo: A Description

The Dirigo Act creates a new, independent Dirigo Health agency within state government,[24] overseen by a board appointed by the governor with senate confirmation. The agency will sponsor health insurance, disease management, and possibly other services for eligible businesses and individuals. All businesses with fewer than fifty full-time employees and self-employed individuals are eligible to enroll. Individuals who work for employers who do not offer insurance coverage are eligible, as long as they have not had employer coverage available for twelve months or longer.

Employers will be required to pay some portion of the participation fees, the exact level to be determined by the board. Low-income enrollees who are eligible for MaineCare will be enrolled in Dirigo along with their coworkers, and will receive additional benefits through the MaineCare program. Enrollees with incomes below 300 percent of the federal poverty level (about $54,000 for a family of four) will be eligible for a discount of their portion of the premium, a cost the Dirigo Program will absorb.

The program encompasses a variety of measures to help reduce the rate of increase in health care costs. Some of these ask for voluntary cooperation from providers and insurers; and some, including a newly expanded and more rigorous Certificate of Need process, are set in place by the new law. One of the shortcomings of the CON process has been its singular focus on hospitals. Setting barriers to capital development for hospitals, but not other medical care settings, encouraged proliferation of high-technology services in ambulatory care settings.

This uneven regulatory approach expanded the health care system in ways that are not necessarily efficient, and created an unfair competitive advantage to entities other than hospitals. Now, the CON process will encompass new technologies and other capital developments that exceed a determined cost threshold, regardless of the setting. In addition, the legislature establishes an annual spending limit for new capital expenditures that require CON review. Henceforth, applications will be reviewed competitively, and the number of approvals cannot exceed the total dollar threshold.

The law further calls for the development of a new State Health Plan, and creates a Maine Quality Forum to build on efforts already underway to enhance patient safety, evidence-based medicine, and health care quality.

In the first year, program administrative expenses and costs of the discounts will be paid through a one-time appropriation of $53 million. In future years, funds will come from an assessment on all insurance premiums in the state. So as not to trigger another round of health-cost inflation, the assessment will be set at a level equivalent to measured savings in the system from reduced bad debt, charity care, and other reductions in the growth of spending. Under no circumstance may the assessment rise above 4 percent.

The Dirigo Program is complex. This summary provides but an outline of a comprehensive reform strategy. The feature that will have the most immediate impact on Maine community members is the low-cost insurance coverage program. Dirigo should dramatically increase the availability of affordable health coverage, particularly for low-wage workers and small business employees.

The most innovative and ingenious component of the reform strategy is the funding mechanism. The program funding is designed to ensure that new money put into the system goes to provide broader coverage, and not to fuel inflation in the health sector. Maine hospitals and physicians currently provide approximately $200 million a year in uncompensated health care services, costs that are recouped through price mark-ups paid by those of us who have health coverage. As uncompensated care costs drop, some part of the $200 million will be plowed back into the system through providing coverage to currently uninsured Maine citizens.

The model creates a win-win situation. To the extent that costs are controlled, businesses and individuals who are already insured will benefit—they will feel the difference in their pocketbooks. System savings will also help support coverage for some of Maine's uninsured citizens. The $200 million in uncompensated care is a substantial resource to put toward *insured* care for the medically indigent. Further, because many individuals and employers who currently pay nothing into the insurance system will pay a substantial portion of their costs, overall resources should grow.

If Maine succeeds in this endeavor, it will be a model for the nation. The elusive goal of universal access and controlled costs is the brass ring; no one yet, in this nation at least, has caught it.

Reflections on Maine's Policy Leadership
Maine has an unusually rich history of innovation and activism in the field of health policy, particularly for a small state with a limited tax base. There may be several reasons that help explain this creativity.

The first might be *Maine's intimate style of politics.* Maine's policy circles are small and cohesive. All the players in an issue area like health care know each other and negotiate issues, time after time. Health policy is complex and it brings many stakeholders to the table. The more stakeholders, the harder it is to reach consensus. In Maine, however—unlike many other states and at the national level—all the stakeholders may fit around a single table, where they may hear each other out. Moreover, it is foolish to make enemies when you may need someone's cooperation the next time around.

Maine is also unusual in *the vibrancy of its consumer advocacy community.* Maine's consumer advocates have large networks that are well-organized and have been tireless in pushing reform for many years. Consumer groups form coalitions and conduct research and grass-roots outreach. They have assured that legislators are acutely aware of how health policy decisions affect their constituents; and their representatives are savvy negotiators in Augusta on behalf of their constituents. Their voices are respected.

Leadership from the governor was instrumental in pushing Maine past its prior pattern of incremental, one-step-at-a-time reform efforts. Governor John E. Baldacci had a clear vision of the outcomes he wanted from the health reform effort. He moved fast, his message was clear and consistent, and he held the line firmly on principles that were important to him—like universal access. He created a framework for negotiations that allowed give-and-take, and established fundamental principles that guided the legislative process.

Finally, *the years of incremental reforms—prior efforts—were not wasted. Maine learned as it went along.* There is an institutional memory; there were strategies that proved ineffective and others that were worth revisiting. The legislative undertaking in 2003 was fully informed by forty years' experience of what has worked and what has not.

The challenges ahead are substantial—intimidating, in fact. Maine must now try to balance the needs of an economically robust health sector with that to restrain costs, so all may afford health care services. Translating savings from averted bad debt and charity care into resources for covering the uninsured will require cooperation from both insurers and providers, in wresting these savings from the system. Consumers, too, will need to change some expectations in order to slow the rate of growth in health care spending. The state health planning initiative will be an opportunity for all Maine citizens to participate in a structured conversation about how to rationalize the distribution of health care resources and spending, to best meet the needs of the Maine community as a whole.

This reflection on Maine over the past fifty years finds the state on the threshold of major change in the health policy sector. How Maine's health system will look ten years hence will depend very much on whether all interested parties can tap into Maine's reserves of community spirit and see this challenge through to a positive and humane restructuring of the financing and delivery of health care services for all Maine people.

E lizabeth Kilbreth is Associate Professor of Health Policy and Senior Research Associate at the Muskie School of Public Service. Educated at Radcliffe College, the Johns Hopkins University School of Public Health, and Brandeis University, Dr. Kilbreth is the recipient of both the prestigious Minkoff Prize in Medical Economics and the John Heinz Dissertation Award. Her research interests embrace health system reform, children's health policy, and medical indigence. She has served on Maine's Health Care System and Health Security Board, charged by the legislature with designing universal health coverage in Maine; and is now directing research and technical support for the Governor's Office of Health Policy and Finance, charged with development of the new, universal Dirigo Health Plan.*

MAINE'S K-12 PUBLIC SCHOOL SYSTEM is today one of the best in the nation due to the dedication and hard work of educators, increased financial commitment from Maine citizens, and passage by the Maine legislature of the Sinclair Act of 1957, the Education Reform Act of 1984, and the Learning Results of 1997. In the last ten years, the cost of providing K-12 education has risen steadily, even while enrollment has decreased. Today Maine school districts face pressure to regionalize and economize, as well as strong local resistance to the idea from citizens accustomed to a high degree of "local control." Looking to the future, Maine faces the challenges of the federally mandated "No Child Left Behind Act," and of funding equitable and accessible education for all students.

6 K-12 Education in Maine
Steering from a Distance

DAVID SILVERNAIL

Maine may take great pride in the changes that have taken place in its public school system in the past four decades. We have come a long way—our teachers are better prepared, our schools are better equipped, our school curriculum is more rigorous, and more and more of our students are challenged to do their best work. Without question, Maine has taken great strides in the last forty years in improving the quality of our public school system, and in expanding educational opportunities for more and more of our children—the children who will be the workers, teachers, and policymakers of tomorrow.

Today, Maine's schools are among the best in the nation. In 1999, the National Education Goals Panel ranked Maine's education system *first* in the nation.[1] In the same year, the Children's Rights Council designated Maine as the best place to raise a child, primarily because of our education system.[2] In 2002 an independent research organization, the Morgan Quitno Corporation, ranked Maine the fifth smartest state in the nation, based on our "commitment to students and teachers, an emphasis on excellence in the classroom, and support of safe, well-run public schools."[3]

How Did We Get Here?

How did we get here? How did Maine's public school system become one of the best in the nation? It was not by happenstance. We got here, in very large measure, because of three things: the continued dedication and hard work of our educators; the increased financial commitment by Maine's citizens to our schools; and by several key legislative actions by Maine policymakers.

The dedication of Maine's educators is not a new phenomenon. Indeed, it is merely a continuation of a very long tradition among Maine's educators going back as far as 1647, the year our public schools were established by law. In reading the annual reports of Maine's state school superintendents, first published in 1853, one encounters example after example of the unwavering dedication of Maine's teachers to our children, under adverse conditions, and for low pay.

This longstanding tradition continues even to today. One has only to visit a few of Maine's schools and classrooms to witness the commitment our teachers make, day in and day out, to educating our children; and they continue to fulfill this commitment at low pay. In the late 1950s, Maine teachers' salaries were 27 percent below the national average;[4] today, they are only 17 percent below the national average, but fully 30 percent less than their counterparts in other New England states.[5]

To use an overused cliché, but one that is appropriate, we could not be where we are today in Maine's public schools without the hard work and dedication of Maine's teachers and administrators. Truly, Maine's children are in very good hands. Policymakers can institute new reforms, they can encourage and even mandate changes, and they can increase the amount of resources in our schools. In the final analysis however, it is the expertise and experience of our teachers and school leaders, and their commitment to their profession and to helping our children, that determine the quality of our education system.

A second explanation of how we got to where we are today is the major financial commitment Maine's citizens make to our schools, a commitment that has increased dramatically in the last four decades. In 1960 the state and local communities together spent, on average, a little over $300 per student to educate our children. This figure is equivalent to about $1,870 per student in 2002–03 dollars. Where are we today? In 2002–03, we spent approximately $8,000 per student statewide. In other words, there has been a four-fold *real* increase in education spending over the past forty years. As one of our legislative leaders, House Speaker Patrick Colwell of Gardiner, put it recently: "Maine is not a wealthy state; but we take care of our own, and we do a lot better than our neighbors when it comes to school funding."[6]

As important as devotion and funding have been—and they have been very, very important—a third factor has contributed greatly to the development and character of Maine's public schools today. This is the passage of three pieces of legislation that have been the principal drivers of the many changes experienced by Maine's public schools in the last forty years. They are the Sinclair Act of 1957; the 1985 Education Reform Act; and the Maine Learning Results in 1997. With these three pieces of legislation, Maine has continued to fulfill its constitutional commitment to its youth and their parents, made significant strides in increasing *equity* of opportunity in and among our schools, and improved *access* to a quality education for more and more of our youth.

What is this constitutional commitment? To quote from Maine's constitution: "A general diffusion of the advantages of education being essential to the preservation of the rights and liberties of the people; to promote this important object, the legislature are authorized, and it shall be their duty to require, the several towns to make suitable provision, at their own expense, for the support and maintenance of public schools."[7] It is the duty of the legislature to ensure that *all* our children, regardless of where they are born or raised in Maine, and regardless of their economic and social station, will receive a quality education. It is, in other words, the constitutional duty of the legislature to *steer the development of our education system from a distance.*

Many reforms have taken place in public education over the past forty-plus years, nationally and here in Maine—reforms such as new mathematics and new science curricula, schools without walls, contract learning, alternative scheduling, year-round schools, transitional kindergartens, and many more. Some of these have come and gone very quickly; others have had a lasting impact on our schools. An important *national* example of the latter is Public Law 94-142, passed by the national Congress in 1975: the Education for All Handicapped Children Act. Today, we take for granted that states will provide a free and appropriate public education for all children, including children with special needs. As late as the mid 1970s, however, this was not the case. Without question, this national piece of legislation has had a lasting impact in all of Maine's schools.

Passage of Public Law 94-142, required *for the first time* that all states provide an appropriate education for children with disabilities, and committed the federal government to provide at least 40 percent of the cost of implementing this act. It is estimated that in the early 1960s, total state and local expenditures for special education in Maine were less than $100,000; in 1978, three years after passage of PL 94-142, Maine spent approximately $14 million dollars, and provided special education services to over 21,000 students. By the late 1980s Maine was serving over 28,000 students, at a cost of $75 million dollars per year.

Today, state and local expenditures for special education equal about $225 million dollars annually, providing educational services to over 36,000 Maine students with special needs, or 17 percent of our public school student population. The federal government, however, pays just 12 percent of Maine's special educations costs, a far cry from the 40 percent promised in 1995.[8] Clearly this piece of legislation has had a major effect on whom we educate, and how we attempt to provide an appropriate education for special needs students mainstreamed into our schools and classrooms.

Maine has instituted many reforms on its own in the last four decades, some short-lived, and others with a lasting impact on our schools. Many could be mentioned, but three are most noteworthy.

The 1957 Sinclair Act

In 1955 the 97th Maine Legislature authorized a study of the needs in Maine's schools. This study, conducted by J. L. Jacobs & Company of Chicago on behalf of a special Legislative Research Committee, found the public school system sadly wanting. The committee reported that per pupil expenditures in Maine were 22 percent below the national average, ranking us eleventh lowest in the country. Average teacher salaries were sixth lowest in the country. A shortage of teachers existed in our schools, and only 45 percent of the teachers employed had an earned bachelor's degree.

A majority of school districts had enrollments under 750 students, and half of our individual schools had enrollments under 200. We had more than 120 high schools with less than 100 students enrolled in them. Teachers in these small schools were paid 30-50 percent less than those in our larger schools. Still, our smaller schools were considerably more costly to run, about a third more costly than was the case of our high schools.[9]

All this led Dr. Mark Shibles, then dean of the College of Education at the University of Maine, to conclude of our high schools: "The program of high school education in Maine suffers from an over supply of unreasonably small, expensive, and ineffective schools.... These small schools present a tragic picture so far as having challenging programs of education to meet the needs of these critical times."[10]

The Jacobs Report concluded, among other things, that:

- "Such substantial inefficiencies as exist in the expenditure of education funds are caused by improper and inadequate organization of school systems at the local level;

- "The existence of the many small town school administrative units, designated as the responsibility of individual town governments, places major handicaps on the establishment of a most effective school finance system, and on the attainment of adequate educational opportunity for all children throughout the state; and

- "The effectiveness with which the state can discharge its responsibilities for an adequate school program is directly related to the degree to which school administrative units are developed of a size and population and financial ability that permit efficient operation."[11]

As one might expect in a state so deeply steeped in local control, the report caused great angst in many towns and hamlets of the state. As one newspaper editorial put it, however:

It is clear that the collective impact of the Jacobs Report recommendations will materially improve the state capacity for meeting its constitutional responsibility for public education through a judicious combination of power and bait with which to coax upward the general performance of the component communities. It is inconceivable that it should be rejected in any of its substantive provisions.[12]

In late 1957, the same year as the launch of Sputnik and under the able leadership of Senator Roy Sinclair of Somerset County and Governor Edmund S. Muskie, the legislature passed the Sinclair Act. This act was a combination of incentives and mandates designed to increase the amount and distribution of state aid to local schools, and to distribute it differently among the towns; to create new and larger school districts by consolidating smaller ones; and to improve teaching conditions in our schools. The act included for the first time:

- Creation of what is known as a "foundation" funding program. Prior to 1957, the state simply reimbursed schools a percentage of their expenditures, and in effect, provided greater support for those school districts that had more resources to spend on their schools. A foundation program, on the other hand, provided funds to ensure at least a minimum level of education funding for all schools across the state. This program not only increased state funds for education, but helped equalize education opportunities by shifting funds to poorer communities.

- Provision of a 10 percent bonus in state aid as an incentive for smaller school districts to consolidate into larger ones;

- State assumption of a larger share of debt for the construction of the new and larger schools; and

- Creation of the first statewide minimum teacher salary.

The Sinclair Act also included provisions to:

- Reduce the amount of state funds paid to communities deemed to have too many unnecessary small schools;

- Require school districts that consolidated into larger ones to have at least one high school of 300 or more students to qualify for the bonus in state aid;

- Require schools to employ only certified teachers, and to adhere to state established teacher-student ratios; and

- Require towns to pay at least the minimum teacher salary, under penalty of loss of state aid.

Passage of the Sinclair Act led to major changes in Maine's public schools. In 1957 over one-third of Maine's youth were attending high schools of 300 or fewer students; by the mid 1960s this had been cut in half. In 1965 per pupil expenditures in high schools of more than 300 students was $66 less per student than in smaller high schools, an amount equivalent to $400 per student today. By 1967 over 230 of the 492 Maine towns, almost one-half, had chosen to reorganize their smaller school districts into larger ones. These towns joined together and formed sixty-four new school administrative districts, most of which still exist today.

Even today, these consolidated school districts created by the Sinclair Act are less expensive than smaller districts. By the mid-1960s, as well, minimum

teacher pay had increased about 60 percent, and the opportunities for students to take a much wider range of high school courses had increased substantially.[13]

These and many more changes that resulted from the Sinclair Act prompted one Maine educator to remark that, for some students, the new school structure was "their first opportunity to work in an adequately equipped science lab; explore in a school library of adequate depth so that real challenge was present; receive a four-year sequence in a second language; have the benefit of instruction from teaching specialists; [and] see and use tools of the industry."[14]

Clearly the Sinclair Act changed the way our schools were organized and run beginning in the early 1960s, and the effects of these changes may still be seen today. The act took Maine several steps closer to creating greater student equity in educational opportunity by creating larger school districts and establishing more comprehensive school programs for more of our children. It provided more funds for education, and it distributed these additional funds among our schools differently, based on need and the ability to pay.

The 1985 Education Reform Act
A second piece of legislation that has played a major role in changing our education system in the last 40 years is the 1985 Education Reform Act, Maine's response to a national movement.

In 1983 a National Commission on Excellence in Education issued the now famous, A Nation at Risk report. It warned that "while we can take justifiable pride in what our schools and colleges have historically accomplished and contributed to the United States and the well-being of its people, the educational foundations of our society are presently being eroded by a *rising tide of mediocrity* that threatens our very future as a nation and a people."[15] (Emphasis added.)

While Guthrie and Pierce have described the report as "...slender in terms of paper, and even thinner in terms of empirical evidence,"[16] the alarm sounded by the report was nevertheless heard all across the country. By one account, more than 700 related pieces of legislation affecting education were passed in the nation between 1984 and 1986.[17]

Maine's principle contribution to the cause was the 1985 Education Reform Act. In 1984, Governor Joseph Brennan appointed a twenty-five-member Commission on the Status of Education in Maine. A year later the Commission concluded that, indeed, our schools needed help; and issued a series of recommendations that many thought would bring about improved performance in our schools by raising standards for students and teacher performance. Most of the Commission's recommendations were incorporated into the reform act, including provisions to:

- Increase the number of credits high school students had to earn in English, mathematics, science, and social studies before they might be graduated from our high schools;

- Require schools to provide guidance and counseling services to all K-12 students, services which were to be provided by trained and certified guidance counselors;

- Require all elementary schools to offer fine arts and physical education programs;

- Establish more rigorous teacher certification standards and require all teachers, for the first time, to pass the National Teacher Exam; and

- Establish a statewide achievement testing program, the Maine Education Assessments (or MEAs). Designed primarily as an accountability tool, the MEAs provided information for the first time for comparing performance of all schools across the state.

The Education Reform Act moved Maine several steps closer toward achieving equal opportunity for all students. Many educators did not then, and to this day still do not believe this was good legislation. Yet, it is difficult to argue with the facts. The reform act did result in more children being taught by more qualified teachers; greater access to support services for all students; and greater accountability for improved academic performance. In many parts of the state, the publication of MEA results has forced local school boards and educators to take a much closer look at what they are doing, and to make needed program changes. As a result of the provisions of the 1985 Education Reform Act, over the fifteen-year period from 1986 to 2000, average performance on the MEAs increased fully 25 percent.[18]

Learning Results

The third piece of legislation that has had a major impact on our schools is passage in 1997 of Maine's Learning Results. Actually, a precursor to this legislation was the development in 1990 of what was called Maine's Common Core of Learning. Unbelievable as it may seem today, prior to Maine's Learning Results there was no expressed agreement among Maine's citizens, policymakers, and educators as to what we wanted our children to know and be able to do when they graduate from high school. The Common Core of Learning took the first step toward forging this agreement by articulating a common vision for education in Maine and identifying four core areas of learning in which all children should be well versed: personal and global stewardship; communications; reasoning and problem-solving; and the human record.

The Common Core was not a mandate, however; indeed, the Common Core Task Force concluded in its report that "we do not believe the types of changes proposed by the Common Core can be mandated."[19] By the mid-1990s, however, views began to change. Maine's legislators and citizens, like their counterparts all across the country, demanded higher standards in our schools and a plan for holding schools accountable for achieving these standards. Thus, in 1997, the legislature codified into law the Maine Learning Results.

The Learning Results established sixty-seven specific standards of learning, in eight different content areas: English language arts, mathematics, science and technology, social studies, modern and classical languages, visual and performing arts, health and physical education, and career preparation. In establishing these standards, the Learning Results Task Force concluded that, "The overriding purpose of the Learning Results is to provide teachers and parents with guidance to improve an existing education system that is already working well for many students in most Maine communities. The adoption of common standards and an accompanying mix of measures which assess learning are widely regarded as the most important next step in improving the quality of public education for all students." [20]

As a result, *for the first time, we had agreement on what we expected our children to know and be able to do by the time they exit our secondary schools*. Additionally, schools had to put in place local assessment systems, to ensure that the students are making progress toward and ultimately achieving these high standards. Equally, if not more importantly, we now had an agreement that *all* Maine's schools are expected to ensure that *all* Maine children are achieving these standards; that is, that in the future we will have *equity in student outcomes*.

While still relatively early in its full implementation, there is already evidence that the Learning Results legislation is bringing about major changes in Maine schools:

- Over 70 percent of Maine's educators report that work on implementing the Learning Results is the top priority in their schools;

- Three-quarters of our schools report that they have aligned their local curriculum to match the content standards in the Learning Results;

- Schools report purchasing new instructional materials to match the Learning Results;

- Teachers report that they are designing their lessons to meet the new standards; and

- Almost two-thirds report that they now have a local assessment system in place to determine if their students are achieving the new learning standards.[20]

Already, then, the 1997 legislation has had a major impact on what now is being taught in our classrooms; how it is being taught; and what is being assessed. Already, development of the Learning Results has had an impact on increasing student equity of opportunities; and it holds great promise for achieving even more in the future.

Where Are We Now?

What has been the combined impact of our dedicated educators, commitment to funding school improvements, and legislative initiatives on behalf of our public school system? Are we better off than we were forty years ago? By many criteria, Maine today has one of the best public school systems in the nation. To mention but a few of our many achievements in the last forty years:

- In the mid 1960s the teacher-pupil ratio was 1:24, meaning on average one teacher for every twenty-four students;[22] today it is 1:14, ranking us sixth best in the nation in teacher-pupil ratio;[23]

- In 1960 there were fewer than 180 school guidance counselors across the entire state; today, there are over 800 guidance counselors and social workers working in our schools, more than four times as many;[24]

- In the mid 1960s, only three Maine high schools—Deering High School, Hebron Academy, and South Portland High School—offered advanced placement courses in the core disciplines;[25] today, over 85 percent of Maine's high schools offer one or more of these courses in the core areas;[26]

- Today we rank twelfth highest in the country in the amount of money we spend per child on education, more than $900 per child above the national average;[27]

- Year in and year out, Maine's fourth and eighth graders score in the top five in the nation on the National Assessment of Educational Progress (NAEP), a series of tests given to samples of students in all fifty states and the District of Columbia;[28]

- On the Third International Mathematics and Science Study, administered to students in over forty countries, Maine ranks in the top ten in performance, ahead of countries such as France, England, Germany, and other states in the United States;[29]

- Maine's high school graduation rate is eleventh highest in the nation;[30]

- Almost 70 percent of our high school students take the SAT tests in their junior or senior year, 20 percent higher than the national average;[31] and

- The National Center for Public Policy and Higher Education ranks Maine seventh highest in the nation for how well we prepare our students for college.[32]

These many accomplishments attest to the fact that Maine has made substantial progress in the last four decades in improving our public school system, and improving it for ever greater numbers of our students.

What price have we paid for these gains, and has it been too great? The economic costs have not been small, by any means, and some argue that by investing so much in our schools, we have neglected other social and economic needs in the state. Others argue that the economic costs have been worth it, but that too much of the burden of funding our schools has fallen on local communities—and the facts support this claim. The economic costs have been *much* greater for our towns. In the last decade alone, expenditures statewide on education have increased approximately 20 percent in real dollars. Yet, while the state's contribution has increased about 10 percent, local communities have increased their share of funding for our schools by fully 30 percent, *three times* as much as the state.[33]

For others, the most important cost has been different in nature: the continuing erosion of local control of our schools—an ever greater shift in power and control of our schools from local communities to the state level. It is difficult to dispute this claim. Prior to the 1960s, towns and districts all across Maine had considerable latitude to decide how much money they would spend on their local schools, whom they would hire, what programs and curriculum they would offer, and whom they would graduate from high school. Today it is quite different. Each piece of legislation discussed earlier, and many others, has resulted in the state having a larger and larger voice in how our schools are organized, who our teachers and school leaders are, what is taught in our schools, and who may be granted a high school diploma.

Has the price been too great? It depends, of course, upon your perspective. As Malen describes it, the proper balance between state authority and local control will continue to be debated, because "neither state nor local governments have a clear corner on virtue. Reasonable, informed, and honorable people can make the case for greater state control and greater local control over education."[34]

Whatever the perspective, the three pieces of legislation described above appear to be very much in line with what the writers had in mind when they crafted Maine's Constitution. The legislature's job was to ensure that the towns provided a good education for *all* our citizens. Recall that the Constitution states that, "the legislature are authorized, *and it shall be their duty to require*, the several towns to make suitable provisions...for the support and maintenance of public schools...."[35] (Emphasis added.)

To put it simply, *equity and access to quality education in Maine was not, is not, and cannot be a local option.*

Where Do We Go from Here?

Given the major strides of the past forty years to improve Maine's education system, it would be easy to develop a false sense of accomplishment and completion. When looking at our public school system, all the accomplishments just described are real; and in the aggregate, they paint a most appealing picture of Maine's public school system. To paraphrase Paul Harvey, however, here is some of "the rest of the story":

- It is true, we do rank very high in performance on national and international tests; we rank first, for example, in eighth grade performance on the reading section of the NAEP. Still, over two-thirds of our students score below the accepted proficiency level, and the same is true for fourth-grade mathematics. In essence, we are first among the mediocre;[36]

- Examination of our own MEA results reveals that we are not yet succeeding in helping *all* our students to achieve at high levels; over three-quarters of our students score below the proficiency levels we have established for our youth in mathematics and science;[37]

- While we have increased educational spending fourfold in the last four decades, the gap between higher and lower spending school districts has not changed significantly; we still have many haves and have-nots. Some districts still can afford to spend 2.5 times more per student on education than other school districts;[38] and

- We often brag about our graduation rate. It is true that we have one of the highest high school graduation rates in the country, but it is also true that the rate has not changed much in over forty years; in 1960 our high school graduation rate was about 74 percent, and today it is 76 percent.[39]

These facts suggest that there is still much to be done to ensure a quality education for *all* our children. Maine' educators, policy makers, and citizens alike have work ahead of them. Equity of educational opportunities is essential to the future well-being of our citizens and the economic viability of the state. Today's jobs will require more education in the future; and more and more of the jobs and careers of the future will require additional education. We have not only a moral, but an economic imperative to ensure equity of educational opportunity for *all* Maine's youth.

So, where will we be in 2010 and beyond? It is difficult to say; the crystal ball is still cloudy. Some key decisions, however—some that are being made now, and some that may be made in the next two to three years—will chart the course of public education in Maine for a long time to come. Each, in its own way, may move us even closer to our goal of student equity for all Maine children. Before we examine these, however, we note the 800-pound gorilla sitting in our classrooms and, indeed, in all classrooms across the country—the new, federal Elementary and Secondary School Act, or "The No Child Left Behind Act of 2001."

The No Child Left Behind Act

Over the last four decades, Maine has received considerable amounts of money from the federal government to support specific school reforms, and with these reforms have come many federal regulations. Prior to 2001, however, the impact of these regulations on the way we run our schools has been limited, with the exception of the PL 94-142, the special education law.

This is all changed with The No Child Left Behind Act (NCLB). Currently the federal government pays for just 7.5 percent of the yearly cost to educate Maine's children, but the NCLB is having and, in all likelihood, will continue to have a major influence on Maine's schools. It includes many reforms, but at the core of the 1,100-page piece of legislation are new assessment and accountability requirements. It calls for yearly testing of all third through eighth graders; it provides a timeline for ensuring that standards are being met by all children; and it calls for sanctions on schools that are not demonstrating adequate, yearly progress.

On the surface, the NCLB is surely laudable; it appears to make us even more accountable for ensuring that *no* child is left behind as we raise standards. Yet, as ever, the devil is to be found in the details; and this act has many, many devils in many, many details. For example, there is no accepted body of scientific knowledge that supports the concept of adequate yearly progress, as it is defined in the law; yet, there are over eighty-five ways a school may qualify as not meeting yearly progress, and the number of ways will double next year. Again, most existing state tests still lack sufficient validity and reliability to ensure fair assessments of student achievement and progress on high-stakes tests. By some estimates, 75–80 percent of our schools nationwide will score poorly on these tests; and, so, will fail to demonstrate adequate yearly progress and be subject to possible sanctions.

Here in Maine we are already beginning to see the effects of this flawed piece of federal legislation. In 2003 over 120 Maine schools were identified as *not* making sufficient progress. This represents 15 percent of Maine's schools, and the percentage will be even higher next year. One only has to review the many newspaper articles listing our so-called failing schools to see the unfortunate impact this national legislation is having on our schools, our teachers, our parents, and our students.

Even while the federal government has promised fully to fund the new requirements of the NCLB, it has to date under-funded it by approximately $8 billion dollars. For Maine, this means $37 million dollars less than is needed to meet the new NCLB targets. These problems have led Maine's Congressman Tom Allen to conclude that:

The No Child Left Behind Act was passed with strong bipartisan support amid great fanfare and hope. It represented a grand bargain. States agreed to implement performance standards to measure annual progress toward learning proficiency goals in math, reading, and other subjects. In return, the federal government pledged an infusion of financial assistance. Today, that bargain is a broken promise. And NCLB is mired in complexity, discredited by inflexible and controversial decisions from the federal Department of Education, woefully under-funded and subject to widespread disillusionment from parents, educators, and state and local officials nationwide.[40]

Maine's experience and that of many other states have led one national analyst to conclude that the NCLB:

is likely to increase the number of dropouts, narrow the curriculum, and label a great many schools as failing—even as NAEP reading and mathematics scores are at very high levels. The effect will not simply be to punish schools and children for failing when they never had a chance. The effect will be that our society accepts a meaner vision of what it means to be educated in America. The effect will be to take money from those schools and those communities that need it most and transfer it to "successful" schools. Ultimately, the effect will be to shift the purpose of schools away from education for a democracy and away from the provision of equal opportunities for all children.[41]

Some will say, "this, too, shall pass," that the NCLB will be nullified in the courts or substantially modified by the U.S. Congress. True, some modifications are likely to occur, but it is important to remember that former President George H. W. Bush and then-future president Bill Clinton both called for the development of *national* student testing as early as 1992. The NCLB, a Republican-backed piece of legislation, was nevertheless co-sponsored by several prominent Democrats and was passed by wide margins in both branches of the Congress. So, even while the No Child Left Behind Act may undergo major changes, it could still have a major influence on how we run our Maine schools for many years to come.

New Maine Initiatives

Returning to the Maine context, what actions are being taken now in Maine that may move us ever closer to equity of opportunity for *all* Maine's children? Three in particular are noteworthy: the so-called laptop program; the school funding formula; and regionalization.

The Laptop Program

In 2002, Maine embarked on a bold initiative, entitled the Maine Learning Technology Initiative (MLTI). The concept of MLTI began with a vision by then-governor, Angus King, Jr., to prepare Maine's youth for a rapidly changing world. In the summer of 2000, the legislature and governor convened a task force and charged it with recommending how to prepare our youth for this new world. The task force concluded:

> We live in a world that is increasingly complex, and where change is increasingly rampant. Driving much of this complexity and change are new concepts and a new economy based on powerful, ubiquitous computer technology linked to the Internet.
>
> Our schools are challenged to prepare young people to navigate and prosper in this world, with technology an ally rather than an obstacle. The challenge is familiar, but the imperative is new: we must prepare young people to thrive in a world that doesn't exist yet, to grapple with problems and construct new knowledge which is barely visible to us today.
>
> It is no longer adequate to prepare some of our young people to high levels of learning and technological literacy; we must prepare *all* for the demands of a world in which workers and citizens will be required to use and create knowledge, and embrace technology as a powerful tool to do so. If technology is a challenge for our educational system, it is also part of the solution. To move all students to high levels of learning and technological literacy, *all* students will need access to technology when and where it can be most effectively incorporated into learning.[42]

In early 2001, the task force issued its report, with the recommendation that Maine pursue a plan to deploy learning technology to all of Maine's students and teachers in the seventh and eighth grade, and then to look at continuing the program to other grade levels. To date, laptop computers have been distributed to over 34,000 seventh- and eighth-grade students and their teachers in all 240 Maine middle schools.

The early evidence indicates that the program has been very effective, not only in improving the technology literacy skills of Maine's students, but in closing the digital divide between the haves and the have-nots. As a result of laptops, more than 80 percent of middle school teachers report that students are more actively involved in their learning, and that they produce better quality work. Teachers report that *all* types of students are more engaged in their learning, particularly at-risk and special-needs children.[43]

Because the program has been so beneficial, Governor John Baldacci has announced plans to expand the program into Maine's high schools and to provide parents access to their children's laptops. If successful, this extension of the laptop program will bring Maine even closer to leveling the educational playing field for all of Maine's adolescents.

School Funding
A second initiative is the reform of Maine's school-funding formula. Clearly, Maine is in need of a new school-funding formula; the current one has outlived its usefulness. While heralded nationally as one of the fairest formulas in the early 1980s, it is now fundamentally flawed. It draws more and more education dollars away from classroom instruction; it encourages the inefficient use of education resources; it increases the gap between the haves and the have-nots; and it is deterring Maine from the goal of having *all* children achieve the new learning standards.

Like most other states, Maine has struggled for many years to create a fairer school-funding formula, one that generates and distributes funds in an equitable fashion and ensures success for all Maine's children, regardless of where they live and attend school. Fortunately, in early 2003 an important first step was taken by Maine's governor and the legislature toward creation of a new formula. It is based on what is nationally known as an "adequacy" model, one being developed in over fifteen other states. As Verstegen has put it, "The current period in American Education may well be remembered as a watershed era, as the states and the nation move from the *old adequacy* of minimums and basic skills to the *new adequacy* of excellence in education for all children at all schools."[44]

In Maine, this adequacy model is called the Essential Programs and Services Model. At its core is the definition of resources needed to provide equal educational opportunities throughout the state.[45] Equally important, the model recognizes that what is considered an adequate amount of resources and dollars may vary depending upon circumstances; the ends are the same, but the means of getting to these ends may require different levels of resources and dollars. All children are valued equally, and all deserve equitable opportunities to achieve common ends—but not all children come to our schools from equal circumstances. Some come to us from resource-rich homes and communities, and some from less affluent circumstances. Some come with special learning needs, and others from non-English language homes.

In spring 2003, the legislature passed, and Governor John Baldacci signed into law L.D. 1623, An Act to Implement School Funding Based on Essential Programs and Services. This act established Maine's new, adequacy-based school-funding formula, one that spells out what it will cost to achieve the Maine Learning Results. It tells us how much more money is needed to ensure that the *all* in our learning results legislation becomes a reality. It establishes, for the first time, that if all Maine's children are to achieve high academic standards, there needs to be a more equitable distribution of Maine's education resources; that is to say, some schools and areas of the state will need more funds than others.

This redistribution of funds is necessary, so that it truly will not matter where in Maine our children are born and raised, and the target for achieving this more equitable distribution of resources is 2010. If we can stay the course and reach this target, we will have substantially increased student equity here in Maine.

Regionalization
The third key area where our actions in the coming years may have a lasting impact on our schools is the area of regionalization and consolidation. We, the citizens of Maine, cannot sustain indefinitely the exponential increase in school funding we have seen over the last forty years. As Richard Sherwood and Deirdre Mageean point out in an earlier chapter, we are becoming older and grayer, and this older population will demand an even larger share of the economic and social services resource pie. At the same time, we must continue to fulfill our constitutional and ethical commitment to our children. We must find ways, then, to ensure that we are using our limited educational resources in the wisest and most efficient ways.

In the last ten years alone, school expenditures have increased over 20 percent in real dollars; at the same time, student enrollment has actually *decreased* over 3 percent. Maine cannot continue this trend in the future. Enrollments are projected to decrease by an additional 10 percent by 2010,[46] a decline of over 18,000 students in six years. At the same time many citizens, policymakers, and educators, alike, are steadfastly attempting to hold onto Maine's many small school districts all across the state.

At present, Maine has 286 separate school districts, to provide education to approximately 208,000 students. This is, on average, one school district for every 730 students, one administrator for every 200 students, and one school board member for every 115 students. The evidence indicates that many of these districts and schools are very costly, in some cases, approximately $400 to $600 more per child than in larger districts.[47] There is evidence that these larger school districts can achieve the same or better results than the smaller ones. Yet, the resistance to regionalization and consolidation, at least so far, has been strong and is deeply embedded in our views of local control.

The good news is that some progress is being made in this area. At least a few communities are beginning to discuss consolidation openly, and Governor John Baldacci has introduced legislation to incentivize "municipal service districts" to consolidate and regionalize local service delivery for greater efficiency and economy. In addition, the governor appointed a task force charged specifically with recommending ways to consolidate school districts and services. After a year of study, the task force concluded that Maine needs "a bold set of strategies like those found in the 1957 Sinclair Act. In essence, we need a Sinclair II Act."

Based on the recommendations of the task force, Governor Baldacci has introduced legislation to create Regional Cooperatives and Regional School Districts. Bold and substantial incentives in the form of increased state aid and staffing, and the state's assumption of a portion of local debt are designed to encourage and assist towns and school districts to recreate themselves as more efficient entities.[48] Make no mistake, this is going to be hard work. It is about shifting and sharing power, a very difficult pill for Maine citizens to swallow. The longer we resist change, however, and do not increase efficiency in our use of scarce resources, the more we place at risk our children and our future.

In summary, Maine has come a long, long way in the last four decades. Our public schools system is stronger, and many more of Maine's youth receive a better quality education. Still, we may not rest on past successes. As we enter the new century, we approach yet another historic opportunity for Maine's policy makers, educators, and citizens alike to rise to the occasion—to move us even closer to the ultimate goal of full equity of opportunity for all our students. Expansion of the laptop program; a new and more fair school-funding formula; and the regionalization of services are crucial steps along the journey. Forty years from now, we may look back and conclude that Maine, in the first half of the twenty-first century, was truly successful in ensuring educational opportunities for *all* our youth.

*D*avid L. Silvernail is professor at the University of Southern Maine's College of Education and Human Development. Educated at Indiana University in philosophy and education, Dr. Silvernail has been at the University of Southern Maine for twenty-six years, in a variety of posts, including associate provost and founder and director of the University Assessment Center. He is now director of the Center for Education Policy, Applied Research, and Evaluation; and co-director of the Maine Education Policy Research Institute jointly supported by the Maine legislature and the University of Maine System. Of late, Dr. Silvernail has been deeply involved in development of the new essential programs and services approach to school funding, and regionalization and consolidation of school districts.

FOR A SPARSELY POPULATED STATE, Maine boasts an exceptional collection of public and private educational institutions; still, rates of higher education participation and attainment in Maine are relatively low. The costs of pursuing higher education remain prohibitive for many Maine students and their families. The structure and largely deregulated governance of higher education in Maine has demonstrated unusual stability compared to other states. Stability has had its benefits; but this also makes higher education a continuing target for reformers and critics, as the changing economy and the decline in numbers of high school graduates put pressure on the system. For these institutions to meet the needs of Maine's citizens more effectively, the state must more closely and effectively link higher education to its overall economic development strategy, improve higher education's operational effectiveness, and strengthen financial aid for low-income Mainers.

7 Higher Education in Maine
Time for Change

TERRENCE MACTAGGART

Maine has much to relish in its system of colleges and universities. Residents of this large and sparsely populated state, if they have the resources, may choose from a variety of public and private, two- and four-year institutions offering an impressive range of programs. Maine hosts some of the nation's best private liberal arts colleges; the University of Maine at Farmington gets high marks in the widely read *U.S. News & World Report* rankings;[1] and the public research university at Orono offers strong undergraduate and graduate programs, including several of national eminence.

Citizens in Maine's larger cities are served by robust institutions like the University of Southern Maine, with campuses in Portland, Lewiston-Auburn, and Gorham; Husson College in Bangor; and the University of New England in Biddeford and Portland. In 2003 enrollments exploded at the state's public two-year colleges coinciding with their transformation from technical colleges to community colleges.

Yet for all the number, diversity and quality of its colleges and universities, still the state suffers from relatively low higher education participation and attainment rates. Roughly half of Maine's high school graduates go on to post-secondary education, and roughly half of those leave the state for colleges elsewhere.[2] While these figures are not as disappointing as those in states in the Deep South, they still put Maine well behind its New England neighbors and the country as a whole. Maine also lags New England and the nation in baccalaureate degree attainment among the working-age population.[3]

Why the gap between this impressive array of higher education opportunities and actual usage by the state's people? Certainly, the costs to attend are a major cause. With high tuition charges by national comparisons, low family incomes, and an inadequate financial aid system, Mainers must expend an unusually high proportion of their resources to afford college.[4] Low aspirations among the state's young people may have contributed to low college attendance in the past, but most high school students and their parents now seem to appreciate the need for advanced education.

The key policy challenge facing Maine political and higher education leaders is how to transform the way Maine organizes, governs, and funds higher education to better prepare more of our citizens for the knowledge-based economy. A powerful cocktail of pressures and trends are coalescing to change the immense stabilizing forces that have prevailed in Maine higher education since 1968. In that year, the state legislature and then Governor Kenneth Curtis chose to harness the state's public colleges and universities under a single board of trustees in the University of Maine System. The present topic goes beyond that System, to be sure; but its creation date offers us a point of departure.

This chapter makes the case that *serious change in the way Maine organizes and delivers higher education is at once likely, timely, and needed.* It first describes the contours of the Maine higher education landscape that make it an anomaly in the United States. These distinctive characteristics display many virtues; but they also represent a culture that will need to summon up its very best qualities, if it expects to meet the serious challenges facing higher education in the immediate future.

Next, it outlines a combination of interests and trends that dovetail to dramatically increase pressure on policy leaders to rethink and redesign the way higher education is offered in Maine. Some of these pressures are new; others have been with us for a while. What makes the current moment different is the density of the forces aligning themselves at the same time.

Finally, it suggests several specific areas that deserve attention if Maine is to make better use of its higher education assets. These suggestions are culled from some of the best practices in other states that have grappled with the problem of making higher education more responsive to the needs of the people.

Put another way, this chapter addresses three questions:

- What are the pros and cons in the distinctive way Maine presents higher education to its people?

- What are the key economic, fiscal, demographic, and other changes that, taken together, compel a rethinking of the way Maine organizes and delivers postsecondary education?

- Where should educators, policy leaders, and engaged citizens concentrate their attention if we are to make positive improvements in the way higher education meets the needs of Maine people?

Higher Education Structure and Expectations in Maine

On the public side, Maine hosts the University of Maine System with seven universities, ten discrete campuses, and many smaller learning centers (university colleges) spread across the state. It is governed by a board of trustees, whose members are nominated by the governor and begin serving when confirmed by the legislature. The Community College System, formerly the Technical College System, also hosts seven institutions, often in the same communities as the universities. It, too, is governed by a board nominated and confirmed like their University counterparts. The Maine Maritime Academy lies outside both systems and enjoys its own board of trustees. According to the New England Board of Higher Education, the public sector served about 70 percent of the 61,000 students enrolled in Maine in 2001.[5]

The private or independent sector includes distinctive liberal arts colleges, several career and professionally oriented institutions, a few proprietary schools and some unique schools offering training in fields from photography to boat-building. The proprietary academic sector is less well developed in Maine, as the major providers continue to focus their attention internationally and on states with larger urban populations.

In sum, for a state its size, Maine supports a great variety of institutions, both public and independent. There is no large private research university like the universities in Rochester, Syracuse, Providence, or Cambridge. The state hosts a large number of schools for its 1.2 million people; and Mainers expect a lot from their higher education institutions. Some of these demands are traditional and enduring, while others are relatively new. Maine people expect:

- Public and private colleges and universities to transform the lives and futures of thousands of students—to teach them in the words of Joseph Conrad, not just what to do, but "how to be."

- Higher education to link students, and to a degree the rest of the population, to the best that has been thought, said, and performed over the centuries.

- Colleges and universities to illuminate the long and sinuous tradition of western culture, as well as the cultures of the world at large.

- A college graduate to be able to think clearly, write forcefully, and engage intelligently with the civic issues of the day.

- Campuses to provide a safe harbor where unpopular and unorthodox ideas can be expressed without fear of reprisal from politicians, an annoyed administration, or even the majority of citizens who hold another view.

- Institutions of higher learning to produce citizen-leaders of all kinds, including politicians, writers, artists, business people, and professionals of all kinds.

- And last on this list, but not least, to field successful teams for women and men in major sports, and to win while still obeying the rules of fair play.

This is a short and more or less classic list of the expectations. With the exception of intercollegiate athletics, which is a distinctly American invention, it would be recognized around the world as the academy's reason for being.

While it is difficult to measure success in achieving this classic agenda, Maine does pretty well on this set of goals grounded in the liberal arts and humanities. Writers like Stephen and Tabitha King, political leaders like George Mitchell, and a host of other highly accomplished people have graduated from Maine's public and independent colleges and universities. Evidence of civic engagement such as high rates of newspaper readership and voter participation also reflect the quality of Maine's college and university graduates, and the social maturity of the population at large.

In order to sustain this traditional agenda, the public institutions at least will need to be successful in serving a newer agenda, as well.

Maine, like many other places around the globe, has added to these noble objectives another stratum of expectations. The newer, and in many cases dominating expectation is that higher education, particularly tax-subsidized public higher education, will become *the engine of economic development*. Institutions and state systems are expected to increase per capita income, salvage communities wounded by the departure of traditional industries, and accelerate growth in already favored urban areas.[6] In some respects, this new mandate is a twenty-first-century version of the land grant mission of the nineteenth. Yet, a key difference is that in varying degrees virtually all public colleges and universities are expected to contribute to the economy in practical ways.

In some states, this new public agenda for higher education goes even further, to give colleges and universities a pivotal role in solving problems like adult literacy, poverty, health care, and the preparedness of high school graduates. Maine has not yet embraced this more ambitious and perhaps unrealistic set of goals.

Under the new mandate, colleges and universities will prepare the workforce of tomorrow for emerging industrial needs; will educate nearly everyone in the society to participate in the new economy; and, in the case of research universities, will produce new processes and products to revitalize mature industries and stimulate new ones. Where knowledge is the essential economic resource, we look to colleges and universities as the source of knowledge and of wealth.

How Is Maine Different?
Resiliency may be the most distinctive feature of higher education in Maine. For example, in spite of nearly constant calls for reform and restructuring directed, it must be said, largely at the University of Maine System, higher education in Maine exhibits unusual stability. Compared to most other states, it is nearly unregulated by the state bureaucracy, but instead has evolved a tradition of informal responses to the demands of governors, legislators, and public opinion. For all the potential conflict among institutions, regions of the state, and competing interest groups, Maine displays a remarkably civil culture. There has never been a strike of unionized employees at the public institutions, though there have been threats from time to time. Nearly all of the potential battles

between public and private institutional interests have been resolved off-stage, rather than in the legislative arena.

Organizational Stability
In the face of criticism from the legislature, activist citizens, editorial boards, angry students, and energized members of the academic community, there has been remarkably little governance or organizational change within public and independent higher education in Maine from the late '60s to the present.

Names have changed in the public sector. The University of Maine at Portland-Gorham has become the University of Southern Maine, and the campus in Orono is heralded (once again) as the University of Maine. Yet, the basic structure of a system with a chancellor and a single board of trustees has prevailed over that period, although participants in the pitched battles over the years remind us that this stability was maintained only following intense debate.

To be sure, a momentous change has occurred in the state's two-year public system, as the former technical colleges became community colleges in 2003. The public universities in Maine, and notably the University of Maine at Augusta, have over the years offered important community-based services through innovative distance education programs. These programs continue to serve large numbers of students. They employ a dedicated television network, numerous sites and larger learning centers, and internet-based courses. The relationship between these efforts and the new Community College System will need to be defined over the next few years. It is remarkable, however, that the recent change in the technical college mission occurred some thirty or more years after most of the rest of the nation established more or less standard community college systems.

In the private sector during this period, a few small schools (Nasson in the south and Ricker in the north) closed and others merged; but the independent sector in Maine remains largely separate from the state apparatus and diverse in mission and reputation. In terms of economic benefit to the state, this sector is becoming increasingly important as several institutions develop a quasi-public mission of educating larger numbers of students for the professions.

At least in the public sector, this equilibrium comes in part from Mainers' predilection for the known versus the untried, from the statewide political balance which Chris Potholm describes elsewhere in this book, and from timely crisis management by boards of trustees and educational leaders. It is worth mentioning that state funding, when measured as a fraction of personal income, has been relatively stable over the years, as well.[7] Anyone especially interested in the political history of the University of Maine System and especially its remarkable buoyancy, should read former Maine State Senator James Libby's *Super U: The History and Politics of the University of Maine System.*[8]

Frequent Criticism and Calls for Reform

While the public sector of higher education in Maine has been among the most stable in the country, it has also been a popular target of critics and would-be reformers. From the unrelenting criticism of the Governor James Longley years, beginning with the 1973 Governor's Blue Ribbon Report on Cost Management, to the so-called Carlisle report of 1996, the University of Maine System, its cost, its structure, and the decisions of its leaders have been the objects of regular attack or at least intense scrutiny.

For example, in arguing for a more market-oriented higher education structure, the Carlisle report echoes the themes of the Longley report written a quarter-century earlier. The Carlisle report asserts that "In most centralized systems [such as Maine's], the bottom line has become so vague as to become indistinguishable...The system creates expensive layers of administration and bureaucracy to fabricate a system of artificial forces.[9]

The vetoing of a bill to establish a medical school, severe budget cuts, and the sudden departure of a chancellor were the outcomes of Longley's term as governor. Aadvisory boards of governors were created for all campuses in the University of Maine System, following the report of a blue ribbon commission established by House Speaker Elizabeth Mitchell. Yet, at the end of the day, it must be said that all of these were changes at the margin.

Civility within Higher Education

Maine is ripe with issues that potentially could drive wedges between the many competing interests within higher education.

The experience of other states is instructive. Minnesota and Pennsylvania, for example, have engaged in political warfare between representatives of the private and public institutions over the state subsidy. Elsewhere, public systems have been torn apart by insurgent campuses seeking either a bigger share of the fiscal pie, as in Nevada and Maryland, or the freedom to go it alone without central coordination, as in New Jersey and Florida.

To be sure, similar pressures exist in Maine; but typically they are resolved short of open warfare. This tendency to put positive working relationships ahead of institutional or regional or group interests may reflect the social maturity of the state and most of its leaders. Civility in the midst of conflict also reflects a recognition that, in the political arena, coalitions typically prevail over the lone wolf.

Civility and respectful relationships are certainly to be cherished. It is fair to ask, however, if Maine leaders too often put peace within the academic community ahead of better service to the people. To paraphrase *Getting to Yes*, have Mainers not gone hard enough on the important policy issues because they wanted to be easy on each other?[10]

Changing Maine

A Largely Deregulated Environment

A university president in Massachusetts once lamented that because of redundant state oversight, he managed to build an $8 million campus building for $11 million! If administrators overspend on construction or anything else in Maine, they have only themselves to blame, because there is little second-guessing by the state.

Maine is one of a handful of states that suffers very little oversight from state bureaucracies. In finance, human resources, capital mangement, contracting, and employee negotiations, the public institutions in Maine enjoy substantial independence to manage as their trustees see fit. One former university chancellor estimated that *not* having to report to a slow-moving state bureaucracy probably equaled a 10 percent budget saving.

Aside from the formidable presence of two system administrations, there is also an unusual absence of formal, statewide governance and coordination in Maine. The one public institution not part of the systems, Maine's highly regarded Maritime Academy, operates like a charter college with its own board of trustees.[11] Unlike the vast majority of states, there is no central planning agency for higher education, much less a statewide coordinating board that would attempt to control duplication, harmonize new initiatives, and nominally at least represent the people's interests when they differ from the academics'.

The public interest is not ignored in Maine; rather, it is addressed through informal means. Assuring that the public's agenda is well served depends more on personal relationships among leaders and trust that they will do the right thing, than on an external, coercive authority.

Informal Solutions

Absent a bureaucratic superstructure which would somehow coordinate the work of the public systems, Maine Maritime, and perhaps in some fashion the independents as well, Maine has evolved *informal*, non-authoritarian ways of responding to legislative or citizen demands. Maine is like Michigan in this respect. Transfer agreements, for example, intended to ease the mobility of students from two- to four-year schools, have been created voluntarily in Maine. In other states, the legislature intervened to require portability of academic credits. Of course, politicians may intervene in Maine as well, if too many of their constituents report problems with credit transfer or other barriers.

These voluntary, informal means of responding to the public interest are essential in a state like Maine, where the key education and political leaders can meet together in the living room in the Blaine House. In effect, the people of Maine entrust the leaders responsible for major educational organizations with responsibility for improving and changing those organizations when the times so require.

Thus, Maine is among a small handful of states where there is literally no formal mechanism, be it a board, a committee, or a state agency, with the leverage to play a strong role in speaking for the people's interest alone. Instead, the state expects its educational and political leaders—its chancellors, presidents, trustees, legislative leaders and the governor—to work together to ensure public needs are met, and the tax payers' investment in higher education is managed as efficiently as possible.

In light of this history and culture, it is legitimate to ask if the somewhat laissez-faire, informal, and personal approach to solving problems will serve in the new era of higher expectations and serious financial and other challenges.

Forces for Change

Two perennial challenges—the changing economy and related limits on state spending—are combining with three relatively new developments to pressure the status quo. The new developments are the transformation of the technical colleges to community colleges; the precipitous decline in the number of Maine's high school graduates; and the expansion of the middle sector of private institutions into more professions.

There is also a wild card in the person of a new governor, John Baldacci, with political savvy, a majority in both branches of the legislature, and the courage to take on tough problems. No one or two of these pressures alone would be enough to bring about change; but the combination of all just might.

A Knowledge-Driven Economy

During the recent (and to too many, the current) recession, Maine led the country in the proportionate loss of manufacturing jobs. This statistic continues a trend that has afflicted the leather, textile, and forest products industries in the state for decades. Jobs that once resided along the Kennebec and the Androscoggin and the Penobscot moved first to the banks of the Mississippi and the Rio Grande, and now move to the Yangtze and the burgeoning cities of China.

Replacing these manufacturing jobs with skilled opportunities in the new economy has been the Holy Grail for Maine and, indeed, for every job-exporting state in the United States. Yet, Maine lags behind most of the rest of the country, not only in educating its own recent high school graduates and the incumbent workforce, but also in producing engineers, computer scientists, and others prepared to lead in the newer technological, knowledge-driven economy. Proportionately, Maine ranks behind states like Mississippi, Alabama and South Carolina in the rate of production of engineers. It is seventh from the bottom in graduating students with degrees in computer and information science.[12]

To many observers, Maine needs to close this gap between the number and kinds of graduates being produced and the kinds and number needed to generate and attract new-economy jobs. Failure to do so leads students to go elsewhere in search of more relevant degree programs and discourages new firms from locating within the state.

Budget Woes

The current budget situation featuring a "structural" imbalance between state revenues and expenditures is really the chronic budget situation in Maine. It is difficult to recall when the state did not enter the new fiscal year without a structural budget gap.

Nor is there reason to believe, when state revenues increase, there will be marked improvement in higher education funding. Voters will continue to resist tax increases. Health care funding—whatever develops in the state's visionary Dirigo Health Plan—is sure to remain a top priority. In the November 2003 referendum, a strong majority supported more state support for local school districts, either immediately or within five years. With popular and legislative support for the community college initiative, it seems safe to say the universities in particular will face an uphill battle before the Appropriations Committee.

The hard reality is that without a new source of revenue, or substantial cost savings elsewhere, there simply will not be enough money to fund bold, new initiatives, such as a Maine version of Georgia's Hope Scholarship or Kentucky's $600 million "Bucks for Brains" investments in research. Nor will there be enough state dollars to keep tuition hikes from averaging, say, double or triple the rate of inflation.

Technical Colleges Become Community Colleges

A few years ago, Professor David Silvernail of the University of Southern Maine's Muskie School, argued that Maine's production of college graduates would increase substantially if the state developed a true community college system. With the transition of the Technical Colleges to Community Colleges in 2003 it appears that Silvernail's predictions are coming true.[13]

Recent double-digit enrollment increases at the former technical colleges strongly suggest that there has been pent-up demand for a true community college option. In the November 2003 bond referendum, voters endorsed additional capital funding for the two-year schools. Likewise, the "racino" proposal for adding slot machines at racetracks includes funding for the community colleges. The governor and legislature have pledged additional operating support in the coming years, as well.

This new system is a major positive development and will increase opportunities for thousands of Maine students over the next few years; but it will also shake up the higher education status quo.

The experience of other states following the initiation of community college systems is instructive. Besides intensifying the competition for dollars and students, the advent of the community college will force greater scrutiny of credit transfer policies among nominally equivalent programs, and of duplicative programs offered in the same or adjacent communities. Differences in tuition and operating costs for similar programs will likely spark interest as well. Tension over these issues elsewhere in the country has led in almost every case to greater state intervention in the management of its higher education systems.

Fewer High School Graduates

Maine is about to experience lean years of declining high school graduation rates. The number of high school graduates drops from just under 15,000 in 2002 to less than 12,000 a decade or so from now.[14] This reality can only exacerbate the competition for traditional-age students.

Currently, about half of the eighteen- or nineteen-year-olds who graduate from Maine's high schools leave the state for further education.[15] Unless this talent drain is reduced, or we can attract more college students from other states, an already shrinking pool of potential college students will decline further.

Demographics is not always destiny; but leaders at the state's smaller, rural campuses— both two- and four-year, public and independent—will need to be especially creative and entrepreneurial if they are to continue to build enrollments in the face of these harsh realities.

The Public Mission of Private Institutions

Maine is recognized nationally for its exceptional, private liberal arts colleges— Bowdoin, Bates, and Colby. With their high rankings in surveys of top colleges, excellent programs, and very selective admissions policies, these schools are a source of justifiable pride to Mainers.

In preparing a large number of Mainers for immediate employment within the state, Maine's middle tier of independent institutions—such as Husson College and the University of New England, to name but two— play an increasingly important role. Husson College, located in Bangor and with learning sites around the state, and the University of New England, which hosts Maine's only medical school and is expanding rapidly into other professional and research areas, provide services that meet the needs of a broad sector of the population. A particularly important segment of the population is the incumbent workforce, which in Maine is relatively less schooled than in the rest of New England and in the nation as a whole.

These schools and others like them perform a quasi-public role, in that their tuition falls near the mid-point between the public and the elite private schools; their admissions policies are generous, and they supply an important percentage of the Maine's need for professionals in health care, teaching, and business.

Clearly, these career-oriented, independent schools are fulfilling public needs not entirely addressed by the premier liberal arts colleges or the public universities. It remains to be seen if this reality will affect the way policymakers look at higher education planning, the distribution of student financial aid, and funding for new programs. Legislative funding for research at private entities like Jackson Labs, the Gulf of Maine Research Institute, and the Foundation for Blood Research creates a precedent for state funding of non-state enterprises.

A New Governor

In virtually all states where higher education's resources have been harnessed to serve a broad public and economic agenda, the governor has led the charge. Zell Miller of Georgia, Paul Patton of Kentucky, Rudy Perpich of Minnesota, and Christine Todd Whitman of New Jersey, as well as several governors in North Carolina and Illinois, were the key actors in bringing about change. States such as Oregon, where higher education leaders and business interests combined to reinvigorate the relationship between the state and the university, find it hard to sustain the change without the support of the state's chief executive.[16]

John Baldacci in many ways fits the prototype of governors elsewhere who restructured their higher education systems to improve their effectiveness. He belongs to the political party that enjoys majorities in both branches of the legislature, is a highly experienced politician with years of service in Augusta and Washington, and has shown the political courage to take on complex and important issues, as his work with health care reform indicates.

Aside from his outspoken support of the community college initiative, the new Governor has not yet shown his hand on other higher education questions. In spite of the current cuts proposed for higher education, in the longer run he may find that the best way to stem Maine's talent drain, to salvage its natural resource-based communities, and to improve personal income will be to redirect the way higher education is delivered in Maine. In addition to leadership, vision, and planning, this change will require new resources as well.

The Direction of Change

Change in Maine's higher education scheme appears inevitable. The economic and demographic trends described earlier are likely to translate into political pressures. If so, the state may intervene in ways it has not since the creation of the University of Maine System in 1968. Even without deliberate state action, the realities of less funding and greater competition for students will themselves require adjustments in the costs charged to students, the amounts of financial aid available to them, and the ability of the colleges and universities to sustain existing programs and mount new ones.

Absent an enlightened, statewide plan of action, the prospects for all but the elite institutions in Maine, and especially for the public ones, is fairly gloomy. Down one path lies a grim future of less public funding, higher tuition, and substandard student financial aid. These inadequacies will contribute to a continuing talent drain from the state, fewer opportunities for the students who need postsecondary education the most, and diminished chances for economic growth. Change is inevitable, but this bleak forecast is not.

If political and higher education leaders in Maine are able to address problems in three broad areas, the colleges and universities they oversee and the state as a whole may experience a much brighter future. Those three areas include the recognition that for Maine and most states, higher education strategy is economic strategy; that operational efficiencies will be a major source of new funding in the future; and that student financial aid policy needs to be linked to the costs passed on to students.

Higher Education Strategy Is Economic Strategy
In the post-industrial world, higher education strategy is economic strategy. To be sure, tax structure, physical infrastructure, location, market size, and cultural variables are critical, as well; but most of these lie beyond the power of policy makers to change in the short term. Designing a more effective higher education strategy is not the work of an afternoon, either; but in a state like Maine, a small number of able leaders may design, secure support for, and begin improvements within a year.

Maine needs to bring together its plans for the future of higher education with a sense of what industries and employment sectors will be dominant in the years ahead, and what the workforce skills and research needs of those industries will be. Most of the information needed to join these two efforts at planning for the future is at hand. State planners have identified target industries. The research initiatives of the past decade are already focused on the state's economic future in such areas as alternative uses for forest products, sensor research, and biotechnology. What is needed is a mechanism for joining the two, so that colleges and universities can support the curricula and produce the graduates and the research essential to the economic future of the state.

To be sure, some will argue that preparing more engineers or computer scientists is tantamount to funding the workforce needs of Massachusetts or any other state that lures Maine graduates. Certainly, some graduates in high-demand fields will seek employment beyond Maine's borders, at least for a time.

Yet, Peter Drucker reminds us, knowledge workers attract knowledge indus-tries.[17] Industries that seek high-skill labor locate where the knowledge workers live. That could be Maine, at least in some specific fields.

There are lessons to be learned from university support of Maine's tradi-tional industries. The University of Maine, for example, is world-recognized for its chemical engineering graduates who work in the forest products industry. The university supports research in cooperation with and with some funding from other natural resource-based industries. Such partnerships exist in bio-technology, wood composites, and sensor research; but more university-industry research partnerships are needed in emerging industries.

Maine's independent institutions already play an important role in preparing these highly skilled graduates. Those private colleges and universities that have the capacity and the willingness to respond to state-identified needs deserve a chair in those Blaine House living room discussions. Occasionally in the past, Maine has invited out-of-state institutions to supply programs not available from Maine's own colleges or universities. It makes sense to engage Maine's own independent sector in the work of planning for the state's economic future.

Operational Improvements

The most unglamorous aspect of reform lies in improving operations, as well as governance and funding patterns; but with little new state funding in sight, this is where Maine must look for the savings to keep tuition affordable and to cre-ate resources for future-oriented initiatives.

Maine faces three key problems on the operational side: too many small units with overlapping programs, a funding mechanism that fails to incentivize strategic growth, and the lack of a means of coordinating the two large systems. Fortunately, there are policy options to address these problems.

Many Small Units

Over 90 percent of the people of Maine are within a thirty-minute commute of some postsecondary educational venue, be it a college, university campus, or a learning center operated by the university or Community College System. For a student living on an island in Penobscot Bay or in rural northern Maine, this proximity is essential. Yet, as economists Thomas Duchesneau and David Wihry have pointed out, the price Maine pays for providing geographic access is a loss of economic access. Because the state hosts so many relatively small, somewhat duplicative units, they argue, Maine suffers diseconomies of scale resulting in higher operating and tuition costs.[18]

The reality of duplication of programs and services will only become more acute as community colleges expand general education programs and offer de-grees parallel to the first two years of the baccalaureate.

There are some promising approaches to getting costs down while sustaining community-based services. One is to clarify the role of the community colleges and that of the university centers located, and sometimes co-located across the state. A second is to create incentives for regional two- and four-year schools to work together, by offering a bonus to a combined effort that serves a thousand or more students with shared management, curriculum, and faculty. The resulting tight consortia of schools have the potential to keep up services across the entire state, to maintain institutional identity, and to improve affordability.

Maine has more experience than many states in offering education at a distance, using technology. With greater access to the Internet, Maine can also call upon its investment in distance education to maintain access at a reasonable cost.

Discussion of the many small institutions in Maine invariably summons up the idea of closing a rural campus. This is an idea that has seldom worked in other states. The experience in Wisconsin and Minnesota, for example, suggests that such action further damages already beleaguered communities, results in little if any cost savings, and is extraordinarily difficult to achieve politically. Moreover, prolonged debate over closing compromises the prospects of improving the campus so it becomes a stronger community resource and attractive to more students. The brilliant turnaround at the University of Maine at Fort Kent, led by President Charles Lyons during the late 1990s, illustrates the potential for other academic gems located in rural Maine.

Funding Mechanisms

The best thinking on funding higher education emphasizes a simple approach which combines a base level of support to maintain institutional capacity coupled with some incentive funding to address state priorities. On balance, Maine handles the capacity part of the equation well; with the exception of special legislative support for research with economic potential, it has less experience with funding for new initiatives. Elsewhere, incentive funds matching public, business, and philanthropic support have delivered institutional payoffs. The spectacular growth of schools like Virginia Commonwealth, Boise State, and the University of Nebraska-Omaha has been fueled with this kind of support.

Taking a cue from other states, Maine could establish incentive funds to increase the enrollment of low income students, increase graduation rates in high demand fields and, as suggested earlier, combine regional programs and services. The University of Maine System's recent proposal to establish an $11 million-student aid fund that includes the requirement to maintain respectable grades illustrates this idea. In general, these "top up" funds would build on existing, market-based incentives to enroll more students, produce more graduates, and reduce costs.

Two Systems with an Increasingly Shared Agenda

To many students and the public at large, both of Maine's systems of higher education share a very similar mission for the first two years. This perception creates both a challenge and an opportunity for the two boards of trustees and their executives. On the one hand, the systems have different expectations of faculty, teaching loads, investments in physical plant and, not surprisingly, different cost and tuition levels. Of course, the university has the unique responsibility for research. Yet, the distinctions between the first two years of general education appear pretty slim to student-consumers, their families, and elected representatives. Where substantive differences in mission and academic programs exist, the burden is on system leaders to make sure that the public appreciates the distinctions. In the business as opposed to the academic operations of the systems, a good case can be made that greater integration would yield substantial savings.

To be sure, the two large systems have worked together to address credit transfer, to combine some services in their learning centers and in requests for private and public funding. With the rapid growth in community college enrollment and programs, the state's chronic revenue problems, and legitimate public expectations, clearly more work on harmonizing the efforts of the systems needs to be done.

Other states offer a variety of models for stronger coordination, but no "off-the-shelf" standard will likely be suitable for Maine. Some states are considering new overarching boards comprised of business, education, and policy leaders. Others, like Florida recently and New Jersey in the early 1990s, did away with statewide boards altogether, in favor of local governing boards. Whatever the structure, the best results come in states that support more effective processes rather than larger bureaucracies. For example, whatever the structure, it makes sense to focus on incentives for systems to work together in achieving public ends, along with an independent means of verifying the effects of that cooperation.

Should Maine's system of community colleges and its university system be merged under a single governing body? To those frustrated by the difficulties in *coordinating* these two large organizations absent a single overarching authority, the idea has great intuitive appeal. Yet, the experience of states which have attempted to restructure their statewide governance systems shows mixed results. In most instances, the costs of statewide governance re-engineering are high, and the benefits slow to be realized. In addition, employee preoccupation with job security diminishes their attention to basic responsibilities, and contributes to a powerful resistance to the change. In combination, these factors make restructuring a questionable first option.[19]

Greater integration, on both the administrative and academic sides, of Maine's two large systems offers educational and economic benefits. Working out a sensible program to achieve these benefits would appear to be a major strategic responsibility of the trustees and executives of these organizations.

Student Financial Aid
Maine received an "F" for affordability in *Measuring Up 2002, The State-By-State Report Card for Higher Education* issued by the non-partisan National Center for Public Policy and Higher Education. Maine does so poorly in this area because financial aid doesn't make up for high tuition and low per capita income. Compared to the best performing states, according to the report, Mainers pay a greater percentage of their income for college costs, Maine offers less state aid for low income residents, and students cross the graduation stage with higher debt.[20]

There have been several initiatives in the past half-dozen years to encourage the most able students to enroll at Maine colleges and universities. The Mitchell Scholars program, supported with funds raised by former Senator George Mitchell, enables top high school students to enroll at Maine institutions, as well as to attend out-of-state schools. The University of Maine's scholarship program for high school valedictorians has sharply increased the numbers of these talented students choosing to enroll at the Orono campus.

Yet, the state needs to do better by its lower income students, as well. Part of the problem is that Maine, like most other states, separates the decisions it makes regarding funding and tuition from financial aid decisions. Thus, the legislature allocates funding to the community colleges and universities with, in the case of the universities at least, limited knowledge of what the consequences will be for tuition and student aid. (The community colleges have voluntarily frozen tuition increases for the past several years.)

As a result, in the university system, Maine finds itself pursuing a policy of higher tuition without compensating increases in student support. This episodic approach means that aid never fully catches up with tuition increases. In future funding requests and decisions, the goal of enrolling lower income students would be better served if the legislature formally linked the state allocation, tuition policy, and student financial aid.

Conclusion
Looking back to the late 1960s, one must be impressed with the n nber and diversity of colleges and universities, both public and independent, v ich have endured and often prospered in serving the people of the state. Thank to capable faculty, many of whom accepted lower compensation in Maine in retu n for the joys of living in the Pine Tree State, these institutions by and large have

delivered on the perennial goals of higher education. Their graduates are as well educated as any to meet the general demands of life and citizenship in the twenty-first century.

Yet, Maine needs to do more to realize the collective benefits to all of its citizens from their investment in higher education. This task is especially challenging in an environment characterized by intense competition for public funding and for students. A better future lies ahead if Maine's leaders can make progress on three prominent challenges: linking higher education's agenda and the state's economic agenda more effectively, finding a way to improve operational effectiveness and especially to harmonize the services of the two systems across the state, and improving financial aid for low income Mainers.

Fortunately, Maine currently employs an exceptionally able group of educational leaders in both of its systems and its colleges and universities. Its new governor, a University of Maine graduate, has shown a willingness to take on tough issues. Working within a tradition of personal, hands-on problem solving, addressing the challenges outlined here ought to be well within the grasp of these leaders.

*T*errence J. MacTaggart *is the immediate past chancellor of the University of Maine System. Educated at Canisius College and Saint Louis University, he is a recognized leader and scholar in American higher education. He is currently University of Maine System research professor, and a former senior fellow with the Center for Public Higher Education Governance and Trusteeship. In addition to his chancellorship of the University of Maine System, he has held this position with the Minnesota State University System. He also served as the campus chief executive (chancellor) of the University of Wisconsin—Superior. Dr. MacTaggart's research and publications focus on higher education policy and management, state-university relations, and economic development. With James Mingle, he recently authored* Pursuing the Public's Agenda: Trustees in Partnership with State Leaders. *In 1995 he served as the editor and lead author of* Restructuring Public Higher Education: What Works and What Doesn't in Reorganizing Public Systems. *He has served as a consultant to numerous colleges, universities, and systems, including the University of Nebraska System, the University System of Maryland, the University of North Carolina at Chapel Hill, the Oregon University System, and the University of Alaska System.*

THE SALES TAX, THE INCOME TAX, and federal aid (especially Medicaid) have funded dramatic increases in state programs over the past four decades, enabling the state to become Maine's primary provider of medical and social services, as well as an equal partner in paying for K-12 education. Hundreds of thousands of Mainers depend on these services; unfortunately, the taxes that support them are highly volatile and respond alarmingly to inevitable market downturns. Maine will have to establish a more stable revenue base by taxing consistent sources (i.e., wealth and property) in order to maintain the level of health and education spending Maine citizens have come to expect.

8 Maine Tax Policy
Lessons from the Domesday Book

PETER MILLS

On Saturday night, the 28th of the June, 1969, the Maine legislature encountered one of its closest showdowns. With the state itself about to shut down for lack of a budget, the issue was whether to pass an income tax designed by Scott Fox, a Falmouth accountant, promoted by the Republican floor leader, Harry Richardson, and endorsed by the leaders of both the Republican and Democratic parties. Despite such support, the tax encountered stiff resistance from rank and file members on both sides of the aisle, including powerful members of the Appropriations Committee.

In an emotional roll call, the bill passed by but a single vote in the house, when one opponent agreed to vote for passage only after he saw that the 100 other necessary votes were already up on the board. When later sent to the senate, the bill failed of passage on first roll call. During a recess, one member was convinced to switch, and it then passed the senate by just one vote, as well.

Because Governor Curtis had supported the bill, he had to fight off a primary challenge in 1970 and came within 800 votes of losing the general election in the fall. However, when the income tax by itself was later forced out to referendum by citizen petition in 1971, it was resoundingly approved by 75 percent of Maine voters.

Maine's original income tax survived because it was fairly structured, simply designed, easily understood, and inexpensively administered. Leaders from across the political spectrum were willing to support the tax and to explain its utility. Most importantly, voters had a sense that the money they were sending to Augusta was being put to good use, that they were getting back something of value for their investment.

I open with this story and highlight its significance because it stands in stark contrast to the present mood of our state and of the nation. To account for this change and to trace its history is one purpose of this chapter.

Why Taxes Matter

> "Under democracy, one party always devotes its chief energies to trying to prove that the other party is unfit to rule. Both commonly succeed, and both are right." —H. L. Mencken

We can not begin to discuss tax policy without first identifying two themes that may, at first, seem diversionary. First, taxes are inseparable from appropriations;

revenue and expense are two sides of one ledger. It is only to support public programs that we must talk about taxes at all. The past four decades have seen dramatic increases in state programs funded by growth in three new revenue sources: the sales tax; the income tax; and federal aid, primarily through Medicaid. These pillars of support enabled the state to assume two new and significant roles: first, as a dominant provider of social and medical services in Maine; and, second, as an equal contributor to K-12 education.

Hard as it is to believe today, for the first two-thirds of the twentieth century, the major function of state government was to build roads and facilitate the expanded use of motor vehicles. Legislators elected in 1960 saw themselves primarily as highway engineers. While the Maine Department of Transportation and the Turnpike Authority continue today to manage major sums of money, they are now dwarfed by two other departments whose budgets outstripped them during the past forty years: the Department of Education and the Department of Human Services. As a result, the two jobs of major significance to today's legislator are these: first, to serve as a co-director of one of the world's largest and most complex health insurers, the American Medicaid system; and second, to raise and distribute taxes as a revenue collector for local schools.

My second preliminary point concerns the complex hierarchy and matrix through which public revenue is raised and disbursed. As our federal system has matured, it has become increasingly difficult to resolve questions of hierarchy— that is, to determine at what level of government our tax money should be raised and at what level it should best be spent, whether by local, regional, state, or federal entities—or, as is increasingly more common, by some blended arrangement among agencies with each of them attaching conditions to the money as it flows from one tier to another.

To take one example, just setting up a child care center or a Head Start program in a local school involves a process so complex that it cannot be funded and managed without the help of professional grant brokers such as those employed by Community Action Programs. Ever since two-income families became the rule, rather than the exception, access to child care has become essential to modern life. School Administrative District 49, the district around Fairfield, provides child care services in each of its four towns. While parents pay a fee for some of the programs based on their ability to pay, the centers are not self-supporting, and could not stay open without substantial public supplements.

Several streams of federal and state grant programs feed into each facility to support Head Start, Early Head Start, and day care. Qualifying parents receive federal vouchers to subsidize day care fees. Pre-kindergarten education programs provided by the school are partially paid for by general purpose aid from the state, because students age four and older are counted under the state's school funding formula. The whole program is administered and sponsored by the school district which supplies building space, utilities, and payroll services. Many of the day care workers are regularly employed by the school district as educational technicians who receive their health insurance and pension plans from the school district and are thus able to moonlight in child care without burdening the program with their fringe benefits.

The recent history of the property tax illustrates further the complexity of current tax hierarchies. As recently as 1951, the last fiscal year before the Maine sales tax, one-sixth of the state's general fund budget was raised through a statewide property tax collected through the towns, as had been done ever since 1820. At the present time, by contrast, the state collects most of its revenue from its own broad-based taxes on sales and income, and sends fully 43 percent of all of it right back to local governments and property taxpayers in the form of school aid, revenue sharing, homestead exemptions, property tax rebates, business equipment tax reimbursements, local road assistance, tree growth refunds, and general welfare assistance.

While many people regard such intricacies as tedious, dry, and without consequence, we need to remind ourselves that poor tax policy was the reason England lost control over its American colonies. Just a decade ago in Maine, tax upheavals caused another revolution that began with a shutdown in state government and led to the imposition of legislative term limits, a complete turnover in political leadership, and the election of an independent governor as a rebuff to both warring political parties. Even more recently, it was the deficient tax structure of our largest state that produced the Terminator's takeover of California.

Tax policy may well be dull stuff; but it matters.

1086, 1820, and All That

> "The nation ought to have a tax system that
> looks like someone designed it on purpose." —William Simon

In framing the U.S. Constitution, the founders of the American republic understood that the states would continue to support themselves primarily through "direct taxes" on people and property, often known as taxes on "polls and estates." Because the commerce clause forbids states from collecting tariffs, either among themselves or against foreign nations, that privilege was left to the federal government, which supported itself until the Civil War primarily through tariffs and customs duties.

Meanwhile, states like Maine collected most of their money by directing towns to send in a portion of the property tax to the state. Our county governments continue to collect their revenue in this way today. While the idea of sending property taxes to Augusta seems foreign to us now, the statewide property tax remained in place from 1820 until 1954, when revenue from a two-cent sales tax replaced it. As a source for school funding reform, the statewide property tax was revived in 1973 as the "Uniform Property Tax," and then repealed at referendum in 1977.

In the year 1086, William the Conqueror sent English public servants out to inventory his nation's property and to create what became the Domesday Book. Its purpose was to equalize the king's property taxes among his subjects after the Norman Conquest. Public employees could well have done very similar work for the State of Maine during our first 130 years of statehood. For, in the intervening millennium, the elements of our state tax structure had changed very little from feudal times.

As both the American republic and the states matured during the nineteenth and twentieth centuries, they became increasingly dependent on excises, taxes that are assessed on various privileges such as forming corporations, conducting certain businesses, transferring real estate, and the like. Maine's insurance premium tax, for example, has been in place since 1874. Beginning in 1934, a significant portion of state revenue came from an excise tax on alcohol and, beginning in 1941, on tobacco. In 1951, the year before the sales tax, the three biggest General Fund taxes were those on statewide property assessments and on alcohol and tobacco; all three were of about equal size.

The biggest tax of all at mid-century, however, was the gasoline tax within the Highway Fund that was, by constitutional amendment, legally and administratively separate from other state finances. Forty and fifty years ago, the Highway Fund regularly accounted for one-third of all state spending. The extraordinary demands on public infrastructure created by motor vehicles required very little sophistication in tax policy. It was enough to impose user fees and not broad-based general taxes. Motor fuel excises, car registration fees, turnpike and bridge tolls and federal subsidies financed highways and their related debt service throughout the century of the automobile.

A Matter of Size: Maine's Great Growth Spurt

"Giving money and power to government is like giving whiskey and car keys to teenage boys." —P. J. O'Rourke

From 1963 to 2002 the highway budget, including federal subsidies, rose from $53.4 million to $422 million, only a little more than the six-fold rate of inflation. During that time, however, the Highway Fund dropped from 32 percent of the state budget to 8 percent, as education and human services mushroomed. Education (both K-12 and higher education) grew from just $31.6 million to $1.25 billion, *six times* faster than inflation. The growth in human services was even more dramatic: the account grew from $16.8 million to $2.22 billion, at a rate *twenty-two times* faster than inflation.

While transportation is funded by user fees, programs in education and social services require general taxes. Expansions in these programs occurred only because the state had new general revenue available from three principal sources: the sales tax, the income tax, and federal matching funds. The sales tax became effective on July 1, 1951, at a rate of two cents on the purchasing dollar. By 1969 the rate was up to five cents, where it is today. In its original form, the sales tax statute contained thirteen paragraphs of exemptions; now, there are ninety such paragraphs, with numerous sub-parts. Despite the narrowness of its base and its failure to include most services, the sales tax grew from $30.1 million in 1963 to $857.5 million in 2003, a rate that exceeded inflation by nearly five times.

The Maine income tax, after its passage in 1969 and validation by referendum in 1971, grew so fast that it eclipsed the gas tax in 1974.[1] In another four years, it exceeded the size of the entire Highway Fund, including federal subsidies. By 1986 combined revenue from corporate and personal income taxes had surpassed the sales tax. The rate of growth of the personal income tax averaged 22 percent per year in its first decade, 15 percent in its second and 6 percent in its third. Since collections began in 1970, the income tax has grown at 7.6 times the rate of inflation.

The third source of new revenue is federal grant money. Invented in 1965 as part of President Lyndon Johnson's "Great Society" program, Medicaid is now a $1.4 billion program in Maine, consisting of one-third state and two-thirds federal money. Child welfare and protective services are similarly subsidized. Ninety-one percent of the payroll in our state Department of Labor is federalized. Most major highways and bridges are built with an 80 percent federal match, as are many sewer plants and other environmental projects. In 1963, the state received $41.6 million in federal grants. In 2002, it received $1.7 billion, representing growth that was 6.8 times the rate of inflation.

Revenue growth from these three major sources has fueled a sea change in people's expectations for state services. We now take for granted that the state is expected to supply, among many, many other services:

- Free health insurance for families with household incomes below roughly the median level for all families;

- Care for most patients in our nursing homes, including many from the middle class who have exhausted their own resources;

- Child care vouchers to enable both parents in working class households to enter the workforce;

- Personal tutoring for any child with an impediment to learning;

- Competent protection for abused and neglected children;

- Round-the-clock support for the mentally ill and disabled now residing in our communities;

- Respite for victims of domestic violence; and

- Environmental protection against a wide array of hazards.

We expected and received little of this in 1963. The state's footprint on the Maine economy is 70 percent larger than it was forty years ago: in 1963, state spending was 8.3 percent of Maine's total personal income; in 2002, it was 13.7 percent.

Today, ours is a society with great and civilized expectations; even reactionary observers foresee no likely retreat from such trends. In 1963 the sexual abuse of children was commonly ignored; it is now recognized as an open and continuing crisis that consumes a wide range of state resources. Highway building, once the king of state appropriations, has been superseded by education and Medicaid. No one is comfortable living in a society where children are not well educated or where people are left to die in crowded charity wards because they cannot afford chemotherapy, coronary by-pass, or nursing home care.

Staying Alive: Hyperinflation in Health Care

"If you think health care is expensive now, wait until you see what it costs when it's free." — P. J. O'Rourke

There is no end in sight for the continuing escalation of health care costs in Maine and the nation. It is probably the most persistent and intractable domestic policy issue all across America. Not only do high costs reduce access to care, but increased premiums paid by employers retard economic development by draining away capital as we compete against others with lower costs.

Health care inflation impacts state governments in a compound way. In the first instance, state government, as a labor-intensive service industry and employer, provides a generous package of health benefits. Maine pays for health coverage for 41,000 employees, retirees and their dependents, over 3 percent of the population. When health care costs escalate, they affect the state as much as they do any private employer. The future unfunded costs for retirees is staggering. At present, the state has reserves to fund an actuarial liability of $1 billion in future costs for retiree health care.

The state is also a major purchaser of care for needy citizens. Providing health care to others consumes fully one-fifth of the state's entire budget. Medicaid pays for 72 percent of all nursing home residents, and one-fifth of all hospital admissions. Medicaid covers over 20 percent of the state's population, including those who are most profoundly sick. The state is the dominant supplier of care for the mentally ill and the developmentally disabled. When provider costs go up, the state must either increase its payments for such services or accept blame for shifting those costs onto private purchasers who buy from the same providers.

Health care inflation also affects state tax receipts. When employee fringe benefits become more expensive, employers hire fewer workers and salaries are crowded out by the added cost of benefits. Taxable wages are reduced and there are fewer business profits to reinvest.

From 1960 to 2002, annual health care costs grew from 5.1 percent of America's gross domestic product (GDP) to 14.9 percent. Because health care is such a "superior good," in the sense that it has greater intrinsic value than nearly anything else we buy, health costs in the future will continue to consume an even greater share of our incomes. Given what we spend to relieve heartburn, is there any limit to what we will spend to cure cancer? It is hard to imagine any product or service valued more greatly than one that keeps people alive and well on this planet.

Three economists writing in the July/August 2003 issue of *Health Affairs* report that real health care spending between 1945 and 1998 grew at rates far greater than GDP, 4.1 percent per year versus 1.5 percent. They project that if health care costs continue to grow even at a very conservative rate, say only 1 percent faster than the rest of GDP, then by 2012, health spending will consume 17.7 percent of GDP. By the year 2075, health care will consume 38 percent, or nearly two-fifths of our nation's total spending.

The authors also assert that these future costs should be rendered affordable by the rate of growth in real income. Even while devoting 38 percent of our economy to health care alone in the latter part of this century, there should be enough money left over to buy everything else that we need or want.

With projected premiums at 38 percent of GDP, it is hard to speculate on what a future insurance system might look like; but it is clear that public spending for health care will dominate the picture to an even greater degree than today. Even at present, there is clearly no private market answer for people whose family incomes are below 200 percent of the federal poverty line.

Ten years ago, the Health Insurance Association of America (HIAA) brought us Harry and Louise ads that killed "Hillary care," the Clinton administration's universal health care initiative. However, only two years ago HIAA publicly agreed that people with incomes as high as 300 percent of poverty lack capacity to participate fully in the health care market without government subsidy. As newfound technologies and longer life spans drive up health care costs, people at ever higher levels of income will require public support.

Health care has become a lot like public education, electricity, the water supply, or safety on airlines: a semi-public utility whose services people expect to receive when needed, regardless of the ability to pay.

Why Is Education So Costly?

"The only thing more expensive than education is ignorance." —Benjamin Franklin

"The schools ain't what they used to be, and never was." —Will Rogers

State spending for education has not grown as fast as health care, but it has grown about seven times faster than inflation since 1963. It surpassed the Highway Fund in 1968. Public support for higher education has grown roughly in proportion to state aid for K-12. Spending by towns on education has grown by less than three times the rate of inflation, even though the property tax base, the value of all taxable property in the state, has grown slightly faster.

The state's contribution to foundation funding for K-12 was only 24 percent in 1963, and is now up to 44 percent, having peaked out at 51 percent in 1989. However, the state has assumed an ever increasing burden of paying for all of the pension costs for retired teachers and 40 percent of their health insurance costs, neither of which is included in foundation school funding. When these are added to the total, the state's level of support for K-12 education is about equal to the local share.

Student enrollments in K-12 peaked at 244,791 in 1971, and have since declined to 204,000; by 2010, enrollments are projected to decline still further to 185,000. It is pertinent to ask why costs for K-12 education have increased so much faster than the rate of inflation since 1963. One reason was the impetus to build new regional high schools under the Sinclair Act, a far-reaching 1957 statute that offered financial incentives for the creation of consolidated school districts. Another reason for growth in costs was an effort to increase teacher salaries during the 1980s; but salaries have since slid back to levels that are disconcertingly low. A recent survey by *Education Week* places Maine at forty-seventh in the nation.

A third reason for increased costs is the trend to decrease class sizes and to enhance opportunities for children with special needs. According to *Education Week*, Maine has the seventh lowest pupil-teacher ratios in the United States for elementary schools (13.1 students per teacher in 2002 versus 16.0 for the nation). During the past ten years, student enrollments have dropped by 6 percent, while the number of teachers has gone up by 10 percent.

The need for more teachers is partly explained by increased enrollments in special education, which have gone up by 26.5 percent in the past ten years. Today 18.1 percent of all Maine public school students are enrolled in special education; the national average is 13.3 percent. Again, this partly explains why Maine is twelfth in per pupil costs ($8,232 versus $7,376 nationally), even though our teacher salaries are relatively low. Maine is number one in the percentage of education costs spent on instruction rather than administration (67.3 percent versus a national average of 61.7 percent).

Envisioning Volatility

> "The 'bungee cord' effect: spiralling increases in funding followed by sharp and potentially severe cutbacks." —Josephine LaPlante and Robert Devlin

Our present revenue system with its reliance on sales and income taxes encountered a big test in the recession of 1991, and it failed. Although the recession was by no means severe in historical terms, its effects on the state budget were devastating and the political fallout, severe. Sawin Millett, who was state budget officer at the time, recalls that revenues began dropping in November of 1990 and then continued to plummet in a sustained free fall from month to month with no predictable limit to the downward slide.

The abrupt downturn traumatized our state to the core, and permanently altered its politics. Combined with the contemporaneous crisis in Workers Compensation, it even closed down government for three weeks. It brought the downfall of the Martin–Pray legislative era, the enactment of term limits, significant alterations to public pension rights, a number of tax increases, and the election of a popular but politically independent governor with only a limited power base and effectiveness. Oversight of state government has since been left to transient legislators who have little institutional memory, who must struggle much harder than their predecessors to survive the door-to-door electoral process, and whose energies are focused mainly on the next campaign that starts sixteen months after the preceding one ends.

Josephine LaPlante and Robert Devlin, after studying the budget crisis of 1991, laid the blame on hyper-elasticity in the state's tax code. Their use of the "bungee cord" metaphor made it possible for every legislator to envision what volatility means. LaPlante and Devlin pointed out that one-third of our sales tax revenue comes from the sale of automobiles and building supplies. When the economy is depressed, few people buy cars or construct a home; when the economy picks up again, these purchases rebound. Because the state does not tax staples like food, home heating fuel, and basic electricity, most revenue derives from the sale of big-ticket items that are deferred when incomes are down. Thus, the sales tax responds in a highly exaggerated way to changes in the economy. The tax lacks an adequate base to carry it through hard times.

LaPlante and Devlin further explained that the state's income tax is similarly volatile because of its large standard deduction and high personal exemption levels, its graduated bracket system, and its dependence on taxes paid by two-income families. In 2001 the state encountered another recession, and we learned that the income tax is volatile for yet another reason: capital gains. The state taxes long-term capital gains as ordinary income, much of it subject to the 8.5 percent top marginal rate. Stock market gains fueled huge surpluses for most states during the last half of the 1990s; but when the markets turned down in 2001, state income taxes for 2002 fell dramatically.

Lincolnville

During the winter of 2001-02, our economic forecasters had predicted a large drop in revenue from capital gains precisely because of the recession and stock market drops that were already in progress; but when tax returns came in during the spring of 2002, capital gains had dropped much further than expected. The resulting loss in revenue caused major state budget crises, not only in Maine, but in nearly every other state with an income tax that piggy-backs the federal system.

While most legislators understand volatility through a vision of the bungee cord metaphor, many assert on faith that volatility can be cured or greatly relieved by altering the structure of our present taxes. They suggest, for instance, that merely by broadening the base of the sales tax our revenues may be stabilized. I have a different view. It seems obvious to me that volatility is intrinsic to taxes based on sales or income, since the revenue is derived from sources that are so intertwined with the instabilities in our market economy. Trying to stop volatility is like trying to dampen tides in the Bay of Fundy.

William the Conqueror knew how to avoid volatility; he taxed wealth and property. So did the State of Maine from 1820 to 1954. As noted earlier, the big three taxes in 1951 (aside from the dominant and protected gasoline tax) were those on property, alcohol, and tobacco. Alcohol and tobacco taxes are notoriously regressive—that is, they are paid disproportionately by poor people—but they are also highly dependable. People continue to buy tobacco and alcohol in a recession. The property tax is also very stable, which is its major attribute. Californians voted to slash their property taxes in 1978 under Proposition 13 and place their faith in the income tax, instead. In 1999 they were awash with silicon capital gains; but in 2001 they were hammered by recession.

One can reduce volatility in sales and income taxes by making them more regressive, for example, by taxing food or by eliminating personal exemptions from the income tax; but even if poor people were willing to be taxed in this way, these taxes will still be highly sensitive to small swings in the economy. We cannot rely on either the sales or income tax to provide consistent support within the frame of a fiscal year. This is unfortunate, because the need for most governmental services, such as those provided by school teachers, firemen, and prison guards, is persistent. In a serious recession, the demands for many safety net services, such as welfare and Medicaid, actually go up substantially. They are counter-cyclical to the economy and to the taxes that support them.

Reaching Our Limits

"People who support unnecessary laws remind me of those who call the fire department to get cats out of trees. Did you ever see a cat skeleton up a tree? They come down when they get hungry." —Rep. Eddie Dexter of Kingfield

"Progress might have been all right once, but it's gone on too long now." —Ogden Nash

Current tensions over tax issues are not fully explained by volatility alone. We seem really to be confronting limits on what present systems will support— not only in Maine, but in most other states. It may not be what we are *able* to do so much as what we are *willing* to do. People are simply in no mood to continue raising state and local taxes.

Our present Democratic governor, John Baldacci, captured the mood in his budget speech to the legislature on February 5, 2003, when he compared our plight to "an economic and financial ice storm—unavoidable and unrelenting.... I believe that raising taxes at this time is the wrong way to go. It sends the wrong message to our citizens and businesses, who, quite frankly, can't afford more taxes.... Now is the time for fiscal restraint and discipline."

Contrast this speech with one given by Governor Kenneth Curtis in 1969. Curtis spoke of Maine as a "Sleeping Giant," then awakening. The preceding year had a set a record for industrial expansion. Four thousand new jobs had been created by fifty-eight new firms in Maine; ninety-eight others had expanded. Tourism had grown by more than 15 percent in one year. New paper mills were going up. General Fund revenues had grown by more than 11 percent, even without raising taxes. The state was able to provide a 40 percent increase in aid for education in 1968, and more was clearly coming.

Curtis confidently laid out a menu of new taxes to enhance programs like Medicaid, the most significant product of Lyndon Johnson's Great Society. He suggested raising the sales tax, increasing the excise on cigarettes, adopting a new tax on soft drinks, removing the automobile trade-in credit, and creating an income tax on individuals and corporations. He listed half a dozen ways in which new taxes might be combined to enhance revenue. If Governor Baldacci had given such a speech to launch his governorship in 2003, he would have been shouted down. If one reads both speeches without knowing the authors, one would conclude that they are not from the same political party. However, they are from the same party; they are simply governors in different times.

During the long run-up in state revenues from 1950 to 1990, people seemed more tolerant of taxation. The availability of new taxes, often leveraged with federal matching money, made possible astonishing changes in the role of state government, primarily in education and social services; but people's willingness to be taxed now seems exhausted. There is also the competitive factor. States are constantly comparing themselves to one another in their efforts to attract business. The phrase "race to the bottom" needs no explication. Grover Norquist and a host of conservative commentators have set the tone by asserting that all taxes are bad. Government in all forms must be shrunk. To slay the beast, cut off what feeds it.

It is not the purpose of this chapter to add yet another voice to the interminable debate over the proper size of state government. As a Republican, I have my own views on a host of things that the government does badly, but my present concern is the lack of stability in state and local revenue. Instability breeds chaos, and chaos leads people to adopt radical and unthinking remedies to complex problems, remedies that are truly pernicious to our society.

Clearly, the states have no new sources of revenue on the horizon; and the two major sources they have developed over the past forty years—sales and income taxes—have proven unstable and unpredictable. They are also limited by competitive pressures among the states. In this climate, what policies should we pursue?

Do Not Flee from Taxing Wealth

> The Domesday Book "was perhaps the most remarkable administrative accomplishment of the Middle Ages." —*Encyclopedia Britannica*

William the Conqueror knew a thing or two about raising revenue. In 1086 he taxed his subjects according to their wealth and did appraisals to tax them fairly. In his day, wealth was tangible and therefore easier to assess. Because most of our wealth today is intangible, because it exists in the form of patents, copyrights, credits at banks, and shares of stock, and because such intangible wealth flows so freely from one jurisdiction to another, people argue that it is no longer fair to tax real estate for anything except the raw cost of the government services that real estate requires—for example, the plowing of roads that lead up to it. It is argued that if we cannot tax all wealth fairly, then we should tax none of it, except for the associated service fees.

People who make this argument ignore the fact that taxation is first and foremost a question of power: the state can tax only that which it controls. A prime example of a tax that failed for lack of power to collect it is the use tax that was passed by most states to complement the sales tax. Passed in Maine in 1951, its purpose is to create symmetry by imposing a substitute for the sales tax when articles are purchased out-of-state and brought into Maine. States have little ability to enforce a use tax on most items, however; to this day, the use tax is seldom paid except on those products—like motor vehicles and boats—where the state asserts its power to collect through mandatory registration of the object taxed.

The fact that Maine cannot effectively collect a use tax on clothing bought in North Conway should not be used as an argument to abandon nearly a billion dollars worth of revenue produced each year by the sales taxes that we can and do collect in places like Freeport and South Portland. By the same token, we should not give up taxing real estate just because we lack power to tax *other* forms of wealth.

Continuing to tax real estate is also justified because the value of real property is largely created *by* the state. Land would be worth little without access to a public road or to a fire department. Think about owning real estate in a jurisdiction without police protection. How much would one pay to buy a dude ranch in Afghanistan outside of Kabul? Its price would have to be discounted by what it costs to hire a standing army to protect it. The presence of a well-ordered state adds value that far exceeds the direct cost of services provided.

A state can only tax what it controls. The people of this state have to tax *something* to support themselves; and what else is Maine known for if not for its highly desirable real estate? It has been our most important attribute since English fishermen opened a store at Damariscove in the summer of 1608. We don't have Alaska's oil, Connecticut's insurance companies, New York's stock exchanges, Wyoming's coal, or California's silicon capitalists; but we do have some of the finest real estate on earth, and lots of it. It is perhaps the biggest reason people move here.

Repairing the Property Tax

> "The smart dollar goes where it is treated best."
> —Anthony Neves, Head of the Maine Revenue Service

It is my long-standing, heretical thesis that *Maine's property taxes, in the aggregate, are not so much too high as they are dreadfully uneven in their burden.* The current average municipal tax rate of 18 mills is the same as it was thirty years ago, when the state first began systematically tracking all realty sales. From my review of town reports going back to the Civil War, I would say that property taxes were about the same 140 years ago in real dollars; but one would have to know more about early assessment practices to make that judgment reliably.

While it is true that revenue from the property tax has increased substantially in recent years, this is not because true value tax rates have changed. It is because property values themselves have risen so much faster than inflation. The total value of all taxable real estate in Maine rose from $7 billion in 1975 to $85 billion in 2001, a rate of growth that was more than three times inflation. York County alone grows every year by an amount that equals the total value of all of Piscataquis County real estate. Hyper-inflation in real estate has aggravated unevenness in the property tax from one town to another.

This unevenness can be relieved by improving three tools that are now in generally accepted use: general purpose aid under the school funding formula; circuit breaker homestead relief; and municipal revenue sharing. All three are feedback systems that use state revenue to relieve inequities; and all three can be made to work better.

To improve school funding, we need to implement a system that defines essential programs and services. This will empower local citizens to know for the first time from an objective source what it should reasonably cost to provide an adequate education for K-12 students and to achieve statewide educational standards known as the "Learning Results." This will provide a more suitable denominator for the school funding formula. While some municipal groups complain that the state has failed to pay its intended 55 percent of foundation costs, it is only fair for the state to require that those total costs be reasonably defined and measured under a uniform standard.

We also need to expand our so-called "circuit breaker" homestead relief program, by which the state refunds property taxes to people with limited capacity to pay. The state should provide better relief to people with middle incomes and burdensome tax bills: fishermen on Chebeague Island; retired people on lakefront property; and the aged, the disabled, and all others whose taxes are rising faster than their limited earnings. This program is by far the cheapest and fairest way to rectify property tax inequities. The money goes only to Maine residents; it goes to renters as well as homeowners; and the amount of relief is proportional to need.

Finally, our municipal revenue sharing system should be converted to what we call "revenue sharing II," which targets state money to service center towns where tax rates are highest, often five to ten mills above the state's eighteen mill average. The most appropriate source for such money is to cut distributions to those communities whose taxes are well below the state average, those fortunate towns and cities that simply do not have a property tax problem. There are many in this state.

With these three refinements, there is no legitimate reason to abandon or limit the property tax, which is a stable source of locally controlled revenue for towns and cities. Furthermore, 20 percent of our residential property taxes are paid by out-of-state owners, probably the highest ratio in the nation.

Much Greater Reserves

"I don't want the cheese. I just want out of the trap." —Spanish Proverb

Preserving the property tax as the base for our local revenue system is an important stabilizing measure; but the ultimate weapon against volatility is an adequate reserve. It is a myth that volatility can be cured through tax reform alone; spreading the base of the sales tax or reducing our dependence on capital gains may help, but only by a little. We might also consciously adopt more regressive taxes, for example by decreasing the income tax standard deduction or by extending the sales tax to more basic necessities, but these are unpopular proposals that would not solve the underlying problem. Volatility will persist because deep swings are fundamental to our new economy and support systems.

The best remedy is to plan for volatility through adequate reserves. States that succeed in managing volatility are happier places in which to live and enjoy more stable politics. Wyoming, the state with the smallest population, carries reserves of over $3 billion, largely derived from taxes on coal and mineral wealth. Alaska is comparably favored with reserves derived from oil. Maine, with a population that is twice as large as either of these wealthier states, entered the last recession with reserves of about $140 million, roughly 6 percent of one year's General Fund revenue. When the recession hit, the reserve was gone overnight.

It is commonly believed that politicians in a relatively poor state like Maine lack the willpower to set aside adequate reserves to weather recessions, but we have succeeded in doing so in other contexts. In the mid-'90s, our unemployment compensation fund had been in crisis for two decades. Reserves had fallen far below safety levels. Benefits were higher than we could afford. The supporting tax system was dysfunctional, and the burdens of the tax were unfairly distributed among employers.

Over several sessions of the legislature, a remarkably gifted bureaucrat in the Department of Labor, Gail Thayer, kept peppering the Labor Committee with suggestions for reform, together with graphs, printouts, and numerous financial projections. After working on the problem for two years, the Labor Committee finally adopted a plan that reformed the system from top to bottom. Organized labor agreed not to oppose the loss of certain benefits; the Chamber of Commerce agreed not to oppose a tax increase; and the burden of the tax was thoroughly redistributed among employers.

Within a short while, reserves rose from $80 million to over $400 million. With such reserves in place, taxes on employers have been reduced to historically low levels. Maine now has the benefit of a well-funded system to protect workers and buffer the state's economy against recession and layoff. This was one of the most remarkable and unheralded achievements of the administration of Governor Angus King, Jr.

The state has achieved a similar degree of resolve to protect pensions for state employees and teachers. In recent decades, the state has accumulated $5 billion in retirement reserves and the legislature continues to contribute $244 million annually, about 10 percent of the general fund budget, toward fully reserving the state's pension obligations. These payments are now being made under the compulsion of a constitutional amendment created by the legislature and endorsed by the public.

If we can create reserves of $400 million to protect the unemployed and $5 billion to protect retiree pensions, it makes no sense to say that the best we could do for the entire General Fund at the peak of the 1999 boom was to save $140 million in a rainy day account. Such a small amount might as well have been a Christmas club.

Curbing the Borrowing Binge

"Now a promise made is a debt unpaid, and the trail has its own stern code."
—Robert W. Service from "The Cremation of Sam McGee"

The legislature also avoids responsibility by borrowing money through bonds. State borrowing has become a perpetual gimmick to unburden legislators from having to raise money they do not have. Issuing bonds transfers the revenue decision onto the shoulders of other legislators, not yet elected. With the advent of term limits, legislators have the lifespan of a fruit fly; no wonder we like to borrow money to postpone the issue of raising taxes!

One can understand why Maine borrowed to support the Civil War and the First World War, to complete highway systems between 1910 and 1965, to build regional high schools under the Sinclair Act in the 1960s, and to construct sewer treatment plants in the 1970s; but why borrow now? We seem to do so as a convenient but sloppy habit carried over from earlier times.

In the spring of 2000, when Maine had surplus funds on hand at the height of the recent stock boom, we were unable to close the state budget without agreeing to borrow $33 million to build a state mental hospital in Augusta to replace one that had been in service for 150 years. The state had no sinking funds or capital reserves from which to contribute money to the cause. Yet when I attend town meeting in Cornville each March, the town report lists several reserve funds to which the town appropriates money each year, in anticipation of replacing equipment or refurbishing buildings that will require future capital. The state also has such reserve systems on paper but does not permit department heads to use them. When revenues drop off, the legislature drains all the money from such accounts, as it did during the recessions of 1991 and 2002.

The legislature has fallen into the habit of putting out a bond referendum each year to fund the entire capital program for highways and bridges. As these bonds have accumulated from prior legislatures, current lawmakers debate interminably over whether to raise the gas tax to pay for what our predecessors spent. In the meantime, we send out bonds of our own for future legislators to fund. If we want the public to validate our capital programs, then the legislature should put such issues on the ballot in a bill that includes the taxes that must be raised to pay for the proposed improvements.

Instead of passing the buck to our political successors, we should, by including the tax increase in the question itself, invite voters themselves to choose whether to pay more for gas or to drive on bad roads and spend their money instead on new tires and tie rods. There is no right or wrong answer to this perennial issue; it is an economic decision that the public should participate in making. Of course, sand and gravel lobbyists do not want the legislature to put these tough questions out to public vote for fear that projects will be rejected when voters must balance them directly against the tax revenue required.

It is good politics for leaders to include voters in decision making whenever feasible, and to frame rational choices for voters to make. The referendum process is as underused by the legislature as it is overused by special interest groups with an axe to grind.

Our Town, Regionalism, and Avuncular Federalism

"As Americans, we sometimes suffer from too much pluribus and not enough unum." —Arthur Schlesinger, Jr.

At present, there is widespread disaffection with our tax systems at all levels of government. Congress is responding by cutting taxes of all kinds, the good ones along with the bad, and these cuts are being made without any regard for their effect on the states whose own tax systems are keyed to the federal. Most states are finding it difficult to conform to the estate tax reductions, and few have conformed to the rapid depreciation provisions that the Congress passed retroactively in response to the tragedy of September 11, 2001.

The popularity of the estate tax repeal has been especially confusing to people like Warren Buffett and Bill Gates who, although highly affected by the tax, also believe that preserving the tax is sound policy. As James Carville, the "Raging Cajun," recently complained, "If we Democrats can't even tax a few dead Republicans, we may as well give up and call ourselves the 'Pro Choice Party,' 'cause dat's de only damn issue we got left." The estate tax is under attack because it was left unattended for so long by Congress. As the rate of tax remained high and exemption levels failed to increase with inflation, small business owners began to perceive the tax as confiscatory.

What is true of Congress's treatment of the states is also true of the state's treatment of municipalities. During the 1990s, the legislature was constantly reminded by the Maine Municipal Association (MMA) of the need for reforms in the complex revenue systems shared by state and local governments. Because those of us who espoused incremental reforms were not able to carry the day, the MMA by-passed the legislature in order to present property tax payers directly with a radical and inappropriate referendum proposal.

If we in the legislature contend that reform and consolidation at the municipal level is crucial to our future, we need to ask why there have been no new school districts created since 1969. If we complain that there are too many firehouses within five miles of Augusta, we need to ask what the state has done to encourage merger and inter-local participation. To avoid political cataclysms, we must create incentives for progress, even if only in small doses, and be ready to reward victory at each stage.

Taxes of any kind do not long survive except by consent of those who pay them. The American Revolution taught King George III that this is as true for monarchies as for democracies. I believe that William the Conqueror conducted his extensive Domesday inventory in 1086 precisely because it was such good politics for him to do so, even though his intrusions were resented. Listing all property in the kingdom was a way of assuring his subjects that they would be taxed evenly. As we know from recently published psychological experiments, a perception of fairness even among monkeys and little children is an instinctual motivator of paramount importance in gaining consent to desired behavior.

Voters are more sophisticated than they are given credit for. Collectively, they know whether they are receiving fair value for the money they invest in the machinery of government; but the choices presented to them are too often limited and inappropriate. Those whom they entrust as political leaders assume a very special burden. I believe that burden includes a duty not only to frame appropriate choices for public decision, but also to propose timely changes to our laws that are responsive to the constant fluidity of our social, economic, and political lives.

The Hon. Peter Mills is a graduate of Harvard College and the University of Maine Law School, and a veteran of the United States Navy. He has been a practicing attorney in Maine since 1973 and is past president of the Maine Trial Lawyers Association. He served as state senator from Somerset County from 1994 to 2002, when he was term-limited out of that seat; since then, he has served in the Maine House of Representatives. During this decade of service, Mills has chaired the legislature's Judiciary Committee and served on the Taxation, Appropriations, and Labor Committees, as well as on numerous task forces including those on Education Funding Reform and on Learning Results. He is known among his colleagues in Augusta as a singularly thoughtful, articulate, and tenacious advocate for educational excellence, fiscal responsibility, social justice, and common sense.

TWO
Toward Greater Community Vitality

MAINE'S STATE AND LOCAL GOVERNMENTS have long struggled with a values clash that may be described as "citizen participation vs. professionalism." As the executive and judicial branches have moved closer to professionalism, the legislature has been impeded in that journey by citizen attempts to retain control through the establishment of term limits and the increased use of citizen-initiated referenda. At the local level, similar battles are waged as municipalities struggle to balance the advantages of small size (participation) with the demands of modern governmental functions (professionalism). Maine's consensus-driven political culture and willingness to innovate will be key factors in determining the state's ability to successfully bridge the divide between the two competing values.

9 Governing Maine
Growing Tensions in the System

KENNETH PALMER

In his authoritative 1959 book, *New England State Politics*, political scientist Duane Lockard devoted a chapter to the government and politics of Maine. Lockard there made an observation that would be much repeated in and out of this state: "In few American states," he wrote, "are the reins of government more openly or completely in the hands of a few leaders of economic interest groups than in Maine."[1]

Looking at Maine politics some forty-five years later, we would, of course, need to alter that assertion. We might now want to say: In few American states over the past four decades have changes in government and politics been more significant—and more far-reaching—than those that have taken place in Maine. Indeed, a *transformation* has taken place since 1960 in government in Maine, and in the relation of government to the lives of our citizens.

This chapter discusses where Maine's state and local governments have come in the past four decades. We will look at changes in the structure and institutions of the states and localities. It is also important to stress political *values*. The contested issues that confront our state and local governments are, fundamentally, conflicts over political values. It is the tension among these values that shapes the continuing debates that rage over government form and governmental policy in Maine, as elsewhere.

Political Values and Policymaking
The values about government that people share grow from the political culture in which they live and endure.[2] Maine's political culture is deeply community-centered; it emphasizes the importance of ongoing participation of citizens in the affairs of their government. This participatory culture grew from the town meeting tradition shared by the other states of New England. Still, Maine is second to none in its embrace of citizen governance. Although modeled after the Massachusetts Constitution of 1780, Maine's fundamental charter of 1819 insisted on a wider suffrage for its citizens, without property qualifications. It also reduced property and religious requirements on persons who might hold the governorship.

Like Massachusetts, Maine created a state legislature and a state executive each with significant powers. This was rare at a time when the state executive office was nearly everywhere else institutionally weak. Still, the legislature had the primary place, consistent with sustaining the value of citizen participation.

The slender Maine executive department established in 1820 contained two administrative officials—the attorney general and the state treasurer—placed in office not by the governor, but by the members of the legislature.

The communitarian value of citizen involvement in Maine governmental affairs has, of course, persisted. For about a century and a half—until the 1960s which is our starting point—Maine's political culture sustained the idea that citizens not only influenced the decisions of government; they also, from their role as citizens, directed agencies of government. The lead symbol is, of course, the town meeting through which members of the town supervised the affairs of the community in a public gathering (historically several times, and then just once a year) aided by a board of town elders (selectmen or selectpersons) who implemented the general mandates to which the community had agreed. It is useful to observe that the town meeting format was carried over into institutions that had much more expansive responsibilities.

Maine's legislature, executive branch, and courts all reflected, despite their differing responsibilities, a value prevalent in nineteenth century America—that of responsiveness or representativeness. It meant that citizen preferences should always be as fully reflected in governmental institutions as possible. One device was the frequent election of public officials. Governors served initially for one year, then for two years. Legislators had a one-year term until 1880; afterward they could remain in office for two years. In its frequent elections for state offices Maine resembled other states.

In its institutional arrangements, however, Maine went beyond the idea of simply representing people. Maine's executive and judicial branches were, in some respects, as much citizen bodies as the state legislature itself. Department heads in state executive agencies were often chosen by boards of citizens; examples were the state education board and the state welfare board. The governor was obliged to work with the officials those bodies selected. In its courts, Maine depended on private citizens to operate many of its trial courts of limited jurisdiction, through the so-called justice of the peace who at times had no legal training.

The Professionalization of Maine Government
These historic arrangements began to shift—and to do so rapidly—about 1960, when all three branches of Maine's government began to undergo a transformation. They moved from the mostly citizen-run bodies, which they had been since 1820, to governmental agencies staffed by persons specifically qualified by skills, education, and experience to perform their assigned functions. In its early stages, the process was generally accepted. The value of professional competence, of assigning persons to governmental positions who could technically fulfill them, did not really conflict with the value of citizen involvement. How-

ever, when the most citizen-related branch, the legislature, began to alter its habits and working style, controversy erupted. A battle between Maine voters and the legislature took place. We look at the institutional changes in the general order in which they occurred.

The Maine Courts

The judicial branch has moved from a fragmented, loosely organized group of courts to a system that is recognized nationally as one of the best coordinated judicial systems in the nation.[3] The first major change occurred in 1961 with the creation of the District Court, to replace an arrangement of about seventy-five municipal and trial justice courts, each with its own authorizing statute. The local magistrates, of course, had knowledge of local conditions. Their verdicts, however, and especially their traffic fines, varied hugely from court to court. Reformers stressed the need for greater uniformity. The new District Court was composed of twenty-five judges, organized into thirteen districts, who held court at thirty-three locations. Maine, for the first time, had professional judges who were serving full-time in all its courts.

Consolidation of the courts continued in other ways. In 1976, the state assumed responsibility for funding of the Superior Court. It had been supported by the individual counties. Court reporters and other personnel were now state employees. To manage the system, the legislature in 1975 created an administrative office of the courts. The office was headed by a director who served under the authority of the chief justice of the Maine Supreme Judicial Court. A chief judge was appointed for the District Court and four regional presiding justices were named in the Superior Court to coordinate the handling of caseloads.

Another interesting change was the end of trial work on the part of justices of the Supreme Judicial Court. Since 1820, members of the top court had been largely, and in some years in the nineteenth century, exclusively responsible for conducting jury trials across the state. As late as the 1920s, Supreme Judicial Court justices handled trials in all but the four counties (Cumberland, Kennebec, Penobscot, and Androscoggin) that had separate justices. After the Superior Court was created in 1929, which provided a trial justice for every county, those responsibilities lessened for the Supreme Court. Nonetheless, until the 1970s, trial activities (sometimes called "single justice work") amounted to about half the working time of the justices. It persisted in Maine longer than in most states, and allowed the justices to maintain unusually close contact with both the public and members of the bar.

Maine's trial courts thus moved to state, not local, control. No longer would a non-lawyer citizen judge hold court in a town, nor would a private attorney individually set the hearing of a civil case in his or her county. The loss of local influence was, one hoped, balanced by greater uniformity of justice across the

City Hall, Hallowell

state. Citizens would, of course, still influence their courts and the way the courts operated. However, they had to do so through influencing the content of the legislative statutes that regulated the courts. The judiciary had become, in the 1960s and 1970s, an integrated, professional state institution.

A different kind of judicial development has been the closer relationship between the Maine Supreme Judicial Court and the U.S. Supreme Court. For many decades, the nation's high Court did not review in full opinion any Maine case. Since 1980, on the other hand, the Court has examined eight cases appealed from Maine's Supreme Judicial Court. Three of them involved provisions in the Bill of Rights in the U.S. Constitution, while the other five tested the constitutionality of federal statutes. Among the more important cases were *Fort Halifax Packing Co. v. Coyne* (1987), which concerned the federal Employees Retirement Income Security Act (ERISA) of 1974; and *Alden v. Maine* (1999), which questioned whether the 11th Amendment to the Constitution barred state employees from using a state court to sue the state government over the application of a federal wage law.[4] Both the *Halifax* and *Alden* cases were very controversial. The U.S. Supreme Court ultimately affirmed the Maine Supreme Judicial Court's settlement in each by a vote of five to four.

Maine's top court may be evolving into a leader among state courts, as a forum for addressing national issues. None of the eight cases that moved to the U.S. Supreme Court reflected situations special to Maine's environment or its political processes; nor did they involve a problem of resistance to federal standards. Instead, they addressed the application of federal law and of the federal Constitution, and could have come from any state. Most of the cases were accompanied by a large number of briefs of amicus curiae, filed by national interest groups, for the U.S. Supreme Court's consideration. As for the outcomes of the cases, the Supreme Court affirmed four of the Maine Court's holdings, and reversed four others—a higher than average "win" ratio, since among the states generally, the Supreme Court has reversed in recent decades about two-thirds of the cases it hears on appeal from state supreme courts.

The Maine Executive

The executive department of Maine government has undergone a transformation similar to that of the judiciary.[5] It has moved from the fragmentation of activities to the coordination of functions under the governor. At the beginning, the few executive offices that existed were filled by constitutional requirement through legislative election. When other executive agencies became necessary, a common practice was to create a citizen commission or board to oversee them.

An example was the State Highway Commission, established in 1915 as the state began to develop a system of paved roads for the automobile. By law, the oversight commission had three members, no more than two of whom by law could be members of the same political party. The commission chairman served a term of seven years, five years longer than the term of the governor. The effect was to make the supervision of the highway system—one of the most important responsibilities in state government—almost entirely independent of the governor's control

After Edmund S. Muskie became governor in 1955, he requested a review of the scattered state executive branch agencies by the Public Administration Service (PAS) of Chicago. The PAS reported that Maine had twenty-nine major operating departments supervised by sixty-two officials, all but four of whom (mostly constitutional officers elected by the legislature) had terms of office—from three to nine years—exceeding that of the governor, who had a two-year term. Nine departments, like the State Highway Commission, were supervised by boards, some of whose members were selected by interest groups directly associated with the work of the department. The remaining twenty departments had single heads, but the governor's control of them was limited by a unique agency, the Executive Council.

The Executive Council was a group of seven officials chosen by the legislature (and who were themselves normally former legislators) to work with the governor in personnel and budget matters. It was sometimes called the "the hidden executive." The Executive Council had the right to "advise and consent" over each gubernatorial appointment. Further, it had powers over changes in the state budget when the legislature was not in session. During the Muskie years—and later under Governor Kenneth Curtis—the Executive Council was always Republican, and nearly always a source of gubernatorial obstruction.

In response to the PAS report, Governor Muskie pushed for reforms, and elements within the Republican party and the existing bureaucracy prevented major change. Still, the executive branch began to modernize. The state approved a constitutional amendment extending the governor's term from two years to four years. The first governor under the new provision was John Reed, elected in 1962 to a four-year term. Additionally, election day was moved from September to November, bringing Maine state elections into line with the rest of the country.

The reforms envisioned in the Muskie years finally took hold in the second term of Gov. Kenneth Curtis. In 1971 the legislature passed a re-organization measure creating twenty administrative departments, each headed by a commissioner nominated by the governor and who served at the governor's pleasure. Shortly after, in 1975, the Executive Council was abolished by constitutional amendment. The change was a product of a legislative compromise in which Republicans endorsed the abolition of the council in return for Democratic support of single-member legislative districts in Maine's cities, which at that time had multi-member districts and whose delegations were usually all-Democratic. The shift allowed Republicans to compete for some city seats.

With the Executive Council gone, Maine for the first time had a true cabinet arrangement in its executive branch. Effective coordination of state executive departments had been a theme nationally for much of the twentieth century, beginning in such states as New York and Illinois in the 1920s. The idea took hold slowly in smaller states, especially those having modest public expenditures where the need for coordination was, accordingly, less pressing. It was probably symbolic that Maine chose the first years of the 1970s to establish the pyramidal form of state administration, with the governor in charge in fact as well as in theory, for that was a period in which important changes in public policy were taking place, as well.

The general direction of Maine was, in the 1970s and afterwards, one of a rather rapid expansion of state public services. Fueling the rise of a service-oriented state government was the enactment of the state income tax in 1969, with bi-partisan support from Democratic Governor Ken Curtis and the Republican legislature. Re-election of Governor Curtis in 1970 and the survival of the tax against a challenge in a statewide referendum in 1971 confirmed the new direction of state government. Among the many new programs was a spate of environmental measures that placed the state at the forefront of the national environmental movement. In education, Maine increased the share of state support for schools, and enacted legislation to create greater statewide equity in support of public schools.

The expansion of state activities could be measured in budget increases. Total general expenditures increased from slightly less than $145 million in 1960 to $373 million in 1970. In 1980, expenditures were $1.326 billion; and by 1990 they had grown to $2.743 billion. Put another way, state government spending was increasing by two to three times each decade. During part of the 1980s, in fact, Maine expenditures rose at a pace nearly twice the national average for states.

The growing prominence of state government altered the citizens' perception of the state's power structure. The interest groups that had once been dominant in Augusta receded in the public's view. Asked in a survey in the 1970s by the *Maine Times* the question: "Who Runs Maine?" the answers centered on the heads of companies such as the Central Maine Power and the Central Maine Railroad. When people were approached with a similar question some fifteen years later, the *Maine Times* found the answers more diffuse, with no one group predominant. As the paper commented, "Maine has progressed from an individualistic to an institutional power structure." Among the institutions particularly cited was the state bureaucracy, which was now seen to be pervasive in all areas of public policy.[6]

The Maine Legislature

The third area of change involves the state legislature itself. Here, the participatory value was historically most entrenched. It was here that the clash between the values of participation and professionalism would grow most acute. We prided ourselves on having a citizen legislature, one that convened for relatively brief sessions to conduct the people's business, had small districts to maintain close ties to constituents, and had high turnover to ensure that policies discussed in Augusta were always aligned to local thinking.

The modifications in the legislature since 1960 have been both more profound and much more controversial than alterations in the courts and the executive. Like the other branches—and like assemblies in other states—our state legislature steadily became more institutionalized. Professional experience and technical skills were stressed. What made that process different was that the key value of citizen participation appeared to get lost. The upshot was a serious political clash—in the early 1990s—over governmental structure. The division was one of the most dramatic Maine has ever experienced, leading to the imposition of term limits on state legislators.[7] So, let us examine the background of that struggle.

Changes in the legislature began rather quickly in the 1960s. First of all, Democrats became a competitive party. They challenged the solid Republican control of both chambers that had persisted for many decades. In 1975, Democrats gained a majority of seats in the House (a margin which they have never relinquished). In 1983 they secured a majority in the state senate.

Additionally, legislators began serving for several terms. The investment of time and money required for political campaigns encouraged members to seek re-election. Their rate of success was high. In the 1970s, turnover in each legislative session dropped from 50 percent to about 25 percent. A corps of career legislators began to appear, especially in the House. The best known was John Martin, representing Eagle Lake. Martin became floor leader of his party in 1973, and speaker of the house when the Democrats won control of the house in 1975. He transformed an office that had customarily turned over every legislative session into the second most powerful position in state government, and elevated the authority of the entire legislature in the process.

At the same time, the greater complexity of lawmaking fostered legislative bureaucratization. The legislature had traditionally relied on groups of legislators, brought together in a Research Committee, to study complex issues between sessions. Other information was drawn as needed during legislative sessions from citizens testifying in hearings before the standing committees and from lobbyists representing interest groups affected by specific bills.

In 1973 policy specialists were, for the first time, made a formal part of the legislative operation. The legislature established the Office of Policy and Legal

Analysis, employing about a dozen professionals to advise its joint standing committees. Soon after, an Office of Fiscal Analysis was established to provide assistance to the appropriations and taxation committees. By the end of that decade, the legislature had enacted a sunset law, under which executive departments underwent formal, periodic oversight by the legislature's Office of Program and Policy Review.

The legislature was changing in other ways, as well. Second legislative sessions—in even numbered years—became the norm in the early 1980s, effectively moving the legislature from biennial sessions to annual sessions. Although officially limited to "emergency" measures, the new second session handled many policy questions carried over from the first session. Further, the standing committees—with more experienced members and the aid of staff—started to occupy a more decisive role in the process. Particularly in complex policy areas, committees began to supplant the party caucuses in framing legislation.

Another innovation was the influence of the Legislative Council, composed of the presiding officers and floor leaders of each party, in each chamber. The council established procedures for the chambers, such as the session date beyond which no bills might be introduced. It also named the legislature's executive director, an official who by the late 1980s was overseeing more than 100 professional and support staff persons.

Despite—or perhaps because of—all these new arrangements, the legislature appeared to be losing its critical link to the voters. Maine still had a turnover higher than many states, and lower compensation for legislators. Nonetheless, an impression grew in the state that the legislature was no longer a "citizen" assembly. Warning signs began to appear in the late 1980s. Evidence could be found in growing media attention to high legislative costs. A more ominous indicator was the frequent use Maine voters were making of the initiative and referendum devices to make law. Between 1909—when the procedure for popular lawmaking was added to the state constitution—and 1969, the state held only six referenda.

In contrast, between 1970 and 1991, the state held a total of 22 referenda. Voters established such policies as a flat-rate telephone service for local calls (1986), indexing the state's income tax to allow the schedules to shift according to rate of inflation (1982), creating a public preserve in the Bigelow Mountain area (1977), and permitting large stores to sell merchandise on Sundays (1990). Voters also occasionally rejected an existing policy. In 1991, for instance, they overturned the legislature's authorization of the Maine Turnpike Authority to widen the turnpike, in a referendum pressed by the Natural Resources Council of Maine. Popular lawmaking—bypassing the legislature—was on the rise in Maine.

Beginning in the early 1980s bills were introduced in the legislature to impose term limits on members. The measures at first found little support beyond a handful of conservative Republicans who regarded term limits as a way of curtailing the authority of Speaker John Martin. However, after the national term limits movement began about 1990, interest in the idea broadened. Then two headline events—the budget crisis in state government in 1991 which shut down state government for three weeks and a scandal in the speaker's office in 1992 which led to a jail term for a top aide of Speaker Martin—dramatically put the idea of term limits into play in Maine politics.

A gulf had emerged between voters and their legislature, which seemed no longer to operate in the fashion of the citizen assembly they had long come to expect. Soon supporters of term limits had collected far more than enough signatures to put the issue to a referendum. After the legislature refused to impose term limits on itself in early 1993, Maine voters endorsed the idea in November of that year by a margin of nearly two to one. The initiative carried in every county and in nearly every town and city. Maine became the only northeastern state to adopt term limits. Beginning in 1996, legislators were limited to four terms (or eight years) of continuous service in the same legislative chamber.

Term limits suggests that the competing values followed in organizing governmental bodies can and do clash. It may be said that Maine voters sought through term limits to restore the value of citizen participation. They tried to reign in the value of professionalism that was threatening to separate the legislature from its constituent base.

Initial research on term limits shows that this goal was achieved, but at a cost.[7] Turnover among legislators has increased, but the legislature as a whole appears to have lost ground in relation to the governor and the executive departments. One reason is the standing committees no longer have the power and expertise they once did to challenge administrative officials in formulating legislation and dealing with budget requests.

Currently, the tension between the two values may become even more prominent at the local and regional levels.

The Growth of Local Government

Measured purely in numbers of units, Maine's local governments have changed little since 1960. We have the same number of counties (16) and almost the same number of towns and cities (492) as we did forty years ago. In contrast, we have fewer school districts, thanks in large part to the Sinclair Act of 1957, which consolidated very small districts—the little red schoolhouses—into larger school administrative districts and, in turn, increased the state's financial aid to schools. School districts diminished from over 400 in the 1950s to the current total of 286. We have, however, seen an increase in other types of special districts, such as water and sewer districts, and we have added regional planning districts to our governmental mix.

Overall, then, Maine continues *rich* in local governments. We are a long way from having the largest number of localities among the states (Illinois has that distinction with nearly 7,000 units). Still, our 827 units are a substantial number. It puts us second among the New England states, which share in the tradition of small towns. There are currently almost 88,000 local units of government in the 50 states. Maine has nearly 1 percent of them. Since our population represents about one-half of 1 percent of the nation, we have about *double* the number of local government entities, measured on a population basis, that is the norm among the states.

An important trend since 1960 is that localities have developed a greater degree of *structural integrity*.[8] They have been given more discretion under state law to frame their own particular arrangements. The key development in this regard occurred in 1969, when the state added a home rule amendment to the constitution. Until then, most communities had only those powers expressly provided them in state law, leaving it to the state legislature to spend time each session dealing with the intricacies of a municipality's government.

The home rule provision stipulates that "the inhabitants of any municipality shall have the power to alter and amend their charters on all matters not prohibited by Constitution or general law, which are local and municipal in character." For some years, Maine courts were inclined to give a narrow reading to those powers. In 1987, however, the legislature revised its enabling act, specifying that "it should be liberally construed to effect its purposes," and the Maine Supreme Judicial Court seems to have followed that direction. In 1993 it held that "municipal legislation will be voided only where (the) legislation would frustrate the purpose of state law."

Currently, about seventy-five towns and cities have charters.[9] The advantage of a charter is that a community may design its own political arrangements subject only to the limitation that it not violate state law. Among other advantages, the charter form has been valuable to communities desiring to adopt a town or city manager form of local government, while preferring to craft a structure that differs from the Enabling Law the state passed in 1939.

Maine has continued in the past four decades to be a leader among states in the use of the town and city manager form of local governmental administration. Currently nearly half of all our towns have managers. Of course, we have attained that number by adapting a form designed and intended for *larger* communities—typically, those of 10,000 or more population, which have managers working with city councils—to suit the purposes of our many, smaller jurisdictions. Town managers serve in Maine with town meetings and boards of selectpersons, as often as they do with elected councils.

Counties have also become somewhat more independent of state government.[10] In the 1970s, the state took over responsibility for the superior court. In the early 1980s, counties gained the authority to formulate and implement their own budgets, a responsibility that had earlier been lodged in the hands of the county legislative delegations.

In the past two decades, counties have been authorized to develop charters and engage county managers. This new authority has not been extensively used and, in some respects, is more circumscribed than the powers granted to municipalities. Only two counties currently employ managers. Further, while counties may adopt charters, unlike municipalities they may not include any power that the legislature has not already granted to them. The legislature has not given the counties the authority to tax citizens, and counties cannot write charters to permit them to do so.

Maine's counties remain among the weakest in the nation, and stand in contrast to counties nationally, which have grown in importance since the 1960s, especially in more urban states. In fact, during the period from the 1950s to the 1970s, bills to abolish Maine's county governments were debated in most legislative sessions. The structural reforms of the 1980s indicated that counties are probably here to stay; but efforts to build them into more significant delivery centers of public services have failed.

Counties continue to have a multiplicity of elected positions that include, in addition to the three county commissioners, the treasurer, sheriff, judge of probate, register of probate, and register of deeds. A long tradition of patronage and partisan politics has surrounded those offices in some counties, which helps account for the reluctance of town and city managers to envision counties as effective service centers following the tenets of management in which they are trained. Here, the value of citizen participation imbedded in county government seems to run against the value of professionalism implicit in the manager form of local government.

Like the three branches of the state government, Maine municipalities have expanded their staffs and developed cohorts of professionally trained persons in policy areas mostly unknown forty years ago, such as environmental protection and technology. Not all their growth, of course, has come from local initiation. State government plays a major role in the governmental arrangements of every municipality. For instance, the responsibilities of positions such as town clerk, tax collector, treasurer, assessor, code enforcement officer, and many others are heavily described by state statute.

Over the period we are examining, Maine's municipalities have grown considerably faster than has state government. This is revealed by a look at the employment levels of the state and localities through two snapshots in time: the year 1960 and the year 2001.[11]

Table 1. State and Local Governmental Employment in the United States and in Maine* (Selected Years)

| | Full-Time Equivalents (FTEs) | | | | FTEs Per 10,000 population | | | |
| | United States | | Maine | | United States | | Maine | |
Year	State	Local	State	Local	State	Local	State	Local
1960	1,410,000	5,159,000	10,428	18,243	79	232	108	188
1970	2,301,963	6,226,271	15,608	25,280	113	306	157	255
1980	3,106,291	7,940,618	18,131	33,361	137	351	161	297
1990	3,840,497	9,239,166	22,012	42,337	154	371	179	345
2001	4,173,400	11,205,524	21,544	53,117	147	393	167	413

Source: *The Book of the States*, selected years.

In 1960, Maine had more full-time state employees per 10,000 population than the national average; we had 108 compared to the 50-state figure of 79. That put us ahead of the national average; but given the nature of the governmental employment statistic we use, a high ranking is fairly typical for large, rural states. The maintenance of a state highway system requires, for example, a certain number of workers-per-mile, regardless of population. Thus, in a sparsely populated state, there is often a high proportion of state employees per 10,000 population—located in various categories of public policy—even if the quality of the services provided is not exceptional.

Looking at 2001, we had risen to 167 state employees, certainly a significant increase but set against a national context, not a particularly large one. Other states had grown at a faster rate, nearly doubling their state workforces by that time; the national average grew from 79 to 147 full-time employees. Maine state government remained ahead, but not as far above the national average as we had been forty-one years earlier. In the light of the great policy initiatives Maine witnessed at the state level during that period, the growth in our state workforce was quite moderate.

The local level tells a different story. In 1960, we had about 20 percent *fewer* full-time local government employees per 10,000 population than other states. In Maine we had 188 employees; the national figure for states was 232 employees. That pattern was consistent with the historic emphasis on citizen governance described earlier. Maine had lots of local government structure, to be sure, but parts of it were in the hands of citizens volunteering their time, and employees serving on a part-time basis.

By 2001, on the other hand, our number of local government personnel had grown to 413 full-time employees per 10,000 population. In the forty-one-year period, Maine's number of local government employees (persons employed on a full-time basis) had considerably *more than doubled*. The 2001 figure now exceeds the average for all states (393 employees at the local level). The rate of growth in Maine showed an increase in municipal employment in the 1990s alone of nearly 20 percent, compared to a little more than 6 percent in the states generally.

An important cause of the growth in Maine's local-government employment is the *spreading of its population*. The state's overall population has risen only modestly since 1960 (in the 1990s it grew by just 4 percent). What has been striking, on the other hand, is the rapid growth of small communities in rural areas. Between 1960 and 1990, the highest rates of growth were in communities approximately 30-35 miles from major towns and cities, some of which witnessed a doubling or tripling in their populations.[12]

Meanwhile, the larger communities remained static or declined in population. The portion that Maine's three largest cities (Portland, Lewiston, Bangor) comprised of the state's population declined from 12 percent in 1980 to 10 percent in 2000. The cost of providing the rapidly growing communities with schools and roads, and with sufficient personnel to mange them, has been high. For instance, Maine state government alone spent approximately $338 million on new school construction in 1975-1995, predominantly in fast-growing towns, even though the state's overall elementary and secondary public school population dropped by 27,000 between 1970 and 1995

The dispersal of population has some political advantages. One is that it tends to reduce differences between geographic sections and between small towns and larger cities. Maine politics reflects little of the sharp rural-urban division that has afflicted some states. Likewise, suburban/central city tensions—where they exist—are more muted than in many other states. Accordingly, legislators throughout the state deal with somewhat similar municipal problems, probably reinforcing the state's moderate, centrist political culture. Yet the costs involved in providing a full array of municipal services across many small jurisdictions are beginning to escalate dramatically, as have the workforces required to administer them

Finding ways to finance and contain the costs of local governments will be a critical issue in this decade. In 2003, the Maine Municipal Association (MMA) and Governor John Baldacci's administration both presented measures at a November referendum proposing to increase state support of local schools, but to do so in different ways and under different timetables. Taxpayer revolts have taken place in some towns; and a citizens' initiative to place a cap on municipal tax increases will be on the statewide ballot in 2004.

Regionalization has been proposed as a solution to cope with the expanding local sector. Towns and cities, it is argued, can and should find ways to share facilities and consolidate the way they deliver services. Considerable cooperation already exists among localities in some areas. Most communities are involved in mutual-aid agreements, especially for fire protection services. Many communities participate in collaborations involving specific officials, such as code-enforcement officers, building inspectors and animal control officers. Joint purchasing alliances among towns are also common.[13]

The dilemma is how best to promote municipal cooperation. Should it continue to grow on a town-by-town basis, in selected functional areas; or should state officials try to mandate a more formal, statewide arrangement in return for increased state financial aid? The latter method was used in the 1950s to consolidate schools into School Administrative Districts. The Baldacci administration in the first session of the 121st Legislature (2003) proposed a somewhat similar concept, styled municipal service districts, which would have had fairly extensive authority. Communities located in them would receive added funds but would relinquish some of their home rule powers. Facing strong opposition from the MMA, the legislature did not endorse the idea in that session.

The Receding Federal Partner

The issues of state and local government cannot be fully understood without reference to the role of the broader federal system. Since 1960 the federal government has, on the whole, been more of a provider of funds for, than a taker of funds from, the state of Maine. In recent years, for every dollar sent to Washington, about $1.30.is returned to Maine. That favorable balance is due to, among other factors, our ranking as one of the lower per capita income states, and to the aggressive pursuit of federal grants in the past forty years by some state administrations. In more recent times, however, the relationship between the states and the federal government has shifted dramatically.

A major change began to take place about 1980, about in the middle of the period under discussion, when the Reagan administration took office. At that time, the target of federal grants-in-aid policy moved from places—that is, from governmental jurisdictions—to people. The "place" emphasis on federal assistance occurred especially during the Nixon and Ford administrations, illustrated by such programs as federal revenue sharing and community development block grants. States and cities received considerable federal dollars over which they had wide spending discretion.

During the life of the revenue sharing program (1972–86), for instance, Maine communities obtained a federal grant equivalent to 8-10 percent of their annual budgets. After 1980, those programs were cut back. Federal dollars went, instead, primarily to groups and classes of individuals who were defined by federal statute as eligible for various types of assistance. The largest of these programs presently is Medicaid, which currently accounts for 25 percent of all federal aid, and which has become the second largest item in state budgets after public education.

The reason for the shift away from aiding places to assisting people is related to federal deficits. When deficits grew in the 1980s, Congress understandably determined that supporting groups of people nationally through redistribution policies was more important than using federal aid to further the economic development efforts of subnational governments. That shrinkage of support has been variously described as "fend for yourself federalism" and "fiscal federalism fizzling."[14] It means that states and their localities are today more on their own financially than they have been in a generation.

It is interesting to note that the current controversy surrounding public school funding in Maine—specifically, about what share of the cost the state should bear—was a major issue some thirty years ago. The previous struggle, however, was fought out against the backdrop of a very different federal system. Then, the federal revenue sharing program, enacted by Congress in 1972, had just gotten underway. In addition to the funds made available to towns and cities, the state government received some $30 million, an amount it turned almost entirely into a new school finance program aimed at equalizing financial resources for school districts throughout the state. That federal partnership ended in the 1980s, with little likelihood of its return.

For the past twenty years, and especially during the administration of President George W. Bush, *regulatory federalism* has taken hold. The national government tries to achieve many domestic policy goals by setting requirements (mandates) on state and localities, often unfunded. The stick, not the carrot, marks intergovernmental relations. So today we are trying to figure out the appropriate financial balance between state and local governments, with the federal government playing a far more limited role.

The changes in the way funds are directed from Washington have highlighted the state's current role as the senior partner in state-local fiscal relations. In 1961 Maine state and local governments each collected, from their own sources, very comparable amounts of revenue—a little over $100 million each. That was, of course, before the state income tax had arrived. In 2001, in a different environment, the state collected almost twice as much revenue from its own sources as localities did from theirs. In 2001, the state also provided a larger portion of its funds to localities to carry out their programs and services.

Conclusions and Observations

Since 1960 Maine state government has changed in ways that could hardly have been imagined at the time. The clash between the values of participation and professionalism have shaped and informed much of that transformation. The three branches are no longer citizen-operated in the way they were at the beginning of the period. The transition of the courts and executive branch into professionally managed structures took place fairly smoothly, while the legislature traveled a more difficult road. Its shift from a purely "citizen-assembly" to one with substantial bureaucratization led to a dramatic rebuff by the voters in 1993, in the form of term limits. In every session since the term limits law took effect (1996), the legislature has confronted burdens owing to the inability of legislators to serve more than four terms in the same chamber. Still, the growth of Maine's state government into a major provider of public services has proceeded successfully, and with only modest conflict.

The question in the present decade is whether a similar story will be told of local governments, as they seek to balance the advantage of small size (participation) with the necessities of modern governmental administration (professionalism). This problem may be inherently more difficult to resolve because of their very numbers: nearly 500 separate municipal jurisdictions. Since 1960 local governments have grown more institutionally and legally separate from the state, especially from the state legislature that, until the home rule amendment in 1969, monitored their day-to-day activities closely. Yet, from a budgetary and financial perspective, they are currently more intertwined with Augusta than ever.

Looking toward the year 2010, the struggle over governing arrangements may well center on state-local relations. That clash will be reflected in debates over the appropriate roles of the state and towns in funding and delivering services in various policy arenas. It will concern decisions over local consolidation and cooperation—that is, how much direction should come from the state and how much the sharing of services should be instigated by individual communities. It will affect the way in which the private and public sectors interact. Ultimately, it will be central to any discussion as to how much government Mainers want, and can afford.

The critical political questions are twofold: *How can we deal creatively with those tensions?* and, *How may we sustain the values of both participation and professionalism in our public life, without inflicting on ourselves damaging, long-term divisions?*

As the debate continues, two features of Maine's governing style should be kept in mind. One is that our state has a basically moderate political culture, one that looks toward *consensus* on most major issues. We tend to eschew extremes in politics and in ideology. The transformation of our state institutions in the past forty years is, I think, revealing of that. Consensus doesn't always prevail: the battle over legislative term limits in 1993 indicated that a serious divide had opened between our citizens and the legislative institution; but it does seem generally to be attainable.

The other quality of Maine governance is our long-standing, pragmatic willingness to *experiment and innovate*, to look for methods and solutions that work and are specific to this state. We see that throughout our state and local government—from legislatively elected executive officers in Augusta, to the hybrid nature of local government management in many smaller communities, where a professional manager works with a town meeting.

These well-established habits of moderation, pragmatism, and innovation bode well for us as we look ahead to the end of this decade of change.

*P*rof. *Kenneth T. Palmer has taught political science at the University of Maine since 1969. He holds a B.A. from Amherst College (1959) and a Ph.D. from Penn State University (1964). He has co-authored several works on Maine government, including* The Legislative Process in Maine *(1973) and* Maine Politics and Government *(1992). His articles have appeared in the* Maine Bar Journal, Maine History, *and* Maine Policy Review. *He has also served as a consultant to the Brookings Institution in Washington, D.C. on the implementation of federal intergovernmental programs, such as the Community Development Block Grant program, in Maine towns and cities. He and two colleagues have recently completed* Changing Members: The Maine Legislature in an Era of Term Limits, *to be published in 2004.*

MAINE HAS A RICH TRADITION of civic organizations at the heart of our community life, where community members have gathered regularly and built a store of "social capital" that may be drawn down to address community needs. Recent development trends across the nation have also affected Maine, contributing to a shift away from this kind of citizen-driven organization to professional third-parties, private and public. Sprawl has isolated people from their neighbors, and two-income families and longer commuting times have discouraged participation in civic organizations of all kinds, including local government. The "two Maines "hypothesis serves further to widen the gap between Maine citizens in addressing statewide issues that require cooperation and sharing of responsibilities. If Maine is to successfully leverage social capital to strengthen communities as in the past, civic duty must be redefined for these times and emphasized in schools and today's community organizations.

10 Maine's Civil Society
An Enduring Strength

MARK LAPPING

The Talmud records this story. A Gentile once appeared before a great rabbi, and said, "I want to be converted to Judaism; but only on the condition that you will teach me all of the Torah while I stand on one foot." The rabbi sent him away. The Gentile went then to another learned rabbi, Hillel, who agreed to the man's request and said to him: "That which is hateful unto thee, do not do unto another. That is the whole Torah; the rest is commentary. Go and study."[1]

Would that it were this straightforward and possible for us to live by the "Golden Rule," for this is the essence of a truly civil and decent society. Alas, this appears not to be the case; and this chapter on Maine's "civil society" is the story of how we do and can live, in a place where our failings at times overwhelm our virtues both as individuals and as a community.

In this chapter, we examine the concept of a "civil society" and its contribution to our well-being; its relationship to what has come to be called "social capital;" some examples of civil society in Maine life; the relationships between civil society and "sprawl," and the stresses of local governance today; some lessons from another country's experience; and, finally, the ongoing education of a civil society.

What Is Civil Society?

To define what we mean by "civil society" in Maine, I turn first to the work of Cynthia Duncan, currently on leave from the University of New Hampshire and directing the Ford Foundation's rural poverty programs. In her most recent book, *Worlds Apart: Why Poverty Persists in Rural America*, Duncan contrasts forms of poverty across the nation through indepth interviews, profiles, and community case studies.

In comparing a Mississippi Delta town and an Appalachian community with the a declining mill town in Maine (one she calls Gray Mountain), Duncan argues that, "the main difference is that when people who are poor in Gray Mountain want to do better, they can find ladders. There are more resources to go around, both because there are fewer poor and because there are more Joanne Martins, Coach Wilsons, and Cassidy Morses," local people who often lend the necessary "helping hand" in times of difficulty. "The problems are less severe, the resources to deal with them greater, and the whole community works differently—partly as a result of the ratio of needs to resources, and partly because long-standing habits of participation, inclusion, and investment have been nourished over the years."[2]

This is as good a description of community civil society as any: high levels of voluntary participation, inclusion of the entire community, and mutual investment and support for one another. How did the Martins, the Wilsons, the Morses, and these "long-standing habits" come about over the years? The answer for Duncan and an ever-growing number of analysts is to be found in a rich civil society suffused with "social capital," numerous networks for the sharing of information and effort, and an authentic commitment to both place and community.

Parenthetically, one might ask whether what Duncan found continues in Maine's mill towns, where the middle management of multinational corporations—which seems to "come and go," and appears to develop fewer ties to the local community—has replaced generations of local ownership. Lloyd Irland speaks movingly to this question in his chapter on the vicissitudes of Maine's forest products industry.

The political philosopher Michael Walzer observes that civil society comprises "uncoerced human association," undertaken for the sake of family, faith, community, interest, and ideology. It is the realm of activity between the marketplace and the state, inhabited by all who engage in voluntary associations that advance the common agenda or public good. It is the place where we actively seek to bring about a balance between the private and the public, between the rights which a free people enjoy and the responsibilities they must execute to maintain these rights.[3] This focus on "uncoerced human association" has become central to almost all contemporary discussions on the nature of civil society.

In her contribution to this book, Dahlia Lynn writes at length about the voluntary sector and how its emergence has changed American life, overwhelmingly for the better. Our traditions of voluntary association run deep in this country and, especially, in New England. Its existence was one of the social characteristics that Alexis de Tocqueville, perhaps the keenest observer of American mores, came to see as fundamental to our democratic life. In his *Democracy in America*, published in two volumes in the 1830s and '40s, de Tocqueville observed that when the English have a problem, they invariably turn toward the crown; and when the French have a problem, they turn toward the state. When Americans have a problem, in contrast, they turn toward one another. De Tocqueville found this "turn toward one another" an essential ingredient of civil society. It was the essence of town life and government in New England, which he touted as the very epitome of American democracy. Again, it is the uncoerced cooperation of American associational life that is the focal point of civil society, the key to its character and accomplishment.

Civil Society and Social Capital

Contemporary discourse on voluntary associations, which has become something akin to a cottage industry, is largely the result of the work of Robert Putnam, of the Kennedy School of Government at Harvard University. Long a student of political culture, Putnam co-authored a decade ago a very important book on Italian politics, *Making Democracy Work*.[4] Here, he attempted to explain why and how some democratic cultures fail, while others grow and flourish, even in times of crisis. Putnam and his colleagues came to the conclusion that democracy is not merely a political system, but also a socioeconomic and cultural system. It implies and demands a sense of community based upon reciprocity, trust, and consistent, face-to-face interaction among citizens, through dense networks that are created and reinforced by a rich and diverse associational life.

Putnam followed his work on Italy with a consideration of our present national situation in the United States. This work resulted in publication of the now-famous 2001 book, *Bowling Alone,* wherein Putnam decries the condition of American civic life and our disassociation from one another as the result of falling membership and participation in organizations; a continuing drop in the number who actively participate in politics; and a splintering of community life, in general.[5] The causes of this unhappy situation he found in such things as increased television viewing—even though we constantly complain that there is nothing worthwhile to watch; an economy that almost compels two-career families, with little time left for family and community life; and suburban sprawl and commuting habits.

In essence, Putnam argues, we still bowl; but we now tend to bowl alone rather than in leagues, as once we did. By bowling alone, he argues, we have lost the contact with one another, the identification with common pursuits, the sharing of information and knowledge, and the bonding which creates trust and opportunity for reciprocity.

Altogether, Putnam equates this decline in community in America with the loss of "social capital," a term first used by the French sociologist, Pierre Bourdieu. Social capital refers to the norms of trust, reciprocity, and concern for mutual well-being that facilitate, even lubricate social exchange. Indeed, Adam Smith, in his *Wealth of Nations*, recognized this kind of trust as the very foundation of capitalism, facilitating economic exchange and increasing its efficiency: a handshake is a promise that renders lawyers needless in transacting business! The understanding of how human interaction creates a larger and more robust community entered the American dialogue through the work of James Coleman.[6]

Bourdieu and Coleman recognized that social capital, compared to other forms of capital, is both intangible and deeply communal; that it exists essen-

Columbia Falls

tially in the heads and hearts of people; and that it requires interaction among people for its creation, sustenance, and renewal. In a sense, social capital is an internalized community norm which, as Alejandro Portes points out, "allows the holders to extend loans without fear of non-payment, to benefit from private charity, or to send their kids to play in the street without concern."[7]

Through his own empirical studies, Putnam came to define social capital as trust, reciprocity, and an abiding concern for the common good. He sees this threatened because we no longer engage in associational life to the extent that we once did, and have lost much of the face-to-face interaction and knowledge of one another that is vital to the maintenance of social capital. His emphasis on associational life as a building block for society has been the point in Putnam's argument that most of his critics have questioned. A number have argued that not all voluntary associations pursue civil or beneficial policies. Nicholas Leeman, for one, wrote a provocative essay, "Kicking in Groups," in which he argues that it is not only not the means but the ends of associations, as well, that determine their utility and impact on the deepening of civil society.[8]

We may remember in this regard that many Maine people once joined the Ku Klux Klan. In the 1920s, it boasted a membership of approximately 50,000, had a substantial headquarters in Portland, and had a real impact on the state's political landscape. Few today would argue that it championed either civility or civic virtue in Maine society. Membership in the Klan reflected a voluntary association based on a corrupt concept of racial heritage, as well as a compelling and ill-informed set of collective fears. It also grew out of a fragmented political environment defined by special interests rather than common concerns, the antithesis of a robust civil society.

The Essence of Maine Civil Society
The quintessentially civil, voluntary association in Maine was, perhaps, the Grange—or, the Patrons of Husbandry. A national organization, the Grange first appeared in Maine in 1873, when the Hampden subordinate grange was established. When farming was a more nearly universal way of life in Maine, the Grange was its ubiquitous and influential voluntary association. As it promoted the modernization of agriculture through lectures, demonstrations, and publications, it also sought to make farm life more tolerable and attractive through the sponsorship of cultural and social events such as lectures, visiting entertainment, dances, common meals, picnics, and rituals.

The location of these functions, as with almost all Grange activities, was the local Grange Hall that served as something of a community center. It brought people together, nurtured a high degree of fellowship and sisterhood, and sponsored activities that involved the entire family. The Grange also involved itself in the political life of the Maine, and often wielded considerable clout. The decline of the Grange mirrors both the decline of agriculture in much of Maine and a shift in the nature of our associational life.

A remarkable example of uncoerced associational life in Maine was the life of one Warren Durgin, farmer and woodsman. Introduced to us in Theda Skocpol's recent essay in the *Maine Policy Review*, Durgin's life is further rounded out in her book, *Diminished Democracy*.[9] Skocpol's husband first came upon Durgin's gravestone while hiking in the mountains of western Maine, and learned from the marker that Durgin was one of the pallbearers for the assassinated President Abraham Lincoln. It was also inscribed that Durgin was a member of the Grand Army of the Republic (GAR), the Kezar Lake Grange No. 440, and the Order of Odd Fellows. Skocpol remarks in her essay that "I could readily understand why Durgin would want to proclaim for all eternity his service as Abraham Lincoln's pallbearer. But ...why add the ties to the Grand Army of the Republic, the Grange, and the Odd Fellows?"[10]

It could not have been otherwise; Durgin was of his place and time, a period when Maine people, and other Americans, freely joined and actively participated in civic organizations that often spanned class divisions, ethnicity, occupational status, and age differences. As Skocpol writes, "Warren Durgin clearly lived in a full-fledged version of Tocqueville's civic America." He was, like thousands upon thousands of Mainers, *obliged* to do these things; to attend meetings, to pay his dues, and to participate actively in the life of the associations he joined—because he simply *had* to do so, to enjoy the rewards and responsibilities that came with citizenship.

Critics of Putnam argue that if Warren Durgin were alive today, he would likely be a member of as many associations as he was during his lifetime, perhaps even more.[11] As Putnam, Skocpol, and others have countered, however, most of today's organizations would be vocational in nature, professionally dominated advocacy groups operating at the national level, non-profit institutions which are minimally "membership" organizations in our meaning of the term, often wedded to the "grants economy," and fundamentally *managerial as opposed to participatory* in nature.

Therein lies the critical distinction: Warren Durgin's affiliations were essentially fraternal and civic, while today our associations tend to reflect our occupational status and political commitments in the broadest sense, and require only our dues rather than our sweat. Even advocacy groups like Common Cause, which is today directed by Maine's Chellie Pingree, are staff-driven, concentrate on lobbying and research, and are managed from the top. They are part of what Skocpol calls the emerging "top-down civic culture."

Others celebrate this development, like Debra Minkoff who maintains that such national-level associations "transcend parochial boundaries based on communities of residence."[12] Please do not get me wrong: I am a member of many of these groups, and think that some do a creditable job. The problem with this conception of civil society is that it is about "doing for, instead of doing with"—as Skocpol puts it—thus contributing to an on-going process of infantalizing the American people and making us ever more dependent upon more distant and nameless "others," rather than upon ourselves and our neighbors.

Some of this is, of course, inevitable and even desirable; but let us recognize that this tendency makes civil society less muscular as we become civic couch-potatoes—experiencing life as television, rather than the endless meetings, hours upon hours of talk, and the "making it up as you go along" that is the very stuff of democratic life.[13]

Civil Society and Sprawl

Among the reasons that social capital has been in decline, according to Putnam, is suburban sprawl. In another chapter in this book, Charles Colgan makes the point that we in Maine increasingly live suburban and work urban. Not only do we spend more time on the road and in our cars than ever before; but the separation between home and work is also growing, fragmenting daily experience ever further.

Sprawl's impact on civil society may be seen in profound ways. As an example, an increasing number of Maine towns are at risk of losing their volunteer fire departments, only to see them replaced by professional departments. On balance this might seem like an advance; in reality, it is something of a retreat from one of the purest forms of Maine's civil society. There was a time when Maine townspeople took turns clearing the snow from roads, building bridges and other infrastructure, providing for the truly needy, and raising money for common civic pursuits through bean suppers and the like. These important local activities were "part and parcel" of the rhythm of the civic experience.

While I do not wish to overly romanticize these sorts of activities, the larger point is that we continue to distance ourselves from the things that must get done if we are to function both individually and collectively. In the case of volunteer fire departments, their diminishment is indicative that as we continue to sprawl, fewer of us work and live in the same space and polity. The inevitable result will be that many of our obligations to one another are becoming ever more tenuous, and passed on to third-party agencies.

Very much more can be said about sprawl, the "smart growth" initiatives that seek to reign it in, the "Great American Neighborhood" movement, and similar matters discussed by Evan Richert in his chapter. Suffice it to say here that whether it is the good work of the "Land for Maine's Future" program, GrowSmart Maine, or Maine's burgeoning land trust movement, Maine people have long realized that how we live upon the land is a reflection of how we choose to live with one another, either in an engaged community or in more privatized settings.

Civil Society and Local Governance

The decline in social capital and civil society may be seen in what I believe to be a true crisis, the survival of towns and their governance. This is a matter quite different entirely from the necessary debate on the regionalization of services that is now taking place. Over the past two decades, we have witnessed a growing number of Maine towns that are compelled to debate and, in some cases, to de-organize or dissolve themselves. In Maine, the very heartland of Tocquevillian America, the very efficacy and viability of local governance and democracy, built on volunteer efforts and traditional notions of civil society, are being challenged.

Towns are "republics in miniature," to use a phrase coined by Ross Stephens and Nelson Wikstrom, the latter a former faculty member at the University of Maine.[14] At present the citizens of Atkinson are debating whether or not to de-organize. In recent times, Alna, Benedicta, Cooper, Coplin Plantation, Madrid, Crystal, Grand Isle, Centerville, Greenfield Plantation, Hammond, Carol Plantation, Elliotsville, Barnard, Sherman, Shirley, Milo, New Sweden, and other communities have examined dissolving local government—or, they have done it. The formal process of de-organization is carefully laid out in state statutes, and requires considerable public discussion and official votes supervised by the State of Maine. Having read accounts of these meetings and attended others, I find that most people approach the question with what can only be called resignation, rather than enthusiasm.

In the case of Greenfield Plantation, former First Selectman Linda Blakeman has said that de-organization "was like a death…. I sat in the car and cried."[15] In Crystal, Selectman James DeAngelo feels that towns no longer matter in the larger scheme of things when he asks, "What decisions do we make? We don't make any decisions. Most are made at the state level now."[16] In the most recent case of dissolution, that of Centerville, Maxine Caler, former school board chair and town assessor, commented that, "I guess people have lost interest in doing things for the town. The younger generations have grown up and gone away. And most of the people just stay to themselves now. Everybody is busy working or doing their own thing."[17]

Lying behind all this is a complex of issues, including rising property tax burdens, the tree-growth tax compensation formula, the loss of a critical mass of residents willing and able to undertake the hard work of local government, rising school costs, and other such matters. In some places, like Madrid, the final vote for de-organization split along lines of "time of residency in town," with relative newcomers voting to disband and long-term residents voting to keep the town government intact.

One can only imagine that what elements of civil society remain in Madrid have eroded further, by a process which highlighted this schism. Of the state's process and procedure of de-organization, Michael Starn of the Maine Municipal Association has made the point that "to do all the things that have to be done to run a town requires commitment to a lofty tradition of service that may be fraying as towns age and change. Money is tight, rules are convoluted, federal mandates governing everything from landfills to disabilities can seem to come from Jupiter, at least in Maine. Everybody's busy, and apathy calls."[18]

Whatever its causes, the significance of town dissolution must be recognized for the gravely disturbing situation that it is. Some communities may well be too small to remain viable, but the loss of self-government is a wound to the entire community of Maine, and a diminution of everyday democracy and civil society. As the regionalization discussion matures, it will serve us all well if, in addition to looking at the efficiency criteria, we also ask questions about how we might enhance and restore vigor and meaning to local government with its human scale and high levels of interaction and connectedness. It *must* be done.

The smartest man I know, who continues to farm well into his eighth decade, has said to me several times that he loves living in his tiny upcountry New England town because "it is so small that you know who all of the SOBs are." There is everything to be said for the scale and the intimacy of the local.

The Good News
The news of social capital and civil society here in Maine is far from all bad. Indeed, we remain one of the healthiest places in the country in terms of the quality and vitality of our civic culture. There are many organizations, formal and informal, and foundations and nonprofits, and community development corporations like Coastal Enterprise, Inc., making important contributions to the maintenance and renewal of community in Maine.

In cooperation with the Maine Community Foundation, one of these marvelous entities, Putnam's Saguaro Seminar in Civic Engagement undertook a survey of the strength of social capital in Lewiston-Auburn, as part of a larger national study. While one may not generalize about an entire state from one case study, the findings are nonetheless revealing and important. Surveys and studies were carried out on the dimensions and depths of local social capital, using variables such as trust levels, political participation, civic leadership, associational involvement, informal socializing and bonding, rates and types of voluntarism and private giving, and engagement in faith-based communities.

The results strongly suggest a Lewiston-Auburn community with a considerable reservoir of social capital: high levels of trust between various groups and municipal government, including immigrants; fewer barriers to social connectedness based on class, when compared with other parts of the nation; strong and visible roles played by women in the fabric of the community and its institutions; and high levels of civic engagement among residents, far exceeding

Changing Maine

national rates. Levels of active participation in faith-based organizations and activities were lower in Lewiston-Auburn than the national average, as was voluntarism among the middle-aged and older residents of the community.

Taken together, the information and stories from the Saguaro seminar should give us pause, at least on the national level, and some degree of cautious pride here in Maine. Putnam came to the conclusion that we all are, simply, "better together"—which phrase became the title of his latest book, as well as his ongoing project to help renew American civic society.[19]

One could mention many more such stories, including how Maine people reacted to September 11, 2001; how Maine people often come together to help those left homeless after a house fire, or to support those facing a catastrophic health crisis; and, of course, the ice storm that held the state in its grip for days upon days. Stories are important because they help us understand our place in the world, and make sense of all we experience. This purpose is reflected in the way that Down East humorists have created the wily, witty, and playful Mainer who enjoys nothing more than fun at the expense of a haughty, arrogant and not-too-bright—"numb" is the proper adjective, as Tim Sample reminds us—visitor from away.

Some Lessons from Estonia

Narratives, then, can have immense power. Let me try to explain this point through a digression. I have spent parts of the last decade working on civil society issues in Estonia, which regained its independence in 1991 from the Soviet Union, to which it had been annexed for more than fifty years. During that era of deep repression and cultural subjugation, one out of every ten Estonians died on the way to, in, or coming back from the Gulag. The Soviets, at the same time, moved some 400,000 ethnic and linguistic Russians into the country. In a small nation of not quite a million people, this was a huge population transfer that changed the dynamics of nearly everything in Estonian life.

Since regaining their independence, both Russian residents in the country and native Estonians have been working toward a new conception of citizenship, one that might allow both communities to come together as a single nation of Estonians, ethnically and linguistically diverse. There are some considerable obstacles in the way of this transformation, but none is more formidable than that Russian Estonians continue to obtain much of their information from Russian sources in the Russian Federation. At the same time, Estonian-Estonians are tied to their own language media.

What has emerged is a nation where a one-third minority has a narrative wildly different from that of the majority. History during the years of Soviet power is recorded and understood in profoundly different ways. The struggles people faced in one community are portrayed in a manner opposite to that of the other community. Contemporary problems are frequently defined and framed in such fundamentally divergent ways as to make them even worse. Instead of a single, unifying narrative, at least two exist, making it extraordinarily difficult for bonding, trust, and reciprocity to take root, develop, and mature. An emerging civil society exists in Estonia, though its roots are not yet deep, and suspicions and fear remain.

While I would hardly suggest that this is happening here in Maine, I have some fears that the continuing portrayal of "two Maines," instead of one, has the potential to undercut our civic enterprise. Our common narrative seems to be fraying at its edges. The roots of the "two Maines" characterization lie in the portrayal of one part of the state as entirely prosperous, while the other atrophies in decline. While this is a stereotypical view of things, it appears to have taken hold in our imaginations and our politics. This narrative sees the first region composed of much of southern and mid-coast Maine, while the remainder of the state comprises the second region. Yet even stereotypes have some element of truth to them, and this one is no exception.

It might be helpful to provide some perspective here, by recognizing that many other states appear to have the same kind of regional imbalance. For almost as long as there has been a Michigan, for example, there has been a strong tension between the Upper Peninsula and the remainder of the state. In Illinois, "upstate" versus "downstate" is a constant political refrain. The western panhandle region of Nebraska actually attempted to secede and join up with Wyoming. However many times one points this out it, does not make the "two Maines" argument any less powerful. We have seen members of the legislature attempt to address these perceived problems in any number of ways, some of which are quite ridiculous.

The possible emergence of two divergent narratives of Maine's fate is potentially dangerous, serving only as an obstacle to making real progress on the public issues we face—stemming the tide of out-migration of the young and well-educated, affordable housing and health services, the creation of high quality job opportunities, and the restoration and revival of hope.

We also must concede that addressing the growing gap in opportunity between Maine's regions is not entirely susceptible of solution in Augusta. We still lack a robust and well-articulated regional economic development policy at the federal level; and President George W. Bush's budget proposals might lead to further cuts in many of the programs that have been most beneficial to regional development and Maine's small towns and rural areas. Yet, this does not take us off the hook. We can choose to allow the two narratives to grow and drive us farther apart as a community; or, we can demand that strategies be enunciated and investments made that build *one* Maine narrative.

The Free Flow of Information

Narrative does not appear out of the proverbial thin air, however. It is constructed from many sources. As a concept, it is closely allied to the long-held American belief that an "informed citizenry" is crucial to the development of civil society. "One of the legacies of the early republic," writes historian Richard D. Brown, is "an informed citizenry that would become a central theme in American public life, encouraging a wide array of voluntary associations such as political parties and promoting a printing industry, the post office, and the development of public education from primary schools through technical colleges and universities."[20] A diversity of sources of information, together with "fair comment," is absolutely essential to the development of our civil society.

One emerging obstacle may be seen in the growth of control of Maine's media by corporations located outside of the state of Maine. This is especially true in the area of radio station ownership where, with very few exceptions, two out-of-state corporations own nearly all of the radio media in Maine. The great exception is, of course, Maine Public Radio. Newspapers appear to be growing in number in Maine, mostly of the weekly and "community" variety, and local community news coverage appears to be strong. In the area of television coverage, we find a mix of in- and out-of-state ownerships; Maine Public Television is an alternative.

Maine is more fortunate than many other largely rural states, where ownership is highly concentrated in out-of-state corporations and coverage of local news and issues has declined. While we presently maintain a reasonable balance in the area of media ownership and coverage, we are losing some of the "fair comment" so essential to an informed citizenry. I am not speaking here about a sudden dearth in the number of editorial pages or television opinion pieces, like those of Fred Nutter here in the Portland area. We have plenty of that. The real loss has been the demise of the *Maine Times* and similar vehicles that have provided in-depth and wide coverage of all things Maine.

I am not arguing here for a revival of that newspaper, though it has been tried several times without success. Much as I wish it were still with us, that does not seem likely. In the demise of the *Maine Times*, we lost a critical perspective, much fair comment, and not a little bit of our narrative as a somewhat contrarian and independent place, with a strong civil society to match.

Learning Civic Culture

Throughout this chapter, I have focused on the infrastructure of civil society and, in particular, on the role social capital plays. We recognize that *democratic citizens are not born; they are made, nurtured by a robust and diverse civil society, and educated into civic practices*. We learn how to act in a civic sense in the institutional settings of our early lives—in our families, schools, churches, and organizations like the Girl Scouts and Boy Scouts. What happens around our youth—especially the attitudes and behaviors modeled by adults—has considerable bearing on what type of citizens they are likely to become.

Critical in this mix are our schools, the civic institution that philosopher John Dewey once called our "laboratories of democracy." We may note with considerable satisfaction that Maine's Learning Results program, which David Silvernail discusses at length in his chapter, has a great deal to say about civic culture. Civil society in this context is closely tied to the social studies curricula.

Building a civil society is not just about a particular subject matter, however; it is, more importantly, about how we are to act and what we are to do in the public realm.

It is, if you will, about teaching and modeling a certain disposition toward daily behavior, with emphasis on practice as well as theory, on form as well as content, on schools as living civil communities, and on the acquisition of the skills that are reported under the category, "playing and working well with others." A Maine document that expresses this splendidly and was developed for Maine's Learning Results program is entitled, "Taking Responsibility: Standards for Ethical and Responsible Behavior in Maine Schools and Community."[21] It is as strong a statement of what our civil society requires as is any available, anywhere.

As this chapter began with a tale of Hillel, so it concludes with his words: "If I am not for myself, who will be for me? And if I am only for myself, what am I ?"[22]

Mark Lapping is Professor of Public Policy and Management at the Muskie School of Public Service. Dr. Lapping grew up on a farm in Vermont; was educated at the State University of New York, MIT, and Emory University; and founded the schools of Rural Planning and Development at the University of Guelph in Ontario, and of Planning and Public Policy at Rutgers University in New Jersey, before coming to the University of Southern Maine to serve as academic vice president and provost for six years (1994–2000) before returning to the faculty. He is the author of eight books and more than 150 scholarly articles and monographs; and consults widely for governments and nonprofits here and abroad, most recently and for over a decade in the nation of Estonia, where he works on issues of rural democracy and community building. Three years ago Mark suffered a kidney failure, and credits the fact that he is alive today to the great generosity of a Maine family who donated a kidney to make him well.

MAINERS' ATTITUDES TOWARD population density make us our own worst enemies when it comes to managing sprawl. Increasingly, as private values like privacy and the desire for a view trump public values, Maine's rural landscape is being transformed into suburban subdivisions, a costly and destructive pattern of development that out-competes the productive uses of rural land. Low-density suburban land makes up the largest, fastest growing category of land use in Maine. The state, however, often treats low-density suburbs like "rural" communities, subsidizing them at the expense of our service centers and truly rural communities. Maine needs to re-evaluate the restrictive zoning that prevents higher density, multi-use development if we are to sustain healthy communities over time.

11 Land Use in Maine
From Production to Consumption

EVAN RICHERT

I am an amateur bird watcher. There are connections between this hobby and my life as a professional planner—namely, concern for habitat, land use, and the like. For example, I have found myself wondering of late: if each part of our terrestrial landscape—the city, the suburb, rural land, and the wildlands—were to be assigned an avian symbol, what would it be?

The city's bird surely would be the rock dove, also known as the common pigeon, with its remarkable substitution of the ledges of city buildings for the wild, rocky areas of its native Europe. Most would probably name the American bald eagle the avian symbol of the wildlands and their rivers and estuaries. For the rural, wooded lands, one might choose from among a host of beauties: wood warblers, chickadees, and thrushes, for example; but my vote would be for the scarlet tanager, one of the spectacularly beautiful indicators of a healthy, rural landscape.

This leaves the suburbs. For its love of shady lawns and golf courses, one might choose the American robin; but, no, the robin does not speak to the essence of today's low-density suburb. That honor goes to the brown-headed cowbird. Let me tell you why.

Organizing Land for Human Use

The 1950s and '60s marked the fading of one era of land use in Maine, and the rising dominance of another. Before I describe this transition, it is useful to think about how and why human beings organize land for their use.

From ancient times in both agricultural and industrial societies, humans have organized some land for the primary purpose of *exchange*. The things being exchanged take every imaginable form. They include goods and services, philosophies and ideas, protection, inventions, rumors and gossip, friendships, fears, mythologies, disease (albeit unwittingly), and, perhaps most important of all, knowledge. These lands were organized as urban places, or cities. On them we put dwellings, stores and market squares, piers and wharfs, places of worship and of pleasure, fuel depots and warehouses, city halls and courthouses, factories to produce the goods for trade, and libraries, universities, and museums to build up and store knowledge for later exchange. All are organized to facilitate rapid and efficient exchange, at scales that match current modes of transportation.

The city is the platform for many functions of society. Lewis Mumford, who explored these functions as deeply as anyone, cited the city's earliest role as a meeting place for ritual; as a memory bank for civilization; and as the venue in which the tensions of society compete, play themselves out, and find new equilibria.[1] In the end, these all involve interactions among people. There would have been no cities if people had no need to exchange things and ideas.

The essential though not the only relationship of the urban land owner or user to the land is one of *speculation*: an investment made in anticipation of a future financial return. The investment isn't just in the form of money, but also in time, energy, emotion, and ideas. In the city, the value of the investment gets translated, more or less universally, into rent, the return to land derived from location. From the city we get such terms as the "100 percent location" and "highest and best use." It is one of the reasons we both revere and fear cities. On the one hand, they are places where much individual and community wealth is created—spawned by the imaginations, investments, and support systems possible only in an urban environment.

On the other hand, cities are places of exploitation. Frank Lloyd Wright captured the sentiments held by many middle Americans in the early twentieth Century. He considered cities the province of the "moneylords" who controlled and collected rent on everything—on land, on money, even on ideas. The city, he concluded, has "made of man a piece of cheap speculative property."[2] We are drawn to cities—indeed, we depend on them—and still we seek to escape them.

From ancient times, both in agricultural and hunter-gatherer societies, humans also have organized land—the largest part of it, in fact—for the primary purpose of *production*. These lands are held and worked to turn natural resources into food, fiber, fuel and energy, and materials. They are organized and managed as rural places: farms, timberland, pits and mines, sources of drinking water, hunting and fishing grounds, and the wildlife associated with them. They embrace, as well, the land required for homes for the producers, and the hamlets and villages that furnish the goods and services needed for daily living.

Even with the urbanization of society, and the physical and psychological distance that now exists between people and their sustenance, rural lands remain the wellhead of human survival. Garrett Hardin estimated that, in addition to the land area that we use for our homes, factories, warehouses, stores, waste disposal, and transportation facilities—an average of 2 to 3 acres per person—each American requires about 4.3 acres of crop- and pastureland and about 2.6 acres of woodland to support our demand for food and other resources.[3]

The relationship of the owner or user of rural land to the land is *active*, whether it be the farmer, logger, or fisherman, earning a living, or the corporate owner or investor, seeking long-term gains. Each applies labor or capital to a natural resource for growing and harvesting or for finding and extracting something for later use.

More recently—dating back some 250 years in Anglo-American history, but in a large-scale way only during the last century—human beings have organized a third category of land, for the primary purpose of *consumption*. This purpose is well documented in the literature of both poets and historians, and now by our own easy observations, as well. Early in the Industrial Revolution, people of means sought to escape the squalor and the dank, dark, noisy conditions of the newly industrialized urban centers. They considered it a moral duty to escape on behalf of their families, which for the first time in history had the luxury to be thought of as social rather than simply economic units.

The land beyond the bounds of the industrial city but within easy striking distance of it came to be organized as a new form of suburb—what historian Robert Fishman has called "bourgeois utopia,"[4] and fellow historian Robert Jackson has labeled the "crabgrass frontier."[5] Whatever it is called, it is organized for consumption. The most obvious manifestation of this is the division of land for the buying of house lots which are separated entirely from places of work, production, and exchange; but that understates the purpose.

Through English poets and other writers, Raymond Williams traced the expanding view of the landscape from one "organized for production, where tenants and laborers will work," to one "being organized for consumption—for the view, the ordered proprietary repose, the prospect."[6] Suburban land is organized above all for the consumption of scenery and privacy; for the view carved out of a landscape needed not for working but for enjoying, and shaped to one's own image or tastes; and for the consumption of a nuclear family oriented way of life.

In contrast to the rural landowner's active relationship to the land, the relationship of the suburban landowner to the land is *passive*. The land exists as a form of buffer from the active and sometimes distasteful rest of the world. This is the dominion of middle class kings and queens who, as much as possible, seek command of their immediate surroundings. One of the tools for exerting this control, the zoning ordinance, may have had its origins in the city; but it was in the suburbs that it was enshrined, and honed into an instrument for erecting barriers between domestic life in the home and anything that might threaten its tranquility.

So, broadly speaking, there are three categories of land organized for different purposes: urban land organized for *exchange*, rural land organized for *production*, and, in between, suburban land organized for *consumption*. There is a fourth category as well, but this is land not organized by or for human beings: wildland. Not much is left in the eastern U.S. Some of what remains today may be found in Maine's North Woods. As Ian McHarg has observed, however, such land is protected principally by poverty and inaccessibility.[7] While Maine and its tourist regions are hardly free of poverty, affluence and accessibility have today claimed most of Maine's once remote wildlands.

Outside Biddeford

The Transition from Rural to Suburb

How much of Maine's land falls into each of these categories of urban, suburban, and rural? Maine contains a little less than 20 million acres of land. At the end of the twentieth century, about 90 percent of it was forested—about the same percentage as in the 1950s, by which time much of the land that had been cleared 100 to 125 years earlier for farming had reverted to trees.[8] Farmland, meanwhile, fell sharply, from nearly 1.5 million acres in the 1950s to fewer than 600,000 acres in the 1990s, a decline of 60 percent. Accounting for the give-and-take between farm and forest, an estimated 88 percent of the land base of Maine may today be considered "rural"—that is, organized for production—though some of this, if a definition were agreed upon, might be called wildlands. Another 4 percent is in fee conservation and parklands and coastal wetlands.

Urban land is but a tiny part of Maine's land base: only about 1.5 percent, less than 300,000 acres; but it is *very efficient*. It accommodates more than 525,000 people, or 41 percent of the state's population, plus much of the state's commercial base. This urban area increased its land base only modestly during the last 50 years—by about 16 percent.[9] Almost all of the growth in development was outside of urban areas, as rural land was converted to suburban use. The amount of suburban land nearly doubled from 1950 to 2000 to approximately 1.2 million acres, or more than 6 percent of land in Maine. This land is occupied by about 600,000 people, or about 48 percent of the population. If these estimates are correct, urban land in Maine (accommodating 1.75 people per acre plus a mix of other uses) is being used at least 3.5 times more efficiently than the surrounding suburban lands (accommodating 0.5 person per acre).

Let us bring this general picture into sharper focus. Most of Maine's rural land—an estimated 89 percent of the forested acres, 73 percent of the farm land, and a large share of the conservation land—is in the nine counties of western, northern, and eastern Maine. Cumulatively, on the order of 98 percent of the land of these nine counties may be considered "rural," and perhaps to some extent wildland. The urban and suburban portions of this region, comprising perhaps 300,000 to 400,000 acres, are concentrated in the Bangor area and in and around the smaller service centers of the territory, such as Presque Isle, Calais, Ellsworth, Farmington, and Skowhegan.

The profile is dramatically different for the seven counties of southern Maine through Androscoggin and Kennebec, and the mid-coast through Knox. These counties are small geographically, containing a total of about 2.7 million acres. Based in part on the recent report of Andrew Plantinga and his colleagues, it can be estimated that a majority of this land, 55 percent to 60 percent, is active or potentially active timberland; another 5 percent is in active farming; and a small share is in conservation and parklands.[10]

Table 1. New and Emerging Suburbs of Southern and Mid-Coastal Maine and Bangor Metro Area.
Excludes "Regional Service Centers"

Name	Acres	1960	1970	1980	1990	2000	2010	Pct. Ch. 1960–2010
		Dwelling Units per 10 Gross Acres						
Suburban Density (At least 1 Unit/10 Gross Acres as of 1970)								
Cumberland	14,865	0.76	1.01	1.33	1.59	1.95	2.38	215.3%
Farmingdale	7,264	0.85	1.09	1.32	1.70	1.88	2.09	144.5%
Kennebunk	23,032	0.82	1.00	1.30	1.75	2.12	2.59	215.1%
Kennebunkport	13,719	0.90	1.11	1.49	1.64	1.80	1.99	121.4%
Owls Head	5,682	0.98	1.15	1.42	1.60	1.77	1.95	98.1%
Suburban Density (At least 1 Unit /10 Gross Acres as of 1980)								
Boothbay	13,089	0.74	0.88	1.13	1.31	1.51	1.73	134.4%
Eliot	13,013	0.84	0.94	1.40	1.55	1.69	1.84	120.2%
Gorham	31,922	0.51	0.69	1.05	1.27	1.53	1.85	264.6%
Livermore Falls	12,620	0.86	0.96	1.19	1.17	1.23	1.30	50.8%
Oakland	16,518	0.73	0.93	1.35	1.50	1.68	1.89	160.7%
Scarborough	31,350	0.85	0.90	1.35	1.72	2.09	2.53	199.1%
Topsham	21,244	0.55	0.78	1.06	1.52	1.67	1.83	232.5%
Windham	35,572	0.62	0.80	1.26	1.46	1.73	2.06	232.7%
Suburban Density (At least 1 Unit /10 Gross Acres as of 1990)								
Friendship	8,153	0.59	0.65	0.80	1.00	1.08	1.15	95.3%
South Berwick	21,057	0.48	0.53	0.71	1.07	1.18	1.30	173.1%
South Bristol	7,847	0.64	0.75	0.94	1.01	1.08	1.17	82.9%
St. George	14,834	0.64	0.69	0.88	1.06	1.12	1.19	85.7%
West Bath	7,890	0.65	0.71	0.98	1.13	1.46	1.88	189.7%
Suburban Density (At least 1 Unit /10 Gross Acres as of 2000)								
Buxton	26,292	0.31	0.38	0.78	0.90	1.05	1.24	299.7%
Gray	31,242	0.42	0.54	0.73	0.91	1.10	1.32	213.3%
Hampden	24,515	0.58	0.61	0.76	0.93	1.10	1.30	121.5%
Sabattus	17,322	0.29	0.37	0.67	0.80	1.06	1.40	385.8%
South Thomaston	8,834	0.46	0.50	0.65	0.79	1.13	1.61	252.7%
Standish	41,140	0.34	0.43	0.72	0.89	1.02	1.16	236.8%
Wiscasset	16,474	0.41	0.46	0.65	0.83	1.14	1.57	283.9%
Suburban Density (At least 1 Unit /10 Gross Acres as of 2010)								
Arundel	15,450	0.20	0.28	0.49	0.67	0.90	1.20	501.5%
Casco	21,034	0.31	0.45	0.58	0.80	0.90	1.02	225.1%
Chelsea	12,516	0.29	0.34	0.57	0.65	0.88	1.21	309.3%
Fairfield	35,201	0.50	0.53	0.65	0.75	0.88	1.02	102.8%
Naples	23,261	0.30	0.35	0.63	0.84	0.99	1.17	291.4%
North Yarmouth	12,373	0.28	0.32	0.49	0.67	0.96	1.37	392.9%
Orrington	17,081	0.52	0.55	0.72	0.81	0.93	1.07	106.0%
Raymond	26,602	0.35	0.53	0.62	0.77	0.93	1.12	222.5%
Waterboro	34,211	0.21	0.26	0.47	0.63	0.79	1.01	373.7%
West Gardiner	15,280	0.28	0.38	0.55	0.69	0.84	1.02	259.0%

| Name | Acres | Dwelling Units per 10 Gross Acres | | | | | | Pct. Ch. 1960– 2010 |
		1960	1970	1980	1990	2000	2010	

Emerging Suburbs

(At least 1 Unit /20 Gross Acres, But Less Than 1 Unit /10 Gross Acres)

Name	Acres	1960	1970	1980	1990	2000	2010	Pct. Ch. 1960–2010
Acton	26,726	0.37	0.56	0.53	0.60	0.69	0.79	111.3%
Alfred	16,765	0.21	0.26	0.47	0.55	0.62	0.71	238.4%
Belgrade	38,233	0.20	0.30	0.36	0.42	0.48	0.55	180.7%
Benton	18,188	0.25	0.29	0.41	0.48	0.64	0.86	245.1%
Berwick	26,849	0.31	0.37	0.57	0.83	0.90	0.97	210.2%
Bowdoinham	23,645	0.17	0.20	0.29	0.37	0.48	0.61	267.4%
Bristol	22,754	0.53	0.60	0.73	0.79	0.88	0.97	81.3%
Carmel	22,209	0.16	0.20	0.27	0.33	0.49	0.73	342.2%
China	33,655	0.24	0.29	0.36	0.50	0.59	0.68	183.7%
Clinton	24,746	0.22	0.25	0.38	0.50	0.60	0.72	225.3%
Corinth	22,519	0.15	0.17	0.28	0.36	0.53	0.79	410.1%
Cornish	13,301	0.22	0.24	0.32	0.38	0.44	0.50	128.0%
Dayton	12,249	0.13	0.15	0.25	0.35	0.44	0.56	344.4%
Durham	23,756	0.14	0.16	0.29	0.43	0.52	0.62	361.1%
Eddington	17,260	0.21	0.29	0.38	0.49	0.57	0.68	227.6%
Edgecomb	11,893	0.26	0.27	0.36	0.44	0.49	0.56	114.6%
Farmington	34,521	0.43	0.50	0.68	0.83	0.89	0.95	119.1%
Georgetown	12,555	0.63	0.45	0.61	0.64	0.70	0.76	21.6%
Greene	23,014	0.25	0.33	0.47	0.63	0.75	0.88	250.6%
Hanover	5,567	0.25	0.25	0.29	0.34	0.44	0.57	128.9%
Harrison	23,385	0.22	0.27	0.41	0.51	0.63	0.79	249.8%
Hermon	25,241	0.26	0.29	0.42	0.56	0.72	0.92	256.8%
Holden	20,230	0.26	0.36	0.55	0.66	0.72	0.80	209.4%
Hollis	20,848	0.21	0.27	0.48	0.60	0.74	0.92	333.1%
Hope	15,280	0.16	0.21	0.27	0.35	0.46	0.60	274.1%
Jefferson	31,675	0.20	0.24	0.30	0.38	0.44	0.51	151.9%
Kenduskeag	10,950	0.15	0.20	0.38	0.41	0.50	0.60	296.8%
Lebanon	36,562	0.18	0.23	0.39	0.48	0.55	0.63	256.8%
Levant	17,693	0.11	0.13	0.16	0.32	0.51	0.80	600.4%
Livermore	25,674	0.22	0.25	0.32	0.36	0.43	0.51	131.4%
Lyman	28,087	0.13	0.24	0.40	0.52	0.59	0.67	426.8%
Manchester	15,775	0.30	0.35	0.52	0.64	0.77	0.92	203.5%
Milford	28,210	0.17	0.20	0.29	0.42	0.50	0.61	257.8%
Minot	19,858	0.13	0.14	0.22	0.29	0.43	0.63	377.9%
Monmouth	24,375	0.37	0.40	0.55	0.63	0.78	0.96	157.7%
New Gloucester	27,406	0.21	0.25	0.39	0.50	0.69	0.96	362.2%
Newport	21,591	0.48	0.50	0.62	0.69	0.75	0.82	73.5%
Nobleboro	15,201	0.25	0.34	0.43	0.59	0.68	0.80	219.4%
North Berwick	23,075	0.29	0.37	0.50	0.63	0.69	0.76	160.9%
Phippsburg	19,813	0.42	0.40	0.53	0.62	0.74	0.89	111.6%
Pittston	20,895	0.19	0.23	0.35	0.43	0.56	0.74	285.2%
Plymouth	17,260	0.09	0.11	0.18	0.26	0.37	0.52	474.3%
Poland	31,799	0.23	0.32	0.47	0.59	0.68	0.79	245.1%
Readfield	20,601	0.22	0.28	0.42	0.49	0.55	0.62	186.7%
Richmond	19,712	0.40	0.45	0.54	0.67	0.74	0.82	103.2%
Rome	21,219	0.13	0.18	0.29	0.37	0.43	0.50	277.9%
Sebago	23,137	0.30	0.35	0.43	0.52	0.58	0.64	112.5%
Shapleigh	25,674	0.35	0.41	0.58	0.63	0.71	0.80	129.8%
Sidney	26,107	0.15	0.20	0.31	0.43	0.63	0.91	512.1%

| Name | Acres | Dwelling Units per 10 Gross Acres | | | | | | Pct. Ch. 1960–2010 |
		1960	1970	1980	1990	2000	2010	
Turner	39,909	0.19	0.23	0.35	0.43	0.54	0.69	267.5%
Union	21,962	0.20	0.24	0.35	0.40	0.46	0.52	156.1%
Vassalboro	33,036	0.27	0.29	0.42	0.48	0.57	0.67	144.4%
Waldoboro	47,996	0.23	0.23	0.34	0.42	0.51	0.62	167.3%
Wales	11,692	0.18	0.23	0.28	0.41	0.48	0.57	219.0%
Warren	31,744	0.20	0.21	0.30	0.41	0.47	0.55	176.9%
Wayne	16,332	0.17	0.24	0.34	0.44	0.49	0.55	216.0%
Westport	5,696	0.31	0.34	0.58	0.72	0.83	0.96	212.3%
Windsor	23,323	0.14	0.14	0.26	0.33	0.47	0.67	389.8%
Winterport	23,095	0.28	0.27	0.44	0.51	0.64	0.81	191.2%

Note: Some "regional service center" densities for comparison:

Portland	26.30
Westbrook	8.39
Lewiston	7.21
Bangor	6.85
Biddeford	4.81
Auburn	2.73
Augusta	2.71

Sources: U.S. Census; projection to 2010 based on change from 1990 to 2000. Calculations by Evan Richert.

These may be overestimates, because they may include blocks of land that have been isolated by development and that alone are too small for farming or forestry. In any case, they mean that a third or more of the region, or more than 900,000 acres, now are organized either for urban or suburban purposes. This is a land mass equal to all of mid-coast Maine; or the equivalent of forty entire towns of average size.

By far the largest and fastest growing part of this land mass is for low-density, suburban use. Since 1960 Maine's year-round population has grown by 300,000. Most of that growth—80 percent, or the equivalent of four cities of Portland—has been in the low-density suburbs of the seven southern counties plus the Bangor metropolitan area. This is the hall mark of change in land use in Maine since the 1960s: what we have come to call *sprawl*.

It is not the decentralization of the population that is new. People have been moving from the urban centers outward for the last century. But in an earlier generation, the decentralization was to compact neighborhoods of distinct human scale, and often within the same municipal boundaries as the urban centers. In Greater Portland these neighborhoods included, for example, Woodfords and Deering Center in Portland, parts of Meetinghouse Hill in South Portland, the northern neighborhoods of Cape Elizabeth, and Wildwood in Cumberland. These places had in common certain telltale features, chief among them: proximity of their physical elements (homes, schools, parks, churches, stores, post offices, etc.) to each other; functional and deliberately planned open space and civic space; and walkability.

What distinguishes the period since 1960 is the way in which the physical elements of the contemporary community have moved away from each other, powered by a combustible mix of the automobile and old, anti-urban sentiments. The physical pieces of community are now connected not by proximity but by ribbons of road. A potent marker of this contemporary pattern of settlement is the sheer *consumption* of land. For example, from 1960 to 2000, the number of new dwelling units in Maine did not quite double, but I estimate that the land occupied by homes nearly tripled.

Data aren't available to estimate a similar multiplier for stores, warehouses and factories; but it probably is much larger, due to their virtually complete switch from vertical to horizontal space, and to the increased ratio of off-street parking spaces per 1,000 square foot of new commercial space. Prior to 1960, the ratio probably did not exceed one or two spaces per 1,000 square feet; since 1960, based on anecdotal information and typical zoning requirements, the ratio probably has increased to four or five spaces per 1,000 square feet.

Little things like parking spaces add up. Each space, including related aisles and driveways, consumes an average of perhaps 350 square feet. It would not be surprising if there are five or six nonresidential, off-street parking spaces for every motor vehicle registered in Maine. With about 1.05 million registered motor vehicles (an increase of 180 percent since 1960), that would be more than 50,000 impervious acres of land devoted to this purpose.[11]

Because so much of Maine is forested, it is hard to appreciate the full impact of the suburbanization of land use. Perhaps this statistic will help: in 1960, fewer than *one in ten* Maine municipalities statewide had hit a threshold of residential density that signaled its end as a rural community—that is, a community organized primarily for production, including forestry, farming, wildlife, water supplies, and the host of natural functions upon which we all depend.[12] Based on the recent 2000 Census, *one in five* municipalities statewide now has hit, or by 2010 will hit, that threshold. (See Table 1.) The maps below, prepared by the Maine State Planning Office, show the long-term trend in forty-year increments from 1940 to 2020.

More impressively, nearly seventy-five towns, or fully *one half* of all municipalities in the seven counties of southern and mid-coast Maine, have passed this threshold; and, except for the urban places among them, are now organized primarily for consumption rather than production. The low-density suburb is expanding at a rate that could cut the number of rural towns in half again, over the next two decades.

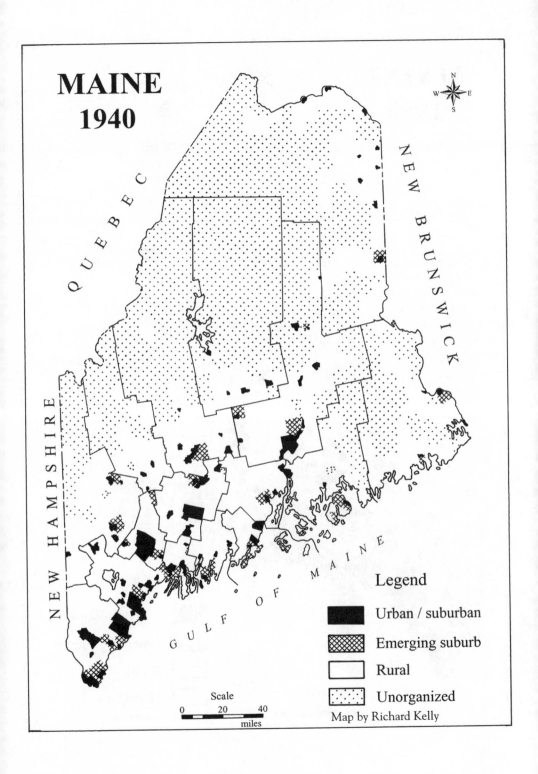

MAINE
1940

QUEBEC

NEW BRUNSWICK

NEW HAMPSHIRE

GULF OF MAINE

Legend

Urban / suburban

Emerging suburb

Rural

Unorganized

Map by Richard Kelly

Scale

0   20   40

miles

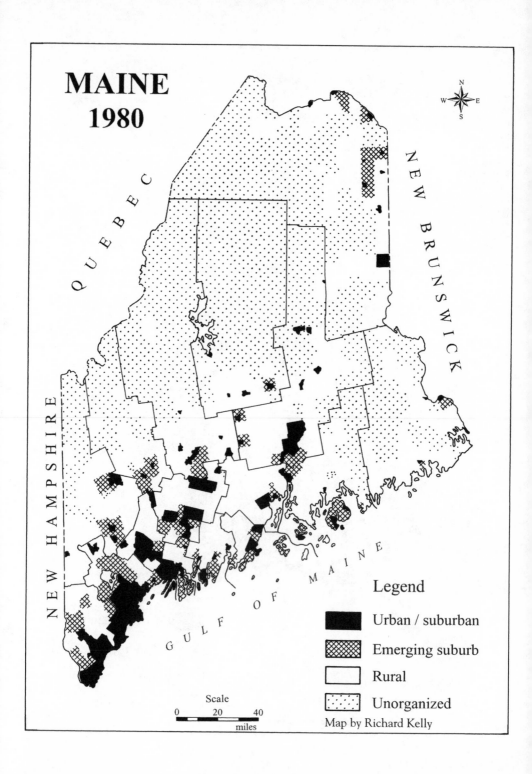

MAINE
1980

QUEBEC

NEW BRUNSWICK

NEW HAMPSHIRE

GULF OF MAINE

Legend

Urban / suburban

Emerging suburb

Rural

Unorganized

Map by Richard Kelly

Scale

0   20   40
                miles

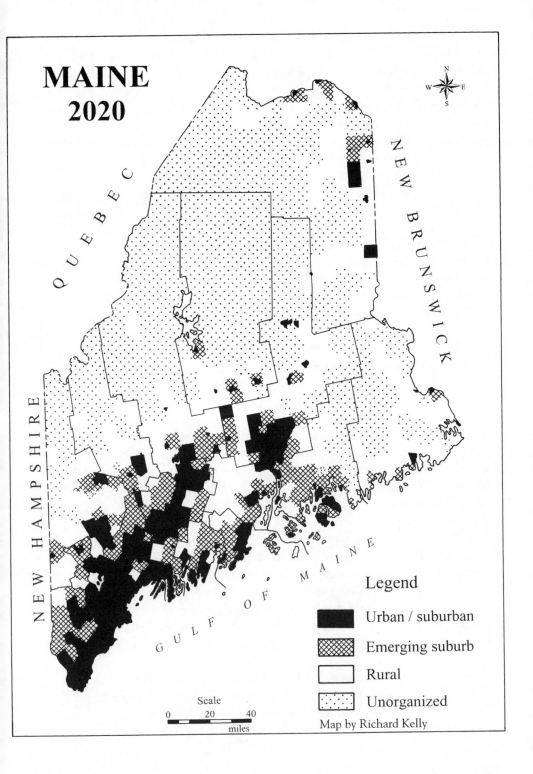

MAINE
2020

QUEBEC

NEW BRUNSWICK

NEW HAMPSHIRE

GULF OF MAINE

Legend

Urban / suburban

Emerging suburb

Rural

Unorganized

Map by Richard Kelly

Scale

0   20   40

miles

"And so what?" you may ask. The answer brings me back to the brown-headed cowbird. The brown-headed cowbird has achieved great evolutionary success, but in a unique way. Biologically, it is wired for deception; it is a *brood parasite*. The female lays her eggs in the nests of other bird species, including several species of woodland warblers and thrushes whose numbers are in decline. The host parents often don't seem to recognize the difference either in the eggs or in the chicks that hatch; they raise the cowbird chick as their own. The cowbird's egg usually hatches a day or two before the host's eggs, which allows the cowbird chick to out-compete the host's chicks for food and space. The result is that one or more of the host's chicks usually perish. The victims often are woodland birds that have nested within several hundred meters of the edge between forest and open country, where the cowbird is active.

This is a pretty good metaphor for the relationship of the low-density suburb to the rural land that it abuts. Because it is low-density—which we may define as not being able to see your neighbor from your window, but usually takes the form of 1- to 5- acre house lots—it has the appearance of being rural. Quite graciously, the host rural community fails to notice the difference and readily accepts this development. Through its tax dollars, it feeds the hungry critter as if it were its own. Soon, this pattern of development is out-competing the host community's true rural character—one that is organized for production—and converts the town into a low-density suburb, a place organized for consumption. It looks deceptively the same as the rural place it invaded. But the market forces, land taxes, and suburban attitudes and expectations that come with land organized for consumption end up driving out the original rural host.

There are many examples of how *state policy* similarly feeds the cowbird with its own subsidies, apparently mistaking the low-density suburbs for poor rural places. Consider school aid in S.A.D. 77 in rural Maine, consisting of the Washington County towns of East Machias, Cutler, Machiasport, and Whiting. Median household income there in 2000 was $29,000, and the rate of poverty was more than 15 percent. Compare this to S.A.D. 51, made up of Cumberland and North Yarmouth; its median household income was more than twice as high at $65,000, and its rate of poverty was one-fifth the rate at less than 3 percent. The Washington County towns are starving for economic opportunity and losing population; our state school funding formula penalizes them for that. Cumberland and North Yarmouth are in the suburban growth belt north of Portland; the school funding formula rewards them for that. It does so in the name of equity.

The increase in students in S.A.D. 51 has greatly outpaced the growth in property tax base, meaning that property tax valuation per student has fallen and local effort to support schools has increased markedly. That triggers an increase in state aid, which measures a community's wealth primarily in terms of property tax base (85 percent property tax base, 15 percent income). The East Machias area, by comparison, appears to the funding formula to be gaining in wealth (or at least not losing as fast as S.A.D. 51)—when, in actuality, the "gain" in property value per student is achieved by losing the region's youth.

In the name of equity, or fairness, school aid for education to Cumberland-North Yarmouth doubled between 1993 and 2003, while aid to the East Machias area fell by 20 percent during the same period. Equity in this case looks a lot like brood parasitism, as suburban interests have learned how to disguise themselves as rural and poor, and out-compete rural interests for limited resources.

Urban places are parasitized as well. Consider Augusta and the adjacent suburb of Manchester. Augusta's median household income at the time of the 2000 Census was just under $30,000. Fifteen percent of its residents lived below the poverty line. Its tax rate is close to $25 per thousand. The property tax burden (property taxes on a median-priced home divided by median household income) is approaching 7 percent. Next door, Manchester's median household income is $52,500. Fewer than 3 percent of its residents live below the poverty line. Its tax rate is under $18 per thousand, and its property tax burden is about 4 percent. When the state reconstructs Route 202, which runs out Western Ave and through Manchester, Augusta will be required to pay a 15 percent match for that portion that is located in the city. Once it passes into Manchester, the state will pay 100 percent and Manchester, nothing.

The brown-headed cowbird does not parasitize other birds' nests maliciously; it is simply doing what it is genetically programmed to do. As long as good habitat remains, the ecological controls that govern species will find a balance between cowbirds and their hosts. It is when such habitat is whittled away that the checks and balances are lost, and the aggressor comes to dominate.

Similarly, there is a place and role for the low-density suburb and the benefits it brings, just as there has long been an honored role for its predecessor—the compact, traditional suburban neighborhood. That form of neighborhood came into its own in the late nineteenth and early twentieth centuries along with the trolley. The trolley suburb changed the city, but the two happened to work synergistically, and an equilibrium emerged. The fixed rail of the trolley served as a constraint on suburban expansion, and it created a two-way relationship between city and suburb, in which suburbanites were economically tied to central business districts. During this time the great city department stores prospered.

In our contemporary, built landscape, however, there are no checks and balances; indeed, from technology to public subsidies and land use laws, there are only incentives to expand—to push the suburban-rural edge ever outward. The result over the last forty years has been a slow and remorseless transition from a landscape organized for production to one organized for consumption. The low-density suburban residential landscape is not necessarily unsightly (though its commercial counterpart always is); but it is a landscape full of risk. It reduces and grossly simplifies wildlife habitat. It pollutes water and air, causes traffic congestion, and drives the consumption of energy and other resources. It demands redundancy in government and public facilities, fuels property taxes, and soaks the treasury. It drains urban places of vitality, even as it places new demands on them from commuters and others who use urban services but pay their taxes elsewhere.

The Suburban Mandate

As of this decade, the statistics show that we still have time to put checks and balances into place. Even in southern and mid-coast Maine, there is still time. Why don't we do so?

For one thing, the impacts accrue very slowly—one cowbird at a time, so to speak. By the time a problem arises, such as high property taxes in a once-rural place, or the closing of a neighborhood school or church in an urban center, enough time has gone by between the inception and the recognition of the problem that we don't connect the dots. When a large Catholic church, a landmark on the Portland peninsula, closed several years ago, who linked it to state school and road subsidies in the emerging suburbs?

Some of the cause-and-effect is direct, but dimmed by time. For example, in 1970 the Town of Standish was still a rural town of 3,100 people living in an area of 64 square miles. It comprised three villages or hamlets with a range of small businesses and services for residents and visitors, and a large hinterland of forest, orchards, and lakes, including the water supply for Greater Portland. It was governed by a board of selectmen, and many town staff wore more than one hat. At the time, local expenditures from tax dollars amounted to about $900 per capita.

Suburbanization was just beginning to expand to the second tier of towns outside of Portland, including Standish. Standish absorbed this growth "at the margin"—that is, making do with the personnel, municipal facilities, and services it already had. By 1984, population had doubled to 6,600; but because it had made do, and with the help of school and other subsidies from state government, the cost of local government per capita from local sources had dropped to about $500.

That is where Standish's costs bottomed out. By 1984, the town's capacity for governance had been saturated; now, it was functionally a suburb, both in services demanded and in its commuter economy. The governmental structure had to change (to a town manager form), and services expanded to meet the new demands; and *per capita* local costs have increased more or less regularly, ever since. By 2000, with population more than 9,000, the expenditures per capita (after adjusting for inflation) had returned to their 1970 levels and were still rising. It is unlikely that those moving to Standish over the last fifteen to thirty years connect their decisions to move with Standish's rising taxes.

Local decision makers, meanwhile, either accept rising costs as the fate of a suburbanizing town or place the blame on outside forces, such as insufficient state school aid. The perspective of state decision-makers, who are preparing to build a multi-million-dollar bypass between Standish and Portland, isn't much broader. In neither case is sprawl identified as the cause for which a solution must be found and aggressively implemented. Only recently has an official body, the Portland Area Comprehensive Transportation Committee, formally drawn the connection, but it has limited leverage over local land use decisions,

The reason for lack of action is more fundamental than this, however; and it has to do with how we think about "density"—or what we think is the right and appropriate number of people or houses to be located near us, within our personal territories. This thinking has not changed over the last forty years; if anything, it has calcified into a mandate to sprawl.

On the one hand, we hold to certain old myths about high density. These are myths about disease, traffic congestion, and social dysfunction, such as crime. These concerns are part of the very rationale for public regulations that mandate a low-density, inefficient, and costly suburban style of land use. Anti-density sentiments are already old in the United States. They especially arose from the abusive heyday of the industrial revolution; and from the racism that accompanied migrations of southern Blacks and eastern European Jews to northern cities during the late nineteenth and early twentieth centuries. It is not a coincidence that American zoning had its origins during this time.

By the 1970s and '80s, most of the industrial revolution's public health and safety concerns had been addressed through building and fire codes, technology, public health and sanitation, and pollution controls including enactment of the Clean Water Act. There were other events in the 1960s, however, with long-term effects on our attitudes toward living compactly. In particular, two great social movements left a legacy that now shapes our cities and countryside. These were the civil rights movement and the zero population and environmental movements. In addition to their enormously important legacies of social justice and environmental consciousness, each had the ironic effects of confirming the density myths and sanctioning sprawl.

The racial unrest of the 1960s in the central cities was interpreted to be not only the result of social injustices, but also of crowding and high residential densities.[13] In Maine this attitude led to prescriptions of lower densities in the suburbs of the southern and coastal regions, in order to exclude both the conventionally accepted notion of crowding and, not incidentally, low-income households, or at least those who could not afford to buy single-family homes

Belfast

financed by the Farmers Home Administration. In 1975, for example, my city of South Portland cut allowable single-family residential densities that had stood for many years by more than half, from a traditional suburban density of six to eight units per acre to two to four units per acre. By 1989, the town of Cumberland had reduced the allowable density for sewered lots by seven-fold, from seven units per acre to one unit per acre, with even larger lots required in the traditional neighborhood known as Wildwood Park.[14]

To many suburban zoners, this seemed the right prescription for the environment, as well: spreading out would lighten the impact on the environment and in any case would slow down growth. It was the terrestrial version of "the solution to pollution is dilution." It also would safely accommodate growth that relied on privately built and maintained underground septic systems, which need space to create safe distances from drinking water supplied by wells. (The state prescribes one-half acre, but most municipalities with zoning or minimum lot size ordinances go multiples larger.)

Spreading out on large lots saved the town from the headache of extending and maintaining publicly financed sewer systems. So there is a strong predisposition against allowing densities of more than one dwelling unit for each one or two acres. But there also is strong predisposition against requiring *very* low densities—say, one home per twenty-five acres—that would so restrict development of rural lands that they would be regarded as a violation of property rights.

Lost in all this is the reality that manmade systems—transportation, utilities, downtowns, affordable housing, and many public and private institutions—require certain thresholds of density in order to function well and economically. All indications are that in the small cities and towns that make up most of northern New England, these thresholds are in the range of three to eight dwelling units per acre. At the same time, natural systems and the production that depends on them need the opposite—very low densities—to preserve their functions. All indications are that they cannot easily tolerate more than one home per 20 or 25 acres, organized to preserve blocks of land at least 100 to 500 acres in size. *Suburban densities fall woefully in between what is required by either manmade or natural systems, severely compromising both.*

Still, suburban densities of one home every acre or two rule the day because they match up perfectly with three sets of values. First, they provide for equal treatment among landowners, allowing each roughly the same opportunity to cash in on his or her land—even if their lands are different in natural capacity and location. Second, they quietly enforce economic exclusion, serving the desire among many homeowners for a sense of security from unwanted uses and people. Third, by segmenting open space into private one- or two-acre chunks, suburban density requirements provide a buffer around individual homes from the nuisances of everyday life—at least until the ATVs show up.

So far, these essentially private values trump public values, such as choice of housing, choice in transportation, lower property taxes, good downtowns, and a sustained natural environment. Perhaps this is because the role of sprawl in eroding these public values is not yet obvious. I refer you back to our earlier discussion of the incremental nature of sprawl and not connecting the dots. Or, perhaps it is a playing out of Hardin's "tragedy of the commons," in which one is more or less aware of the eventual public consequences but, lacking outside constraints, is compelled by much more immediate self-interest to make what appears to be a rational individual decision.

In any case, the rationales of the 1960s' worries about moderate densities leading to crowding, social pathologies, and environmental damage persist to this day. They have provided the necessary legal cover to justify uniform, one-size-fits-all, low-density zoning, to sanction its spread everywhere, and to resist any reasonable checks and balances.

Responding to the Challenge

This is not to say that between 1960 and today no one has recognized the problem; many have. The fact that they (that is, we) have not made much of a difference yet does not mean Mainers will fail to take corrective action over the next decade. The cumulative impacts of sprawl began to be noticed in Maine in the mid-1980s, and since then several foundations for change have been laid. Among the most important are the following five, in rough chronological order:

First was enactment in 1988 of the state's Growth Management Act during the administration of Republican John McKernan. Though it evolved into a largely voluntary piece of legislation, it elevated the role of local comprehensive planning. It specifically set as a goal in state law the prevention of development sprawl, and it re-established a legitimate state interest in town planning and development. Of particular note are these provisions of the law:

• Municipalities are not required to have zoning or land use regulation beyond basic shoreland zoning and review of subdivisions. However, if they choose to have townwide zoning or similar regulations, they must first adopt a comprehensive plan that the state finds consistent with the ten statewide goals contained in the law. This includes the goals of orderly development, efficient use of public facilities, and preventing development sprawl.

• To be consistent with the law, a comprehensive plan must, among other things, designate "growth" areas and "rural" areas. The growth areas are intended to match up with the best development conditions and available public services in the town. The rural areas are intended to be protected from significant new development, so that they may continue to support an array of rural and natural resource functions. Since the early 1990s, suburban and suburbanizing communities have done an increasingly good job of identifying such areas in their plans; but no more than a handful, and perhaps not even that many, have meaningfully implemented them.

- Until recently, there has been no consequence for failing to implement a plan. However, the law set January 1, 2003, as the deadline by which all provisions of townwide zoning ordinances, impact fee ordinances, and rate of growth ordinances must be consistent with approved and adopted comprehensive plans. Any provision that is not consistent "is no longer in effect."[15] This requirement of the law is not self-executing. However, an aggrieved property owner (or other person with standing) may sue in court to nullify an inconsistent provision of one of the subject ordinances. The first such suit was filed in the Fall of 2003 to allow a "traditional," compact neighborhood development to proceed in the Dunstan Corner area of Scarborough, as prescribed by the town's comprehensive plan but prohibited by the zoning ordinance.

- The Growth Management Act also includes a directive that the state has given itself. In 2000, the legislature amended the act to require that state office and civic buildings and certain other state "growth-related investments" must be located in downtowns and other locally designated growth areas. Such facilities had been leaking out to the edges of towns for many years, stimulating the very growth patterns that the Growth Management Act tries to slow or reverse. The 2000 amendments were a statement that the state intended to get its own house into better order. Since then, regional human services offices, courthouses, and other state facilities and investments have been redirected to a variety of downtowns.

Second in the chronology of important actions and trends has been the rise of local and regional land trusts as forces in the land preservation movement. Though a number of local land trusts have existed for years, they came into their own during the 1990s. Besides statewide organizations such as The Nature Conservancy and the Maine Coast Heritage Trust, there are now ninety-five local land trusts. They are evidence of the public's commitment to funding land preservation, including $88 million through the Land for Maine's Future Program since it was established in 1987.

The land trusts are not yet effective agents for stemming sprawl. Their focus has been on unique lands or lands of particular natural resource or amenity value, not on the greenbelt-types of purchases that will contain sprawl. Sometimes they have been motivated more by a NIMBYism that promotes rather than contains sprawl; but the network of land trusts holds enormous potential to check the unbridled conversion of rural land to suburban use.

Third was an environmental risk project sponsored by the state and carried out in the first half of the 1990s by the organization Eco-Eco. Eco-Eco is a coalition of environmental and business interests sponsored by the College of the Atlantic and directed by Theodore Koffman, now a state legislator and co-chair of the Natural Resources Committee. Though the results of Eco-Eco's analysis of environmental risks are fading with time, it produced a lasting result. For the first time it fixed in the minds of the major environmental organizations of the state that our spreading-out pattern of development underlies several of the high-risk areas of the environment, including pollution of groundwater, fertilization of lakes and estuaries, nonpoint source air pollution, and loss of wildlife habitat.

Each of the organizations now has sprawl on its agenda. Meanwhile, a new statewide organization, GrowSmart Maine, whose members include some of the same mix of environmental, natural resource, and business interests who made the environmental risk project possible, has made finding alternatives to sprawl its sole mission.

Fourth is the political organization of the *service center* communities. As a whole, these communities have property tax burdens and rates of poverty well above their suburban neighbors. Yet public policy treats them as if they were still centers of personal wealth, and the suburbs as if they were still poor country cousins. The taxpayers of the hub communities are called upon to subsidize many of the suburban demands for services—from sheriff patrols to new schools—while also carrying their own. There are signs that the hub communities have had enough. In 2001 they formally organized into a political coalition.

As it turns out, the self-interests of the service center communities line up well with the goal of reducing suburban sprawl. They are arguing that the state should level the financial playing field among municipal governments; that is, that urban-to-suburban subsidies should be reduced; and certain costs that service centers bear disproportionately on behalf of the larger regions they anchor—such as special education costs and services to property tax exempt institutions—should be relieved or reimbursed. They endorse a reorganization of the delivery of public services to achieve efficiencies; and they advocate lowering barriers to compact, mixed-use developments.[16]

Fifth is the rebirth of one form of compact, mixed-use development, what has come to be known as the Great American Neighborhood. If there is to be a check on sprawl, the public has to be convinced that there is an alternative—one that doesn't just say "more density," but also says, "good design." The alternative to sprawl cannot be sold if it means sacrificing the goals of the suburbanite: control over one's surroundings, access to open space, and a good place to raise a family.

The State Planning Office, drawing on the tradition of many good neighborhoods in small-town Maine, as well as the "new urbanist" movement in small-town design elsewhere in the country, has introduced such a blueprint. Developers want to build it and the market is ready to buy it.[17] The hallmark of the Great American Neighborhood is a mix of homes, civic buildings, and neighborhood businesses, arrayed around open spaces and along protected, interconnected streets—all within a ten-minute diameter.

One of the remaining high hurdles is the suburban zoning ordinances that systematically ban such new neighborhoods. To lift the ban, towns will need to allow at least moderate residential densities (two to eight units per residential acre) in town centers and other appropriate areas; repeal the current stock of dimensional standards that end up creating tract subdivisions (such as frontage requirements, setbacks, and street specifications), and replace them with more carefully considered design and open-space standards; and allow a modest variety of everyday, small-scale activities within walking distance of people's homes.

How do you know if you've achieved a small town Great American Neighborhood? Landscape architect Anton Nelessen uses the "Grandpa and Jennifer" test. Good design requires that you should be able to answer "yes" to three questions:

- Can Grandpa and Jennifer live in the same community at the same time?

- Can Grandpa and Jennifer walk downtown safely and comfortably? and

- Will Grandpa find a safe, convenient place to sit down and meet his friends, while Jennifer finds something to keep her occupied?"[18]

Being able to answer "yes" doesn't sound so dangerous that municipal zoning ordinances should ban it.

Conclusions
Whether an effective counterattack on sprawl takes shape over the next decade depends on seeing the low-density suburb in a more complete light. The low-density suburb is a middle landscape where Maine's personal wealth is now concentrated, an attribute of which is a lifestyle that emphasizes family, privacy, open space, and sameness; has the power to out-compete rural uses like woodlots, farms, and wildlife habitat, and will whenever the opportunity arises; still depends on urban centers for jobs and services; and has the political power and, as a rural impostor, the guise and guile to extract subsidies from its neighbors, even those that are less well off—subsidies that feed the cycle of sprawl.

If we, as a state, wanted to find three ways to build in checks and balances in this suburbanizing landscape, they would be:

- *First, squeeze the state subsidies out of sprawl.* This will be politically difficult and perhaps impossible because the balance of political power now rests in the suburbs. It will happen only if rural legislators finally see the difference between rural and suburban—if they finally spot the cowbirds among them— and ally themselves with service center legislators out of common interest to form an urban-rural majority.

- *Second, plan, tax, and regulate land on a regional basis,* at a scale that gives the low-density suburb its due but that also protects expanses of rural lands and keeps hub communities vital. These need not be large regions that create distance between the people and their local governments. Small groupings of municipalities, treating land under a single set of rules and tax policies, will work. In the spring of 2003, Governor John Baldacci proposed a frame-work for such small, voluntary regional governments as a strategy for lower-ing the cost of local government.[19] Efficient, lower-cost government and "smart growth" have much in common.

- *Third, reform exclusionary zoning ordinances to increase the choice of housing and lifestyle.* If necessary, we should enact state law to end the ban on well-designed, environmentally responsible, traditional neighborhood develop-ment—developments we have no business prohibiting under the guise of protecting public health, safety, and welfare.

In 1829 Moses Greenleaf, in his *Survey of the State of Maine,* wrote that there would come a time when the population of Maine would no longer be able to "diffuse itself at pleasure."[20] He didn't predict when that time would come; but, 175 years later, it has arrived. The way a society uses its land is the best reflection of the values that it holds dear. From now on, the public debate must be about the right balance between often conflicting values—values bound up in lands organized for production and exchange versus land organized for consumption.

*E*van D. Richert, AICP, is associate research professor in the Muskie School, where he directs the Gulf of Maine Program of the Census of Marine Life, teaches graduate courses in community planning and development, and is a consultant to state and local governments. From 1995 to 2002, Evan served as director of the Maine State Planning Office, where he also chaired the Land for Maine's Future Board and the Land and Water Resources Council. Prior to his appointment to the State Planning Office, he was co-owner and president of Market Decisions, Inc., a planning consulting firm, and was planning director for the City of South Portland, Maine.

M AINE HAS A LONG-STANDING REPUTATION as an inspirational
environment for artistic creation, beginning with the rich artisan
tradition of Maine's Native Americans. As a state of artists, craftspeople, and institutions that support them, Maine has nurtured writers,
visual artists, performing artists, musicians, and artisans in communities
all across the state. In the last third of the twentieth century, growth in
the state's arts community was stimulated by the creation of the National Endowments for the Arts and the Humanities under President
Lyndon B. Johnson. The Maine Arts Commission, created in 1965,
channeled state and federal resources into support for arts organizations
in Maine's communities. The result is a strong, statewide arts and culture infrastructure, one that positions Maine communities to take
advantage of the emerging national focus on the "creative economy."
Support for the arts translates into dollars, and trends indicate that
Maine's economic future will be closely tied to continuing investment
in the state's artistic and cultural heritage.

12 Maine Arts and Culture
The Emergence of a New Force

ALDEN WILSON

In this chapter I will consider the growth of the arts in Maine over the past forty years and the challenges faced by artists and by the arts and cultural community. I will look at this growth in terms of the roles played by artists, arts and cultural institutions, community interests, and the public sector. Second, I will look at the emergence of what is today known as the "creative economy," and how Maine is providing leadership in forwarding a new agenda to connect our state's arts and cultural community to Maine's future economic well-being. Finally, I will offer some suggestions for how Maine's cultural life may play a greater role in the state's well-being in this first decade of the twenty-first century, as we enter what is a new beginning for cultural affairs in Maine.

While this chapter is primarily about the arts, and particularly our public arts sector, I hope in its course to show the linkages among all our cultural sectors: the fine, applied, and performing arts; our libraries, museums and archival concerns; historic preservation of our architectural heritage; and the legacy of history and the humanities.

In the Beginning

Let me begin with consideration of Maine's rich cultural history. Maine is a state of artists and craftspeople and the institutions that support them. It has always been this way; it is a part of our heritage and our abiding sense of place. Our indigenous people of the Abenaki created useful items of hand manufacture for clothing, industry, hunting, and fishing that are now treasured as objects of great beauty. The state's Native American basket-making tradition, for example, prospers to this day in large part thanks to the Maine Indian Basketmakers Alliance, which not only encourages the continuity of the tradition, but also develops marketing strategies to bring more attention to Maine's rich native traditions, similar to what has been done in both the American Southwest and Northwest.

These Native American traditions have been maintained through mentoring and apprenticeship programs that have not only passed on the basket-making traditions but also begun to reach other areas of Native American arts and industry, such as birchbark canoe-making. So, too, has Maine Native American language, song, and dance been preserved through the simple process of mentoring younger generations to carry on traditions thousands of years old. This Native American work has provided a successful mentoring model for other folk traditions in Maine, such as Franco-American fiddling and step-dancing; song, storytelling, and carving from the Maine woods; and expressions of art forms by Maine's new immigrants from Southeast Asia and Africa.

Following European exploration and settlement in Maine, the new arrivals' arts and cultural expressions were created early on. An unknown English artist painted a young Native American woman in 1605, and the portrait, now in England, may be the first European portrait of a Mainer. A sketch by John Hunt depicts the 1607 settlement at the mouth of the Kennebec River; the settlement lasted but one year. In 1766 a subscription library was founded at Falmouth Neck (now Portland). In 1785 composer Supply Belcher settled in Hallowell and later in Farmington, and published a collection of musical compositions in 1794, *The Harmony of Maine*. Maine's first theater opened in Portland in 1794. Sally Wood of York wrote Maine's first novel in1800.

In the performing arts, the Handel Society of Maine was founded in Hallowell in 1815, becoming the then District of Maine's first district-wide cultural organization. In the same year, the Maine Charitable Mechanic Association was founded by craftsmen, and the organization began the new state's first arts, craft, and invention exhibitions in 1826. The Maine Historical Society was founded in 1822 and the Portland Society of Art—later to become two organizations, the Portland Museum of Art and the Maine College of Art—was established in 1882.[1] Maine state government also recognized the need for opinions about arts matters, and in 1933 created an advisory body, the Maine Art Commission, to advise the governor on the selection or purchase of art.

Until recent decades, Maine's artistic life may have been best known by the artists whose work relates directly to the landscape and the sea. We think of naturalist John James Audubon, who came to Maine in the first half of the nineteenth century; or of Thomas Cole, whose dramatic landscapes helped to attract the "rusticators," Maine's first tourist trade, to Bar Harbor. It would be difficult to think of Maine's mark in the world without John Marin, Andrew Wyeth, Berenice Abbott, Marsden Hartley, Fairfield Porter, Louise Nevelson, Edna St. Vincent Millay (who won the Pulitzer Prize in 1923), or Edwin Arlington Robinson (who won three Pulitzers).

In 1960 Maine had several college museums with important collections, a few summer theaters, and two year-round, if not yet professional symphony orchestras, but not one year-round commercial art gallery or community arts council.[2] Maine was then best known nationally for its superb summer arts institutions, training schools, and places to experiment with new art that even today attract the best faculties and students in the arts. In the visual arts, the faculty and students of Skowhegan School of Painting and Sculpture, founded in 1946, reads as a who's who of movers and shakers in the visual arts at a time when America was leading the world in contemporary painting and sculpture.

Haystack Mountain School of Crafts, founded in Montville in 1950 as an off-shoot of the 1920s and 1930s hand-crafts revival movement, relocated to a new campus on Deer Isle and quickly became a leader in the nascent movement of craft as art.

In the performing arts, there were institutions of equal stature. The Domaine School, founded by Parisian Conductor Pierre Monteux in 1943, opened to train conductors and orchestral players. Kneisel Hall, founded by internationally acclaimed violinist Franz Kneisel, has roots to 1903, and continues a tradition of chamber music training steeped in artistic excellence.

These summer-based institutions have had much to do with the changing image and nature of the artist community in Maine—from the image of the summer artist "from away" to a year-round community of artists who chose to stay and settle here. Consider the case of one internationally prominent artist, Robert Indiana, one of the creators of the Pop Art movement, and whose "LOVE" with tilted "O" is one of the best known symbols in American art. Robert Indiana came to Maine by train in the 1950s to attend the Skowhegan School. In a recent ceremony at the state house, where Indiana's works were exhibited in both the governor's and legislative galleries, Governor John E. Baldacci introduced Indiana and celebrated his many productive years in Maine.

Indiana has been based on Vinalhaven Island for over twenty-five years, a longer term period, he observes, than in his native Indiana or New York City. He is, no doubt, one of the state's best-known, year-round resident painters and sculptors. As Christine Vincent, president of Maine College of Art, has stated, "In terms of its present-day artistic legacy, Maine has few equals…. It stands with the Hudson Valley, Santa Fe, and Northern California as a place where artists have been inspired. Is there a state in the nation whose identity has been more defined in the eyes of the world by artists than Maine?"[3]

Culture Puts Down Roots
In the 1970s, Maine's arts and cultural scene became more community-based and visible throughout the state. This growth came rapidly. The Portland Symphony Orchestra that had professionalized in the early 1960s became one of the state's largest cultural institutions. Just a few of the institutions that emerged during this period were the Shakespearean Theater at Monmouth, in 1971; Maine's first local government-sanctioned community arts council, L/A Arts in Lewiston-Auburn, in 1973; and the year-round Profile Theater Company, now Portland Stage Company, in 1975. Both the newer and older organizations became more professional in terms of the quality of their artistic endeavors and their business practices.

This growth has continued to the present time. In literature, for example, *The Beloit Poetry Journal*, with deep roots in Maine, has been located here for two decades. It is regarded as one of the chief outlets for emerging as well as established poets in America. Similarly, Alice James Books, originally established in 1973, moved to Maine in 1994 and has achieved a reputation for publishing poetry of extraordinary literary quality. Continuing the tradition of Maine's summer institutes in the arts, Stonecoast Writers Conference in Brunswick and Freeport celebrates its twenty-fifth year in 2004, as it continues to bring well-known and developing writers, poets, and teachers to its summer training sessions and offers a MFA program.

Bates Dance Festival, at Bates College in Lewiston, brings together an international community of choreographers, performers, educators and students dedicated to the practice and presentation of the best in contemporary dance. Music traditions established by the Domaine School and Kneisel Hall continue with the Bowdoin International Music Festival, now with a new name and mission, and with performance-based organizations such as Saco River Festival in Kezar Falls, the Sebago-Long Lake Chamber Music Festival, and the DaPonte String Quartet, which had its Maine beginnings in1995.

There also developed the beginning of *communities of interest* within arts and cultural disciplines. Maine Preservation was founded in 1971 to advocate for the preservation of Maine's remarkable architectural heritage. In the museum and historical society field, the Maine League of Historical Societies and Museums became dormant in the 1980s and was revived in the last decade with a new structure, Maine Archives and Museums, that added the concerns of archivists. The Maine Alliance for Arts Education was founded in 1973 to provide an advocacy voice for statewide arts education. Similarly, to serve growing numbers of artists and their needs to communicate among themselves and with the public, the Maine Writers and Publishers Alliance was created in 1975, and the Maine Crafts Association, in 1983.

Perhaps it is obvious, but since the 1970s cultural organizations have sprung up in *all* parts of the state—not just in the expected locations in southern Maine, Portland, Bangor, and the midcoast, but also in many other communities like Eastport, Calais, the St. John Valley, Dover-Foxcroft, Norway-South Paris, Gardiner, Lewiston, and Waterville. So, too, is arts and cultural activity prevalent throughout Maine in all the artistic disciplines of the performing arts, the visual arts and crafts, the literary arts, and multi-media. Artists live in every county in Maine. While there is a concentration of artists in our cities, along the coast, and near the locations of the artist-training institutions such as Haystack Mountain School and Skowhegan School, artists in rural areas are as much a part of the Maine cultural community as are our more visible communities of artists.

A study of Maine's nonprofit cultural organizations, conducted by the New England Foundation for the Arts for the year 2000, shows that the nonprofit creative sector comprised some 1,284 organizations; provided 4,056 full-time equivalent jobs, of which 2,338 were artists; and had attendance at events of 4,223,509 people, or about four times the state's population. These institutions also enjoyed the leadership and hard work of over 18,000 volunteers. They spent a total of $146 million, of which $49.9 million was for salaries and $96.1 million was for other operating expenses. They received $179 million in income, of which $69.3 million was private contributions, $29.9 million was government contributions, and $79.7 million derived from other sources. Of the total, 24.3 percent came from out-of-state sources. The total economic impact of the nonprofit arts and culture segment in Maine for 2000 was $211.6 million, including indirect and induced spending of $65.6 million.[4]

The Federal Stimulus and Influence

Much of the growth in Maine's arts community was stimulated by President Lyndon B. Johnson's Great Society program, and the creation of the National Foundation for the Arts and Humanities in 1966. The foundation consisted of two publicly funded endowments: the National Endowment for the Arts, and the National Endowment for the Humanities. A vital provision of the law set aside funds for the states to create their *own* governmental state arts agencies; and a percentage of the total congressional appropriation to be allocated by formula directly to those state arts agencies. In 1964 just nine states had state arts agencies; by 1967 all fifty had a state arts agency with some degree of effectiveness, most with enabling legislation, and over half with state appropriations.[5]

Maine's state arts agency, the Maine State Commission on the Arts and the Humanities, now the Maine Arts Commission, was established in 1965, with $25,000 from the National Endowment and $10,000 from the state's General Fund. With the exception of the state of Vermont, which to this day has a nonprofit organization as its designated state arts agency, a direct funding and program planning relationship now existed between the federal government and the new state government arts agencies. Most states, including Maine, patterned their programming and decision-making after the National Endowment for the Arts, itself. Programming included support for programs and projects of excellence, and arts education and decisions were made by peer review panels in the arts disciplines.

As state arts agency collective appropriations came to outstrip federal allocations, however, some state arts agencies moved away from the federal program support; still, all have retained some form of peer review and a close planning partnership with the National Endowment. Maine's approach, especially in recent years, has been radically different from other state arts agencies in order to meet the special qualities that drive Maine's state and local community interests.

The National Endowment for the Humanities developed a somewhat different relationship with the states. Three initial structures for state-based programs were established, one each with state agencies such as Maine's state arts and humanities commission; universities; and independent, nonprofit organizations.

From the beginning, the humanities programs were much more directed from the National Endowment. Upon my arrival at the Maine State Commission on the Arts and the Humanities in 1971, for example, the humanities program was *required* to address public policy issues in the humanities. Since the arts programs enjoyed more flexibility and a larger constituency than the humanities, tension arose between the two program areas. This was deepened by the more directed program control placed on the humanities program from the National Endowment for the Humanities than was the case with the arts.

By 1974 a different accommodation for the humanities needed to be created. In June of that year, by invitation of the National Endowment for the Humanities, the humanities program was separated from the Maine State Commission on the Arts and Humanities, and became an independent public enterprise bearing no organizational relationship to state government.

In 1975 the Maine Humanities Council was established as a nonprofit organization. What is now the Maine Arts Commission retained "humanities" in its title but carried out minimal humanities programming or support for historical concerns. In 1986 the legislature authorized a name change to make a clear distinction between the state government agency for the arts, the Maine Arts Commission, and the private, nonprofit Maine Humanities Council. In the intervening twenty years the arts and humanities agencies have, nonetheless, retained a close working arrangement, especially in the last decade with the able leadership of Dorothy Schwartz, the Maine Humanities Council executive director.

The Maine Arts Commission

As federal and state financial resources grew, the Maine Arts Commission put its efforts into helping existing arts institutions, through a program of matching grants. Typical grants in the 1970s and '80s included support for the exhibitions or performances of the Portland Symphony Orchestra, the Bangor Symphony Orchestra, Portland Stage Company, the Portland Museum of Art, Bay Chamber Concerts in Rockport, Maine State Music Theater in Brunswick, and the Maine Maritime Museum in Bath.

Some institutions received substantial funding, in excess of $20,000, a large amount given the resources available at the time. With special funding and encouragement from the National Endowment for the Arts, Maine embarked upon a matching grant program to bring artists in all disciplines into Maine's public schools for short- and long-term residencies. As with institutional funding, the Maine Arts Commission accepted applications from throughout the state, and awarded grants based on program and artistic merit.

By the early '90s this system of support, used by most state arts agencies, showed major signs of strain. The arts community had grown in the number of organizations vying for limited resources. When the Maine Arts Commission's grant programs were first established, there were no community arts councils; now, there were over twenty. The performing and exhibiting arts institutions had grown dramatically, and had greater expectations of the commission to provide support on an ongoing basis, as opposed to a project basis.

It grew clear that the commission was not reaching the entire state with its artist-in-education programs; the schools with the best grant writers were the ones receiving the funding. While high-quality arts programs continued to be funded, the arts community was increasingly dissatisfied with a system that had become so highly competitive that it was difficult to judge one grant project over another. Most importantly from a state perspective, the old system was doing nothing to build a *statewide* community in the arts and culture. In fact, quite the opposite was taking place: given the existing funding mechanisms, one organization was pitted against another.

The "Culture Wars" of the '90s

By the mid-1990s two other developments had taken place, with a major impact on how the Maine Arts Commission would provide support for the state's arts community. The first, colloquially known as "The Culture Wars," was a direct result of the reaction by certain congressional leaders to projects funded by or thought to be funded by the National Endowment for the Arts. Photographer Andreas Serrano's *Piss Christ*, an image of a crucified Christ figure in a container of urine, and Robert Mapplethorpe's homoerotic photographs became the bellwether images for congressional attacks on the National Endowment.

The National Endowment's budget was slashed, and the states suffered the consequences. Since 40 percent of the program funding for the National Endowment is allocated by formula to the state arts agencies, the Maine Arts Commission lost $400,000 overnight, and a similar amount was lost in *direct* National Endowment grants to Maine arts organizations.

A second development had to do with the state budget crises that took place shortly after The Culture Wars. In the early '90s, Maine state government faced the most serious state budget fiscal situation in a generation, precipitating major cutbacks in services and funding. The Maine Arts Commission lost 30 percent of its staff and 40 percent of its General Fund appropriation.

This led to a series of public meetings and a controversial decision, in 1995, to postpone grant-making as it had been known and devise a new way of supporting the arts and culture in Maine. At the heart of this change, as it evolved, was the principle of *investing in local cultural development, by helping communities to define themselves culturally.*

The Maine Arts Commission began to see its role less as a funding agency and part of the arts community, and more as a cultural community development agency that could assist in community-building through the arts and culture. The commission made the policy change from competitive grant-making, not without considerable displeasure within the arts organizations the commission had supported in the past. This policy change, now nearly ten years old, distinguishes the Maine Arts Commission from other state arts agencies, and has led to increased visibility for the arts in Maine, more state funding, and greater national attention.

Discovery Research

The most significant program development since the commission's change in direction has been the Discovery Research process. This program has helped communities develop cultural inventories, strategies, and structures that serve to sustain the community's cultural development. The Discovery Research effort, now embracing over 60 percent of the state geographically, provides in-depth information about artists, arts organizations, and arts- and culture-related businesses; and builds greater communication and collaboration among these cultural interests.

Discovery Research communities publish directories of cultural resources and establish websites about these resources. Increasingly, they organize to learn from one another, and web-based technology is being developed to assist this communication. The publication of directories and creation of websites often seem the most tangible products of Discovery Research, but the most significant outcome is the coming together to identify common community concerns that may be addressed through the arts and culture.

Aroostook County, for example, has completed three Discovery Research projects, one in the Houlton Area, a central Aroostook project centered on Presque Isle, and a third in the St. John Valley, where Discovery Research has led to a focus on better interpretation of Acadian culture for visitors to the area. Among the products is a cultural tourism guide for service vendors—waiters and waitresses, service station attendants, and shop clerks—on the interpretation of Acadian heritage and the location of historic sites. It is a handy reference guide when these vendors are asked questions by travelers. Brunswick's Discovery Research has developed a family arts festival and a holiday gallery weekend, and attracted both office space and an appropriation from the town government.

Other participants in Discovery Research are Bridgton, southern York County, Waldo County, Knox County, Hancock County, Piscataquis County, part of Washington County, Portland, Waterville, Lewiston-Auburn, Bangor,

Lincoln, Biddeford-Saco, and two regions of western Maine. Communities of interest have also participated. A recent grant was awarded to the Center for Cultural Exchange in Portland, to conduct an inventory and assessment of needs within the Latino community. The clay community, from historic brick-works to contemporary pottery making, was studied by another of Maine's internationally known summer-arts training institutions, Watershed Center for the Ceramic Arts in Newcastle. From this, the "Mudmobile" was created and now travels with expert teachers to schools and workshops throughout Maine.

As we will see later, Discovery Research has become an important link to Maine's involvement with the developing creative economy. Through Discovery Research, we have learned about cultural resources throughout the state, in both an empirical and anecdotal manner. This information demonstrates that not only are the arts and culture located everywhere in the state, but that they are vital in all their manifestations: America's artistic heritage, contemporary arts practice, the passing down of folk traditions, and the respect for classical traditions from other cultures.

Maine Public Leadership

Before I turn to activities shared among a broad range of Maine's cultural interests, it is appropriate to cite how our elected officials have exercised leadership in cultural affairs. In 1979, the legislature created Maine's Percent for Art Law, which provides that 1 percent of public building construction be used for the commissioning or purchase of works of art. Since then, the cities of Portland and Bangor have created their own public art policies and procedures. About half of the fifty states now have public art laws, but Maine's differs in that public schools may participate at their option. About 95 percent of Maine's elementary and secondary schools opt to commission Maine artists' works in their new or renovated buildings. Since the law was passed, over $7 million in commissions has been allotted to more than 400 projects statewide.

In the late '70s, the legislature made it illegal to deface works of art in public settings. The legislature also made it possible, in 1979, for the heirs of artists to pay state inheritance taxes with works of art, rather than in dollars. This deals with the problem of heirs who may have had large inventories of an artist's work but insufficient funds to pay inheritance taxes. Prior to the law, heirs often had to flood the market with art, at prices far below what fair market value would normally bring. The law helped the heirs and Maine both to benefit from art placed in public locations throughout the state.

It would be inaccurate to claim that the public sector led private sector development in the arts and culture; but it is unlikely that the reach of cultural development in Maine would have taken place without state leadership, a statewide process, and subsequent public-private collaboration. Perhaps nowhere is this more evident than in the creation in 1989, as the result of a Joint Select Study Committee on Cultural Resources, of the Cultural Affairs Council. The Cultural Affairs Council was initially comprised of the Maine Arts Commission, Maine State Library, Maine State Museum, and Maine Historic Preservation Commission, bringing the state's major cultural agencies under one umbrella. The council was subsequently expanded to include the Maine State Archives, Maine Humanities Council, and Maine Historical Society.

The enabling legislation maintained the independence of each agency's programs, many of which are federally mandated, centralized business and personnel functions, and made two simple requirements: that the council plan its separate programs together and that it present their budgets jointly to the legislature. The statute balances the need for specificity in cultural fields—the need to understand library science, how records and objects should be preserved, how historic buildings should be restored, and how literacy may be enhanced and creativity fostered—with the needs to create strong, statewide alliances and to speak with one voice on cultural matters.

The most visible example of what the Cultural Affairs Council has achieved is the New Century Community Program. This program, created by the legislature in 2000, provided $3.2 million for the council to use in outreach grants and services to strengthen the state's cultural infrastructure. The next year, another $1 million was added. For the first time, the members of the Council and their broad constituencies joined in one legislative plan and spoke with one voice. An extensive grassroots advocacy effort combined with sponsorship from legislative leaders to assure passage of the legislation.

The products of the New Century Community Program are extraordinary. Buildings are restored, records and objects are preserved, library services reach a broader public, and arts and humanities programs strengthen local organizations that deliver cultural services. From the initial $3.2 million appropriation, 742 projects and services were supported in 183 communities in every region of the state. These grants and services leveraged another $9 million in local cash-match and $1.3 million in in-kind services.[6]

Others beyond Maine took notice of not only Maine's cultural achievements, but also of the manner in which a coordinated approach at the state level had made these achievements possible. The Pew Charitable Trusts found Maine's collaborative, statewide service program to be of such value that it cited it as one of ten exemplary public policy initiatives in the country. In reference to Maine's work, Pew Charitable Trusts stated, "there are common ingredients in success: collective action, grassroots advocacy, and unified messages that communicate public benefits. Cooperation among leaders from the separate cultural fields is a proven way to gain more clout at the state policy table."[7] The program also attracted national funding from the Charles Stewart

Mott Foundation and a special citation from Harvard University's John F. Kennedy School of Government.

Lingering Issues

This great growth of Maine's cultural resources and organizations has been remarkable; but it does not mask lingering problems. Maine's scores of local historical societies are constantly challenged by inadequate technical know-how and financial resources to care for the state's historical record. Public schools struggle to maintain sequential arts education programs and other arts learning activities, even while studies show that studying and practicing the arts are not just helpful, but essential to learning and development. A recent National Governors Association publication, *The Impact of Arts Education on Workforce Preparation*, explains that, "the arts can provide effective learning opportunities to the general student population, yielding increased academic performance, reduced absenteeism and better skill building."[8]

Maine now has scores of year-round galleries; there are forty in Portland alone. It is still difficult, however, for visual artists to make a living, unless the connections are made to sell their work outside Maine in the nation's arts centers or on the Internet. The same applies to performing artists, many of whom need to have sophisticated booking arrangements beyond Maine to live here. Maine's nonprofit arts organizations often exist in a precarious state, with slim annual budget margins and no significant cash reserves to fall back on in lean economic times.

A review of publicly accessible Internal Revenue Service form 990s, filed annually by nonprofit organizations, tells us that with some exceptions Maine's arts institutions do not have large unrestricted endowments to produce income for annual operations. While in nearly every case these organizations' revenues exceeded expenses in 2003, there still exists a pressing need for substantial annual giving and increasing unrestricted endowments for the state's arts organizations to prosper and grow. This is especially the case since admissions and ticket sales account for only a part of arts institutions' annual operating costs. Maine's cultural resources, ubiquitous as they are, lack collective visibility. *It is a supreme irony that that which provides so much of our sense of place often goes unnoticed, or is taken for granted.*

Like most Maine problems, our cultural challenges could be alleviated by more money; but Maine is a state that has a relatively high number of nonprofit organizations and relatively low charitable giving. Based on 2003 figures compiled by the Maine Philanthropy Center, Maine ranks forty-ninth among the fifty states in charitable giving.[9] This is not to say that our population is not generous; individuals and our corporations, foundations, and local businesses do give. A relative new comer, the twenty-year-old Maine Community

Foundation has greatly increased its assets and our ability to serve Maine's overall community development needs.

Still, Maine has a limited resource base in both the public and private sectors. We are all familiar with state budget woes—and there are no Fortune 500 companies in Maine. Maine arts institutions often have to raise funds for annual operations from a population base of less than 50,000; an arts institution of similar size in another state might draw on a population twenty times that size. We need to think creatively about how to build a stronger financial base for Maine cultural affairs, and about why public and private decision-makers will believe it is important to do so. This takes us to the creative economy.

The Creative Economy

It comes as no surprise that Maine's economy is today changing from a manufacturing base to a service economy—one that needs to find new ways to produce goods and services, to satisfy human needs, and to employ people. Today, the arts and culture play a vital role in Maine's changing economy; and they will play an even greater role in Maine's future, as we begin better to understand and build upon the emerging, "creative economy."

The national buzz about the creative economy centers on the work of Carnegie Mellon University economist, Richard Florida, author of the book, *The Rise of the Creative Class*.[10] Florida tells us how the creative economy is transforming the patterns of work throughout the United States. His study encompasses artists and musicians, engineers and architects, software designers, scientists, and anyone else who uses creativity as an input factor in business, education, healthcare, and the other professions. Florida's work focuses on how, why, and where people choose to work; his research shows that, "people [are] not slavishly following jobs to places. Their location choices [are] based to a large degree on their lifestyle interests, and these [go] well beyond the standard quality of life amenities that most experts thought were important."[10]

Florida goes on to describe that these lifestyle interests require vital community centers with, among other amenities, an active cultural life. It is, he writes, these very types of communities that attract people, especially the young and mobile workforce of the twenty-first century, the same people we want to keep in Maine and to attract here. Florida's work is primarily urban-based; and while he is no stranger to Maine, with two trips here previously and two more planned for 2004, we expect to hear more from him about Maine's small city, town, and rural nature, and how his findings apply to Maine's demography and settlement patterns.

In 2000 the New England Council and the New England Foundation for the Arts published *The Creative Economy Initiative: The Role of the Arts and Culture in the New England Economy*.[11] The New England Council is an alliance of business, academic, and nonprofit organizations, formed in 1925 to promote economic growth and a high quality of life in New England. The New England Foundation for the Arts supports the arts in New England and conducts research on regional arts needs, employment, and economic impacts.

For the first time, *The Creative Economy Initiative: The Role of the Arts and Culture in the New England Economy* looked at not only the nonprofit arts sector, but also at profit-making organizations and artists within the creative economy; in the past, only the nonprofit sector had been studied. This work defined the creative economy for the region as having three components. The first is *creative workers,* who may or may not be employed by cultural organizations, yet are involved in creative work. Fine and commercial artists, educators, architects, and designers are all examples of the creative workforce. The creative workforce is composed of individuals whose jobs require a high level of skill in the cultural, fine, or applied arts.

The second component is the *creative cluster,* including industries that have a concentration of workers such as furniture makers, graphic and textile designers, filmmakers, and boat builders. The creative cluster includes nonprofit institutions, commercial businesses, and individual artists who together reinforce and support one another. The third component is *creative communities,* where there is a concentration of creative activity. These communities value cultural assets, support diversity and innovation, and understand that quality of life is directly connected to building concentrations of creative workers and creative

Figure 1. The Creative Economy

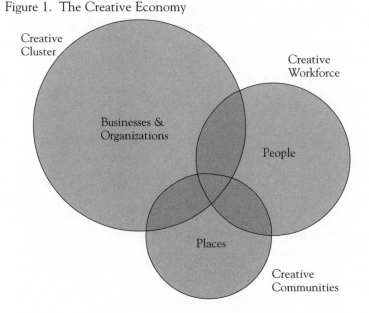

industries. These communities are not only a powerful draw to tourists, but also contribute to the economic vitality of New England.[12]

While some of the employment statistics cited in the study are now out of date, a number of the principles remain valid. The creative cluster, for example, brings significant revenues into the region, from the sale of cultural goods and services, and private foundation and federal sources. The creative workforce is highly entrepreneurial and has many of the qualities required to compete in today's economy, such as creativity and initiative, design and technical skills, advanced conceptual skills, and the ability to respond rapidly to change. Creative communities continue to be catalysts for attracting businesses and revitalizing downtowns. They are present throughout New England, in both our small towns and our urban centers, as New England continues to be recognized nationally for its arts and creative activity.

In Maine, the creative economy has taken on a new dimension with the personal commitment of Governor John E. Baldacci. In his campaign for governor in 2002, candidate Baldacci made the creative economy one of his core themes and issues. When elected, Governor Baldacci moved swiftly on this agenda. On the second day of his term he delivered a public address on the subject to a large group assembled at the Center for Maine Contemporary Art in Rockport. Shortly thereafter, the governor appointed arts, government, business, and creative economy leaders to a steering committee for the Blaine House Conference on Maine's Creative Economy, May 6 and 7, 2004, at the Bates Mill in Lewiston.

In charging the committee with its responsibilities, Governor Baldacci asked that the group help inform the general public and publicize the creative economy concept and case studies; develop strategies and policies to use the creative economy approach in the state's community and economic development efforts; and adapt the urban creative economy model to our rural state. "The creative economy," Governor Baldacci said, "is a catalyst for the creation of new jobs in Maine communities. People who create jobs want to live in places that have a diverse cultural mix and an educated and innovative workforce. Maine will be competitive economically if we continue to capitalize on the synergies between entrepreneurship, education, the arts, and our quality of life."[13]

To prepare for the Blaine House Conference, the steering committee held eight regional forums around the state in fall 2003 and winter 2004. The purpose of the forums was to learn from communities about interest in the creative economy concept; and, based on this information, to plan the conference. The meetings were in such demand that they quickly doubled in number and reached over 900 Maine artists, arts organizations, economic developers, elected and appointed local officials, legislators and interested citizens. From the forums, we learned that Maine people wanted to know how the creative economy was already working in Maine, and how it was working elsewhere. Forum attendees wanted to know in specific terms how the creative economy might work or work better in their own communities, and what "next steps" might move the creative economy initiative forward.

In specific terms, what does the creative economy mean for Maine? Recent research by the New England Foundation for the Arts tells us that in 2002, there was growth in Maine in a number of areas of creative employment, particularly in the visual arts fields, and a decline in the performing arts.[14] Total creative economy employment in 2002 was slightly more than 9,500 individuals. What is significant about the creative economy, however, is less its absolute size than its synergistic effects. John Rohman, of WBRC Architects and Engineers in Bangor, and co-chair of the steering committee for the Blaine House Conference, refers to the creative economy as "the little engine that could."[15]

In Maine, the "little engine" brings with it a long train of cars that metaphorically include safe places to live and work, an unparalleled natural environment, a three-season climate, outdoor variety, and sports and adventure activities. In a state that cannot promote itself as having low taxes and energy costs, the little engine of the creative economy and its train cars provide one of the most promising alternatives for Maine's economic future.

Some Examples of the Creative Economy

Let us take a look at the creative economy in action in Maine, because the creative economy is happening now. An excellent example of a creative community is Bangor. A once-dying downtown has been enlivened through civic and private commitment to the arts. The Discovery Museum for children opened in the old Freese's Department Store. The University of Maine Museum moved to an extraordinary space downtown, one that gives a sense of being in a large, urban gallery district. The Bangor Public Library made a major, architecturally significant addition to its downtown building. The Penobscot Theater moved into the old Opera House. The National Folk Festival, a coveted prize for any city, came to Bangor instead of Los Angeles, and the festival attracted over 100,000 people in its second year. All this development has been driven by creativity, combined with committed civic and private sector leadership.

Another example is in the Camden-Rockland area, where the coalition of a major corporation, MBNA, the Wyeth family, and the Farnsworth Museum have expanded the Farnsworth and created a catalyst to fill the downtown with shops, restaurants, and galleries. Wisely, the Farnsworth Museum opened both its entrances onto Main Street, opening the museum to street-level commerce. Downtown Dover-Foxcroft is restoring its old theater, and there is a new restaurant in town, and another is on the way. The western Piscataquis County region also supports the Highlands Guild, a marketing organization that brings

Wyeth Center, Farnsworth Art Museum, Rockland

the products of Maine's rural artisans to a wider public.

Maine is blessed with remarkably intact nineteenth- and twentiety-century downtown centers, architecturally rich buildings, and spaces that have benefited over the past thirty years from the guidance of Earle G. Shettleworth, Jr., and the Maine Historic Preservation Commission. More recently, the Maine Downtown Center has provided financial and consulting resources to improve the economy and viability of Maine downtowns. The creative economy is a part of each of these local improvement projects. Artists' housing and work space needs are part of Biddeford's and Saco's development plan. In Norway, revitalization of the former Opera House remains a goal, and the Fare Share Market, an unusual cooperative food market and adjacent art gallery, is front and center on the downtown main street. Eastport and Waterville have identified the arts as a natural, creative niche for their downtown revivals.[16]

In the for-profit field, Transformit, Inc., of Gorham is representative of Maine's best kept secrets: the many small creative businesses that are located here and have national and international markets for their products and services. Transformit creates stretched fabric sculptural forms over welded aluminum frames for exhibition presentations and to define space for commercial use. Transformit's installations were commissioned for the Barcelona Olympics, and you may see them today in Nordstrom's department stores in the nation's West and Midwest. Transformit employs stitchers who formerly worked in the textile industry, as well as MFAs who are designing computer graphics. Transformit's founder and owner, Cynthia Thompson, came to Maine in the early 1990s to start her business because, she says, of the spirit of Maine. She began her business with no government or private sector assistance. Today Thompson employs fifty people.

Transformit is an example of the kind of business we want to encourage to grow, to locate or expand in Maine: "green" businesses where creativity is central to their purpose. There are many of these businesses in Maine today, located throughout the state. Angela Adams Designs and Doug Green's Furniture have national markets, and Maine Oxy in Auburn trains welders in sculpture techniques as well as traditional fabrication, through its New England School of Metalwork. In the nonprofit sector, the Center for Furniture Craftsmanship in West Rockport recently quadrupled the size of its workshop and exhibition facilities, and brought greater attention to the well-developed tradition of fine furniture-making in Maine

What is changing in Maine, and what we are beginning to see with the emerging creative economy, is that *the nonprofit and for-profit fields do not exist separately from one another—and from creative individuals, artists and entrepreneurs.* If considered as a sector, or as a series of sub-industry sectors such as design or filmmaking, the creative economy is part of what Maine needs for its future economic health. The creative economy cannot be the only solution, a miracle if you will, to change Maine overnight, but it is one of the elements that Maine can promote in this decade to diversify its economic base with resources that are already here and do not need to be imported. Considered broadly within the context of the creative economy, cultural resources are not only about a sense of place, important for our identity as a state, but also about livelihood and jobs as well.

Some Recommendations
In order to capture the energy from a generation of Maine's remarkable growth in the arts and culture, and to build upon the new work of the creative economy, I offer the following three recommendations:

- Support and grow the creative economy;

- Brand Maine as the "Creative Economy State"; and

- Create a private organization to advocate for cultural affairs and the creative economy

I begin with the first and most obvious, to support and grow the creative economy. More people need to know about the creative economy, which is why the Blaine House Conference on the Creative Economy will be held. Clearly it is important to continue to conduct research on the creative economy. The arts and culture is a field that has not traditionally invested in research on itself. Available funds have gone for programming; and while this is as it should be, we need now to make room for more hard data about the creative sector. In the Discovery Research process, much information has been gathered on the local level, including information about numbers of artists in a region, arts-related businesses, and nonprofit organizations. This information was gathered with the goal of encouraging communities to come together around the arts and culture, as a community-building process; it was not intended as an economic research initiative.

We need to know more about the often elusive cultural sector, about its practitioners in the profit-making and nonprofit fields, about the size of the cultural industry and, most important, about its effect on other areas of the economy and Maine life. Likewise, we need to organize and strengthen the creative clusters, and connect the profit-making and nonprofit fields. In design, for example, it is very difficult to build a design industry if there is not communication and organization within the design sector itself.

Further, we need to expand work already begun with public-private partnerships. Projects such as the seven-institution Maine Art Museum Trail tourism promotion project need to be the norm, rather than the exception. This project brought Maine's leading art museums together in a joint promotional effort to increase museum visitation. As a result, visitation at some museums jumped 15 percent, and the Maine Public Broadcasting Network subsequently embarked on an hour-length feature on each art museum.

We need to build upon partnerships to revitalize our downtown and community centers. Coordination among the private sector and the Maine Historic Preservation Commission, Maine Arts Commission, Maine Downtown Center, and the Maine Housing Authority can use our extraordinary architectural heritage, civic spaces, and contemporary arts to bring new life, new people, and new investment to our community centers. These are the very qualities that some Maine communities have embraced, and they are the same qualities that Richard Florida tells us we *must* have to attract and keep the young, mobile workforce of the twenty-first century. And, finally, what better way to slow the rate of sprawl than by investing in our downtowns?

My second suggestion is to identify and brand Maine as the Creative Economy State. Given the cultural resources here and our quality of life, this sector can grow and attract cultural resources from elsewhere. We can export more Maine creative products in both the fine and manufactured arts, and be savvy about the use of the Internet to do so. We can learn from other examples, such as the incentives for artists' living and working spaces in Providence, Rhode Island, and the effective incentives provided to artists in Ireland. We need to think about how Maine may strengthen public incentives and private financing to support the creative economy, as Maine has supported other business ventures. Buoyed with better information, we can create a toolkit of resources for creative economy practitioners.

In addition, we can consider ways in which arts institutions themselves can strengthen their financial bases. Programs like National Arts Stabilization have made remarkable differences in the finance of leading arts organizations in Baltimore, Cleveland, and the state of Arizona, by advancing a bottom-line approach to arts organizations' business practices and building endowments. Maine could benefit from a similar approach, statewide. All these efforts require greater visibility of the creative sector in general. If we can bring the various sectors into closer communication and partnership, we will be able to utilize the creative economy as a new means to market and develop Maine, a way in which to brand our state as a place where the creative economy is vigorous and welcome.

The third recommendation is structural, and a means to achieve the first two. By way of explanation, it is useful to compare cultural development in Maine with the movement to preserve our natural environment. Maine's cultural development bears a remarkable similarity to the movement to preserve Maine's natural environment—except that, politically, cultural development is at a place where the environmental movement was thirty years ago.

A generation ago, private organizations devoted to preserving the Maine environment came together with state government leadership to create a public-private support network that is today a model for others to emulate. In the cultural field, we have seen tremendous growth in cultural activity, and more local and regional organization in cultural affairs. Maine is recognized for its leadership in state cultural policy through the work of the legislature and the Cultural Affairs Council. Maine's current chief executive has made the creative economy a priority in his economic and social agenda.

In the private sector, however, we do not have the coming together that took place in the 1970s around environmental matters. We will need this for arts organizations, artists, and the creative economy to prosper. This is not to imply that Maine does not have effective, statewide cultural service groups. The Maine Library Association, Maine Preservation, Maine Alliance for Arts Education, and the Center for Maine Contemporary Art are among the many highly effective constituent groups.

To move forward with a coordinated and powerful message, however, we need a private, statewide Creative Economy Council with several key elements: participation from Maine's traditional business, creative economy businesses, and cultural and academic institutions, and close liaison with state government programs designed to assist the creative economy's growth. The steering committee for the Blaine House Conference on Maine's Creative Economy possesses many of these characteristics; it is an insightful, committed, and dynamic group of twenty-three individuals from across all sectors. It is not too great a leap from this steering committee to a statewide organization with a broad, gubernatorial mandate to promote the creative economy.

Curiously, Maine's cultural resources are often best appreciated by those who do not live here. We possess, as a state, a world-renowned artistic legacy, authentic cultural traditions, distinctive community centers, and an abiding spirit of entrepreneurship. We have now begun to connect these resources with a developing new economic model. More of this will probably happen, whatever we do. People from away will continue to find Maine's scenic, outdoor adventure, and cultural attractions. Creative businesses will start up. Young people will grow increasingly proud of being Mainers and want to stay here. However, the likelihood of positive growth through Maine's creative and cultural sector will be diminished without greater attention to the sector itself.

Maine, then, has a choice, much as it did with environmental policy in the 1970s: namely, to promote a policy of managed cultural growth and financial vitality through the creative economy, or to let matters take their own course. The wise path is the former, to help chart Maine's destiny with resources that are right here before us.

Changing Maine

*E*ducated at Colby College in art history and music, Alden C. Wilson served in 1971 as a National Endowment for the Arts management intern at the Maine Arts Commission. Three years later, in 1974, he became director of the commission. (There is a moral in this for all our students reading this today!) Alden is today the longest-serving arts agency director in the nation. He has served on the board of the National Assembly of State Arts Agencies, and is one of just ten recipients of the prestigious Gary Young Award for outstanding service in the state arts agency leadership field. Alden is a board member of the New England Foundation for the Arts (NEFA), where he has served as board president. In the nation, he has conducted site reviews for the National Endowment for the Arts in Ohio, Florida, New Hampshire, Louisiana, and New Mexico. Here in Maine, Alden has served on the Governor's Tourism Council, the Governor's Committee to Expand the Retirement Industry, the Maine Film Commission, and the steering committee for the May 2002 Blaine House Conference on the Creative Economy.

I N RECENT DECADES, nonprofit organizations have become an
indispensable part of our communities' well-being all across the
nation. These "third sector" entities provide an enormous range of
social services, artistic and cultural productions, political advocacy,
and environmental preservation activities. As a rural state with an
environmental conservation ethic, artistic and creative traditions, and
an increasing demand for social services, Maine has the fourth highest
number of nonprofit organizations per capita in the nation. While
nonprofits have become an integral part of life in Maine, they face a
number of challenges which threaten their viability, including slow
growth in private charitable giving, limited support for nonprofit capacity building, and the lack of comprehensive data on their nature
and operation. These challenges require attention to the Maine nonprofit sector and, by extension, to Maine communities if they are to
thrive in coming years.

13 Maine's New "Third Sector"
The Emerging Nonprofit Landscape

DAHLIA LYNN

From the very beginning, we Maine people have concerned ourselves with the health and well-being of our private market sector and, if skeptically, the public sector of government; only in recent years have we begun fully to appreciate the significance of the not-for-profit sector and its many contributions to our state. It is no exaggeration to suggest that Maine's past, present, and future are inexorably linked to the vitality of our charitable and nonprofit community. Indeed, one may argue that no understanding of Maine history is complete without reference to what we may now call, with very good reason, Maine's "third sector."

In this chapter, I will consider the great tradition of nonprofit service in Maine, the role of the third sector as an employer of significance, and the sector as an extension of our unique environment. I will attempt to identify what lies ahead for the more than 4,000 charitable organizations that call Maine home. Finally, I will suggest some steps we might consider to address the changing nonprofit landscape and strengthen the social and economic fabric of our communities in this time of change and uncertainty.

The "Lost Continent" of Non-Profits

"It has long been clear to sensitive observers that Maine is a more caring and compassionate, a more sane and sensible place than the nation of which we are a part. The values of Maine are best illuminated for us…not by those who deal in the currencies of profit and power but of symbols and spirit." These words, written by Richard Barringer in the first *Changing Maine* series in 1990, capture the essence of the third sector's contributions to Maine.[1]

Before I begin discussion of the changing nonprofit landscape in Maine, however, let me take a few moments and give you a sense of the nonprofit sector throughout the United States. Nonprofit and charitable organizations constitute a distinctive sector in the nation's economy, in that they engage us in collective purposes outside both the marketplace and the state. Nonprofit organizations are independently organized and self-governing. They are voluntary, in that membership in them is not legally required, and they attract some level of voluntary contribution of time or money. They are also not profit distributing, in that they do not return profits to their managers or to a set of "owners."

This said, nonprofit organizations are characterized by tremendous diversity in their origins, size, finances, the types of activities they undertake, the people they serve, and the means they use to reach their goals. Nonprofit causes include, among countless others, environmental preservation, health education, the arts, and the care of the elderly. Some nonprofit organizations aim to benefit their own members, while others aim to promote broader well-being among the public, including the opportunity for democratic participation in the life of the communities in which they are found.

The products of nonprofit organizations include artistic and cultural productions, political advocacy, spiritual guidance, and care for the poor, sick, and disabled. As new social problems emerge and are recognized, new agencies are created to meet the need: agencies for runaway youth, shelters for battered women, hospices for AIDS patients—just to name them is to chart the development of the nation's social welfare agenda in recent decades.

In addition to their service functions, nonprofit organizations play economic and political roles, as well. Alexis De Tocqueville recognized the powerful contributions of voluntary associations to the country's political and intellectual life; and voluntary associations still enable citizens to express their collective interests and solve community problems. Because of their unique position outside the market and state, their connections to citizens, their flexibility, their capacity to tap private initiative in support of public purposes, and their newly rediscovered contributions to building "social capital,"[2] civic organizations have surfaced as strategically important participants in the search for a middle way, between sole reliance on the marketplace and the state as service providers.

As the nonprofit scholar Lester Salamon has commented, however, "the nonprofit sector remains the lost continent on the modern landscape of modern society, invisible to most policy makers, business leaders, and the press, and even to many people within the sector, itself."[3] What we know about the charitable sector is largely limited to those public-service serving organizations that are eligible to receive tax-deductible donations. These include all those registered with the Internal Revenue Service (IRS) under section 501(c)3 of the Internal Revenue Code, which embraces not-for-profit hospitals, clinics, colleges, universities, elementary schools, social service agencies, day care centers, orchestras, museums, theaters, environmental organizations, homeless shelters, animal welfare organizations, and many more.

Throughout the United States, the nonprofit sector is comprised overwhelmingly of small, community-based entities with relatively meager resources. Even among those meeting the threshold for IRS reporting, most have modest budgets, use only volunteer labor, and operate locally. At the same time, financial resources and employee numbers are highly concentrated in the largest organizations, chiefly hospitals and universities, which often dominate national statistics on the nonprofit sector.

The ebb and flow of larger economic and political forces affect the numbers, growth rates, strengths, and viability of nonprofit organizations. An estimated 40 percent of public charities suffered a decline in inflation-adjusted income in the recession-dominated years between 1989 and 1995. A similar number operate today on a slim margin, with net worth less than or equal to three months of expenses. Nonprofit revenues are a complex mix of private and public dollars raised through grants, contracts, fees for services, sales, donations, investment income, special events income, and income from commercial ventures.

In general over the last few decades, the proportion of private donations has decreased, and program service fees have become the nonprofit sector's largest source of revenue. Over the past several years, government revenues in absolute terms have increased slightly, mainly fueled by Medicare and Medicaid payments to hospital and other health-care providers; but they have decreased for social and legal services, for arts and culture, and most substantially for civic, social, and fraternal organizations.

At the same time, a vibrant nonprofit sector has become a necessity—to give expression to citizen concerns, to hold governments accountable, to promote community, to address important social needs, and generally to improve the quality of American life. The story of Maine is in great measure the story of these vibrant organizations; and I hope to shed light here on the importance of this sector to the State of Maine.

The Tradition of Nonprofit Service in Maine

First, however, a story of "the opera house and the hamlet." If you ask why four New Yorkers bought and restored a ninety-one-year-old opera house in a remote fishing village on Penobscot Bay, the answers given by the owners are not only about living a good life but also about doing what you think it is important and giving something to the community. Built in 1886, the Stonington Opera House on Deer Isle was long the cultural center of town. In 1910 a fire ravaged Stonington, on the very day the first fire hydrant was installed. While the hydrant saved much of the town, the Opera House was gutted.

In 1992 the building was on the National Register of Historic Places, but an eyesore; yet, as one of the current owners remembered, "we stood in the dark peering into the smelly building and said, 'we can do this.' At the time, I didn't even know what was the cause; but I had a sense possibility, a sense that this was the right thing to do."[4] This sense of possibility, the belief in the right thing to do in our communities, is at the heart of the tradition of nonprofit service in Maine.

The nonprofit sector in Maine is large and diverse, and fills a number of significant roles: as tools for community building, fostering civil society, and strengthening the social fabric of our communities. The development of the nonprofit sector in Maine has a deep and rich connection to religious, economic, and social movements within the state, and to larger historical movements within the nation. The society and culture which Maine people have created has been characterized as one aimed at linking the material and the spiritual in harmony, while achieving a modest, independent competency in life.[5] Indeed, Mainers have been described as the "forgotten children" of the French and English empires, left behind after the French and Indian Wars and the American Revolution, in a state often considered a place apart from the mainstream of American society.[6]

Mainers are considered a hardy people who persist largely through their own ingenuity, in a region of abundant natural resources, in what can be a harsh, uninviting climate. The image of Maine, as both a "Vacationland" and a frontier removed from the national mainstream, has influenced the development of the state and our efforts to manage the tides of social change, the excesses of market competition, and the occasional stresses of social polarization.

The role of individuals in volunteer service in Maine was alive and well long before the formalization of the nonprofit sector, as such. Religious institutions often undertook education and healthcare services: to teach, to nurse the sick, to care for orphans and the elderly, to feed the hungry, and to respond to emergencies. There has also been the connection to humanitarian movements, as charitable groups developed to address the impact of the industrial revolution, the abolition of slavery, waves of immigration, and persistent poverty.

The history of Maine is, in many ways, the history of its nonprofit sector. It is the story of a sector that has reflected the growing importance within the state of community standards, and created the infrastructure to make good on social commitments, the promise of education, the needs of immigrants, and the health of our land and waters. Nonprofit organizations have provided an opportunity for a wide variety of artistic, religious, cultural, ethnic, and social expressions that add richness to community life. They have also helped foster social capital, the bonds of trust and reciprocity that appear to be crucial for the healthy functioning of a democratic polity and a market economy.

Today in Maine, the nonprofit sector encompasses an enormous range of organizations engaged in education, health care, research, the arts, religion, the environment, civil rights and human service. In them, Mainers affirm their belief in humanity by providing services to thousands of their fellow citizens every year, day in and day out.

Employers of Significance
Nonprofit organizations are critical service providers to Maine's communities, and a major force in the state's economy and in each of its regional economies. The significance of the nonprofit sector as a source of jobs and wages is often

overlooked when we consider economic development, as well as education and job training efforts. Greater understanding of the economic contributions and the impact of the nonprofit sector throughout Maine will heighten appreciation of the stake Maine's citizens have in the sector's health.

In 2000 there were a total of 1,809 reporting charitable nonprofits in Maine. In addition to these "501(c)3s," there were over 2,500 small, charitable nonprofit organizations registered with the IRS but not required to file—including booster clubs, local PTAs, youth soccer, and other small organizations. Their expenditures in 2002 totaled some $4.6 billion, representing fully 12 percent of the gross state product. This is significantly higher than the national average of 7.8 percent. In that year Maine's charitable nonprofits held $7.9 billion in assets, almost a three-fold increase since 1990 ($2.8 billion); and Maine's nonprofits paid $3.5 billion in payroll income.[7]

As a contributor to Maine's economic engine, the nonprofit sector represents almost 12 percent of total employment in the state, or one out of every eight workers and over 14 percent of all non-governmental employment in the state. This puts Maine, significantly above the U.S. average in terms of the nonprofit share of total employment (7.2 percent). Nor is nonprofit employment restricted to any one region in Maine; rather, it is found in every county.

Like Maine's population, however, most of the state's nonprofit employment is located in our urban areas. Sixty-two percent of Maine's nonprofit employment is located in four counties: Androscoggin, Cumberland, Kennebec, and Penobscot. (Cumberland County, with the state's largest city of Portland, employs 28 percent of the state's nonprofit workers.) Twenty-three percent of the state's nonprofit employment (approximately 17,000 workers) is located in the more suburban counties of Hancock, Knox, Lincoln, Waldo, and York. The remaining 15 percent is located in the more rural counties, including Franklin, Oxford, Aroostook, Somerset, and Washington. Nonprofit organizations play a critical role in Kennebec and Hancock counties, accounting for nearly 20 percent of total non-governmental employment there.[8]

The nonprofit sector in the state employs nearly three times as many people as state government; almost three times as many people as the state's transportation industry and its wholesale trade industry; and more than twice as many workers as the state's construction, finance, insurance, and real estate industries combined. Finally, the nonprofit sector employs more people than all local governments combined; and almost as many people as the state's entire manufacturing sector.

The nonprofit sector also accounts for the lion's share of non-government employment in a number of key fields. This includes over 97 percent of all private hospital employment; over 96 percent of higher education employment; over 90 percent of elementary and secondary education employment; close to three-quarters of all private residential care and individual and family service employment; and more than half of all private child day care employment.

Health service organizations represent 19 percent of all nonprofit organizations, but account for nearly half of all of Maine's nonprofit jobs. Health services organizations include hospitals, nursing and personal care facilities, and home health care organizations; and employ almost 35,000 people, representing 49.7 percent of total nonprofit employment.

Social and human services organizations make up the largest proportion of Maine's reporting nonprofits (33 percent), and represent 28 percent of all nonprofit jobs in Maine (almost 10 percent greater than the nation, at 18 percent). These include employment in individual and family services, job training and related services, child day care services, residential care, youth development, and disaster relief.

Sixteen percent of all nonprofit organizations in the state are involved in educational services—including elementary and secondary schools, colleges and universities—and represent 11 percent of all nonprofit employment in Maine (as opposed to 15 percent nationwide). Twelve percent of these organizations are in the arts, culture, and humanities, but account for only 1.3 percent of all nonprofit employment in the state (as opposed to 4 percent nationwide). Overall, the distribution of nonprofit employment in Maine is similar to the national average, although Maine has a larger share of nonprofit employment in social services and a smaller share in health, education and the arts.

As a Reflection of Our Environment.
We are a state often short on resources, and long in the belief that being removed from the national mainstream serves only to strengthen our resolve to maintain the well-being of our communities.

On the face of it, Maine appears to be the third most rural state in United States, with 55 percent of its citizens living outside Census-designated urban areas. In terms of population density, Maine has a scant thirty-six people per square mile. Like many "rural" states, communities in Maine face more than a few obstacles:

- Rural per capita income is 24 percent below urban income;

- 56 percent of the state's poor live in rural areas;

- 60 percent of Maine's unemployed live in rural areas;

- The elderly represent the fastest growing segment of Maine's rural population. It is projected that by 2020 Maine will have the fifth largest percentage of population sixty-five and older; and

- While 76 percent of Maine's rural adults have completed high school, just 40 percent of these adults have any post-secondary education.

For all this, Maine ranks fourth nationally in the number of nonprofits per capita. The high ratio reflects a number of factors: as a relatively poor state with dispersed populations often far from our service centers, there is a significant demand for social services, a niche that has been filled by nonprofit providers.

In 1960, 24 percent of Mainers earned an income below the poverty line. The household poverty rate for Maine as a whole stood at 10 percent in 1996 and at 11.5 percent in the Census 2000 report. The combination of regional poverty, rural isolation, unemployment, and an aging population places a high demand on the services traditionally provided by nonprofit organizations.

In addition, the recent Poverty in Maine report issued by the Margaret Chase Smith Center for Public Policy identified the large proportion of below-poverty households consisting of people living alone (45 percent) as one of the most striking features of poverty in Maine.[9]

Funding, Volunteerism, and Philanthropy

We may not discuss the nonprofit experience in Maine without addressing the realities of funding, volunteerism, and philanthropy. Private giving and volunteerism have long been vital parts of Maine life, and the lifeblood of the third sector. In 1999, 9 percent of the total revenues for reporting nonprofits in Maine were contributions from individuals, corporations, and foundations.

The major source of revenues, 91 percent, comes from user fees and charges, government support and investment income. Our nonprofits do not subsist on government largess, however. True, some nonprofits receive government grants and contracts; but most use a variety of funding mechanisms to support their operations. Vital as it is, direct government funding accounted for less than 28 percent of nonprofit income in 2000.

In terms of individual giving, Maine is often portrayed as ranking near the bottom nationally. The average charitable contribution of those who itemize deductions was $2,181 in Maine, almost $1,000 less than the national average. Yet, the percent of income, 2.9 percent, is only somewhat less than the national average of 3.5 percent, and Maine is tied with Vermont for the highest percentage of total income contributed to charities among New England states. While we may contribute less in total dollars, we give a higher percentage of our income to charities than all New England states but one![10]

We find other ways to contribute, as well. Our state is fortunate that the percentage of adults who volunteer is significant; our citizens are involved in both *sustained* volunteer work (mentoring, coaching, hospice, firefighting, etc.) and *episodic* work (walkathons, clean-up days, playground construction, and food drives as examples.) Results of the 2001 Citizen Survey conducted by the Maine Development Foundation[11] found that fully 39 percent of all survey respondents assisted in public schools or community organizations that assist youth; 27.3 percent contributed their time towards organizations which assist the needy; 13 percent of Maine's citizens contribute voluntary efforts to environmental organizations; and 22 percent volunteer in organizations that assist the elderly. On a personal level, for example, in 2000:

- 48 percent of high school students in the state said they volunteered in their schools or communities;

Former MBNA Buildings, Camden

- 8,165 citizen volunteers served as mentors, teachers, water quality monitors, safety educators, and members of fire departments;

- 34 private consultants contributed at least 10 hours annually to advise and assist small volunteer service organizations across Maine, as part of the Maine Service Exchange; and

- 22 volunteer projects were carried out by 991 youth in conjunction with Martin Luther King Day.

Among civic leaders in Maine, a discussion on the future of corporate philanthropy or "giving" in the state has been sparked by the increasing number of Maine companies that have merged or been purchased by national corporations in recent years. This transformation—from an economy that was largely owner-occupied forty years ago, to one governed increasingly by distant, corporate owners—has created apprehension in the nonprofit community that absentee owners will be less responsive to the compelling needs of Maine and its nonprofit organizations. To the discussion of absentee ownership and its impact on the philanthropic community is added the fact that total corporate giving has shown a steady decline relative to profits.

The nonprofit sector, in Maine and most of the United States, is comprised overwhelmingly of small, community-based entities with relatively meager resources; and in the world of organizations, size *can* matter. Large nonprofit organizations have the luxury of addressing issues in ways that mirror corporate practices: they provide health care benefits and annual leave, upgrade computer systems, consider the child care needs of employees, pay their utility bills on time, and, perhaps most importantly, see to it that there is someone to shovel the walkway and parking lot when it snows.

The opposite is often true for smaller nonprofit organizations. Like their Maine predecessors, they are undaunted in overcoming every obstacle, because they believe so deeply in the work they are doing: if they fail, people will suffer. Facing their clients every day, they do not take much vacation time because the staff is not large enough to provide coverage for client services. They worry about making payroll and paying for the electricity. They cannot afford the time or cost for professional development, accept cast-off computers, and have a sign-up sheet for shoveling the snow. The vast majority of the nonprofit organizations in Maine are the latter, and not the former.

What Lies Ahead?

What lies ahead are diverse pressures, including political and economic forces affecting the growth rate, strength, and viability of Maine's nonprofit organizations. While assets of nonprofit organizations in the State of Maine have grown from $2.8 billion in 1990 to $7.9 billion in 2002, as my colleague Charles Colgan noted in an earlier chapter, the principal problem associated with prosperity is keeping it.

In 2000 the average nonprofit human service provider operated with a 3 percent cushion—enough to tide the typical provider over for about three weeks. Two in five human service providers operated in the red, and most groups had little slack in their budgets to meet unexpected demands or emergencies. The demand for services has increased, and revenues are down; the nonprofit sector in Maine is once again under pressure to do more with less. Unlike the federal government, the nonprofit sector cannot disguise deficits; and unlike the private sector, it cannot easily streamline itself by simply eliminating unprofitable product lines.

The commitment to mission is at once the nonprofits' greatest strength and weakness. Mission gives nonprofit employees the energy to keep going under trying circumstances, at low pay, in often under-funded and under-equipped organizations. On the other hand, the commitment to mission can invite exploitation and futility. Nonprofit organizations are often willing to skip paychecks, cut supply and training budgets, defer needed maintenance and hiring, and even sell capital assets to keep the mission alive. Despite the important contributions nonprofit organizations make to the State of Maine, these organizations find themselves today in a time of testing.

The third sector in Maine has experienced a significant fiscal squeeze, not only in the decline of actual dollars from federal and state government, but also in the form this funding takes. Government grants and contracts that offer direct support to nonprofit service providers are giving way to client vouchers. Since 1996, 70 percent of all federal support to nonprofit organizations has taken the form of these consumer-side payments. While vouchers maximize choice for their recipients, nonprofit organizations' stream of funding becomes more uncertain as clients choose among options for service provision.

The rise of managed care in health and social service fields has likewise added to the competitive and financial pressures on nonprofits. Private philanthropy has not kept pace either with the growth of the overall economy or the nonprofit sector. Giving has declined steadily as a share of personal income, and the recent recession of 2000–02 has reversed the asset growth nonprofit organizations saw in the late 1990s. Nonprofit organizations face increased competition from for-profit firms that have entered fields once dominated by the nonprofits. Fields such as rehabilitation services, mental health services, home health, hospice care, and childcare have seen increased competition, in part from the growth in the government's consumer-side payments.

In the face of increased competition, nonprofit organizations in Maine also confront rising pressures to demonstrate their effectiveness. Earlier notions of the inherent trustworthiness of nonprofit organizations have given way to a pervasive accountability environment in which performance must be proved. In response, organizations like United Way of America have launched elaborate efforts to establish performance measures for its funded agencies, and a new venture philanthropy model has taken root, encouraging grant funders to insist on measurable results.

Futurist Atul Dighe suggests that the unique demographic, technological, and cultural transformations facing the United States today have special implications for America's nonprofit organizations, because of their commitment to innovation, their vulnerability to shifts in other sectors, and their involvement in many of the fields such as health care and education where the pace of change is especially fast.[12]

Among the forces shaping the future of the nonprofit sector in Maine, perhaps the easiest to predict are the demographic. America is being transformed into a country where a majority of its citizens will be non-Euro-Americans by the middle of the twenty-first century. This transformation has significant implications for Maine, as well. We need look no farther than the communities of Portland and Lewiston-Auburn to understand the important roles nonprofit organizations play in the areas of refugee resettlement programs.

Longer life expectancies are also producing a more complex mix of social commitments. As the Maine population ages, we face the continued loss of many of our younger citizens throughout much of Maine. Family structures are more diverse and complex, as traditional models of families are increasingly replaced by an array of living arrangements; and as families look for alternatives to traditional family responsibilities, such as childcare, adult day care, transportation needs, and after-school supervision. These shifts have immense implications for nonprofit organizations in Maine. As a result, many nonprofit organizations will play vital roles in creating community in a context of ethnic diversity, and will stand to benefit from the growing need for elder services and family support functions.

Technological change also seems likely to create challenges as well as opportunities for nonprofit organizations in Maine. As secondary education moves increasingly towards a more expansive learning model, nonprofit educational institutions will push the boundaries of classroom walls and traditional service delivery mechanisms, rethinking what time and distance mean for learning.

New technologies are likely to transform medical care, as well. New care models will engage our thinking about the way we provide for the newest and oldest members of our state. New diagnostic tools may enable those with chronic long-term care needs to remain more independent with the support of nonprofit health care providers.

The Internet facilitates new forms of social activism that can empower nonprofit advocacy on a statewide, if not national level. The recent campaign to abolish bear-baiting was led by nonprofit animal welfare organizations that utilized the Internet to launch petition drives, arrange public meetings, and connect volunteers and funders.

Maine citizens reflect the profile of volunteers across the United States. The majority of adults volunteers five or fewer hours per month, and there is a growing shift of volunteers away from sustained involvement in a specific community program to episodic volunteering with a shorter commitment to a greater variety of charitable organizations. The nonprofit sector may be vulnerable not only to the lack of growth in philanthropic contributions, but also to civic disengagement, especially among lower income people. Outside of religious congregations, participation by the less well-off in community associations and in the political process is more limited than for those who are more affluent. This participation level poses a major challenge, as involvement in civic activities increases with education and income.

Nonprofit organizations also face market pressures to work more effectively. Applying the business model of the for-profit sector to the nonprofit arena may be a good thing; but one must use caution in its application. For, community building, rather than business oversight, may be a more appropriate goal in a sector where responsiveness and accountability and not the bottom-line of profit are the objective.

Creative and realistic solutions to the social problems of community require a realistic understanding of the role and capacity of nonprofit organizations. As the demand for alternative service delivery and an enhanced expectation of nonprofit providers grow, we must first acknowledge both the strengths and limitations of nonprofits. As a nation, we have clung for a quarter century to the notion of an independent, charitable social safety net that is able to offset decreased government support for social services. This myth has persisted, as nonprofits are expected to become less dependent on a shrinking government sector and more businesslike, lean, efficient, and effective.

Some Recommendations

In this time of constant change, how might the people of Maine envision the future of this critical sector—one that represents so much of what is important to this state? I have four suggestions that I will leave the reader to consider.

First, however, I would share with you "the rest of the story" about the opera house and the hamlet. The Opera House was part of a dream, and resulted in the forming of the Opera House Arts, a nonprofit corporation to purchase the building. The day after the closing, the new owners entered a float in the Fourth of July parade, and handed out popcorn and fliers announcing their plans to reopen the building the following summer. Local workers and volunteers installed bathrooms, created fire exits, refurbished the seating, and repaired the stage. On July 8, 2000, the Opera House opened with a season that included eight professional performances. Last year, financial contributions totaled more than $200,000, and almost all performances were sell-outs.[13]

Meanwhile, in nearby Deer Isle village, a performing arts center has been built, further affirming the vision of the performing arts on the island. The Opera House owners are spending more time in Maine and plans proceed to winterize it. When that is done, the owners hope to attract regional theater companies looking for a quiet setting. "We could do this anywhere else," the owners said, "but there is a particular energy here in Maine that's unique. We don't know if it's the granite, in the water, or what."

My first recommendation to strengthen Maine's third sector at this time is to encourage corporate-nonprofit collaborations and partnerships. This might involve an action as simple as a corporate sponsor sending a check to a non-profit, or as complex as sharing corporate facilities or executives with a non-profit organization. Strategic collaborations could be encouraged where private firms realize benefits while advancing social welfare, such as in the sponsorship and donation of equipment and products; or, commercial collaborations that are designed to increase revenue for both the private entrepreneur and the non-profit organization. This effort must also extend to municipal and state agencies, and involve the exploration of partnership agreements with nonprofit organizations. The existing state-university system partnership for research and training might serve as a model.

The second recommendation addresses the serious shortage of resources needed to succeed by a significant number of nonprofit organizations in Maine. Internal capacity building cannot occur when the utilities need to be paid. In 2000, there were 266 foundations in Maine with total assets of over $792 million and whose giving totaled over $46 million. The collective strength of these foundations could be harnessed to establish an incentive fund for non-profit organizations throughout Maine, enabling them to improve internal and external communication, increase training, enhance technology, support professional skill development, initiate new collaborative efforts and undertake strategic planning. Organizations such as the Maine Community Foundation, the Maine Association of Nonprofits, the Maine Development Foundation, and the Maine Philanthropy Association could partner in this effort, as well.

The third recommendation focuses on the importance of gathering both data and narrative stories regarding the nonprofit environment in Maine. An effort should be undertaken to produce a "state of the nonprofit state" report, to more fully understand and address the host of challenges facing the state's private, nonprofit organizations.

Finally, we need to increase awareness of the sector's importance as a partner in the delivery of social services, as builders of social capital, and as major contributors to the economic welfare of Maine. This might best be accomplished in a Governor's Blaine House conference or summit to address the sustainability of Maine's nonprofit sector. A number of such information-gathering and policymaking initiatives have been undertaken by Governor John E. Baldacci; among the various economic sectors being examined, however, none is more deserving of attention or filled with promise for Maine people than the new "third sector" emerging on Maine's landscape.

Educated at Florida International University, Dahlia Bradshaw Lynn is Associate Professor of Public Policy and Management at the Muskie School of Public Service, where she serves as chair of our Public Policy and Management Program. Dr. Lynn's teaching and research interests include civil service reform, human resource management, collaborative leadership, and faith-based social service delivery. Her most recent publications include the editorship of a symposium on human resource management in nonprofit organizations for the Review of Public Personnel Administration; and she is soon to have a book chapter published by Jossey Bass as part of an edited volume on the evolution of public personnel systems. Dr. Lynn's background also includes fifteen years of practice in the field of human resources and service on numerous nonprofit boards of directors.

THEIR EMPLOYMENT OPPORTUNITIES were listed in the "Help Wanted: Female" section of the newspaper; they earned about fifty-nine cents for every dollar earned by men; domestic violence was not recognized as a crime; birth control was rarely prescribed for unmarried women; and abortions were illegal, expensive, and often dangerous. The world inhabited by Maine women in the early 1960s is practically unrecognizable to young women today, thanks to changes brought about by the women's movement and the dedicated, persistent efforts of women in Maine and the rest of the nation. Maine organizations like the Mabel Wadsworth Women's Health Center, the Maine Coalition to End Domestic Violence, and the Maine Women's Lobby have worked for three decades to improve the quality of life and equality of opportunity for women in Maine. While significant discrimination still exists, a great deal of positive change has transpired since 1960. By fully understanding the magnitude and the history of the changes that have taken place, today's women may more successfully address the inequities that continue to plague Maine society today.

14 Maine Women's Changing Roles
Hard Work and Some Progress

MARLI WEINER

I wish to begin by describing some of the circumstances girls and women in Maine—and the nation—generally faced in 1960.[1]

1960: Limited Options

Girls born in 1960 were wrapped in pink blankets. As they grew older, they were given dolls and easy-bake ovens to play with; usually, they were warned against running, jumping, climbing trees, and other varieties of rough-and-tumble play. If they did, they might get their dresses dirty. Girls in those days did not wear pants to school, to church, downtown, or many other places. Skirts fell to the knee or below. Physical play was considered unseemly, not part of the repertoire of appropriate behavior for young ladies, no matter what their class or background. The books from which they learned to read had Dick running, jumping, and otherwise doing things, while Jane and Sally watched.

A young woman in high school in 1960 was far more likely than her brother to be taught typing, shorthand, and other secretarial skills. She took classes in home economics and sewing, while he took shop; there was no possibility of crossing the gender line. While she would have been told in many different ways that it was her responsibility to save herself for marriage—with her "self" equated with her virginity—our young woman might well find herself facing pressure from her boyfriend to have sex (that is, to "go all the way") with him. Doing so would threaten her reputation; "nice girls" were presumed to be asexual, and told that it was their responsibility to curb male lust. If she did relent in spite of the risk to her reputation, she would find getting access to birth control difficult, unless the man was willing to ask the pharmacist for condoms. Few young men were so brave.

While the birth control pill was introduced in 1960, few doctors were willing to prescribe it for unmarried women, and few young women were brave enough to ask. In 1960 most doctors in Maine and the nation were men. Whether our young woman was married or not, should she find herself pregnant, obtaining an abortion would prove virtually impossible—unless she were very lucky, well-connected, *and* had access to a sizable amount of ready cash, because abortion was illegal except to save the woman's life. Even if she were able to find someone to perform one, it was usually a humiliating experience—and not necessarily safe. Unmarried women who were unwilling or unable to arrange abortions might find themselves suddenly at the altar or shuttled off to a home for unwed mothers, where they were likely to be pressured to give up the child for adoption, often without ever seeing it.

In 1960 non-heterosexual women would have difficulty even finding a name for what they were, and just as much difficulty finding others like themselves. For a woman to reject marriage and motherhood was almost unthinkable; to be a lesbian meant rejecting both, and often brought stigma and shame.

When it came time for our young woman to look for a job, she would find the columns in the newspaper headed "Help Wanted—Male" and "Help Wanted—Female." She would have known better than to apply for a job in the former category. Under Help Wanted—Female, she would find listings for jobs as a secretary, as a clerk in a store, as a hairdresser, at the telephone company, and in light industry. Nearly all would be in sales or service; few paid well; few offered much in the way of benefits; few offered significant mobility. Hardly any of the jobs she might get were unionized, and even if she were a union member, the union was not likely to address women's workplace concerns.

If she went to college, she might aspire to a job as a teacher or a social worker; if she did not go to college, she might become a nurse. In 1960 few young women were admitted to law or medical schools, few studied science, fewer still engineering. Whatever job she did get would pay wages that were significantly less than those paid for the jobs in the Help Wanted—Male columns. She might or might not work full time, be given benefits like health insurance, accumulate a pension; if she did, she would not be encouraged to take her job seriously enough to consider it a career.

Women who became pregnant, married or not, were likely to face discrimination in the workplace. They were treated paternalistically by their doctors, who did not consider them capable of making decisions about their bodies. Women gave birth in hospitals with only medical staff present, while fathers paced in waiting rooms and older children remained at home. Women were discouraged from nursing their babies and those who did would never have dreamed of doing so in public. Few if any public rest rooms had changing tables. There were few child care centers and no financial support or tax credits for women who used them. Raising children was widely understood to be a mother's responsibility, with little assistance from the father or anyone else.

A working woman with children in 1960 was likely to be in the same kinds of jobs as the young woman just starting out, and not likely to earn very much more money. The numbers vary a bit, depending on who is doing the counting, but the best estimates suggest that even when she worked year round and full time, she earned 59 cents for every dollar that men earned, mostly due to the kind of job she had and her lower level of education. Working year round and full time was extraordinarily difficult for her. It meant scrambling to find some kind of child care for her children. It meant doing a second day's work—housework—when she finished her work for wages. In 1960 men generally did not do much cooking or cleaning or grocery shopping or laundry or taking care of children. Working outside her home meant dealing with social pressures that told her she was not a good wife, not a good mother, that she was neglecting her home and her family.

A woman who did not have a husband was likely to experience some combination of pity and blame, as well as significant economic hardship. Women with children who could not make ends meet might qualify for welfare. Receiving welfare was usually a humiliating experience. Men could not be present in the household, which meant that women's sexual activities were open to scrutiny by caseworkers, as were their abilities as mothers. Welfare did not pay enough for women and their children to live with any margin of safety, never mind a degree of comfort. Welfare payments came at the cost of stigma and shame, usually delivered by the very individuals who administered it, as well as by the larger culture.

Women who could not attract and keep a husband—and a husband able to support them—were widely perceived as insufficiently feminine, as having something wrong with them. Even if a woman did not need welfare, to be divorced—no matter what the circumstances that led to it—was to be suspect. Jokes about divorcees—like jokes about old maids, about mothers-in-law, about grasping career women, and about desperate singles—were heard everywhere.

All women, no matter what their age or marital status or their income, found getting loans or credit in their own names difficult, if not impossible. As a result, women often could not get loans to start small businesses, mortgages to buy their own homes, or even credit cards separate from their husbands. Women rarely had life insurance, either as a benefit of employment or on their own.

A woman of retirement age in 1960 was far less likely than the men in her neighborhood to have a pension of her own. If she had been married, she would have access to Social Security through her husband. Few women earned enough during their working lives to live decently off their own Social Security and few could accumulate significant savings of their own. Older women were invisible in the culture; hardly anyone paid attention to their needs, tried to sell them anything, or portrayed them in movies.

Women of any age who were raped first had to convince the police that a crime had occurred—that they had not been "asking for it." In 1960 most police in Maine and the nation were men; so were most lawyers and judges. A woman who was raped would be asked about her previous sexual experiences by the police and in court. Few rape cases were brought to trial even if there was a witness, which many considered necessary to get a conviction. Should a rape case go to trial, the woman's sexual history was fair game for defense attorneys intent upon discrediting her story, as was her clothing. Judges did not think it necessary to instruct juries to disregard such testimony. In 1960 a husband could not be accused of raping his wife, because marital rape was not a crime. Nor was sexual harassment, at school or in the workplace, a crime; in fact, there was not yet even a term to describe it, nor was it a violation of civil employment laws.

Domestic violence was also not understood as a crime. Women who called the police for protection were most likely to find their complaints not taken seriously and the police siding with the men involved, both assuming that these women "were asking for it"—that they deserved what they got. The police did not consider domestic violence a serious problem, nor did they believe that what happened within families was their responsibility; to consider it so would be interfering. As in cases of rape, should a case of domestic assault be brought to court, the woman's behavior was open to scrutiny, with few restraints by judges either in allowing testimony or instructing juries. There were no domestic violence shelters in 1960, no rape crisis centers. Women who called on doctors (remember, doctors were men) or on clergy (also men) fared no better than women who called the police.

Of course, there were exceptions to this portrait of women in Maine in 1960. Throughout the state, some women defied the odds, did not conform, forged their own paths. Luck and determination had something to do with their success; so, often, did family support and money. Still, the women who in 1960 worked as doctors or lawyers, scientists or politicians, journalists or professors did so *despite* the dictates of their society, not with its blessing. Many of Maine's young women who aspired to these careers found that they had to leave the state for the opportunity—and anonymity—of Boston, New York, or beyond.

A Long, Hard Struggle for Autonomy

Clearly, many things have changed between 1960 and today even while some things have not. This picture of women's lives in 1960 certainly feels unfamiliar to us today. Before turning to Maine women's lives and roles today, I will spend some time exploring how we got from there to here. Part of the reason that the experiences of women forty years ago seem so different from our lives today is, simply, that *women here and in the rest of the nation worked very hard and long to create these changes*, in an amorphous and complex set of activities collectively called the women's liberation movement at the time, and now more commonly referred to as "feminism."

Historians of women generally date the beginning of the modern feminist movement to the social change movements of the 1960s. That is certainly justified, although Maine (like the nation) has, in fact, a long tradition of activist women. This dates back at least to the mid-nineteenth century, when women in the state became active in the abolitionist movement to end slavery and in other reform movements. Later, they worked together to support the Union effort in the Civil War. During the war and after it was over, a few traveled South to nurse the sick or teach the freed slaves.

Still later, Maine women joined together in a host of organizations dedicated to improving their own lives and those of their families and communities, including the Women's Christian Temperance Union, the Maine and General Federation of Women's Clubs, and the Maine and National American Woman's Suffrage Associations. They campaigned for public health reform, worked for child welfare, became environmental activists. Their effort to convince male voters to extend suffrage to them was defeated in 1917. When they were granted the right to vote in 1920, however, they set to work to educate themselves politically. Today, Maine women share with men one of the highest voter participation rates in the nation. These voters have a long tradition of electing women to local, state, and national office, including Margaret Chase Smith and our two current United States senators.

Maine women's tradition of activism extended to the economic realm as well, although perhaps as much by necessity as by choice. Throughout the nineteenth and twentieth centuries, women did what was necessary to help their families survive. Sometimes this meant harnessing traditional Maine values of thrift ("use it up, wear it out, make it do, or do without") by growing and preserving food, or by sewing, knitting, and recycling clothing, for example. Sometimes it meant taking jobs in the seasonal or part-time economy, such as canning, making Christmas wreaths, or serving summer tourists. For generations of mostly young women, it meant working in the textile mills in Lewiston, Biddeford, and Westbrook; many of them were the daughters of French Canadian families. This work was often dangerous, offered little mobility, and was poorly paid.

Maine's traditional industries of fishing, lumbering, and paper-making offered relatively few opportunities for women to gain the full-time, year-round, well-paying jobs that men had access to, although the wives and daughters of these men appreciated the stability and comforts these jobs could provide, despite their dangers. Maine women have long been more or less willing participants in the economy, if only to make ends meet, although the importance of their participation has scarcely been recognized.

Despite these generations of activism and economic participation by Maine women, their lives in 1960 remained circumscribed. Historians generally attribute more fundamental social change in the modern era to three concurrent and more or less interrelated movements: the Civil Rights movement, the New Left, and the counterculture. We credit the Civil Rights movement with creating an understanding and a vocabulary of oppression, helping even white women to understand that doctrines of fairness and equality of opportunity might be applied not just to African Americans, whose exclusion was overt, but to themselves as well. The Civil Rights movement also offered women experience in organizing, which they would later apply to organizing themselves, and a vision of what was called the "beloved community," in which people theoretically worked together as equals, sharing the hardships and the excitements of day-to-day struggle. We credit the New Left, that conglomeration of anti-Vietnam War and social-change groups, with continuing the analysis of oppression and opening opportunities for women to develop the skills of grassroots community organizing.

Men in both movements, however, relegated women to making coffee and running mimeograph machines most of the time. Women rarely were listened to when it came time to make policy and were denied the opportunity to make speeches. Women were often expected to be sexually available to male leaders and were castigated as "uptight" if they refused. At about the same time, the counterculture offered women encouragement to reject the morals and mores of middle class society, allowing them to "tune in, turn on, drop out" along with men. Here, too, however, women were expected to be sexually available to men, as well as to make the coffee.

The introduction of the birth control pill in 1960 contributed to what was at the time called the "sexual revolution," which simultaneously encouraged women to explore their own sexual pleasure, often outside of marriage or monogamy, and increased the pressure on them to be sexually available to men. All three movements encouraged women to see their lives as restricted by the limits placed on their self-definition and autonomy, as well as on their opportunity. Together, they inspired women to think about their own needs, their own circumstances—and to come together to change what they did not like about those circumstances—in the movement we now know as feminism.

In Maine women came together in a number of different ways. Thirty years ago in Bangor, for example, a group of women concerned about domestic violence came together to form Spruce Run, now the third-oldest domestic violence project in the nation. Spruce Run was founded not by professionals, social workers, or legal experts determined to help women out of their professional expertise, but by ordinary women, some of whose personal experiences with domestic violence and efforts to escape it helped them to perceive the need. In addition, some of the founders' backgrounds in social justice activities gave them the determination and skills to try to do something about that need.

In the early years, members of Spruce Run offered support and advice to women trying to leave their marriages. They helped women obtain *pro se* divorces, which did not require the assistance or expense of a lawyer. They set up a hot line that women in abusive situations could call for help, to strategize plans to leave, or just to talk about their options. They worked with the police, training them to respond to calls for aid with tact rather than ridicule, with help rather than neglect. They orchestrated testimony before the legislature, bringing battered women to describe their experiences, hoping to convince legislators to enact better laws and provide funds to support their work. They established a shelter to house women and their children in a safe place until they could establish themselves on their own. They trained women, some of whom had themselves been battered, to speak in schools, to community groups, in churches, as well as to the legislature—to anyone who would listen. They worked with women in other parts of the state to establish similar projects, so that no woman would have to travel far for assistance.

In turn, these projects have created a statewide clearing house, now the Maine Coalition to End Domestic Violence, to work together to lobby and raise awareness about domestic violence. Collectively, all of these activities helped save the lives and restore possibility and the spirits of large numbers of women and their children, who otherwise would have had few resources to escape dangerous situations. They also helped the people of Maine to understand domestic violence as a problem, which had not previously been the case, and to develop solutions to ameliorate it.

Spruce Run has helped to shift public understanding of domestic violence away from the situation in 1960, when the subject was rarely discussed in public, women had no resources to speak of, and were widely assumed to be "asking for it." Today, too many women and children are still battered, too many killed, and resources are still inadequate compared to the need, but there *are* resources and, just as important, understanding of domestic violence as an issue of public concern and not the fault of the individual woman.

Another example of how Maine women have come together to create change is women's health. In 1983, again in Bangor, a group of people connected with the local family planning program became increasingly concerned about the Reagan administration's plans to restrict discussion of abortion in facilities that accepted federal funding; this was known as the "gag rule."

These women recognized that all women's access to legal abortions, made possible by the U.S. Supreme Court's *Roe v. Wade* decision, was being seriously undermined by an administration not sympathetic to choice in family planning. They worried about a political climate that might limit discussion of other issues, especially lesbian health care needs in the early years of AIDS. They wanted, in the words of one of the founders, "a platform to stand on, to talk about health rights for all people"—a way to provide health care services that paid attention to *all* women's needs, without fear of government intervention.

In 1984 the group incorporated as the Mabel Wadsworth Women's Health Center, with three key goals: to educate women about their bodies and their health, to provide medical services, and to engage in political advocacy for women's health issues. In the early years they engaged primarily in education, offering talks on lesbian health, on abortion, on menopause, and the like to community groups, colleges, and at day-long conferences. In 1992 they opened a clinic, at first with a paid coordinator and volunteer providers.

The Mabel Wadsworth Women's Health Center today offers a full range of women's health services, including pre-natal care and abortion. Women from all parts of the state use its services, in part because it is one of the few providers of abortion aside from private doctors. Organized as a private non-profit entity, the center still does not accept government funding. It continues to work to educate women about their bodies and their health. It continues to advocate, providing an important voice at the state level and beyond, especially for lesbians whose health care needs are too often neglected. Today, it is perceived as a community resource in Bangor, working with physicians, with Eastern Maine Medical Center, and with the city council to provide training for doctors, training in lesbian health care, and reacting to threats to women's health care. It also continues to be a resource for women themselves.

The Mabel Wadsworth Women's Health Center is the only private, free-standing, non-profit women's health center in Maine, one of fewer than twenty in the nation. Like Spruce Run, it has helped to shift the circumstances of women in Maine from what they were in 1960. Today, not all the doctors are men; women providers are available to care for other women. Now, women do not have to summon their courage to address their health concerns, no matter what those concerns might be.

A third organization that has helped to create change for Maine women is the Maine Women's Lobby, based in Augusta. Founded twenty-five years ago, the Maine Women's Lobby was inspired by the experiences of the state's delegation to the 1977 National Women's Conference in Houston. This conference brought activists of all beliefs together, to share ideas and strategies for change, and inspired many participants to renewed efforts to improve the quality of women's lives through attention to difference, coalition building, and a wide range of public policy initiatives.

Looking for ways to implement what they learned, Maine women who had been to Houston focused first on domestic violence. They worked on a bill to fund shelters for battered women and received an array of assurances of support as they guided it through the legislature, only to find that the legislation was killed on the appropriations table after they had gone home. They were told that this had happened because women were not represented as an interest group. As a result, they decided that women needed a full-time lobbyist to monitor legislation affecting them. They raised money, founded a non-profit organization, gathered supporters, and hired a lobbyist for the 1979 legislative session. (I make this and the other work that women did sound easy, but this kind of work is never easy.) In that session, the bill to fund shelters for battered women passed and was funded.

The Maine Women's Lobby worked for many years with the lobbyist as its single paid staff person; it continues today to work to increase social, political, and economic opportunities for Maine women and girls through public policy and leadership development. It focuses on issues in four areas: health care, including reproductive rights; violence prevention; non-discrimination; and economic security. Over the years, it has successfully lobbied not only for funds for domestic violence shelters, but also for legislation to make marital rape a crime (1985 and '87), to create employment and training programs for women on welfare, to ensure implementation of federal Title IX opportunities, and to ensure that women have access to choice regarding abortions.

More recently, it has lobbied for civil rights for gay men and lesbians, to remove derogatory terms for Native American women, and to remove firearms in certain cases of protection from abuse orders. It focuses on increasing women's economic opportunities and security, including for part-time workers; on jobs creation; and on allowing women family medical leave when necessary.

Increasingly, the Maine Women's Lobby has also focused on women's leadership development, through an internship program for a student at the University of Maine School of Law and through the Girls' Day at the State House program, which each year brings one hundred seventh- and eighth-graders to Augusta to meet the governor and learn about lawmaking. The Maine Women's Lobby works with other groups to develop strategic partnerships and coalitions to advance the women of the state. The organization has had and continues to have tremendous impact on the lives of women in Maine.

One of the reasons the description of life in 1960 seems so unfamiliar to us today is the work women in these three organizations—three among many— have done to create change. One organization out of the many others in Maine is the Maine Women's Fund. Founded in 1990 as a non-profit corporation, the Maine Women's Fund "supports programs, policies, and practices that empower Maine women and girls." It has awarded $900,000 in grants since 1990, mostly in relatively small amounts. It created a New Girls' Network of women leaders in their twenties and thirties. It works with other groups to help make the state a place where women of all ages can be "full participants in every area of society." If money makes a difference, the Maine Women's Fund is helping to enhance opportunity for Maine women by making it available.

These are just a very few of the multitude of women's organizations in Maine, nearly all of which were created or reinvigorated in the past three decades. Organizations like the YWCA, the League of Women Voters, the National Organization for Women, the American Association of University Women, the Maine Centers for Women, Work & Community, the Maine Lesbian/Gay

Political Alliance, Women Unlimited, which trains women to do construction work—a whole host of organizations for girls, for displaced homemakers, for victims of rape, for disabled women, for lesbians, for working women, for working women in specific occupations, for working women in male-dominated trades, for business women—*all these and many more have been forces for change for women of the state.*

Together and separately, they have worked for women's issues including access to education, to jobs, to health care, to child care, to business opportunity, to rights and opportunities of all sorts. The good will and commitment with which women have approached working on them has been overwhelming; they have had a significant impact on women's lives in the state, helping to account for the changes from 1960 to today.

Significant Changes in the Policy Realm

Other changes were legislated by the federal or state government, most often because women pushed hard for them, or were the result of decisions by various courts. In 1964 Congress passed the Civil Rights Act, Title VII of which prohibited discrimination in employment for people with a variety of characteristics, and established the Equal Employment Opportunity Commission to enforce the law.

One of those characteristics was sex (others were race, color, religion, and national origin), which opened the door for women to demand access to jobs and to seek redress if denied. Sex was added as a category at the suggestion of a conservative Virginia congressman, who intended it to discredit the bill and the civil rights assumptions behind it; to his chagrin the bill passed. The law applied in Maine as well as the rest of the nation, offering women access to jobs from which they had previously been excluded, and putting employers on notice that they could not continue to discriminate.

Congress also passed Title IX of the Education Amendments of 1972, which prohibited discrimination in any educational institution that received federal funding. Not only did this force previously all-male schools to open their doors to women, it transformed the nation's athletics program as well. For the first time, schools and colleges were required to provide equivalent (although not identical) benefits to male and female athletes; as a result, the numbers of women athletes in high schools and colleges in Maine and elsewhere soared, as did the amounts of money available to them in athletic scholarships.

Still other changes to laws affecting women were made at the federal and state levels in these decades. During Lyndon B. Johnson's presidency, the executive branch explicitly extended civil rights provisions to women and began issuing guidelines for affirmative action, so that hiring by federal contractors, including universities, would not discriminate against women. Marital rape was defined as a crime; later, in the 1994 Violence Against Women Act, so was rape within cohabiting relationships. This act also recognized that people had "the right to be free from crimes of violence motivated by gender" and established domestic violence and sexual assault as potential violations of the victim's civil rights.

Other changes affecting women's lives were the result of court decisions. The Supreme Court declared unconstitutional laws (found mostly in southern states) that prohibited interracial marriage (*Loving v. Virginia*) and a Connecticut law that made it illegal for physicians to prescribe birth control, even to married couples (*Griswold v. Connecticut*). A lower court prohibited references to sex in employment want ads. In 1973 the Supreme Court prohibited unequal benefits for male and female members of the armed services (*Frontiero v. Richardson*); in the same year, it struck down laws prohibiting abortion during the first trimester of pregnancy (*Roe v. Wade*). In 1975, the court declared that women had to be automatically included in jury pools (*Taylor v. Louisiana*), overturning a 1961 decision that had accepted a Florida law requiring them actively to put their names onto jury lists. Together, these cases and others like them ensured that women would have more freedom in their daily lives and greater opportunity to participate in civic life.

Not all changes proposed in public policy or law in the decades since 1960 have become a reality, most notably, the Equal Rights Amendment. First proposed in Congress in 1923 and regularly reintroduced thereafter, it was again introduced in 1970 and passed by Congress two years later. Although thirty-five of the necessary thirty-eight states had ratified it by 1978, no additional states joined them and the deadline for passage lapsed. It would have guaranteed that "equality of rights under the law shall not be denied or abridged by the United States or by any state on account of sex."

In addition, some changes enacted by laws or made possible by court decisions have subsequently been eroded. Nowhere is this more evident than in women's access to abortion, as many states, including Maine, and the federal government have passed restrictions that have been upheld by the courts. Congress has refused to pay for abortions for women receiving Medicaid, even when medically necessary and in cases of rape or incest. The Supreme Court, in the 1989 *Webster* decision, said that states could prevent public funds and facilities from being used for abortions; it has also upheld waiting periods and parental consent laws. Congress recently banned late-term (so-called "partial birth") abortions, even when the woman's life or health is at stake.

The outcome of these restrictions, along with the polarization of public opinion on the subject, has in practical terms limited doctors' willingness to perform abortions and women's access to them. The Mabel Wadsworth Women's Health Center in Bangor is regularly picketed by anti-abortion protestors. In the spirit of making lemonade out of lemons, it has used this to inspire a fund-raising campaign, asking donors to pledge money for every day the picketers appear.

In spite of the limits of policy change and a changing political climate, the women's movement has had a dramatic impact on the state, as well as on the individuals within it. Sometimes, women who began activist careers as volunteers in social change organizations have moved into paid staff positions within them; others have gone on to positions in state government or other public agencies. Laura Fortman, for example, became the first staff person of the Maine Women's Lobby, and is today Maine's commissioner of labor. Other activists became attorneys, state legislators, and public administrators. These women have helped to institutionalize the changing attitudes about women and their place in society that their activism both represented and encouraged.

Assessing the Effects of Change

It remains, however, to assess the impact of these changes, to explore the ways in which women's lives today are similar to and different from those of the women of 1960. To do so, I want first to look at Maine women's lives in the aggregate, and in the process compare them to men and to women in the rest of the nation. Then, I will attempt to put the present into context—not an easy task for an historian, but one in keeping with the spirit of this book.

Maine women have come a long way from 1960, according to most measures of change. Educational opportunities are no longer rigidly gender-based; young women (and men) now take classes in school according to their interests, not their gender. Bowdoin College and Maine Maritime Academy opened their doors to women, and women may now major in forestry at the University of Maine. The curriculum in many respects has been broadened to include the accomplishments of women and Jane and Sally no longer watch Dick do things. Almost all the state's institutions of higher learning offer degrees or programs in women's studies.

Maine women have roughly the same educational accomplishments as the state's men, with roughly equal percentages completing high school and college; women lag behind men only in the percentage holding post-graduate degrees, although the numbers are relatively small for both sexes. Maine women compare favorably to those in the rest of the nation in terms of educational achievement, with more of them completing high school and roughly the same percentages attending and completing college. Even so, in higher education, women are under-represented as both faculty and students in science and engineering, as they are in programs that teach the traditionally male skilled trades.

Economic opportunities and earnings tell a more complex story. Women still earn less than men do, even when we compare full-time and year-round workers—although the gap has narrowed from the fifty-nine cents for every dollar that men earned in 1960. In 1995 Maine women still earned just under sixty-nine cents for every dollar that men did, very close to the national figure.[2] The increase is partly because women's educational level is today more similar to men's, and partly because women have been in the workforce for longer periods of time, allowing them to increase their wages. More women than ever before are employed in the better paying occupations, as well. Sixty-nine cents is certainly better than fifty-nine, but women in Maine and the nation still have a long way to go to achieve economic parity with men.

In 1990 Maine women stood thirty-first in the nation in terms of their median annual earnings. Maine women continue to be over-represented among part-time and seasonal employees, sometimes voluntarily and sometimes not, and under-represented in unionized jobs. Seasonal jobs especially revolve around tourism and tend not to offer high wages, although they do offer women more time with their children. More Maine women than ever before own their own businesses, although a slightly smaller percentage of businesses are owned by women in Maine than in the rest of the nation, and the businesses themselves tend to be smaller in scale. The vast majority of these businesses are in services and retail trade.

Although women's overall earnings compared with men's have improved since 1960, women continue to be over-represented in the sales and service sectors of the economy, in jobs referred to as "pink-collar," and under-represented in heavy industry, in forestry, and in production—in blue-collar jobs. They are also under-represented in high-status professional and technical occupations. Women's jobs are less likely than men's to offer what the Institute for Women's Policy Research calls "economic autonomy"—that cluster of factors that offer women "the ability to act independently, exercise choice, and control their lives." Too many Maine women work in jobs that do not pay enough to allow them to cover the costs of a "basic needs budget."

According to Stephanie Seguino, who studied Maine women's economic circumstances and their ability to provide for their families, in 1993 "on average, Maine women earned less than three quarters of the average hourly wage required to meet a basic needs budget."[3] This means that many Maine women and their children live in poverty. Poverty can mean homelessness and hunger, no health care, no dental care, no transportation, and no security. Too many Maine women still do not have health insurance, although that is changing. Too many women do not have access to adequate and affordable child care, one of the key factors that makes their participation in the labor force so problematic. Many women still rely on public assistance, now called Temporary Assistance to Needy Families, to help them to make ends meet, but life continues to be a struggle for such women.

Two-parent homes are less the norm today than they were in 1960. In 1990 59 percent of Maine households consisted of married couples, with or without children, somewhat more than in the rest of the nation; somewhat fewer Maine families lived in female-headed or single-person households.[4] Not surprisingly, the members of those female-headed households, especially those with children, are more likely to live in poverty than those with men present. Women who do not live with men—whether single by choice, divorced, widowed, or lesbian, as well as those who are raising children on their own—are subject to less social stigma than they were in 1960, although this stigma has not disappeared. Maine's repeated refusal to pass legislation to ensure the civil rights of gay men and lesbians suggests that discrimination has not disappeared, although in many cases it may be less overt than before.

The Glass: Half Empty or Half Full?
We are left to make sense of all of this change. A girl born today is still likely to be wrapped in a pink blanket, although it may also be yellow, green, or blue. Like her brother, she may be dressed in overalls; like him, she will be encouraged to jump, run, and play, without worrying too much about getting dirty. In school, her textbooks show men and women, boys and girls taking active roles in society. She will be more likely than the girl of 1960 to be encouraged to raise her aspirations, to study math and science, to participate in politics. She can be inspired by many women in positions of power and influence, including two senators and many state legislators.

Our young woman today is more likely than the woman of 1960 to be encouraged to go to college, to follow her interests no matter what these might be, to think about developing a career. She has more choices about what that career might be. Even so, she is still not likely to study science or engineering, to gain training in the trades, to go to some kinds of professional schools.

A young woman today may still feel pressure to have sex with her boyfriend, as her mother did in 1960. She is much more likely than her mother, however, to understand herself as a sexual being and be able to make choices about her body. She will not be valued primarily for her virginity, or for her ability to be a good wife and mother, rather than for her self. She is likely to be informed about the consequences of the choices she makes about her body and able to protect herself against sexually transmitted diseases and unplanned pregnancy—although she may not always act on this information.

When she seeks medical care, she may have access to information about contraception and abortion, offered by a provider who may well be a woman. Young women today tend to take this access for granted; they are sometimes surprised to learn that access to abortion was not always legal, is still not always available, and continues to be under threat.

If a woman today is attracted to women, she will be more likely than in the past to name herself lesbian, more likely to find others like herself, less likely to be stigmatized. Her high school may well have a civil rights team to address the discrimination and hate she may experience as a lesbian—or as a member of any other minority group, for that matter. Some Maine cities and towns have passed ordinances extending civil rights protection to gay men and lesbians, and some employers offer domestic partner benefits to same-sex couples. Maine has passed legislation restricting marriage to one man and one woman, however; and the federal Defense of Marriage Act allows a state to refuse to recognize marriages performed in another.

Young women today face pressures that those of 1960 rarely experienced, and they sometimes respond to these pressures in new ways. Messages from the mass media about how to look and behave are more relentless than ever. While the climate in classrooms may be less overtly hostile to young women's intelligence and aspirations, peer pressure may be worse. The term for date rape did not exist in 1960, but knowing the language today does not protect young women from the experience. Too often young women today respond to these pressures by developing eating disorders or depression, or by cutting themselves, all of which are sometimes considered to occur in epidemic numbers.

Young women looking for jobs today, no matter how much education they have acquired, may have a difficult time finding one, though not necessarily more difficult than their brothers; the problem today is the economy, not necessarily job discrimination. Sex discrimination in employment is now illegal, and women who think they have been discriminated against can seek redress. Many young women today recognize that they will need to work to support themselves, and possibly their children, for much of their lives. Many recognize that combining work and family remains challenging, sometimes from watching their own mothers struggle to do so. Still, they are committed to finding ways to "have it all," in spite of the difficulties, where "it" refers to work, marriage, motherhood—whatever they believe necessary for self-definition and autonomy.

Women in the middle of their work lives today are still likely to be found in pink-collar jobs, in service and sales. They still earn less than men do, even when they work year round and full time. Their jobs are less likely than those of men to carry benefits, including health care and pensions. They are still under-represented in the trades, in unionized jobs, and in many professions. Women who do have professional jobs find themselves hitting their heads against the glass ceiling, unable to rise into the highest levels of authority. Even today, women are under-represented at the highest levels of government and business in Maine and the nation.

Women still struggle to combine work and care for children, with the double day. However, women who support themselves and their children without

Deb Bickford, Garfield

the presence of men are less likely than before to be criticized for their failures or stigmatized by their neighbors. Temporary Aid for Needy Families may not be as demeaning as welfare, but women who depend on it find arranging for nearly every aspect of life difficult: housing, transportation, food, medical care, and clothing.

Those who are married are more likely to negotiate with their husbands about important decisions, once the sole purview of men, including such matters as where to live and what car to buy. They are also more likely to negotiate about sharing housework and child care, although it is difficult to assess the results. Most of the time, women still assume primary responsibility for domestic life.

Women of retirement age today are still less likely than men to have pensions of their own or sufficient Social Security on which to live comfortably, in part because of their more traditional career trajectories. Elderly women live disproportionately in poverty, even as they live longer than men. They remain largely invisible in society.

Women today who are raped or battered have far more resources available to them than they did in 1960. They are more likely to be taken seriously by the police, some of whom are women. Their rapists and abusers are more likely to be prosecuted and convicted, although women who have been raped still find their sexual behavior and even their clothing subject to public scrutiny. Convicting men accused of rape remains difficult. Women who have been raped can call rape response hotlines and other resources for assistance, however, including support in dealing with hospitals and the police.

Similarly, battered women can now obtain protection from abuse orders, although that does not guarantee their safety, and can seek assistance and shelter in any one of a number of locations throughout the state. Violence against women, in the form of domestic violence and sexual harassment, as well as rape, is now clearly against the law and women have access to both criminal and civil courts for protection and redress.

Women subject to sexual harassment—like those who believe they have been discriminated against in the workplace, in employment, in housing, in education, in credit, or in access—can also call for help, including help from the Maine Human Rights Commission.

Learning from the Past, for the Future
So, we are left to decide whether the glass is half empty or half full. Clearly, a great deal has changed since 1960. Whether enough has changed remains open for discussion, as does the direction of change in recent years. Is the situation for Maine women now getting better or worse? Are our circumstances becoming more like those of 1960 than they once were? As an historian, I am far bet-

ter equipped to look at the past than to make predictions about the future. Nevertheless, I want to take a stab at some guesses, taking comfort in the fact that only time will tell whether I am right or wrong.

Women in Maine today, particularly young women, have little sense of how much has changed in what historians can only describe as a very short period of time. Even those of us who remember 1960 do not often step back and reflect on how different it is from today. This breeds complacency. *We tend to think, if we think about such things at all, that the rights we enjoy today will always be there—have always been there—without recognizing the dedication, the hard work, and the commitment that made them possible. We do not want to see these rights as vulnerable, as alienable.*

We take for granted that there will be help available if we are raped, battered, harassed, or discriminated against. We prefer to see ourselves as equal to men, in terms of access to education, jobs, credit, housing, benefits. We like to think that Maine and the nation are becoming ever more fair, ever more open; that, as women, we are ever more equal.

This is the side that sees the glass half full, if not more than half full. Yet another side warrants attention, one that worries about slippage and loss of hard won rights and opportunities. Here, we need to recognize that some of the most fundamental problems facing women—particularly how to combine work and family life—remain perplexing, that we still fall far short of solutions. Women and their children still too often live in poverty; women still work the double day. Careers and children are hard to attend to simultaneously. Discrimination in every aspect of life still exists, although it is usually far more subtle than ever before, and this makes it more difficult to pinpoint and combat.

The consequences of discrimination remain powerful. Rights that we have taken for granted are today threatened by a federal administration determined to limit women's access to reproductive choice; to define marriage and the social and economic benefits it conveys in strictly heterosexual terms; to support only the most traditional rather than broader definitions of the family. Public policies are being written that define family in ways that impose penalties on women's choice of any but conventional, heterosexual behaviors.

I cannot tell you which view of the present is more convincing; no one can, because we do not yet have a vantage point from which to decide. I will end, however, by making a case for history, for understanding the past as a way of understanding—and changing—the present.

It is only when we have a clear sense of where we have been, where we have come from, and how we arrived here, that we may understand who we are today—as individuals, as a state, and as a nation.

Only when we understand the limits of women's opportunity and autonomy in the past may we treasure what we have available to us today.

Only when we know how hard women have worked, individually and collectively, to change their lives may we appreciate their accomplishments and value the impact they have had on us and on our society.

Only when we understand the past and the fragility of progress itself, may we change Maine and make it a better place for girls and women.

When we understand the problems and the ways in which women have worked to solve them, only then may we build the kind of society in which *all* will be able to thrive.

---

*E*ducated at the Johns Hopkins University, Sarah Lawrence College, and the University of Rochester, Marli F. Weiner is Professor of History at the University of Maine. She is editor of the important and soon-to-be-released work from the University of Maine Press, Of Place and Gender: Women in Maine History. Among her many contributions to Maine life and scholarship, Marli has served for a decade on the Maine Humanities Council, which she now chairs. Of especial interest to this audience, she recently led one of the council's many, successful public seminars for Maine citizens, on Alexis deTocqueville and civic leadership. Her writings range across issues of wellness, race, gender, and morality in this country, from pre-Civil War times to today.

B ASED ON TREATIES ESTABLISHED with the government of the Commonwealth of Massachusetts in 1796 and 1818, and later determined to be invalid, Penobscot Nation Chief Barry Dana argues that Maine's Indian tribes at statehood owned fully two-thirds of the land now called Maine. In 1975 the federal government sued the State of Maine on behalf of the tribes, and the resulting Settlement Act of 1980 has shaped life over the past quarter-century for the members of the Penobscot, the Passamaquoddy, the Micmac, and the Maliseet tribes living within Maine's borders. While the Settlement Act recognized the tribes as a defined "sovereign," legitimizing tribal government, Maine state government has often refused to recognize the tribes' sovereign status and treated them instead as a political subdivision of the State of Maine. Chief Dana shares his personal memories of growing up as a Native American in Maine, and candidly discusses the 1980 Settlement Act, the casino debate, and Indian development prospects from the perspective of Maine's Native American tribes.

EDITOR'S NOTE: At the time of this writing, the State of Maine and the Penobscot and Passamaquoddy tribes are each appealing (for different reasons) a delegation of authority by the U.S. Environmental Protection Agency (EPA) to the state, to issue National Pollution Discharge Elimination System permits under the Clean Water Act. The recent EPA decision (January 2004) delegated permitting authority to the state for all dischargers in the Penobscot and St. Croix river watersheds, except those located on Indian Island in the Penobscot River and at Pleasant Point (or, Sipayik). The tribes argue this circumscribes their sovereignty rights, while the state is concerned it violates provisions of the Maine Indian Land Claims Settlement Act. When the EPA originally proposed the delegation of authority to the state, the tribes objected, arguing that the rivers should be looked at more expansively in terms of tribal jurisdiction or sovereignty, and expressing concerns over the state's environmental standards. The paper companies involved requested all the information the tribes had provided to the EPA in their challenge to the delegation, and the tribes declined, again citing issues of sovereignty. The tribes did not turn over documents for some time, but the information was eventually submitted under court order. For background on this and other recent Indian issues in Maine, and the history of Indians in Maine from earliest times, see Neil Rolde, *Unsettled Past, Unsettled Future: The Story of Maine Indians* (Gardiner, ME: Tilbury House, 2004).

15 Native American in Maine
Toward a New Relationship

Barry Dana

It often comes as a surprise to people who do not know Maine well that there are Indians and Indian reservations in Maine. I am living proof that the tribes have been here since 1960 and long before, that we are here today, and that we plan to be here in 2010 and beyond, so long as the Penobscot River flows.

There are more than 2,000 members in the Penobscot Indian Nation. Some 400 tribal members reside on Indian Island, one of more than 200 islands in the Penobscot River that comprise our reservation. Another 500 or so members live within an hour's drive of Indian Island. The Penobscot are one of four federally recognized Indian tribes who live within the borders of the State of Maine. The Penobscot, the Passamaquoddy, the Micmac, and the Maliseet tribes are the remnants of a once powerful confederacy known as the Wabanaki. Wabanaki is derived from our native language, and means "people that dwell in the land of the dawn."

From American Independence to the Settlement Act

Like many of the tribes of the eastern United States, the Penobscot until recently had no formal relations with the federal government; at first we dealt directly with the colonies and, later, with the states. In fact, our tribe had no relationship with the federal government until the 1970s. The treaties that delineate our reservation were entered into with the Commonwealth of Massachusetts in 1796 and 1818. In 1820, when Maine became a separate state, a treaty was entered into between the Penobscots and Maine, and the terms of the 1818 treaty were adopted. Ironically, this situation formed the basis for the Penobscot and Passamaquoddy tribes' later claims to ownership of two-thirds of the State of Maine.

Because we had no formal dealings with the federal government, these treaties never received the approval of the United States Congress, as required by the federal Trade and Non-Intercourse Act of 1790. Due to this lack of federal approval, the treaties were invalid, and all of our historic territory was, therefore, legally still owned by the tribes.

Because the State of Maine enjoyed sovereign immunity, we could not bring suit directly against it; only the federal government may bring suit against a state. Because of the historic lack of dealings with the Maine tribes, the federal government was reluctant to act on our behalf, but on June 2, 1972, the tribes filed suit in the Federal District Court in Portland to force the federal government to bring suit on the tribes' behalf against the State of Maine for the illegal taking of our lands. The Federal District Court of Maine determined in *Passamaquoddy v. Morton* that the Maine tribes, despite never having established a formal relationship with the federal government, were, indeed, Indian tribes within the meaning of the Trade and Non-Intercourse Act of 1790; therefore, the federal government owed a trust obligation to us.

This decision was affirmed by the United States Court of Appeals for the First Circuit in 1975. Shortly thereafter, the federal government initiated a suit against the State of Maine on behalf of the Penobscot Indian Nation and Passamaquoddy Tribe, which case was later settled by the parties. This negotiated settlement came to be known as the Maine Indian Land Claims Settlement Act of 1980 and was later ratified and confirmed through federal legislation and a companion state act.

Prior to the Settlement Act, the State of Maine claimed full authority over the Maine tribes. In fact, the state created laws that governed every aspect of tribal life on the reservation, from the structure of our government to the licensing of dogs. These laws were codified in Title 22 of the State of Maine Statutes, entitled, "Indians." Not until the court cases in the 1970s that led to the Settlement Act was it determined that the state had wrongfully exercised authority over the tribes all those years.

Unfortunately, the time between these court cases and the signing of the Settlement Act left little opportunity for the state to appreciate that the Maine tribes are separate governments, with sovereign powers exclusive of the state. The state leaders' interpretation of the act is that it returned the tribes to a subordinate relationship with the state. We do not agree with this interpretation of the act, and never will.

During the period in which the state claimed ascendancy over the tribes, it had illegally sold four townships that the Penobscots owned in the Millinocket area. The proceeds from these so-called Indian Purchases were placed in trust with the state, and provided funding for state services to Penobscot people. Unfortunately, any claim by the tribe for this illegal sale was relinquished as part of the 1980 Settlement Act.

Personal Recollections
Before we proceed, let me offer some personal perspectives on life growing up on the reservations.

Tribal members were not allowed to vote in federal elections until the 1950s, and in state elections until the 1960s. My great uncle, Donald Francis, fought on behalf of the United States in World War II and was killed in action. It has always bothered me that he was deemed citizen enough to go to war and die for this country, but not enough of a citizen to have ever voted in a federal or state election.

A single-lane bridge connecting Indian Island to the mainland was built in the early 1950s. Prior to construction of the bridge, tribal members accessed the mainland across a sawdust trail over the ice in winter, and by ferry when the waters flowed. My great-grandfather, Sylvester Francis (Donald's father), was the last ferryman for the tribe.

For my grandmother, the bridge was a major technological advance for the tribe. She grew up when there was a ferry and no bridge. Her father ran the ferry at one penny a person, and when he had a full load, all the kids would jump in because they didn't want to spend that penny. In winter, to travel across, the tribal members made a sawdust bridge to keep the ice from thawing, and people would actually drive cars across the ice bridge. There was one family my grandmother talked about who had a car, the only one on the reservation. They would pack the car up on Saturday and drive to Bangor with everybody's shopping list.

My grandmother was a sweet-grass braider. It was her job to do the braiding for the many basket-makers in the community, and they would barter. There wasn't much money on the reservation back then, so she would trade baskets for her sweet grass. Then, when she had a lot of baskets saved up, she would go and sell them. She continued this into her seventies. When my aunt moved to New Mexico, my grandmother would travel there each year with a huge suitcase full of baskets and bring back turquoise and braided rugs. She was very instrumental in my growing up; I spent a lot of time with my grandmother.

I also spent a lot of time with my grandfather. He was a log-driver and an expert canoe man, if that's the right terminology (I can think of it in Penobscot, but it's hard in English). He would give us grief if we used canoeing strokes that resembled today's racing techniques. His was all one side, one-handed, and he could move a canoe with a moose packed up in it, silently and efficiently. We used to talk about great feats of physical ability, so I really got inspired not only to match those feats, but maybe go a little further. They used to run from Indian Island to Lincoln Island (or, Mattanawcook), which is thirty miles, and be there by lunch, so we had to try it, too. We got there by supper, but we got there. This was the impetus for what some of you may know as the "Katahdin 100."

The 1960s and '70s

In the 1960s, we were a very small community, with no general store; everything purchased or bought would be done in town. If you had no money, and few of us did, you would go see the Indian agent, Ray Ellis. "Uncle Ray" was a non-Indian in an office building with one room and a phone. It was always neat to go down there because you would hear his phone ring—it was this incredible sound that many of us didn't have in our own homes. *I* was my mother's phone, which was the way I got into long distance running, I suppose. Every time she wanted to talk with somebody, *I* was her voice and would have to run. Or, I would run to the store, as she had no car.

When it was time to go to school, all of us would go down to see Uncle Ray. We children thought of him fondly, because to a very young child, here was this man giving money to our mothers so we could go into Old Town and get school clothes or a food order. Little did I know that, at the time, the money that Ray Ellis was giving out was money that was put in trust by the State of Maine for the tribes. This sounds nice, until you realize where the money came from.

The state—from one office to another, I suppose—deeded to itself four townships of tribal land in the area, land that was not disputed. No permission was given from the tribe, whatsoever. Simply, "Could you sign this?" "Sure!" The deal is done, four townships. It was helpful to find this out, because, as I was growing up, I was very upset to think that my ancestors somehow, through treaty, gave away or relinquished title to our most sacred place on this planet, Katahdin. But now I know that the state did this on its own, without permission. There was money set aside from this deal, and not knowing the full story, we felt like we were fine, we could have clothing and food on the reservation.

We had an elementary school on the reservation that went to fifth grade. In sixth grade, I went to school in Old Town, and that was quite the culture shock. It was the first time I ever had to get into fist-fights three or four times a day, so that I could maintain the pride that I had been given through my grandparents and my parents. Growing up on the reservation, I never heard the words, "You dirty Indian" or, "You lazy thief"; but in sixth grade, in the non-Indian school, I did. When you are a sixth-grader, and you grow up kind of tough, anyway, there's only one way to resolve it. So, for the first month, all the kids from the Island were getting into these fights. Once we proved ourselves and people got to know us, the fights went away, and we all got to be friends. We went into junior high school in "Mill Town," and then on to high school.

In high school, things got relatively easy for me. I was in the band; I played trumpet; I was in academics; I ran with a crowd of people who were motivated, somewhat intellectual. I don't consider myself intellectual, but I managed to get the grades to get into college, and I was on the sports teams. So things moved rapidly for me. But I also witnessed a different story for many of the people I grew up with, people who chose to keep their hair long, who chose not to stand at the Pledge of Allegiance, because they did not feel that the American flag represented their interests. I watched them being sent to the office on a daily basis—a total misunderstanding of cultures. They managed to get through, but it wasn't easy; for me, personally, it was easy. I was just way too busy with homework and having to do this, that, and everything else, to be overly concerned about such issues then.

In the late-1970s it came to a point where I had to say something. I was in a Maine literature class, and the teacher was reading aloud from a book. At "the early explorers learned medicines from the savages," I raised my hand and said, "Who are the savages?" The connotation today, I suppose, is somewhat different from the time the book was written; for the sake of discussion, let's work in today's concept.

She said, "Well, I suppose it would be the Indians. Do you have a problem with that?"

I said, "Yes, well, I do. I'm Indian. I'm Penobscot, I know a lot of Penobscots, and I don't consider them to be savages." And the room just fell dead silent.

"We didn't know you felt that way."

"Well, you do now."

I think it is important when these situations arise, we address them so that stereotypes are put away through education. If I had been running the classroom that day, I would have thrown down the book and said, "Now we can start teaching! Because we've got something worth talking about, instead of this book that is 200 years old!"

The point that I brought up that day was quickly dismissed, however, and the teacher moved on. So, I was left with this, "Wait a minute, I'm at the front line of this war here, and the battle's gone." The thing is, so were the rest of the students in the class. You know—thirty students all looking at me, going, "What's up? Talk to us. Let's talk about this."

I was happy to talk about it. I think it's important. There are many issues today that still need to be talked about—Redskins, Big Squaw Mountain, things of this nature. "Why can't you guys get over it?" I hear people say, "When is it going to end, this political correctness road?" My answer is, "When all the damage has been rectified." So, we're going to have to keep talking about these things.

The 1980s

When 1980 came along, that is probably when most people realized, "Wow, there are Indians in this state! I didn't know that!" Some of that came about when the tribes had to bring suit in federal court to sue the State of Maine for what was rightfully ours—two-thirds of the State of Maine. There was no dispute to that.

Even today, I have people come up to me and say, " You know, I was working at such-and-such bank, and we were getting ready to do such-and-such transaction, and everything stopped"—because title was threatened. But it was tribal land—two-thirds of the State of Maine! What were you going to do? People were living there, and they had to settle this thing. There were many proposed settlements put before the tribe, and all were rejected. A timeline was being used as a tool to force us to decide prematurely. I suppose that's the definition of a settlement: when both parties disagree, they have to meet in the middle somewhere.

If you were the State of Maine, how would you deal with these people who think that two-thirds of the state is theirs; yet, legally, you don't have a leg to stand on? What were you going to do about it? It just put the whole state in a total crunch. I was in high school at the time, having to listen to comments in the community.

"What are you Indians going to do with all that land, anyway?"

"Well, give it back, and we will see." And that was the end of the conversation.

The last discussion I remember the tribe having was, "Ronald Reagan is going to be in office, and he won't sign this thing. We have to get it passed now." I said, "Who is Ronald Reagan? I don't care who Ronald Reagan is. I care about this document in front of me that starts off saying, 'All past illegal takings of Indian land are hereby okayed.' That is not right."

This is about illegal transactions. It's simply a case where land had been illegally taken from the tribes, and now we were being asked by this document, by signing this 1980 Settlement Act, to ratify it, to say it's okay.

I was nineteen years old; I was not about to give in to that. But my tribe did, by way of an "advisory" vote. If there is anybody who was around at the time who is Penobscot or Passamaquoddy, and who remembers, it was considered an advisory vote, not a legally binding Penobscot vote.

Crunch time had come, however. The deadline had arrived, and it was the last chance for the tribe to take a vote. I don't know the numbers, but the "Yes" side won, accepting the Settlement Act. The state took this as the tribe's position, it went forward, and President Jimmy Carter signed the Settlement Act.

The Penobscot and Passamaquoddy "team," as it was called—the negotiating team—came back from several Washington trips to meet with us, the community. We asked about one word in the language of the act: "What does this word mean, 'municipality?'" "Oh, don't worry about that. The State of Maine has said that they would recognize us like a municipality, so we can receive funding. So, don't worry about that, that's only for funding purposes." Like your "Star Spangled Banner," those words rang loudly on my face: "For Funding Purposes Only."

Now, when law is being disputed, you do what? You go back to the intent. Our negotiating team came back from Washington, where they had gone for the sole purpose of asking Congress about this "municipality" status. "This is for funding purposes only. This settlement package strengthens tribal sovereignty." Those were the words of the Congress: "strengthens tribal sovereignty." Cool! Maybe this deal isn't so bad after all. I would still vote against it, but maybe it wasn't so bad after all, because at the time the state refused to recognize tribal sovereignty.

The State of Maine had passed laws in Augusta dictating life on reservations even while admitting they had no legal right to do so. The tribes had said, "Well, we need a set of laws, these will work for now, and until we change them, we'll operate under them. They seemed to work for Old Town. You know, we'll get our dog license and car license, things of that nature."

"For Funding Purposes Only!" So, the tribe went forward with the concept, because the intent was that we remain a federally recognized sovereign nation. Now, a sovereign nation, if you want to put it in the context of countries, is different for tribes. It is not like we are the nation of Canada within the United States; we do not have that status. We have federal recognition, which is as a defined sovereign. *There is federal government, there is state government, and there is tribal government.* It receives its own status.

The State of Maine has repeatedly refused to recognize that status. We were of the understanding that because of the intent, because our negotiating team came home and reported after each visit to Washington that we are sovereign, we were given "municipal status" because we need to plow the roads—we are going to get the snow off the roads, and they are going to help us with some money to do that. Even to this day, that's about all we get. We do have other programs that we have initiated and worked on with the state, but not as a result of the Settlement Act.

That was probably the biggest thing right there, the 1980 Settlement Act, which changed the status of the tribe. First of all, it gave us status in the State of Maine because, as Richard Barringer has previously stated, we were a forgotten people. *We* did not forget who we were; but we were not there. To this day, I still have people come up to me and say, "You know I grew up here, and I didn't know there were tribes in Maine." I was at Colby College recently, and they did not know that forty-five minutes north there is a reservation with its own people. So, the educational process is ongoing.

Maintaining Culture and Autonomy
After 1980, the tribes sort of calmed down. We went about trying to create a life for ourselves while still maintaining our culture. Now, you want to talk about *two* heavy burdens: create housing, create economic development, make sure our kids are going to school—and, at the same time, retain our culture. A lot of my cultural traditions—the language, the ceremonies, the activities—had to diminish, because of the demands of college. But while I was in college, I

maintained hunting, going to see elders, and doing my language; that's my excuse for only getting Cs in college. I had to be diverse, plus play sports; that is the life for native people.

We work hard in two worlds. We are asked to be Indian, and, at the same time, we are asked to be non-Indian, because of lifestyle. I think a lot of that comes from our having to ask ourselves to be that way, because if you don't understand the dominant society, it will run you over!

We have become educated—we have doctors and lawyers and individuals in every walk of life—but that does not mean we have lost our traditions. We maintain a really strong sense of who we are. This is where you will find conflict—in a culture that views life one way, versus a culture that views it a different way. This conflict is evident almost daily. If you really want to see it at its highest point, you can go to Augusta and hear, "Here we are, we have these people: what do they want all these special rights for?" This is what you hear: "They don't want to be subject to the same laws as the rest of the state."

The Settlement Act clearly defines certain things, and it makes zero mention of others, and the zero-mention means that that which was not discussed, was not relinquished. We did not talk about spirituality. We did not talk about sacredness. We did not want to relinquish it! Our form of government—we did not give it to the state, because we did not want to relinquish it, nor our title to the river, or our title to lands. There are many things that are not in the Act. The problems, though, are the things that are in the act, where you find words like "Unless otherwise provided."

Now, it is easy to run over that phrase really quickly: "Unless otherwise provided, the laws of the State of Maine shall apply on the reservation."

So, you think, "Wow, that is pretty powerful. The laws of the State of Maine shall apply on the reservation. Gee, that doesn't sound very good."

"Well, mister nineteen-year old college kid, don't forget 'unless otherwise provided.'"

"Well, what does that mean?"

"That is somewhere else in the act."

"Okay, take me to that. Read it to me."

We did this. We had these huge public hearings. People would come and we would shred this thing, word for word; I could have gone to law school from that.

"Unless otherwise provided, you are acting as a tribal government."

"Oh, sovereignty!"

"Yes. Congress said it will strengthen sovereignty." There it is.

"OK, I suppose it's not that bad, after all; hopefully, we can live with it."

In every case where these two phrases come into discussion—"sovereignty," and "unless otherwise provided"—the tribe takes one view, and the State of

Maine takes the opposite. "Unless otherwise provided" means to us that our tribal government is an internal affair, and shall not be subject to the laws of the State of Maine.

If I have documents that are created in my office and I am the chief of the tribe, would you consider these documents to be part of my tribal government? Would you not take the minutes from our council meetings, and consider them to be documents created as a part of tribal government? I would. If you disagree, I have to live with it. And there are many who disagree—the State of Maine is one. The court system tried to say, "You have this municipality over here; you are a municipality!" But they realized they couldn't say it this way, because, in fact, we are not a municipality, we are a tribal government. You cannot be an orange if you are an apple. So how are we going to word that? Ah-ha! "A tribal government, when acting in its municipality status, shall be subject to Maine's Freedom of Information law."

When the apple is acting in its capacity as an orange, I guess we should peel it! We don't know. Hopefully, someone is going to take this and appeal it, because it doesn't make any sense to us. How could it, when the chief justice, or one of the justices told the lawyers for the state and the paper mills, "It is none of your business!" The tribes took that to mean it is none of their business what we do or what we say, especially when the documents they were looking for were documents between my office and EPA, a federal agency, which is bound by federal law to produce those documents when asked for them.

You should understand that I operate with a certain amount of common sense in life.

"Now hold on, you are telling me those people requesting the documents, the lawyers representing industry on the Penobscot River, can go to EPA, request them, and they'll get them?"

"Yes."

"Then, why are they coming to us?" The attorney general's office for the state filed such requests with the EPA, and the EPA complied with that request. In Augusta are fourteen feet of documents. The request that went from the state attorney general's office was identical in wording to the request that the tribes got from lawyers representing industry. Identical! The law firm representing the mills was in Portland; the law firm representing the State of Maine was in Augusta. How is it they had identical wording? So, when the tribe received this document, this request for our documents, we denied it.

We are not a political subdivision of the State of Maine! Read the law. Read Maine's Freedom of Information law: all political subdivisions of the State of Maine shall comply with this law. Go to Augusta, go to Portland, go to these towns, and demand whatever it is you are looking for! You do not go to the Town of Indian Island—that is, to the Penobscot Nation, a federally recognized sovereign—and demand documents. You may *request* them; as a matter of fact, for those who have requested documents in the past, we asked them in, we sat them down, and we talked to them. We have always had an open-door policy. The information requested in the documents has been offered as a gesture of good neighbors living and working on the same river. But now they didn't want that.

All this happened as the result of the tribe's opposing the State of Maine's authorization from the EPA to administer the Clean Water Act here in Maine, in Indian waters. If you go onto the reservation, no one is going to tell you different: the river is ours! It always has been, it is, and it always will be. This was not relinquished. If there's going to be a pipe going into that river, directly into the river, we want to know what is in that pipe. We want to know the results. We have a complete department, the Water Quality Department, and our people are out there every day, monitoring the water. Guess who is *not* out there every day, monitoring that water: *your* Department of Environmental Protection. We share the results with them, so they *do* know what is in the water. We have a collaborative, good neighbor policy.

Of course, we want them to know what is happening to the eagle. It was very important that we have the EPA retain oversight authority on these permits. There was a permit issued to one request that allowed enough toxins to be discharged into the river that would accumulate in eagles to the point where there would be "not more than five eagle deaths per year." These permits are public knowledge. You can go in, as we did, and say, "Let us see these permits; we want to know what is going on." And when we saw that allowance for pollutants, we fought that. We got the EPA involved and the permits were revoked, protecting the eagles. Not even the Audubon Society knew about this. We knew about it because it is our tradition to know about the river and to protect it.

To The Present

With this request for documents and our opposition to the State of Maine's handling of pollution permits in our waters, you have probably heard the tribe's name in the media of late, not to mention that "other" project of ours. This brings me to the present.

When I am not dealing with all of this, back on the reservation I am dealing with who is applying for what job, and what are the policies and did we follow them, and who got hired, and they shouldn't have been hired because I do not like them, and they got their master's degree and I knew him when he was a kid, and I didn't like him then, and, besides, we have all these cats running around and we have to take care of them, and we are licensing our dogs so why not do the same with these cats, and who is going to take care of the garbage, and who is going to do what—so, I am a little busy. There is no issue that is not important, because if you do not take care of that garbage, it builds up. Speaking of garbage, do you know that there is a landfill right next door to the Penobscot Nation that we are getting involved in, as well? That is another story.

What else are we doing? We have a Boys and Girls Club. It is getting national acclaim, and with that status comes money. We have redone our gymnasium with a beautiful wooden floor, six baskets, a room divider, and a computer lab with twenty-five computers. Kids are there every day, fifteen to twenty kids in that one room, doing their homework every night, because we have a paid staff person who does homework with them.

This May we are creating an elderly abuse tribal law to protect our elders in all agencies and in community planning. We are trying to bring our culture into our policies, into agency decisions and things of that nature.

At a recent press conference, I challenged the Maine Department of Environmental Protection (DEP) to show me in their regulations and in their standards for water quality, the word "sacred"; it *is* in ours. We are being asked to surrender to the State of Maine this protection of the eagle and the fish and the dragonfly and the turtle; yet, in *its* policy, in *its* water quality standards, you don't see the word "sacred." I don't know if I can sleep well with that; this is part of the issue.

The other issue is, *a sovereign entity regulates itself*; a sovereign entity enforces those regulations. If you want to get into a whole other topic, you may go to DEP, sit in its office for weeks as we have done, and you will read documents and find out what level of enforcement takes place in the State of Maine, and you will be educated. Because, if you are an industry and you pollute way above and beyond those standards, and there are numerous fish kills a year, and your comment as a departmental agent is, "Why worry, when there are no fish left to kill?" *I* worry; and I think all Maine *ought* to be worried. Whether or not DEP gets this authorization, every Mainer ought to be asking, "Is that water being protected? Are we going to live by the status quo, and allow standards to be created but not lived up to?"

You ought to go to the DEP hearings when someone is there requesting a permit. I have been there, I have seen it; it is ridiculous. The permit is written before the hearing; the hearing is a formality to justify the permit. I went because one such permit was in the Penobscot Nation's waters, and I had to stop the fellow and say, "I'm sorry if I don't understand all the terminology, but what is this 'mixing zone?' Mixing zone is the portion of river figured in cubic feet per second?" That was my assumption.

"No, I'm sorry, it is figured in miles—how many miles of river it is going to take to identify these certain toxins, and dilute them to the point where downstream we cannot detect them."

So, when you hear the phrase, "non-detect pollutant," it is because you are so far down river that you have had miles of river volume to dilute it to the point where you cannot find it.

If I seem a little upset, a little angry, it is because I have to live up to a tradition of thousands of years, a mandate that I protect that river and *all* its inhabitants. Not just for *my* use. We as humans are the most selfish creatures on this planet. *I* want to go fishing; *I* want to go camping; *I* want to go swimming. Beautiful, we should want that; but there is a *higher* purpose. I do not see that in the regulation, either.

"Well, Chief, don't worry; we've written it in so you can go fishing."

"'You can go fishing.' Well, does that mean, eat the fish?"

"Oh, well, we're not going to talk about that."

We are going to take this topic and put it on the shelf for now? Well, I am not. I want to talk about that right now, because sustenance fishing is not "catch and release." Sustenance fishing is *eating* the fish.

Finally, let me ask some questions. [At this point in the public lecture, Chief Dana posed a series of questions to his audience and asked for responses, one at a time. Nearly all of the audience did not know the answers.] Did Columbus call us "Indians" because he thought he was in India? Are we called "Redskins" because of the color of our skin? Did the Pilgrims create Thanksgiving? Do the tribes pay no taxes? Did Maine give the tribe millions of dollars in the 1980s, and we squandered the money? I ask these questions because, along my trail, these are the things I still hear. Now, let me take a moment to give you the other perspective on all this.

In 1492, there was no such word as "Indian." There was this country, India, and it was called Hindustan. Columbus was in search of whatever he found. It happened to be this particular place that had people he called "Indios." In Latin there is a word for "Indios," but not "Indian." "Indios" means "People of God." All of a sudden, "Indian" is not quite so bad.

"Redskin" is not the color of the skin; it is the color of the scalp when you take it off the head. My tribe and many other tribes had bounties on their heads, where it was so many pounds for a male scalp, a female scalp, and a child's scalp, and you would have to produce the scalps to receive payment. There were many people in those days who got plenty rich. We have the bounty proclamation on the wall in our council chambers, because there are certain things that we will never forget.

Pilgrims were in fact *invited* to a particular ceremony that happened every year, and still does; we called it "giving thanks." I guess you flip-flop it, so it has become "Thanksgiving."

Tribes pay many taxes, most of what you pay. We don't charge taxes to ourselves, however; we will not go so far in the acceptance of European culture, that we will tax ourselves. We pay taxes to the state, and we pay income taxes. Many people who live on the reservation do not pay a property tax to the state; nor do they pay a property tax to the tribe. As a matter of fact, we provide many things to them for nothing. We do not have a tax base, yet we give them services.

In 1980, with the signing of the Settlement Act, the federal government gave the tribes $81 million, or something like that, for the purpose of buying land, and that we did. The land had to be converted to Indian territory. For the Passamaquoddies, most of that has happened; for the Penobscots, we are still in the process. The Settlement Act states that we had a certain time to buy all the land and convert it to Indian status, and then they created a hundred-step process for converting it—which included that if there is a town government involved, *they* have to approve it, too. Talk about challenges!

Now, I have already gone on longer than I ever have before. Questions and answers are great, because they allows me to find out where you are coming from, and that way I can speak to your thoughts.

Questions and Answers

Q: *Is there diminished legal status for members of the tribe? Can they run for legislature? Where do the lines get drawn?*

A: I would like to know that, too. Where do the lines get drawn? In Maine, the Penobscot Nation is in such a grey area that we'd like to identify exactly this distinction between when we are a state and when are we strictly a tribal animal. Can we vote? Yes. Can we run for offices outside the reservation? Yes. As a matter of fact, our non-voting representative to the Maine legislature is now running for the state senate, and we wish her a lot of luck.

Ours is not a diminished status, however. If you are on the Penobscot reservation talking to people, they will tell you that we are a sovereign people, that we have been here for ten thousand years, that we have been who we are and never anything else. Our goal is to get Maine government and courts to understand that. When you read the letter of the law and you come to these gray areas, there is nothing to turn to except the intent. You have to go over all these legal documents. We feel strongly that, even there, it supports our position 100 percent. For any entity to think otherwise is to disregard a lot of history.

Q: *You mention a landfill near Indian Island. In terms of economic development, is this something the tribe is considering?*

A: Economic development does not mean the destruction of our most precious resources. Tribal members work in these mills. The landfill in question, however, will be huge. We are not convinced, from the research put forth by the state and the company, that they have a good handle on the science. We have readings of high levels of arsenic in water wells close to the site, as it is. This site is upstream from our reservation, and I have mentioned catching fish. Fishing is not catch-and-release for us; it is sustenance. If we are convinced beyond a doubt that a facility upstream will not be harmful to us, then fine; but we *have* to be convinced.

The amount of time given to the public to fully understand this landfill is so short. The water quality person brought in the application, and it was in a box two and half feet long with huge three ring binders. We have eighteen people in our department who are going over this, and they don't have time. The public hearing is next week, and the final permit will be written a week thereafter. This is the process that is used in giving permits. They give you the hearing and such a short amount of time that you and a staff of eighteen people are not going to be able to do it. We are not opposed to it until we know for sure; we are desperately trying to move toward being sure right now.

Q: *What is the source of your money to start development efforts?*

A: If you come onto the reservation, you will see a couple of really nice buildings and a beautiful school. I'm going to guess that 90 percent of what we have been able to do on the reservation is the result of contract money from the federal government, Bureau of Indian Affairs. It is specifically targeted, so we may not use that money for economic ventures; you have to use the money for services you've requested. We have high stakes bingo, though, and seven times a year people come from as far south as Rhode Island and play high stakes bingo on the reservation. That is our one profitable, money-making venture right now. Economic development is quite the challenge. We are looking to create a credit union, so the money we do have we can keep under our control and generate interest for ourselves.

Q: *About gambling: after the election of November 2003 and the defeat of casino gambling, I believe your first words were, "We haven't lost; we just haven't won yet." Is this still your thinking?*

A: Absolutely. If you are hungry, you do not give up looking for food until you find it. On an economic basis, we do not know how far into the future our high stakes bingo is going to be able to feed us. Like a family that has a budget, we have a budget; but if a family is operating on a shoestring budget, paycheck to paycheck, what happens when the furnace breaks down? You are without, because you do not have a capital source to go to. That is what it is like for the tribe today. We are able to meet our needs, but that is just it. We cannot create things on top of that; we do not have the capital. We are working on it; but should we never get gaming, we will still work on it, and we will always be okay. We are survivors. We have survived a whole lot in the last 500 years, and we will be here for the next 500.

When it comes to gaming, if you look around Indian country, all around America, it is the absolute number-one way that tribes have turned things around overnight. With that as the model, we are certainly going to look at it as a means that we hope to develop, as well. We are not caught up on the morality question. We have been to Indian country, we have seen these casinos, we have seen tribal governments, we have talked with thousands of people, and we have read the government reports on related crime, and so on. We looked at every avenue and convinced ourselves beyond any doubt that this was a good project to get involved with. That is when we went ahead. We did our homework. It was not like we just wanted to bring this evil thing into Maine.

Q: *You speak about the tribe's desire for acknowledgement of your concept of the sacred, and for this to become part of the way we all do business and make policy in Maine. What do you say to Mainers for whom gambling is immoral, and would like the tribe to recognize their concept of what is sacred?*

A: That is easy. Look at the religions of the world. If you put the religious leaders, each one representing his or her faith, in one room, and asked them to come out with one philosophy, what would happen? Is it happening across the world today? What is the result? Instead of talking to one another, they kill each other. That is how strong their beliefs are. Their perception, their faith says, If you do not join me, I will kill you—and they do it. That is the extreme example, of course; but it is real, it is happening today.

Morality is a question of faith. What you view as moral is good for you. What others view as moral is good for them. As long as the two do not harm one another, what is the harm? We tried, in talking about gaming, to discuss this question of morality in terms of gaming. We looked around the tribe; this was our first study group, and we wanted to get a feel for who would be harmed by gaming. So, we asked, "Who is gaming today?" "So-and-so usually buys a lottery ticket, so-and-so goes to every church bingo in the area; and so-and-so goes to Foxwoods twice a year, three times maybe." We had a fairly good look at who was participating in gaming today.

Now, out of that population, who is adversely affected? How many divorces; how many child beatings; how many loss of jobs; who's now in jail because of it? Zero! It is a form of *entertainment* for these people. Do I go to Foxwoods? Do I play the lottery? I did once, but I never checked my numbers; so I never played it again. I personally do not participate in gambling, but it is not for me to say, "Neither can you." It is like saying, "My faith is this, so should not yours be this?" No. Mine works for me, and yours works for you.

For you to take away the tribes' opportunity, *that* is immoral. Your morality works for you, let ours work for us. Don't take this away from us. It is just unfortunate, given the terms of the 1980 Settlement Act, that we are in this mess as it is. Other tribes do not have to deal with a "settlement"; they don't have a "settlement" with their state. They are free to have gaming, and they have it: overnight, jobs; overnight, education; and overnight, adequate housing. I have been there, I have seen them. I have talked to the elders of the Onieda Nation. I have done my homework.

Q: *There was a lot of talk about the harm of gambling in the 2003 election. The governor spoke out about it, but now in the spring of 2004 the state is broke, and he is proposing that we join Powerball, which is like a high-stakes lottery. I am wondering, did you take that as a slap in the face?*

A: I try to be very political when I answer this with the media. I did not say I consider it a slap in the face; I said, "If you ask people here in Augusta, the words I am hearing are, 'What a slap in the face!'" I'd like to take it a step beyond that. If you looked at our proposal, and if you counted every projected dollar that was an offshoot of the gaming facility itself, if you have close to 5,000 jobs in the facility, and because the facility works with entities elsewhere in Maine you are creating other jobs, and you look at income taxes, and you look at what is being purchased, the total income was $400 million a year to the economy of Maine. Powerball is going to create $9 million. I think that is a slap in the face to the entire state. You are going to have to cut programs if you are not going to raise taxes. If you are not going to raise taxes, you have to create revenue. I have yet to hear of a solid plan to create that kind of revenue.

Q: *People come to Maine for tourism and to explore the wilds and the museums; and some say there is an opportunity for the tribes to show themselves and their history to their advantage, for a profit. Do you buy this notion? [Another member of the audience spoke up to say that this idea was offensive, akin to suggesting setting up a "petting zoo."]*

A: In my answer, I hope to explain how both points of view are valid. That is, for us to stand up and be recognized, to display ourselves in our own voice—not a non-Indian speaking on our behalf, which is what has happened to this point—taking the credit, the glory, and the proceeds. We are going through this right now on the reservation; it was not on the agenda, but it kept us up until midnight: what are the native people in Maine, the Penobscot Nation, going to do if it does not like non-Indians doing it on our behalf? We need to do it.

Did we want to do it twenty years ago? No. I went to my tribe as a very young man and asked permission to start my own business, because I was getting phone call after phone call from people, mainly in our schools, asking,

"Could you come to our school and talk about your culture?" Being fairly young, I said, "Why would I want to do that? Ah, no! You stole everything from us, and now you want to steal everything else." That was the perception, growing up on the reservation. Leave us alone, and that is all there is to it. I underwent an extreme process that I put myself through, thinking, "Wait a minute; if we do not, who is going to do it?" I went to the tribal council. Oh, goodness! It was a great discussion, and they granted me permission, through the discussion of, "If we do not, who will? If he is willing, let us support him."

I went into the schools, and took baskets and things of that nature, because that is what people wanted to see; but I also took every opportunity to talk about the stereotypes.

"Well, how did you get here?"

"My Subaru."

"Do you live in a house?"

"Yes."

"Well, we thought you lived in teepees."

"Well, I do. Remember that 'teepee' is Lakota for house, and 'wigwam' is Penobscot for house. Do you live in a wigwam?"

"Oh, no!"

"Do you live in a trash can, or what?" Students who got it would giggle.

What I am hearing is a need and an opportunity for native people to stand up and take control of our own fortunes. If we do not, someone else will.

*T*he Hon. Barry Dana, Chief of the Penobscot Nation, was born and raised on Indian Island, in a one-room house by the Penobscot River. At Old Town High School he earned All-State football honors, then traveled to Orono for his college education, the first person in his family to go to college. "It was only three miles," he says of the journey; "but it was a world away for me." While at the University of Maine at Orono earning degrees in forestry and education, Dana co-founded the Native Americans at Maine club, and he has not stopped working since on matters of Native American education, cultural heritage, and economic self-sufficiency. In 1981, before the start of his senior year in college, Dana paid homage to the ancient Penobscot tradition of making long-distance treks to Katahdin. He ran the 100 miles from Indian Island to the mountain and, upon his return home, told others of the experience. Thus began a new tradition, the Katahdin 100, which today draws 100 or more people each Labor Day to run, walk, or paddle all or part of the way to Katahdin. Those who make the journey describe themselves as "spirit athletes."

Having taught Native culture for fourteen years at the Indian Island Elementary School, Dana started his own small business, Native Studies, to teach Native skills to children at his outdoor camp in western Maine. He, his wife Lori, and their nine-year-old daughter Sikwani, live in a log house in Solon, where he keeps a garden, cares for his sled dogs, and makes birch-bark baskets and canoes for sale. "I continue making them," he says, "because when I do, I love it. I love making baskets, and I really love making canoes." In Chief Dana's time as leader of the Penobscots, the tribe has actively pursued not only the question of casino gaming in Maine, but, as well, a small business incubator in an empty factory building on Indian Island, for self-employed Penobscots, especially craftspeople and artists; the feasibility of commercial windpower on tribe-owned mountains in western Maine; and a bottled water enterprise on tribal lands in the Carrabasset Valley.

MAINE'S POLITICAL TRADITION offers a great deal to be proud of, including a preference for feisty, independent-minded legislators with a national view; a culture of political honesty and civility; and a political system that remains remarkably open to talent and malleable. In the past fifty years Maine has produced such national leaders as Margaret Chase Smith, Edmund S. Muskie, William Cohen, and George Mitchell, elected two independent governors, and sent more women to the U.S. Senate than any other state. All the while, rising standards and increasing professionalism have made Maine elections more competitive, if more costly. The future of Maine electoral politics is being shaped by national trends in campaigning, especially the identification and targeting of "psychographics" and the enormous cost-driver of television advertising.

16 Electoral Politics in Maine
Recent Trends, Enduring Archetypes

CHRISTIAN POTHOLM

The last forty years have witnessed great and significant changes in Maine's electoral politics; some have been minor, others have been profound.[1] Yet, amid all the changes, there have been several patterns and archetypes that have endured. In this chapter, I underscore the most enduring trends discernible since 1960, including the abiding power of the "center" in Maine politics; the rise in costs and professionalism of Maine political campaigns; the enduring archetype of the moderate, independent, national senatorial model; the rise of the Franco-American voter; the increasing importance of the ballot measure and its democratization of the political process; and the increasing importance of psychographics in Maine politics. I conclude with some observations concerning the many positives that continue to be present in both the process and style of Maine politics.

The Power of the Center in Maine Politics

One of the overarching themes of the last forty years in Maine politics has been the pattern of increasing costs and professionalism in Maine elections, leading to a competitive partisan balance that was not present in earlier eras of Maine political history.

A review of Maine politics since World War II shows that when it comes to the elections for governor, Congress, and the U.S. Senate, the Republican domination of the 1940s and early 1950s soon gave way to a Democratic ascendancy from the mid-1950s until the early 1970s, as the Muskie revolution of 1954 propelled the Democrats from obscurity to center stage. So strong was the Democratic momentum that in 1972, had not William (Bill) Cohen won the 2nd District seat for the Congress, the Democrats would have controlled both Senate seats, both congressional seats, and the governorship in that year.

In turn, the Cohen counter-revolution helped to restore balance to the political scene; and the last twenty years has been characterized by Republican, Democratic, and Independent successes, with the Green Party adding an important dimension to the mix in several important elections.

Just as Edmund S. (Ed) Muskie had built up the Democratic Party and attracted a variety of strong candidates, Cohen's style and campaign tactics attracted a number of young, energetic, and moderate Republican office-seekers. The result was a highly competitive political system. In fact, at century's end, the Congressional delegation was balanced with two Democratic Congressmen

(Tom Allen and John Baldacci) and two Republican Senators (Olympia Snowe and Susan Collins), together with an Independent governor (Angus King, Jr.).

This end-of-century balance was also reflected in ongoing voting patterns. There were more unenrolled (or, Independent) voters (38 percent) than either Republicans (29 percent) or Democrats (33 percent); but because Independents are less likely to vote than their enrolled counterparts, the electorate might be thought of as basically in a one-third—one-third—one-third balance. As a practical matter, this means that any candidate must today garner substantial support from parties other than his or her own, to be successful. This is why successful major party candidates in general elections in Maine are almost always nominees who are not from the far left (if Democrat) or far right (if Republican) of their respective parties. For Maine, over the last forty years, "the center holds"; and this is very much in the Maine historical tradition.

Other political forces may have an impact, as well. While it has just 1 to 2 percent of the registered votes in the state, the Maine Green Party, founded in 1984, often delivers 5 to 10 percent of the general election vote for its candidates and causes. It thus played an important role in such close electoral contests as the 2nd Congressional District race of 1992, when it helped Republican Olympia Snowe hold off the challenge of Democrat Patrick McGowan; and in the gubernatorial contest of 1994, when it siphoned off votes in Portland and undercut the campaign of Democrat Joseph Brennan. Its 1994 showing of 6.5 percent of the vote was enough to qualify the Green Party as an official party in Maine, the first recognized Green Party east of the Mississippi.

A Time of Rising Costs and Professionalism
This rough parity in voter turnout between Republicans and Democrats has been buttressed over time by a dramatic increase in the professional operation of campaigns.

Democrats began to use television for campaign purposes in 1954, and it took the Republicans nearly twenty years to catch up to its potential. Today, both major parties and their Independent and Green counterparts have access to superior local and national television talent for use in Maine campaigns. Added to this, the rise of professional polling—again with both local and national players of note—means that all successful, and many unsuccessful candidates have had access to assistance beyond the imagination of their counterparts from the 1940s and 1950s.

All this professional talent required considerable expenditures of money, of course, and overall costs of successful campaigning in Maine have skyrocketed. Whereas someone could run for Congress in the 1960s or 1970s and spend just tens of thousands of dollars, by century's end successful candidates were obliged to raise $300-400,000 for contested races. Major party candidates today routinely spend $2-3 million for Senate and gubernatorial races; and in 2002, the Green Party, electing to go with public financing in the gubernatorial race, was able to spend over $900,000 of taxpayer money.

By far the largest and most expensive element in the mix is the cost of television time. Whereas the 1954 Muskie gubernatorial campaign could buy a half-hour of television time for several hundred dollars, and get a good reach for its message, the same market penetration in 2002 cost $125,000! The thirty-second television commercial has become the staple of political campaigns for Congress, governor, and the U.S. Senate, and its quality and quantity often accounts for success or failure in the current Maine political environment.

This is a far cry from the 1960s, when candidates expected—and were expected—to spend the bulk of their campaign time meeting voters face-to-face. Today, such activity goes by the name "retail politics;" and while it is still important in the rural areas of Maine, it has been diminished by the overwhelming demands of the television effort, often referred to as the "air war." Despite the passage of Maine's so-called "Clean Elections Act" of 1996 (which affords candidates the choice of public financing in gubernatorial races), most candidates continue to spend inordinate amounts of time and effort raising money, both within and outside the state.

This rise in cost and professionalism has not dimmed the general enthusiasm for politics, however. The 2002 election cycle saw nine Democrats and four Republicans vying for the open 2nd Congressional District seat, when incumbent John Baldacci ran for governor; and every two years, dozens of Maine citizens offer themselves up for public scrutiny and possible service.

An Enduring Archetype

In the midst of these changes in the rhythms and demands of political campaigning in Maine, it is interesting and, indeed, comforting to note the persistence of sturdy political archetypes in the Maine tradition. As we open the twenty-first century, none is so discernible as that of the election of strong-willed, independent U.S. Senators (and, at the moment, we could add, Republican and female).

In 1960 Senator Margaret Chase Smith was at the height of her political power, nationally, and running for President of the United States, the first woman ever to do so. Elected to Congress in 1940 following the death of her husband, Congressman Clyde Smith, Margaret Chase Smith quickly established herself as a feisty, hard working, shrewd campaigner; she won four elections within six months of each other, during a six-month period in 1940.

In 1948 Smith decided to run for the U.S. Senate, challenging a very popular, sitting Republican governor, Horace Hildreth; a World War I hero and former governor, Sumner Sewall; and a highly regarded minister, Albion Beverage. Her upset victory in the Republican primary of 1948 thrust her onto the national stage; and her follow-up victory in the September general election, as well as two successful re-election campaigns, solidified her position in the Maine and national political firmament.

Much more importantly for the course of Maine politics in general, Smith established herself in Washington as a strong, independent, national voice. In doing so, she was often at odds with her Republican president. In fact, for as much as six of the eight years Dwight D. Eisenhower was in the White House, she was out of favor with her own president.[2] Smith's independence, national stature, and legislative power—as the ranking Republican on the Armed Services and Appropriation committees—established a model that was followed by Ed Muskie, Bill Cohen, and George Mitchell; and that today is personified in Maine's two Republican senators, Olympia Snowe and Susan Collins.

For his part, Ed Muskie was often at odds with Democratic President Lyndon B. Johnson, and Bill Cohen even voted to impeach Johnson's Republican counterpart, Richard M. Nixon. Today, both Snowe and Collins are often in the press for opposing one or another of President George W. Bush's policies. Both continue to acknowledge their debt to Senator Smith; and it is not difficult to see the latter's archetypal impact and hear echoes of her style and personality in their political activities. Maine likes feisty, independent senators!

It is now an enduring part of our Maine political heritage that while we assume our Congressmen and women will be faithful to their party and their presidents, we expect, even demand that our senators fit the model of being independent, national in outlook, and willing to both tell truth to power and be a little self-righteous in the bargain. For students and practitioners alike, the persistence of such an archetype is a fascinating insight into Maine politics.

Many people in other states frankly prefer other models for their senators. In lieu of national stature, they often expect elaborate political patronage and "bringing home the bacon"; think, for example, of Senator Robert Byrd of West Virginia, who managed to bring a major Coast Guard facility to his landlocked state; or of Senators James Eastland and Trent Lott of Mississippi, who have routinely taken ships that might be built in Bath and carted their contracts off to Mississippi. In Maine, the political culture expects, even demands both national outlook and performance.

In Maine we expect our senators to play a national role and, at least on occasion, to sacrifice Maine's parochial interests for the greater good of the nation; Maine's two current senators are well within this tradition. Both also exhibit the competitive streak that made Ed Muskie want to top Margaret Chase Smith, Bill Cohen to top Ed Muskie, and George Mitchell to top Bill Cohen. Maine citizens praise cooperation among the Maine delegation, but they also appreciate competitive zeal on the national stage. They simply expect their senators to play a national, as opposed to a purely representational role; they expect their senators to fit the modern model of Margaret Chase Smith. This is simply the persistence of a previously featured and, for Maine people, a most satisfying archetype.

The Rise of the Franco-American Voter

Yet, another important trend in Maine politics, one that intensified in recent decades, is the rise of Independent candidates, and their considerable electoral success. In 1960, Independents never came close to being elected to major office, although Neil Bishop, a rural Republican populist who ran as an Independent Republican in the general election, helped Ed Muskie defeat the incumbent Republican governor, Burton Cross in 1954.

James Longley, Sr., was the first Independent governor in the United States, following his victory in a hotly contested, three-way race in 1974 against Republican James (Jim) Erwin and Democrat George Mitchell. Political insiders were not surprised by the defeat of Jim Erwin, for he had already run for governor twice and lost both times; they were, however, stunned by Longley's upset of George Mitchell. Mitchell, the protégé of Ed Muskie and a veteran of many political battles on behalf of the Senator, saw his late and large lead eclipsed by a surprising surge the last weekend of the campaign, which put Longley over the top.

Both the accomplishments and antics of Longley in office lie beyond the scope of this chapter; but in terms of politics in Maine, he served as a role model for many citizens who wished to imitate his efforts. More than a dozen Independent and third party candidates ran for governor from the period 1974 to 2004. John Menario and Sherry Huber each received 15 percent of the vote in 1986, their totals setting the high-water mark in the twenty years following Longley's precedent-setting performance.

None of these Independent candidates succeeded in winning, however, until Angus King, Jr., did so in 1994, fully twenty years after Longley. Anyone who knew both Longley and King, with their differing temperaments, public philosophies, and personalities will no doubt be surprised to learn of the identical nature of the political coalitions that elected them. Both benefited from relatively poor campaigns run by their opponents, had a strong inner faith in the righteousness of their quests, and shared a strong sense of their own superiority.

Most importantly, however, both Longley and King were elected by exactly the same voting coalition: an unusual combination of urban, Franco-American Democrats and small town, Yankee Republicans. Of the dozens of Independents who ran for governor, only these two were able to put together the necessary demographic combinations to emerge victorious. The explanation requires some background. Much has changed in this regard since 1960.

Until 1972 Maine had straight-ticket party voting, which meant that a voter could check off a single, large box at the top of the ballot, and vote thereby for *all* the candidates of the party she or he chose. This was called the "Big Box" system; and it played a very important role in making it easy for the party faithful, Republican and Democrats, to vote a "straight" ticket. It is very difficult to imagine circumstances prior to 1972 in which the major parties would have seen the significant defections necessary to propel an Independent into office.

Both parties had generally assumed that the Big Box helped their cause. However, following the very close race for governor in 1970, when Democrat Kenneth Curtis narrowly defeated Republican James Erwin, there was a great deal of scrutiny of the voting patterns; and the definitive assessment was done by none other than George Mitchell, on behalf of the Democratic Party.

In a widely read piece for the *Maine Sunday Telegram*, Mitchell proved conclusively that there was a rural-urban split in Maine voting patterns, with urban dwellers much more likely to vote Democrat and the rural voters much more likely to go for Republican candidates. This prosaic notion fit the assumptions both parties had long made. What raised eyebrows and political tempers, however, was Mitchell's further findings that Democratic voters were much more likely to use the "Big Box" than their Republican counterparts; and that, most importantly, Franco-Americans, the bedrock of the Democratic coalition, were most likely to use the device.

Taking a position which he took to be pro-democratic (as opposed to pro-Democratic), Mitchell called for the elimination of the Big Box. Reaction was swift, ironic, and more than a little important for the future of Maine politics. Democrats resisted all attempts to eliminate the Big Box; but Republican activists seized on Mitchell's article as proof that the system needed reform. Various legal and political machinations followed, but it was left to Robert (Bob) Monks, Sr., a Massachusetts transplant who wanted to run for the U.S. Senate, to organize and fund a referendum to eliminate the Big Box. The referendum was successful in June of 1972, and set the stage for a Republican resurgence led by Bill Cohen.

Cohen would win his congressional race the Fall of 1972, in large part because of his ability to attract Franco-American voters, especially from Lewiston, getting them to split their ticket by voting for Democrat Bill Hathaway over Senator Margaret Chase Smith, and then for him, over Democrat Elmer Violette. Cohen was thus able to keep Violette's margin down in Androscoggin County and win the seat, the only Republican to win major office that year. From 1972 onward, then, Franco-Americans (18 percent of the electorate), who had traditionally been Democratic voters and the most stalwart of that Party, were now "in play."

Before 1972 Republican defeats had been something of a self-fulfilling prophecy, as their candidates did not bother to campaign in the Franco-American cities like Biddeford, Lewiston, Sanford, or Waterville. Now, it was both imperative and rewarding for Republicans and Independents to campaign there.

This, then, was the background for Longley's historic victory as he put together the first coalition of urban Francos and small town Republicans. While Longley did not capture a majority of Franco-American voters statewide, he did well enough in his home of Lewiston-Auburn to defeat George Mitchell narrowly, despite (or, rather, because of) Mitchell's major get-out-the-vote effort in Lewiston in November 1974. Mitchell had driven them to the polls, where they voted for Longley!

Following Longley's success in 1974, more than a dozen Independent or nontraditional party candidates would seek the governorship in the coming decades; but none came close to winning, in part because none recognized the only, potentially winning, coalition. Indeed, even having the model was not enough, because putting that particular coalition together required that the major parties field either poor candidates or good candidates who lacked the resources or strategy to run good campaigns.

Only twenty years later, Angus King, Jr.—running not as the Democrat he had been for his adult life, but as an Independent—was able again to put together this seemingly strange alliance. It was, of course, not a strange alliance, at all, if one takes into account the worldview of many Franco-American voters in Maine. Unlike Irish-American voters, who in large numbers tend to champion bigger governmental programs and more social engineering, Franco-American voters are more likely to agree with so-called Republican issues, such as small business and less government regulation in their lives.

King's successful campaign targeted both these urban, small Democratic business operatives and also, of course, the small town Republican voters who had long supported small business and opposed greater state and federal intrusion into their realm. While King's overall margin of victory was smaller than Longley's, he actually captured a plurality of Franco-American voters statewide, defeating both Democrat Joseph Brennan and Republican Susan Collins in 1994.

So, the Franco-American community in Maine has gone from being a "safe" and often unrewarded part of the Democratic coalition, to a more powerful and influential demographic force, both in terms of candidate campaigns and in ballot measures, as well. The election of the first avowed Franco-American in modern times to major office took place in 2002, when Michael Michaud of East Millinocket won the 2nd Congressional District seat over Kevin Raye of Washington County. Interestingly, Margaret Chase Smith was of French Canadian background, but did not know of, or acknowledge it until late in her life, after her loss of the Senate seat to Democrat William Hathaway in 1972.

Increasing Importance of Ballot Measures

A fifth major change in the Maine political landscape in recent decades has been the rise of the ballot measure, or referendum process. While there were numerous referenda in Maine in the 1960s and 1970s, and a few (such as the referendum on the income tax in 1971) were of considerable importance, these were mostly somewhat low-key, in-state contests.

All this changed with the 1980 Maine Yankee shutdown referendum, which altered the Maine political landscape with force and vigor; and the politics of the state has not been the same since. From 1960 to1980, there were just a half-dozen citizen-initiated referenda, while from 1980 to 2000 there were nearly thirty. Not only did these ballot measures come with greater frequency, but they increasingly became issues either brought from outside the state or financed (on one or both sides) primarily by outside interests.

The Maine Yankee effort was the first Maine ballot measure to break the $1 million spending mark. Previously, the most expensive efforts had been the 1973 public power authority referendum, which cost less than $250,000, and the 1976 bottle bill, which cost less than $500,000. Later ballot measures, like their candidate counterparts, rose in cost and duration. For example, campaigns over the Forest Compact and the clear-cutting ban cost well over $1 million. The gay rights struggle of 1995 cost $1.3 million, while the 1999 fight over "partial birth abortion" cost $2.4 million, and that over physician-assisted suicide cost $4 million. The battle over the proposed casino in Sanford in 2003 broke all previous records, with over $10 million spent.

The casino vote shows why it should be noted that, in a referendum as in a candidate campaign, *having the largest budget is no guarantor of success*. The pro-casino "Think About It" effort of 2003 spent more than twice as much money as did the "Casinos No!" campaign, which won the vote. In each of referenda that included the bottle bill of 1976, the effort to widen the Maine Turnpike in 1991, the local measured service (telephone) campaign, the anti clear-cutting campaigns of 1997 and '98, the gay rights battle of 1998, and the physician-assisted suicide contest of 2002, the side with substantially greater financial resources lost.

Ballot measure campaigns also extended the campaign time frame. Whereas those in the 1960s had been of two or three months' duration, by the end of the century they often ran twelve to eighteen months. The Maine Municipal Association, for example, seeking an estimated 15 percent local property tax cut by having the state fulfill its 1984 commitment to pay 55 percent of the cost of K-12 education, began their campaign early in 2002 for the election of 2003.

Ballot measure campaigns did more than simply extend the duration of the political season in Maine, however; they enabled citizens to much more directly influence public policy in a way they had never done before. During the period under review, more citizens and organizations began to view the referendum process as both a legitimate tool and an operational necessity. If stymied in the legislature, they could go outside that process relatively easily (only 40-50,000 signatures are required to put a measure on the ballot) and quickly (by gathering all the signatures needed on a single general election day).

The 2003 referenda on casino gambling and property tax reform reflect citizen initiatives to go around the legislature when that body refuses to deal with these issues in a fashion acceptable to their supporters. This democratization of the political process had been largely ignored, or under-reported, or even missed entirely by many observers of the Maine political scene.

Maine has changed, however, from a state where election day saw primarily candidate and bond issues on the ballot, to one where it usually sees one or more referenda on the ballot and, equally importantly, one's friends, neighbors, and strangers seated at small card tables asking for signatures for the next round of ballot measures! I believe that as many people sign petitions because of the friendly faces offering pens and coffee, as of the causes, themselves. Of course, political consultants and their allies and kin sign the petitions out of a desire for their full employment possibilities!

A Threat to the Ballot Measure Process
There is today, however, a major threat to the democratization of the ballot measure process, the last several election cycles having witnessed a most pernicious change in this dimension of the Maine political climate. There has been a discernible rise in censorship within the ballot measure process. Fortunately, it is unlawful in candidate campaigns.

Television is the principle driver of ballot measure outcomes. Therefore, free and unfettered access to television is the *sine qua non* for competing ideas in referenda. Now certainly, television stations must have some standards of what is acceptable and what is not, when it comes to thirty-second commercials; and few would suggest that the body politic would be well served if outright lies were allowed to permeate the airwaves.

What has evolved, however, is a far cry from fair and reliable standards. Today, the station managers in Maine television stations take it upon themselves to pass judgment on virtually every ballot-measure commercial that comes their way, subjecting it to scrutiny and a personal standard seldom, if ever, applied to their commercial advertisers.

For anyone not on the inside of political campaigns, what follows may be hard to imagine. Occasionally, there are well publicized cases of stations taking a commercial off the air; but here, the self-serving comments of the station managers are taken at face value, because the campaigns fear they will be discriminated against even more when they submit their next commercial. Most of the current censorship goes on out of sight of the public, however, and with few exceptions has gone unnoticed.[3]

The present censorship and vetting process conducted by television station managers is arbitrary, capricious, and pernicious in the course of democratic politics. Station managers can and do decide which commercials are acceptable, and which are not. All political sides have to marshal legal talent to present their cases; all have to provide masses and masses of "supporting" documents for all claims; and all know that the station managers are playing this game, so they in turn mount challenges to any and all of the opponents' commercials.

The resulting process is messy, arbitrary, and unfair to the citizens, because it means they get only those images, thoughts, and facts which the station manager deems acceptable or appropriate to the issue. Moreover, there is no recourse if one's commercial is pulled. Most readers may be shocked to find out that the fairness doctrine no longer applies in referendum situations (as it did prior to the Reagan presidency); so, the station managers end up being the only arbiters of the process.

Some station managers reject commercials because they contain the word "will" instead of "could" or "might." Some prefer commercials with no verbs! Some reject commercials because they don't like the subject. Some reject commercials because they don't like the treatment of the subject. Some reject commercials because their stations have editorialized against the side putting up the commercial. Some reject commercials on whims.

In the last decade, then, ballot measure campaigns have had to develop "pressure strategies," because if one campaign does it, the other must produce a countervailing influence. So, batteries of lawyers are engaged, campaigns send reams and reams of documents, and the station manager continues to have the last word, and there is no appeal process possible. As a result, campaigns end up having to put pressure on stations in other ways, by having their supporters pull commercial sponsorships. It is ironic that station managers are most likely to fear the withdrawal of car advertising, not any political retribution.

All of this is quite a change from 1960! And not a change for the better, for it denies the voting public a chance to hear all sides unfettered and uncensored. Capricious censorship, indeed unfair or arbitrary censorship of any kind, has no place in a free society. The free exchange and clash of ideas will always lie at the heart of the democratic process, and we must all work to restore balance and integrity and predictability to the process.

The Rise of Psychographics

Perhaps the biggest change in Maine's political landscape, and one which flows directly from use of the referendum process and television, is the rise in importance in election campaigns of "psychographics," as opposed to demographics.

324   Changing Maine

The term psychographic needs some explanation in this context. Originally used in advertising and marketing to denote lifestyle and consumer preferences, we have increasingly found it a useful tool in understanding Maine politics. As used in this chapter, "psychographic" refers primarily to the psychic imagery around which voters make decisions. It is a shorthand way of describing the "inner landscape" of the voters.

Psychographics turn out to be highly useful in determining why voters vote a certain way on certain issues at certain times, and then another way at other times. Part of this has to do with the basic and existing mind set of the voters— that is, what imagery they bring to a particular referendum; and part of it has to do with the ability of various campaigns to reinforce, change, or obliterate the existing imagery by substituting new images and giving new meaning to older cognitive maps.

In the 1991 referendum to stop the widening of the Maine Turnpike, for example, opponents of the widening were highly successful in the run up to the election, in providing powerful word pictures of wetlands. These "sacred wetlands," as they became known, and the wonderful ecosystems they supposedly contained, were actually the drainage ditches to the side of the proposed wider highway. Even though the "wetlands deficit" was to be offset with other created wetlands elsewhere, the power and majesty of the "sacred wetlands" imagery overrode more pedestrian notions of what was at stake for many people. The up-scale voters in the Portland suburbs, for example, voted against the widening in large part because of their environmental concerns.

In 1996, when the issue was reintroduced to the voters, proponents of the widening superimposed another, more powerful image onto the sacred wetlands. This was the notion of traffic jams and the danger to one and all. Powerful and evocative commercials showing emergency workers trapped in traffic on the Maine Turnpike convinced voters that safety and emergency access were more important than worrying about the drainage ditches. The fact that so many of the upscale voters who had voted against the widening in 1991 had been stuck in traffic on their way to Boston in the intervening years didn't hurt either.

Again, take the example of the North Woods; here, I have traced two archetypes over the past twenty years. The first is that of "The Wild, Wild East" of wilderness and forests where hunting and fishing is in a grand tradition, the scenery is magnificent, and the trees are tall and cut, if at all, individually. The second is that of "The Industrial Forest," best captured by a Wilderness Society film featuring a gigantic, house-sized machine coming through the woods, not only cutting every tree but literally picking them up by the trunks and shaking out the dirt from the roots.

The various debates over clear-cutting in the woods have taken place within the context of these two images. Psychographically, people tend to vote based on the archetype they start with and retain, or which can be superimposed on their initial image. The Forest Compact went down to defeat primarily because of the powerful imagery used at the end by its opponents, which featured chemical spraying of the woods and its implied threat to life and limb, children and grandchildren. Conversely, in the forestry referendum of 2002, the carefully and lovingly tended plots of small woodlot owners evoked a more positive and nostalgic look at the Maine woods, and offered them as Maine's best defense against the dreaded "sprawl."

The industrial forest psychographic won the first referendum, while the Wild, Wild East took the second. Inside voters' heads, the negative imagery of clear-cutting first drove out proposed modest changes in forest practices; while later images of small wood lots acted as a persuasive buffer against sprawl. Wherever else sprawl might be found, it was found in voters' minds as much in the North Woods as in the suburbs of Portland.

These competing lifestyles and dispositions residing in one's inner worldview are also at the heart of the debate over the proposed Indian gambling casino in Sanford. This contest became one not just about gambling, or the specifics of the project, but between different images of Maine held by the voters.

On the one hand was the notion of a grand resort casino bringing progress, prosperity, and modernity, tied up with images of Las Vegas and urban life. On the other was the carefully crafted world of L. L. Bean's and its tie-in to the psychic imagery of the Wild, Wild East. The inner landscape of Maine people was not, at least in 2003, holistic enough to include both powerful images; and the Sanford casino was overwhelmingly defeated. Still, the more modest, bucolic-appearing "racino" in Bangor—with its traditional imagery of horsemen and women, county fairs, and an agricultural lifestyle—was approved by voters on the same day.

The psychic images and inner mind-scapes of Maine people and the connotations they provide, continue to help determine the outcome of the public policy decisions made at the ballot box, as much if not more than party registration, economic status, or other demographic considerations. As the twenty-first century proceeds, and there are more ballot questions and public policy issues decided each November, the role of psychographics will only increase. Individuals, groups, parties, and corporations will only ignore these important realities at their peril. These interior landscapes, these cognitive maps, increasingly give texture and meaning to the state's political decisions.

Maine: The Way Politics Should Be
We in Maine have many things to be thankful for when we think about our political system: the quality of our candidates; the ease of entry into the political process; the willingness of our citizens to change their minds during cam-

paigns; the careers in politics open to talent, not just as candidates but as political operatives; and the ease with which citizens can bring their causes to the marketplace of political ideas.[4] Too often, analysts of the Maine political scene decry its shortcomings to the exclusion of a well-deserved emphasis on its politics. It is not possible to look at the last forty years of Maine's political history without being struck by a number of considerable positives in the process.

Maine politics remains tremendously *open* to talent. People from all walks of life enter politics and get elected to major offices in the state. Congressman Michael Michaud was a blue-collar worker; Governor John Baldacci worked in his family's restaurant; and Susan Collins was a congressional staffer. She and Olympia Snow are self-made political successes in the tradition of Margaret Chase Smith. On all levels, Maine people literally walk in, off the street, to get involved and play major roles in the campaigns which shape the state's destiny.

Maine politics also remains tremendously *accessible*. The past forty years has seen many candidates and ballot measure campaigns succeed simply because of the quality of those campaigns as campaigns. Some Maine people put together their time, effort, and scarce resources in more appropriate and effective ways than others. There is little that is "pre-ordained" in the Maine political process.

Personal *honesty and civility* remain hallmarks of Maine politics. Despite the increasingly negative tone of our national politics, and the unpleasant intrusion of national negative ads and styles into our state, Maine candidates continue to exhibit honesty, integrity, and civility in equal measures. In general, it is hard to dislike most of the people who run for higher political office in Maine, even if we disagree with their stand on issues. They tend to treat each other the way we, and they, would prefer to be treated. Character assassination and personal vitriol remain very much the exception in Maine politics.

We have much to be thankful for in these early years of the twenty-first century, and it remains for us to pass on this cherished, positive legacy to those who will come after us.

Christian Potholm is DeSilva Stanwood Alexander Professor of Government and Legal Studies at Bowdoin College and the author of over a dozen books on politics. His latest work (2003) is "This Splendid Game" Maine Political Campaigns from 1940 to 2002. His previous books on Maine politics are The Delights of Democracy (2002), An Insider's Guide to Maine Politics (1998) and "Just Do It!" Political Participation in the 1990s (1993). He is also the founder and president of Command Research, a national polling firm that during the last twenty years has polled in all of the forty-eight contiguous states. His consulting group, The Potholm Group, specializes in ballot measure initiatives. Some of his political campaigns have included Bill Cohen for Congress and Senate, Angus King for Governor, Maine Won't Discriminate, Maine Yankee I and II, Sunday sales, the moose hunt referendum, Land for Maine's Future I and II, widening the Maine turnpike (1991), NO on One (assisted suicide) and NO on Two (forestry), and various tax cap referenda.

THREE
Toward Greater Ecological Integrity

MAINE'S CURRENT APPROACH to environmental protection developed over the last four decades in a remarkable display of public leadership, grassroots organization and efforts, and bi-partisan political action. Forty years ago the Androscoggin River was identified as one of the ten most polluted rivers in the nation. Today, Maine boasts pioneering environmental legislation in water pollution control, land use and preservation, shoreland zoning, and solid waste reduction. While the condition of Maine's environment is surely much improved since 1960, the state still faces the daunting problems of Maine Yankee's low- and high-level nuclear waste, poor air quality, and land-use sprawl. To address this "second generation" of environmental challenges, new approaches will be needed that go beyond governmental "command and control" and recognize personal responsibility. Maine must also develop and hew to an environmentally acceptable energy policy to ensure that the state is prepared to weather the inevitable future energy crises.

17 The Law and Maine's Environment
Toward a New Ethic

ORLANDO DELOGU

Almost fifty years ago, Maine's environmental movement was jolted into action by the shameful featuring of the Androscoggin River on the cover of a national news magazine, under a banner headline describing it as one of the ten most polluted rivers in the country. The backup story indicated that it carried the population equivalent (a measure of pollution load) of over a million people—this at a time when the population of the entire state was not yet a million people. This was not the sort of factual reality and attention that a proud Maine people wanted or would long abide.

New political winds were already blowing, however, winds that would make Maine forevermore a two-party state, and that would bode well for the environment. A young legislator out of Rumford, Maine, Edmund S. Muskie rose to serve as Maine's governor from 1954–58. Though little that could be characterized as modern environmental legislation was passed at this early stage, Muskie and the Maine legislature began the dialogue: a Water Improvement Commission was created, and the groundwork for more effective pollution control was laid. Ed Muskie, of course, went on to serve Maine in the United States Senate where for the next twenty years his name would become synonymous with environmental leadership and legislation for an entire nation.

The Early Years

In the early 1960s, the first significant state appropriation to facilitate the work of the Water Improvement Commission was authorized, and in 1964 the legislature passed and the voters approved the first of several bond issues, in the unprecedented amount of $25 million, for municipal wastewater treatment plant construction. More importantly, the state had the courage to pre-fund the federal share of these treatment plants when federal appropriations fell behind the pace of construction. The federal government eventually honored its commitment, and Maine's construction programs moved steadily forward, but there were several nervous years in which Maine laid out both its share and the federal share, and waited patiently for reimbursement. We had, indeed, begun what was to become a long and costly journey that has not yet run its full course.

In the late '60s and through the early '70s, the rush of events from these modest beginnings was breathtaking; it is the story of a relative handful of men and women, events and institutions that shaped an environmental blueprint and a legacy of concern for the environment that lasts to the present day. We didn't always get it right, and, as we shall see, we took a step backwards, a time or two; but for the most part there is much to be proud of, and there is a good foundation to build upon as we move into the twenty-first century.

A second stirring of both alarm and hope was found in an unlikely place, and was the product of an unlikely spokesperson. Bowdoin College was the setting, and John McKee, a Maine photographer, became a voice that produced both anguish and hope. His deftly mounted photographic exhibit, "As Maine Goes," was proudly and prominently hung by the college's art museum in the early fall of 1966. In large black and white photographs, the despoliation of Maine was there for all to see.

Skillfully juxtaposed with this tragedy, McKee presented his counterpoint: equally large color photographs of Maine's unsurpassed beauty. Artistically, the point was made and key questions were asked: What are we doing to ourselves? How long will it go on? In an introduction to the museum's catalog of the exhibit, Supreme Court Justice William Douglas declared that, "...new standards are needed that control the relation and attitude of man toward the land, the air, the waters, and the life of this earth."[1] These controls were not long in coming to Maine.

If more by way of incentive was needed, a string of one-time and on-going publications brought home the dangers of environmental harm, the degree of corporate excess in fostering this harm, and the timidity of all but a few of our political leaders in addressing these problems. In 1962, Rachel Carson (not a Mainer, but with strong ties to Maine) published *Silent Spring*, a book that documented the dangers of DDT and our penchant to misuse and overuse pesticides, to our long-term detriment.

Closer to home, and almost a decade later, a young Portland lawyer, Richard Spencer, working with University of Maine law students, published *The Company State* under the auspices of Ralph Nader's Center for the Study of Responsive Law. This volume documented not only the environmental harms wrought by Maine's pulp and paper industry, but the corporate and political power wielded by this industry group in its efforts to maintain the status quo.

Finally, 1968 saw the beginning of a new weekly publication, the *Maine Times*. Irreverent and committed to the environment, Peter Cox and John Cole were hands-on publisher and editor, first-rate journalists, and relentless in their journalistic pursuits. They assembled a dedicated staff of like-minded individuals; and for the next decade and a half, issue after issue examined the economic, environmental, cultural, and political life of Maine in depth. A wealth of information, ideas, and good, old-fashioned muckraking journalism poured out, all with an eye to protecting Maine's long-term quality of life which they saw as threatened. Few corporate or political leaders of the day were spared the sharpness of their analysis, or of their journalistic tongues. The paper became "must" reading, alike, for those who feared the new and growing environmental movement, and for those for whom it could not come fast enough.

A Burst of Environmental Legislation

On the political front, the late 1960s found another young Maine governor, Kenneth Curtis, in the right place at the right time. He had surrounded himself with a staff of bright and ambitious young men—Peter Bradford, Kermit Lipez, P. Andrews Nixon, and Walter Corey, to name just a few. Long before the first Earth Day in 1970, Maine's legislative wheels were churning; a strengthened Water Pollution Control Act was passed in 1967, and expanded in 1969; a new Air Pollution Control Act was passed in 1969.

These legislative enactments, modeled after federal legislation, focused on the quality of waste water and air emission discharges, and required the licensing of individual dischargers.[2] The old Water Improvement Commission was now the Water and Air Environmental Improvement Commission, a body that would subsequently become the Board of Environmental Protection.[3] A Maine Mining Conservation and Land Rehabilitation Act was passed in 1969;[4] an Act to Regulate the Alteration of Wetlands was passed in 1967, and revised and strengthened in 1969.[5] A revised Pesticides Control Law was put in place in 1969, strengthening first-generation legislation dealing with these issues put in place in 1965.[6]

The pace was dizzying. Perhaps of greatest long-term significance, an Act to Create a Land Use Regulation Commission (LURC) was passed in1969.[7] A tribute to the vision of many, though none more than the late James Haskell, LURC has enabled the state to bring comprehensive planning, zoning, and development controls to the increasing range of activities taking place on the state's nearly 10 million acres of Unorganized Territory, an area encompassing nearly one-half the state. Given the many thousands of miles of haul-roads and growing development pressures in the Unorganized Territory, LURC's activities today are even more important than they were thirty-five years ago, when this creative instrumentality was fashioned.

Maine's burst of legislative energy with respect to the environment both contributed to and drew strength from the national momentum of the day. April 22, 1970, marked the first Earth Day, and, as if to commemorate the event, Maine, on May 9, 1970, passed two landmark pieces of legislation: the Site Regulation of Development Act, enabling state-level review of major development activities; and an Act Relating to the Coastal Conveyance of Petroleum, enabling the state not only to regulate this hazardous undertaking, but establishing a fund to compensate the state and third parties who might be damaged as a result of oil discharges.[8]

Bond Brook Fish Ladder, Augusta

A year later, the Maine legislature became only the third state in the nation to put in place a Mandatory Shoreland Zoning and Subdivision Control Act, requiring comprehensive planning and the careful control of development in these fragile areas.[9] Continuing to lead the nation, Maine in 1976 was one of only a handful of states to deal with solid wastes, by passing a bottle redemption bill.[10] Though few states have followed our lead, we have shown this to be a viable strategy to control litter, reduce the volume of solid wastes, and bring a practical, citizen-oriented approach to recycling strategies.

Administratively during this period, Maine largely resisted the pressures brought by the first OPEC oil embargo. Get-rich schemes—some by fly-by-night entrepreneurs and some by major energy producers—for oil refineries and oil storage facilities, were turned back in Portland, Searsport, and Eastport. Maine people need to be convinced by hard data before they will accept schemes that look too good to be true—particularly when offered by people from "away"; this penchant stood the state and its environment in good stead. We were not as fortunate or wise with respect to Maine Yankee, however. The beguiling appeal of cheap energy and a home-grown company, Central Maine Power, led us in 1972 to accept nuclear energy. We didn't know what to do with the wastes then, or now. The risks associated with the facility prompted us to close it earlier than its designed useful-life would have allowed; but in heightened risk and dollars, we have paid a high price for our venturesomeness; and it's not over yet.

Throughout this period and well into the 1980s there were, of course, other environment-related legislative enactments. Some might characterize these as "lesser" pieces of environmental law, but each dealt with some aspect of these highly interrelated issues; all remain important today. In 1965, for example, the Allagash Wilderness Waterway was created, under the control of the Maine State Park and Recreation Commission; and important protections and land use controls were put in place to preserve this unique white water resource and its immediately adjacent land corridor.[11] In 1973 a Department of Conservation was created, merging several natural resource agencies for purposes of better resource management.[12] Again in 1973, Maine undertook an aggressive program to clarify ownership claims to, and to take more effective control of, publicly owned offshore islands; to this end, a Maine Coastal Island Registry was established.[13] In 1977 comprehensive and significantly strengthened billboard restrictions were adopted;[14] and in 1979, ground waters and aquifers were more fully protected.[15]

During the period 1977–1981, the state put in place a variety of complementary energy conservation strategies: the Energy Conservation in Buildings Act;[16] an act requiring the creation of energy efficiency performance standards for all residential, commercial, and industrial buildings;[17] and an act regulating energy audits.[18] The legislature's concern with energy policy issues continues to the present day: in 1999 the State Planning Office was vested with authority to review, coordinate, and submit to the governor and legislature every two years a resources plan which is to include conservation programs.[19] In 2001 an Energy Resources Council was established;[20] and in the same year, a revised provision of the Electric Industry Restructuring Act was adopted that requires energy providers to adopt conservation programs.[21]

In this historic era of environmental lawmaking, note must be made of an array of important state-level planning and land use control (including land acquisition) enactments. In 1989 the shared role of the state (with municipalities) for comprehensive land use planning was laid out; state planning goals were for the first time articulated; a mechanism for state-level review of local comprehensive plans was fashioned; and an array of sophisticated land use control tools was expressly authorized, as well as procedural safeguards to insure the fair use of these tools.[22]

In 1987 a Land for Maine's Future Board and fund were created; subsequent bond authorizations have committed tens of millions of dollars to the acquisition of unique, scenic, park, and open space areas in all parts of the state. These acquisitions have included conservation easements, easements of access, and the outright purchase (in fee) of 115,000 acres of Maine land for the benefit of future generations of Maine citizens. It is remarkably far-sighted, one of but a few such programs in the nation.[23]

The point is amply made: the period encompassing the late 1960s through the 1980s was extraordinary. In any number of areas of environmental concern, Maine men and women have fashioned and amended an array of laws; lobbied individual proposals through to enactment, sometimes in the face of powerful and opposed interest groups; and, for the most part, seen to the successful implementation of these enactments over a considerable period of time.[24]

Two factors seem central to this achievement. The first is the fact that the protection of Maine's environment was never and is not today seen in partisan political terms. In the late '60s, a Democratic governor, Kenneth Curtis, and his staff worked readily with Horace Hildreth, Jr., and Harrison Richardson, two leading Republicans of the day, to fashion the legislative majorities needed for passage of many of the above-noted measures.

Second, grassroots environmental organizations arose in Maine to carry the fight from every corner of the state to city halls, town meetings, and to the legislative and administrative halls in Augusta. The Natural Resources Council of Maine, Maine Audubon Society, Maine Coast Heritage Trust, Maine Chapter of the Nature Conservancy, Sierra Club, Conservation Law Foundation, PIRG, and many others have played vital roles. Most importantly, these organizations and the cadre of environmental lawyers they spawned have persisted over the years; they remain today to protect the environmental legacy for our children.

Some Mistakes Were Made

Before I am accused of seeing Maine's environmental movement through rose-colored glasses, let me return to a point made earlier: some mistakes were, indeed, made, and we took a step backward a time or two. Some of these mistakes are irretrievable, and we must live with the consequences of our bad judgment. The building of Maine Yankee is an example. We compounded this mistake, particularly as it relates to nuclear wastes, in the way we responded to federal legislation requiring states to find low-level nuclear waste disposal sites.[25]

"Compact" arrangements were encouraged, and we initially expressed a willingness to join with New York and other New England states, to find a suitable (or, "least harms") site that would serve a six or seven state region. While signaling our willingness to participate on one hand, however, we at the outset informed the other states in the region that if the best regional site turned out to be in Maine, we would not accept it. How realistic was that? How fair? With such unbalanced ground rules, the other states quickly cut Maine loose, and we wound up partnering with Vermont to send the low-level radioactive wastes of our two states to Texas, at a horrendous price.[26]

In short, fearful of the very wastes we had created and benefited from through the operation of Maine Yankee, we struck a "Faustian" bargain to send our low-level wastes to a poor, rural, largely Hispanic corner of Texas, thought to be "suitable" for such disposal facilities. Time-lags in this field being what they are, not a lot of money has been paid out to date, and Texas is rethinking its position, but Maine's approach to these issues was not our finest hour. The problem with low-level, much less high-level radioactive wastes has not gone away. Low-level wastes continue to be generated by a variety of medical, industrial, and scientific activities, not the least of which is the Maine Yankee decommissioning process, and thousands of spent fuel rods remain entombed over a fault zone in Wiscasset.

Another environmental mistake that is correctible, but may prove to be very difficult to change or correct, is the too exclusive or singular approach we have taken to major point sources of water pollution. In an effort to reduce pollution loads by large, measurable amounts, it certainly makes sense to go after large corporate polluters first: they have no right to pollute, and their pollution loads can and should be reduced. Moreover, they often have the resources to pay for the required pollution control equipment. They do not, however, represent the whole of the problem.

In many water pollution settings, the major point sources represent no more than half the problem. The remaining pollution load comes from a thousand (nay, tens of thousands of) camps and cottages, farm and forest activities, and small businesses located in every nook and corner of the state. Individually, their pollutant loads are small; but in the aggregate, they are half (in some settings more than half) of the problem, and we do little to insist that these pollution loads be responsibly dealt with. Indeed, we "grandfather" many of them.

In sum, then, Maine people want a clean environment; but we are unwilling to impose heavy burdens on ourselves, on people we perceive to be the "little-guy," even when it is clearly demonstrated that the aggregate of little-guy pollution loads are a *big* part of the problem. One is reminded of the Pogo comic strip wherein he says, "I have met the enemy, and he is us." We have got to begin changing here: "grandfathering," for other than short transition periods of time, must end, and all forms of non-point source pollution must be subject to meaningful regulations that are enforced.

An air pollution control equivalent of this same mistake involves our backing away from motor vehicle exhaust emission testing. Again, we vigorously pursue and license major, in-state point-source emitters, and we should. We fruitlessly pursue in the courts Midwest public utilities whose airborne wastes land on our doorstep. Yet we refuse to acknowledge that the literally hundreds of thousands of trucks and cars that ply Maine roads are a significant contributing factor to the quality of the air we breathe.

Worst of all, we had it right at one point in time; a motor vehicle emissions testing program that would have reached thousands of Maine vehicles was in place;[27] contracts between the state and testers had been entered into; the growing pains of launching the program were being worked out. Then, as auto emissions testing became linked with air emissions trading strategies, we lost our will—and we lost our way. At the critical juncture, there was a failure of gubernatorial, legislative, state agency, and painfully, Natural Resources Council of Maine (NRCM) leadership. Faced with the possibility of a repealing referendum, the legislature in 1995 killed the auto emissions testing program.[28] Pogo redux.

Another mistake we continue to make is to over-rely on "command and control" regulatory measures. Notwithstanding the success we have had with the "bottle bill," which relies on a small economic incentive to achieve a desired environmental objective, we quite irrationally resist the broader use of market (or, economic incentive) strategies to achieve Maine's environmental goals. Bear in mind, it's not an either/or choice; other countries, other states see regulation and market strategies as complementary tools, and so should we.

Economic self-interest is a powerful motivational tool used in countless settings in our market economy; it can be, and should be harnessed to achieve a broad range of environmental objectives. For example, air emission reduction credits (resisted by the NRCM in the early '90s) are authorized by the 1990 Federal Clean Air Act; they are today bought, sold, and traded in many parts of the country, in settings that induce many emitters to do far more than regulations alone would require. By allowing these emitters to profit from their readiness to exceed clean air standards, the air is cleaner than it otherwise would be. *In fact, there is almost no environmental problem for which a market incentive strategy could not be developed*—a strategy which, when combined with regulation, might achieve the environmental goal more fully than either approach on its own.[29]

Two unfortunate mistakes in the land use area have had, and continue to have adverse environmental consequences for Maine. The first involves the state's commencement and then abandonment of funding for the development and updating of municipal comprehensive plans.[30] Nothing by way of rational land use control and environmental protection can be put in place without the overarching public involvement, data gathering, and fashioning of policy that comprehensive plans represent. Short-term state budgetary considerations in the late '80s and early '90s led us to a funding cutback that has imposed long-run costs on many municipalities in the form of poorly located development, higher than necessary infrastructure costs, and a wide variety of harms and environmental damages that must at some point be remediated.

Second, we succumbed somewhere in the '70s to the belief that large-lot zoning would protect Maine's suburban and rural environment from despoliation. One-, two-, or three-acre minimum lot sizes were idealized as part of "the good life," and if this was good, five- or ten-acre lot sizes would be even better! How this view took hold, and who is to blame is neither important nor fully knowable at this point. What must be recognized is that this pattern of sprawling development is incorrect and inherently destructive of both village centers and the suburban/rural landscape we would preserve.

We have come to characterize it as "sprawl," and we have begun (if haltingly) to address it; but not all of our fellow citizens realize just how damaging the past thirty years of large-lot zoning has been. It has created an automobile dependency, which in turn creates another range of road construction and transportation problems; it has imposed huge public utility infrastructure costs on society; it has been and still is environmentally harmful; and it destroys the social fabric, the small town feel and sense of community that Maine and northern New England cities and towns have cherished for over 200 years.

A last mistake of relatively recent origin was the failure of environmental organizations, key legislative and state agency personnel, and responsible voices in the forest products industry to come together to fashion sound, workable forest management practices and strategies that would see us well into the twenty-first century. Like too many cooks, too many egos seemed to get in the way, and a singular opportunity for compromise and consensus was lost in the failure to adopt the Compact for Maine's Forests in 1996 and again in 1997.[31] Maine forests will surely survive in some form; but the fact is, they are less well-managed and protected than they ought to be, particularly from the more rapacious within the forest products industry.

The Law and Maine's Environment

Kokadjo, T1 R12

Some Environmental Goals for the Early Twenty-First Century:

Perhaps at the outset, one should state the obvious. Not all of the mistakes of the past need be continued. If some mistakes are irremediable, others are correctible. We can begin dealing with all forms of non-point source pollution or, put more broadly, all the more diffused forms of environmental harm. Individual citizens can and must come to feel that they have a stake in Maine's environmental future; that there are steps they can and should take beyond just returning bottles to protect that future.

Motor vehicle emissions testing can be resumed; and a range of market strategies to address a wider range of environmental objectives can be fashioned.[32] The state, using its funding and regulatory powers, can also begin to play a more positive, a more active, and a more equally shared role with municipalities, in dealing with planning and land-use control issues, in ending or at least minimizing sprawl. Finally, the state can and should take the lead in broadly based discussions aimed at formulating a new forest management compact. With some additional effort and compromise, the benefits that eluded us in the late '90s remain achievable early in this century; the need is surely still there.

There is perhaps no more important task, however, than simply to "endure;" to continue to foster in Maine the non-partisan atmosphere and approach to environmental issues that has characterized Maine's environmental past. We must continue incremental improvement of the existing framework of environmental laws dealing with the traditional problems of air, water, solid wastes, and land use; and, more importantly, we must consistently enforce these laws, day in and day out, indefinitely into the future.[33] There is a tendency to grow tired, particularly when big environmental quality leaps are no longer likely or possible. Succumbing to this tendency simply plays into the hands of those who would exploit or despoil the environment; they will take whatever is given them. In short, environmentalists in the twenty-first century must play a long and patient game.

At the same time, there are three or four relatively new issues and specific steps that are worth pursuing. First, we need to fashion a consensus with respect to a major state or national park in some part of the forested region of northern Maine. At present, we seem of several minds on the idea, and we are simultaneously pursuing several strategies that are not altogether consistent. For example, some want no park of any type at all; they urge no, or at most limited, public land acquisition in Maine's North Woods. Some are committed to a widened use of conservation easements, as a way of precluding large scale development while preserving both public access and traditional, forest-related activities. Millions of scarce public and private dollars have already been spent in pursuit of this strategy.

A third group sees this approach as a costly and temporary solution. Easements expire, and leave the land in private hands; restrictions may be interpreted ever more broadly over time, to allow development activities we may not be altogether comfortable with. These people would coordinate and increase public and private fee simple acquisition of unique or critical forested areas. Fee simple holdings are permanent; they could become part of a loosely linked state (or federal) park system, or they could focus on expanding existing holdings, such as Baxter State Park.

As this short discussion suggests, there is much to talk about here, but the point is that those of us who call ourselves environmentalists seem quite divided on the question of how to move forward in this area of concern. The character of northern Maine over the next 100 years, and beyond, turns on decisions that will be made in the next five to ten years, perhaps less; we need to talk more openly, more constructively with one another about these issues.

A second initiative that is worthy of our attention grows out of the Maine Supreme Judicial Court's decisions in the so-called Moody Beach cases.[34] In a nutshell, public use rights in sand beach areas were interpreted very narrowly; the rights of upland owners, including the right to exclude the public from these beach areas, were interpreted broadly. The likelihood that federal law will overturn these holdings, or that the Law Court will revisit these issues is remote to the point of non-existent. Consequently, I would reiterate a plea made almost a decade ago:[35] that Maine, working with those towns that have sand beach areas, set about the task of systematically acquiring all of these areas; that they work with and through public and private instrumentalities (land trusts, and the Land For Maine's Future Board);[36] and that they use government's spending powers to accomplish the acquisition of these properties.

Our experts tell us there are but 35 to 40 miles of sand beach in this state with over 3,000 miles of foreshore; the symbolic, tourist industry, and recreational value of publicly owning and providing adequate year-round access to all of these sand beach areas seems incalculable. We should commit ourselves to this task immediately; the costs of acquiring these properties will only rise with the passage of time.[37]

In looking to Maine's environmental future, a third issue that must be confronted is our energy future. I cannot help but believe that it is only a matter of time, perhaps a relatively short period at that, before the next energy crisis is upon us. We are no better prepared to deal with it today than we were in the early '70s. We love our trucks and SUV's; we want the lights to go on with the flip of a switch; we want to be warm in winter and cool in summer; we don't want regulations that would make gas-guzzlers or multiple car ownership more costly. We don't want most forms of energy production: nuclear power is too hazardous and produces wastes we can't deal with; wood stoves are unhealthy;

wind farms and transmission lines are unsightly; fossil fuel burning or trash-to-energy facilities are dirty and pose air emissions problems; solar energy is too costly; liquefied natural gas (LNG) facilities[38] and gas pipelines are too dangerous; and hydro-electric dams block fish passage.

In short, unless "muddling through" can be called a policy, we have no energy policy to address the next energy crisis. We have rejected virtually all options, often on environmental grounds. Here, again, I urge that we begin to talk with one another; we may need to have several conversations. What energy sources, even if less than perfect, are we prepared to live with and actively support? What conservation steps should we insist upon now? What mass transportation alternatives—bike, bus, and train—should we subsidize now, even though less needed today, because they will be sorely needed at some point in the future? These are questions worth asking and answering; and it is the environmental community that should lead this discussion.

Finally, the state's role must be expanded to deal with large-scale development proposals with economic and environmental consequences that are of regional or statewide importance. At times, the state's role may be only regulatory; in other settings, the state may need to play an entrepreneurial role; and sometimes the state must play both roles simultaneously. Many such developments cannot be built, expanded, or maintained by private corporations acting alone, particularly if they face resistance at the municipal level of government; and many such developments involve facilities that are economically beneficial or necessary and important to our environmental well-being.

The proposed LNG facility in Harpswell is but one example. Development of recycling facilities, waste disposal facilities, wind-driven energy facilities, energy transmission facilities, and tank farms likewise come to mind, and are especially vulnerable. In short, when the private sector cannot act, will not act, or is prevented from acting by local regulations or attitudes, but action is necessary and environmentally appropriate for the public good, the state *must* become an actor, a market participant, the entrepreneur of last resort.

There is at least one recent example of the state's stepping in to perform this essential role. In 2003 the legislature authorized the state, acting through the State Planning Office, to "...acquire, own, and cause to be operated an existing...solid waste disposal facility in the City of Old Town...."[39] The former private owner of the facility was apparently no longer able to operate the facility; it is an essential repository for a variety of industrial and municipal wastes; some remediation of relatively minor environmental damage at the existing facility is needed; some expansion of the facility to meet future public and private waste disposal needs appears both necessary and capable of being accomplished in an environmentally safe manner; the costs of state acquisition can apparently be born in what is referred to as a "revenue-neutral" manner, i.e., tipping and/or licensee fees can be set at a level that will amortize acquisition costs;[40] and the daily operation of the facility may be transferred to a licensee of the state who must be selected "...through a competitive bidding process...."[41]

This sort of direct state involvement in acquiring, improving, expanding, and operating needed environmentally related facilities should not be frequently or lightly undertaken by the state, but when it is necessary to advance the general welfare, the state should not fail to act. The model provided by the state's approach to the Old Town waste disposal facility is useful; it can and should be refined and utilized in the future whenever circumstances and environmentally driven needs dictate.

Conclusion

I am certain there are environmentally significant events and people, legislative initiatives and administrative actions that I have failed to note in these brief remarks; for this, I apologize. Enough is presented, however, to underscore the point made at the outset. We have made progress. Our air and waters are cleaner today than they were in 1960. We are thinking more clearly and carefully about development and the use of our land. In many environmental settings, we have acted with courage.

Yet, it is not over; in fact, it will never be over. There are mistakes that need correcting. Second and third generation environmental problems and issues need to be confronted. The costs of acting responsibly will mount and need to be paid. Those who would exploit the environment will not go away, and must be faced down.

These facts underscore the last point I would make: environmentalism is not something we do and, like baking a cake, it's done; it is instead, an ethic, an attitude, a way of life, an approach to working and living in a finite world. It is a way of enduring far into the future, rather than burning brightly and extinguishing ourselves in the technology and excesses of the moment. In my view, it is a worthy, necessary undertaking for any or all of us.

Orlando E. Delogu is Professor of Law at the University of Maine School of Law. Educated at the University of Utah and the University of Wisconsin, Professor Delogu served on the Governor's Committee on Pollution Abatement in 1966–67, and on the Maine Board of Environmental Protection from 1969–74. For almost forty years he has served as consultant to federal, state, and local government agencies, planning firms, and law firms in the areas of land use, environmental, and natural resources law. He has written and lectured widely on environmental issues and concerns in Maine, throughout the United States, and abroad. Here at home, in the past decade he has served as an elected member of the Portland City Council and as an appointed member of its planning board. Orlando Delogu was, literally, present at the creation of the environmental movement in Maine and he has not gone away since—in his writings, in his activities, and in his devotion to the cause of saving the planet from ourselves.

I N THE PAST FORTY YEARS, reaction to outside influences and events has shaped Maine's energy policymaking far more than any pro-active planning efforts; as a result, the state has failed to achieve a long-term, sustainable energy policy. Like the rest of the nation, we react to short-term price increases by finding greater efficiencies and diversifying sources, then neglect or abandon these efforts when prices fall. We fail to recognize the true costs of energy consumption, costs that are paid in environmental damage, increasing health problems, and threats to industries that depend on healthy, natural ecosystems. Maine's natural beauty is one of the state's greatest assets; to protect this resource and create a sustainable energy policy, Maine must increase energy efficiency and diversify energy sources.

18 Maine Energy Policy
More like the Nation

CHERYL HARRINGTON

Energy policy, in Maine as in most places in the world, is at once a story of natural resources, technology, politics, culture, the environment, economics, and above all else, dynamic if sometimes repetitive change. It is also a story of rascals and saints, though there is often disagreement as to who belongs in which category. The saints of one decade often look like the rascals of the next.

In 1927, for example, Walter Wyman, president of the Central Maine Power Company, sold majority ownership in the company he had carefully built to Samuel Insull, the inventor of the electric utility holding company. Insull was building an empire of electric utilities and using their revenues to support investments in unrelated businesses, such as street trolleys. For his part, Wyman was looking for capital to expand CMP's service territory, and to invest in a few affiliated businesses of his own. Insull was a high flyer, and one suspects there must have been a moment when Wyman felt like he was hanging onto the ropes of a hot-air balloon, rising from the ground, too late to let go, and not at all happy with the direction the balloon was taking.

Insull acquired and borrowed against his acquisitions throughout the U.S., and was moving into Europe when, in the early 1930s, he became stretched so thin that his empire crashed down into bankruptcy. It was very much the ENRON of the era. Walter Wyman, having lost control of his beloved company, did hang on and managed to repurchase CMP out of the Insull bankruptcy, restoring himself to full control of his company – and undoubtedly as a wiser man.[1] The U.S. Congress promptly passed a law prohibiting a replay of Insull's use of ratepayer funds to expand into unrelated businesses, the Public Utility Holding Company Act of 1935.[2] This law is today subject to repeal in the Energy Bill submitted to the Congress by the Administration of President George W. Bush.

Thinking about Energy

There are many ways to tell Maine's energy story over the past forty years. For example, one might think about energy in terms of the resources or fuels used to *produce* it: oil, coal, gas, and plutonium, as well as water, wind, sun, woods, and other biofuels. These are often broken into three groups: fossil fuel, nuclear, and renewable resources. Maine's early energy sources were, of course, renewable. Wood and water power were at the center of Maine family and economic life long before the days of organized power companies; and these fuels remain an important part of Maine's energy mix today.[3]

Another way to think about energy is the various ways in which we use it; this is called the *end use* analysis of energy. Generally, no one really needs a kilowatt hour of electricity, or even a gallon of gas, as an end in itself. What we need, want, and are willing to pay for is the end use we get from energy: light, heat, and cooling; movement from place to place in our cars, trucks, and fishing boats; power for our computers; industrial motor power to run our manufacturing equipment, and so on. In particular, Maine uses more energy per capita than most states—we are tenth nationally, and tenth in motor fuel use per capita. This is due primarily to our home heating and motor transport needs.[4]

End use analysis leads directly to another important energy source in a complex economy like ours: *energy efficiency*. Strategies and technologies that allow us to get the same of amount of end use from smaller and smaller amounts of energy are, in a very real sense, a source of energy, themselves. For example, modern refrigerators use *half* the electricity they did in the 1960s and 1970s, to produce the same amount of cooling; and many of them come with very nice added amenities. The same is true of light bulbs, oil furnaces, cars, air conditioners, washer and dryers, and a whole host of end-use products—though for many appliances and products, including passenger vehicles, many already existing efficiency gains have yet to be incorporated into the models we buy today.

So, end use and efficiency are important. Maine's economy has become more energy efficient in recent years. For example, between 1985 and 2000 our Gross State Product increased 40 percent (in real dollars), while our total energy consumption increased just 26 percent.[5] Unfortunately, some of that change reflects a loss of manufacturing industries, rather than an increase in efficiency itself.

One may also think about energy in terms of the *technology* used to create the energy: large hydro dams to capture and hold water, run turbines, and produce electricity; thermal-steam plants, or as one of my colleagues calls them, giant teakettles, that burn coal, oil, or nuclear fuel to boil water, use the steam to run turbines, and produce electricity; combustion turbine engines which apply the principle of the jet engine to the production of electricity; wind mills and solar cells; and so on.

We use *all* these sources in Maine, though not all of them on a commercial level. We have seen steady movement, first, to ever larger, capital-intensive technologies associated with hydropower and the large steam-driven power plants; and then to the smaller, cheaper-to-build, combined-cycle combustion turbine technologies (CCCT) associated with the increased availability of natural gas.

The most common way of thinking about energy, of course, is in terms of *cost* and *price* (which are not always the same thing); the opportunities for job production or loss; and other economic impacts, such as that on the family budget. Yet another, repeating set of *economic concerns* is how much we should

Changing Maine

rely on markets, and how much on regulation and state policy action to assure that the energy we need will be there when we need it, at affordable prices for all Maine citizens.

We may also think about energy in terms of the *environmental impacts* by which various energy sources and technologies can be measured: How much lung disease? How much habitat destruction? How much risk of climate change? Accepting that energy and the environment are *inextricably linked* was perhaps the most important energy lesson of the past forty years and possibly will remain the most important lesson of the next forty years, as well! These issues—the economy and the environment—have a strong link to the highly political nature of energy and energy policy mentioned earlier.

Having identified the various ways we can think about energy, we may now look at what the past forty years or so have brought to Maine, and what we may expect to find ourselves concerned about in the years ahead, as we think about energy matters in Maine.

The 1960s: They Seemed Good at the Time

Whatever their other problems, which were many, the 1960s seemed a pretty good time for energy in Maine. Many Maine people had good jobs in manufacturing and natural resource-based industries; many Maine households had cars; and there were many Maine roads that had been expanded and improved throughout the 1950s. It was fun to drive, and gasoline was cheap—how about 25 cents a gallon? Our relentless increase in driving and motor fuel consumption had begun. We used 8.9 million barrels of motor fuel in 1965;[6] by 1970, that number was 10.8 million barrels, a 21 percent increase in just five years. Mainers have enjoyed the same love affair with their cars and trucks and boats as the rest of America; in fact, as noted earlier, we love them above average, and drive more than most of the rest of the country.

In the electricity sector in the 1960s, the investor-owned utilities—Central Maine Power, Bangor Hydroelectric, and Maine Public Service—were thriving businesses serving thriving businesses. Shoes, textiles, and wood products all required electrical energy. Not least among utility customers were the pulp and paper mills, which no longer needed to be supported with loans from the power companies to stay in business, as they had in the 1940s and '50s.[7] Though some mills produced their own power, they were also customers of the utilities.

By the '60s, most Maine residential dwellings and commercial establishments were hooked into the local power grid. Home amenities such as refrigerators, washers, and dryers were becoming commonplace, not to mention such luxury items as dishwashers and the occasional air conditioner. This was the era of the electric knife, for those who remember that strange instrument. We were all encouraged by then actor Ronald Reagan to "live better electrically;" and, in fact, we did.

The real price for electricity was falling, tracking the falling costs of power production, as generators of larger and larger size captured economies of scale. The electric companies in Maine stayed ahead of the growing demand curve by diversifying their generating sources, having already moved in the mid-1950s from mostly hydro generation to add coal-burning stations (Mason Station), then oil burners (Yarmouth Wyman station), and, finally, into the nuclear age. As the nation's experts described nuclear power as "too cheap to meter,"[8] Maine's utilities laid plans for the first nuclear power station to be constructed in Maine, in the town of Wiscasset: the Maine Yankee Atomic Power Company.

The electrical utilities were at the very center of Maine economic power, in close connection with the pulp and paper industries; and this put them at the heart of political power, as well. The 1970s were probably the height of the dual influence of the power and timber industries in Maine politics—power which yielded only slowly over the following decades as first regional, then national, and, finally, global changes worked their way into Maine's economy.

We should mention that the power companies were in many ways at the heart of Maine's social culture, as well. The utilities continued to play a central role in many small towns through their local district offices, where you could buy your appliances or pay your bills.[9] The bills of many social, sporting, cultural, and civic events, in turn, were paid by the utilities, often donating ratepayer money. People knew their power company representatives. They were your good neighbors, and their executives and managers were among the first citizens of their communities and the state.

This being the '60s, however, upset was on the way. It arrived first in the form of the Northeast Power Blackout of November 9, 1965. (Yes, there has been more than one northeast blackout; this is why it is important to know your region's history.) Thirty million people in the northeastern United States and Canada went without electrical power for as many as thirteen hours. The direct outcome of this event was the formation of the New England Power Pool, or NEPOOL, which became operational in June of 1970. The significance of NEPOOL is that for the first time Maine, except for northernmost Maine, became fully integrated into the single power grid which served all six New England states. Key decisions regarding dispatch of plant production, use of major transmission lines, as well as need for new power plants and lines, now occurred within the Power Pool, where Maine utilities participated as minority voters.

For all practical planning and operational purposes, the region was treated as though it were a single service territory. NEPOOL created significant economies of scale for all of New England, as well as the sought-after increase in system reliability. The Maine Public Utilities Commission (PUC) continued to exercise authority over the dollars invested by Maine's utilities through its setting of retail rates; but the engineering dynamics and economics of electricity began to be dominated by the regional architecture of the system. This was the first step toward the regional electricity market we participate in today; but it was also a giant step in ceding local control to regional decisionmakers.

1970s: Turmoil and New Ideas

The '70s was a decade of truly unprecedented events for energy in Maine and the rest of country. First, we should note that Maine Yankee was completed and came on line in 1972. The power system planners at NEPOOL envisioned a network of *sixteen* or more nuclear stations throughout New England—including others in Maine, such as at Sears Island—to serve as the backbone of the regional grid. Only seven of these plants were ever constructed, as economic costs and environmental concerns mounted.

The national environmental movement had begun to coalesce in the early '70s. In Maine, it soon began to demand that energy decisions reflect environmental impacts. This played out in two interesting cases which dominated the news for much of the decade. The first was the proposed decision by the Army Corp of Engineers in 1972 to build two dams on the St. John River, one each at Dickey and Lincoln schools, to provide 800 MW of peaking power for New England. The project was to be paid for by the U.S. taxpayers, and would be a "public power" project—that is, a facility not owned by the existing utilities, but rather by a public entity along the lines of the Tennessee Valley Authority.

The second environmental case-in-point was the attempt by private interests to build a major oil refinery in Machiasport, to serve the oil and gas needs of the entire Northeast.[10] Both of these were "mega" projects that, if built, would have had major impacts on both the landscape and the economics of Maine for decades to come. Both required federal approval, however, and the ensuing battles, while vigorously joined by Maine citizens, businesses, and politicians, were fought out largely in Washington, DC.

Needless to say, the environmental movement came of age opposing these two nearly forgotten projects. As to Dickey-Lincoln, the environmentalists had allies in the investor-owned power companies, who were not interested in the prospect of a public power entity competing in New England power markets. Interestingly, some of the advocates of public power later found their way into the electric industry mainstream, as independent sellers of generation services.

By the end of the decade, both projects had failed; neither was built. Considering the beauty of Starboard, Maine, where the oil refinery was to have been built, and the pristine St. John River corridor, now preserved as wilderness, it is difficult to regret the failure of the two projects. In both cases, priceless Maine ecosystems and scenery have been preserved for the contemplation and pleasure of future generations. Unhappily, however, the need to figure out *what* parts of our landscape might properly be made available for energy development remains unresolved to this day. Where do we want to locate wind power? Do we want to use our ports to import liquefied natural gas? Ought we to think about designating energy development zones before projects are proposed and pitched battles are engaged?

In 1973 the growing dependence of the U.S. on imported oil and the sales embargo by Middle Eastern OPEC producers rapidly escalated the cost of energy, reaching crisis proportions first in 1974 and then, again, in 1978. Crude oil, which had been selling for $3.40 a barrel in 1970, tripled to $9 a barrel in 1974; increased to $12.46 in 1978; and was at $28 a barrel in 1980 (nominal prices). Respected forecasters anticipated $60-80 a barrel by the mid-eighties, and $100 per barrel prices by the decade's end.[11]

State and federal energy policies reacted to these increases with a variety of strategies and incentives to reduce reliance on oil, increase energy efficiency, and diversify to other fuels. In 1978, the federal Public Utilities Regulatory Policy Act (PURPA)[12] was enacted, requiring investor-owned utilities to buy cogenerated energy and power from small, renewable energy projects whenever it could be acquired for less that the utilities' own, going-forward costs for expanding and optimizing the electrical system (that is, their so-called "avoided" costs). Maine passed its own, indigenous energy resources law, The Small Power Production Act,[13] which carried very similar requirements. These two laws set the stage for many of the electric energy policy decisions, investments, and controversies in Maine in the 1980s.

Finally, in reviewing the electric industry in Maine in the 1970s, we must mention the bizarre bombing in 1974 of the new CMP corporate offices on Edison Drive in Augusta. Domestic terrorism, strange as it seems today, had come to Maine. The late '60s and early '70s had been a time of social turmoil throughout the nation, much of it in protest of civil rights and the Vietnam War. In at least one twisted mind, lashing out at a public utility was a blow against established authority. Fortunately, the two bombs that exploded in the library and mailroom did not result in personal injury. It did lead to tightened security in the building, however, and in many other facilities within the electric system.[14]

In the transportation sector, federal fuel-efficiency standards (CAFÉ)[15] were enacted. Drivers in Maine began moving to cars with better fuel efficiency, as gas prices spiked, then settled at levels double those in the early years of the decade. The change was somewhat slow, however, due to our tightwad tendency to hang on to old cars. Ride-share programs also became popular, with the state acting as surety for van purchases and providing convenient parking lots for ride-sharing commuters. Motor-fuel use in Maine had climbed to 12.5 million barrels by 1975, and then dropped to 11.6 million barrels in 1980, the only such drop in this forty-year time period.[16]

At home, Mainers installed woodstoves and turned to the forests for fuel. Wood had been on the decline as a fuel since the mid-'60s; but as fuel oil prices doubled and then doubled again, it seemed that all that cutting, stacking, carrying, and burning was worth it. Maine hobby-horsed from burning 322,000 cords of wood for residential use in 1965, down to 222,000 cords in 1970, and up again to 356,000 cords in1980.[17]

1980s: The Rise of the Independents
The 1980s saw the implementation of many of the energy policies established by legislation in the late 1970s, primarily in response to the oil crisis. This was particularly true for electricity. Both federal and state law required wholesale purchases of electricity from qualifying independent power producers when the cost was lower than the power provided by the regulated utilities, known as the "avoided cost." These companies would in time become known as the non-utility generators of power, or NUGs.

The utilities themselves proposed to invest in major, capital-intensive facilities such as Seabrook (New Hampshire) Units 1 and 2, as well as other nuclear units in New England; a coal plant, to be located on Sears Island; a new dam on the Penobscot River at Veazie; and, later, large power purchases imported from Hydro-Quebec. When the "avoided" costs for these proposed facilities were put to bid, qualifying independent producers offered power at less cost, thus creating an historic shift in who would build and produce the next generation of power plants in Maine. It also introduced new players into Maine's energy politics who, at least in part, balanced the political role of the investor-owned utilities. Some of these turned out to be the large pulp and paper mills, who were now in the energy-selling business.

Many of the new power plants built by independent producers were biomass facilities burning wood waste, and located in northern Maine counties. Municipal trash-to-energy facilities were built in cities in central and southern Maine. As mentioned, other successful competitors were pulp and paper mills that were already producing large amounts of power for their own use. Since the 1980s, the cost of power from these non-utility facilities has taken a great deal of abuse for being well above the current market cost of power in the '90s.

It is important to remember, however, that the facilities and investments proposed by the utilities would have been even *more* expensive than the non-utility power. The development of the independent power industry had a strong, beneficial effect on the northern Maine economy,[18] one of the intended effects of the Maine law. By the end of the '80's, fully 40 percent of Maine's electrical

Waste-to-Energy Generating Plant, Biddeford

energy was coming from renewable resources, by far the largest such figure for any state in the nation!

State policy also required energy *efficiency* investments by electric utilities, again when the cost of efficiency was below the utilities' "avoided cost." As most efficiency measures were then substantially below avoided cost, a lot of energy efficiency investments were made by the utilities among *all* customer classes. The supply-oriented utilities, however, were not happy with the new state policies, which were hard to swallow after so many years of previous political success before both the legislature and the Maine PUC.

One unexpected outcome of these realigned regulatory relationships was the replacement of senior CMP management, after a vice president lied under oath to the PUC to hide the political nature of questions appearing on a CMP customer-satisfaction survey. Power company relations with the PUC remained strained throughout the decade, as the utilities viewed the implementation of competitive power and energy efficiency policies as a threat to their core business interest of producing and selling ever more electricity.

Meanwhile, oil and gasoline prices had declined substantially by the mid-1980s. The average price for a barrel of crude oil in 1984 was $24; in 1985, it was $12. Once again, and not surprisingly, we saw renewed growth in the use of motor fuels. Mainers consumed 11.6 million barrels in 1980, climbing to 12.3 million barrels in 1985, and 13.4 million barrels in 1990. Again, as prices dropped, we were driving more.[19]

Environmentally, we voted twice at public referendum on whether to close the Maine Yankee nuclear power plant, once in 1982, and again in 1984; both questions failed to pass. We voted in 1986 on whether to require approval by public referendum for the storage of low-level waste; that one passed. Clearly, a significant portion of Maine's voters were concerned about the environmental impacts associated with the operation of Maine Yankee and the storage of its nuclear wastes.

Climate change issues also came of age in the late '80s, as scientific evidence mounted that human activity was impacting our global atmosphere. In particular, the emission of carbon, a byproduct of burning fossil fuels, had been identified as one of the primary culprits. In general, coal emits twice the carbon per BTU as oil; and oil, twice the amount of natural gas.

Following the collapse of world oil prices, energy policies began to tilt *away* from energy planning and *toward* greater reliance on markets. This trend accelerated following the fall of the Communist Bloc in the early 1990s: planning was out; markets were, once again, in. The lesson for us all is clear: *Only the certain prospect of resource scarcity will motivate the human species to plan thoughtfully and deliberately for the future!*

Changing Maine

The 1990s: Greater Reliance on Private Markets, Again

The energy policies of the '80s began to run into trouble when they hit the recession of the '90s; and the embedded costs of producing electricity were once again higher than falling market prices.

Aside from fuel prices, much had been happening in the electricity arena. The economies of scale that had been realized with the big steam-kettle technology throughout the '60s had stalled out by the '70s, and slowly gave way to new, greater economies in the smaller, "jet engine" combustion turbine (CT) units. The military and aerospace development of these large engines and the opportunity to turn them on end and use them to produce electricity set off a revolution in power plant construction. The capital cost of constructing a CT unit fueled by natural gas was a fraction of the cost of the large, capital intensive thermal units, generally powered by coal and oil. No one was proposing new nuclear construction or any large hydro production.

With the low cost and a seemingly unending "bubble" of available natural gas, the cost of producing electricity dropped dramatically. The difference between the low cost of power from CT units which could be built by anyone, and the higher-cost power developed in the '70s and '80s, created irresistible pressure to restructure the highly regulated electricity markets. Maine's electric power costs represented the old, higher cost technology.

However, the growth of the independent power industry in Maine and elsewhere demonstrated that the production of electrical power need not be a regulated monopoly. Instead, electricity could be a competitive enterprise in which regulation would focus on market structure and rules, rather than on setting prices. Electricity policy at the state and federal level, from the mid '90s on, concerned itself with creating the right conditions for the new wholesale electricity markets.

The Maine Electricity Restructuring Act of 1997 adopted the new, competitive model for both wholesale and retail sales of electricity in Maine.[20] Wyman Dam, the once proud symbol of Maine energy and ingenuity straddling the Kennebec River at Bingham, Maine, was sold to the Florida Power and Light Company, along with most of Central Maine Power's other generating assets. The generating facilities owned by Bangor Hydroelectric and Maine Public Service were also sold. The assets with positive market value were sold with proceeds benefiting ratepayers; assets such as the Maine Yankee and the NUG contacts with negative market value were retained, paid for by ratepayers.

At this same time, it became clear to CMP and its co-owners of Maine Yankee that costs of needed repairs to its vast system of pressurized pipes would cause power from that unit to exceed the market value of power. The decision was made to cease power production and dismantle the facility, the first dismantlement of a major nuclear power plant in the nation.

Maine utilities would no longer produce power; their business would be limited to the *distribution* of power purchased elsewhere. Next, the utilities, themselves were sold to out-of-state and out-of-country corporations. The electric utilities were no longer in the hands of Maine owners and managers. Maine became an outpost of larger empires. The social, cultural, and political roles that had been played by the utilities throughout the twentieth century were dramatically and forever altered on the eve of the twenty-first.

The construction of the natural gas pipeline across Maine, bringing natural gas to New England markets from the Canadian Sable Island field, provided the state with much-needed, additional fuel diversity, and allowed new CT units to be built in Maine. Because natural gas emits far less carbon dioxide than coal, it became the fuel favored by those who did not want more coal burned to serve the power needs of the Northeast. Indeed, natural gas became the favorite fuel of the entire electric industry.

Meanwhile, with oil prices as low as they had been in the 70s, Mainers stopped burning wood at home, and for much of the 90s forgot about energy efficiency. The reformed power companies gleefully resumed promotion of KWH sales. In transportation, the '90s were a driver's and boat owner's heyday. In real dollars, gasoline prices were as low as they had been in the '60s. Motor fuel used for transportation grew from 13.9 million barrels in 1990 to 16.2 million barrels in 2000, just about double the use in 1960.[21]

2000 and Beyond

This brings us, finally, to the current decade. What do we now face by way of energy challenges? Well, the heavy reliance nationally on natural gas for new electricity generation has finally absorbed the gas "bubble;" and prices for natural gas have recently doubled, as natural gas production from new wells falls short of compensating for losses from old, exhausted wells.[22]

The heightened demand for natural gas throughout the U.S. has led to great interest in importing liquefied natural gas (LNG) from the Middle East, Africa, Asia, and elsewhere. This will require significant infrastructure investment, estimated to be 200 billion dollars.[23] Of course, an investment of this size might go a long way if applied to energy efficiency and renewable resource development. The recently announced interest in construction of a facility for receiving LNG at Sears Island is a part of this growing national interest in LNG.

As the reader may have gathered by now, Sears Island, with its prime location at the top of Penobscot Bay, has had an amazing history as the site of one energy proposal after another, each defining its own decade: oil refinery, nuclear plant, coal plant, and now LNG facility. An LNG facility also has been proposed at a location in Harpswell. Both proposed sites will undoubtedly face intense environmental scrutiny—even while many who care for the environment would encourage the increased use of natural gas, due to its lower emission of carbon when compared to coal or oil.

In Maine, our competitive retail electric markets seem to be working for industrial customers, but not for residential and commercial customers, almost all of whom remain on a regulated rate. Oddly, for those who were on the losing side of the public power debates of the 1970s, the PUC now contracts with competing wholesale suppliers for the electricity sold to retail customers, a function which used to be performed by private utilities. The question of how these non-industrial electricity customers will be best served over the long run has not yet been finally answered. The current practice of relying on single contracts of short duration heightens customer exposure to volatile electricity markets, which are becoming more volatile as the shortage of natural gas drives up prices in peak hours of electricity use.

Short-term contracts of one to three years' duration encourage the market to invest in new natural gas-fired power plants, and not much else. We simply may not want all of our eggs in the one natural gas basket. On other hand, relying solely on long-term commitments might lead to the cost imbalances of the 1990s. Careful portfolio management is required that manages risk by using a diversity of fuels, multiple contracts of various commitments, and energy efficiency. Efficiency, too, has become a function of the PUC, rather than the utilities. *The State of Maine, through its PUC, now plays a role on both the demand and the supply sides of the electric markets, as well as participating in its regulatory oversight.* An odd turn of events, indeed!

In transportation, our confirmed driving habits have continued to grow, exacerbated by the love affair with SUVs that burn a lot more fuel to get where they are going than standard sedans. Our motor fuel use in 2000 was 16.2 million barrels.[24] Nationally, and most probably in Maine, transportation is the fastest growing contributor to global-warming gases. Becoming efficient in our transportation energy use remains a significant challenge for Maine.

Finally, there are the costs of trying to keep the Middle East a peaceful, reliable supplier of energy, as well as our ongoing concerns for climate change. These are energy-related costs that remain largely *external* to the calculations of those who make energy investment decisions. The price we pay for oil does not reflect the costs of military involvement needed to protect oil sources in the Middle East. (Have I mentioned that after Russia, Saudi Arabia has the largest known reserves of LNG? Or, that Iran is a close third?) Nor do the prices we pay for other fossil fuels reflect the full cost of environmental and health impacts that occur from burning these fuels in our cars, homes, and power plants.

The cost of the harm is real; and it is borne by all of us through increased health costs and loss of woods, agricultural productivity, wildlife habitat, and scenic places like the view from Cadillac Mountain. Can we adopt a "no regrets" policy that will lead us to greater use of renewable fuels and energy efficiency, as a hedge against Middle East military involvement and catastrophic climate change? Are we ready to learn the lessons of source-diversity and energy-efficiency all over again?

Governor John Baldacci recently created the Office of Energy Independence (independent from what, I am not certain), with a mandate to draw public policy attention back to the development of indigenous renewable resources and energy efficiency. This is a step to be applauded. On December 3, 2003, the Energy Office filed with the legislature a Draft Report, setting forth a series of policy recommendations that, if adopted, will help Maine move in the right direction on energy.[25]

So, what have we learned in the past forty years? I believe we have learned that:

- We have slowly ceded much control over energy decisions to regional, national, and international events and decisionmakers;

- Many of the true costs of energy remain external to the prices we pay, distorting our energy choices;

- We do not have the political will to internalize these true costs of energy;

- We forget to diversify our energy sources;

- We buy more and more when prices drop, ignoring history;

- We engage in patchwork, catch-up remedies when energy prices rise, and forget about them when prices fall;

- We love to drive;

- In short, Maine looks very much like the rest of the country these days when it comes to energy.

Because energy supply decisions are today so profoundly affected by events outside of Maine, I believe Maine must concentrate its policy attention on the *demand side* of the equation. We are what we buy. We *can* be considerably more efficient while enjoying the lifestyle and conveniences all Americans want to enjoy. Adoption of energy efficiency standards for many appliances and vehicles, and convincing our sister states to join us would be a good first step.

Rewarding our distribution utilities for encouraging conservation, and penalizing them for promoting sales of kwh is another needed step. Maine must also become a savvy electricity purchaser, insisting upon a portfolio of diversified sources, and refusing to ride the volatility of an all natural gas-driven electricity market. We can choose to invest more in new, renewable energy development. Finally, we have to stop deluding ourselves that energy is cheap; it isn't.

In closing, it is my hope that Maine might just be the first state to figure out how private markets and state action can work together to give us the energy we need, at prices we can afford to pay, without doing unnecessary damage to this beautiful world we call home.

Cheryl Harrington is the co-founder and director of the Regulatory Assistance Project (RAP), a non-profit organization formed in 1992 to foster regulatory policies for the electric industry, which encourage economic efficiency, protect environmental quality, assure system reliability, and allocate system benefits fairly to all customers. RAP has worked with public utility regulators in forty-five states, Washington D.C., and in several other countries including China, India, Indonesia, and Brazil. Before founding RAP, Cheryl was a regulator herself, serving as a member of the Maine Public Utilities Commission from 1982 to 1991. She has advised committees of the U. S. Congress on the subjects of energy efficiency, the relationship between efficiency and global warming, and the economic and environmental benefits of a national energy strategy that embraces energy efficiency. Ms. Harrington is a lawyer by training; prior to serving on the Maine PUC, she served in the Maine Attorney General's office as division chief for consumer and antitrust litigation.

THE WAYS IN WHICH we use Maine's forests have changed signifi-cantly since 1960, with dramatic implications for employment and community vitality in much of the state. In the 1960s "lumber and wood products" was a labor-intensive industry with growing markets that were largely insulated from foreign competition. Sawmills and woodworking and paper mills could be found in nearly every town across the state, providing stable and well-paid employment for gener-ations of Mainers. The forty years since have brought the environmen-tal movement, increased mechanization, global economics, and land-use sprawl. Together, these developments have forced enormous changes in Maine's forest-based industries. While forest management practices have been honed and developed, large-scale mill employment may well be gone for good. Maine communities must find new ways to leverage our forest resources to yield a living in the new economic setting.

19 Maine's Forest Industry
From One Era to Another

Lloyd C. Irland*

This chapter addresses how the forest products industry of Maine has changed since 1960, and the ways in which these changes have affected Maine people and communities.[1] The topic requires comment on the ownership and condition of the forest resource itself. Forest policy and the state's civic culture are noted, as well, and their prospects considered. We begin with some "snapshots" of the industry, as background to our story.

Some Historical Vignettes

1640s: Maine is not just an exporter of raw materials; it is already shipping value-added wood products—house frames and barrel staves—to the Sugar Islands of the Caribbean.

1869: A survey of Maine's water power reports that water-powered establishments along Gardiner's Cobbossee Stream employ 410 hands, mostly year-round. There are thirteen sawmills and wood plants, two small papermills, and a number of metalworking shops.

1920s: South Paris enjoys a national reputation as "Toy Town," the nation's largest concentration of producers of toys, including wooden sleds and many other items.[2]

1950s: Great Northern Paper Company produces one-third of all U.S. newsprint output; owns and manages an empire of some 2 million acres across the Maine woods; and is one the state's leading private employers.

Early 1970s: Great Northern builds the "Golden Road," to connect Millinocket and the Quebec border. Horses are still widely used for logging in the Maine woods.

Late 1970s: The four-lane Interstate Highway 95 arrives in Houlton.

Fall 2002: Strong loses its wood products plant, Forster Manufacturing, which invented the toothpick and many other specialty items.

Winter 2003: Great Northern, shrunken by sales, re-sales, and asset disposals, declares bankruptcy after its modernization efforts fail in weak product markets.

Pittston

Where We Were

In 1960, Maine was a quiet, backwater place. It shared with other rural regions of the country a slowly growing economy, and growing desperation over whether there would be a future for its young people. At the time, the footwear business was at the peak of its employment in Maine. The Maine Turnpike reached Augusta only in 1955, and the interstate highway to Houlton remained but a dream. Trains still carried passengers, and a lot of pulpwood. The Allagash, a stream of wildness and myth, had more than a century of legend behind it, but its public ownership was in the future. Maine's forests were growing back from the budworm outbreak of the World War I era. The woods were spreading slowly over southern Maine's landscape. From more and more of the low hills, the view was being engulfed by growing woods.

The Maine woods were busiest during logging season, except for established locations like Greenville. Only a few intrepid canoeists dared the rips and rapids of the Allagash. All-weather road access to the woods was limited. Even by the late '70s, entire towns lacked haul-road access, which greatly hindered rapid response to the budworm epidemic. Much of the North Woods' pulpwood harvest was moved by water. Skidders remained in the future. From the stump to the landing, horses hauled much of the wood up north, and plenty of it in southern Maine, as well.

Sawmills and wood products plants were numerous and small. The post-World War II period had unleashed nationwide economic growth, and a considerable outbreak of entrepreneurism. New plants were opened everywhere. Of 1,829 wood-manufacturing plants noted in the 1954 federal Census of Manufacturers, only 27 had more than 100 employees; 83 percent had fewer than 10.[3] In 1960, it was really true that Maine was a manufacturing state, with 38 percent of non-farm employment in manufacturing. The decline in that percentage since then has been truly dazzling (Table 1).

The geography of the industry was different then, as well. In 1955 Aroostook County was the leading lumber county but produced only 50 million feet annually,[4] less than one large mill can saw today. In second and third place, and very close behind, were Oxford and Cumberland counties. In 1960, the lumber industry was everywhere, with its hundreds of small mills, often run seasonally. The entire solid wood products industry, however, was dominated by Penobscot County, with almost 25 percent of total value of production. Penobscot, Somerset, and Oxford together accounted for 54 percent of the state's total.

In 1960, footwear (termed "leather" in the official statistics) led Maine in manufacturing employment. The average annual wage for all manufacturing workers was $4,023. Paper workers did *far* better at $5,647. Workers in lumber and wood did less well at $3,326, but far better than leather or apparel at $2,917 and $1,415 respectively. My wife's grandmother worked all her working life in a

Table 1. Maine Non-Farm Employment, 1940–2000, by Industry

| | | | Pct. of Mfg. | |
Year	Total	Manuf.	SIC 24	SIC 26
1940	100%	45%	n.a.	n.a.
1950	100%	43%	18%	16%
1960	100%	38%	16%	17%
1970	100%	33%	13%	16%
1980	100%	27%	12%	16%
1990	100%	19%	11%	17%
2000	100%	14%	13%	15%

Note: Total is all nonfarm employment; manufacturing was 45 percent in 1940. SIC 24 is the lumber and wood products industry; SIC 26 is the paper and allied products industry. n.a. indicates not available. Source: US BLS website.

Lewiston "shoe shop," walking to work each day. She and many of her generation told their grandchildren, "Get an education so you'll never have to work in a shoe shop."

Maine's days as a national lumber leader were in the distant past. Technology had not arrived to bump up the production and improve quality; most of the product was sold green. Everybody knew fir wouldn't make good lumber, and you couldn't sell hardwood pulpwood. The Maine paper companies were *paper* companies; no sawmills for them. Not only were they paper companies, they were the reigning leaders of a national industry. Spoken of as "The Northern," "The Diamond," or "The I-P," they had clout in town, in Augusta, and in Washington. They seemed, back then, as permanent as the very mountains.

Mechanization and improved techniques meant that a worker could produce a lot more over the years. From 1952 to 1979, jobs per million feet of logs in the solid wood sector went from 32.8 to 13.3, and continued falling after that. In pulpwood, jobs per million cords went from 7,900 in 1952 to 5,700 in '79.[5] In these plants—some still there in the late '70s—*the managers were the owners*. They knew how to use a wrench and drive a forklift. Skilled millwrights built their own machines; there were not enough clothespin plants in existence nationally for the suppliers to do it for them. Leading families were into a diversity of local businesses, and played important roles in these communities.

It looked like a level of stability all could count on for the indefinite future; but times were changing. A new impetus came for environmental improvement; and rising uses of wood began to clash with new needs and new political forces. Instead of stability, then, what we saw was anything but. (Table 2)

Table 2. Maine Forest Industry Dimensions, 1960 and 2000

	1960	2000	
Timber Cut			
Sawlog Harvest (5 key spp) (MM ft)	470	1,237	(1)
Pulpwood harvest (MM cords)	2.1	3.0	(2)
Lumber Production (MM ft)	303	1,225	(3)
Paper Production (M ton)	1,756	4,061	(4)
Employment (paper & lumber) (Thousands)	35	24	(5)
Wage & Salary Income ($ MM current)			
FPI Total	179	1,182	(6)
Percent of all Mfg.	39.8%	34.3%	

Notes:
(1) Spruce-fir rose from 124 to 725 MMbf
(2) Peaks of 3.5 MM in 1985, 1995
(3) Peaked in '95 at 1.3 MM ft
(4) 2000 was all time high
(5) See Table 1.
(6) FPI = Lum & Wood, Furn & Fixt, and Paper & Allied

Sources: MFS, 2003; Irland, unpub. compilations of Census data;
American Forest and Paper Association.

A Changing Forest

During the 1970s and early '80s, increasing timber inventories, growing demand for quality printing papers, and stricter environmental regulations provided incentives to modernize. The mills, for the most part, did; those that
didn't, closed. Technology came along to make a 2x4 out of an astonishingly
small log, and sawmills began to get a lot larger. The paper companies bought
themselves some. Maine and nearby areas began to become more prominent in
the northeastern lumber business, as a result. When the western national forests were essentially shut down in the early 1990s, at a time of booming demand, lumber prices boomed and so did log stumpage prices. For the first time
in postwar days, Maine stumpage rose relative to inflation.

At the opening of this period, Maine's forest was underutilized, and hence
growing in inventory volume. What we think of today as active forest management barely existed; what did exist was largely on small individual lots and on
progressive family lumber company tracts. By the mid-'70s, the inventory
reached unsustainable levels due to its large supply of short-lived balsam fir, all
nearing harvest age at once. Then the spruce budworm, a native pest, caught
up with it, along with rising lumber demand. The result was that, for the first
time since about 1910, Maine's wood-using industry had to contend with tim-

ber supply limits that were coming fast. The spruce–fir inventory actually declined substantially for two and one-half decades, though it now appears to have stabilized. The story of the changes in timber supply and the roles of budworm, intensive management, spraying, and landowner policies may be followed in a series of state reports and related papers.[6]

In the late '80s, Diamond International was acquired by an overseas financier, Sir James Goldsmith, and later broken up. The sale of its regional landbase, including more than 600,000 acres of lands in New York, New Hampshire, and Maine, created a major regional stir in 1986. In 1990, Great Northern Paper was acquired by the Georgia Pacific Corporation. Subsequent land sales raised concern about the stability of ownership in the region. In the years after 1990, major corporate holdings were restructured, and longtime corporate names literally vanished from the landownership roster.[7] Two federal studies were funded to look into the issue. Land acquisition efforts by the states were increased, especially with the creation and funding of the Land for Maine's Future program in 1987.[8] Federal programs were tapped more vigorously. The most dramatic development was the rise of private conservation funding, focused on large-scale conservation easements and outright purchases.

A dramatic announcement in early 1999 told the world that the heirs of David Pingree, owners of a holding dating back to pre-Civil War days, planned to sell a conservation easement to the little-known New England Forestry Foundation. This represented not only a huge increase in the scale of efforts to address development pressures, but also triggered an increase in land conservation activity without precedent in the entire country. In short order, The Nature Conservancy purchased 175,000 acres of International Paper Company timberland along the St. John River, and allocated 40,000 acres to wilderness status. A bewildering array of cooperative projects emerged. In late 2003, Roxanne Quimby, a successful entrepreneur, acquired a township near Baxter State Park, declaring that she planned to use it and other smaller tracts as a nucleus for a new National Park. What was striking about these efforts was the declared intent, in nearly every instance, to maintain a "working forest." Of course, how to define a working forest engendered considerable debate among specialists, interest groups, and funders.

Where We Are Now....

By the year 2000, a great deal of water had gone over the dam. In fact, one of the dams, itself, in Augusta, was about to be gone! Forest output was strikingly higher, as Table 2 above shows. The number of people engaged had shrunk, of course, but not in proportion to total manufacturing in the state; the industry's importance to the manufacturing sector had not diminished. In 1997, a paper worker made an average wage of $47,585, compared to the average manufacturing wage of $31,721. Workers in lumber and wood made $24,448, due to the many labor-intensive secondary plants. The number of plants had fallen dramatically. Many small towns and crossroads had ceased to be mill towns. Some substantial communities, like Winslow, lost their papermills and sizable portions of their employment and tax base. Striking changes in these forty years include the loss of as many as a *thousand* small woodworking plants and sawmills, and the construction of a series of new, large, modern mills. As a result, lumber production grew almost threefold from 1960 to 2000. Paper production increased dramatically.

After the mid-'70s recession, Maine's economy slowly began to shift away from its heavy reliance on natural resources and manufacturing, and to take on the characteristics of the rest of the country—that is, relying more on trade and services. We may now see that the employment in lumber and wood products hit its peak in the mid-'50s, relying on labor-intensive techniques and a growing national market largely untouched by foreign competition. Changing technologies, maturing North American markets, unfavorable exchange rates, and international investment flows placed Maine mills increasingly at a disadvantage. Few industry experts can even remember the last "greenfield" papermill built in the U.S. The trade papers tell of billion-dollar pulp projects in South America and China. The cost of just *one* of these could likely buy the entire Maine paper industry during a spell of weak markets.

By the mid-'80s, it was clear that employment had been sustained by a rising log harvest, and that this could not continue indefinitely. The state's production statistics show the peaking of log harvests, and the employment numbers after 1990 show the effect on jobs. The forest resource is not growing in total area to any extent, and is being whittled away at the edges. Active subdividers are giving homeowners what they say they want across southern Maine. Efforts to shift the incentives away from sprawl and toward more rational land use seem to be failing. To the north and on the semi-rural fringes of the North Woods, the liquidators happily chop up parts of entire townships, to sell to speculators and visitors coming up the interstate from "the flatland."

Most disturbingly to some, some paper companies declare that they have no need to own the woods anymore. One of the biggest, Georgia Pacific, sold all its lands and then took out ads in the *Wall Street Journal* satirizing those who kept their lands: "Money does not grow on trees," they said. At this point, four of the state's largest papermills own no land at all and buy on the open market or through long-term supply contracts.

We are buying cabinet doors of radiata pine, cut from plantations across the world and sold at prices our pine mills here could not imagine meeting. The furniture store increasingly carries top-end furniture made in China. Nationally, we are in a true crisis of change in rural areas as small plants close. Maine is part of this, and the wood sector is not immune. Our extensive forest cannot shelter us from the chill winds of international competition.

The Wood Products Towns

In the nineteenth century, virtually every Maine town had a mill, often a combined saw and grist mill. Many of these ran seasonally, on spring high water, and met limited local needs. Until steam power and higher volume methods arose at mid-century, there were few sawmill towns. The principal exceptions were the mill complexes at locations like Bangor, Fort Kent, and Calais, where river drives brought logs in huge volumes on the spring flood.

A good deal of the woodworking was in tiny shops, many in urban areas. Carpenters dressed much of their lumber on the jobsite, working up timber framing from logs delivered there by teamsters, and profiling millwork on site. By the late nineteenth century, however, woodworking mills had clustered in centers like the Norway-Paris area and nearby. They built upon the labor surplus released by shrinking farming and supplied by immigration, on the expanding forest, and on proximity to urban and small-town markets.

In a detailed wood industry survey in 1912,[9] it was found that woodworking plants consumed 84 million feet of white pine, the premier wood for packing as well as high-quality worked items. Virtually all was grown in Maine. In that year, 59 million feet went into boxes and crates. Eighteen different categories of industry used white pine, some in tiny amounts, to be sure. When the boxboard market vanished, wiped out by the cardboard box made from southern pine, Maine farmers and industry foresters could no longer thin their pine stands.

A specialty peculiar to Maine was the diversified industry built on white birch, which used 38 million feet in 1912. Seven categories of industry used more than a million feet each, the largest being shuttles, spools, and bobbins, which took almost half the total. Mill owners believed that Maine's birch was superior to that grown elsewhere. Perhaps so; but perhaps, instead, it was superior craft, millwrights, and marketing that kept this industry going.

About 1800 small wood products plants spread across the Maine landscape in the mid-'50s (Table 3, Fig 1). Some were too small, or too seasonal, to have a noticeable influence compared to the shoe plant, the cannery, or the metalworking shop in town. A few of these grew over the generations into larger businesses, but most simply left a circle saw, an old skidder, and other gear rusting in a side-yard. Nearly 200 plants in 1954 employed more than 10 workers; even the smallest of these could play a role in a small crossroads village and contribute something to the tax base. Such a plant would employ perhaps twice as many workers around the county in getting in and hauling wood. The Maine Forest Service reported in the 1970s that some *1,400 different items* were being made of wood in the state.

International Paper Mill, Bucksport

Table 3. Number of Plants, Lumber and Wood Products Industry, 1949-97

1949	399	State Mfg. Census
1955	1,829	Peck, P., based on federal sources
1960	1,006	State Mfg. census
1992	812	"
1997	779	"
2000	784	US DOC—County Bus. Patterns

Note: Sources differ. 1949 is most probably an undercount. These numbers include "logging camps and contractors," which are grossly undercounted in this statistical source.

The steady growth of spruce–fir production, following a rebounding forest resource, shifted the lumber business northward. New and expanded mills at places like Passadumkeag, Nashville Plantation, St. John Plantation, and Woodland brought a new round of wood products employment to towns that had seen little of it for two generations. Most of this growth is a product of the 1970s housing boom, the re-growth of the forest, the budworm salvage period, and the new technology for making 2x4s out of small logs that once went for pulp or stayed in the woods.

In 1960 Maine was known as a center for toothpicks, dowels, clothespins, and a host of turnery and related items. This industry had grown up around the growing white birch resource, a tree favored by gone-back farms, small timber cuts on small lots, and occasional fires. At one time, the white birch of good grade was our most valuable wood. A bustling industry kept tiny towns from Bryant Pond to Old Town and across southern Maine busy, cutting up the birch bolts for products sent far away. After the 1972 Forest Service inventory was done, it was thought desirable to have a special analysis of the wood availability for just this industry.[10] It found that the amount of birch used was about the same as it had been in 1912, and the total consumed by the turneries was more than 90,000 cords. In a prescient observation, the authors noted that imports could pose a long-term threat to this industry.

These plants were labor intensive, as was the preparation of the bolts in the woods. They were built on the ingenuity of proprietors, often of several generations, who were handy with metal and machines. They had to be; nobody sold clothespin machines. In town after town, small birch plants provided employment and supported town services. In the late '40s, some of the biggest plants ran three shifts. Things were changing by 1960, but only slowly. This was a period when manufacturing, retailing, and distribution were of small scale. The

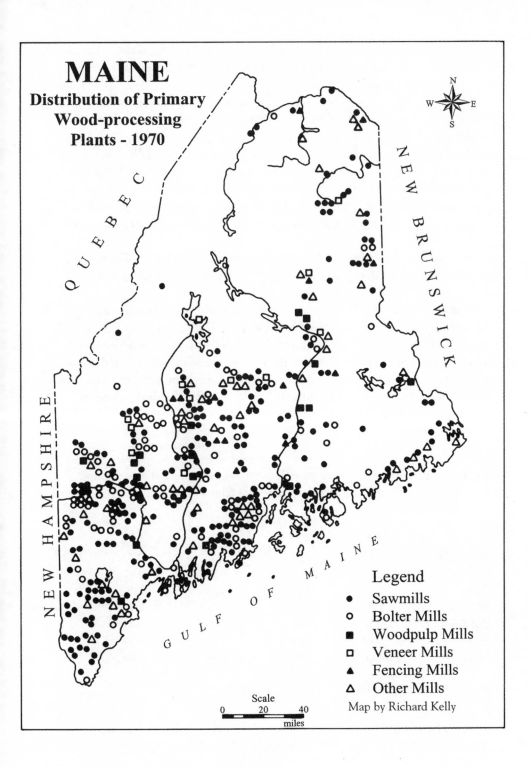

MAINE

Distribution of Primary Wood-processing Plants - 1970

QUEBEC

NEW BRUNSWICK

NEW HAMPSHIRE

GULF OF MAINE

Legend

- ● Sawmills
- ○ Bolter Mills
- ■ Woodpulp Mills
- □ Veneer Mills
- ▲ Fencing Mills
- △ Other Mills

Map by Richard Kelly

Scale
0   20   40
miles

materials of the nineteenth century had not been replaced by modern chemicals and plastics; and the wood products sector of the tropics was still doing little but exporting mahogany logs.

More and more homes would have washing machines and electric dryers; clothespins came to be seen only at Grandma's house. Later, plastics came to dominate the bulk markets for golf tees, toy wheels, and much else. Still later, offshore woods came to be used for many of these items. Ironically, it was not a matter of price competition as far as the consumer was concerned. Tongue depressors and coffee stirrers go out for free. How many golfers know the price of a golf tee? The costs were felt by the huge distributor who bought in massive quantities. For a savings of a few percent on an order of clothespins, the order goes to Asia now.

As these jobs have dwindled, population structure has shifted. The number of young people has declined, even as the populations in retired age brackets increase. (See Table 4.)

Today, there are small companies succeeding in the wood business in Maine, though they seem rarely to make the newspapers. They often pick up distressed assets of failing firms and make a go of the viable pieces. So, there remains ample scope for entrepreneurship in the Maine woods and wood-based industries. Small-town life in many parts of Maine will never be the same, however. Wood products jobs were among the last to leave, after the food processing moved to Delmarva and the "corn shops" (local corn-canning plants) closed.

Table 4. Changing Age Structure, Selected Communities and Age Groups: Ratio of Year 2000 to 1960 Population in Age Class

	Age Class			
	0-5	15-34	65+	All
Millinocket	0.17	0.44	2.15	0.7
Phillips	0.51	1.29	0.91	0.97
Strong	0.82	1.61	1.53	1.29
W. Paris	1.01	1.77	2.92	1.71
Old Town	0.38	0.97	1.45	0.94
Bethel	0.54	1.06	1.26	0.99
Portland	0.46	1.56	0.88	0.89

Source: US Census of Population.

There is much more to this period than one table can show, and many local factors affect these trends.[11] (For more, see Mageean, AvRuskin, and Sherwood, 2000.)

After textiles went to North Carolina and the shoe plants went to the Dominican Republic and Malaysia, the small wood plants were still there. There was a relation to land, however imperfectly glimpsed at times. Out for a drive to town, you drove past your raw material.

Tiny towns had something for the high school graduate and the young person home from the navy. The wages weren't much, but for people who wanted to stay near family, it was possible. A modest house could be dreamed of, though it would take some years of saving. Lots were cheap. Thrifty people could make the old Ford run a long while. For those who preferred not to go down to Hartford, it offered a choice. Let's not romanticize it, however. There were backs crushed from heavy lifting in the woods and on the loading dock. There were missing fingers and worse. There were few trips to Florida. Firewood was not used for heat because it was "green" or stylish; these families never gave it up in the first place. For retirement, there was only social security.

It is easy to see a story of exploitation here. Certainly, profits were made, and indifference to workers was not uncommon. Many of these workers knew well what "being poor in Maine" is like.[12] Especially in logging, bad working conditions, low wages, and the absence of fringes were standard. Unions were virtually absent. At one time OSHA identified logging and wood products manufacturing as "target industries," though I recall few people noticing their doing much about it. Probably it is useful to ask: if there was exploitation, what permitted it? I think there are many answers, but chronic labor surpluses in the rural regions, especially nearby Quebec, go a long way toward explaining it.

Maine is the worse off for the passing of small-scale, independent industries like this one, which used local raw materials and met a need for jobs. The owners lived nearby, and had relatives on the plant floor, driving trucks, and out in the woods running the skidders. A community was a place where something was produced; it was not just a place where people come home from the office in a distant city to have dinner. As Cohen and Zysman say, "Manufacturing Matters."[13] A 1992 report by the Mainewatch Institute was subtitled, "Improving prosperity through the secondary wood products industry in the western mountains of Maine;"[14] unfortunately, the subsequent decade brought just the opposite of prosperity to many of these towns.

Looking at this, warts and all, what will replace it? What kind of a society will it be? Before thinking of implications, let's look at another social phenomenon of Maine, the papermill town.

The Paper Mill Towns

A paper mill town, as I use the term here, is a small community, the economy of which is dominated by a primary paper or pulp mill. (There are a few towns similarly dominated by "converting" plants, but I do not consider those here.)

In 1906, near the peak of paper mill building, there were about fifty-one mills in Maine, counting about a dozen then in construction. These were owned by twenty-seven companies. After the newsprint tariff came off during World War I, just a few new mills were built in Maine, examples being Seaboard at Bucksport in the early 1930s, and the International Paper mill in Van Buren, closed by the mid-'50s. The Somerset mill built by Scott Paper Company in the late '70s is the last "greenfield" mill built in Maine.

So, there are a number of former papermill towns, already; and there are several whose mills have endured since the early twentieth century, and have employed several generations in some families. There are a number of paper mills at the edge of very large cities, which do not have mill town traits because of their more diverse economies; Westbrook, Winslow before 1999, and Brewer are examples. Old Town, in ready commuting range of Bangor and adjacent to a large university town, is an intermediate case.

Paper mill towns (Figure 2) offered secure employment for several generations of Mainers, at rising living standards that were the envy of other Maine workers. Increased investment and production kept job counts rising at many mills until the 1960s and '70s. At about that time, populations of the true mill towns hit their peaks, for the same reason. Since the '70s, increased mechanization has caused productivity to rise. The stringent limits on timber supply, as well as competitive factors, have prevented capacity increases. The result is declining headcounts, at mill after mill. Reflecting these changes, many mill towns peaked in population by 1960. A few have declined dramatically since their peaks (Table 5). Not only mill towns lose population, though; Portland's population is below its 1920 level, partly for the same reasons: the direct and indirect effects of losing its industrial base.

Mill town status is related to a number of social and economic traits that are distinctive (Table 6, Fig. 3). Many of these revolve around the high wage levels, the effects of shift work, and the limited economic diversification of such towns.[15] (See Irland, 2002.) These issues have never been thoroughly studied, and generalizations must not be allowed to mask considerable variation among these communities.

The dwindling of high wage jobs has changed the population age structure in these communities. Millinocket may be an extreme case. For the mill, the workforce is heavily skewed toward workers older than fifty. For the community, school enrollments decline, and the supply of entry level workers—for whatever occupation—decreases. With the mill downtime in 2003, Millinocket entered the winter with 25 percent unemployment, which has had severe effects on the area economy as well as the individuals and families involved.

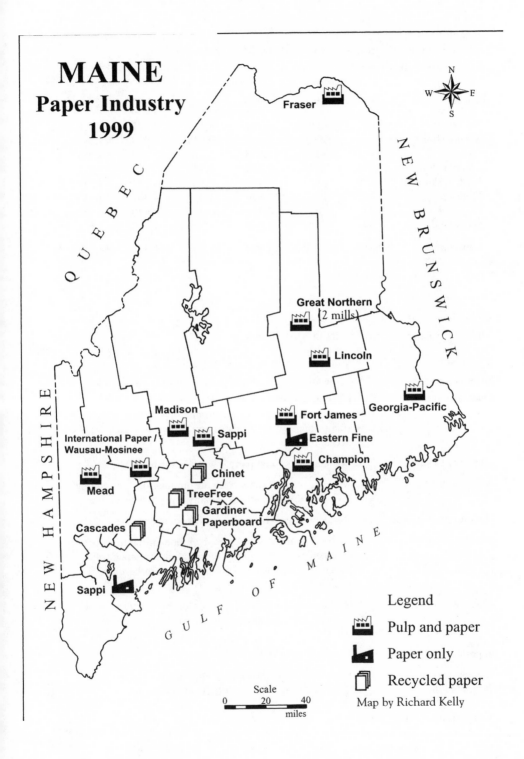

MAINE
Paper Industry
1999

Fraser

QUEBEC

NEW BRUNSWICK

Great Northern
(2 mills)

Lincoln

Georgia-Pacific

Madison

NEW HAMPSHIRE

International Paper /
Wausau-Mosinee

Sappi

Fort James

Eastern Fine

Champion

Mead

Chinet

TreeFree

Gardiner
Paperboard

Cascades

Sappi

GULF OF MAINE

Legend

Pulp and paper

Paper only

Recycled paper

Map by Richard Kelly

Scale

0   20   40

miles

Table 5. Population Trends, Selected Paper Mill Towns and
Portland for Comparison

Town	1900	1920	1940	1960	1980	2000
Bucksport	2,339	1,906	2,927	3,466	4,345	4,908
M't-E. Mlnkt	n.a.	5,920	7,886	9,845	9,939	7,031
Jay	2,758	3,152	2,858	3,274	5,080	4,985
Lincoln	1,731	2,452	3,653	4,541	5,066	5,221
Madawaska	1,698	1,933	4,477	5,507	5,282	4,534
Madison	2,467	3,700	3,836	3,935	4,367	4,523
Rumford	3,770	8,576	10,230	10,005	8,540	6,472
Woodland	1,096	1,120	1,298	1,372	1,369	1,403
Portland	50,415	69,272	73,643	72,566	61,572	64,249

Source: US Census and Maine SPO

Table 6. Socioeconomic Traits of Mill Towns

Ethnic Mix	Varied by region within state
Geographic Isolation	Some are compact, some draw from wide labor markets.
Outdoor Culture	Fishing, hunting, snowmobiling are strong in mill towns. Paperworkers have the means and opportunity to own small camps, often on paper company leases; conflict over access is common.
Employer Dominance	Some are true "company towns;" many are not.
Shift Work	Working on shifts affects friendship relationships, family life, civic engagement, and many aspects of social life.
Commuting Patterns	Residence near the mills remains common.
Job Tenure	In the past, many spent careers in one mill; mill work was regarded as secure; there were many multi-generation paperworkers; town had essentially no similar industrial work at similar pay levels.
Aging Workforce	In many mills, a high proportion of the workforce is older than age fifty; significant effects on all aspects of social life.
Importance of Union	Key institution in local life.
Worker Role in Political Life	Increasing over time; now, a paperworker sits in Congress. (Rep. Michael Michaud of Millinocket)

Source: Irland, 2002,. unpub.

Figure 3. Millinocket Age Structure, 1960 and 2000

Population

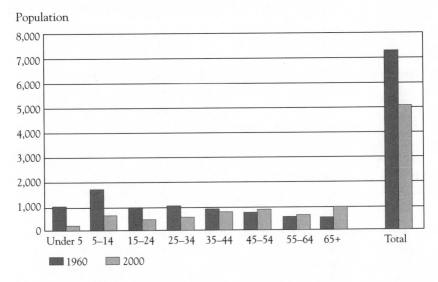

Source: U.S. Bureau of Census, Census of Population.

Who Will Cut the Wood?

In 1960, horses continued in use in logging, on small operations in southern Maine for the birch plants and pine mills, and on a large scale in the North Woods to supply pulpwood to the paper mills. In the North Woods, many of the loggers were Canadians, coming to work season by season for the winter. Many of the contractors were based in Quebec. A map of the woods in the winter of 1960 would show three and four camps in each town, each camp with 100 men and even more horses. The Canadian role provoked two generations of controversy and contention. In the late 1950s there were about 6,000 "bonded" workers in Maine's North Woods; by the early years of this century, there were fewer than 600.[16] Despite rising demand for wood, there were too many loggers and machines out there. Mill wood buyers regularly rationed the "tickets" to bring in wood. The wood came to them; they did not have to go out and scratch for it.

A rising flow of wood was provided by rebuilding the capital structure of the logging industry—not once, but twice since 1960. From the early '70s, skidders ruled the woods, becoming ever larger and more capable. The last of the horses were gone by the mid-'70s, with only occasional exceptions. A new generation of machines appeared during the late '80s, much more powerful and expensive. Large, well capitalized contractors bought fleets of trucks, and invested in huge, hydraulically operated "bunchers," "limbers," and cut-to-length (CTL) processors.

These new behemoths in turn drove out many of the skidders, pushing them into specialized roles or work on small lots. It was said in 1999 that in Jackman, the logging town *par excellence*, not a single skidder was owned. There was, throughout, too much logging capacity. Despite periodic price boomlets in pulp and lumber, long-term returns for the large companies were squeezed. Changing contracting methods shifted returns toward landowners, as they struggled to maintain modest incomes in a period of rising costs.

Then, in late fall 2003, the Louisiana Pacific Company announced that they would temporarily close an OSB (structural panel) mill at Woodland, because they could not get enough wood. A season of difficult logging weather had depleted mill log-piles everywhere, and mills were paying panic prices to get wood. This was at a time of unprecedented highs in OSB prices. It later emerged that the problem was getting the loggers to cut and haul the wood. Industry observers began to wonder if the long-expected crisis had arrived; if a decade of falling contract rates had finally driven out enough capacity to fatally undermine the industry's wood supply chain.

University of Maine forestry professor Andrew Egan conducted a survey of loggers.[17] He found that many of them did not expect their sons to enter the business. This reinforced indications from an earlier study, and kept the question before us: who will cut the wood?

Changing Civic Culture and New Policies
Looking back to the political culture of the state in relation to forestry in 1960 feels something like walking through the Maine State Museum, and walking past interiors of square-rigged ships, Lombard log haulers, and nineteenth-century artifacts. It was a *long* time ago. There was no pressure for change; stability in the woods was assumed. There was no budworm, no herbicide controversy. The Allagash referendum was in the future. In their history of the state, Judd, Churchill, and Eastman name their chapter on this period, by R. Condon, "Maine Out of the Mainstream."[18]

There was no tree growth tax, and the state's forestry program was small. Very little was asked of it. An industry committee concerned with fire protection in the North Woods (the Maine Forestry District, or "MFD") essentially appointed the state forester and oversaw his work.[19] Maine's public reserved lands entailed long-forgotten "timber and grass rights" on patches of land all across the region, and the state took care of some 40,000 public lots in the plantations. The state park system at the time was minimal.

The level of wood production was low, traditional forest practices were benign, the economy was changing slowly, and so far as pollution and hydropower were concerned, the rivers belonged to big industry, power companies, and big city sewers. This began to change, slowly at first, in the late '60s as new environmental priorities pushed their way into the political process. Hardly noticed at first, Maine's economy shifted more to a service and retail base, as traditional manufacturing stood still until the 1990s, and then shrank dramatically.

Maine suburbanized at a rapid rate. National groups for the first time began to take an interest in Maine affairs, and local environmental groups grew their memberships, sharpened their tactics, and developed allies in the legislature and the press. Political candidates, however conservative, would declare themselves "environmentalists." A political system for forest policymaking, built on decades of one party control and on limited public involvement, entered a prolonged struggle for control over policy against these emerging forces.

In 1960 few people knew what a land trust or conservation easement was, or had any reason to care. A series of legislative leaders began bending history in a new direction in the late '60s, partly aided by new activism in Washington.[20] For too long on environmental matters, the states had exercised their prerogatives by doing nothing, and stubbornly resisting federal action. The Maine Land Use Regulation Commission came into being in 1969, to serve as a state-level zoning body for the unorganized territories—the 10 million acres of Maine with no local government. The Tree Growth Tax law was adopted in 1973.

Governor Kenneth Curtis re-organized state government from a wilderness of independent agencies almost beyond counting, to a manageable number of fewer than twenty departments. In the bargain, the Department of Conservation was created by the merger of five baronies—the Land Use Regulation Commission and the Bureaus of Public Lands, Parks and Recreation, Forestry, and Geology. Three of these had previously been overseen by citizen boards, and one (LURC) would continue to be. State government crept closer to the position of an independent actor in the Maine woods, a situation not always to everyone's liking.

Ralph Nader's people came along and told us that Maine was a "paper plantation." The state banned log driving after 1976; the last drive was on the Kennebec River. A major spruce budworm epidemic then spread from Ontario to Nova Scotia and beyond, engulfing Maine in a long, costly, and contentious spraying program in an effort to staunch the losses.[21]

In the 1990s, the state encountered a series of highly polarized issues, culminating in the divisive referendum campaigns of the late '90s, to ban clear-cutting. This put previously centrist environmental groups on the spot; and gave new impetus to conservative and property rights advocates who sought to recover and then cement control over the various trade and resource groups. The declines in the spruce–fir inventory; the escalating rate of land sales by companies that seemed in 1960 to be enduring features of the landscape; and the escalating distrust of paper companies created fertile ground for the appeals of the clear-cut ban proponents. Polarization, however, did not achieve a clear resolution of some of the most difficult issues, which continue to this day.

Largely due to paper company investments from the late '70s to the present, some 800,000 acres of intensively managed Maine forests are occupied by managed stands, some of natural origin, that are growing back in the wake of the heavy clear-cutting of the '80s. Many of these stands are growing at *twice* the rate of unmanaged natural stands, some even faster. The cumulative private investment involved exceeds $100 million. This does not include the large public and private outlay for budworm spraying from the '70s to the mid-'80s.

State government has a full agenda ahead of itself. Recommendations are at hand, from past efforts (e.g. Peck 1957; Rice 1999; Irland 2003) as well as from the extensive effort that culminated in Governor John Baldacci's Blaine House Conference on Natural Resource-Based Industry.[22] The Blaine House conference recommended that state government focus on the areas of logging capacity and forest industry infrastructure; energy and transportation costs; business climate and tax policy; connections between managed forests and tourism; branding and certification; the competitive advantages of Maine species and carbon finance opportunities; improved sharing of information; and federal trade policy—a daunting agenda, indeed!

Study committees and outside contractor research projects are under way on a number of issues.[23] Finally, and of critical importance, Maine voters in 2004 will face a major bond issue to continue the important land acquisition work of the Land for Maine's Future program.

Prospects
The ills of the wood sector today reflect the widespread shrinkage of manufacturing in our society—from a high of 25 percent of personal income in Maine in 1960, to just 11 percent in 2000.[24] The trends, however, are not just a matter of statistics; they reflect changing opportunities for once-rooted families to remain rooted. They mean fewer opportunities for multi-generational families to be in touch, to regularly see their grandchildren. Schools are closing, and small rural hospitals are under stress. Compared to 1960, the pace of change has accelerated dramatically; stasis recedes, change prevails.

There is a blind spot engendered by the fairly small percentage of total gross state product (or jobs) that now is contributed by the forest-based sector. The sense appears to be that if the percentage is small, then it doesn't matter; but it does matter! *It is a matter of the future of rural small towns statewide; and for these places, and for the families who live there, it does matter!*

Changing Maine

How the wheel has turned! In late 2003, a group of legislators issued a report calling for more entry-level jobs to retain Maine young people in the state.[25] The report clearly echoes the concerns of the '60s and '70s, when the economy was not generating jobs sufficient to keep our children here. Over the generations, small woodworking plants and logging supplied such jobs in tiny towns across the state. Summer jobs there helped put many young people through college. These jobs often did not make a career; but they enabled a person with just a high school diploma to start one. Today, policymakers in Augusta and economic pundits have finally noticed—a little bit late, it would seem—that these jobs counted for something.

Unhappily, simple solutions do not appear to be at hand. Some things seem fairly clear, however:

- The forces shrinking U.S. manufacturing have not fully played out, and there is little Maine can do to influence them. In common with farming and fishing, our state is undergoing a dramatic and permanent shift away from resource dependence for its economic base. Despite arguments to the contrary, I am unable to see that tourism, recreation, or other economic activities will ever be able to offset what has been lost—national park, or no national park.

- The age of a few large organizations owning and managing the Maine woods in huge tracts—and for extremely long periods of time—is over. We do not even see, much less understand, all the implications of this fundamental fact.

- A new age of conservation ownership is upon us, in which ownership interests are split in novel ways, and funding comes from novel sources. The number of actors is increasing. We do not understand all of the implications of this, either.

- Sprawl and wasteful, inefficient land use will continue to eat away at both the private and public values of the forest. Recent efforts to "immunize" large areas against subdividing will be of permanent benefit to our descendants. We need to be doing more of this in southern Maine—much more.

- Maine's forests have a number of important values—as cultural asset, timber base, economic sector, biodiversity haven, wildlife habitat, recreational resource, and real estate. All of these values will increase in importance over time.[26] No one of these values should be allowed absolutely to dominate any one of the others, much less all of them.

Through much effort and controversy, we know how to manage the Maine forest a good deal better than ever before. What is now unclear, however, is whether we can sustain the private ownership institutions, a supportive public policy environment, and the public support necessary to carry this forward into the future.

We are at times nostalgic for the simpler life of 1960, when all seemed so stable, conflict was minimal, and so readily resolved. Yet, our economy will face still more challenges, and our political system, which often appears badly adapted for making tough choices, may continue to face polarization and division. The policies of the past seem less and less applicable to the challenges of the future; and there are but few new ideas out there.

Yet amid all the change, we may remember that a key trait in the Maine character has always been adaptability. We hope for a future filled with vibrant, small communities, entrepreneurship, and businesses based on renewable raw materials produced here, in the Maine woods. To reach this future, there is much to do.

*E*ducated at Michigan State, Arizona, and Yale Universities, Lloyd Irland has been active in Maine forestry affairs for almost thirty years—ten of them in state government, as director of the spruce budworm management program, director of the Bureau of Public Lands, and economic advisor to Governor Joseph Brennan. As president of the Irland Group for more than fifteen years, he has balanced consulting with industry, government, and the nonprofit sector in the U.S. and Canada, with teaching at Yale University and within the University of Maine System and, as well, with a research program that has produced more than three hundred publications. The topics of his writings range across all the values of forests, from ethics to wilderness and water, to recreation and commercial timber, to sustainable forestry and its scientific requirements. Recently identified as one of the top thirty foresters in the United States, Dr. Irland is a Fellow of the Society of American Foresters. He is frequently asked to address legislative committees on questions of forest policy and management, and has twice delivered major addresses to the Society of American Foresters national convention. Most recently, he has been an outspoken leader in the effort to eliminate cut-and-run or "liquidation" harvesting in the Maine woods. A resident of Wayne, Maine, Lloyd is married, the father of four children, and the grandfather of a brand new grandchild.

RECENT REPORTS IN THE MAINSTREAM PRESS portray a Maine agriculture in steady decline, as dairy and potato farmers struggle to compete with much larger commodity growers elsewhere in the nation. These reports mask a new and emerging trend which offers great promise for Maine agriculture in particular, if it is nurtured and developed effectively. Industrialization has profoundly impacted agricultural economies all across the nation and, as a result, farm size has grown while the number of farmers has declined precipitously. The news may sound bleak, but emerging evidence suggests that Maine's agricultural sector has been steadily moving in a different direction from the rest of the country since the 1970s. A dual agricultural structure is evolving in Maine, with more diversified, small scale farms producing for local consumption. Through more sophisticated techniques of production and marketing, these farms are establishing themselves as a new, if more complex model for agriculture in Maine. While the commodity system will continue to expand and comprise a large portion of the state's agricultural production, "local agriculture" offers new promise for farmers and new options for consumers.

20 Maine Agriculture
Adapting to a More Complex Setting

STEWART SMITH

A reader of the daily press is likely to assume that Maine agriculture today is in deep trouble.

We read that the dairy industry, which supports much of the open space in central Maine, is threatened by new federal policies that expose Maine dairy farmers to a market increasingly dominated by new and large farms, primarily in the nation's Northwest and Southwest. The governor and legislature acted to help dairy farmers through the turmoil of last year, and they seem prepared to provide longer-term support this legislative session.

Potato farmers appear headed towards another difficult year, with abundant national supplies depressing market prices, and with difficult growing and harvesting weather challenging more farm families. Three blueberry processors are financially threatened by a court decision that rejects the way they pay their grower-suppliers. Imports of apple juice concentrate from China and South America depress apple prices so severely that most Maine orchardists can no longer compete in U.S. wholesale markets.

Drought reduces crop yields throughout much of Maine, triggering a federal disaster declaration; excessive wet-weather during harvest triggers calls for another declaration. Traditional water supplies for irrigation are no longer readily available to many Maine farms, even as irrigation becomes increasingly critical to farm viability.

These are the stories most of us read in the daily press, and they contribute to the public definition of Maine agriculture—one that all too often suggests pessimism and decline.

There is another Maine agriculture story, however—one that is often unrecognized and, until quite recently, largely under-reported. It is the story of what is being called "local agriculture," built around local food systems where farmers produce food for consumers, rather than commodities for market. In this story, farm numbers are increasing, farms are more connected to their local communities, and optimism reigns.

This story may be less obvious, because it represents a steady, persistent movement toward a dual agricultural structure in Maine—a fork in the road, if you will. This chapter on Maine agriculture considers this fork, how we got here, where it may take us, and what we may want to do about it, if anything.

An Emerging Paradigm

Let me illustrate this dual agriculture by describing some farms that are taking the newer path in the road; the reader may be familiar with some of them. About mid-century, Jan Goranson's parents moved from Aroostook County to Dresden, carrying their potato-growing skills with them. The Goransons developed a fine potato farm between the banks of the Kennebec and Eastern rivers. Jan returned from college to help out at the farm when her father became ill, intending it to be a short stay. While at the farm, she started to grow a few crops other than potatoes and sold them at farmers' markets. At the time, she met Rob Johanson, who was growing melons and mixed vegetables and producing maple products in Whitefield.

As Jan became increasingly attached to the farm—and to Rob, as the relationship grew into a family—Jan and Rob determined that the days of producing potatoes for wholesale prices at their scale in Dresden were doomed. They did not have enough land to produce the volume necessary to compete in the conventional market. Since Jan liked the farmers' markets and Rob had the skills to manage a diversified farming system, they started to transition the farm from one producing commodity potatoes to one producing food for consumers. If you visit the Goranson Farm today, you will see a diversified farm producing a number of vegetables, small fruit, and livestock (chickens and pigs); a maple syrup facility; greenhouses; and a farm store—a far cry from the potato farm that Jan and Rob took over nearly two decades ago.

While the numbers of farm families making this transition from producing commodities to producing food for local consumers is not yet large, the story is repeated numerous times in Maine. In Bars Mills, for example, John and Ramona Snell have transitioned the Snells' apple farm to a diversified mixed vegetable, fruit, maple, and greenhouse farm, selling product at their farm store and farmers' markets. It is repeated at Nezinscot Farm in Turner, where Gregg and Gloria Varney transitioned the Varney dairy farm to an organic dairy farm with a retail store and café that sells their own organic vegetables, meat products, bakery products, fabrics, preserves, and a number of purchased whole food items.

Other farms were started as diversified, high-value farms from the beginning. On King Hill Farm in Hancock County, Dennis King and Jo Barrett operate what started as an oversized home garden with livestock. Dave and Christy Colson operate New Leaf Farm in Durham as a biological system of crops and livestock, and grow a number of vegetables and greenhouse products that are sold directly to restaurants, stores, and consumers.

These farms represent a relatively new direction in Maine agriculture, one that is growing in significance to Maine people but that represents only *one* component of Maine agriculture. To understand the totality of changes taking place, we need to view the totality of Maine agriculture today.

An Important Distinction

Maine agriculture can be viewed from two perspectives. The more conventional and common picture is of an industry that produces agricultural commodities; in Maine, we commonly refer to this as *commodity agriculture*.[1]

In this view, we see Maine agriculture as potatoes (about $100 million sales per year), milk (~$100 million), eggs (~$60 million), blueberries (~$30 million), nursery (~$25 million), vegetables (~$20 million), cattle (~$15 million), apples (~$10 million), and a number of commodities with lesser sales.[2] Most of this production is destined for regional, national, and international markets, often through commodity processors. More than half the Maine potato crop is processed into frozen fries and potato chips. More than half our milk is bottled in four processing plants in-state; most of the rest is bottled out-of-state. Seven freezing plants process practically all of our blueberry production.

Altogether, commodity sales at the farm level totaled $419 million in 2001.[3] Thirty years ago, from this perspective, Maine agriculture would have been, in order of sales volume, potatoes, broilers, eggs, and milk, with apples, blueberries, cattle, and other commodities, all totaling nearly $400 million. While the mix of commodities has changed somewhat, the nominal value is quite similar, reflecting a decline in real value of about 50 percent since the mid-1970s. (See Table 1.)

Table 1. Maine Cash Farm Receipts without Aquaculture
(Selected years in nominal dollars, millions)

	1973	1975	1980	1985	1990	1995	2000	2001	Composite (1973–2001)
Potatoes	141.8	88.1	96.0	79.9	139.5	97.1	114.8	101.8	107.4
Milk	50.8	61.1	91.6	91.1	91.9	88.3	93.2	105.8	84.2
Eggs	79.2	90.1	104.6	79.4	90.0	73.8	56.4	56.6	78.8
Other Poultry	86.8	91.1	85.7	35.0	4.6	3.9	3.6	3.0	39.2
Blueberries	5.9	3.2	8.1	11.4	27.7	21.0	44.3	23.0	18.1
Cattle	9.7	6.3	14.5	20.3	19.7	16.4	17.4	17.0	15.2
Green/Nursery	3.0	3.5	6.6	8.9	18.8	28.6	23.9	24.4	14.7
Vegetables	4.2	3.4	4.3	4.3	13.6	18.4	27.0	24.4	12.5
Apples	13.9	7.5	12.5	13.0	15.3	10.2	9.9	9.2	11.4
Other	3.3	12.7	11.0	30.5	28.7	47.5	51.1	54.0	29.9
Total	398.6	367.0	434.9	373.8	449.8	405.2	441.6	419.2	411.3

Source: Economic Research Service. 2003. Farm Cash Receipts, 1924–2002.
Accessed at www.ers.usda.gov/Data/FarmIncome/Finfidmu.htm.

In addition to farm sales, commodity agriculture includes the *processing* sector mentioned earlier, which converts raw agriculture products grown in Maine into processed products for sale to consumers, or for further processing—especially with milk, blueberries, and potatoes. This industry segment represents about $500 million of sales, or about 50 percent of total food processing in the state, and is vital to the viability of commodity farming. Taken together, the agricultural commodity production and processing sector have an economic impact of nearly $1.4 billion in the Maine economy.

Goranson Farm, Dresden

An alternative perspective on Maine agriculture is of a state *food and agricultural system*, whereby agriculture is *an industry that provides food and related products to human consumers*. This perspective is usually referred to as *local agriculture*. In this view, we may see Maine agriculture as an integrated system with direct economic activity of about $3.3 billion. Agricultural production comprises about 13 percent of that system (~$435 million); food processing, 30 percent (~$1 billion); and food distribution and retailing, 57 percent ($1.9 billion).[4]

Food distribution and retailing is, by far, the largest component of the Maine food and agricultural system. As more Maine farms find global commodity markets less attractive, opportunities to provide marketing services *within* the Maine food and agricultural system become more attractive.

While these perspectives—commodity and local—are laid out here as two distinct systems, it is important to recognize that many Maine farms fall along a continuum between these two systems. Still, the distinction between Maine agriculture as a commodity producer/processor system, or as the Maine food and agricultural system, is a useful and compelling one when considering the historical context, future direction, and policy implications of Maine agriculture.

Let me turn now to the question of how we got to where we are—to the industrialization of agriculture.

The Process of Agricultural Industrialization

Commodity agriculture is the product of agricultural industrialization, a process that has dominated U.S. agriculture for the past 150 years, and especially for the past 50. In the industrial process, farmers seeking more income adopt technologies that allow them to produce more. As their production increases they sell more commodities and increase their net income. Not surprisingly, other farmers see this happening, and adopt similar technologies. Eventually, the commodity supply increases and prices decline, eliminating the increased income of the earlier adopter. To make up for the new loss of income, the early adopting farmer looks for other technologies that will allow him to increase output and income again.

This process has been termed the "technology treadmill" by Willard Cochrane, a well-known agricultural economist and historian; it represents a constant search for new technologies that provide short-term gains, and the subsequent and inevitable loss of this gain for the adopter. Since the early adopter had a period of increased income, he has the financial resources to purchase the farm of the late adopter who has earned no similar financial cushion, but is faced with the same lower prices. This creates Cochrane's "farm cannibalism," which accompanies the technology treadmill.[5]

An alternative, although not inconsistent view of the industrialization process is offered by Goodman, Sorj and Wilkinson, in their 1987 book, *From Farming to Biotechnology: A Theory of Agroindustrial Development.*[6] Their work suggests that the industrialization process is driven by *non-farm firms* seeking to increase market share, rather than farmers seeking greater income gains. Non-farm firms develop products that are purchased and used by farmers, and displace farm labor and management.

Goodman and his colleagues refer to this process as "appropriationism"; and they demonstrate that the result of this process is a shift of economic activities,

Changing Maine

and accompanying returns, from the farming sector of the food and agricultural system to the *non-farm input sector*, from farm labor and management to purchased inputs. A similar process, coined *substitutionism*, is taking place at the other end of the farming process, where food manufacturers are continually searching for ways they can use less costly raw farm products by creating specific characteristics of the final product with further processing. The Goodman model explains *the shift of economic activities and returns from the farming to the non-farming segments* of the food and agricultural system that we see in the industrialization process.

Both models explain how the industrialization process simplifies farming operations by replacing farm management and labor with purchased products. *Simplification*, usually derived from specialization of production, allows farmers to operate larger farming units that capture economies of scale. By capturing economies of scale, larger farms can accumulate capital and expand by buying smaller farms.

The so-called *mechanical revolution* dominated agricultural industrialization from the late nineteenth century to about 1950. During that time, tractors driven by fossil fuels displaced horses on most Maine farms, releasing large amounts of acreage from growing feed for horses. The reduced acreage simplified farming operations, but resulted in a larger share of farm income going for purchased inputs, especially equipment purchases, maintenance, and fuels.

The mechanical revolution was then followed by a *chemical revolution*, dating from about 1950 to the 1990s, in which pesticides rid farmers of crop pests that had previously been managed by crop rotation. With no need to rotate crops, some farms could focus entirely on producing a cash crop, thereby increasing their output of cash crops substantially for their given land and management resource base. In both cases, farm operations were simplified and output was increased, but economic activities per unit of production were shifted from the farm to the non-farm components of the food and agricultural system.

The process continues today, with biotechnology products, for example. Recent work by one of my graduate students estimated the shifts in economic activities and returns from the adoption of rBST, or recombinant bovine somatotropin, the artificial growth hormone introduced in dairy cattle to increase milk production. rBST has received recent attention from the lawsuit brought against Oakhurst Dairy of Portland by the Monsanto Corporation, which manufactures a brand of rBST. (Oakhurst advertising indicated that it did not buy milk from farmers using artifical growth hormones for their cattle.) This study estimates that the use of rBST in dairy farming shifts about 9 percent of farming sector returns to the non-farm input sector, primarily to pharmaceuticals. Regardless of its other impacts, the general use of rBST will result in fewer farms, farming activities and farming returns, and more non-farm activities and returns.

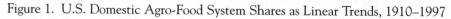

Figure 1. U.S. Domestic Agro-Food System Shares as Linear Trends, 1910–1997

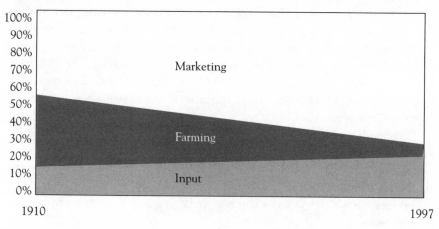

Source: Stewart Smith

At the national level, between 1910 and 1997, farming activities and returns constantly declined due to industrialization, while marketing and input activities and returns, those associated with the other components of the food and agricultural system, increased. As a proportion of the domestic food and agricultural system, farming returns declined about 65 percent, while the marketing share increased by 35 percent and the input share by 40 percent. (See Figure 1.) The Maine picture is quite consistent in terms of these shifts, with the input sector claiming less than 50 percent of farm revenues in 1950, but 70 percent in 1997.[7]

Let me now turn to the impact of all this on farming in Maine.

Agricultural Industrialization and Farm Types
Agricultural industrialization, in addition to shifting economic activities and returns from the farming sector to the non-farm sectors, promotes specialization of production and economies of scale. Farms can produce few commodities in large volumes, resulting in fewer but larger farms. These trends could be seen in Maine and nationally in the first three-quarters of the last century. In Maine, average farm size increased from 105 acres in 1910, to 221 acres in 1978. In constant dollars, the average sales per farm increased nearly 500 percent from 1910 to 1978. (See Table 2.)

Specialization may also be seen in Maine from the shifting of commodities to particular areas of the state, leaving commodity production unevenly spread across the Maine landscape. Most Maine potatoes are produced in Aroostook County; most milk is produced in a seven-county dairy belt, centered on Ken-

Table 2. Size Consolidation of Maine Farms
(Selected Years, 1880–1997)

	1880	1910	1978	1997
# of Farms	64,309	60,016	6,775	5,810
Acres/Farm	102	105	221	209
Sales/Farm ($1992)		17,026	97,226	71,110

Sources: Ahn *et al.*, MAFES *Technical Bulletin 182*; S. N. Smith

nebec County, and most blueberries are produced in Washington and Hancock counties. These areas are particularly vulnerable to price and yield fluctuations and other unforeseen impacts on their commodities.

This regional specialization is the result not just of nature, but of industrialization, as well. Aroostook was the largest dairy-producing county in the state in 1910. Potatoes contributed just half of total farm revenues in Aroostook then, but increased to 83 percent in 1997 after the dairy industry concentrated in central Maine. Dairy, the largest individual commodity produced in Kennebec County now, contributed just 15 percent of county farm revenues in 1910, and 45 percent in 1997.[8] *Consolidation, concentration, and regional specialization based on agricultural industrialization shaped the structure of Maine agriculture throughout the past century.*

In recent years, however, the stories in Maine and the nation have diverged, as a result of that fork in the road I noted above. Since 1978 average Maine farm size has leveled off to 209 acres in 1997, down about 5 percent, and per farm sales in constant dollars have declined nearly 20 percent since then. The leveling off of farm sizes and farm numbers in Maine since the mid 1970s is not the result of changes in the trends of commodity agriculture. Rather, it is the result of the entry of new, smaller, more diversified farms that are usually participating in local agriculture. Unlike most states, Maine farm numbers remain quite stable while average farm size declines, even as commodity farms continue to get larger and fewer.

The Rise of a More Complex Agriculture

The increase in smaller, more diversified farms since the 1970s, generally under the rubric of sustainable agriculture, suggests a growing and potentially sustainable farming sector for Maine. This agriculture appears in at least two forms.

One is the relatively small but quite diversified farm that sells its output to the final consumer, who usually is a local resident or visitor, or to a local institution. These farms are likely to be near population areas, and are substantially integrated into the local community.

Another farm type seems to be proving viable at the mid-size range, by alleviating some of the dependence on economies of scale. This farm is moving away from the strict commodity model on the production side, but not completely away on the marketing side. It maintains its commodity marketing while it accesses some higher value markets with new production. Costs are reduced with more complex production systems, including integrating crops and livestock enterprises. Dairy farms adding high value vegetable enterprises represent one type of this new farm.

While both these farm types generally produce less than a specialized commodity farm in total farm output, on a per unit basis they can leave more net income for the farm, generate more value added for the total farming sector, and often integrate more actively into their local community. They often sell their output to local consumers who may visit the farm as part of the purchasing process. In the case of community-supported agriculture farms, or CSAs, consumers participate to some extent in the farming process itself.

A recent survey of Maine farms that I am now analyzing demonstrates some interesting differences between local agriculture farms and commodity farms. The survey represents a cross section of Maine agriculture, except for blueberries and large egg producers. Respondents were almost evenly spit between commodity farms and local agriculture farms. Slightly more than half, 52 percent, indicated that their farm better fit the commodity profile; 48 percent indicated they better fit local agriculture.

Not surprisingly, local agriculture farms had significantly more enterprises, and used significantly more practices than commodity farms; they are more complex and are operated as holistic systems. They are also twice as likely as commodity farmers to provide public access to their farms, with much of that access involving the sale of products. Local agricultural farms are relatively small; commodity farms are fifteen times larger in sales, and twelve times larger in crop acres.

While commodity farms sold slightly more than two-thirds of their output to wholesale markets, local agriculture farms sold two-thirds of their output directly to consumers. About two-fifths of commodity farms relied on farming to meet their families' financial needs, compared to less than one-fifth of local agriculture farmers. Still, farming was an important contributor of family livelihood, although not necessarily the sole income source, to nearly 60 percent of local agriculture farms and more than 80 percent of commodity farms. Off-farm work was a more integral part of local agriculture farms, where nearly three-quarters had at least one member working off-farm, compared to about half for commodity farms.

The two farm types are also different in experience and education of the farm family. Commodity farmers indicate they have been farming, on average, twenty-eight years, while local agriculture farmers indicate seventeen years. While all farmers have more formal education than the state average, with 65 percent of farmers and spouses having college degrees, local agriculture farmers have more formal education than commodity farmers. Eighty percent of local agriculture farmers and spouses have schooling beyond high school, with over one-quarter having schooling beyond college. This compares to 60 percent of commodity farmers and spouses with education beyond high school, and one-eighth beyond college.

The profiles of the two types of farming in Maine help to paint the picture of Maine agriculture. While commodity agriculture remains dominant in terms of cropland used and value of sales per farm, local agriculture farms are becoming nearly as numerous. Local agriculture farms are more complex, and are operated as integrated biological and community systems. Local agriculture farmers are younger with more formal education, and rely less on farm income to sustain the family; but the farm is an important component of their family livelihood.

Maine today, then, appears to be moving toward a viable, dual agricultural structure that has important implications for state agricultural policy. Let me turn to this question now.

Some Policy Implications
This profile of a new Maine agriculture suggests new policy directions, if we wish to maintain farm numbers and farm families. As long as commodity agriculture efficiencies are driven by economies of scale, commodity farms, if they are to remain competitive, must continue to get larger and fewer, even as production is maintained or increased. With Maine's limited land base, the number of commodity farms must decline if size is to increase. Without a fundamental change in agricultural technology development, century-long trends suggest that within two generations we will be counting dairy and potato commodity farms in the dozens rather than the hundreds, just as two generations ago we counted them in the thousands.

On the other hand, we see growth in the numbers of small and moderate-sized farms that become part of the local food system. While my crystal ball is blurred by the lack of historical data on these farms, I would not be surprised to see substantial growth in local agriculture farming in the next generation, especially if it receives adequate public support. Because local agriculture farming is a substantively different farming system, built around biological and community systems rather than efficient production of commodities, transitioning our farming resources from commodity to local systems will be a daunting challenge to many farmers. *For many farmers and communities, the success of this transition will depend largely on the preference that local consumers express for maintaining a local agriculture, and on sound, supportive public policy.*

I was pleased to hear Governor John E. Baldacci in his January 2004 State of the State address announce that he was directing the Department of Agriculture to develop a program to support local agriculture. Let me offer some suggestions for the content of this program.

First, it would be wise to determine the extent of the potential for local agriculture. None of us knows exactly how large it might be; but we do know some parameters. According to our economic development models, of the $3.3 billion spent for food by Maine consumers and institutions, only about $120 million, or 4 percent, goes to Maine farmers; and a third of that is for dairy. Surely, that can be increased substantially.

Some, and maybe much of that increase would be from farm sales made directly to local consumers. We do not know the full potential for those sales; but I believe past sales have been greater than those reported by the Agricultural Census.[9] According to the census data, Maine farmers sold somewhat over $5 million of food products directly to consumers in 1992, and over $8 million in 1997. While we do not know what the 2002 Census (available later in 2004) will show, my own data generated from farm surveys suggest those numbers are too low, and that direct food sales to consumers in 2002 were close to $50 million.

Considering that, on a national basis, about 20 percent of consumer expenditures in the domestic food system goes to U.S. farmers, it does not seem unreasonable to establish a goal of 10 percent of Maine consumer food expenditure going to Maine farmers. This would represent an increase in revenues to Maine farmers of $210 million, and would generate a substantial amount of new economic activity in rural Maine. *It will likely require a concerted policy effort to support Maine farm production and sales destined for local consumers.*

Second, Maine farmers will need both technical and financial assistance in transitioning to these systems, which are complex and require very different management skills from commodity farms. I know a number of farmers who contemplate the transition but find it very difficult to keep the commodity component financially viable while building the local agriculture component.

For many of these farms, I suspect, it will require a partnership relationship, where farm management responsibility is split between commodity and local agricultural production. In some cases, those responsibilities may be split among family members. We see some of these arrangements now, where one member manages the commodity side and another, the local agriculture side. In other cases, non-family members may have to share the management responsibilities,

Changing Maine

providing additional challenges to farmers who, by tradition, value their independence deeply.

As I suggested above, managing local agriculture systems is very different from managing commodity systems; and many existing management models are less than ideal for the more complex systems. Models that conceptualize farm management decisions as selecting the proper amounts of inputs and outputs are not particularly useful in managing complex farming systems. Models based on complex system science, rather than input-output relationships, will be more appropriate.

A local agriculture development program will need to offer both technical assistance and financial assistance, including both loan and grant-funding support. Support needs to be targeted to systems that are viable in their specific setting. Unlike commodity farms that can use standardized practices because they use standard purchased inputs and sell to external markets, local agriculture systems are site-specific, from both a production and a marketing perspective.

On the production side, a combination of crop rotations and placements are used to provide plant nutrients and to manage pests. While certain agronomic and pest dynamic principles apply generally, the effectiveness of selected practices is substantially affected by the resource base of the specific farm. Further, since many of these farms are selling to local customers, the crop and livestock choices are heavily influenced by the income, tastes and preferences of the local consumer base, and by production from similar, neighboring farms.

Maine's Potato Market Improvement Fund (PMIF) and the Farms for the Future (FFF) programs are excellent models for a local agriculture development program. The PMIF supports the adoption of specific technologies that promote the marketing of Maine potatoes. It provides for industry input in judging the appropriateness of proposals. The FFF supports farmer adoption of changes that are more appropriate to the current market environment. The FFF program requires business planning as a first step in farming system change.

Third, the needed technical assistance will require support from the research community. In the past, most agricultural research has focused on industrial agriculture. The University of Maine has made a good start, especially on the cropping side, in redirecting research capacity to sustainable agriculture systems. It is critically important that the university continue and extend that effort.

A proper state development program would be expressed in a number of ways. It would support both consumers and farmers. Local food networks could make local foods more accessible to local consumers. These might take the form of community facilities for year-round farmers' markets, as other states have, or the development of more farm stores that are accessible to more consumers. It would support the development of further processing of farm production before sales in local markets. It would support farmers who are already doing local agriculture, but need to upgrade; or, it could provide support to those farmers who want to enter local agriculture farming, either from an existing commodity farm or as a new farmer.

In any case, the program support would have to be carefully targeted since, unlike commodity agriculture, markets are relatively narrow and supply must be balanced with demand. The resources required for supporting this change enhance more than an agricultural sector that must change in order to survive and thrive. An adequate development program also provides substantial public benefits in the form of open space, fresh foods, and vital communities.

Addressing Cost Disadvantages

Drawing the distinction between commodity agriculture and local agriculture is critical to developing a sound agricultural policy for Maine. Still, local agricultural development cannot be the sole element of a state strategy to support a viable but changing Maine agriculture. Commodity agriculture will continue to use most of the agricultural land base in the state, and to produce most of the output—even as commodity farms get larger and fewer, and as sales of local agriculture grow much more significant. Maintaining the viability of commodity farming must also be a component of a state strategy; and a number of factors work against the competitiveness of commodity agriculture in Maine today.

In November 2003 attendees at the Blaine House Conference on Maine's Natural Resource-based Industries identified and discussed a number of cost-competitive issues that Maine commodity agriculture must address to maintain its vitality.[10] Some issues may be mitigated or even eliminated through policy measures; others may only be recognized, and overcome strategically. An agricultural land base that is limited in both quantity and quality, for example, is a challenge that cannot be eliminated, but must be addressed strategically.

With the exception of Aroostook County's farming area, the Maine landscape is one of forestlands with occasional fields, often along river valleys. For the most part, contiguous farming fields are in the tens of acres, rather than the hundreds or thousands of acres found in other parts of the nation. This limitation will become increasingly critical for commodity farmers, who must compete in regional and national markets by capturing economies of scale. As future efficiency-gains call for 2,000-acre potato farms and 1,000-head dairy farms, fewer and fewer Maine farms, especially outside Aroostook, will find the land base to remain competitive—although some will capture certain economies of scale with production units in multiple locations.

Again, outside of Aroostook County and some valley intervales, the quality of the land base is challenging. The soils are naturally acidic, and many are stony and shallow to bedrock. Substandard soil quality in many areas increases the cost of production for many cropping options.

Patrick Shea, Jefferson

While Maine's climate and our relatively short growing season challenge some agricultural pests—and so provide some advantages to organic and pesticide-limiting farming systems—they also limit crop choices. Degree-days in Maine are low, compared to most agricultural areas in the U.S., substantially limiting our choice of crops and crop varieties. We can grow grain corn; but Maine farmers cannot use the late-maturing varieties that produce high yields and low per-unit costs. Aroostook County's comparative advantage is in potato production; but the short growing season limits production protocols that produce high yields like those in the Pacific Northwest, for example.

Despite significant natural rainfall, Maine agriculture also faces limited water supplies that increasingly threaten the viability of farms, especially those in competitive markets. We lack the large, easily accessible aquifers found in many agricultural states; and we have no river systems dammed to provide irrigation for agriculture. Concern for wetlands protection requires farmers to build costly reservoirs from which to irrigate. With an increasing need for supplemental irrigation, and without effective policy support this lack of water access will place Maine agriculture in a deteriorating competitive position.

These natural resource challenges—a limited base of land and water and a short growing season—cannot be removed; they must be recognized, and managed strategically. It is critical to the future of Maine agriculture and to the vitality of Maine's rural communities that our good agricultural land be available for future farming use. In 1997 Maine had 1.2 million acres in farmland, a decline of more than 50 percent since 1964. Of that, 534,000 were in cropland, compared to 894,000 in 1964. In 1997, one-third of Maine's cropland was in Aroostook County, while five counties—Androscoggin, Cumberland, Oxford, Waldo, and York—each had between 3.5 percent and 5.5 percent of Maine's cropland, much of it in areas under heavy development pressure.[11]

According to the State Planning Office, between 1992 and 1997 Maine converted 33,500 rural acres *each year* to development, a rate four times that of the previous decade, and a figure greater than all the cropland in nine Maine counties. This has resulted in the loss of a substantial volume of the land used by the livestock industry to pasture animals and produce feed crops.[12]

Nor is development pressure localized in any one area; it extends the length and breadth of Maine, boosting land values above those supported by agricultural production. In the northern areas, the demand is for individual house lots and seasonal homes, rather than commercial development; but the impact on fragmenting the agricultural landscape and increasing farming costs is similar statewide.

Besides increasing the incentive for farmers to sell their land for development, especially when they leave farming, development pressures also increase production costs from increases in the valuation of farmland for property tax assessment. The Farmland and Open Space Tax Law is designed to relieve this cost pressure by providing for the valuation of classified farmland based on its current use as farmland or open space, rather than its potential value for more intensive uses.

Owners of farmland must, however, work with their town's assessor to enroll in the program. While the penalty for withdrawing from the program was reduced by the 119th Legislature so that, upon withdrawal, farmers only pay five years of tax savings plus interest, the program is still misunderstood and underused. This results in sporadic requests for automatic assessment of all farmland at current-use values, or other similar initiatives, to reduce the property tax burden on Maine farms. Taxation of farmland remains an important and unresolved cost issue for many Maine farmers.

To address the problem of farmland loss, the Maine Department of Agriculture, Food and Rural Resources recently published *Saving Maine's Farmland: A Collaborative Action Plan*, the result of a two-year planning process that offers a number of farmland protection program options.[13] Donation or purchase of development rights in exchange for agricultural conservation easements is the primary technique currently used in Maine to permanently protect farmland. The Land for Maine's Future program (LMF), with a mandate to spend up to 10 percent of its resources on farmland protection, is the primary state financing mechanism.

The LMF is complemented by the USDA Farm and Ranch Lands Protection Program (FRPP), which provides a cash match of up to 50 percent of the appraised value of the development rights. While support from the LMF and FRPP have helped the Maine Department of Agriculture gain some notable success with protecting specific farmlands in southern and central Maine, more resources are needed to develop and implement a comprehensive farmland protection program that may assure the future land base for a viable agricultural industry throughout Maine.

The commitment of Governor John E. Baldacci to a substantial bond issue ($100 million over five years) to continue the good work of the Lands for Maine's Future program is a welcomed indication that the state may be able to play a critical role in maintaining farmland and open space. We must be sure, however, that an appropriate portion of these monies is devoted to agricultural land protection, and that it is used in ways that will best maintain a viable and sustainable farmland base for Maine agriculture.

The lack of adequate water for crop irrigation must also be addressed strategically. While we have more natural rainfall than some areas, buyers of Maine products, both for fresh use and processing, today demand consistent quality of product across seasons. The low financial margins experienced by many farmers, and the increasing demand for product consistency associated with commodity markets, makes supplemental irrigation increasingly essential to the financial success of Maine farmers.

In the past, Maine farms received higher profits per unit of output, making episodic losses from drought less critical; today, losses from one year of drought can wipe out several years of gains. Over one-third of crop losses in the past three years have been from drought, which is now considered the single most important risk management factor facing Maine crop farmers.

This comes at the same time that Maine farmers are losing access to historical water supplies. In the past, farmers have often pumped water directly from streams, or have dammed streams to provide irrigation. Today, alternative uses and regulations reduce the opportunity for farmers to use those water sources, and Maine has limited access to alternative water supplies. With the increasing need for supplemental irrigation, lack of access to water will put Maine agriculture in a deteriorating competitive position if policy support is not adequate.

The state needs a clear policy on agricultural water use and programs to assure that farmers have adequate water availability and appropriate user techniques within that policy.

In response to the severe droughts in 2000 and 2001, the Department of Agriculture and concerned commodity groups supported legislation to create a cost-share program for farm water reservoirs. The program to date has invested just under $1 million to provide irrigation to 2,838 farmland acres and prevent nearly $9 million of crop losses. A recent survey indicates the need for an additional $15 million over the next five years. There is also a need to extend and formalize authority for the program. In addition to developing water sources consistent with state policy, many farmers will need cost-share assistance to develop efficient irrigation systems. The state must offer appropriate grants and loans to support farmer development of appropriate water sources and irrigation technology.[14]

If we cannot eliminate our short growing season and relatively harsh winter, we should turn them to our advantage. While the short growing season limits certain crop production options, when combined with our relatively long and cold winters it can substantially limit pest pressures. A number of pests do not survive our winters, and the short growing season limits the number of pest generations per season; pest management options are increased, allowing for reduced costs. More importantly, it also provides the potential for producing and marketing "green" products, thereby capturing market share and price premiums associated with green marketing.

Other competitive challenges may be eliminated or mitigated by policy. Much of Maine agriculture, for example, suffers from high input costs, especially for labor and purchased inputs, that place Maine farmers at a competitive disadvantage. Most purchased inputs carry relatively high transportation costs, and labor costs, compared to some other major agricultural areas, are high especially in the central and southern parts of the state.. Some farmers experience labor shortages because of their difficulty paying competitive wages and benefits. In other cases, cropping systems have heavy seasonal requirements that make it difficult to find adequate labor for short periods. Participants at the Blaine House Conference on Natural Resource-based Industries urged the state to review tax and regulatory policies that might mitigate these cost disadvantages.

Finally, the farm is not the only part of the food system where policy can assist cost-competitiveness. Most farm production from the commodity system in Maine gets to market through food processors. These processors are now the key to Maine farmers' competitiveness in commodity markets. With certain exceptions, the Maine food processing industry is reasonably strong and contributes to the global competitiveness of Maine's commodity agriculture.

While just one major frozen fry plant remains in Aroostook County, it now supplies the fast food market, the premium market for frozen fries unavailable to Maine farmers in the past. The plant takes the largest share of the nearly 50 percent of the annual potato crop that is processed in Maine each year; and it is part of a large, privately held Canadian food processing firm. A number of smaller firms process an array of other potato products.

In the dairy sector, about one-half the milk produced on Maine farms is processed in one of the state's four processing facilities, two of which remain independent and locally owned. The other plants are owned by national milk processing firms that have, themselves, been purchasing local and regional processors to achieve a dominant market position. Two of the plants are located within the city of Portland; a third is a relatively new facility on the outskirts of Bangor; the fourth and smallest is in Aroostook County.

Most of the wild blueberry crop is processed by one of the seven established freezers in Washington and Hancock Counties. One of those is Canadian-owned, with plants on both sides of the border, and one Maine-based firm has a processing facility in Canada. Blueberries move freely across the international border during the freezing season.

Especially in the potato and blueberry sectors, Canadian interests are today an integral and important component of our food processing sector. Canadian management and capital support a substantial portion of the frozen fry processing capacity in the Maine potato industry, and part of Maine's wild blueberry processing. While there is considerable episodic tension between Canadian and U.S. agricultural interests, it is likely the Maine food processing infrastructure will be greatly disadvantaged without access to Canadian management and capital.

To maintain a vital commodity farm sector, state agricultural policy must support the sector that processes Maine farm commodities, even as increased efficiency results in fewer jobs. Most Maine commodity farms cannot prosper without a competitive processing sector.

And in Conclusion—

Maine agriculture faces a new century, and it is challenged to change with the times. The commodity system that has offered most of the farming opportunities of the past half-century will continue to dominate the Maine landscape; and commodity farmers will continue to expand farm size, in order to remain competitive in national markets. Opportunities for new farmers in commodity production, however, will continue to decline.

At the same time, local agriculture will offer new opportunities for farmers old and new, as long as Maine consumers value local farms and state policy is supportive. In exchange for this support, Maine residents will gain access to fresh, local foods, the maintenance of our cherished open space, and more vibrant Maine communities.

Stewart N. Smith is Professor of Sustainable Agriculture Policy at the University of Maine. Dr. Smith has been involved in agriculture his entire working life, much of it in Maine. After graduating from Yale University, he started farming potatoes in central Maine. While building a potato marketing business, he served as president of the Maine Potato Council, now the Maine Potato Board, and in the 106th Maine Legislature, representing his farming community. He later pursued graduate work, receiving his M.S. and Ph.D. in agricultural economics from the University of Connecticut. During the administration of President Jimmy Carter, Smith served as associate administrator of the Agricultural Stabilization and Conservation Service (now the Farm Service Administration) and vice president of the Commodity Credit Corporation, where he managed a $6 billion program budget. He returned to Maine to serve as Governor Joseph Brennan's agriculture commissioner. During his government service, Smith became increasingly interested in the nascent, alternative agriculture—and later sustainable agriculture—movements. He pursued those interests at Tufts University's School of Nutrition as the Henry Luce professor and as a senior economist at the Joint Economic Committee of Congress. He continues that pursuit in his work today with Maine farmers, including serving as executive director of the Maine Sustainable Agriculture Society.

SINCE THE 1970S, MAINE'S FISHING INDUSTRY has been marked by erratic booms and busts. Poor management, unenforceable or un-enforced regulations, and inadequate understanding of and attention to marine ecosystems contribute to extensive over-fishing and rapid stock depletions, leading to a "tragedy of the commons." The notable exception to this has been the lobster fishery, where fishermen have developed a strictly enforced ethic of self-regulated conservation. The other fisheries may learn from this example. Successful management of a sustainable fishery requires effective social, not just technical solutions, as well as decentralization of authority and shared decision-making at the local, regional, state, and federal levels.

21 Maine's Fisheries
Learning to Govern Effectively

JAMES WILSON

Our fisheries are among Maine's most cherished icons. People tend to think of them, especially the lobster fishery, as quaint, traditional, the very symbol of the independent yeoman facing off against a difficult and unruly nature. This is a comfortable romantic vision of the fishery. There is another side to our fisheries, however; they are very complicated and deeply fascinating. Most of all, they are a marvelous case study of the difficulties we have adapting human activity to the needs of the natural environment.

Let me explain these difficulties with a little story from the fishery for sea urchins. The history of the Maine urchin fishery is short and sour. Not long ago, this was the second most important fishery in the state; it is no longer.

In the mid-1980s, after the depletion of the West Coast urchin fishery, Japanese buyers began purchasing Maine urchins (the exclusive market for urchins is for sushi). At the time, urchins were extraordinarily abundant along the Maine coast. My colleague Bob Steneck refers to sea urchin barrens—large areas of the bottom where all you could see when diving at the time was sea urchins. Prices were high, urchins were easily harvested, and we had a minor "gold rush." Itinerant divers from all over the country showed up and had one hell of a party for several years. By the mid-'90s, the fishery had peaked; today, there is only a remnant fishery Down East. This episode was a classic case of over-fishing, played out in a very short period of time.

The memory of this period that stands out most in my mind is a series of intense conversations with a couple of fishermen and one of the buyers for the Japanese, George Parr. They saw the end coming long before there was any official concern, were all looking for some way to forestall that end, and were all frustrated. It was the same story we have played out in most of our other fisheries: some people see the problem, while most people don't or don't want to, or do and don't give a damn.

The problem is not an easy one. Fisheries are always highly variable, and sorting out natural variability from human impacts is often very difficult. It is also extremely difficult to negotiate a reasonable set of fishing restraints, especially if you cannot agree on the probable cause. Today, we have lost the urchin fishery for all practical purposes. Time and time again, we play out this "tragedy of the commons." We do it in a different way in each fishery, and only rarely do we create a sustainable social *and* biological regime.

Figure 1. Maine Sea Urchin Landings and Value

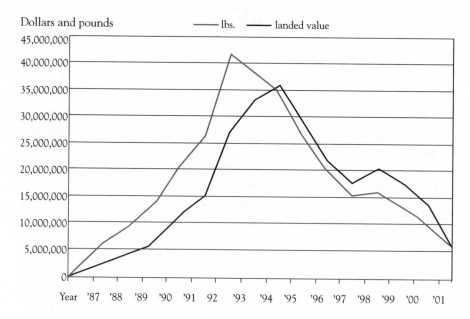

In this chapter, we examine the history of three of our other fisheries—groundfish, lobster, and herring—with a keen eye toward *the common threads* that contribute to this usually dismal result. After these brief histories, we turn to the major themes of the chapter: Have we learned anything about sustaining our fisheries and ocean ecosystems? Is there anything we can do to avoid a continuing tragedy of the commons?

The Groundfishery
We start with the groundfishery. The fish in the groundfishery are cod, haddock, flounder, monkfish, and a variety of other species. Most of these fish are found near or on the floor, or the "ground," of the ocean. Today, there are basically two kinds of boats that work in the groundfishery: draggers (or, trawlers) that tow a large, funnel-shaped net along the bottom of the ocean, and gillnetters, generally smaller boats, that place stationary nets also at the bottom of the water column.

The commercial groundfishery has a long history in Maine, some 400 years. Richmond Island, Monhegan, Damariscove, Pemaquid—all these places were used as fishing stations just before or after the European settlement at Plymouth. The history of the fishery since then has many fascinating chapters;[1] but what I wish to emphasize here is the fairly recent history, or what might be called the modern fishery. There are a number of important waypoints in this history.

The modern groundfishery in Maine begins in the 1920s and '30s, with the introduction of the dragger fleet. Then, we really had two separate fleets. One was the small boat, in-shore fleet, operating out of over a dozen harbors along the coast. The other was the redfish fleet based in Rockland and Portland. The vertically integrated redfish fleet, with its processing and marketing arms, was the height of modernity at the time it was introduced in the early '30s.

Redfish are a deep-water species that yields a fairly homogenous catch, with few unwanted species. They are well suited for freezing and were one of the first food products to take advantage of Birdseye's new freezing technology. Processing took place ashore; and the frozen product was shipped largely to the Midwest, where it first competed with and then replaced the supply of lake perch. Redfish is known in the Midwest as ocean perch. The redfish boats worked mostly in what are now Canadian waters. The fleet went out of existence in 1984 for reasons made clear below.

The small dragger fleet worked the near-shore waters of the coast. Near-shore dragging came a little late to Maine, mostly because it is very difficult to fish the rough bottom of the Maine coast without tearing up nets. In the 1930s and '40s, in fact, and through the '70s, dragging was restricted to well-known areas of relatively smooth bottom, referred to as "good tows."

The difficulty of knowing safe places to tow restricted the early draggers to a fairly small portion of the bottom. This was good for conservation in some ways, and a disaster in others. It helped, because it maintained a large part of the Gulf of Maine as an unintended sanctuary. It became problematic because of the way cod behave, and the way draggers work. When cod spawn, they do two things that make them great targets for draggers: they form dense aggregations, and they generally move to smooth mud bottoms. This makes them very easy to catch, even for boats with no electronic navigation or sounding gear.

Ted Ames, a good friend and fisherman who lives in Stonington, has done an extensive and extraordinarily interesting set of interviews with many of the now-retired fishermen who worked on these early draggers.[2] From these interviews, it appears the dragger fleet probably extinguished well over a dozen local spawning groups of cod and haddock along the coast. After sixty to seventy years, these spawning groups have either not returned or are present only in very diminished numbers. Whether these stocks are present today or not, it is fairly clear that these early dragger activities strongly impacted the abundance of cod and haddock as well as the basic structure of our coastal ecosystems.

Waypoint 2: In the mid-'60s, huge year-classes of cod and haddock showed up on Georges Bank and in the Gulf of Maine. Shortly after, the Soviets, the Germans, even the Bulgarians—indeed, almost everyone imaginable—showed up on our doorsteps with a very large fleet of very large factory trawlers. Within five or six years, the fisheries of New England had been decimated—not only the groundfish, but also the herring. The ecosystems were badly distorted.

The following decades, the '70s and '80s, saw huge blooms of sand lance and eventually the growth of very large populations of dogfish and skates; at one point, these species were estimated to account for nearly three quarters of the fish biomass on Georges Bank and the Gulf of Maine—another significant perturbation of the ecosystem

Waypoint 3: By the early '70s, it had become very clear to the United States and to most all other coastal nations that we could not maintain our ocean resources without some sort of control over fishing. In 1976 and '77, a tipping point was reached, and almost all the major coastal nations of the world rushed to extend their political jurisdiction to 200 miles offshore.

When the U.S. extended its jurisdiction, Congress made a strong commitment to manage our living ocean resources so that they might be made sustainable. At the time, there was confidence that we could sustain the stocks *and*, at the same time, provide much greater economic value from the resource—what was termed "optimum yield."

A number of tax and other incentives were put in place to encourage the development of a modern fleet and, thereby, to enhance the economic side of this equation. These incentives, along with the expectation of restored stocks, worked well and quickly; but the fleet built up too quickly and too much, at least in retrospect. On the biological side of the "optimum yield" equation, the first action of the New England Fisheries Council—created to manage the new federal fisheries under the extended jurisdiction—was to impose quotas designed to rebuild the stocks that were still recovering from foreign over-fishing.

By 1981 it was clear that the quota approach completely lacked credibility in the industry and was unenforceable. At approximately the same time, there was a growing sense that the U.S. fleet was more than adequate to the available resources. Two major problems were beginning to become apparent: the difficulty of controlling fishing effort, and the need to consider the ecosystem effects of fishing. The New England Fisheries Council shifted gears and embarked on an "interim plan," designed to give everyone time to rethink our approach to managing the fishery.

Waypoint 4: In 1984 the World Court established the U.S./Canadian maritime boundary, awarding the best fishing grounds, the Northeast Peak, to Canada. The Hague Line, as it is called, bisected Georges Bank, leaving the Northeast Peak, always one of the most important fishing areas for the New England fleet, to Canada. Canada quickly excluded U.S. vessels from this territory. The U.S. fleet, including what was left of the redfish fleet, was forced to retreat into a much more restricted area; as a result, there was a large increase in the fishing effort expended on U.S. stocks. Populations that appeared to have been holding steady and perhaps even increasing, quickly reversed direction. The downward trend has continued with occasional blips of abundance to the present day.

Waypoint 5: Two years after the establishment of the U.S./Canadian maritime boundary, the Portland Fish Exchange opened. For North America, this was a radical new way to sell fish. Fish at the Exchange are displayed and sold in small lots, through a competitive auction. It was the first time the U.S. fishing industry had had an open and transparent market. The Exchange drew boats from as far away as Delaware, and became a model for similar (mostly unsuccessful) efforts in New York, Gloucester, San Francisco, New Bedford, and Vancouver. Portland quickly moved from the third to the most important groundfish port in New England. Unfortunately, groundfish stocks continued to decline, and closures and other rules imposed by the New England Fisheries Council have increasingly come to favor fishing out of Massachusetts.

Waypoints 6 and 7 occurred at the beginning and the end of the 1990s. They were precipitated by legal challenges initiated by the conservation community. These suits demanded that the council take steps to fulfill the often-renewed congressional commitment to sustainable fisheries. The conservation groups won both suits. At the moment, the fishery is in the midst of the deep uncertainties surrounding Amendment 13, which is the council's attempt to respond to the mandate of the court to fulfill the congressional commitment to sustainable fisheries.

The proposals before the council today are not appetizing. Indeed, they are mostly patches and quick fixes that may keep the fishery afloat for a while, but do not address the fundamental problems recognized way back in 1981, namely, finding meaningful ways to restrain fishing and figuring out the ecosystem impacts of our activity.[3]

Currently stocks are at a very low level: there appears to be growth in some of the important groundfish stocks, but the picture is mixed. Many people see light at the end of the tunnel; I am much more pessimistic.

The Lobster Fishery
We turn now to the lobster fishery, one with a stikingly different history and sociology. Today, landings in the lobster fishery are at historic highs. Eighty to ninety years ago, the fishery was in abysmal shape. In the 1920s and '30s, landings were below 5 million pounds. After World War II and into the mid-'80s, landings stabilized at around 20 million pounds per year. Today, they are in the neighborhood of 60 million pounds. There are several waypoints that are important in this history, as well.

In the late '30s and continuing through the '60s and '70s, the industry made an important social and political transition. In the early part of the period, the population of lobstermen appeared to have had a heavy sprinkling of outlaws. There was an active short-lobster trade, and other indications of a studied disregard for any conservation measures. By the end of the period, however, things had changed. Somewhere along the line, there occurred a collective decision that conservation was important and necessary. There was a new *ethic of conservation*: the laws were enforced, the fishery recovered, and landings increased.

We are not sure just how and when this came about; but it expressed itself in the resolve of ordinary fishermen, buyers, and co-ops. They were willing to confront the people selling the short lobsters; and they were willing to collaborate with the state's Marine Patrol. This made it possible to enforce the rules effectively. This ethic continues, and is perhaps even stronger today.[4] Stories are common of how fishermen often engage in local "enforcement initiatives." Sometimes it is with a quick knife, but mostly it is much more subtle and graduated. However it occurs, it is critical to the functioning and prosperity of the fishery.

Still, there is a dangerous balance here between vigilantism and the community's interest in resource conservation. The state—that is, the Marine Patrol—plays an important role in this balance. The patrol has to know when to collaborate with these local "initiatives," and when to restrain their vigilante impulses. What is remarkable about the lobster fishery—indeed, what sets it off from most other fisheries—is how well this balance works. Mainly, this is due to the fact that the Marine Patrol knows the local context in which it is working, and is able to avoid the impersonal bull-headedness that sometimes characterizes law enforcement.

The next important waypoint for lobster was the sudden increase in landings and apparent population, beginning in the late-1980s.[5] From an annual average 20 million pounds, the fishery moved quickly to 60 million pounds. Even the strongest proponents of the current management system will not claim that this surge in landings was the result of management. Management may have avoided the destruction of the fishery before the late '80s; but it is not the reason for the current abundance.

It is much more likely that this change is due to significant, human induced shifts in the structure of the ecosystem—in this case surprising and fortuitous shifts. The fact is, however, we do not know enough about the structure and dynamics of the Gulf of Maine ecosystem to do anything other than guess at the source of this current good fortune. The other side of this good fortune is the unknown consequences of losing many of our other inshore fisheries—groundfish, urchins, and herring. The next surprise for the lobster fishery may not be so pleasant.

Changing Maine

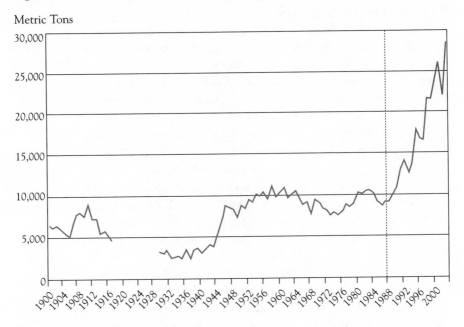

Figure 2. Maine Lobster Landings 1900–2002

Metric Tons

The third and final waypoint for lobster was the establishment of the system of lobster zones in 1997. This is a dramatic experiment in the democratic, local governance of a natural resource. There are seven zones along the coast; each has a council elected by the fishermen in the zone. The zone councils can propose changes in rules that affect things local. A change in the rules requires a two-thirds approval by the fishermen in the zone, as well as ratification by the state commissioner of marine resources.

The idea behind the zones is both simple and complex. There are many aspects of the fishery, both biological and social, that vary greatly from Kittery to Eastport. Some are local in nature; some have a much broader scope. When the fishery was managed as a single, statewide fishery, we could not take those local differences into account. For twenty-five or more years the, legislature (and the federal government) tried to deal with trap limits and limits on the number of fishermen.

These are very difficult matters of culture and equity; for twenty-five years the legislature and the federal government failed to resolve them. What was acceptable in Casco Bay was an outrage in Jonesport, and vice versa. Interestingly, within a year of their start-up, all seven zones had put in place trap limits, but these were trap limits that they felt fit their local circumstances. Within three or four years, the seven councils went to the legislature to ask for the right to control entry into the fishery; and, when given that authority, five of the seven promptly did just that.

The lesson is important: *by learning to manage at multiple scales—local, state, regional and national—we can partition our conservation problem into more manageable components.* We can fit ourselves into the environment in a way that is better for us *and* for the environment. Too often, our fisheries and environmental policies have been top down, undemocratic, and without a clue about local circumstances, either biological or social.

The next important waypoint for the lobster fishery has not yet been reached. The big question facing everyone in the fishery is, "How long will the current levels of extremely high abundance last?" Southern New England has experienced an epidemic of shell disease, and landings have dropped by 30 percent. We have not seen significant instances of shell disease in Maine, but we know we are working in a destabilized ecosystem. It is probably true that the only reasonable expectation we can draw is that we are going to be surprised; how and when are not at all clear.

The practical problem is this: there are a lot of lobstermen with large mortgages on new houses and boats; they cannot afford to stop fishing hard. Many of them have never seen a bad year, and are not prepared in either their head or their pocketbook, should one appear. When and if a significant, unpleasant surprise hits the lobster fishery, these people will become a significant political force, resisting any change in the way fishing takes place. The real test of the lobster zones will be their ability to overcome this political reality, and react in an appropriate way.

Will we once again destroy the fishery? Will we have to re-learn the difficult lessons of the last century? I am not sure what the outcome will be if a downturn occurs; but I am fairly sure that the ability to respond appropriately is much more likely with the zones in place than with only the legislature or the federal government trying to make the decision.

The Herring Fishery
The last fishery we quickly survey is herring. The herring fishery in Maine began in the mid-1800s. For nearly 150 years it supplied canneries and a large trade in salted and smoked fish. The latter supplied the tavern trade and virtually disappeared with the advent of prohibition; the canning part of the industry remains intact but greatly diminished. At the close of World War II, we had close to fifty canneries; today there are but a handful.

Until the 1970s the industry caught mostly juvenile fish with weirs and stop seines—passive gear that cannot chase down the fish. (Weirs are permanent, shallow-water traps made of stakes and nets that are used to herd the fish. Stop seines are nets used to close off a narrow cove.) In the 1970s a shift to purse seiners and mid-water trawlers began. These are boats and gear that search out schools of herring in open water and set encircling nets (in the case of purse seiners) or tow large funnel shaped nets (in the case of mid-water trawlers). The fishery now catches both juvenile and adult fish and has gained a new, major market—lobster bait—which replaced redfish frames after the loss of the redfish fishery. Today, only a handful of weir and stop seine operations remain, almost all along the Cutler and Perry shores Down East.

Beginning in the 1970s we also saw a significant shift in the spatial structure of herring populations. For some time it has been known that herring have a complicated population structure. There are spawning groups on Georges Bank, along the Scotian shore, and in the Bay of Fundy. Until the 1970s or '80s we had had, apparently, a host of localized spawning sites in the bays along the coast, and maybe offshore from mid-coast to Down East. We have gradually lost the bay-spawning populations, and have only a small residual left Down East. Spawning apparently occurs on some of the offshore ridges.[6]

In spite of these depleted conditions inshore, landings and the estimated biomass of fish have remained in the same range as we have seen historically, and on that basis alone one might judge the fishery to be in good shape. In fact, the National Marine Fisheries Service, which does a combined assessment of the Georges Bank and Gulf of Maine stocks, is very explicit in its judgment that this is *not* an over-fished fishery.

Nonetheless, there is a fairly strong presumption that we have *many* stocks of herring, not one. Consequently, the loss of our inshore stocks in the last twenty years or so, is a disquieting reminder of what has happened to almost all our fisheries—that is, significant changes in population structure and abundance either in response to major shifts in the ecosystem or to the effects of fishing.[7]

The Problem of Scale

What, then, have we learned about sustainable fisheries in the last twenty-five years? Is there anything we can do to forestall the tragedy? The answer, I believe, lies in the single, admittedly large thread running through all these histories: the problem of scale, as it affects both scientific uncertainty and the building of public (or industry) resolve to take effective conservation action.

The essence of the problem of scale is that both people and fish adapt to their *local* circumstances. When we ignore this fundamental ecological and social fact, we erect unnecessary scientific and social/political obstacles to the sustainability of our resources. *The point is not that we should do everything at a local level; the point is that we need to operate at several scales, not simply at a single, large scale, as we tend to do now.*[8]

Unfortunately, we tend to think about ocean conservation at a large or broad scale almost exclusively. We do not pay much attention to finer-scale biological and social phenomena. When we think of cod, it is the cod in the Gulf of Maine, not the cod that spawn off the Sheepscot River or in Machias Bay. The same is true of herring. In the lobster fishery, we were hung up for years trying to manage with one-size-fits-all rules for the entire coast, from Kittery to Cutler. In the urchin fishery, we completely ignored local aspects of the population and the fishermen.

This preoccupation with large-scale phenomena and events blinds us to both the critical biological *and* social aspects of the fishery. We are not really sure why lobster are doing so well; we don't know why the cod have not come back to the old spawning areas along the coast; we don't know if we have impaired the population structure of herring; and even though we know there have been substantial shifts in the structure of the ecosystem, we don't know the ecological mechanisms behind those shifts, or ways that they might or should be repaired. The list could go on for a long time.

On the social side, we are essentially oblivious to the finer-scale organizational and incentive problems that immobilize the management process. Basically, the problem is that when there is a heterogeneous biological and social environment, one-size-fits-all rules create horrendous allocation and scientific problems. The politics around these rules are nasty and inconclusive, especially in the groundfishery. All the public and private incentives encourage doing as little as possible. To do more would seriously disadvantage someone in the system, without giving others appreciable advantage.

The result is not quite deadlock, but something very close and almost as ineffective. I wish to emphasize that I do not see evil intent in all this. It is a difficult problem, and most of the people involved would like to find a reasonable solution. Solutions just have not been forthcoming.

Our inability to match the scale of our social institutions to the scale of the biological and social aspects of the system is a major reason for these difficulties. By emphasizing only the large scale, we disarm our science, slow down our learning, and make our political process almost intractable. To address these problems, we have to decentralize our management institutions. We have to divide the problem up into manageable local and manageable regional pieces.

The ironic part of all this is that this country, of all the countries in the world, has been the first to apply these principals to almost everything we do. The federal system of governance is multi-scale management. The U.S. Senate does not decide when to plow the streets here in Portland; neither does the legislature in Augusta. Over the years, we have learned how to fashion an uneasy but workable balance between local and larger scales of governance, to suit the requirements of the problem at hand.

Our industrial empires have pioneered the decentralized management of economic activity; the chairman of General Motors does not oversee the installation of alternators in each car. For a thousand years, the Roman Catholic Church has organized itself according to the principle of "subsidiarity," pushing all decision-making as far down in the organization as is consistent with the needs of adequate information and fairness.

We simply have not applied these obvious lessons to our fisheries. So, the point is this: *We have to start decentralizing, running experiments like the lobster zones, finding ways to adapt our human activities to the ecology of the ocean; technical solutions are important, but social solutions are paramount.*

Some Policy Implications
If this analysis is correct, it has important policy implications for the governance of Maine's fisheries.

The Groundfishery
Most importantly, *federal regulatory processes have proven unable to balance biological and human needs. The result of this imbalance is a death spiral for Maine's groundfish industry.*

Regulation and biological scarcity have reduced the number of boats, and are leading to a further consolidation of the fleet. As the harvesting sector declines, necessary infrastructure loses its economic base and disappears. Even core market institutions such as the Portland Fish Exchange are endangered. If the exchange were to fail, a transparent, competitive market would disappear. This would increase even more the incentives for consolidation of vessel ownership, various forms of vertical integration and, very possibly, the physical consolidation of the fleet at a central location in Massachusetts. The Maine economy—fishermen, boat owners, processors, buyers and suppliers—would lose greatly. There is little reason to believe that the patterns of ownership and market structure created by a transition to a vertically (or quasi-vertically) integrated industry would be reversible, even if groundfish stocks achieve their former abundance.

This situation points to a core set of priority policies that the state should adopt and actively develop. Basically these are policies intended to maintain a viable cluster of economic activity in the groundfishery.

First is the maintenance of a competitive market, the Portland Fish Exchange. Without a competitive market, even those boats that might pursue the "industrial" route will find themselves in a seriously disadvantaged position. Small boats unable to contract with substantial buyers will be forced to sell by consignment which is always a risky and unfavorable way to sell. In both instances, the node of product consolidation will shift more strongly to the south, and processors will have an increasingly hard time obtaining product without going (expensively) to the point of consolidation.

Second is the continued presence of essential industry infrastructure. On the input side, this means unloading docks, berthing space, refrigerated storage, trucking and shore-side businesses that service vessels and sell ice, fuel, and gear. On the output side, it means processors and distributors. Without infrastructure, the costs of fishing in Maine will rise, and fishing will be inconvenient and expensive even for those boats that survive the current period.

Third is the assurance of continuing access of Maine boats to the groundfish resources of the Gulf of Maine. Consolidation of fishing rights in response to the current scarcity of the resource carries with it the very distinct possibility

York Harbor

that only a very few boats will retain rights to future access. On the other hand, without consolidation, a high percentage of the boats fishing today will have a very hard, probably unsuccessful time surviving in the next few years.

The state must find a way to allow leasing, or some sort of cooperative means for pooling days-at-sea, without at the same time shutting off future access for those boats that wind up not fishing. If those future rights are lost, there will not be enough economic activity to support a viable economic cluster; the once prosperous groundfish industry east of Portland will not rejuvenate; and the overall volume of activity in the state will be inadequate to support a viable service industry, processing, and the Exchange.

Fourth, the state must initiate and fight for policies, especially in the federal arena, that will develop the institutions needed to balance biological and human needs. In particular, this means finding ways to improve the governance process, preferably through decentralization. The "game" has to end; poor resource management has led us to this situation and will keep us there.

Fifth, the stakeholders in the industry must come together and begin to build a consensus, or at the least to have a constructive dialogue, about how they want the fishery to be managed. The Department of Marine Resources must develop or search out a mediated forum in which people can discuss these issues openly and without the need to consider their strategic posture in the "game."

Beyond these core policies, the state and the industry are faced with two starkly different, possible policy strategies. The first is one that acknowledges and encourages the process of consolidation and transition to a vertically integrated industrial structure, while taking whatever steps might be necessary to protect the interests of Maine boat owners, buyers, processors and suppliers. This is essentially a strategy that accepts the basic thrust that follows from a scientific view of "homogeneous" fish stocks that range over a broad scale—as, the Gulf of Maine—and the economic consequences that are consistent with that view. It assumes that further reductions in fishing effort under the current approach to management will restore fish stocks and the economic fortunes of the industry.

The alternative is a strategy that attempts to retain a fairly diverse, independent, family-owned fleet and infrastructure operating in a transparent, competitive market. This strategy is consistent with a scientific view of "heterogeneous" fish stocks that are adapted to relatively local circumstances—as, Penobscot Bay.[9] It will also require reductions in fishing effort, in order to restore fish stocks. An essential element of this strategy is some form of decentralized, area management for basic conservation and long-term economic viability. *If* this strategy were adopted, it would be necessary to add a sixth core policy:

Sixth, then, the state, industry, and federal regulators must come together and develop some sort of decentralized Gulf of Maine management unit as part of the current Amendment 13 process.

This is a difficult time for the state's groundfish industry. The social, economic, and biological conditions in the groundfishery all point to a fundamental turning or tipping point. The patterns of access to the resource, the operation of transparent competitive markets, the continuing existence of essential infrastructure, and our scientific approach to management may *all* change dramatically in the near future.

The New England Fisheries Management Council will make basic decisions as part of the Amendment 13 process in the next few months. To influence that process effectively, the state needs to know what it wants to do and get its political ducks in line within the state, with the other New England states, and in Washington. It needs to put in place quickly a consultative process for the discussion of the industry and state's alternatives and preferred policies. The five or six basic policy priorities outlined here need to be fleshed out with specifics. This can only be done through an active and timely consultative process.

The Lobster Fishery
By far the largest problem facing the industry is that of fishing effort. This is a classic common property problem. Because no one owns the resource until they catch it, there are strong incentives to race to catch the resource before someone else gets it. When everyone succumbs to this strategy, an on-going escalation of fishing capabilities ensues. Equally important, the process puts in place a dynamic that threatens the biological basis for the fishery.[10] Clearly, what is needed is some kind of equitable, effective, collective solution.

Unfortunately, the clarity of solutions to this and similar commons problems is lacking. As with the disease problem, there is uncertainty about the extent of the problem, especially the biological problem; there is uncertainty about the biological and economic outcomes of any policies we might put in place; and, especially, there is uncertainty about the appropriate distribution of the costs (who bears the burden) of policies we might undertake to solve the problem. And, just as with the threats of disease and/or court action, we have to put in place ways to make these decisions in a timely and reasonable way.

In the last few years, the industry and state have taken significant steps towards solution of the classic commons problems this fishery faces today. Zone councils were established in 1997. They were (or are) a large step in the direction of ending the game being played. Within a year or so all seven zones voted for trap limits and within four years five of the seven zones had voted for various forms of license limitation. These same items had been on the legislature's agenda for almost twenty-five years without any resolution!

The point is that the decentralization of decision-making created the political conditions under which difficult conservation decisions were made. Even if the initiative for these decisions comes from higher up, the creation of a policy dialog at the local level and the ability to adapt broad policies to local circumstances greatly increases the probability of action.

This process is new and far from perfect, and the state can take steps to strengthen it. Realistic solutions to the problems of the fishery have to come from a broad and varied constituency: scientists, fishermen, bureaucrats, and interested citizens. Creating an effective governance process that brings in the knowledge and interests of these constituencies is probably the strongest foundation we can lay for an uncertain future. In practical terms this means:

First, we need more and better science. Science can give us a better understanding of the lobster population and the ecosystem in which lobsters reside; it can give us better ways to observe and monitor the behavior of that system; it can give us more timely warnings of imminent surprises; and it can give us pretty good ideas about the kinds of policies that might and might not work.[11] It forms an essential foundation for good management, but we should not expect it to deliver a silver bullet.

Science can be especially helpful to local-zone decision-making if fishermen are actively engaged in the process of doing the science, in the discussion about science, in at-sea work, and in cooperative research projects. The state and the industry have to acquire the resources necessary to bring science into the zone discussions. Cooperative science has expanded greatly in the last few years; however, the state and the industry have made few efforts to bring the science discussion down to the level of the zones.

Finally, the DMR, its lobster advisory committee, and the leadership in each zone need to take deliberate and persistent steps to invigorate a public dialog about the science, about equitable ways we can respond to possible problems like shell disease and other downturns in abundance, and ways we can improve the governance process. The zone councils will work well in the face of crisis and will make the state's regulatory role much easier, but only if there is a widespread prior and informed discussion of the issues.

And in Conclusion

We in Maine face a fundamental, overriding problem in our fisheries today—a governance process that works *against* fishermen's collective, rational interest in resource conservation. Decisions about conservation are usually avoided, because no one can capture the benefits and, in addition, because we don't have (and probably never will have) the scientific knowledge to know exactly the right thing to do.

The result for the state has been the effective loss of most of its fisheries, as well as the impoverishment of the ecosystem of the Gulf of Maine. Even the fisheries that remain viable, such as the lobster fishery, are continually at risk because of the loss of ecosystem integrity. We have to address these issues. That process has begun in the lobster fishery, but it needs to be strengthened there and adapted and expanded to our other fisheries. If we do not do this, we will never solve the conservation problem, and are very likely to have no viable fisheries in the near future.

James A. Wilson is Professor of Marine Sciences and Resource Economics at the University of Maine. Educated at the University of Wisconsin, he has been a respected and influential presence on the Maine fisheries scene for three decades. In 1975, with Robin Alden of Stonington, he initiated the annual Maine Fishermen's Forum, which each March brings the entire Maine fishing community together to learn from one another, to have fun, and to make some trouble for the politicians. A decade later, in 1986, his research in market economics led to the creation of the Portland Fish Exchange, which permanently changed the marketing of the Gulf of Maine's products and saved the Maine fishing community from marginalization. More recently, he helped initiate the current lobster zones within Maine, as well as a comparable, larger-scale system for all of New England. For the past decade, and most importantly for Maine's future, he has conducted extensive research in fisheries management and the governance of complex, adaptive systems—for both the U.S. and the Swedish national academies of science, the University of Michigan, and others.

Tourism revenues in Maine have grown five-fold since the early 1970s, making tourism now the second largest sector of Maine's economy, generating $5.4 billion annually. Because Maine tourism relies critically upon our renewable natural and cultural resources, it offers great potential for sustainable economic development. Still, Mainers have historically remained lukewarm toward tourism, due to its negative side effects such as summer traffic congestion, soaring waterfront real estate prices, frequently low-wage jobs, and sprawling development. For Maine to benefit more substantially from tourism, greater investment is necessary in its planning and development, and in education, research, and extension efforts. If Maine is able to shape its tourism growth in ways that realize its potential benefits, tourism may emerge as a powerful and welcome economic driver for all regions of the state.

22 Tourism in Maine's Expanding
Service Economy

DAVID VAIL

This chapter offers a portrait of Maine tourism "the way it was," from the late 1950s to the early 1970s. Then, emphasizing major continuities and changes over the past three decades, it will take an extended look at today's tourism patterns and prospects. This snapshot highlights tourism's major challenges as well as the exciting opportunities we may look forward to in the rest of this decade. While parts of the story are critical, it is based on an optimistic premise: that every tourism problem poses a challenge; and every challenge is an opportunity for Maine.

Why optimism? Because tourism—in contrast to such resource-based sectors as bulk commodity agriculture, ground fishing, and paper products—offers great promise for sustainable economic development in Maine. If planned, promoted, and developed effectively, selective tourism growth can contribute to social and economic revitalization of our rural communities and enhance all Maine residents' quality of life. The opportunities are real, but success is not guaranteed. The state must make a major commitment, and go about it with energy, caring, and imagination.

First, however, to get an idea of the possibilities for sustainable Maine tourism, we might look forward to the end of this decade.

Looking Forward

The year is 2010. In Atlanta, Georgia, fifty-something suburbanites, Betty and Bill Jones, are planning their upcoming summer vacation, when they catch an eye-popping, thirty-second TV ad featuring moose, mountains, lobsters, and lighthouses, with the tag line, "It Must Be Maine!" Recalling the traffic jams and sweltering heat on last summer's trip to New Orleans, they decide to check out the Maine Office of Tourism's web site. There, they discover Maine's stunning variety of coastal and inland landscapes, outdoor recreation opportunities, cultural and heritage attractions, and world class lodging and dining. They are amazed by what Maine offers:

- The Office of Tourism's on-line service to facilitate all their arrangements for a ten-day visit;

- The "Explore Maine" transportation network, where trains, buses, vans, and ferries let visitors roam the state without need to put foot to a gas pedal once there;

- Diverse trails networks, ranging from wildlife to landscape gardens, from mountain biking to forest history; and

- Maine's unique, certified ecotourism, a public-private partnership that brings environmental education and nature conservation together with the premier quality services offered by whitewater rafting outfitters, sporting camps, windjammer cruises, fishing guides, and many others.

Betty and Bill are hooked. Their *biggest* challenge is deciding how to fit everything they'd like to do into a nine-day trip. Space doesn't allow a detailed recounting of Betty and Bill's Maine itinerary, but their postcards to friends back in Atlanta's brutal 95° heat hit the high points: cool breezes on the high-speed ferry from Rockland to Bar Harbor, an Acadian fiddling contest at Calais's Downeast Heritage Center, loons calling in the twilight at their cabin on Grand Lake Stream, a whitewater rafting adventure in the Kennebec Gorge, a Gulf Hagas hike followed by moose steaks at the Appalachian Mountain Club's Little Lyford Pond Camps, and, on their final evening in Portland, the Center for Cultural Exchange's dazzling multicultural arts festival.

By the time Betty and Bill board the plane back to Atlanta, they are already planning their next Maine trip: maybe they will return for fall foliage and moose viewing in the western mountains, maybe for a few days of lodge-to-lodge cross-country skiing along Maine's famous Mahoussocs-to-Moosehead trail.

Betty and Bill's "excellent adventure" offers a snapshot of Maine tourism as it *can be* in 2010, if we do things *right*. For a sense of how we can get from here to there, we first must rewind the Maine tourism story back to 1960, and then run it forward to 2004.

Visiting Vacationland: A Special Kind of Export Industry
"Vacationland." For decades, our license plates have advertised one of Maine's core industries. In 2001, tourist spending generated nearly 7 percent of Maine's gross state product (GSP), more than any other sector save health care and forest products. Tourism's 78,000 full-time equivalent jobs made it Maine's largest source of employment.

I speak of tourism as an industry, but it is a peculiar sort of industry, in three important ways. First, unlike paper or banking, tourism is not a single economic sector turning out a limited range of well-defined products. Rather, it is a web of thousands of businesses, most of them very small, that derive some or all of their income from sales to Maine visitors. Tourism-dependent businesses span an enormous range: from whale watches to hunting guides, from ski resorts to clam shacks, and from gas stations to grocery stores.

Second, Maine tourism is in essence a nature-based industry. Beyond our obvious natural attractions, like Sebago Lake and our extensive snowmobile trails, the tourist's experiences of shopping for camping gear, eating a lobster, or visiting a local historical society are enhanced by Maine's beautiful, natural, largely unspoiled surroundings. Unlike other resource-based sectors, however—such as fisheries, agriculture, and forest products—tourism does not *extract* material goods from nature. Rather, its services flow from and require healthy natural systems. As Evan Richert points out in his chapter in this book, tourism is organized not for active production, but for passive consumption of the landscape.

Third, tourism is Maine's number two export industry. Visitors "from away" bring nearly $4 billion dollars to spend here each year. Tourism is very different from an export like computer chips or potato chips, which we produce and then ship to customers out of state. With tourism, the customers—about 26 million a year—come to us. They share our our wilderness areas, our beaches, our autumn leaves, our restaurants, our roads, and our parking lots. As a result, tourism has pervasive side effects on scores of "host communities" and their residents, often for the better and sometimes for the worse. This is especially true of tourism's "hot spots"—those times and places where tourist concentrations come to dominate local life. Examples come quickly to mind: Bar Harbor's "Fourth of July flush" (as the locals call it), Rangeley on Snodeo weekend in January, and the Saco River's summer weekend, floating beer parties.

Tourism's downside was already clear to observers back in 1974, when the Maine Travel Analysis Committee reported "lukewarm public support" for tourism and even "public resentment of crowds and congestion."[1] Back then Maine hosted just 3 million out-of-state visitors per year; now, it is 26 million.

Looking Backward

Maine has a storied history as a destination for leisure travelers. From the time of Henry David Thoreau's sojourns to the Maine woods in the mid-nineteenth century, "sports" have hired Maine guides and used remote sporting camps for their "hook-and-bullet" adventures. With the coming of the railroads after the Civil War, wealthy East Coast urbanites turned Bar Harbor into a summer colony. By the 1890s trainloads of working-class Boston day-trippers made York and Old Orchard beaches their weekend and holiday playgrounds. In terms of sheer numbers and economic magnitude, Maine tourism has always been heavily concentrated in the summer and on the coast, a pattern that persists in 2004, despite decades of public and private efforts to market the hinterland and the state's four season attractions.

Tourism underwent momentous changes between the turn of the twentieth century and 1960. In her fascinating tourism history, *Inventing New England*, Dona Brown documents the profound impact of public road investments and automobiles following World War I.[2] Previously, most tourists traveled to a single Maine destination, by train or steamer, and stayed put for the duration. Resort hotels and rooming houses thrived, as did seasonal homes for the affluent along the coast and inland lakes and ponds. All this began to change with construction of U.S. routes 1 and 2 in the 1920s, and completion of the Carleton Bridge across the Kennebec in 1928 and the Waldo-Hancock Bridge over the Penobscot in 1932.[3] In 1941 the Maine Turnpike Authority was created; in 1955, the turnpike reached Augusta; and, in 1965, Interstate Highway 95 (I-95) reached Houlton.

Tourism in the present epoch, then, is a central feature of America's love affair with the automobile. Automobile tourism to and through Maine grew rapidly, and with it two phenomena we will encounter repeatedly: surging numbers of short-term visitors and sightseers (whom we now call "general tourists"), who visit several attractions and destinations. From the 1920s onward, campgrounds and the ubiquitous motels were built to meet mobile travelers' growing demand. By 1972 general sightseers were the largest single category of Maine tourists, and motel users accounted for over one-third of all tourist spending.[4]

As signs of the changes brought by the "car culture," Bar Harbor ferry services ended in 1932. Maine's train passenger traffic plummeted 75 percent between 1920 and 1931, and, in 1964, the Maine Central Railroad ended passenger service altogether. Auto travel's near monopoly, in combination with a prolonged tourism bust during the Great Depression, sounded the death knell for the old tourism model centering on lengthy summer stays at hotels and boarding houses. The grand hotels at Poland Spring, Samoset, and Kineo were sold off or torn down.

Post-World War II affluence brought tourists back to Maine in droves and enabled Mainers themselves to increase their leisure travel in the state. This ushered in a half century of nearly continuous tourism growth. State agencies commissioned studies of tourism as early as 1959,[5] but our clearest image of those times comes from an Arthur D. Little study commissioned by the Maine Vacation Travel Analysis Committee (VTAC) and published in 1974 as the report *Tourism in Maine*. The Legislature created VTAC to overcome, "the lack of knowledge concerning tourism in the State," and "to plan effectively for future tourism development."[6] The next few paragraphs draw a statistical sketch of Maine tourism three decades ago, based largely on the VTAC report.

In 1972–73, Maine hosted just over 10 million (10.2 million) leisure and business travelers, a number that was up about 50 percent from 1960.

• 3.1 million tourists visited from out of state, which means that Maine's one million residents made the remaining 7 million tourist trips, for an average of 7 per person;

- Most non-resident visitors were drawn from a fairly narrow base of nearby states and provinces—30 percent from Massachusetts alone, and 65 percent from five northeast states;

- Fully three-quarters (7.7 million) of all tourist trips were day trips—with important implications for the economy and for growing seasonal congestion, which are explored below; and

- Over half of all trips (53 percent) were concentrated in the three summer months.

Direct tourist expenditures were $1.1 billion (in 2003 dollars) in 1972–73, less than one-fifth of today's level.[7]

- While non-residents made just one-third of all tourist trips, they accounted for four-fifths of total spending—a fact with important economic and promotional implications;

- Spectacular nature and a unique culture and heritage may have been Maine's prime tourist attractions, but they were largely un-priced public goods; thus their *direct* economic contribution was comparatively small. It is important that nearly ninety cents ($0.87) of the tourist dollar was (and is today) spent on the "big four" services: lodging, dining, transportation, and shopping;

- It is not clear whether L. L. Bean was already Maine's biggest tourist destination, as it is today, but shopping—accounting for 15 percent of all tourist spending—was already taking off as a tourist activity;

- The wages, business proprietors' income, and state revenues generated by tourism ($550 million at 2003 prices) amounted to just over half of total tourist spending. This means that the other half of the tourist dollar did not benefit Maine's own economy, but rather "leaked" out of the state in the form of tourist businesses' purchases of inputs produced elsewhere— for example, restaurant equipment, hunting gear, insurance fees, vehicles, and fuel;

- Tourism directly contributed roughly 5 percent of Maine's gross state product in 1972 ($490 million in 2003 dollars).[8] As incomes generated by tourism were re-spent in local economies, they had an additional *multiplier effect*; and

- Today, state agencies boast about the tax *revenues* generated by tourism. The VTAC study, in contrast, also estimated the state's direct and indirect *costs* of supporting tourism—from road maintenance, to state police, to marketing. They found that *more than half* of the state's $120 million in tourism revenues ($61 million in 2003 dollars) was absorbed by its costs.[9]

In 1972–73, tourism and recreation supported roughly 21,000 full-time equivalent jobs, or 6.5 percent of the state's employment.

- The A. D. Little statistics on wages and employment offer an early indication of a chronic social and economic problem facing tourism-dependent economies: low average wages. Although tourism accounted for 6.5 percent of Maine's employment, tourism workers received just 4 percent of the state's aggregate wages and salaries.

Even today, the, the VTAC report's data reveal intriguing glimpses into tourism's seasonal and regional tourism patterns, which have evolved dramatically since 1972–73. Back then, well over 1 million people (1.142 million) par-

The Maine Outlet, Kittery

ticipated in hunting and freshwater fishing, a number that has shrunk steadily in recent decades. For Maine's interior regions, the yearly spending of $69 million by fishers and hunters (in 2003 dollars) was the principal source of tourism income and jobs in the spring, summer, and fall seasons.[10] To be sure, there were then some bus tours for fall foliage viewing; but "leaf-peeping" was still a minor market segment.[11]

The winter season lagged badly, with just 11 percent of the state's yearly tourists; but it was poised to take off. Alpine skiing was just starting a twenty-five-year surge, after the opening of Sugarloaf's first rudimentary facilities in 1955. Recreational snowmobiles had also been introduced in 1954; and in 1972–73, the state was just beginning to build the landowner–snowmobile club partnership that has since shaped an extraordinary 13,000-mile trail network

all across Maine. Then as now, long distances and few transportation options limited the number of non-resident winter sports participants. Sixty-one percent of skiers, and 94 percent of snowmobilers were Mainers. Combined 1972–73 revenues from these two activities ($42 million 2003 dollars) were just 4 percent of total tourism spending. Today each is a $300+ million dollar activity, and together they generate 10 percent of Maine's tourism spending—on a par with fishing and hunting.

In many ways, A. D. Little's analysis of Maine tourism's problems and VTAC's recommended solutions read as if they were written in 2004, not 1974. Looking at the big picture, they stress that "*congestion* is the primary cause of serious social and environmental impact…. Maine suffers from seasonal congestion (summer) and locational congestion (most notably the southern coast)." Even in 1974 these were not new concerns. They echoed an alarm that had previously been raised at a 1966 Bowdoin College conference on coastal congestion.[12]

To address these and other issues, VTAC urged Maine to move beyond piecemeal policy measures and adopt a concerted tourism development strategy, including special state initiatives to boost interior Maine's limited and highly seasonal tourism. In a sign of the times, VTAC expressed grave concern about the vulnerability of Maine's car-dominated tourism to energy shortages. This was, of course, in reaction to the 1973–74 Arab oil embargo and U.S. energy crisis. From a 2004 vantage point, their alarm about the adverse impact of gasoline price spikes might seem irrelevant. However, the weakness of Maine's tourism economy since the September 11, 2001, terrorist attacks reflects our continuing vulnerability to "outside shocks," particularly shocks emanating from the Middle East.

Many 1974 VTAC recommendations still resonate, even in 2004. I will highlight two clusters: one, focusing on promotion of regional tourism development; the other, on the need for the state to assume a leading role. (Two other VTAC emphases that continue to preoccupy tourism promoters are encouragement of general sightseeing and business and convention travel.)

VTAC believed that Maine's western lakes and mountains should be the prime focus of tourism growth, founded upon development and marketing of four-season attractions. The big winter drawing card would be ski resorts; for the summer and fall, it would be lakeside second homes. The record of growth in these activities over the 1960s prompted VTAC's optimism. (From the end of World War II to the early 1970s, the average workweek was shrinking and vacation time was increasing in America.)

It was assumed that Maine's lakes and mountains could attract a larger share of people with ample time for extended stays. VTAC recommended the creation of a Rangeley–Flagstaff Development Authority, to design and direct the western mountains tourism strategy. (Parenthetically, in that era of "rogue snowmobilers," VTAC expressed serious reservations about encouraging the spread of sledding and other motorized backcountry recreation. In addition to vandalism and other violations of landowners' rights, these vehicles, it stated, "create pollution of all types—air, water, noise, and visual."[13])

VTAC's proposals were made in a period when several grandiose, recreational development schemes were afoot in western and northern Maine. One envisioned a string of elaborate ski resorts, running from Saddleback Mountain to the Bigelow Range, that would rival the Colorado Rockies. Another would have carved a million-acre recreation complex out of the upper St. John and Allagash watersheds. The construction of what is now a 25,000-mile North Woods logging road network would have facilitated such mass tourism undertakings in what had previously been remote areas, accessible only to dedicated and hardy recreationists. The specter of such mammoth North Woods develop-

Access by Snowmobile

ments gave rise to a conservationist backlash, contributing to the formation of the Land Use Regulation Commission (1971) and the successful voter referendum to protect the Bigelow Preserve (1982).[14]

In VTACs vision, the state's Department of Commerce and Industry (predecessor to today's Department of Economic and Community Development) would have been assigned a far more active role in tourism planning and development. This would have included more state support for community and regional tourism development efforts, based on the proposed Rangeley–Flagstaff prototype. VTAC also urged that the state's extremely limited tourism marketing and promotion functions be strengthened and rationalized, by creating a "quasi-governmental" organization similar to today's Maine Office of Tourism. In the event, most of VTAC's recommendations gathered dust in the 1970s, as governors Kenneth Curtis and James Longley and successive legislatures did *not* make the proposed new state investments in tourism development, promotion, and organizational infrastructure.

In this sense, the VTAC report can be seen as one phase in a sad half-century tradition, whereby tourism's challenges have gotten onto Maine's public policy radar screen at roughly fifteen-year intervals. In a continuing pattern, reports have been commissioned, blue ribbon committees have been formed, ambitious recommendations have been offered, and comparatively little has been done to implement them. The precedent was set with the 1959 Department of Economic Development report, cited above.[15]

A decade after the 1974 VTAC report, the tourist economy was revisited in a trio of new studies.[16] In 1986 a Maine Vacation Travel Commission reported to the legislature, and the following year Governor John McKernan received a report and recommendations from the Tourism Subcommittee of the Governor's Taskforce on Economic Development.[17] Again, this round of activities had little impact on actual policy or public investment. Today's round of tourism analysis and strategic discussion centers on the Maine Tourism Commission's Natural Resources Committee, created by the legislature in 2003, as well as the November 2003 Blaine House Conference on Maine's Natural Resource-based Industries. These initiatives, and their prospects for a kinder fate, are discussed more fully below.

Because of space limitations, we now make a quarter-century leap from Maine tourism in 1974, and the state's tourism *non*-policy, to the twenty-first century. This by no means implies that nothing new happened in Maine tourism over the intervening decades. On the Maine coast, for example, we saw the establishment and growth of cruise ship visits, whale watches, and sea kayaking. In the interior, the Allagash Wilderness Waterway was created, whitewater rafting took off, the moose hunt was introduced, and the combination of skiing, snowmobiling, and fall leaf-peeping were firmly established as major tour-

Changing Maine

ism "season extenders." Shopping, already a big deal in 1974, became a billion dollar-a-year part of the tourist economy, with L. L. Bean's the state's most popular tourist destination.

In addition, Maine tourism again showed its vulnerability to large scale forces outside our control—not the escalating gas prices VTAC had feared; but stagnant tourist spending during two national economic recessions in the '80s, and a drop in Canadian visitors in the '90s as the falling Canadian dollar priced many of our neighbors out of the Maine market.

Maine Tourism Today: Dealing with Unevenness

The overwhelming impression one gets by comparing Maine's past and present tourism statistics is one of truly *dramatic growth*. Today's 45 million yearly tourist trips are more than four times the number reported for 1972/73. Recall that even then, summer coastal congestion was considered a serious problem. The average yearly increase in tourist visits has been nearly 5 percent. Our 26 million non-resident visitors are more than eight times the 1972–73 number. More than half of them—14 million—are now day-trippers from nearby states.[18]

Tourist spending has grown five-fold since 1972–73, to some $5.4 billion/year, faster than Maine's overall economy. Tourism's direct contribution to our gross state product is five times larger, at roughly $2.5 billion, after netting out leakages. As a share of gross state product, it has risen from 5 percent to nearly 7 percent, dwarfing all of Maine's other resource-based industries except for paper. Tourism employment, now pushing 75,000 full-time-equivalent jobs, has jumped from one of every fifteen Maine workers to one in nine.[19]

In many rural Maine communities, growing economic dependence upon tourism has been met with mixed reactions. Nevertheless, tourist spending has been one of their principal buffers against the impacts of long-term decline in traditional resource-based and manufacturing industries, such as food processing, shoes, textiles, and secondary wood products. Tourism has helped to sustain local commerce, the property tax base, a clientele for public services, and, of course, jobs. Tourism growth, however, as well as tourism's benefits and costs, have been *uneven*. This unevenness, and what we can do about it, are the focus of the rest of this chapter.

Coastal Maine

With its lighthouses, lobsters, and L. L. Bean, the Maine coast Down East to Mt. Desert has a potent brand image in national as well as regional markets. Forty-three percent of overnight visitors really do eat a lobster; and L. L. Bean's 3.5 million customers each year make it Maine's most visited destination. Maine's nine most visited tourist destinations are all on the coast. The coast attracts first-time visitors and enjoys a high rate of return visits. Its diverse and closely spaced attractions play well in this era of growth in general touring, especially among affluent retirees and baby boomers like Betty and Bill from Atlanta. The coast's big challenge, as all know who live there, continues to be the unresolved problem of severe summer congestion—the danger that we will "love it to death."

Maine has neither a coherent state or regional growth management strategy, nor one to manage the flow of tourists in and around coastal hot spots. Shoe-horning 22 million visitors into a narrow strip of land each summer inevitably has consequences. Some of these are obvious: crowded parking lots, boat ramps, beaches, restaurants, public restrooms, and bumper-to-bumper Sunday traffic. There are also less obvious impacts: soaring real estate prices that contribute to the loss of working waterfronts and affordable housing; increased strip development and sprawl; a higher incidence of violence and property crime; and stress on public services and budgets in host communities.[20] No wonder, then, that many residents continue to be "lukewarm" toward tourism (in VTAC's terms), and react skeptically to any announced plan to expand tourist attractions and facilities.

Individual towns are coping; for example, Kennebunkport, with restrictions on town-center tour bus parking; and Freeport, with its "green lined," noncommercial zone. Even the most stringent town-level initiatives are inadequate, however, because sprawl and summer tourist congestion, in particular, tend to spill over from one town to another. Effective, regional "crowd control" is still lacking.

The inescapable fact is that 92 percent of non-resident visitors arrive in Maine by car (compared to 78 percent car travelers, nationally). Easy I-95 access from the south and the effective lack of alternative transportation modes have led to an explosion of summer day-trippers, who not only intensify road and parking congestion but also spend less than half as much each day as do overnight visitors. (Day-trippers average $61/day compared to $136/day for overnighters.[21]) A recent *Maine Sunday Telegram* feature story on the aging tourist magnet, Old Orchard Beach, chronicled the downward trajectory of its tourist reputation, on what analysts euphemistically call the "tourism development cycle."[22]

A sign that coastal tourism may be nearing its saturation point is Maine's stagnant share of the national, overnight tourist market since 1995 and our declining share of the Northeast's overnight market.[23] Maine tourism also continues to be vulnerable to outside forces. This can be seen in the sector's sluggish performance over the past three years, under the twin impacts of a national economic slowdown and the tourism chill following September 11 and the war on terrorism.

Interior Maine

Shifting our focus to interior Maine, it also has a share of renowned tourist destinations, and even some hot spots that come to mind: the crowded summits of Mount Katahdin and Tumbledown Mountain in August; peak-season congestion of Kennebec–Dead River whitewater rafting and Allagash Waterway campsites; and popular segments of the ITS snowmobile network, during Presidents' Week. In contrast to the coast, however, it is *underutilized* capacity, not congestion, that characterizes most interior tourist attractions, most of the time.

For the most part, nature-based tourism in the North Woods and Down East Lakes regions continues to be a compatible, secondary use of working landscapes, just as it was a century ago. This complementarity among land uses is demonstrated vividly by snowmobiling, which has seen eleven-fold growth into a $300 million-a-year business since 1972–73. Sledding is now a key to winter social and economic vitality in numerous towns, from Fryeburg in the west, to Greenville in north-central Maine, and Fort Kent in the far north. Over 90 percent of Maine's outstanding 13,000-mile trail network runs across private lands.[24] Unfortunately, snowmobiling and several other outdoor recreation activities may be vulnerable to the dramatic land ownership changes that are now taking place in Maine's Unorganized Territories.

In these vast and remote landscapes, tourism's growth potential is constrained primarily by limits to demand, not supply capacity— although I would emphasize that the limited supply of top-quality tourism facilities and activities is one reason for interior Maine's limited appeal to potential first-time visitors. Inland and upland, the growth in tourist numbers and spending appears to be limited by several key factors:

- Long driving distances on a less-than-excellent road system, coupled with the national trend toward shorter day and weekend trips;

- Declining participation in traditional backcountry activities, particularly fishing, hunting, and wildlife watching. Maine's 1991 total for those three activities was 1.22 million; by 2001, it had declined more than 20 percent to 0.96 million;[25]

- Limited development and promotion of diverse, high-quality activities, marketed as "packages" that might compete effectively in the growing general tourism market; and

- Capacity limits at our best-known outdoor adventure attractions, such as whitewater rafting and climbing Katahdin;

In sum, the North Woods and Washington County lack what tourism analysts call "destination drivers"—that is, prime attractions, backed by an outstanding promotional effort that will give them a marketing edge over more effectively "branded" competitors, such as the White Mountains, the Adirondacks, and the Rockies.[26]

Quality Jobs

Finally, Maine must face tourism's job quality problem, hinted at earlier. Certainly, tourism offers thousands of rewarding and well-compensated career opportunities in occupations as wide-ranging as fishing guides, executive chefs, whale watch captains, ski instructors, motel managers, museum curators, and craftspeople. On the whole, however, tourism is a "low end" service sector, nationally as well as in Maine. Median earnings are very low in comparison both to Maine's average earnings, and to the Maine Economic Growth Council's "livable wage" standard.

As mentioned above, Maine tourism involves thousands of businesses, most very small and many seasonal. Our "best practice" tourism businesses—outfitters, inns, hotels, craftspeople, farm B&Bs, restaurants, etc.—offer premium quality goods and services and have won awards testifying to it. However, the "average practice" among tourism businesses falls well short of our best practice models. Low labor productivity in such businesses is at the heart of the compensation problem. The tourism occupational mix, dominated as it is by hourly wage-earners in dining, lodging, and retail sales, is also part of the problem.

An assessment of pay scales in tourism occupations suggests that, at most, 40 percent of tourism workers attained the Maine Economic Growth Council's "livable wage" standard in 1999, compared to 68 percent of all Maine workers. (The standard was $10/hour in 2000). Further, just one in four hourly paid hospitality workers received health benefits.[27] More recently, the Maine Department of Labor estimated the average earnings of full-time "leisure and hospitality services" workers at $13,320 in 2002, less than half Maine's average private sector earnings ($29,239).[28]

Many tourism workers also face high commuting costs because affordable housing has disappeared from tourism centers, and many must hold multiple jobs to make ends meet. Low wages and poor benefits, combined with unattractive working conditions, long commutes, and limited career prospects are among the key reasons for Maine's much-publicized tourism labor shortage, a recruitment problem that affects even high unemployment areas like Greenville and Millinocket.

A picture emerges: tourism has been a powerful engine of job creation, but not now a very potent source of quality, livable wage jobs.

Changing Maine

Maine Innovations

This snapshot of Maine tourism today might appear without hope; however, it omits two important and promising signs. The first is an array of exciting private, public, and non-governmental initiatives that can serve as building blocks in a strategy for sustainable tourism development. The second is a renewed awareness among Maine policy-makers of tourism's social and economic importance and of the critical need to fashion a farsighted strategy for its development.

Cultural and heritage tourism initiatives, supported by the Maine Office of Tourism and the Maine Arts Commission, are taking off in all of Maine's eight tourism regions. They range from art and craft shows to logging museums, and from refurbished town centers to garden tours. Their geographic scope extends from western Maine's Mountain Counties Heritage Network (supported by the Sandy River Foundation) to Washington County's new, multi-million dollar Down East Heritage Center in Calais (supported by the Libra Foundation). Such attractions are publicized online and in brochures like the "Maine Guide to Crafts and Culture," and "The Kennebec-Chaudière International Corridor."

Maine does not have world class cultural and heritage attractions like, say, historic Boston and Williamsburg, Virginia. By themselves, they do not have the drawing power to bring large numbers of new tourists to the state. They are, however, excellent complements to Maine's outdoor recreation opportunities and key components of general touring packages. Cultural and heritage resources also have two special benefits. First, they induce visitors to travel beyond major tourist hubs and spend some time and money in out-of-the-way communities. Second, they enhance local residents' quality of life, as well as the tourist experience.

Stronger links are being cultivated between tourism and Maine farmers and fishers. In its simplest form, this involves increased farm sales to inns and restaurants, and through Maine's sixty farmers' markets. In Hancock County, this niche market even includes farms' supplying fresh produce for windjammer cruises. At a deeper level, the Maine Department of Agriculture and the university's Cooperative Extension Service are assisting enterprising farmers to develop on-farm tourist services, as a complement to their crop and livestock production. Niche opportunities range from farm bed-and-breakfasts to hay and sleigh rides, cross-country ski trails, and maple sugaring events. On the coast, some fishing businesses have added profitable sidelines like wharfside restaurants and nature cruises.

Across the state, communities and tourism planners have eagerly embraced the trails concept, offering tourists with particular interests an opportunity to sample Maine's diverse offerings. At the local level, dozens of towns now offer self-guided walking tours. On a much larger scale, the 325-mile Maine Island Trail runs from Casco Bay to Machias Bay, and offers recreational access to over 100 private and public islands. The Kennebec-Chaudière Corridor highlights nature and Francophone culture from Quebec City to Pemaquid Point. The Maine Landscape Garden Trail loops through much of the state.

Several new trails, in the planning stage, will have the potential to attract first time visitors to interior Maine. They include the 180-mile Mahoussocs-to-Moosehead cross-country ski and mountain bike trail, featuring lodges at convenient locations; the Northern Forest Canoe Trail, which will stretch from New York's Adirondacks to the St. Croix River on Maine's New Brunswick border; the Appalacian Mountain Club's planned "family friendly" loop trails, in the underutilized 100-Mile Wilderness region between Moosehead Lake and Baxter State Park; and a proposed, car-accessible bird-watching trail. Like Maine's cultural and heritage attractions, each of these trails will benefit Mainers as well as our "customers" from away.

An accredited ecotourism model is being shaped through a collaboration among the Maine Island Trail Association (MITA), the Maine Department of Inland Fisheries and Wildlife (IFW), the Bureau of Parks and Lands (BPL), and the Maine Sea Kayak Guides and Instructors (MASKGI). MITA and BPL have recently completed a ten-year plan, establishing carrying-capacity limits and management guidelines for camping and day use on more than forty publicly owned islands along the Maine Island Trail. MASKGI is committed to a "leave no trace" approach to island use and certifies sea kayak guides in sustainable practices. MITA and MASKGI, rather than the state, have the major responsibility for monitoring island use and enforcing good stewardship.

After nearly a forty-year gap in passenger rail travel from the Northeast megalopolis to Vacationland, the Downeaster has revived service from Boston to Portland. This could be the first key link in a multi-modal transportation network that would give tourists convenient alternatives to the automobile. On Mount Desert Island, the Island Explorer bus service has demonstrated how effective convenient public transportation can be in reducing road and parking congestion, when upwards of 2 million summer visitors converge on Acadia National Park. Scores of cruise ships have added Portland and Bar Harbor to their itineraries, becoming an important fall tourism season extender.

Nearly a decade ago, the Maine Department of Transportation unveiled its visionary Explore Maine tourism transport plan. It featured carefully linked long-distance and local travel options by train, ferry, bus, van, and taxi (not to mention moped and bike). In view of Maine's two serious tourism transportation constraints—coastal road and parking congestion, and excessive travel times to North Woods and Down East destinations—Explore Maine merits a serious new look.

Perhaps most exciting of all, the Land for Maine's Future program and land trusts are making wonderful investments that will protect Maine's prime recreational landscapes, through a mix of land purchases and conservation ease-ments. Dozens of these initiatives have been local—for example, the Town of Brunswick and the Brunswick-Topsham Land Trust's collaboration to acquire key parcels for an Androscoggin River-to-the-Sea trail corridor. In terms of their potential to boost the tourism economy of distressed rural communities, however, it is large-scale acquisitions and easements in the North Woods and Down East Lakes regions that offer the breakthrough opportunities.

Like jewels in a crown, these new acquisitions and easements may be art-fully combined with existing state parks and public lots to create high-profile destinations for environmentally friendly outdoor adventure activities, as well as for more contemplative recreation. I have more to say below about the plan-ning methods, infrastructure investments, and promotional strategies needed to shape premier three-season destinations in the North Woods.

Sustainable Tourism Opportunities
Despite all these exciting initiatives, Maine lacks what could be called a coher-ent tourism strategy. Developing such a strategy is imperative, because Maine faces stiff competition for tourists like Atlanta's Betty and Bill Jones, from other U.S. states, Canadian provinces, and foreign nations. In this era of globally integrated markets and Internet communications, the high-spending, overnight traveler can choose from literally thousands of competing destinations.

Barring major changes in Maine's tourism strategy—and unforeseen shocks to the national economy, energy prices, or national security— the broad pat-terns described above are likely to hold between now and 2010. In other words, summer congestion will limit coastal tourism growth. More summer coastal tourism, if it occurs, and especially if it means an increase in day-trippers, will only intensify the social and environmental costs of tourism, which have been recognized for many decades. In North Woods and Down East regions, the lack of potent "destination drivers," backed by a unique and compelling brand im-age, will limit growth on the demand side. Many small tourism businesses will continue to fall short of the service quality, resource productivity, and market-ing support they need to grow, prosper, and offer high quality jobs.

The November 2003 Blaine House Conference on Maine's Natural Resource-based Industries addressed these and other challenges facing Maine tourism. Governor John Baldacci's Maine Woods initiative, announced in late 2003, and his State of the State address in January, 2004, emphasized several of the conference's core recommendations. These recommendations comprise a core set of policy initiatives and public investments that might move Maine onto a path toward economically, socially, and environmentally sustainable tourism growth. They might even convince Atlanta's Betty and Bill Jones to choose Maine for their summer vacation in 2010.

First, we must establish a substantial state tourism planning and development capacity. The Maine Office of Tourism (MOT), within the Department of Economic and Community Development, is the logical lead agency. The MOT appears to be quite effective at fulfilling its present limited mandate, which focuses primarily on marketing and promotion (including marketing assistance to the state's eight tourism regions). Adding planning and development capabilities would bring tourism up to a par with Maine's other natural resource-based industries—agriculture, forestry, and marine resources—which have long had state agencies dedicated to their long-term planning and development.

In several respects, however, tourism is different from other resource-based industries. First, it encompasses many diverse economic sectors; second, it depends critically on access to healthy and diverse land and sea environments that are primarily dedicated to other types of production; and third, it has economic linkages to all the other resource industries. Effective tourism planning will, therefore, require an especially high level of inter-agency and public-private collaboration.

Second, if we accept that Maine's prime tourism strategy objective is to compete more effectively for high-end tourists by offering world-class services, then the university and community college systems must offer coming generations of tourism professionals degree programs that go beyond their current limited (and shrinking) hospitality and recreation offerings. In addition, meeting the goal of helping hundreds of existing tourism businesses toward best business practices will require substantial research and extension efforts. Two existing University of Maine programs—in Parks, Recreation, and Tourism, and in Resource Economics and Policy—are already staffed by talented natural and social scientists. What they need is a clear mandate and the requisite resources to fill tourism knowledge gaps that are identified in the collaborative planning process.

In the realm of extension services, technical assistance, and off-season training to the hospitality and recreation sectors, we might learn from the University of Minnesota's highly regarded Tourism Center.[29] Short training courses for tourism's front line employees—and their supervisors—will be important to meet the goal of creating thousands more quality jobs with livable wages. The task is to improve workers' skills and attitudes in such areas as problem-solving, teamwork, multi-tasking, self-supervision, and service quality. The Maine Community College System has earned a reputation for quality employee training programs; these can be adapted to tourist services.

Third—"where the rubber hits the road," or the tourist hits the beach—Maine's communities and regions will need better data and planning models, as well as knowledge about effective policy instruments, to plan and manage local tourism growth. The State Planning Office, in partnership with University of Maine researchers and the Maine Tourism Commission's Natural Resources

Committee, is the state agency best able to develop user-friendly techniques, so communities can assess the social and environmental impacts of proposed tourism developments.

Hot-spot communities, in particular, need methods to estimate carrying capacity, and management tools to keep tourist pressures within capacity limits. One specific capacity-expanding challenge is to develop a convenient, multi-modal tourist transportation network. Maine needs to reduce severe summer traffic congestion that both turns off prospective tourists and erodes residents' quality of life and their support for the tourist economy. In addition, we need transport options to overcome the long driving times to interior destinations.

Fourth, Maine needs a sharply focused effort to *brand* the North Woods and Down East Lakes region as attractive, four season destinations, particularly for two fast-growing demographic groups—middle-age general tourists and outdoor adventure seekers. This means developing powerful images and themes for these regions, and investing much more in promoting them. The still bigger challenge is to conceptualize and invest in the clusters of tourist attractions that will make interior Maine destinations stand out from their many competitors.

The non-profit organization, RESTORE the North Woods, has articulated one model that could very well create both potent destination drivers and a potent branding message: a Maine Woods National Park.[30] Given widespread opposition to the national park concept among North Woods residents and Maine's elected officials, however, the challenge is to frame an alternative vision and strategy that will capture similar economic development without federal ownership and management. Some exciting ideas along these lines are currently under development or discussion, including:

- Weaving natural attractions together with cultural and heritage assets (plus great food and lodging) to create attractive general touring destinations. The collaboration between the Maine Highlands tourism region and university researchers to develop a Piscataquis County tourism initiative exemplifies the effort to shape tourist destinations around diverse attractions, in one of Maine's most economically distressed regions;

- Developing a Maine ecotourism accreditation program. In many parts of the world, ecotourism certification is protecting natural environments and educating tourists about nature conservation, while opening up profitable niche market opportunities for certified tourism businesses and strengthening the brand image of entire regions and nations. Maine, and particularly its interior tourist destinations, might get a powerful marketing boost by being the first Northeast state to adopt an official ecotourism accreditation system, with high performance standards and third-party evaluation of applicants. Certification advocates envision a public-private ecotourism partnership, perhaps building on the existing, three-way collaboration among the Department of Inland Fisheries and Wildlife, the Maine Island Trail Association, and the Sea Kayak Guides;

- Developing major summer events that can attract thousands of first-time visitors. Maine is very good at inducing past visitors to make repeat trips, once we get them here; but we are less effective at attracting new visitors.[31] It is an inescapable reality that rural Maine is not on the radar screen of many potential tourists, including millions who visit the coast but do not venture inland. It is problematic, of course, to propose mass tourism events as a promotional tool, if what we seek is nature-based tourism that will be environment- and community-friendly. We should, however, recognize the economic boost that Maine derives from well-planned events such as Common Ground Country Fair, the recent National Folk Music Festivals, and even the Pfish concerts. These draw thousands of first-time visitors to Unity, Bangor, and Aroostook County. In addition to the event-goers' direct spending, a significant proportion of them stay in Maine for additional days, sampling other attractions, and many return again and again. Such events also serve to advertise interior Maine by attracting national media attention; and

- Creating a recreational strategy around the vast array of old and newly acquired state lands, trust lands, and conservation easements. An outstanding example is the outdoor recreation strategy being framed for the region connecting Moosehead Lake with Baxter State Park, and including the 100-Mile Wilderness, Katahdin Iron Works, Gulf Hagas, Little Lyford Pond camps, the Debsconeags, and other outstanding natural attractions.

The Blaine House Conference recommendations and their affirmation by Governor John Baldacci lend confidence that we are beginning to "get it" in Maine:

- To understand tourism's tremendous economic importance for the state and its untapped potential for sustainable growth;

- To recognize that tourism has a downside and develop measures to mitigate it; and

- To combine our promotional efforts with farsighted planning and complementary public investments.

If all this is accomplished, we will pass on to our children and grandchildren a Maine that is both an exceptional place for them to live, and an exceptional "Vacationland" for visitors like Betty and Bill Jones from Atlanta.

*D*avid Vail is the Adams-Catlin Professor of Economics at Bowdoin College, and a participant-observer of Maine tourism since his family moved to Brunswick from East Africa in 1970. He began to study tourism's contributions to community development some six years ago, when he co-authored the Maine Center for Economic Policy's influential monograph, "Tourism and Maine's Future." Since then, his articles on the subject have appeared in the journals Ecological Economics, Current Issues in Tourism, and the Maine Policy Review. His tourism research has been featured on National Public Radio's "Living on Earth" series and, as well, on Radio Sweden's "World of Science" program. In the past year, Professor Vail served on the planning committee for the Blaine House Conference on Maine's Natural Resource-Based Industries, for which he prepared its important background paper on the challenges and opportunities confronting Maine tourism. He was recently named to the Governor's Steering Committee on Resource-based Industries and is a board member of the Maine Center for Economic Policy.

Notes

ACKNOWLEDGMENTS

1. Richard Barringer, ed., *Changing Maine: The 1989 Robert R. Masterton Lectures* (Portland, Maine: University of Southern Maine, 1990).

INTRODUCTION

1. For a fine sociologist's interpretation of this era in American history, see David M. Potter, *People of Plenty: Economic Abundance and the American Character* (Chicago: University of Chicago Press, 1954).

2. Michael Harrington, *The Other America: Poverty in the United States* (New York: Penguin Books, 1962).

3. See Robert Putnam, *Making Democracy Work: Civic Traditions in Modern Italy* (Princeton, NJ: Princeton University Press, 1993). For a more concise statement, see "The Prosperous Community: Social Capital and Public Life," *The American Prospect*, vol. 4, no. 13 (March 21, 1993).

4. See *Fishing, Farming, and Forestry: Resources for the Future* (Augusta, ME: Maine State Planning Office, 2001), p. 21; and Fulton, Pendall, Nguyen, and Harrison, *Who Sprawls Most? How Growth Patterns Differ Across the U.S.* (Washington, DC: Brookings Institution Survey Series, July 2001).

5. Aldo Leopold, *A Sand County Almanac* (New York: Oxford University Press, 1949), pp. 210 ff.

6. Rachel Carson, *Silent Spring* (Boston: Houghton Mifflin, 1962).

7. Richard Barringer, *A Maine Manifest* (Portland, ME: Tower Publishing Co., 1973).

8. For the first systematic evaluation of the Maine's legislative term limits law, especially with reference to the goals of its proponents, see M. C. Moen, K. T. Palmer, and R. Powell, *Changing Members* (Lexington, MA: Lexington Books, 2004).

9. Duane Lockard, *New England State Politics* (Princeton, NJ: Princeton University Press, 1959), p. 79.

10. In his remarks at the Muskie School inaugural on November 30, 1990, the late Edmund S. Muskie characterized the essential responsibility of democratic leadership as "to explain, to justify, to persuade." I characterize the nine essential *functions* of leadership (as opposed to management) as: challenging the status quo; inspiring through a shared vision; meaning-making through storytelling; enabling through collaboration; emboldening through risk-taking; empowering through achievement; encouraging through celebration; trust-building through modeling behavior; and communicating through listening. The seven essential *skills* of leadership identify active listening, imagination, reflection, courage, commitment, communication, and an ethical point of view.

11. For a liberal perspective on the role of leadership, see Arthur Schlesinger, Jr., *The Cycles of American History*, Ch. 14, "Democracy and Leadership" (Boston: Houghton Mifflin, 1986); and for a conservative view, see Irving Babbitt, *Democracy and Leadership* Boston: Houghton Mifflin, 1924).

12. From "The Road Not Taken," in Robert Frost, *New England Anthology of Robert Frost's Poems*, with an introduction by Louis Untermeyer (New York: Washington Square Press, 1946).

13. For the most influential and enduring statement of this last point, see John Kenneth Galbraith, *American Capitalism: The Concept of Countervailing Power* (Boston: Houghton Mifflin, 1968).

14. Garrett Hardin, "The Tragedy of the Commons," in *Science*, vol. 162, 1968.

15. World Commission on Environment and Development, *Our Common Future* (New York: Oxford University Press, 1987). Also see Herman E. Daly and John B. Cobb, Jr., *For the Common Good* (Boston: Beacon Press, 1989).

16. Charles Colgan, "Sustainable Development and Economic Development Policy: Lessons from Canada," *Economic Development Quarterly*, vol. 11, no. 2, 1997.

17. President's Council on Sustainable Development, *Sustainable Communities: Task Force Report* (Washington, DC, Fall 1997).

18. Adam Smith, *An Inquiry into the Nature and Causes of the Wealth of Nations* (London, 1776). For a contemporary interpretation and context, see Robert L. Heilbroner, *The Worldly Philosophers: The Lives, Times, and Ideas of the Great Economic Thinkers*, 6th ed. (New York: Simon & Schuster, 1992).

19. Robert Putnam, *Making Democracy Work*. See also Leonard Cottrell, "The Competent Community," in Kaplan, Wilson, and Leighton, eds., *Further Explorations in Social Science* (New York: Basic Books, 1976).

20. See Malcolm Gladwell, *The Tipping Point: How Little Things Can Make a Big Difference* (Boston: Little Brown & Co., 2000).

21. For more on the idea of a "sustainable" Maine, see Richard Barringer, ed., *Toward a Sustainable Maine: The Politics, Economics, and Ethics of Sustainability* (Portland, ME: University of Southern Maine, 1993); and *Sustainable Maine: Integrating Economy, Environment & Community—A Primer* (Portland, ME: Sustainable Maine, 1996).

ONE

Sir Arthur Conan Doyle, *The Memoirs of Sherlock Holmes* (Pleasantville, NY, and Montreal: The Reader's Digest Association, 1988).

Merritt T. Hemminway, *Maine's Disappearing Youth: Implications of a Declining Youth Population* (Augusta, ME: Maine Education Leadership Consortium, 2002).

Deidre M. Mageean, Gillian AvRuskin, and Richard Sherwood, "Whither Maine's Population?" *Maine Policy Review*, vol. 9, no. 1 (2000), pp. 28–43.

Maine Department of Human Services, *Maine Vital Statistics*. Selected Years.

Maine State Planning Office, *The Cost of Sprawl* (Augusta, ME, 1997).

Maine State Planning Office, *Economic Distress and the Changing Nature of Rural Maine* (Augusta, ME, 1979).

Maine State Planning Office, *Why Households Move* (Augusta, ME, 1999).

Maine State Planning Office, *A Golden Opportunity II: How Maine Can Enhance the Retirement Industry* (Augusta, ME, 1999).

James E. Tierney, *Diversity in Maine: An Opportunity*. http://www.umehon.maine.edu/documents/tierney.htm (April 22, 2002)

U.S. Census Bureau, *Census of Population and Housing*. 1960 and 2000.

U.S. Census Bureau, *Intercensal Estimates of the Total Resident Population of States*. 1960 to 1999.

U.S. Census Bureau, *Population Projections for States by Age, Sex, Race, and Hispanic Origin: 1995 to 2025*. 1996.

U.S. Census Bureau, *Statistical Abstract of the U.S.* Selected Years.

TWO

1. While the reference date for the chapters in this book are 1960–2000, all of the principal regional economic data series begin in 1970, so that is used as the base year for data discussions in this chapter. Trends described in this chapter generally apply to the period from 1960 on, so the discussion of trends since 1970 are reasonable approximations of trends since 1960.

2. See Kenneth Jackson, *The Crabgrass Frontier: The Suburbanization of the United States* (New York: Oxford University Press, 1985).

3. Luis Suarez-Villa, "High Technology Clustering in the Polycentric Metropolis: A View from the Los Angeles Metropolitan Region." *International Journal of Technology Management*, vol. 24, no. 7/8, 2002, pp. 818-42.

4. Joel Garreau, *Edge City: Life on the New Frontier* (New York: Doubleday, 1991).

5. See Edgar Hoover, *The Location of Economic Activity* (New York: McGraw Hill, 1948).

6. Sam B. Warner, *Streetcar Suburbs: the Process of Growth in Boston, 1870-1900* (New York: Atheneum, 1962).

7. Source: Bureau of Economic Analysis. Gross state product used as the measure of value added. Employment is wage and salary employment.

8. Joseph Wood, *The New England Village* (Baltimore: Johns Hopkins University Press, 1997).

9. See www.roadrail.com

10. This regional perspective was spurred to a significant degree by federal law which requires metropolitan-wide planning for transportation.

11. Maine State Planning Office. *Reviving Service Centers: Report of the Task Force on Service Center Communities* (Augusta, ME: Maine State Planning Office, 1998).

12. William Barnes and Larry Ledebur, *The New Regional Economies: the U.S. Common Market and the Global Economy* (Thousand Oaks, CA: Sage Publications, 1998).

THREE

1. "Poverty Level in Maine is Problem for Everyone." Lewiston *Sun-Journal* Magazine Section, July 26, 1969.

2. U.S. Census Bureau. *Poverty Thresholds for 2002*. http://www.census.gov/hhes/poverty/threshld/thresh02.html The poverty threshold, used to calculate poverty rates, is slightly different from the federal poverty guidelines, which are a simplified version of the poverty threshold issued by the U.S. Department of Health and Human Services and used for determining eligibility for certain federal programs. The guidelines are frequently referred to as the federal poverty level.

3. U.S. Census Bureau. http://www.census.gov/hhes/poverty/poverty01/povage01cht.gif

4. Barbara Ehrenreich, *Nickel and Dimed: On (Not) Getting By in America*. (New York: Metropolitan Books, 2002), p. 199.

5. *Minimum Wage History. Nominal and Real Minimum Wage*. Oregon State University. http://oregonstate.edu/instruct/anth484/minwage.html

6. Lawrence Mishel, Jared Bernstein, and Heather Boushey, *The State of Working America, 2002/2003*. (New York, NY: Cornell University Press, 2003), p. 197.

7. Ibid., p. 198.

8. Lawrence Mishel, Jared Bernstein, and John Schmitt, *The State of Working America, 1998/1999*, (New York, NY: Cornell University Press, 1999) as cited in Jared Bernstein, et al., *Pulling Apart: A State-by-State Analysis of Income Trends*. (Washington, DC: Center on Budget and Policy Priorities and Economic Policy Institute, April 2002), p. 41.

9. Economic Policy Institute. *EPI Issue Guide on the Minimum Wage*. http://www.epinet.org/Issueguides/minwage/MinimumWage_IssueGuide.pdf

10. Jared Bernstein and John Schmitt, *Making Work Pay: The Impact of the 1996-97 Minimum Wage Increase*. (Washington, DC: Economic Policy Institute, 1998).

11. Economic Policy Institute. *EPI Issue Guide on the Minimum Wage*.

12. Lisa Pohlmann and Christopher St. John, *Getting By: Maine Livable Wages in 2002* (Augusta, ME: Maine Center for Economic Policy, July 2003, p. 28).

13. Maine Department of Labor, *Maine Occupational Wages, 2003* (Augusta, ME).

14. Data sources for "Maine Livable Wage Compared to Other Benchmarks": TANF and Food Stamps, Maine Department of Human Services; Federal Poverty Threshold, U.S. Census Bureau; Minimum Wage After Taxes, Author's calculations; Livable Wage Income, Pohlmann and St. John, *Getting By*; Median Family Income, Economic Policy Institute analysis of Current Population Survey.

15. Bernstein, et al., *State of Working America, 2002/2003*, p. 159.

16. Ibid., p. 49.

17. Unpublished tabulations of Panel Study of Income Dynamics by Peter Gottschalk in Lawrence Mishel, Jared Bernstein, and John Schmitt, *The State of Working America, 2000/2001*. (New York, NY: Cornell University Press, 2001), as cited in Bernstein, et al, *Pulling Apart*, p. 36.

18. Bernstein, et al, *Pulling Apart*. Maine State Fact Sheet.

19. Ibid., p. 15.

20. Ibid., p. 67.

21. Ibid, p. 21.

22. Michael R. DeVos, *Ending Homelessness: Maine's Strategic Plan. A Report to Governor Angus King* (Office of the Governor, Senior Staff Committee to End Homelessness, March 2002), p. 16, http://www.mainehousing.org/download/homelessness.pdf

23. See Dennis Raphael, "Health Inequities in the U.S.: Prospects and Solutions, *Journal of Public Health Policy*, 2000, vol. 21, no. 4, pp. 394-427; Alvin R. Larlov and Robert F. St. Peter, eds., *The Society and Population Health Reader: Volume II: A State and Community Perspective*. (New York: New Press, 1999).

24. See Kim Lochner, et al., "State Level Income Inequality and Individual Mortality Risk: A Prospective, Multilevel Study," *American Journal of Public Health*, 2001, vol. 91, no. 3, pp. 385-99; Ichiro Kawachi, Bruce P. Kennedy, and Richard G. Wilkinson, eds., *The Society and Population Health Reader: Volume I: Income Inequality and Health*. (New York: New Press, 2000).

25. See, for example, Ichiro Kawachi, and B. P. Kennedy, *The Health of Nations: Why Inequality Is Harmful for Your Health*. (New York: New Press, 2002).

26. Susan Korenman and Jane E. Miller, "Effects of Long-Term Poverty on Physical Health of Children in the National Longitudinal Survey of Youth," in Greg Duncan and Jeanne Brooks-

Gunn, eds., *Consequences of Growing Up Poor*. (New York: Russell Sage Foundation, 1997), p. 71.

27. Judith R. Smith, Jeanne Brooks-Gunn, and Pamela K. Klebanov, "Consequences of Living in Poverty for Young Children's Cognitive and Verbal Ability and Early School Achievement," in Duncan, et al., *Consequences of Growing Up Poor*, p. 164.

28. Rand D. Conger, Katherine Jewsbury Conger, and Glen H. Elder, Jr., "Family Economic Hardship and Adolescent Adjustment: Mediating and Moderating Processes," in Duncan, et al., *Consequences of Growing Up Poor*, p. 302.

29. Jay D. Teachman, et al., "Poverty During Adolescence and Subsequent Educational Attainment," in Duncan, et al., *Consequences of Growing Up Poor*, p. 415.

30. Michael Harrington, *The Other America: Poverty in the United States*. (New York: Penguin Books, 1962).

31. Sheldon Danziger and Robert H. Haveman, eds., *Understanding Poverty*. (New York: Russell Sage Foundation. 2001), p. 1.

32. James J. Mikesell, et al., *Meeting the Housing Needs of Rural Residents: Results of the 1998 Survey of USDA's Single Family Direct Loan Housing Program*. (USDA Economic Research Service. RDRR-91), p. 1. http://www.ers.usda.gov/publications/rdrr91/rdrr91a.pdf

33. Michael Harrington, *The New American Poverty*. (New York, NY: Holt, Rinehart and Winston, 1984), p. 29.

34. Danziger and Haveman, *Understanding Poverty*, p. 4.

35. Harrington, *The New American Poverty*, p. 36.

36. Danziger and Haveman, *Understanding Poverty*, p. 3.

37. Lisa Pohlmann. *Welfare Reform: Lessons from Maine* (Augusta, ME: Maine Center for Economic Policy, March 2002), p. 19.

38. Rebekah J. Smith, Luisa S. Deprez, and Sandra S. Butler, *Parents as Scholars: Education Works* (Augusta, ME: Maine Equal Justice Partners, March 2002).

FOUR

1. David Birch, *America's Housing Needs: 1970 to 1980* (Joint Center for Urban Studies of the Massachusetts Institute of Technology and Harvard University, 1973), p. 3–4.

2. All data cited in this section is from the U.S. Census. For a good overview of historical state housing statistics, see http://www.census.gov/hhes/www/housing/census/histcensushsg.html

3. See http://factfinder.census.gov/servlet/QTTable?geo_id=04000US23&ds_name=DEC_2000_SF3_U&qr_name=DEC_2000_SF3_U_QTH7&_lang=en&_sse=on

4. *The State of Maine's Housing 2002* (Maine State Housing Authority, 2002), data available by housing market area. See http://www.mainehousing.org/reports.html

5. See http://factfinder.census.gov/servlet/DTTable?geo_id=04000US23&ds_name=DEC_2000_SF3_U&mt_name=DEC_2000_SF3_U_PCT026&_lang=en&_sse=on

6. See http://factfinder.census.gov/servlet/QTTable?geo_id=01000US&ds_name=DEC_2000_SF3_U&qr_name=DEC_2000_SF3_U_QTH14&_lang=en&_sse=on

7. *Maine Housing Trends, 1950–1980* (Maine State Housing Authority, 1984), p 4.

8. For general information on differing housing markets, see *The State of Maine's Housing, 2002*. For information on Kittery-York's ranking, see http://www.nahb.org/fileUpload_details.aspx?content ID=535

9. For a general discussion of differing housing market conditions and their public policy implications, see *The State of Maine's Housing, 1999* (Maine State Housing Authority, 1999), pp. 20–23, also at http://www.mainehousing.org/reports.html

10. "Going through the Roof," *The Economist*, May 28, 2003, also at http://www.economist.com/displaystory.cfm?story_id=1057057

11. Federal Reserve Bank of Boston, *New England Economic Indicators*, November 2003, p. 17; also at http://www.bos.frb.org/economic/neei/current/neei.pdf

12. Community Current and MLRD, *City of Gardiner Housing Assessment*, November, 2002, p. 22. http://www.gardinermaine.com/Public_Documents/GardinerME_EcDev/housinginput

13. See http://www.census.gov/prod/2003pubs/censr-12.pdf

14. A fuller treatment of the issue of housing and economic development can be found in: Frank O'Hara, *Houses, Jobs and Maine People: 2001* (Maine State Housing Authority, 2001), at http://www.mainehousing.org/reports.html

15. For a news article describing the session, see "Residents Share Vision of Town's Future," *York County Coast Star*, April 25, 2002, also at http://www.seacoastonline.com/2002news/yorkstar/ys4_25c.htm

16. See *The Cost of Sprawl*, Maine State Planning Office 1997, especially p. 12. On the web at http://www.state.me.us/spo/landuse/docs/CostofSprawl.pdf

17. For a discussion of how this can take place, see *The Community Visioning Handbook*, Maine State Planning Office, 2003, at http://www.state.me.us/spo/landuse/docs/visioning/visioning.pdf

18 . Harold Clifford, *Maine and Her People* (Bond Wheelwright Company, 1976), pp. 59–60.

19. The Chisholm story is related in an out-of-print company publication *The Oxford Story: A History of the Oxford Paper Company, 1847–1958* (Oxford Paper Company, 1958).

20. From the Rumford Bicentennial website, http://www.geocities.com/Heartland/Garden/9556/bicentennial3.html

FIVE

1. Information available online at the website of Maine's Bureau of Health, www.state.me.us/dhboh/ophep/ophepdocuments.htm

2. G. Grog, *From Asylum to Community*, (Princeton, NJ: Princeton University Press, 1991), pp. 157–80.

3. *Augusta Mental Health Institute History*, available online at www.maine.gov/bds/amh/history/html .

4. The AMHI Consent Decree was signed in 1990 and committed the State of Maine to meet specified conditions by 1995. In 1994, 1996 and 2002, the court found the state to be in violation of various provisions of the decree. For the most recent court order, see *Paul Bates, et al. v. Lynn Duby, et al.*, available online at www.courts.state.me.us/opinions/superior/2003.htm

5. For a thorough discussion of recent mental health policy in Maine, see D. Rooks, *Darkness to Dawn: Maine's Mental Health System* (Maine Center for Economic Policy). Accessible online at www.mecep.org/affhealthcare/MHSystemReport.htm

6. Personal Communication, Steve Michaud, executive director, Maine Hospital Association.

7. P. Starr, *The Social Transformation of American Medicine* (New York: Basic Books, 1982), pp. 343–47.

8. *Health, United States, 2003, With Chartbook on Trends in the Health of Americans*, (Hyattsville, MD, National Center for Health Statistics, Centers for Disease Control and Prevention, U.S. Department of Health and Human Services). Available online at www.cdc.gov/nchs/hus.htm

9. Quoted in J. Morone, *The Democratic Wish* (New York: Basic Books, 1990), p. 262.

10. This language is reminiscent of the language in the new Medicare Drug Benefit Act which forbids the government from negotiating prices with the pharmaceutical industry.

11. Statistics for 1960 from Henry J. Aaron, *Serious and Unstable Condition* (Washington, DC: Brookings Institute, 1991), p. 39. Per capita spending is presented in 1990 dollars. Statistics for 2003 from Katharine R. Levit, Director, National Health Statistics Group, Center for Medicare and Medicaid Services, U.S. Department of Human Services, news release (2004).

12. The hospital payment system, known as the DRG system, is far more complex than indicated in this summary description. Payment rates take into account a patient's secondary conditions that may complicate treatment, for example, and some types of hospitalizations are exempt from the system because costs are too variable to establish a rational, "average" costs. For a good discussion of the DRG system and its strengths and weaknesses, see R. Ellis, "Hospital payment in the United States: An overview and discussion of current policy issues, a paper prepared for Colloque International, June, 2001. Available online at http://econ.bu.edu/Ellis/Papers/Ellishosppayment.pdf

13. Under the Bush administration the name of the HCFA was changed to the Center for Medicare and Medical Services (CMS).

14. Maine Department of Human Services, *Annual Medicaid Report, 2003*, (Augusta, ME, 2004).

15. Aaron, *Serious and Unstable Condition*, p. 39.

16. Maine's program came under the rubric of the National Health Planning Act of 1974, a federal law that required the formation of local health systems agencies and state planning boards and that mandated the establishment of Certificate of Need programs.

17. The slower growth rate in regulatory states was apparent up to the time that Medicare instituted a prospective payment system for hospitals at which point, hospital increases in all state dropped. C. J. Schramm, S. C. Renn, and B. Biles. "New Perspectives on State Rate Setting," *Health Affairs*, vol. 5, no. 3, Fall 1986.

18. E. Ziller and B. Kilbreth. *Uninsured in Maine: A Household Survey* (Portland, ME: Institute for Health Policy, Muskie School of Public Service, University of Southern Maine, 2003).

19. R. D. Deprez, B. D. Curran, and M. A. Spindler. *A Study of Maine's Catastrophic Illness Program, 1975–1980* (Augusta, ME: Medical Care Development, Inc., 1983).

20. A. Martin, L. Whittle, K. Levit, et al. "Health Care Spending During 1991–1998: A Fifty-State Review," *Health Affairs* (July/August 2002), pp. 112–26.

21. State Health Facts Online, Henry J. Kaiser Family Foundation, www.statehealthfacts.kff .org.htm

22. Information reported on the website of Maine's Bureau of Insurance. www.state.me.us/pfr/ ins/ins_index.htm

23. See, *The Cost of Health Care In Maine: Report of the Year 2000 Blue Ribbon Commission on Health Care*, available from the Maine Development Foundation, Augusta, ME.

24. Information on the Dirigo Plan is available on the governor of Maine's website at www.state.me.us/governor/baldacci/healthpolicy/launching_dirigo_health/index.html

Six

1. National Education Goals Panel, *The National Education Goals Report: Building a Nation of Learners*, 1999 (Washington, DC: US Government Printing Office, 1999).

2. Children's Rights Council, *Fifth Annual Ranking of Best State to Raise a Child* (Washington, DC, July 19990.

3. *State Rankings 2002* (Washington, DC: Morgan Quitno Corporation, 2002).

4. R. S. Barth, *School Reorganization and Public Education in the State of Maine* (Cambridge, MA: Harvard Graduate School of Education, August 1967).

5. *Report Card on American Education: A State-by-State Analysis 1976-2001* (Washington, DC: American Legislature Exchange Council, 2002).

6. Patrick Colwell, "School Funding and Property Tax Relief," *Bangor Daily News*, September 20, 2003.

7. *Constitution of the State of Maine* (1820). Article VIII, Part 1, Section 1.

8. Data provided by the Maine Department of Education, Augusta, Maine.

9. *School Finances and Needs* (Augusta, ME: Maine Legislative Research Committee, January 1957, no. 98-2).

10. M. Shibles, *Portland Press Herald*, January 7, 1958.

11. *School Finances and Needs*, p.11.

12. R. S. Barth, *School Reorganization*, p. 29.

13. R. S. Barth, *School Reorganization*.

14. R. S. Barth, *School Reorganization*.

15. National Commission on Excellence in Education, *A Nation at Risk: The Imperative for Educational Reform* (Washington, DC: U.S. Department of Education, 1983).

16. J. Guthrie and L. Pierce, "The International Economy and National Education Reform: A Comparison of Education Reforms in the United States and Great Britain. *Oxford Review of Education*, 1990, vol. 16, no. 2, pp. 179–205.

17. B. Furtrell. "Mission Not Accomplished: Education Reform in Retrospect." *Phi Delta Kappan*, 1989, vol. 71, no. 1, pp. 8–14.

18. Data from the *Maine Education Assessment* (Augusta, ME: Maine Department of Education).

19. *Maine Common Core of Learning* (Augusta, ME: Maine Department of Education, 1990), p. 32.

20. *State of Maine Learning Results* (Augusta, ME: Maine Department of Education, July 1997).

21. *Task Force to Review the Status of Implementation of the System of Learning Results* (Orono, ME: Maine Education Policy Research Institute, University of Maine Office, March 2003).

22. R. S. Barth, *School Reorganization*.

23. *Report Card on American Education*.

24. Data provided by the Maine Department of Education.

25. R. S. Barth, *School Reorganization*.

26. P. B. Gravelle and D. L. Silvernail, *The Condition of K–12 Public Education in Maine, 2004* (Gorham, ME: Maine Education Policy Research Institute, University of Southern Maine Office, 2004).

27. "Quality Counts 2003." *Education Week*, January 2003.

28. "National Assessment of Educational Progress," *The Nation's Report Card* (Washington, DC: National Center for Education Statistics, 2003).

29. *Third International Mathematics and Science Study*. US TIMSS National Research Center (East Lansing, MI: Michigan State University, 1999).

30. "Chance for College by Age 19 by State in 2000." *Postsecondary Education Opportunity*, September 2002, No. 123.

31. Gravelle and Silvernail, *Condition of K–12*.

32. National Center for Public Policy and Higher Education, *Measuring Up 2002: The State-by-State Report Card for Higher Education* (San Jose, CA, November 2002).

33. D. L. Silvernail and J. Sloan, *Growth in Total State and Local Expenditures for Education in Maine* (Gorham, ME: Maine Education Policy Research Center, University of Southern Maine Office, February 2003).

34. B. Malen, "Tightening the Grip? The Impact of State Activism on Local School Systems." *Educational Policy*, May 2003, vol. 17, no. 2, pp. 195–216.

35. *Constitution of the State of Maine*.

36. *The Nation's Report Card* (2003).

37. Data from the *Maine Education Assessment*, Maine Department of Education.

38. D. L. Silvernail and W. L. Bonney, "Essential Programs and Services: The Basics for a New Approach for Funding Maine's Public Schools." *Maine Policy Review*, Winter 2001.

39. "Chance for College by Age 19 by State in 2000."

40. Press release by U.S. Representative Tom Allen (January 8, 2004). United States Congress, House of Representatives.

41. W. J. Mathis, "No Child Left Behind: Costs and Benefits." *Phi Delta Kappan*, May 2003, vol. 84, no. 9, pp. 679–86.

42. *Task Force on Maine's Learning Technology Endowment* (Augusta, ME: Maine Legislature, Office of Policy and Local Analysis, 2001).

43. D. L. Silvernail and D. M. Lane, *The Impact of Maine's One-to-One Laptop Program on Middle School Teachers and Students* (Gorham, ME: Maine Educational Policy Research Institute, University of Southern Maine, February 2004).

44. D. A. Verstegen, "Judicial Analysis During the New Wave of School Finance Litigation: The New Adequacy in Education." *Journal of Education Finance*, Summer 1998, vol. 24, no. 1, pp. 1–68.

45. *Equity and Adequacy for Funding to Improve Learning for All Children* (Augusta, ME: Maine State Board of Education, January 1995).

46. R. Sherwood, *Projected Public School Enrollments* (Augusta, ME: Maine State Planning Office, 2001).

47. *Report of the School Administrative Unit Task Force* (Augusta, ME: Maine State Board of Education, December 2003).

48. *Final Report of Task Force on Increasing Efficiency and Equity in the Use of K-12 Education Resources* (Augusta, ME: The Governor of Maine Office, January 2004).

Seven

1. "America's Best Colleges, 2004," *U.S. News & World Report* (Washington, 2004), p. 186.

2. Frances Lindemann, "Higher Education for All Maine People," *Report of the Maine Center for Economic Policy* (Augusta, ME, 2002), available at www. mecep.org/higheredforall/.

3. Ibid., p. 3.

4. *Measuring Up 2002, The State-by-State Report Card for Higher Education*, (San Jose, CA: The National Center for Public Policy and Higher Education, 2002), available at http://measuringup.highereducation.org/2002/stateprofilenet.

5. "Annual Directory of New England Colleges and Universities, 2004," *Connections: The Journal of the New England Board of Higher Education* (Boston, 2004), vol. 18, no. 3, p. 55.

6. Terrence J. MacTaggart and James R. Mingle, *Pursuing The Public's Agenda: Trustees in Partnership with State Leaders*, (Washington: The Association of Governing Boards of Colleges and Universities, 2002), pp. 1–9.

7. "State Investment Effort in Higher Education, FY1962 to FY2003," *Postsecondary Education Opportunity: The Environmental Scanning Research Letter of Opportunity for Postsecondary Education* (Dec. 2002), vol. 126, p. 4.

8. James D. Libby, *Super U: The History and Politics of the University of Maine System*, (Rockport, ME: Picton Press, 2002).

9. Peter Carlisle, et al., "The University of Maine System: A Time of a Change [*sic*]," unpublished manuscript, cited in Libby, *Super U*, p. 126.

10. Roger Fisher, William Fry, and Bruce Patton, *Getting to Yes: Negotiating Agreement Without Giving In*, 2nd ed., (New York: Penguin Books, 1991).

11. Robert O. Berdahl and Terrence J. MacTaggart, *Charter Colleges: Balancing Freedom and Accountability* (Boston: Pioneer Institute, 2000), p. 13.

12. National Center for Higher Education Management Systems, *Report to the South Carolina Board of Higher Education*, December 8, 2003.

13. David L. Silvernail, "Increasing Postsecondary Enrollments in Maine," *Maine Policy Review*, vol. 6 (1997).

14. Philip Trostel, "Ending Maine's Brain Drain," *The Bangor Daily News*, July 16, 2003, p. A9.

15. Lindemann, "Higher Education," p. 1.

16. MacTaggart and Mingle, *Pursuing the Public's Agenda*, p. 10.

17. Peter F. Drucker, *Post Capitalist Society* (New York: Harper Collins, 1993), pp. 1–16. See also Philip Trostel, "The Long-Term Effects of Declining State Support for Higher Education: Are States Shooting Themselves in the Foot?" a paper and presentation at Wisconsin Center for the Advancement of Postsecondary Education, Madison, WI (October 15, 2003).

18. Thomas D. Duchesneau and David Wihry, "Financing Public Higher Education in Maine: Patterns and Trends," *Maine Choices 1997: A Preview of State Budget Issues* (Augusta, ME: Maine Center for Economic Policy, 1997).

19. Terrence J. MacTaggart, *Restructuring Higher Education: What Works and What Doesn't in Reorganizing Governing Systems* (San Francisco: Jossey-Bass, 1996), pp. 230–36.

20. "Measuring Up, 2002."

EIGHT

1. As an aside, I would note that the original American income tax was invented in 1861 by a New Hampshire Republican, Salmon P. Chase, who helped found the Republican Party and served as treasury secretary under President Abraham Lincoln. In 1994 Mr. Chase's great-great-grandson, Christopher St. John, founded the Maine Center for Economic Policy, which has had a major impact on tax policy here in Maine.

Compendium of State Fiscal Information, from the Office of Fiscal and Program Review (287-1635), summarizes the recent history of all major sources of operating revenue and expenditures plus debt obligations and per capita comparisons with other states.

The first volumes of the *Governor's Budgets* submitted in January of 2001 and 2003 contain helpful pie graphs and analytical material on budget issues.

Any recent Maine General Obligation Bond, available from the state treasurer (287-2771), contains a large quantity of fiscal information about the state, much of it in narrative and graphic form addressed to potential investors.

Reports of the Maine State Revenue Forecasting Committee, available from the State Planning Office (287-3261), outline four-year projections for revenues and the economic assumptions upon which they are based.

Summary of Major State Funding Disbursed to Municipalities and Counties, from the Office of Fiscal and Program Review (287-1635), summarizes the recent history of all sources of state support flowing to Maine's municipalities.

Municipal Valuation Return Statistical Summary, published by the Property Tax Division of Maine Revenue Services (287-2011), contains a complete profile of the property tax for every town plus aggregate figures by county and state.

Commissioner's Recommended Funding Level, published each December by the Maine Department of Education (624-6790), contains a complete outline and recent history of the K-12 school funding formula which accounts for 30 percent of the General Fund budget.

Medicaid in Maine, an annual report from the Bureau of Medical Services of DHS (287-2674), the state's largest health insurer, outlines recent trends in Medicaid spending broken down into components. The state's share of Medicaid accounts for one-sixth of the General Fund budget and is leveraged with a two-to-one match from the federal government.

Maine State Retirement System Annual Report outlines the recent history of all state, teacher and local pension systems administered by MSRS (287-3461) including investment returns on $7 billion of assets. State and teacher pensions cost about 10 percent of the General Fund. The state's unfunded liability is $1.9 billion, nearly an entire year's General Fund tax revenue.

Maine Tax Incidence Studies, printed in December of 2000 and 2002 by the Research Division of Maine Revenue Services (287-6965), explains where state and local tax revenues come from and who pays them. It includes comparative data from other states. Economist Michael Allen is the bureau's chief analyst.

A Golden Opportunity II, published by the Maine State Planning Office (287-3261) in December 1999, outlines how Maine can enhance the retirement industry. A valuable part of the document is Appendix C, a report entitled *Taxes and Retirement in the State of Maine* prepared for the Libra Foundation by the Kennedy School. This study contains an insightful general profile of Maine's state and local tax structure and addresses how Maine's wealthy retirees interface with high taxes and cold winters.

The Maine Policy Review, published three times a year by the Margaret Chase Smith Center for Public Policy at the University of Maine, contains a wealthy analytical history of policy issues relevant to our work as Maine legislators. Past articles are available in the Law Library and can be downloaded from www.umaine.edu/mcsc/mpr.htm

Maine Center for Economic Policy (622-7381) and the Maine Municipal Association (623-8428) are constantly publishing fresh and valuable analytical work of use to Maine legislators. Of recent note is Frank O'Hara's *Maine Revenue Primer*, published by MECEP in April of 2003, a lucid explication of Maine's revenue sources.

Dollars and Sense by Josephine LaPlante and Robert Devlin published by the Muskie Institute in 1993 is an encyclopedic analysis of how Maine raised and spent revenue during the decade of the 1980s and what went wrong in 1991. The authors' recommendations are still relevant and largely unfulfilled.

Health Affairs, published six times a year with supplements on the web, is the nation's preeminent clearinghouse for policy studies on health care. Recent articles on cost trends include: "Increased Spending on Health Care: How Much Can the United States Afford?" by Chernew, Hirth and Cutler in vol. 22, no. 4 (July/August 2003); "Health Spending Projections for 2002-2012" by Heffler, Smith, Keehan, Clemens, Won & Zezza in the Web Exclusive Series (published February 7, 2003); and "Is Technological Change in Medicine Worth It?" by Cutler and McClellan in vol. 20, no. 5 (September/October 2001).

NINE

1. Lockard, Duane, *New England State Politics* (Princeton, NJ: Princeton University Press, 1959), p. 79.

2. These ideas are adapted from Herbert Kaufman, *Politics and Policies in State and Local Government* (Englewood Cliffs, NJ: Prentice-Hall, 1963).

3. For changes in Maine's courts, see Harriet P. Henry, *The Maine District Court: A Quarter Century of Progress* (Tower Publishing Co., 1987) and *Administrative Unification of Maine State Courts* (Boston, MA: National Center for State Courts, 1975).

4. Kenneth T. Palmer, "The Maine Supreme Judicial Court and the U.S. Supreme Court: Two Decades of Review," *Maine Bar Journal*, vol. 15, no. 2 (April 2000), pp. 86–90.

5. For changes in Maine's executive departments, see *Organization and Administration of the Government of the State of Maine* (Chicago, IL: Public Administration Service, 1956) and *Toward a More Responsive and Effective State Government: A Report by the Governor's Task Force on Government Reorganization* (Augusta, ME: Office of the Governor, 1969).

6. Phyllis Austin, "Who Runs Maine?" *Maine Times*, July 22, 1988, p. 8.

7. Matthew C. Moen and Kenneth T. Palmer, "Maine: The Cutting Edge of Term Limits," in *The Test of Time: Coping with Legislative Term Limits*, edited by Rick Farmer, John David Rausch, Jr., and John C. Green (Lanham, MD: Lexington Books, 2002), pp. 47–59.

8. G. Thomas Taylor and Kenneth T. Palmer, "Maine" in *Home Rule in America: A Fifty-State Handbook*, edited by Dale Krane, Platon N. Rigor, and Melvin B. Hill, Jr. (Washington, DC: CQ Press, 2001), pp. 183–90.

9. Geoffrey Herman, "Municipal Charters: A Comparative Analysis of 75 Maine Charters." *Maine Townsman*, August 1992, pp. 5–15.

10. Kenneth T. Palmer, G. Thomas Taylor, and Marcus LiBrizzi, *Maine Politics and Government* (Lincoln, NE: University of Nebraska Press, 1992), ch. 13

11. Statistics are drawn from *The Book of the States* (Lexington, Kentucky: Council of State Governments, 1962–63 and 2003) .

12. See Maine State Planning Office, *The Cost of Sprawl* (Augusta, ME: Maine State Planning Office, 1997).

13. MMA's State and Federal Relations Staff, "Regionalization: The Rhetoric vs. The Reality," *Maine Townsman* (November 2002), pp. 12–19.

14. John Kincaid, "Is Fiscal Federalism Fizzling," in *The Book of the States, 2003* (Lexington, KY: Council of State Governments, 2003), pp. 26–31.

TEN

1. Rabbi Alexander Feinsilver, ed., 1980. *The Talmud for Today* (New York: St. Martin's Press, 1980), p. 124.

2. Cynthia M. Duncan, *Worlds Apart: Why Poverty Persists in America* (New Haven, CT: Yale University Press, 2000), p. 184.

3. Brian O'Connell. 1999. *Civil Society: The Underpinnings of American Democracy* (Hanover, NH: University Press of New England and Tufts University).

4. Robert D. Putnam, Robert Leonardi, and Raffaella Y. Nanetti, *Making Democracy Work: Civic Traditions in Modern Italy* (Princeton, NJ: Princeton University Press, 1994).

5. Robert D. Putnam, *Bowling Alone: The Collapse and Revival of American Community* (New York: Simon and Schuster, 2001).

6. James Coleman, *Foundations of Social Theory* (Cambridge, MA: Belknap Press of Harvard University, 1998).

7. Alejandro Portes, "Social Capital: Its Origins and Applications in Modern Society," in Eric J. Lesser, ed., *Knowledge and Social Capital: Foundations and Applications* (Woburn, MA: Butterworth-Heinemann, 1998), pp. 43–67.

8. Nicholas Leeman, "Kicking in Groups," *Atlantic Monthly* (1966), vol. 227, no. 4, pp. 22–26.

9. Theda Skocpol, "Warren Durgin's Gravestone and the Renewal of American Civic Democracy," *Maine Policy Review* (2000), vol. 11, no. 2, pp. 8–11; Theda Skocpol, *Diminished Democracy: From Membership to Management in American Civic Life* (Norman, OK: University of Oklahoma Press, 2003).

10. Skocpol, *Diminished Democracy*, p. 5.

11. Dietland Stolle and Thomas Rochon, "Are All Associations Alike? Member Diversity, Associational Type, and the Creation of Social Capital," *American Behavioral Scientist* (1998), vol. 42, no. 1, pp. 47–65; Carla M. Eastis, "Organizational Diversity and the Production of Social Capital: One of These Groups is Not Like the Other," *American Behavioral Scientist* (1998), vol. 42, no. 1, pp. 66–77.

12. Debra C. Minkoff, "Producing Social Capital: National Movements and Civil Society," *American Behavioral Scientist* (1997) vol. 40, pp. 606–07.

13. Francesca Polletta, *Freedom is an Endless Meeting: Democracy in American Social Movemeents* (Chicago: University of Chicago Press, 2002).

14. G. Ross Stephens and Nelson Wikstrom, "'Republics in Miniature' and Other Toy Governments." Paper presented at the Annual Meetings of the American Political Science Association, Philadelphia, August 29, 2003.

15. Quoted in John Hale, "Property Tax Load Becoming Heavier, Cuts in Federal, State Aid Adding to Local Burden," *Bangor Daily News*, August 21, 2003.

16. Quoted in Wayne Brown, "Crystal Votes to Continue Process to De-Organize Town," *Bangor Daily News*, January 19, 1995.

17. Quoted in Katherine Cassidy, "Region's Tiniest Town De-Organizes: Centerville Residents Grew Tired of Responsibilities of Self-Government," *Bangor Daily News*, November 6, 2003.

18. Quoted in Amy Zimet, "No More Town, Madrid Lost Much. Now It Loses Its Being," *Portland Press Herald*, November 21, 1999.

19. Robert D. Putnam and Lewis M. Feldstein, *Better Together: Restoring the American Community* (New York: Simon and Schuster, 2003).

20. Richard D. Brown, *The Strength of a People: The Idea of an Informed Citizenry in America, 1650–1879* (Chapel Hill, NC: University of North Carolina Press, 1996), p. xiii.

21. *Executive Summary*, Maine State Department of Education, February, 2001.

22. Quoted in Abba Eban, *Heritage: Civilization and the Jews* (New York: Summit Books, 1984), p. 82.

ELEVEN

1. Lewis Mumford, *The City in History* (New York: Harcourt Brace Jovanovich, 1961).

2. Robert Fishman, *Urban Utopias in the Twentieth Century* (Cambridge, MA: The MIT Press, 1988), p. 125, quoting Wright.

3. Garrett Hardin, *Living within Limits: Ecology, Economics, and Population Taboos* (Oxford: Oxford University Press, 2000), pp. 122–23.

4. Fishman, Robert, *Bourgeois Utopias: the Rise and Fall of Suburbia* (New York: Basic Books, Inc, 1987).

5. Kenneth Jackson, *Crabgrass Frontier: The Suburbanization of the United States* (New York: Oxford University Press, 1985).

6. Williams, Raymond, *The Country and the City* (London: Chatto & Windus, 1973), p. 124.

7. Ian McHarg, *Design with Nature* (Garden City, NY: The Natural History Press, 1969), p. 19.

8. These calculations were derived from Lloyd C. Irland, *Maine's Forest Area, 1600-1995: Review of Available Estimates* (Maine Agricultural and Forest Experiment Station, University of Maine, Miscellaneous Publication 736, February 1998); Andrew J. Plantinga, Thomas Mauldin, and Ralph J. Alig, *Land Use in Maine: Determinants of Past Trends and Projections of Future Change* (United States Department of Agriculture Forest Service, Pacific Northwest Research Station, Research Paper PNW-RP-511, June 1999); United States Census, 2000, Standard File 1, Table GCT-PH1, Population, Housing Units, Area, and Density; "Maine Vision Plan: Natural Resources Summary," found at http://www.umass.edu/greenway/Me/Vision/ME-VP-nat-sum.html; and Maine Department of Environmental Protection, *Maine's Wetlands: Their Functions and Values*, September 1996.

9. Plantinga, et al., *Land Use in Maine*.

10. Ibid.

11. Maine Department of Transportation, *Keeping Maine Moving: Long-Range Transportation Improvement Plan, 2003-2025*, November 2003, p. 16.

12. Author's calculations based on land area and housing unit data from the United States Census. Based on observation of the form and functions of Maine's municipalities, the threshold between "rural" and "emerging suburb" appears to be approximately 1 dwelling unit per 20 gross acres of land in the municipality; and between "emerging suburb" and "mature suburb," it appears to be approximately 1 dwelling unit per 10 gross acres of land. Urban communities in Maine tend to have at least 1 dwelling unit per 3 gross acres. Gross acres include all land, whether devoted to residential uses, commercial and industrial uses, transportation systems, civic uses, parks and open spaces, utility corridors, farms and woodlots, or other activities. Of course, as discussed earlier, suburban and urban are not simply different in degree—as represented by residential densities—but in kind.

13. See, for example, Ian McHarg, *Design with Nature* (Garden City, NY: The Natural History Press, 1969), pp 193–94, in which a leading ecologist and planner accepted and applied to urban environments research on "crowding" that was discredited by virtually all subsequent research. See Irwin Altman, *The Environment and Social Behavior: Privacy, Personal Space, Territory, and Crowding* (Monterey, CA: Brooks/Cole Publishing Co., 1975); Jonathan L. Freedman,, *Crowding and Behavior* (New York: The Viking Press, 1975); Andrew Baum and Paul B. Paulus, "Crowding," in *Handbook of Environmental Psychology* (New York: John Wiley & Sons, 1987); Frans B. M. De Waal, Filippo Aureli, and Peter F. Judge,, "Coping with Crowding," *Scientific American*, May 2000, pp. 77–81.

14. Eugenie Moore, "Wildwood Park, Cumberland Foreside, Maine" (unpublished, Fall 2002).

15. Title 30-A, Maine Revised Statutes Annotated, Section 4314.

16. Maine Tomorrow, *A Strategic Plan for Reviving Maine's Service Centers*, (Hallowell, ME: March 2003).

17. Evan Richert, *Markets for Traditional Neighborhoods* (Augusta, ME: Maine: State Planning Office, 1999).

18. Anton Clarence Nelessen, *Vision for a New American Dream* (Chicago: American Planning Association, 1994), p. 139.

19. L.D. 1629, 121st Legislature of the State of Maine, 2003.

20. Moses Greenleaf, *Survey of the State of Maine*, reprint edition of 1829 text edition (Augusta, Maine: Maine State Museum, 1970).

TWELVE

1. William David Berry, "A Timeline of Maine Arts and Culture," Maine PBS's *Home: The Story of Maine*.

2. Edgar Allen Beem, *Maine Art Now* (Gardiner, ME: The Dog Ear Press, 1990), p. xv.

3. Christine Vincent, excerpt from email to Alden Wilson, January 26, 2004.

4. *New England's Creative Economy, The Non Profit Sector, 2000*, New England Foundation for the Arts, May, 2003.

5. Edward Dickey, "History of the Federal-State-Regional Arts Partnership, A Selective Chronology," unpublished, December 2003.

6. *The New Century Community Program, Building a Cultural Policy for Maine*, Cultural Affairs Council, September 2002, p 1.

7. Christine Dwyer and Susan Frankel, *Policy Partners: Making the Case for State Investment in Culture*, Pew Charitable Trusts, p. 10.

8. *The Impact of Arts Education on Workforce Preparation*, NGA Center for Best Practices, May 1, 2001, p. 1.

9. Maine Philanthropy Center, *2003 Generosity Index*.

10. Richard Florida. *The Rise of the Creative Class* (New York: Basic Books, 2002), p. x.

11. *The Creative Economy Initiative: The Role of the Arts and Culture in New England's Economy*, New England Council, June 2000.

12. http://www.nefa.org/

13. *A Blaine House Conference: Maine's Creative Economy*, Maine Arts Commission, January 2004.

14. http://www.nefa.org/

15. John Rohman, Blaine House Conference Steering Committee Meeting, 2003.

16. Darcy Rollins, email correspondence, January 30, 2004.

THIRTEEN

1. Richard Barringer, ed., *Changing Maine* (Portland, ME: University of Southern Maine, 1990), p. 2.

2. R. Putnam, *Bowling Alone: Collapse and Revival of the American Community* (New York: Simon and Schuster, 2000).

3. L. M. Salamon and H. K. Anheier, *The Emerging Nonprofit Sector: Vol. 1*. The Johns Hopkins Nonprofit Sector Series (Manchester: Manchester University Press, 1996), p. 2. L. M. Salamon, "The Rise of the Nonprofit Sector," *Foreign Affairs* (1994) vol. 74, no. 3, pp. 94–116.

4. A. Anstead, "Saving an Opera House for a Hamlet in Maine," *New York Times*, August 20, 2003.

5. K. Lockridge. "New England's Generation: The Great Migration and the Formation of Society and Culture," *Journal of Social History*. (1993) Vol. 26, No. 3, pp. 671–77.

6. _____. "Cheese Curls and Potatoes: Poor Whites in Maine," *The Economist* (US). (1992) vol. 325, no. 27.

7. L. M. Salamon and S. L. Geller. "Maine Nonprofit Employment," *Nonprofit Employment Bulletin Number 12*. (2003) The John Hopkins Nonprofit Employment Data Project. (Baltimore: Johns Hopkins Center for Civil Society Studies, Johns Hopkins University), http:www.jhu.edu/ccss.

8. D. Freeman. *The Maine Charitable Nonprofit Sector, 2000 Report*. The Maine Association of Nonprofits and the Unity Foundation in collaboration with the Urban Institute's National Center for Charitable Statistics and the National Council of Nonprofit Associations.

9. _____. *Poverty in Maine* Executive Summary, 2003. Margaret Chase Smith Center for Public Policy, University of Maine. http:www.umaine.edu/mcsc/Research/HeaSocPol/Poverty/Exec_Sum.htm

10. _____. *Maine Information*, 2001. Forum of Regional Association of Grantmakers. Connecticut Council for Philanthropy.

11. _____. *Maine Development Foundation 2001 Survey of Citizens and Businesses*. "Survey results do not reflect the views of the Maine Development Foundation." http://www.mdf.org

12. A. Dighe, "Demographic and Technological Imperatives." In L. M. Salamon (Ed.), *The State of Nonprofit America* (Washington, DC: The Brookings Institution Press, 2002).

13. Anstead, "Saving an Opera House."

FOURTEEN

1. I wish to thank many people whose conversations and suggestions helped to make this a stronger essay than it otherwise would have been. First, members of the writers' group at the University of Maine, whose suggestions about writing and content were extraordinarily helpful. The group's commitment to improving women's lives helped me to clarify my thinking about the present as well as the past. They are: Mazie Hough, Sue Estler, Amy Fried, Kristin Langellier, Pauleena MacDougal, and Elizabeth Allan. Several women shared information about organizations, including Sharon Barker, Ruth Lockhart, and Sarah Standiford. Finally, I wish to thank Harriet Henry, Deedee Schwartz, and Ann Schonberger for their fine examples of women's leadership.

2. Institute for Women's Policy Research, *The Status of Women in Maine: Politics, Economics, Health, Demographics* (Portland, ME: Women's Development Institute and the Young Women's Christian Association of Greater Portland, 1996), p. 11.

3. Stephanie Seguino, *Living on the Edge: Women Working and Providing for Families in the Maine Economy, 1979–1993* (Orono, ME: Margaret Chase Smith Center for Public Policy, 1995), p. x.

4. Institute for Women's Policy Research, *Status of Women in Maine*, p. 34.

SIXTEEN

1. I have tried to capture a good deal of the flavor and consequences of these changing campaign patterns in some detail in *This Splendid Game: Maine Politics from 1940 to 2002*. (Washington: Lexington Books, 2003). See also, L. Sandy Maisel and Elizabeth Ivry, "If You Don't Like Our Politics, Wait a Minute: Party Politics in Maine at the Century's End," in Jerome M. Mileur, ed., *Parties and Politics in The New England States* (Amherst: Polity Publications, 1997), pp.15–35, as well as the very important Kenneth T. Palmer, G. Thomas Taylor, and Marcus A. Librizzi, *Maine Politics and Government* (Lincoln, NE: University of Nebraska Press, 1992). Richard Condon and William Barry also cover this general topic in their "The Tides of Change, 1967–1988," in William W. Judd, Edwin A. Churchill and Joel W. Eastman (eds.), *Maine: The Pine Tree State from Prehistory to the Present* (Orono: University of Maine Press,1995), pp. 554 –71.

2. Over the last decade, there has been something of a boom in scholarly writing about the nation's first woman senator elected in her own right. See especially Janann Sherman, *No Place for a Woman: A Life of Margaret Chase Smith* (New Brunswick: Rutgers University Press, 2000); Patricia Ward Wallace, *Politics of Conscience: A Biography of Margaret Chase Smith* (Westport: Praeger,1995); and Patricia L. Schmidt, *Margaret Chase Smith: Beyond Convention* (Orono: University of Maine Press, 1996). For reasons not clear to this author, there has not been a comparable level of interest in Ed Muskie. In fact, not only has there been no major work since the 1970s when Muskie was in the national spotlight and the subject of David Nevin's *Muskie of Maine* (New York: Random House, 1972) and Theo Lippman and Donald Hansen's *Muskie* (New York: W.W. Norton, 1974). Moreover, Chris Beam at the Muskie Archives at Bates College indicates that there is no biography under way using those documents. This seems a pity.

3. A special thanks to those scholars and activists who have commented on drafts of this chapter. These include Dick Morgan, Jean Yarborough, Joel Moser, Maria Fuentes, Ken Palmer, Erik Dodds Potholm, Sandra Quinlan Potholm, and Richard Barringer, friends all and most helpful critics.

4. See, for example, Jim Brunelle, "TV Stations Managers Shouldn't Be Censoring Political Speech," *Portland Press Herald*, October 3, 2003, p. 17A. I have also explored this outrage in "A Clear and Present Danger," in *The Delights of Democracy* (New York: Cooper Square Press, 2002), pp. 49–54.

SEVENTEEN

1. Bowdoin College Art Museum, "As Maine Goes," 1966.

2. Maine Laws of 1967, Chapter 475 and Maine Laws of 1969, Chapters 431 and 474, see MRSA, tit. 38, §411 et seq. and MRSA, tit. 38, §581 et seq.

3. Maine Laws of 1967, Chapter 475 and Maine Laws of 1969, Chapter 499, see MRSA, tit. §341-A et seq.

4. Maine Laws of 1969, Chapter 472, see MRSA, tit. 10, §2201 et seq. This legislation was subsequently expanded and incorporated into Maine's Site Location of Development Act, see Maine Laws of 1979, Chapter 466, and f.n. 8 *infra*.

5. Maine Laws of 1967, Chapter 348 and Maine Laws of 1969, Chapter 379, see MRSA, tit. 38, §480-A et seq.

6. Maine Laws of 1965, Chapter 447 and Maine Laws of 1969, Chapter 479, see MRSA, tit. 22, §1471-A et seq.

7. Maine Laws of 1969, Chapter 494, see MRSA, tit 12, §683 et seq.

8. Maine Laws of 1969, Chapters 571 and 572, see MRSA, tit. 38, §481 et seq. and MRSA, tit. 38, §541 et seq.

9. Maine Laws of 1971, Chapter 535, see MRSA, tit. 38, §435 et seq.

10. Maine Laws of 1975, Chapter 739, see MRSA, tit. 32, §1861 et seq.

11. Maine Laws of 1965, Chapter 496, see MRSA, tit. 12, §661 et seq .

12. Maine Laws of 1973, Chapter 460 (combining for the first time the Departments of Forestry, and Parks and Recreation, the Maine Forest Authority, the Maine Mining Bureau, the Keep Maine Scenic Committee, the Allagash Wilderness Waterway, and the Land Use Regulation Commission), see MRSA, tit.12, §5011 et seq.

13. Maine Laws of 1973, Chapter 616, see MRSA, tit. 33, §1201 et seq.

14. Maine Laws of 1977, Chapter 494, see MRSA, tit. 23, §1901 et seq.

15. Maine Laws of 1979, Chapter 472, see MRSA, tit. 38, §401 et seq.

16. Maine Laws of 1977, Chapter 320, see MRSA, tit. 5, §1761 et seq.

17. Maine Laws of 1979, Chapter 503, see MRSA, tit. 10, §1411 et seq.

18. Maine Laws of 1981, Chapter 597, see MRSA, tit. 32, §8021 et seq.

19. Maine Laws of 1999, Chapter 336, §2, see MRSA tit. 5, §3305-B.

20. Maine Laws of 2001, Chapter 630, see MRSA, tit 5, §3327 (Supp.).

21. Maine Laws of 2001, Chapter 624, §3, see MRSA, tit. 35-A, §3211-A et seq.

22. Maine Laws of 1989, Chapter 104, subpart 6-A, see MRSA, tit. 30-A, §4301 et seq. This legislation originally provided a generous level of state funding to municipalities to facilitate the planning process and the adoption of first-generation comprehensive plans; in 1991, however, ongoing budgetary difficulties required a sharp scaling back of this state funding commitment and the rewriting of some of the mandatory provisions of the original legislation; see Maine Laws of 1991, Chapter 622. Notwithstanding this setback, large portions of the 1989 act remain in place to the benefit of the state, local governments, and the environment.

23. Maine Laws of 1987, Chapter 506, see MRSA, tit. 5, §6200 et seq.

24. For a good general overview of Maine's panoply of environmental laws, see Verrill & Dana Env. Law Group, *Maine Environmental Law Handbook,* (Gov. Inst. Inc.,1990). Though the bulk of statutory environmental legislating in Maine can be said to be accomplished, the task of fine-tuning and adjusting to new data and/or technological innovations and newly perceived problems is unending.

25. See federal Low-Level Radioactive Waste Policy Act, 42 USC §§2021b-2021j, also Maine's response thereto, MRSA, tit. 38, §1501 et seq.

26. See Texas Low-Level Radioactive Waste Disposal Compact, MRSA, tit. 38, §1545 et seq.

27. Maine Laws of 1993, Chapters 418 and 683, codified as MRSA, tit. 29-A, §403.

28. Maine Laws of 1995, Chapters 49 and 50.

29. See Stewart, "Economics, Environment, and the Limits of Legal Control," *Harvard Environmental Law Review,* vol. 1 (1985), p. 9; Mikkelson, "Earning Green for Turning Green: Executive Order 12291 and Market Driven Environmental Regulation," *Kansas Law Review* vol. 243 (1993), p. 41.

30. See f.n. 22, *supra,* and accompanying text.

31. In 1995 the Maine legislature was presented with a citizen's initiative spearheaded by Jonathan Carter that would (along with other provisions) ban clear-cutting; Governor Angus King, Jr., working with the legislature, the Maine Forestry Service, the forest products industry, and environmental organizations, crafted a competing measure, the Compact for Maine's Forests. In November 1996, because of the sizable number of votes cast against both measures, neither of the measures received a majority of the votes cast; thus, neither became law. The compact did receive the largest number of votes (of the three alternatives presented) and more than one-third of the votes cast; thus, in accordance with the state constitution, it was resubmitted to the voters in November 1997; in a straight up or down vote, the compact was defeated by a relatively narrow margin.

32. For example, incentives to insulate one's home could be developed; inducements to buy smaller vehicles, more fuel-efficient vehicles, to limit multi-car ownership could be fashioned by appropriately designed incentive and disincentive mechanisms; in the same vein the appropriate disposition of old tires, batteries, paint cans, no-longer-needed appliances, computers, etc., could all

be encouraged by "bottle bill" type incentives. A limited and underfunded pilot program to incentivize the turning in of an older (more polluting) vehicle and the purchase of a newer more fuel- and emissions-efficient vehicle existed briefly in Maine; but again we lost our courage. It was repealed two years after passage, see Maine Laws of 1999, Chapter 684, repealed by Maine Laws of 2001, Chapter 714 §JJ-1, also MRSA, tit. 10, §393 et seq.

33. See f.n. 24, *supra*.

34. See *Bell v. Town of Wells*, 510 A2d 509 (Me. 1986) and *Bell v. Town of Wells*, 557 A2d 168 (Me. 1989).

35. See Delogu, "An Argument to the State of Maine, the Town of Wells, and Other Maine Towns Similarly Situated: Buy the Foreshore–Now," *Maine Law Review*, vol. 243 (1993), p. 45.

36. See f.n. 23, *supra*, and accompanying text.

37. With this in mind, it is worth noting that Governor Baldacci in his 2004 State of the State address committed himself to a further and significant level of additional bond funding, $60 million, for the acquisition of property interests by the Land for Maine's Future Board. No earmarking of these funds was suggested, but a commitment to utilize a significant portion of these funds to acquire the state's sand beaches for public use (a goal that enjoys wide public support) might go a long way towards securing passage of the referendum authorizing these bonds.

38. The LNG facility currently being proposed in Harpswell, Maine [and more recently in other coastal communities], exemplifies the dearth of our thinking with respect to energy policy and facilities; proponents cite a range of energy and economic benefits; opponents cite a range of real or imagined environmental harms and risks. Who is to be believed? Who is right? Who will prevail? Moreover, projects of this size and scope expose another weakness in our approach to these issues; critical (probably dispositive) decisions affecting the state as a whole will not be made by a technologically sophisticated, broadly based, non-partisan state instrumentality; instead, they will be made by referendum in the Town of Harpswell or by some other municipal voting mechanism. This is not a sensible way to proceed; it asks too much of towns thrust into Harpswell's position. Do they have (can they quickly find) the technological skills necessary to evaluate proposals of this sort? Can they overcome NIMBY and/or more parochial decision making instincts. On occasion the answer to these questions will be, Yes; more often, the answer will be, No. Either way, the present procedure is inappropriate; proposals of this size and magnitude require early and direct state intervention. Harpswell and its residents, the residents of nearby towns, the entire surrounding environment should be protected, but projects with a regional or statewide impact, like the LNG facility presently on the table, require evaluation, approval (with stringent conditions, if necessary), or denial by a statewide body; this body should listen carefully to the host municipality, but the host municipality (whether Harpswell, Searsport, or Cumberland) should not have a "veto" power over the project.

39. Maine Laws of 2003, Resolve, Chapter 93.

40. Ibid., para. 1.

41. Ibid., para. 3.

Eighteen

1. Clark Irwin, *The Light from the River*, Central Maine Power Company 1999; William B. Skelton, *Walter Scott Wyman*, www.wyman.org/Stories/WalterScott_Content.htm

2. 15 USC 79 et seq. See also, *The Public Utility Holding Company Act: It's Protections Are Needed Today More Than Ever*, American Public Power Association, February 2003.

3. C. Hazen Stetson, *From Logs to Electricty*, Maine Public Service Company 1984. This book is a wonderful description of the early days of water power and electricty in northern Maine.

4. Data from U.S. Department of Energy, Energy Information Agency, http://tonto.eia.doe.gov/oog/info/state/me.html; and California Energy Commission, 2002, http.energy.ca.gov/gasoline/statistics/gasoline-per-capita.html

5. U.S. Department of Commerce, Bureau of Economic Analysis: Regional Economic Activity, http://www.bea.gov/bea/regional/gsp/action.cfm; Energy Information Agency, State Energy Data, Energy Estimates by Source, Selected Years 1966-2000, Maine, http://tonto.eia.doe.gov/oog/info/state/me.html This source will be referred to as "EIA Data" hereafter.

6. EIA data.

7. Stetson, *From Logs to Electricity*.

8. Admiral Lewis L. Strauss, Chairman, U.S. Atomic Energy Commission, Address to National

Association of Science Writers, September 16, 1954, New York City.

9. Irwin, *Light from the River*. CMP closed its last appliance stores in the late 1960s.

10. Peter A. Bradford, *Fragile Structures: A Story of Oil Refineries, National Security and the Coast of Maine* (Harpers Magazine Press, 1975).

11. EIA data.

12. P.L. 95-617. (92 Stat. 3117) 116 U.S. Code Sections 2601

13. 35-A MRSA 3301 et seq., repealed. The Small Power Production Act

14. Irwin, *The Light from the River*.

15. Corporate Average Fuel Economy, 49 USC 329.

16. EIA data.

17. EIA data.

18. Mainwatch Institute, *Energy Choices Revisited: An Examination of the Costs and Benefits of Maine's Energy Policy* (Hallowell, ME: Mainwatch Institute, 1994), pp. 1–6.

19. EIA data.

20. 35-A MSRA 3210-3217 Electric Industry Restructuring

21. EIA data.

22 *Balancing Natural Gas Policy*, National Petroleum Council Study, September 2003 www.npc.org

23. Daniel Yergin and Michael Stoddard, "The Next Prize," *Foreign Affairs*, November/December 2003.

24. EIA Data.

25. *Maine Energy Policy: Overview and Opportunities for Improvement*, December 3, 2003. www.state.me.us/spo/energy/energycouncil/docs/Energy Report Text.pdf

Nineteen

My thanks to Richard Barringer for support and editorial advice, and to Kelly Coleman, Yale School of Forestry and Environmental Studies graduate student, for research assistance

1. J. Kusel, "Assessing Well Being in Forest-Dependent Communities." Linda Kruger, ed. *Understanding Community-Forest Relations* (Portland, OR: USDA Forest Service Pacific Northwest Research Station [PNW-GTR-566], 2003), pp. 81–103. An excellent literature listing is C. W. Richardson, compiler, "Stability and Change in Forest-Based Communities: A Selected Bibliography," *USDA Forest Serv. Pac. Northw. Research Station. Gen. Tech Rept. PNW-GTR-366*. 1996.

2. Charles Francis, "The Grand Trunk comes to Paris," *Discover Maine*, vol. 1, no. 3 (2003), p. 51.

3. Austin H. Peck, *The Wood Products Industries of Maine: A Report to the Department of Economic Development* (Orono, ME: University of Maine at Orono, 1957), p. 27.

4. Ibid., p. 115.

5. Lloyd. C. Irland, "Future Employment in the Maine Woods: Situation, Forces, and Outlook," in *Proceedings: A Forest-Based Economy — Carrying a Tradition into the Future* (Augusta, ME: Maine Department of Conservation, Blaine House Conference on Forestry, 1984), pp. 78-108).

6. Citizens' Forestry Advisory Council, *Forest for the Future: A Report on Maine's Forest to the Legislature, the Governor, and the People of Maine* (Augusta, ME: Maine Department of Conservation, 1988); Charles J. Gadzik, James H. Blanck, and Lawrence E. Caldwell, *Timber Supply Outlook for Maine: 1995–2045*, (Augusta, ME: Maine Department of Conservation, 1998); Maine Department of Conservation, *The 2001 Biennial Report on the State of the Forest: Report to Joint Standing Committee of the 120th Legislature On ACF* (Augusta, ME: Maine Department of Conservation, 2001); Kenneth M. Laustsen, Douglas M. Griffith, and James R. Steinman, *Fourth Annual Inventory Report on Maine's Forests* (Augusta, ME: Maine Department of Conservation and United States Forest Service, 2003); P. E. Sendak, R. C. Abt, and R. J. Turner, "Timber Supply Projections for Northern New England and New York," *Northern Journal of Applied Forestry*, vol. 20, no.4 (2003), pp. 175–85.

7. Background can be found in Irland Group, *Forest Industry and Landownership in the Northern Forest: Economic Forces and Outlook* (New York: Open Space Institute, 1999).

8. Background on the Board is supplied in Lloyd C. Irland, "Policies for Maine's Public Lands" in *Maine Choices 1999* (Augusta, ME: Maine Center for Economic Policy, 1999) pp. 7–21, and documents cited there.

9. J. C. Nellis, "Wood-Using Industries of Maine," *1912 Annual Report of the Forest Commis-*

sioner (Waterville, ME: Sentinel Publishing Company, 1912), pp. 85–188).

10. E. H, Wharton, R. L. Nevel, and D. S. Powell, *Supply and Demand of Timber for Wood Turning in Maine,* (Broomall, PA: U.S. Department of Agriculture, Forest Service, Northeastern Forest Experiment Station, Bulletin NE-RP-589, 1977).

11. D. Mageean, G. AvRuskin, and R. Sherwood. "Whither Maine's Population." *Maine Policy Review,* vol. 9, no.1 (2002), pp. 28–43.

12. Lisa Pohlmann, "Being Poor in Maine: 1960-2010," *Choices,* vol. 9, no. 8 (2003), pp. 1–8.

13. Stephen S. Cohen and John Zysman. *Manufacturing Matters: The Myth of the Post-Industrial Economy* (New York: Basic Books, 1987).

14. Mainewatch Institute, *Families and Forests: Improving Prosperity Through the Secondary Wood Products Industry in the Western Mountains of Maine* (Hallowell, ME: Mainewatch Institute, 1992).

15. Lloyd C. Irland, "Papermaking in New England's Flannel Shirt Frontier: Social Change in the Paper Mill Towns." In a forthcoming book edited by Mark Lapping.

16. Pan Atlantic Consultants and The Irland Group, *Maine Logging Industry and the Bonded Labor Program: An Economic Analysis* (Augusta: Maine Department of Labor, 1999).

17. Andrew A. Egan and D. Taggart, "Who Will Log? Occupational Choice and Prestige in New England's North Woods," *Journal of Forestry,* vol. 102, no 1 (2004), pp. 20–25.

18. Richard W. Judd, Edwin A. Churchill, and Joel W. Eastman. *Maine: The Pine Tree State from Prehistory to the Present* (Orono, ME: University of Maine Press, 1995).

19. A. H. Wilkins, *Ten Million Acres of Timber,* (Woolwich, ME: TBW Books, 1978).

20. See Richard W. Judd and Christopher S. Beach, *Natural States: The Environmental Imagination in Maine, Oregon, and the Nation.* (Washington: Resources for the Future, 2003).

21. A compact summary of these times can be found in Neil Rolde's *The Interrupted Forest: A History of Maine's Wildlands* (Gardiner, ME: Tilbury House, 2001) and in Judd, Churchill, and Eastman, *Maine: The Pine Tree State,* ch. 23.

22. See, Peck, note 3 above; Lloyd C. Irland, "This Evergreen Empire: Maine's Forest Resources and Industries in a New Century," in *Blaine House Conference on Maine's Natural Resource-Based Industry: Charting a New Course, Conference Report, 17 November 2003* (Augusta, ME: Maine State Planning Office, 2004), pp. 97–113; Robert W. Rice, "Task Force to Increase Primary and Secondary Forest Products Manufacturing, Final Report" (abridged), *Maine Image Analysis Lab,* May 2003; R. Barringer and R. Davies, *Blaine House Conference on Maine's Natural Resource Based Industry: Charting a New Course* (Augusta: State Planning Office, Feb. 2004) pp. 32–34.

23. Barringer and Davies, Note 22 above, p. 31.

24. Patricia M. Flynn, Ross J. Getell, and Norman H. Sedgley. "New England as the Twenty-First-Century Approaches: No Time for Complacency." *New England Economic Review* (Nov. 1999), pp. 41–53.

1. *Presiding Officers' Task Force on Creating a Future for Youth in Maine. Final Report* (Augusta: Office of the Speaker of the House, Jan. 2004. 2d reg. sess., 121st Legislature).

26. Lloyd C. Irland, "Maine Forests: A Century of Change, 1900–2000," *Maine Policy Review,* vol. 9, no.1 (2000).

Twenty

1. Note that *commodity* as used here is quite different from its use by the USDA, where "commodity" refers to grains and other crops specified in certain federal legislation. There, potatoes and blueberries, two of the largest crops in Maine commodity agriculture, are identified as "specialty" rather than "commodity" crops.

2. This does not include aquaculture sales, which totaled $64 million in 2001.

3. New England Agricultural Statistics Service, *2002 New England Agricultural Statistics* (Concord, NH: National Agricultural Statistics Service, 2003).

4. Jesse Gandee, *Economic Impact of the Maine Food System and Farm Vitality Policy Implications.* A Report to the Joint Standing Committee on Agriculture, Conservation and Forestry of the 120th Maine Legislature. Augusta, 2002.

5. Willard Cochrane, *The Development of American Agriculture.* (Minneapolis, MN: University of Minnesota Press, 1979).

6. David Goodman, Bernardo Sorj, and John Wilkinson, *From Farming to Biotechnology: A Theory of Agroindustrial Development* (Oxford, UK: Basil Blackwell,1987).

7. Stewart Smith, "Leaks, Leaps and Struggles: Farms and Farming in Maine from 1910-1997."

Proceedings of the Maine Rural Development Council Annual Forum. Orono, ME, 1999.

8. Smith, "Leaks, Leaps and Struggles."

9. SoEun Ahn, William Krohn, Andrew Plantinga, Timothy Dalton, and Jeffery Hepinstall, "Agricultural Land Changes in Maine: A Compilation and Brief Analysis of Census of Agriculture Data, 1850-1997." *MAFES Technical Bulletin 182* (Orono, ME: University of Maine, 2002).

10. United States Department of Agriculture. *Census of Agriculture* (Washington, DC, 1997).

11. See R. Barringer and R. Davies, *Blaine House Conference on Maine's Natural Resource-based Industries: Charting a New Course—Conference Report,* Augusta ME, 2004. Recommendations, pp. 16–28.

12. Maine State Planning Office. *Fishing, Farming and Forestry: Resources for the Future.* (Augusta, ME, 2001).

13. Maine Department of Agriculture, Food & Rural Resources. *Saving Maine's Farmland: A Collaborative Action Plan* (Augusta ME, 2003).

14. The needs and response strategies are presented in *Growing Agriculture: Sustainable Agricultural Water Source and Use Policy and Action Plan,* prepared by the Maine Agricultural Water Management Advisory Committee and issued by the Department in 2003.

TWENTY-ONE

1. S. Baird, *U.S. Commissioner of Fish and Fisheries Report of 1883* (Washington,DC, 1883) pp. xi–xiv. J. R. Collins and W. C. Rathbun, "Fishing Grounds of the Eastern Coast of North America," in G. B. Goode, ed., *The Fisheries and Fishing Industries of the U.S.* (Washington, DC: U.S. Government Printing Office, 1987). W. M. O'Leary, "Maine Seafisheries, 1830–1890," thesis, University of Maine, Orono, 1981. W. H. Rich, *Fishing Grounds of the Gulf of Maine* (Washington, DC: U.S. Commissioner of Fisheries, 1929).

2. E. P. Ames, "Cod and Haddock Spawning Grounds of the Gulf of Maine from Grand Manan to Ipswich Bay," in *The Implications of Localized Fish Stocks* (Ithaca, NY: NRAES, 1997), pp. 55–64. E. P. Ames, "Atlantic Cod Stock Structure in the Gulf of Maine," *Fisheries,* 2004, vol. 29, no. 1.

3. Spencer Apollonio, *Hierarchical Perspectives on Marine Complexities* (New York: Columbia University Press, 2002).

4. James Acheson, *Capturing the Commons* (Lebanon, NH: University Press of New England, 2003).

5. R. S. Steneck and C. Wilson, "Large-scale and Long-term, Spatial and Temporal Patterns in Demography and Landings of the American Lobster, Homarus Americanus, in Maine." *Marine Fisheries Resources,* 2001, vol. 52, pp. 1303–19.

6. David Libby, Maine Dept. of Marine Resources, personal communication, 2003.

7. Apollonio, *Hierarchal Perspectives.*

8. James Wilson, "Scientific Uncertainty, Complex Systems and the Design of Common Pool Institutions," in *The Drama of the Commons,* Paul Stern, Elinor Ostrom, Thomas Dietz, and Nives Dolsak, eds., National Research Council, Committee on Human Dimensions of Global Climate Change, 2001, pp. 327–60. See also James Wilson, "Maine's Fisheries," in Richard Barringer and Richard Davies, *Report of the Blaine House Conference on Maine's Natural Resource-based Industries,* Augusta, ME, 2004.

9. For a more elaborate discussion of the "homogeneous" vs. "heterogeneous" nature of groundfish stocks and its implications, see James A. Wilson, "Maine's Fisheries," a background paper in R. Barringer and R. Davies, *Blaine House Conference on Maine's Natural Resource-based Industries: Charting a New Course—Conference Report,* Augusta ME, 2004, pp. 89 ff.

10. What sets apart competition in the fisheries from competition in other industries is the distinct possibility that fisheries competition might lead, eventually, to the destruction of the resource upon which the industry is based. This leads to the presumption that government or some other form of collective action might improve upon a competitive market result. Scientists and economists have always drawn this conclusion in the context of a particular species, e.g., we over-fish cod, or whatever. There is mounting evidence however, that the relevant damage from fishing is the unrealized destruction of ecosystem structure and functions. Sometimes the short hand for this is "fishing down the food-web."

11. The industry is extraordinarily tight fisted about support for science. This probably comes about because of the ill-considered claims of silver bullets by many scientists and by the equally ill-

considered idea held by many fishermen that the taxpayer should pay for activities that principally benefit the lobster industry. The typical full-time lobsterman lands product worth over $100,000 per year from this publicly held resource. For this opportunity he pays between $150 and $250 dollars per year.

TWENTY-TWO

1. Arthur D. Little, Inc., *Tourism in Maine: Analysis and Recommendations*. Report to Maine Vacation Travel Advisory Committee (Boston, 1974).

2. Dona Brown, *Inventing New England: Regional Tourism in the Nineteenth Century* (Washington, DC: Smithsonian Institution Press, 1995).

3. Robert York, "The Maine Economy: 1900-1940," *Thomas Business Review*, vol. 3, no. 1 (1975), pp. 21-31, Waterville.

4. Little, *Tourism in Maine*, p. 6.

5. William Hatch, "Tourism," *Thomas Business Review* vol. 3, no. 2 (1976), pp. 35-38, Waterville.

6. Little, *Tourism in Maine*, p. 1.

7. Because of price inflation over time, comparison of past and present monetary magnitudes requires a conversion of past values to current (2003) dollars. Conversions have been made using J. McCusker, "Comparing the Purchasing Power of Money in the United States from 1665 to Any Other Year," Economic History Services, 2001, URL: http://www.eh.net/ppowerusd/

8. The $490 million contribution to GSP is less than the $550 contribution to gross income because $60 million of state expenditures to support tourism are netted out

9. Little, *Tourism in Maine*, Appendix C.

10. Little, *Tourism in Maine*, p. 98.

11. Maine League of Historical Societies and Museums, *Maine: A Guide "Downeast"* (Rockland, ME: Courier-Gazette, Inc. , 1970).

12. Hatch, "Tourism," p. 35.

13. Little, *Tourism in Maine*, p. 10.

14. Richard Judd and C. Beach, *Natural States: The Environmental Imagination in Maine, Oregon. and the Nation* (Washington, DC: Resources for the Future, 2003).

15. Hatch, "Tourism."

16. Center for Survey and Marketing Research, *Maine Tourism Study 1986-87 Economic Analysis*. For the Maine State Development Office (Kenosha, WI: University of Wisconsin-Parkside, 1988). Thomas Davidson, *The Maine Growth Model: Promoting Maine Tourism*. For the State Development Office, 1987. Davidson-Peterson Associates, USTDC (US Travel Data Center), *Maine Tourism Study, 1984-85, Volumes I & II* (Maine State Development Office, 1985).

17. Maine Vacation Travel Commission, *Maine's Tourist Industry: A Potent Force for Economic Development*. Presented to the Maine State Legislature. Tourism Subcommittee, 1986. *Economic Development Opportunities in Tourism*. Governor's Taskforce on Economic Development. Augusta, 1987

18. Longwoods Associates, *Travel and Tourism in Maine—2000 Visitor Study* (Augusta, ME, 2001)

19. David Vail and T. Heldt, "Institutional Factors Influencing the Size and Structure of Tourism," *Current Issues in Tourism.*, vol. 3, no. 4 (2000), pp. 283–324.

20. David M. Vail, M. Lapping, W. Richard, and M. Cote, *Tourism and Maine's Future* (Augusta, ME: Maine Center for Economic Policy, 1998).

21. Travel Industry Association of America, *Expenditure Patterns of Travelers in the US—2002 Edition* (Washington, DC, 2002).

22. Barbara Walsh, "Old Orchard Beach: Is 'Vacationland' in Trouble?" *Maine Sunday Telegram*, July 6, 2003.

23. Longwoods, *Travel and Tourism*.

24. David Vail, "Snowmobiling in Maine: Past Successes, Future Challenges," *Maine Policy Review*, Winter 2003, pp. 130–40.

25. U.S. Fish and Wildlife Service, *2001 National Survey of Fishing, Hunting, and Wildlife-Associated Recreation—Maine*. FHW/01-Rev. (Washington, DC: US Department of the Interior, 2003).

26. David Vail, "Sustaining Nature-Based Tourism in Vacationland, in *Proceedings of the Blaine House Conference on Maine's Natural Resource-based Industries*, Augusta, 2004.

27. David Vail and W. Kavanaugh, *Livable Wages in Maine Tourism?* (Augusta, ME: Maine Center for Economic Policy, 2000).

28. Maine Department of Labor, "Average Annual Wages in 2002," *Labor Market Digest,* June 2003, Augusta.

29. University of Minnesota Tourism Center, *Overview and Programs.* CD-MI-3518 (St. Paul, MN: 1998).

30. Thomas Power, *The Economic Impact of the Proposed Maine Woods National Park and Preserve* (Hallowell, ME: RESTORE the North Woods, 2001). David Vail, "Ecotourism and Sustainability." *The Bath-Brunswick Times Record.* "Sustain Maine" series. June 27, 2003.

31. Longwoods, *Travel and Tourism.*